Magazine Markets
for Children's
Writers 2011

Writer's Institute
Publications

D1119550

Acknowledgments

The editors of this directory appreciate the generous contributions of our instructors and students, and the cooperation of the magazine editors who made clear their policies and practices.

SUSAN TIERNEY, Editor in Chief

BARBARA COLE, Associate Editor

SHERRI KEEFE, Associate Editor

VICTORIA O'CONNOR, Editorial Assistant

CHERYL KAUER, Editorial Assistant

Contributing Writers: SUSAN ANDERSON, KRISTEN BISHOP, CAROLINE LaFLEUR, SUSAN TARRANT

Cover Design: JOANNA HORVATH
Cover illustration supplied by iStockphoto

International Standard Book Number 978-1-889715-55-1

1-800-443-6078. www.writersbookstore.com
email: services@writersbookstore.com

Printed in Canada

Contents

Step-by-Step through the Submissions Process

This section offers tips and step-by-step instructions for researching markets; writing queries; preparing manuscripts and bibliographies; following up; and understanding copyrights, permissions, and other common publishing terms.

Gateway to the Markets

Listings
New listings in this year's edition are indicated by ❗ .

51

How to Use the Listings
A section-by-section description of the listings.

52

Listings of Magazines

54

Additional Listings
Includes short listings of additional markets.

231

Contests and Awards
Provides basic guidelines for 46 magazine writing contests and awards.

289

Writers' Resources
A completely new section with 44 resources useful for writers on writing, career, children, and research.

303

Indexes

317

2011 Market News
Identifies new listings and deletions and name changes.

318

Fifty+ Freelance
Lists magazines that rely on freelance writers for at least 50% of the material they publish.

320

Category Index
Lists magazines under selected categories according to the type of material they are interested in acquiring.

321

Index
Cross references all magazines, contests, and resources listed; provides page references.

369

Step-by-Step through the Submissions Process

Selling Your Big Idea

Do you have a big idea? The editors of every one of the 20,000 magazines in North America are in search of big ideas on a daily basis—and yours could be one of them. The right idea can be your entrée into magazine publishing, but only if you know how to sell it.

Contrary to what you might think, your first job as a freelance writer is to sell your idea, not your article. (In fact, most professional writers don't write the article until they've already sold their idea.) Whether you've written the article already, or if you've just done the necessary research to be sure you can deliver on your idea, the first step on the road to publication is marketing.

Marketing Smart

Just as market research is an essential part of any successful business, it plays an equally significant role in selling your writing. Even if you've come up with an article idea that takes a fresh perspective on a particular subject, your idea won't sell unless you market it correctly. Magazine editors are always looking for the perfect match between a writer's idea and their magazine; if you can make that connection, your chances for making a sale will dramatically increase.

But making the perfect match often involves more than just finding a magazine that publishes articles like yours. It also means making smart submissions that are well researched and maximize your sales potential.

For example, you may know a young volunteer in your community who would make a great subject for a profile article. Without doing any market research you might conclude that *American Girl* is a good fit, based on your familiarity with the magazine and its articles. It probably is a good fit for this idea, but take a close look at the listing: 4% of the magazine is written by nonstaff writers, and it publishes only 5 freelance submissions yearly, 2% of which are written by unpublished writers.

Further research might reveal other, more promising markets, particularly for unpublished writers. *Girls' Life*, written for a similar age group, has a continuously running department that features profiles of real girls. It is 25% written by nonstaff writers, and publishes 40 freelance submissions yearly, 10% of which are by unpublished writers. And depending on the slant and subject of your article, deeper research may yield some additional, unexpected potential markets. *Hopscotch*, a magazine designed to be both "entertaining and educational," is aimed at 5- to 14-year-old girls. *Hopscotch* is 80% written by nonstaff writers, and publishes 100 to 120 freelance submissions yearly. Check its upcoming themes and read a few recent issues. If your idea fits with this magazine's style and editorial mission, then you may have found your perfect match at last.

With this directory in hand, you already have one of the best tools available to help market your work. The rest of your marketing strategy depends on crafting the right idea to begin with, starting with its very foundation: the topic.

Choosing a Topic

Whether your topic is fiction or nonfiction, you'll increase your publication odds if you know what topics interest children. For example, an article about the basic principles of electricity would be more interesting for kids if presented through the eyes of the famous magician, Jean Eugéne Robert-Houdin. This approach also connects the past to the present, a learning concept that appeals to classroom magazine editors. When you're thinking about ideas, consider how a young person views the world. What is their typical day like? What kinds of things are they interested in? Questions like these can produce a number of interesting subject leads.

Another way to find an appropriate subject is to review current publications. Start by surveying the categories of magazines in *Magazine Markets for Children's Writers*. The category index on pages 325–368 is an excellent guide to finding magazines that publish the types of articles or stories you write on the subjects that interest you. You'll find everything from general interest publications, like *Boys' Quest* or *Highlights for Children*, to special interest periodicals on topics such as sports, careers, crafts, current events, parenting, geography, health and fitness, and more.

> **To build your credibility, consider specializing in a particular subject area. Think about what subjects you have specialized knowledge or interest in, and develop a portfolio of articles within that field.**

Continue your research online or at libraries. What magazines are out there, for what ages, and what subjects do they cover? Along with magazines targeted specifically to children, be sure to check parenting, educational, and regional magazines.

You'll find that each magazine covers numerous subjects from month to month or year to year, even special interest publications that cover a niche more deeply than widely. Read several issues of each magazine to find out which subjects a potential target magazine has covered recently and how it has approached particular subjects in the past. Begin to make a list of the magazines that cover subjects of interest to you.

Targeting Your Readers

Subject and audience often go hand in hand, though many subjects can be geared toward a variety of audiences, with the right treatment. Select a subject slant that is age-appropriate for your intended audience and your potential market. For example, if you'd like to take on the subject of architecture you might write a story on the basics of building design for younger readers, or cover the more complex slant of conservationist/green design for high-school readers. Both articles vary in the amount and complexity of information offered, and in tone. Determine each magazine's target age and how the publication speaks to that age, through voice and purpose.

To learn more about the developmental level of your intended age range, go to the Internet and other media, as well as to schools and children's activities. For example, at the Google Directory (www.google.com/dirhp) click on Kids and Teens. Look at the topics under preschool, school time, teen life, and other categories. The arts section in particular has many interesting sites that relate to every age group.

Understanding the Magazine

Once you have a good handle on your subject and your audience, start doing in-depth research for those magazines you intend to target. Create a magazine market file for publications that seem to match your interests. Use index cards, a notebook, or your computer to develop a file for each magazine for your initial list of publications.

Sample Guidelines Request

Name
Address
City, State ZIP

Date

Dear (Name of Current Editor):

I would like to request a copy of your writers' guidelines and editorial calendar. I have provided a self-addressed, stamped envelope for your convenience.

Sincerely,

Your name

Review the Writers' Guidelines

If the listing for a particular magazine indicates that it offers writers' guidelines, either send a letter to the publication along with an SASE (see the sample on page 7) to request the guidelines, or check the magazine's website. (The listing will specify where to look for this information.) Writers' guidelines, editorial calendars, and theme lists may give you specific topics to write about, or they may be more general.

Either way, follow the guidelines carefully, or your submission could be rejected by the editor. Guidelines are key to the needs of publications and often new writers give them too little weight.

Some guidelines are more detailed and helpful than others, but virtually all will tell you something about the readership, philosophy, and voice, as well as word length requirements, submission format, and payment. More than that, some guidelines give writers specific insight into the immediate needs of a magazine. For example, *Adoptive Families* magazine has thorough guidelines that include a listing of its departments, instructions on how to submit your work, subject areas editors are looking to cover, and suggestions for writers, such as "have a clear sense of your central theme," and "focus on choices made and strategies used to deal with a particular situation." *Pack-O-Fun's* guidelines offer a detailed list of the kinds of crafts its editors are looking for year-round.

Depending on their level of detail, some guidelines may also indicate the rights a publication purchases, payment policies, and many more specifics—factors you'll consider as you get closer to submission. Many experienced writers do not sell all rights, unless the fee is high enough to be worth it; reselling

Magazine Description Form

Name of Magazine: *The Science Teacher*   **Editor:** Megan Sullivan
Address: 1840 Wilson Blvd., Arlington, VA 22010-3000

Freelance Percentage: 100%   **Percentage of Authors Who Are New to the Magazine:** 50%

Description
What subjects does this magazine cover? Science education, biology, Earth science, computers, social issues, space, technology, and sports medicine

Readership
Who are the magazine's typical readers? Science educators of grades 7–12

Articles and Stories
What particular slants or distinctive characteristics do its articles or stories emphasize? New and creative ideas for the secondary science classroom that provide practical help for teachers. Classroom activities, teaching techniques, and scientific research are all areas of interest.

Potential Market
Is this magazine a potential market? Yes. My article fits with an upcoming theme, and *Science Teacher* welcomes freelance writers and new writers.

Ideas for Articles or Stories
What article, story, or department idea could be submitted? My article focuses on the use of Earthcaching in the classroom. In addition to teaching students how to use a GPS receiver, Earthcaching requires them to take that knowledge outside the classroom to visit a local Earthcache site, which could include anything from fossil sites and canyons to caves and hot springs.

articles or stories for reprint rights can be an additional source of income. (See the discussion of rights on page 27.)

Review Sample Issues

Get sample issues of the magazines and read them, either by requesting them from the publisher; finding copies at the library, the bookstore, or through friends; or by reviewing articles on the magazine's website. The listings in *Magazine Markets for Children's Writers* will tell you if writers' guidelines, an editorial calendar, or a theme list are available, as well as the cost of a sample copy requested directly from the publisher.

Review each of the magazines in more detail for subjects similar to yours. You should also check the *Readers' Guide to Periodical Literature* in your library to see if a target magazine has covered your topic within the past two years. If so, you may want to find another magazine or, depending on the publication, develop a new slant if you find that your subject is already well covered.

Use the Magazine Description Form (see page 8) to continue your detailed analysis of the publications, especially those you're beginning to hone in on as good matches. Evaluate how you could shape or present your manuscript to improve your chances of getting it published. If you're new to a particular magazine, a good way to get your foot in the door may be to pitch a short article for the front pages or a particular department, rather than a full-length feature article. If a particular idea or target magazine doesn't work out now, it may in the future—or it may lead to other ideas, angles, or possible markets. Review your market files periodically to generate ideas.

Your review of sample magazines and guidelines should include:

- **Editorial objective.** In some cases, the magazine's editorial objective is stated inside the publication, on the same page as the masthead, where the names of the editors are listed; it is also usually stated on the website. For example, the editorial objective of *Highlights for Children* is summarized in its simple subhead, "Fun with a Purpose." Does your story or article fit your targeted magazine's purpose?

New Angles, New Audiences

A substantial amount of research goes into writing magazine articles, and it's to your advantage to make the most of this time. In many cases, the research for one article can be used for other articles, as long as they reach different audiences and have fresh angles. To find additional sales opportunities, consider other markets that might be interested in the information—religious publications, arts and crafts magazines, science magazines, etc. Then investigate angles that would be of most interest to them. Make a list of the possibilities, like the ideas below, and keep it handy for future reference.

Subject: Shadow Drawings

Magazine	Audience	Slant
Pack-O-Fun	6- to 12-year-olds	How to make shadow drawings
Chicago Parent	Parents	"Short Stuff" column about a local teacher who used shadow drawings as part of a summer enrichment program; include directions on how to make the drawings
Science and Children	Science teachers	How to teach concepts of light and shadow through the classroom activity of making shadow drawings

- **Audience.** What is the age range of the readers and the characters? For fiction, is your main character at the upper end of that range? Kids want to read about characters their own age or older. For nonfiction, take a look at the advertisements, which have been expertly tailored to the target audience. They can offer valuable clues about the magazine's readers and their interests.

- **Article and story types.** Examine the types of articles in the issue, paying special attention to article construction. Are the articles informal, or are they filled with facts and statistics? Are they interactive? Do they use anecdotes or personal experience stories to illustrate a point? Has your topic already been covered by this magazine recently? For fiction, what genres does it cover? What is the average story or article length?

- **Layout and formatting.** Examine the overall look of an article. Are sidebars, subheads, and/or other elements included? Is the magazine highly visual or does it rely primarily on text? Will photographs or illustrations be a consideration for you? Will your article work using the magazine's preferred format?

- **Style.** Become familiar with the magazine's editorial style, and how it is impacted by the age of the audience. Does it strive for a conversational, energetic style, or a straightforward, educational one? Are the sentences simple or complex, or a mixture of both? Are there numerous three-syllable words, or mostly simple words? Do the writers speak directly to the readers or is the voice appropriately authoritative?

- **Editor's comments.** Very often the writers' guidelines include insight from the editor about the feel of a magazine. For example, *Instructor* magazine's guidelines state, "Write in your natural voice, as if you were talking to a colleague. We shy away from wordy, academic prose." *Breakaway* magazine's guidelines describe it as "fast-paced," "compelling," and "out of the ordinary."

Magazine Markets for Children's Writers includes a section called Editor's Comments in each listing. Study this section carefully for similar remarks about what editors want to see, or don't need.

> When you're ready to query, use the information from your sample issue review to show the editor that you're familiar with the publication. Pitch your article to a specific section of the magazine, or mention a recent article in your query.

Refine Your Magazine List

After you analyze your selected magazines, rank them by how well they match your idea, subject, style, and target age. Then return to the listings to examine other factors, such as the magazine's freelance potential, its receptivity to new or unpublished writers, rights purchased, and payment.

Not only should your decision to submit be based on how well your idea matches a particular publication, you should also consider which publications match you as a writer. An examination of magazine business policies—not just current editorial needs—can reveal significant details about the magazine that you can use to your advantage as a freelance writer. For example, many published writers prefer magazines that:

- respond in one month as opposed to three or more;
- pay on acceptance rather than on publication;
- do not purchase all rights (see the rights discussion on p. 27);
- publish a high percentage of authors who are new to the magazine.

If you're not yet published, however, writing for a nonpaying market or taking risks in other areas (such as signing a work-for-hire contract or agreeing to payment on publication rather than on acceptance) may be worth the effort to earn the clips needed for future submissions. Once you've acquired credentials in these markets, you can list these published pieces in your queries to other markets.

Submitting Your Work to an Editor

Submission policies vary across the board; some magazines accept queries only, others accept complete manuscripts or queries, while others want queries accompanied by writing samples, a synopsis, an outline, or other information. A query may be sufficient for some editors; others prefer to get a more complete sense of you and your work before making a determination. To know for sure what to send, check the writers' guidelines for the publication you're interested in. Expect that the editor who accepts a complete, unsolicited manuscript may require even more revisions or rewrites than if you had queried first.

The Right Stuff

So you've looked it up, and the guidelines of your target magazine say to "query with outline, bibliography, and clips or writing samples." In this case, you should send the following:

- One-page query letter
- Brief outline of article topics
- Bibliography of research sources
- Selected clips (published writing) or writing samples (unpublished writing, such as blog entries, Web content, letters to editors, etc.)
- SASE

For nonfiction submissions, it's always a good idea to include a bibliography of your research sources, whether you're sending a query letter or a complete manuscript. A well-rounded bibliography with a variety of sources demonstrates a professional approach. For complete manuscript submissions of both fiction and nonfiction, include a cover letter that briefly introduces the work (see p. 19). And unless you're submitting via email (see below), an SASE is a necessary part of any submission package.

Email Submissions

Email is an efficient means of communication in business today, but publications still vary widely in their policies regarding email submissions: Some publishers prefer to receive submissions via email, others accept both print and email submissions, and still others avoid email submissions altogether. The only way to know for sure is to check each publisher's guidelines.

Before you submit via email, be sure that your electronic query is as carefully crafted as a print one. Email queries by nature are slightly less formal, but not sloppy, and the content of your query should be as informative and engaging as a traditional one. Beware, however, the conversational, too-familiar tone of many emails, which is inappropriate for queries and submissions. Your query is your first contact with an editor, so write in a professional manner. Pay close attention to grammar and punctuation and avoid using cutesy email addresses and emoticons. And remember—email does not always mean faster response times, so be patient with the editor and respect his or her time.

Before you hit the send button, check that you've complied with any guidelines specific to email submissions, such as:

- *File formats:* Should the submission be included in the body of the email or as an attachment? Should files be sent in Microsoft Word or Rich text format?
- *Subject line:* Should your subject line say "Query" or "Submission," and include your name or the title of the work?
- *Contact information:* Your name, address, email address, and telephone number should be included below your "signature."

Crafting a Query Letter

The query letter is a writer's most important marketing tool: In the same way the back cover blurb of a book draws in potential readers, your query must intrigue an editor enough to make him or her want to see your work. While writing a query can be challenging, it's an art worth practicing—good query letters are few and far between, and a standout will make an editor take notice.

There are several advantages to using a query letter. First, it is the preferred submission method of many publications. Editors are deluged with pitches, and queries offer a quick, easy way to identify those with potential. Also, many query letters are written before the manuscript. Whether or not this is the case, phrase your letter as if the article is in the planning stage. Editors prefer pieces written specifically for their publication; early involvement also allows them to mold the piece to their specifications. Some writers even find that crafting a query pitch helps keep them focused while writing.

Essential Elements of a Query

Editors always appreciate a well-written query that catches their interest and gets to the point quickly. The following elements are part of every good query letter, though some elements may be emphasized more than others.

Article/story summary. The purpose of a query is to pique the interest of an editor, not to provide a detailed outline of your nonfiction article or in-depth coverage of your story's plot. More important at this stage is getting across the basic idea of your piece—what it is about and who are the key players—in a lively, professional manner. Start your letter with a lead-in that hooks the editor, and state your article or story's unique point of view upfront. Remember to include the approximate word count of the article, as well as any sidebars or other elements, in your letter.

Your qualifications. Pitching yourself—not just your article—is another key component. List your publishing credits if you have them; if not, don't mention it at all. Even if you haven't been published, you may have experience in some other area that proves relevant to the topic you're writing about. For example, if you're pitching an article to a children's

Query Checklist

❏ Direct your query to a specific editor. Verify the spelling of the name and address.

❏ Begin with a lead paragraph that "hooks" the editor and conveys your slant.

❏ Include a brief description of your article that conveys your central idea.

❏ Show how your idea meets the editorial goals of the targeted magazine.

❏ Indicate approximate word length of main article, along with any sidebars.

❏ Provide specific details about the content—compelling anecdotes, case histories, relevant personal experience stories, etc.

❏ Cite sources and planned interviews to show that you have access to sources.

❏ Include a unique, attention-grabbing title.

❏ If applicable, indicate number and type of photographs or illustrations available.

❏ List your publishing credits, or emphasize your relevant or unique experience.

❏ Close by asking if the magazine is interested; mention whether your query is a simultaneous submission.

❏ Include other information if requested, such as an outline, bibliography, or resume.

science magazine on how bees make honey and you once worked as a researcher in this area, you are particularly qualified to write such a piece even if you've never been published before. Note any background or experience you have that gives you credibility in writing this piece for this particular audience.

Knowledge of the market. Know your audience, and know the magazine you're pitching to inside and out. Tailor your idea to work specifically for that publication. Know the word limit the magazine prefers and whether or not it requires a bibliography of sources. Know its tone and style, and mold your article to match. For example, if the magazine only publishes how-to articles and interviews, pitch a unique article in one of those categories. Or, if the magazine often includes information from an expert's perspective, find an expert who's willing to participate in an interview for your article and include his or her name in the letter. Understanding a magazine's "personality" will help you make a convincing argument as to why your article will benefit that publication.

Professional presentation. Some editors stop reading a query altogether after finding a mistake, so take a few extra minutes to make sure your letter is ready to send. Proofread for grammar, spelling, and typos throughout. Double-check the spelling of the publication, the address, and the editor's name. Use a letter-quality printout, with crisp, dark type, single-spaced, and a font close to Times Roman 12-point. Make sure your contact information is included, along with a self-addressed, stamped envelope or postcard for the editor's reply.

Use this list of essentials to determine if your query is getting the point across in the most effective and professional manner possible. A good query letter is short and to the point. If you can't get your idea across in one page or less, your article may not be as tightly focused as it should be. Similarly, if you've sent out the same query many times with no response, it may be that your article or story's basic concept is the problem, not the query.

Article Appeal

If you're pitching a nonfiction article, one of the ideas below might be just what your manuscript needs to get noticed.

- ***Photographs.*** While most publications don't require photos with a submission, most welcome them. To add visuals to your article, you can either take pictures yourself and send them with your query, or search online for images. Government sources, PR departments, museums, and historical associations are all good places to search. Let the editor know that you've located good-quality, accessible photos and where. A submission with a visual component is more likely to get an editor's attention.

- ***Sidebars.*** Magazines specialize in serving up small bits of information, and one way to "chunk" your manuscript is through the use of sidebars. The contents of a sidebar may include fast facts, checklists, instructions, definitions, quizzes, quotes, or crafts to support the article. Sidebars offer readers an additional point of entry to the larger article, and serve as a visual element. Sidebar titles, concepts, and word counts should be mentioned in your query as an optional addition to the main article.

- ***Unusual formatting.*** There are many ways to present facts, and the traditional narrative format is just one of them. Some magazines are very visual, and prefer art-driven pieces, relying heavily on charts, photos, games, captions, etc. Other innovative formats include Q & A's, profiles, interviews, quizzes, lists, and crossword puzzles. Use your imagination to think of alternative formats that might be appropriate for your subject.

Sample Query Letter

Address
Phone Number
Email
Date

Cobblestone Publishing
30 Grove Street, Suite C
Peterborough, NH 03458

Dear Editor,

Imagine yourself being up to bat. Fans are screaming your name, up on their feet cheering and chanting. You're in the zone. You can't hear any of it. You've got your head in the game. You think you're tuned out to the sound because you're focused? Not in this case. You can't hear it because you're deaf.

I am proposing a profile on William "Dummy" Hoy, a major influence in baseball history who doesn't seem to get a lot of attention. This 712-word profile aimed at ages 7-12 provides interesting history on William Hoy's silent but strong influence on major league baseball. This Cincinnati native has affected several aspects of the sport, including the uniforms and why they don't have pockets! I believe this article would fit very well with your focus on history as stated on your website.

I've also included a 55-word sidebar that highlights other deaf professional athletes including Lance Allred of the Cleveland Cavaliers basketball team.

I have been published in *Highlights* and *Stories for Children.com*. I have submitted this article to other publishers as well.

Thank you for your time. I look forward to hearing from you.

Sincerely,

Katherine Ruskey

Sample Query Letter

Address
Phone Number
Email
Date

Ms. Christine French Clark
Highlights for Children
803 Church Street
Honesdale, PA 18431-1895

Dear Ms. Clark:

Consider the drinking straw: a simple, functional, benign object.

But the history of the drinking straw shows us that while it may always have been simple and functional, it has not always been benign. In ancient times, a drinking straw was, well, made from a piece of straw (or reed), and imparted its own flavor to drinks. After a few sips, it became a soggy mess, like the paper straws of the 1900s.

I am an archaeologist who works with teachers, and my colleagues and I recovered many plastic drinking straws from an excavation we carried out on the grounds of an elementary school. Thus, I was spurred to research this most mundane of artifacts: What could we tell the students about drinking straws? My research led me to the Middle East, then to a tavern in our nation's capital, and even to a chemical laboratory in England.

If you think your young readers would be interested in an 800-word nonfiction article about the history of the drinking straw, entitled "Sippin History," I would be pleased to send it to you for your review.

Sincerely,

A. Gwynn Henderson
Archaeologist/Education Coordinator
Kentucky Archaeological Survey

Sample Query Letter

Address
Phone Number
Email
Date

Boy Scouts of America
Paula Murphey, Senior Editor
1325 West Walnut Hill Lane
P.O. Box 152079
Irving, TX 75015-2079

Dear Ms. Murphey,

Divers weave through a forest of marine life after a long day of studying coral and fish. They're heading home. However, they're not heading to the surface. Their home is underwater.

My article entitled, "Getting Their Feet Wet" (793 words), showcases Aquarius, an underwater ocean laboratory that recently took on its 100th mission. Aquarius is not only dedicated to protecting one of Florida's most valuable marine resources, but it will continue to expand our knowledge of coral reefs, our oceans, and our planet. I think young readers will be as fascinated as I was to learn that Aquarius lies 60 feet deep in the ocean, and is the size of a large mobile home; and that aquanauts are underwater for days and must endure 17 hours of decompression to return to the surface.

I consulted with Dr. Ellen Prager, the chief scientist at Aquarius. Dr. Prager can provide high resolution digital photos and there is no fee for photo use.

I've had numerous articles published in *Stories for Children Magazine*, and have forthcoming articles in *AppleSeeds*, *Focus on the Family Clubhouse Jr.*, and the Institute of Children's Literature's Web resource, *Rx for Writers*. I'm also a member of SCBWI.

Thank you for your time and consideration.

Sincerely,

Lori Calabrese

Enc.: Article outline, Bibliography, SASE

Sample Query Letter

Address
Phone Number
Email
Date

Elizabeth Crooker Carpentiere, Editor
FACES
Cobblestone Publishing
30 Grove Street, Suite C
Peterborough, NH 03458

Dear Ms. Carpentiere:

Ever write a story about your family? Draw pictures of someplace special you visited on a family vacation? Taken a picture of a favorite aunt you haven't seen in a while? The native people of Southern Alaska did the same thing hundreds of years ago, but in a very different way. Instead of using paper and markers or snapping a digital photo, they carved images into the wood of ancient red cedar trees.

I am proposing a 650- to 700-word article, tentatively titled "Totem Poles: An Ancient Alaskan Art." I'd like to incorporate a craft activity into the piece for making a mini 3-D totem pole. A photo of the completed project is available upon request. An optional sidebar could include a key to the meanings behind the traditional symbols used by the Inuit people.

I am enclosing a detailed outline of the proposed piece as well as a bibliography.

Previously my short stories and articles have appeared in publications both in print and online.

If you are interested in seeing the finished article, I would be happy to submit it for your consideration. I have enclosed an SASE and I look forward to your reply.

Sincerely,

Ruth Schiffmann

Sample Query Letter

Address
Phone Number
Email
Date

Elizabeth Lindstrom, Editor
Odyssey
Carus Publishing
30 Grove Street, Suite C
Peterborough, NH 03458

Dear Ms. Lindstrom:

In math classrooms, students seem to understand the concepts in class only to turn around and fail a test given the next day. What's the deal? The majority of students don't know how or what to study for math tests because studying for math is totally different than studying for other school subjects.

I've prepared a 966-word article tentatively titled "Passing with Flying Colors: How to Ace a Mathematics Test" that outlines specific tips to help students receive an excellent grade on any math test. The article begins with a brief conversation between study partners to grab attention. Following this, I cite math test-taking tips such as active daily learning, using flash cards, studying over time, and taking a practice test.

As a middle-school math teacher, I witness the common studying mistakes that students make. By using the tips mentioned in the article, teenagers can learn how to prepare and study for a math test and wow their teachers and parents with their grades.

If you are interested in seeing the finished article, I would be happy to submit it for your consideration. I have enclosed a self-addressed, stamped envelope and I look forward to your reply.

Best regards,

Janae Rosendale

Enc.: SASE

Preparing a Manuscript Package

The following guide shows how to prepare and mail a professional-looking manuscript package. However, you should always adhere to an individual magazine's submission requirements as detailed in its writers' guidelines and its listing in this directory.

Cover Letter Tips

Always keep your cover letter concise and to the point. Provide essential information only.

If the letter accompanies an unsolicited manuscript submission (see below), indicate that your manuscript is enclosed and mention its title and word length. If you're sending the manuscript after the editor responded favorably to your query letter, indicate that the editor requested to see the enclosed manuscript.

Provide a brief description of the piece and a short explanation of how it fits the editor's needs. List any publishing credits or other pertinent qualifications. If requested in the guidelines or listing, note any material or sources you can provide. Indicate if the manuscript is being sent to other magazines as well (a simultaneous submission). Mention that you have enclosed a self-addressed, stamped envelope for return of the manuscript.

Sample Cover Letter	Address
	Phone Number
	Email
	Date

Boys' Quest
P.O. Box 227
Bluffton, OH   45817-0227

Dear Editor:

Twenty-five percent of the population has a sense of taste that is three times stronger than most. These people are commonly referred to as 'supertasters.' This is the topic of an article I have enclosed for consideration in an upcoming issue of *Boys' Quest*.

The piece titled "Do My Taste Buds Have Super Powers?" is 483 words, not including a crossword puzzle and an activity on how to determine if you're a supertaster. The focus of the article is to explore what it's like to be a supertaster and to better understand why they don't enjoy certain foods.

The article is intended for intermediate readers, suitable for your target audience. It received an honorable mention in the December 2007 Short Article Contest for *ByLine Magazine*. Note: *ByLine* does not routinely print winning entries, allowing the author to sell first rights later.

Thank you for your consideration, and I hope you enjoy the article. I have enclosed a bibliography, copies of the sources cited in the bibliography, photographs, and an SASE for your convenience.

Sincerely,

Julie M. Smith

Encl.: Manuscript, Bibliography, Source copies, Photographs, SASE

Subject/ Specifications: A brief description of the topic and its potential interest to the magazine's readers. Word lengths, age range, availability of photos, and other submission details.

Closing: Be formal and direct.

Standard Manuscript Format

The format for preparing manuscripts is fairly standard—an example is shown below. Double-space manuscript text, leaving 1- to 1½-inch margins on the top, bottom, and sides. Indent 5 spaces for paragraphs.

In the upper left corner of the first page (also known as the title page), single space your name, address, phone number, and email address. In the upper right corner of that page, place your word count.

Center the title with your byline below it halfway down the page, approximately 5 inches. Then begin the manuscript text 4 lines below your byline.

In the upper left corner of the following pages, type your last name, the page number, and a word or two of your title. Then, space down 4 lines and continue the text of the manuscript.

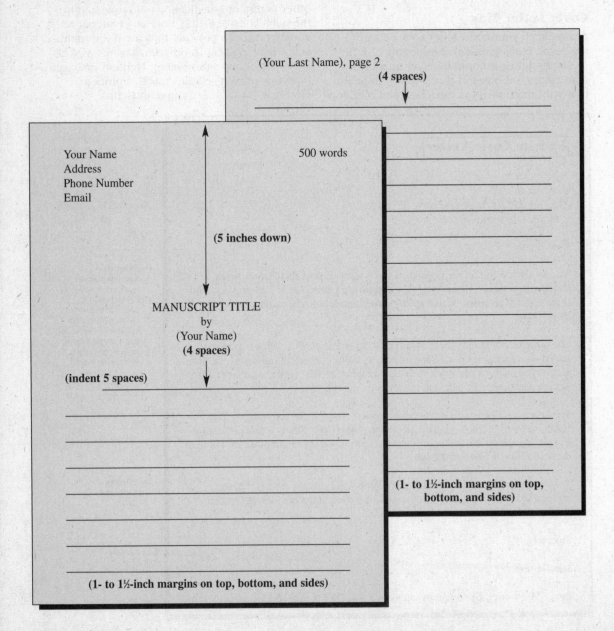

(Your Last Name), page 2

(4 spaces)

Your Name
Address
Phone Number
Email

500 words

(5 inches down)

MANUSCRIPT TITLE
by
(Your Name)
(4 spaces)

(indent 5 spaces)

(1- to 1½-inch margins on top, bottom, and sides)

(1- to 1½-inch margins on top, bottom, and sides)

Sample Cover Letter

Address
Phone Number
Email
Date

Submissions Editor, *Cricket*
Carus Publishing
70 East Lake Street, Suite 300
Chicago, IL 60601

Dear Editor,

Eleven-year-old Aden returns to his favorite fishing spot early one spring afternoon only to find all the fish lying dead upon the shore. What caused this horrible tragedy? How did the fish die? Will Aden's favorite spot ever be the same again? As one clue leads to another, Aden and his friend Sammy scramble to solve this science-based mystery and save the fish.

Touching on the potential loss of the fish and of one child's special place, this 1,130-word story is sure to capture the interest of young readers ages 8 to 10. In addition, this story is based on a true ecologic crisis, the invasion of the zebra mussel that has recently occurred in many parts of the United States. A sidebar with factual information about nonnative zebra mussels and how they are affecting local ecosystems like the one in this story can easily be included for even greater interest.

As a high school science teacher, former park ranger, and environmental educator, ecological mysteries and animal adaptations are a favorite teaching topic of mine. Enclosed you will find a copy of "The Mystery of the Dead Fish" for your consideration.

I look forward to hearing from you and I have included an SASE for your convenience. This manuscript has been sent exclusively to you at this time.

Sincerely,

Eliza Bicknell

Sample Cover Letter

Address
Phone Number
Email
Date

Suzanne Hadley
Focus on the Family Clubhouse Jr.
8605 Explorer Drive
Colorado Springs, CO 80920

Dear Ms. Hadley:

Max has made a mess and blamed it on his brother Seth. Seth is only two and can't tell Mom that Max lied. Seth wouldn't get in any real trouble. So what's the harm? Will Max's conscience catch up to him?

I have enclosed a lively story entitled "Max's Mistake" for 4- to 8-year-old children. Along with my manuscript, I have enclosed an SASE for your reply.

Thank you for your time and I look forward to hearing from you.

Sincerely,

Casey Brown

Enc: Manuscript, SASE

Sample Cover Letter

Address
Phone Number
Email
Date

Editor
Boys' Quest
P.O. Box 227
Bluffton, OH 45817-0227

Dear Editor,

Don't think you can enjoy your favorite pastime of fishing in the dead of winter? Well, think again. Unbelieveably, fishing on a frozen lake is possible and fish can be plentiful. Not only is it exciting to learn a new way to fish, you will also enjoy the great outdoors in a very different way.

For many years my father took me on ice fishing trips. I always found it amazing that you could drill holes in the ice and catch live fish out of the frozen lake.

Enclosed for your consideration is a 500-word article on ice fishing entitled, "Fishing Through a Frozen Lake." The article includes information on safety tips, equipment, clothing, and tips for ice fishing. As per your writers' guidelines, I have included two black-and-white photos, which I have the JPEG files for if you are interested. I have also included a bibliography for your review.

I am a graduate of the Institute of Children's Literature and a member of SCBWI. My writing has been published in *Stories for Children Magazine, A Long Story Short, Kid Magazine Writers,* and *The National Writing for Children Center.*

Thank you for your time and consideration. I look forward to your response. An SASE is enclosed for your reply.

Sincerely,

Donna M. McDine

Enc: Ms, bibliography, B&W photos & SASE

Sample Outline

ARTICLE OUTLINE FOR "GETTING THEIR FEET WET"

I. Underwater home
   A. In Key Largo, Florida, scientists wake up, brush their teeth, and eat breakfast underwater.
   B. Dr. Ellen Prager has been studying coral reefs and marine science for years and is now chief scientist at Aquarius.
   C. Aquarius is an underwater ocean laboratory based at Conch Reef in the Florida Keys National Marine Sanctuary.
   D. Recently, Aquarius took on its 100th mission called Teacher Under the Sea.

II. Why study these habitats?
   A. Coral is an animal, but it creates a rock called limestone.
   B. Most corals are colonies of tiny animals called polyps. Over time, polyps grow and build up into underwater structures called reefs.
   C. Coral reefs provide food and shelter for a whole community of marine animals.
   D. The reefs protect beaches from waves that would wash the sand away, and the fish around reefs provide food to many countries.

III. How are the scientists able to live underwater?
   A. Aquanaut trainees undergo five days of training before each mission.
   B. Divers must know their depth at all times.
   C. Since they're underwater for days, their bodies fill with gas due to the higher pressure at the surface.
   D. Aquanauts must go through 17 hours of decompression before returning to the surface.

IV. Just like home
   A. The pressure inside Aquarius is the same pressure as the water outside.
   B. Air is piped in from the surface, so the aquanauts can breathe.
   C. The entryway, called the moon pool, remains open as the air pressure inside prevents the water from flowing in.
   D. Aquarius provides living and working space for a six-person crew.
   E. Amenities include air conditioning, a hot water shower, toilet, cooler, and microwave.

V. Conclusion
   A. Aquarius is not only dedicated to protecting one of Florida's most valuable marine resources, but it will continue to expand our knowledge of coral reefs, our oceans, and our planet.
   B. Perhaps Aquarius shows what life might be like in the future.

Bibliography

A thorough bibliography is particularly valuable to editors, who use these source lists as a way to determine how extensively a manuscript has been researched. In fact, many nonfiction editors review the bibliography even before the manuscript. A well-rounded, diverse bibliography not only shows that you've properly acknowledged and credited your sources of information, but that the finished piece is likely to present an original point of view that is supported by credible sources.

Some magazines require a bibliography as part of a submission package for nonfiction articles. (Bibliographies are rarely required for fiction, with the possible exception of historical fiction.) Unique research methods are required for every project but, in general, the bibliography should be made up of resources that are both historical and current, target adults and children, and cover primary and secondary sources. Search museums, libraries, and other organizations for primary documents such as naval reports, maps, bills of lading, court documents, song lyrics, and more. Your bibliography should also show that you plan on culling information from other sources, such as interviews with experts or other relevant individuals (a profile subject and those who know him or her, for example). It's also a good idea to mention your research in your cover letter, to explain your main sources and any other research-related issues.

Citation styles vary greatly, but several references are available and generally accepted for bibliographic format. Among these are: *The Chicago Manual of Style*; *Modern Language Association (MLA) Handbook*; or handbooks by news organizations such as the *New York Times*.

> To find expert sources to interview, read newspapers, magazines, and journals with articles about your topic. Current articles may include the names of specialists who are doing work in your area of interest, some of whom may be available for interviews.

Sample Bibliography

Bibliography for "Doctor Dog" by Jennifer Mattox

"Animal-Assisted Therapy Brings Patients One Step Closer to Healing," *Columbus Parent Magazine*, March 2007.

"Canine Companions for Independence," www.caninecompanions.org.

"Columbus Children's Hospital Staffs Full-Time 'Medical Dog' In New Animal-Assisted Therapy Program," March 2007, www.columbuschildrens.com.

Lundine, Jennifer. Telephone Interview. March 31, 2007. Speech pathologist at Children's Hospital, Columbus, Ohio.

Mehus-Roe, Kristen. *Working Dogs: True Stories of Dogs and Their Handlers*. Irvine, California: BowTie Press, 2003.

Writing Your Résumé

Many publications request a résumé along with queries or sample clips. You may have a résumé you use for job-hunting, but it isn't likely to address the needs of an editor, who is only interested in your writing experience. By reviewing a résumé, an editor can determine if a prospective writer has the necessary experience to research and write material for his or her publication.

If you have few writing credits, format your résumé so that your writing-related skills and experience appear first, such as writing a company newsletter or reports, or creating volunteer materials. Then briefly list your work history and educational information, followed by awards and professional memberships such as SCBWI. Pertinent job experience should always be highlighted, both on your résumé and in your cover or query letter.

Many writers tailor their résumé to be most relevant to the particular job or opportunity they are seeking. For example, if you're querying an educational publication, emphasize your experience as a writing instructor or a teacher; for a nonfiction editor, highlight any nonfiction writing credits first.

No one style or format is preferred, but make sure your name and email address appear at the top of the page. Keep your résumé concise—it should not be more than one page.

Sample Résumé

Joanna Coates
Address
Phone
Email

EDUCATION:

	University of Missouri, Columbia, MO
1980	M.Ed. Reading
1975	B.A. English Education

Missouri Certified Teacher of English and Reading Specialist

TEACHING EXPERIENCE:

1997–present	Instructor
	Adult Continuing Education ESL Classes
	Springfield College, Springfield, MO
1981-1995	Classroom Teacher
	Middle School English and Reading
	John Jay Middle School, Thornfield, MO

EDUCATIONAL MATERIAL PUBLISHED:

	Educational Insights
1995	FUN WITH READING II
	Story/activity kit
1993	FUN WITH READING I
	Story/activity kit

MEMBERSHIP:
Society of Children's Book Writers and Illustrators

Copyright and Contracts

Just like the movie you watched last night and the CD you listened to on the way to work this morning, your magazine article is one of many creative works that is afforded the protection of copyright. As one of the nation's "copyright-based industries," publishing relies heavily on the concept of obtaining legal ownership of written works. When you write an article, you own the legal rights to the manuscript, as well as the right to decide how it is reproduced and, for certain works, how it is performed or displayed.

As of 1998, your heirs can also enjoy the fruits of your labor: That's when Congress passed the Copyright Term Extension Act, which offers you copyright protection for your work created during or after 1978 for your lifetime plus 70 years, until you choose to sell all or part of the copyright for this work.

Do You Need to Register Your Work?

Thanks to copyright law, your work is protected from the moment it is recorded in a tangible medium, such as a computer file or on paper, without any need for legal action or counsel. You don't even need to register your work with the United States Copyright Office; in fact, most editors view an author's copyright notice on manuscripts as the sign of an amateur. A copy of the manuscript and a dated record of your submission will provide proof of creation, should the need arise.

If you do decide to register your work, obtain an application form and directions on the correct way to file your copyright application. Write to the Library of Congress, Copyright Office, 101 Independence Ave. S. E., Washington, DC 20559-6000. These forms and directions are also available online at: www.copyright.gov/forms. Copyright registration fees range from $35 (online) to $65 (paper).

If you have registered your unpublished manuscript with the Library of Congress, notify your editor of that fact once it is accepted for publication.

Rights Purchased by Magazines

As a writer and copyright holder, you have the right to decide how your work should be shared with the world. By agreeing to publication in a magazine, you also agree to transfer some of your rights over to the magazine so that your article can be printed and distributed as part of that publication. A publisher is restricted, however, on when, how, and where he or she may publish your manuscript—terms that are set down in a publishing contract. Below is a list of common rights that are purchased by magazines:

- **All World Rights:** The publisher purchases all rights to publish your work anywhere in the world any number of times. This includes all forms of media (both current and those which may be developed later). The publisher also has the right to all future use of the work, including reprints, syndication, creation of derivative works, and use in databases. You no longer have the right to sell or reproduce the work, unless you can negotiate for the return of certain rights (for example, book rights).

- **All World Serial Rights:** The publisher purchases all rights to publish your work in newspapers, magazines, and other serial publications throughout the world any number of times. You retain all other rights, such as the right to use it as a chapter in a book.

- **First Rights:** A publisher acquires the right to publish your work for the first time in any specified media. Electronic and nontraditional markets often seek these rights. All other rights, including reprint rights, belong to you.

- **Electronic Rights:** Publishers use this as a catch-all for inclusion in any type of electronic publication, such as CD-ROM, websites, ezines, or in an electronic database.

- **First North American Serial Rights:** The publisher can publish your work for the first time in a U.S. or Canadian periodical. You retain the book and North

American reprint rights, as well as first rights to a foreign market.

- **Second or Reprint Rights:** This allows a publication non-exclusive rights to print the material for the second time. You may not authorize second publication to occur until after the work has appeared in print by the publisher who bought first rights.

- **One-time Rights:** Often bought by regional publications, this means the publication has bought the right to use the material once. You may continue to sell the material elsewhere; however, you should inform the publisher if this work is being simultaneously considered for publication in a competing magazine.

You should be aware that an agreement may limit a publisher to the right to publish your work in certain media (e.g., magazines and other periodicals only) or the agreement may include wider-ranging rights (e.g., the right to publish the manuscript in a book or an audiocassette). The right may be limited to publishing within a specific geographic region or in a specific language. Any rights you retain allow you to resell the manuscript within the parameters of your agreement.

It is becoming increasingly common for magazines to purchase all rights, especially those that host Internet sites and make archives of previously published articles available to readers. Unless you have extensive publishing credentials, you may not want to jeopardize the opportunity to be published by insisting on selling limited rights.

Contracts and Agreements

Typically, when a publisher indicates an interest in your manuscript, he or she specifies what rights the publication will acquire. Then usually a publisher will send you a letter of agreement or a standard written contract spelling out the terms of the agreement.

If a publisher does not send you a written contract or agreement, you need to consider your options. While an oral agreement may be legally binding, it is not as easy to enforce as

Get It in Writing

If you've been offered a publishing contract, it's smart to make sure that all the details are down in writing. The following is a partial list of items that may seem obvious to both parties, but that should be clearly noted in your agreement:

- Are any expenses, i.e. telephone, gas, etc., covered for research purposes?
- Will you be able to see the article before publication?
- If the article will be accompanied by artwork, who is responsible for finding the art and/or paying for it?
- In what form does the magazine expect the manuscript to be delivered? On paper? Disk? Via e-mail?
- What is the due date?
- What is the length of the work?
- Are payment terms according to word length, time spent, or another measure?

a written one. To protect your interests, draft a letter outlining the terms as you understand them (e.g., a 500-word article without photos, first North American serial rights, paying on acceptance at $.05 a word). Send two copies of the letter to the editor (with a self-addressed, stamped envelope), asking him or her to sign one and return it to you if the terms are correct.

Every writer has the right to negotiate contract terms, so take a close look at yours before you sign. For example, payment may be an issue, but before you start negotiating you should know exactly what the job is worth to you. Put a monetary value on your time: How long will it take you to produce the work? Calculations like these can help determine an appropriate rate of pay, and help justify your request for additional money.

If you do need to negotiate, always be professional, and act as a partner with the editor, working toward terms that will benefit both parties. If you don't understand something, ask. Most editors work with freelance writers on a daily basis and are willing to make changes. If an agreement can't be reached, you always have the option of not signing—and selling your work somewhere else.

Work Made for Hire

Another term that is appearing more frequently in contracts is *work made for hire*. As a freelance writer, most editors treat you as an independent contractor (not an employee) who writes articles for their publication. Magazine editors can assign or commission articles to freelancers as works made for hire, making the finished article property of the publisher.

Under current copyright laws, only certain types of commissioned works are considered works made for hire, and only when both the publisher and the commissioned writer agree in writing. These works typically include items such as contributions to "collective works" such as magazines. A contract or agreement clearly stating that the material is a work made for hire must be signed by both parties and be in place before the material is written. Once a writer agrees to these terms, he or she no longer has any rights to the work.

Most writer organizations recommend not signing a work-for-hire agreement in any situation, but there are some instances in which work-for-hire contracts may be appropriate. The ideal is to sell as few rights as possible, leaving the magazine to re-negotiate with you if it wants to purchase additional rights. This scenario ensures that you won't lose out on any compensation related to future use of your work. Before you refuse a work-for-hire arrangement, however, consider the market, the article topic, and the pay. If the initial pay is very good, or if chances are slim that you'll be able to sell the article elsewhere, signing might be your best option.

Note that a pre-existing piece, such as an unsolicited manuscript that is accepted for publication, is not considered a commissioned work.

Guidelines for Permission to Quote

When you want to quote another writer's words in a manuscript you're preparing, you must get that writer's permission. If you don't, you could be sued for copyright infringement. Here are some guidelines:

- Any writing published in the U.S. prior to 1923 is in the public domain, as are works created by the U.S. government. Such material may be quoted without permission, but the source should be cited.
- No specific limits are set as to the length of permitted quotations in your articles: different publishers have various requirements. Generally, if you quote more than a handful of words, you should seek permission. Always remember to credit your sources.
- The doctrine of "fair use" allows quoting portions of a copyrighted work for certain purposes, as in a review, news reporting, nonprofit educational uses, or research. Contrary to popular belief, there is no absolute word limit on fair use. But as a general rule, never quote more than a few successive paragraphs from a book or article and credit the source.
- If you're submitting a manuscript that contains quoted material, you'll need to obtain permission from the source to quote the material before it is published. If you're uncertain about what to do, your editor should be able to advise you.

Resources

Interested in finding out more about writers and their rights under the law? Check these sources for further information, and look into some of the other writers' career aids in the Writers Resources section, starting on page 303:

- The Publishing Law Center, www.publaw.com/legal.html

- *The Copyright Handbook: What Every Writer Needs to Know,* 10th Edition, by Attorney Stephen Fishman. Nolo, 2008.

- *Copyright Companion for Writers,* by Tonya Evans-Walls. Legal Write Publications, 2007.

Last Steps and Follow Up

Before mailing your manuscript, check the pages for neatness, readability, and proper page order. Proofread for typographical errors. Redo pages if necessary. Keep a copy of the manuscript for your records.

Mailing Requirements

Assemble the pages (unstapled) and place your cover letter on top of the first page.

Send manuscripts over 5 pages in length in a 9x12 or 10x13 manila envelope. Include a same-size SASE marked "First Class." If submitting to a foreign magazine, enclose the proper amount of International Reply Coupons (IRC) for return postage. Mail manuscripts under 5 pages in a large business-size envelope with a same-size SASE folded inside.

Package your material carefully and address the outer envelope to the magazine editor. Send your submission via first-class or priority mail. Don't use certified or registered mail. (See Postage Information, page 34.)

Follow Up with the Editor

Some writers contend that waiting for an editor to respond is the hardest part of writing. But wait you must. Editors usually respond within the time period specified in the listings.

If you don't receive a response by the stated response time, allow at least three weeks to pass before you contact the editor. At that time, send a letter with a self-addressed, stamped envelope requesting to know the status of your submission.

The exception to this general rule is when you send a return postcard with a manuscript. In that case, look for your postcard about three weeks after mailing the manuscript. If you don't receive it by then, write to the editor requesting confirmation that it was received.

If more than two months pass after the stated response time and you don't receive any response, send a letter withdrawing your work from consideration. At that point, you can send your query or manuscript to the next publication on your list.

What You Can Expect

The most common responses to a submission are an impersonal rejection letter, a personalized rejection letter, an offer to look at your material "on speculation," or an assignment.

If you receive an impersonal rejection note, revise your manuscript if necessary, and send your work to the next editor on your list. If you receive a personal note, send a thank-you note. If you receive either of the last two responses, you know what to do!

Set Up a Tracking System

To help you keep track of the status of your submissions, you may want to establish a system in a notebook, in a computer file, or on file cards (see below).

This will keep you organized and up-to-date on the status of your queries and manuscripts and on the need to follow up with certain editors.

SENT QUERIES TO THE FOLLOWING PUBLICATIONS

Editor	Publication	Topic	Date Sent	Postage	Accepted/ Rejected	Rights Offered

SENT MANUSCRIPTS TO THE FOLLOWING PUBLICATIONS

Editor	Publication	Title	Date Sent	Postage	Accepted/ Rejected	Rights Offered

Frequently Asked Questions

How do I request a sample copy and writers' guidelines?

Write a brief note to the magazine: "Please send me a recent sample copy and writers' guidelines. If there is any charge, please enclose an invoice and I will pay upon receipt." The magazine's website, if it has one, offers a faster and less expensive alternative. Many companies put a part of the magazine, writers' guidelines, and sometimes a theme list or editorial calendar on the Internet.

How do I calculate the amount of postage for a sample copy?

Check the listing in this directory. In some cases the amount of postage will be listed. If the number of pages is given, use that to estimate the amount of postage by using the postage chart at the end of this section. For more information on postage and how to obtain stamps, see page 34.

Should my email submission 'package' be different than a submission via snail mail?

In general, an email submission should contain the same elements as a mailed one—i.e. a solid article description, sources, etc. In all cases, writers' guidelines should be followed to the letter when it comes to sending writing samples, bibliographies, and other requirements, either as separate file attachments or embedded in the email text.

What do I put in a cover letter if I have no publishing credits or relevant personal experience?

In this case, you may want to forego a formal cover letter and send your manuscript with a brief letter stating: "Enclosed is my manuscript, (Insert Title), for your review." For more information on cover letters, see pages 19–22.

How long should I wait before contacting an editor after I have submitted my manuscript?

The response time given in the listings can vary, and it's a good idea to wait three to four weeks after the stated response time before sending a brief note to the editor asking about the status of your manuscript. You might use this opportunity to add a new sales pitch or include additional material to show that the topic is continuing to generate interest. If you do not get a satisfactory response or you want to send your manuscript elsewhere, send a certified letter to the editor withdrawing the work from consideration and requesting its return. You are then free to submit the work to another magazine.

I don't need my manuscript returned. How do I indicate that to an editor?

With the capability to store manuscripts electronically and print out additional copies easily, some writers keep postage costs down by enclosing a self-addressed, stamped postcard (SASP) saying, "No need to return my manuscript. Please use this postcard to advise me of the status of my manuscript. Thank you."

Common Publishing Terms

All rights: Contractual agreement by which a publisher acquires the copyright and all use of author's material (see page 27).

Anthology: A collection of selected literary pieces.

Anthropomorphization: Attributing human form or personality to things not human (i.e., animals).

Assignment: Manuscript commissioned by an editor for a stated fee.

Bimonthly: A publication that appears every two months.

Biweekly: A publication issued every two weeks.

Byline: Author's name credited at the heading of an article.

Caption: Description or text accompanying an illustration or photograph.

CD-ROM (compact disc read-only-memory)**:** Non-erasable compact disc containing data that can be read by a computer.

Clip: Sample of a published work.

Contributor's copies: Copies of the publication issue in which the writer's work appears.

Copyedit: To edit with close attention to style and mechanics.

Copyright: Legal rights that protect an author's work (see page 27).

Cover letter: Brief letter sent with a manuscript introducing the writer and presenting the materials enclosed (see page 19).

Disk submission: Manuscript that is submitted on a computer disk.

Early readers: Children 4 to 7 years.

Editorial calendar: List of topics, themes, or special sections that are planned for upcoming issues for a specific time period.

Electronic submission: Manuscript transmitted to an editor from one computer to another through a modem.

Email (electronic mail)**:** Messages sent from one computer to another via computer network or modem.

English-language rights: The right to publish a manuscript in any English-speaking country.

Filler: Short item that fills out a page (e.g., joke, light verse, or fun fact).

First serial rights: The right to publish a work for the first time in a periodical; often limited to a specific geographical region (e.g., North America or Canada) (see page 27).

Genre: Category of fiction characterized by a particular style, form, or content, such as mystery or fantasy.

Glossy: Photo printed on shiny rather than matte-finish paper.

Guidelines: See **Writers' guidelines.**

In-house: See **Staff written.**

International Reply Coupon (IRC): Coupon exchangeable in any foreign country for postage on a single-rate, surface-mailed letter.

Kill fee: Percentage of the agreed-upon fee paid to a writer if an editor decides not to use a purchased manuscript.

Layout: Plan for the arrangement of text and artwork on a printed page.

Lead: Beginning of an article.

Lead time: Length of time between assembling and printing an issue.

Libel: Any false published statement intended to expose another to public ridicule or personal loss.

Manuscript: A typewritten or computer-printed version of a document (as opposed to a published version).

Masthead: The printed matter in a newspaper or periodical that gives the title and pertinent details of ownership, advertising rates, and subscription rates.

Middle-grade readers: Children 8 to 12 years.

Modem: An internal device or a small electrical box that plugs into a computer; used to transmit data between computers, often via telephone lines.

Ms/mss: Manuscript/manuscripts.

One-time rights: The right to publish a piece once, often not the first time (see page 28).

On spec: Refers to writing "on speculation," without an editor's commitment to purchase the manuscript.

Outline: Summary of a manuscript's contents, usually nonfiction, organized under subheadings with descriptive sentences under each.

Payment on acceptance: Author is paid following an editor's decision to accept a manuscript.

Payment on publication: Author is paid following the publication of the manuscript.

Pen name/pseudonym: Fictitious name used by an author.

Pre-K: Children under 5 years of age; also known as *pre-school*.

Proofread: To read and mark errors, usually in printed text.

Query: Letter to an editor to promote interest in a manuscript or an idea.

Rebus story: A "see and say" story form, using pictures followed by the written words; often written for pre-readers.

Refereed journal: Publication that requires all manuscripts be reviewed by an editorial or advisory board.

Reprint: Another printing of an article or story; can be in a different magazine format, such as an anthology.

Reprint rights: See **Second serial rights.**

Response time: Average length of time for an editor to accept or reject a submission and contact the writer with his or her decision.

Résumé: Account of one's qualifications, including educational and professional background, as well as publishing credits.

SAE: Self-addressed envelope (no postage).

SASE: Self-addressed, stamped envelope.

SASP: Self-addressed stamped postcard.

Second serial rights: The right to publish a manuscript that has appeared in another publication; also known as *Reprint rights* (see page 28).

Semiannual: Occurring every six months or twice a year.

Semimonthly: Occurring twice a month.

Semiweekly: Occurring twice a week.

Serial: A publication issued as one of a consecutively numbered and indefinitely continued series.

Serial rights: See **First serial rights.**

Sidebar: A short article that accompanies a feature article and highlights one aspect of the feature's subject.

Simultaneous submission: Manuscript submitted to more than one publisher at the same time; also known as multiple submission.

Slant: Specific approach to a subject to appeal to a certain readership.

Slush pile: Term used within the publishing industry to describe unsolicited manuscripts.

Solicited manuscript: Manuscript that an editor has requested or agreed to consider.

Staff written: Prepared by members of the magazine's staff; also known as *in-house*.

Syndication rights: The right to distribute serial rights to a given work through a syndicate of periodicals.

Synopsis: Condensed description or summary of a manuscript.

Tabloid: Publication printed on an ordinary newspaper page, turned sideways and folded in half.

Tearsheet: A page from a newspaper or magazine (periodical) containing a printed story or article.

Theme list: See **Editorial calendar.**

Transparencies: Color slides, not color prints.

Unsolicited manuscript: Any manuscript not specifically requested by an editor.

Work made for hire: Work specifically ordered, commissioned, and owned by a publisher for its exclusive use (see page 29).

World rights: Contractual agreement whereby the publisher acquires the right to reproduce the work throughout the world (see page 27); also known as *all rights*.

Writers' guidelines: Publisher's editorial objectives or specifications, which usually include word lengths, readership level, and subject matter.

Writing sample: Example of your writing style, tone, and skills; may be a published or unpublished piece.

Young adult: Readers 12 to 18 years.

Postage Information

How Much Postage?

When you're sending a manuscript to a magazine, enclose a self-addressed, stamped envelope with sufficient postage; this way, if the editor does not want to use your manuscript, it can be returned to you. To help you calculate the proper amount of postage for your SASE, here are the U.S. postal rates for first-class mailings in the U.S. and from the U.S. to Canada based on the latest increase. Rates are expected to increase again, so please check with your local Post Office, or check the U.S. Postal Service website at usps.com.

Ounces	9x12 Envelope (Approx. no. of pages)	U.S. First-Class Postage Rate	Rate from U.S. to Canada
1	1–5	$0.88	$1.03
2	6–10	1.05	1.29
3	11–15	1.22	1.55
4	16–20	1.39	1.81
5	21–25	1.56	2.07
6	26–30	1.73	2.33
7	31–35	1.90	2.59
8	36–40	2.07	2.85

The amount of postage and size of envelope necessary to receive a sample copy and writers' guidelines are usually stated in the magazine listing. If this information is not provided, use the chart above to help gauge the proper amount of postage.

How to Obtain Stamps

People living in the U.S., Canada, or overseas can acquire U.S. stamps through the mail from the Philately Fulfillment Service Center. Call 800-STAMP-24 (800-782-6724) to request a catalogue or place an order. For overseas, the telephone number is 816-545-1100. You pay the cost of the stamps plus a postage and handling fee based on the value of the stamps ordered, and the stamps are shipped to you. Credit card information (MasterCard, Visa, and Discover cards only) is required for fax orders. The fax number is 816-545-1212. If you order through the catalogue, you can pay with a U.S. check or an American Money Order. Allow 3–4 weeks for delivery.

Gateway to the Markets

Spin Science Facts into Gold

By S. M. Ford

"There are no seven wonders of the world in the eyes of a child. There are seven million."
Walt Streightiff

Kids and science writers are curious as the proverbial cat. The world is full of fascinating facts and amazing details to explore. No question is too small to ask. The typical four-year-old's natural inclination to ask *why?* is a positive attribute for science writers who can satisfy the desire to discover that is inherent in young readers. *Why, how,* and *what if* questions are the straw that science writers can turn to gold.

Cricket Editor Lonnie Plecha makes the point clearly when he says, "A good science story for children is one that would also hold the attention of an intellectually curious adult."

Questionability

Exploration of the world has no better avenue than either the Socratic method or the scientific method, both based on questioning. If you want to find science topics to write about you might begin by asking: What have I always wondered about? What concepts, actions, events, or things do I not understand? What have I seen or heard that has sparked my interest? What am I afraid of, and do I know why? Find out.

Rosanne Tolin, Editor of *Imagination-Café,* says that for her, the ideal science submission is "something that's either a  gross-out piece (kids love that!), or that answers all those *why* or *what* questions (Why do cows moo? What are clouds?)."

Managing Editor Jude Isabella of *Yes Mag,* a science magazine for ages 9 to 14, says, "We like articles to be focused on something new in the world of science, not just how *neat* something is. Our sci/tech department focuses on reporting new discoveries. Our themes might not be topical (in current news), but we find the latest research in the field. Or we seek to overturn assumptions about a topic. We like science profiles when researchers do exciting things in the field, with good photos." Recent themes of *Yes Mag* have included medieval science, the science of magic, urban wildlife, and cycling.

You may know answers to a child's *why*, but validate your knowledge with research from three or more sources. Nothing turns off an editor faster than inaccurate information disguised as fact. Another benefit of research is it often leads to more ideas.

The Internet is helpful to begin research, but verify information you discover with print and primary sources. *Yes Mag* expects writers to interview scientists. "We prefer primary sources, researchers, and their research papers." Isabella says he receives "too many animal stories, or just plain newsy things I read in the *New York Times* science section every Tuesday."

Do not forget to check out science museums, zoos, aquariums, science societies, universities, and government agencies, as well as specialized libraries, which can all lead you to experts. An interview with a scientist, museum curator, or professor can also provide human interest if you investigate the struggles and successes they have experienced. Their enthusiasms can fuel yours.

Another approach is to research potential markets to find the subjects that are of interest to them—especially if they work with themes, like *AppleSeeds* and *Odyssey*. "Since *AppleSeeds* is a social studies, not a science magazine per se, our ideal submissions place science topics in a social studies context," says Editor Susan Buckley. "We are interested in the human aspects of science more than the how-to aspects."

Interview your experts in person, by phone, or by email. Many are willing to talk about their areas of interest. Do not expect them to start at the beginning, however, and do not waste their time with your lack of knowledge. Learn as much as you can about your subject, and then prepare a short list of intelligent questions.

Discover what makes your expert passionate about what he does, what she has discovered, or how something works. Be prepared for the interview to go off

> **"A good science story for children is one that also holds the attention of an intellectually curious adult."**

topic into something you never would have thought to ask. If you are doing a face-to-face interview, take good notes and, after requesting your source's permission, consider recording the conversation. Your last question in an interview should always be, "May I contact you again if I have further questions?"

Star-Forming

Once you have gathered all your research material, narrow your focus. Sight in on one specific person or discovery. Do not provide informational panoramas. Instead, zoom in on a particular aspect of the topic that you determine will be the most interesting, and new, for your audience. For example, do not write about all galaxies, or even about the whole of the Milky Way. Write, perhaps, about the new star-forming regions of our galaxy discovered in 2010.

If your subject matter is not related to a recent discovery, use a fresh or unique angle that will draw in editors and readers. Consider the article forms that appeal to you and to your potential readers, and that will best suit your topic:

- a profile or interview of a scientist
- a report on a new discovery
- how something works
- a science experiment
- a practical application piece
- what is coming in the future
- how to get involved
- a "why" piece
- a personal experience

The slant you take can make all the difference between a successful article and a rejection. Select the appropriate angle for each magazine you pursue. "A *Cricket* science article is centered around a problem, issue, or question, and is not just a recitation of known truths," Plecha says. "Our stories tend to portray the pursuit of knowledge—not a collection of settled facts. We believe *Cricket* readers will identify with the incessant curiosity about the world that drives working scientists." Isabella describes *Yes Mag* this way: "Slightly cheeky, irreverent but also full of wonder while prodding readers to think critically."

Symbiosis: Readers and Magazines

Eureka moments, or amazing facts that wow you, make you laugh, or gross you out—all the ones that make you want to know more—are means of inviting readers into your universe. Grab hold of them with your title, and especially with your lead.

Write with the appropriate tone for the market you have chosen. Like drinking buttermilk when expecting whole milk, an article with a different tone than the rest of a magazine jars the reader. *Nature Friend,* for instance, is a conservative Christian nature magazine for children ages 6 to 12. Its subjects, articles, and tone will be quite different than for, say, Scholastic's *Science World.*

Editor Kevin Shank of *Nature Friend* says, "God's Word will not pass away, so it is the litmus test for any science article written" for them. The goal of this publication is "to partner with like-minded writers who help us fulfill our goal of honoring God while educating children in the realm of nature."

Yet another tone and direction is preferred at *Imagination-Café,* which Tolin calls "factual, kid-friendly, interactive, and fun!" She wants neither preaching nor "too much editorial voice."

Lively, clear, and age-appropriate writ-

> ## "Our stories tend to portray the pursuit of knowledge—not a collection of settled facts."

ing keeps readers' attention all the way through. Make your article a joy to read through surprising facts, strong narrative, personal interest, humor, or language, in the form of imagery, puns, turns of phrase, and so on. Challenge your readers with questions, and interesting things to consider.

Do not inundate readers with scientific terminology, but also do not hesitate to use correct terms and explain them well, but briefly. Depending on the word and your audience age, consider a glossary and a pronunciation guide. You want your material to be clear and make sense without condescending.

Use comparisons with the familiar to

explain the unfamiliar. You might compare the size or length of an everyday object, or another fact, to present something new to readers. For example, explain the deepest part of the ocean, the Mariana Trench, by saying you would have to take the equivalent of seven round trips between New York and Los Angeles before reaching the bottom.

In science, observation is golden. When possible, explain scientific concepts and unusual facts to young readers with comparisons to the smell, taste, sound, or touch of an ordinary item.

For scientist profiles, make the person feel real to readers. Individual foibles, eccentricities, and dedication provide interest. Highlight what the person says when trying to prove a point, share excitement, or display character. If you know something about your subject's childhood that relates to the age of your audience, communicate that fact or story.

Customize

Science is a field in which accuracy is absolutely essential—which offers a reminder to writers that it is truly as important in their field. Inspect your article for unnecessary words or paragraphs, clarity, and accuracy in quotes and facts. Revise your article to meet the required word count.

"Many authors of unsuccessful submissions simply do not take writing science for children seriously enough, and fail to invest the same discipline and energy as would be expected in writing for adults," says Plecha. "Too often,

potentially interesting topics are given a quite cursory treatment; explanations are superficial, vague, or imprecise; authors presume too much or too little background knowledge of our readers; and, much too frequently, the author's facts turn out not to be facts at all, so the manuscript contains inaccuracies or partial truths that need correcting."

Remember one article does not fit all, so beyond accuracy of fact, check your accuracy in targeting a market. Customize your material for each magazine you choose to approach.

For *AppleSeeds*, science topics must relate to social studies—history, geography, sociology, economics. "Environmental and geographical topics are especially relevant, also technology," says Buckley. A bibliography is not required. Send queries only.

At *Cricket*, says Plecha, "We are open to whatever an author finds genuinely interesting. Short, newsy reports on the latest discovery, however, would be for a more topical science magazine than for *Cricket*." An article on a working scientist needs to focus on his or her work—the compelling area of inquiry. "Childhood experiences that shaped the adult scientist can help children connect with the article, so that it seems not just to be about another accomplished adult but what the child might aspire to become." *Cricket* requires that a solid bibliography accompany submissions. "Also, we appreciate a short cover letter highlighting any relevant qualifications in science the author might have or any working scientists who were consulted."

Imagination-Café has a Creature Feature department that showcases "nonfiction articles and trivia about animals, both the unusual and adorable," explains Tolin. She would like to see articles on how things work, discoveries, and science experiments. Remember, she says, "We're not a beginner's market; study the site before submitting!"

If you have experience writing about science for six- to nine-year-old children, *Know*, a companion magazine of *Yes Mag*, invites you to contact Editor Adrienne Mason with samples of published work. *Know* does not accept queries or unsolicited submissions.

Nature Friend needs science projects for ages 8 to 16. In addition, Shank says, "We tend to run short on stories of families or children interacting with nature. Stories may be true or fiction. We generally have plenty of essays about nature." Check out this magazine's goals and the "objectionable words and ideas" in its online writers' guidelines.

Yes Mag highlights Canadian science and scientists. "Due to the requirements of a Canadian government grant, at this

A to Z List of Science Studies

Anemology: the study of winds

Bacteriology: the study of bacteria in relation to disease and agriculture

Cytology: the study of the structure, origin, function, and pathology of cells

Dioptrics: the study of light refraction

Entomology: the study of insects

Fluviology: the study of watercourses

Geophysics: the study of physical and geological properties of earth, minerals, and rocks

Heliology: the science of the sun

Koniology: the study of atmospheric pollutants and dust

Limnology: the study of lakes

Metrology: the science of weights and measures

Noology: the science of the intellect

Oneirology: a scientific study of dreams and their contents

Philology: the science of language and linguistics

Rheology: the study of the deformation and flow of matter

Somatology: the science of the properties of matter

Thalassography: the science of the sea

Virology: the study of viruses

Zymology: the science of fermentation

time we are only accepting queries from Canadian writers." For new writers, Isabella says bibliographies should be included with articles.

Photographs, sidebars, or additional materials such as an activity or experiment often clinch a sale because they round out and deepen an article. But as always, know your market and its preferences.

Cricket wants every article to stand on its own, and it finds photos for articles. *Nature Friend* has specific and detailed photo guidelines. For *AppleSeeds,* says Buckley, "Ideas for sidebars and activities are welcomed but should not be written. We appreciate all links or ideas for photo sources, and will accept digital images, after the query." Tolin says, "Sidebars that are hands-on, such as experiments, are awesome" for *Imagination-Café.* She likes jpegs of quality photos to accompany these sidebars. Sidebars, lists, and digital photos are pluses for *Yes Mag.*

If you find a science topic interesting or unique, and can convey the details in a kid-friendly way, you will sell your work to magazine editors. So go out and spin straw—uhhmm, facts—into gold.

Sample Science Subjects

- *AppleSeeds,* ages 6 to 9
  - "Eww, Gross!" (bubonic plague)
  - "Eat Your Candy!" (hydroponics)
  - "Where Does It Go When You Go?" (digestion)
  - "All Wrapped Up: The Many Tasks of Mummymakers"
- *Cricket,* ages 9 to 14
  - "Dragon Spit" (Komodo dragons)
  - "The Life of the Loggerhead"
  - "New York's First Air Train"
  - "Why Is It So Hard to Get Ketchup Out of the Bottle?" (thixotropic solutions)
  - "A Bright Idea" (why light bulbs burn out, at the atomic level)
- *Imagination-Café,* ages 7 to 12
  - "How's Your Taste, Bud?"
  - "You Don't Say!" (body language)
- *Know,* ages 6 to 9
  - "The Sweetest Scoop" (ice cream)
  - "Sticky Science"
  - "The Winter Olympics"
- *Nature Friend,* ages 8 to 16
  - "The Princely Pileated Woodpecker"
  - "In Our Skies" (comets, asteroids, meteors)
  - "The Diet of Our Lungs"
  - "Rats to the Rescue"
- *Odyssey,* ages 9 to 14
  - "Blood Stains Be Gone!"
  - "Robot Scientist"
  - "Mysterious Space Blob"
  - "Hyena Poop Hairballs"
- *Yes Mag,* ages 10 to 15
  - "Food Fraud Investigators"
  - "When Grizzlies Go Polar"
  - "Hocus Focus: The Science Behind Magic"

Writing to a Theme:
Unusual Pairings, Creative Takes

By Katherine Swarts

Magazine theme lists can be useful to writers stuck for query ideas. But some writers limit themselves by assuming that a given theme may be incompatible with a certain category or approach. What can the music historian say about the theme of time, or the poet about mathematics?

You might be surprised how much.

Matchmaking

"Try to make connections between disparate areas—machines and recipes, biography and checklists, poetry and math," says Jamie Bryant, Founder and Editor in Chief of *Kiki*, for 8- to 14-year-old girls. "One of my favorite examples is *Mathematickles*, by Betsy Franco, a book of haiku about math concepts. See if you can create fun out of two elements normally not associated with each other."

Carus Publishing's Cobblestone division publishes themed magazines almost exclusively. "Because our issues usually cover a country or region," says Editor Elizabeth Carpentiere of *Faces*, for readers ages 9 to 14, "authors who love to write about sports should be able to find a sport that is unique or important to a culture. The same goes for art, music, and science."

"I urge writers to be creative and imaginative," says Susan Buckley, Editor of Cobblestone's *AppleSeeds*, whose readers are 6 to 9. "We welcome unusual takes. For an issue on time, someone proposed an article on how the concept of time is integral to music. I never would have thought of that!"

Some writers have the opposite problem: Their interests are too obviously connected to the topic. If you love bird-watching and a magazine announces an issue on outdoor hobbies, your first impulse may be to propose an article on using binoculars or field guides. With over 45 million bird-watchers in the United States alone, hundreds of writers will share that first impulse. Even if your query arrives first, the editor's reaction may be "been there, done that."

Editor Lynn Gilliam of *Pockets* advises writers to identify "the first thing you think of when you think of that theme—and don't write about that! I've just finished putting together an issue on serving others. There were several well-written stories under consideration, but it was difficult to pull the issue together because almost every story was about a child serving at a homeless shelter. That's a strong aspect of the theme, and I wanted one good story on that. But I'm not going to choose four stories for one issue with that as the setting! There are so many ways kids can serve others."

Carpentiere agrees: "We recently did an issue on the U.S. West Coast. I told writers at a workshop that I would immediately throw away any queries about the general history of Hollywood. We brainstormed and came up with numerous articles that would allow us to cover Hollywood in a less clichéd manner. As it turned out, one of those writers wrote a piece for the issue on non-conventional Hollywood jobs: special effects makeup artist, software engineer, assistant director of animation."

"Writers might take a two-pronged approach I call 'meat and potatoes meets blue sky,'" suggests Steve Rabey, Editor of *YouthWorker Journal.* "Submit two story proposals. First, for meat and potatoes, find an angle or personal story that covers the fundamental aspects. This lets the editor know you grasp the key topic. Then, for blue sky, use your imagination or spend some time on directed Google searches to find a unique and different approach." Doing it this way "doubles your chance for making a sale and lets the editor know you can do both basic stories and more complicated assignments."

If It Doesn't Fit, Don't Force It

Another mistake—especially common among those eager to break in at a high-prestige magazine—is forging ahead with an idea even after it becomes clear that the idea and the magazine or theme list are ill-matched. Bryant offers a list of warning signs that an author is trying to force a square-peg topic into a round-hole theme:

- "The piece becomes repetitive or unnecessarily wordy." If you spend

> **"Take a two-pronged approach I call 'meat and potatoes meets blue sky.' It will double your chance for making a sale."**

three-fourths of an article explaining what you are talking about, rethink your topic.

- "The proportion of the piece that feels tightly connected to the theme is small compared to the rest of the article." Writing an article on Denver skyscrapers and slipping in a two-paragraph anecdote from a tenant's Caribbean trip does not make it an article on cruise ships.
- "It's easy to go off on a tangent." If you are quickly distracted from your article's supposed thesis, that may be a warning you are not committed to the theme.
- "You spend too long working on a single block of text." Heavy editing is a part of writing, but if you just cannot seem to get a section right, that may be because it is in the wrong article.
- "If you can't have a conversation with a person in that age range about the topic, the article probably won't work." The topic itself may be too mature, or too childish, for the audience. "If you're writing a piece for 8-year-olds, try talking to an 8-year-old about it. Be aware of how engaged the child is," concludes Bryant.

"The biggest problem I encounter," says Carpentiere, "is writers trying to fit adult topics into a children's magazine without modifying them to make them age-appropriate. Presenting a topic for children does not just mean using smaller words. You have to realize which aspects of the topic will appeal to children and which aspects will go right over their heads or worse, bore them." Or frighten them.

The Exotic Topic

Now, we all have passions. It might be collecting lunch boxes from the 1960s, Mexican folk art, beagles, or the green revolution. If your life's passion is totally unfamiliar to the general public, you have to work harder just to find markets in the first place.

"It's easier to place content for some topics than for others," admits Bryant. One idea she suggests can help: "Use a thesaurus to see how many words connect to your area of interest. For example, *sewing* may link to *craft, fiber, stitching, darning, dressmaking, embroidering, mending, needlecraft, needlework, patching, seaming, stitchery,* and *tailoring.*"

The typical theme-oriented periodical has an overall focus on a fairly broad subject area (hobbies, spirituality, science, etc.), so if your interest is a narrow one, consider the larger categories into which it falls. Do not stop at the obvious here. *Chemistry experiments* would work in children's science magazines, but also in parenting magazines ("Play Chemistry with Your Kids"), educational or home-schooling magazines ("Fun, Winning Strategies for Science Fairs"), and even craft and family magazines ("Hot Stuff: The Chemistry of Cooking").

"Almost every idea has components that match other interests," says Lou Waryncia, Cobblestone Publishing's Editorial Director. "If the theme is the American Revolution and your interest is food, what did soldiers eat on the battlefield? How did they cook? How

---

My Target Market Doesn't Have a Theme List . . . Or Does It?

Even magazines without official theme lists may replay certain topics often enough to make those subjects, categories, or formats especially good bets for queries. "Read through an entire year of back issues," says Lou Waryncia, Editorial Director of Cobblestone Publishing. "Libraries are a good source. Is there a certain type of article that appears in every issue no matter what the theme is? Does the time of year influence the type of articles published? Do certain themes or ideas repeat themselves in different ways? Look for these situations and you can figure out what types of articles might happen in the future."

Once you develop a basic understanding of a magazine's mission and focus, it rarely hurts to ask a question directly. "Never underestimate the willingness of an editor to help," says Waryncia. "Send an email asking for advice and direction on themes. Offer some suggested themes based on your study of the publication. If you approach an editor in a professional, maybe-I-can-help-you way, you should get some response—or an assignment."

was food stored, carried? Look for the human characteristics of a theme and you'll find many different ways to approach a topic. A good example: *Odyssey* did an issue on art in science. There was an article on a cell phone orchestra—unexpected, but perfect."

"A writer should always keep eyes open for potential markets," notes Carpentiere. "The more a writer researches and works on a topic, the more ways of presenting it he or she will uncover."

Redirect

Stretch your personal limits and typical perspectives. "One of the best places to start is at a kid's level," says

Waryncia. "What seems obvious to adults is often a mystery for kids. What was the kid's perspective of a particular event or time? What were the contributions of kids? How was life different for children?"

"Think in terms of a college course catalogue," suggests Bryant. "If you like gardening, think about what college students need to cover to get a degree in horticulture." Most colleges post their course lists online. "Seeing the menu of classes required for that degree could give you insights into other fields that connect to yours, and by extension, other publications that might be interested in your work."

Seeing what other magazine markets have already published can be helpful, but do not get too caught up in trends that seem of high interest yet are already arcing down. "Spend time at a news-

What Do These Topics Have in Common?

Try this exercise for matching topics with seemingly dissimilar themes. Make a list of five article titles for each pair of items listed below.

● Terrorism and humor: *Example:* "The Five Most Outrageous False Alarms Ever"
● Computers and fine art: *Example:* "Would Leonardo Paint with Pixels?"
● Natural disasters and mathematics: *Example:* "How Scientists Count a Season's Hurricanes in Advance"
● Health and energy efficiency: *Example:* "Are Weatherproofed Windows Poisoning Your Air?"
● Archaeology and the modern urban lifestyle: *Example:* "What 1970s Garbage Tells Us"
● Biography and quizzes: *Example:* "Could You Be a Martha Washington?"
● Work vehicles and recipes: *Example:* "Birthday Cakes That Thrill the Young Truck Lover"

stand," advises Waryncia. "You can pick up hundreds of magazines, brimming with information. And, buying magazines helps the industry grow and provides more markets."

Bryant advises subscribing to magazines that interest you as a writer, too, "so you have a sense of the material that has been recently published. By seeing what has been done in the past couple of years, you'll have a better sense of what the magazine won't want." Not only will you avoid sending ideas or queries that repeat what a magazine has already done, you will have the plus of gaining a feel for whether its overall style (humorous, conversational, scholarly, partisan) is compatible with yours.

Ultimately, being true to a theme is not enough. No magazine wants an article that does not strongly reflect its focus and mission—and no magazine fails to value thoughtful writing that enhances its reputation.

Many magazines do not have a formal theme list, but have a default set of interests related to the year or the times: winter-related topics in winter, subjects related to the next Olympics, or the anniversary of a major historical figure's birth or death or a critical event.

Return to timeliness and your own true passions when ideas seem not to be coming. "Research events that connect with your area of interest," says Bryant, such as "upcoming art exhibits, anniversaries of kid-oriented organizations, and cultural festivals. As you read adult newspapers and magazines, shop for ideas that could be repurposed for children. As you see trends in the larger world, you'll be better able to anticipate things that could translate to children's magazines."

Make a file now for upcoming subjects in magazines you like, and start collecting materials and formulating ideas. Some may pan out, and some may not, but if one idea does not work for one publication, it may for another.

Calling All Boys —
And Writers for Boys

By Sue Bradford Edwards

Getting busy boys to read is often difficult, but some magazines make it their goal—and accomplish it with top-notch fiction. They may, like *Cadet Quest,* be geared exclusively to boys, but general interest magazines like *Cicada* also target male readers.

Executive Editor Deborah Vetter says, "For *Cicada,* we run a mix of stories featuring male and female protagonists. It's that old adage, which may or may not be true, that girls will read stories with male protagonists but guys won't read stories with girl protagonists." But snagging male readers goes beyond your character's gender right to the writing itself.

Action and Emotion

It should not have to be said, but emphasis is needed: First and foremost, you have to write good fiction. "In the most essential ways, the elements for successful boy fiction are the same elements that make for any good fiction," says Kerri Majors, Editor of *YARN* (Young Adult Review Network), an online literary publication for readers 14 and up.

Author Kurtis Scaletta agrees. "Some of the elements (in stories for boys) belong to any good fiction: compelling characters, an interesting premise, and a good story," he says. "With middle-grade readers, the audience I write for, the protagonist is even more important. Your main character has to be likable and believable and have a strong voice. Whether he's a wizard or the son of Perseus, he has to feel like the kid next door."

Likable is not as necessary in YA. "In any genre, an authentic, compelling voice is the baseline. Readers have to believe in the main character, and be willing to follow him for the length of the work," says Majors. "We don't necessarily have to like the character, but we must find him interesting enough to want to read on."

Fiction for boys is often action-oriented. Tyrannosaurus Press and *The Illuminata* Editor Bret Funk says, "I think that younger boys prefer stories with strong external conflict—cowboys and Indians, cops and robbers, knights and dragons. It really doesn't matter who the protagonists and antagonists are; boys just like to see lots of fighting, fleeing, and overall action."

Boys also appreciate humor, but keep it in check. "Like a writer I know recently said, it doesn't have to be all 'farts and firetrucks,'" says Scaletta. "The humor can be mild and character-driven. Boys can appreciate dry humor more than you might think. Similarly, the action doesn't have to be over-the-top battles for the fate of the world. I've seen boys respond just as well to sports or minor scuffles with bullies. I don't mean to imply there's no room for quieter, more serious books, either. Boys are all different and want to read different things."

Humor plus action cannot come at the expense of other elements. "This doesn't mean that characterization or internal conflict shouldn't be a factor," says Funk, "though in short stories, it's often very difficult to include both (internal and external) conflict."

The key is to balance action and emotion, and emotion is present in stories for and about boys. "Look no further than the novels of Barry Lyga, John Green, or Matt de la Peña for proof of that. But whereas in a work of fiction for girls the emphasis is on the emotional dilemma of the female character, in boy fiction, the emotions often creep in around the edges; sometimes they take over the story and sometimes they stay on the margins, but they always influence the outcome," says Majors. Emotion drives action and so a writer must reveal something of the emotional motivations of the characters in order for the story to ring true.

Scaletta includes both action and emotion in his own work. "I try to find a mix of tried-and-true, boy-friendly themes like sports and snakes, but also poke a little at the expectations: Maybe there can be a little romance, or lessons about friendships and family. The

Just for Boys

No two boys are created equal so it is not surprising that magazines cater to boys with various interests. Here are a few that target boys in niche markets.

- *Boys' Life:* Cub Scouts, Boy Scouts, or Venturers, ages 8 to 18
- *Boys' Quest:* Ages 8 to 10
- *Cadet Quest:* For members of the Calvinist Cadet Corps, ages 9 to 14
- *JAKES:* Published by the National Wild Turkey Federation, covering wildlife, hunting, and camping, for ages 10 to 17
- *Slap:* Online YA magazine for skateboarders
- *Thrasher:* Skateboarders and snowboarders, ages 12 to 20

Know boys in the target audience and remember the differences that come at different ages. "The most common mistake I see is fiction that is not age-appropriate. I see stories of boys driving cars and hanging out with their youth groups. Our readership is ages 9 to 14, so they don't drive and most are not part of youth groups," says *Cadet Quest* Editor Dick Broene. Don't try to appeal to the niche at the expense of realism. "Some Christian writers feature young boys who are eager to share their faith. In real life, there are very few children who go out of their way to be Christian witnesses." If you can write for niche audiences, it is worth your while. "Alaskan author Douglas DeVries has been a regular contributor to us for 20 years now. Each year he sends us a series of stories involving the same characters throughout a single year. An example of his work is 'Trouble For Wily,' in the March 2010 issue," says Broene, who is also on the lookout for new authors such as Glenn Haggerty, whose "Fishing Lesson," appeared in the January 2010 issue.

kinds of themes that are typically put in girls' books really are part of every kid's life," he says.

> **"In boys' fiction, emotions often creep in around the edges; sometimes they take over, and they always influence the outcome."**

Souped-Up Superboys

One of the biggest problems editors see in boys' fiction involves characterization. Including emotion can help. Says *Highlights for Children* Associate Editor Joëlle Dujardin, "Character growth is important in all kinds of fiction. While boy fiction might emphasize emotions less, the internal struggle and development should still be apparent—perhaps shown primarily through actions rather than through thoughts or dialogue."

Growth adds to character depth, and helps avoid generic figures. "I have seen hundreds of stories where you could substitute Dennis the Menace or Han Solo or Conan into a particular character's place and not realize that they were never intended to be there from the start," says Funk. "In reality, every person is unique, even when they share many similarities with the people around them. The more individuality that writers instill in their characters, the more believable they make their characters, the better the story will be, and the greater the appeal to readers."

Part of creating believable characters is having them act like real boys, not souped-up superboys. "Authors sometimes go over the top in trying to reach out to boys through the gross-out factor or

the *boys-rule, girls-drool* mentality, and the boy characters come off seeming flat or stereotypical, or the language feels condescending," says Dujardin. Just as problematic are characters who could just as easily be girls. "Sometimes authors simply replace a girl character with a boy, so the language and point of view end up sounding too passive or subtle, or the conflict doesn't seem relevant to a boy's experience." Solve this by knowing how boys act.

"If you don't have boys in your life, go somewhere you can observe them. Watch what and how they play and interact," says author Susan Uhlig. "Remember boys are more physical. A seven-year-old boy and a seven-year-old girl might both be interested in an unusual insect on the ground, but the boy is more likely to stomp it or say, 'Kill it!' Boys are generally less fearful. Just watch boys in a playground or park. Who is more likely to push to the edge, walking on the narrow wall beside the sidewalk? Look at who is doing the tricks at a skate park."

Note how behavior varies with the audience. "Watch how the boys in your math class behave; listen to what they say at family gatherings. Eavesdrop at Starbucks. Do you notice a difference between how boys talk around their guy friends, and how they talk to their girlfriends? Their parents?" says Majors. "Then, think about what you've seen and heard, and try to invent stories around it.

What would motivate a guy to do that, or say that?"

Do not take the differences between boys and girls too far. "I've seen manuscripts that go out of their way to show the writer has done his or her homework on boys. The hero loves pizza, video games, and lists his favorite pop songs and baseball players. I don't think you need to do all that," says Scaletta. "Instead of asking, 'What are boys like?' ask, 'What is this boy like?' What makes this boy different? Why is he special? What are his interests besides pizza and video games? How does he interact with his friends? Show him doing those things, pursuing his interests, bantering with his buddies."

Funk agrees. "The easiest thing to do is to base characters on people you know, or to at least observe the behavior of similarly aged individuals. In the end, the biggest secret is not to worry about it too much. I just write what seems the natural response for the character in any given situation. I try not to dwell on (boy versus girl) too much, because, in the end, the differences between men and women pale in comparison to the similarities we all have as human beings."

Whether you are writing for the play date set or your audience is dating, know them and what they are like. You will discover a variety of boys and young men with far-reaching interests, all available to people your fiction and entertain audiences of like-minded males.

Study Up

"Read fiction written by men for boys," advises Joëlle Dujardin, *Highlights for Children* Associate Editor. Read novels, read stories. You can start with these authors:

Sherman Alexie
M. T. Anderson
Andrew Clements
Eoin Colfer
Bruce Coville
Chris Crutcher
Roald Dahl
Neil Gaiman
Jack Gantos
Dan Gutman
Bruce Hale
Carl Hiassen
James Howe
Jarrett Krosoczka
Gary Paulsen
Rick Riordan
Louis Sachar
Jon Scieszka
Brian Selznick
Maurice Sendak
David Shannon
Jeff Smith
Rob Thomas
Mo Willems
David Yoo

Listings

How to Use the Listings

The pages that follow feature profiles of 675 magazines that publish articles and stories for, about, or of interest to children and young adults. Throughout the year, we stay on top of the latest happenings in children's magazines to bring you new and different publishing outlets. This year, our research yielded over 77 additional markets for your writing. They are easy to find; look for the listings with an exclamation point in the upper right corner.

A Variety of Freelance Opportunities

This year's new listings reflect the interests of today's magazine audience. You'll find magazines targeted to readers interested in nature, the environment, computers, mysteries, child care, careers, different cultures, family activities, and many other topics.

Along with many entertaining and educational magazines aimed at young readers, we list related publications such as national and regional magazines for parents and teachers. Hobby and special interest magazines generally thought of as adult fare but read by many teenagers are listed too.

In the market listings, the Freelance Potential section helps you judge each magazine's receptivity to freelance writers. This section offers information about the number of freelance submissions published each year.

Further opportunities for selling your writing appear in the Additional Listings section on page 231. This section profiles a range of magazines that publish a limited amount of material targeted to children, young adults, parents, or teachers. Other outlets for your writing can be found in the Selected Contests and Awards section, beginning on page 291.

Using Other Sections of the Directory

If you are planning to write for a specific publication, turn to the Magazine and Contest Index beginning on page 369 to locate the listing page. The Category Index, beginning on page 327, will guide you to magazines that publish in your areas of interest. This year, the Category Index also gives the age range of each publication's readership. To find the magazines most open to freelance submissions, turn to the Fifty+ Freelance index on page 320, which lists magazines that rely on freelance writers for over 50% of the material they publish.

Check the Market News, beginning on page 323, to find out what's newly listed, what's not listed and why, and to identify changes in the market that have occurred during the past year.

About the Listings

We revisited last year's listings and, through a series of mailed surveys and phone interviews, verified editors' names, mailing addresses, submissions and payment policies, and current editorial needs. All entries are accurate and up-to-date when we send this market directory to press. Magazine publishing is a fast-moving industry, though, and it is not unusual for facts to change before or shortly after this guide reaches your hands. Magazines close, are sold to new owners, or move; they hire new editors or change their editorial focus. Keep up to date by requesting sample copies and writers' guidelines.

Note that we do *not* list:

- Magazines that did not respond to our questionnaires or phone queries. Know that we make every effort to contact each editor before press date.
- Magazines that *never* accept freelance submissions or work with freelance writers.

To get a real sense of a magazine and its editorial slant, we recommend that you read several recent sample issues cover to cover. This is the best way to be certain a magazine is right for you.

Babybug

Cricket Magazine Group
70 East Lake Street, Suite 300
Chicago, IL 60601

Who to contact —— Associate Editor: Jenny Gillespie

DESCRIPTION AND INTERESTS

Profiles the publication, its interests, and readers

This magazine is designed in board book style for the littlest readers. Its brightly colored pages feature stories, poems, words, and concepts that help young children discover the world around them. It is part of the Cricket Magazine Group. Circ: 50,000.

Audience: 6 months–2 years
Frequency: 9 times each year
Website: www.babybugmagkids.com

FREELANCE POTENTIAL

100% written by nonstaff writers. Publishes 30–40 freelance submissions yearly; 50% by authors who are new to the magazine. Receives 2,400 unsolicited mss yearly.

Designates the amount and type of freelance submissions published each year; highlights the publication's receptivity to unpublished writers

SUBMISSIONS

Provides guidelines for submitting material; lists word lengths and types of material accepted from freelance writers

Send complete ms. Accepts hard copy and simultaneous submissions if identified. SASE. Responds in 6 months.

- Articles: 10 words. Features material that conveys simple concepts and ideas.
- Fiction: 4–6 short sentences. Simple stories.
- Artwork: By assignment only. Send sample tearsheets, photoprints, or photocopies to be kept on file.
- Other: Parent-child activities, to 8 lines. Rhyming and rhythmic poetry, to 8 lines. Action rhymes, 4–8 lines.

SAMPLE ISSUE

24 pages (no advertising): 4 stories; 4 poems; 1 activity. Sample copy, $5. Guidelines available at website.

- "Kim and Carrots." Story features a little girl who likes to draw alongside her mother.
- "My Letter." Story tells of a young girl making and then sending Valentine's Day cards to her grandparents.
- "Play Dough." Poem looks at the fun of playing with play dough.

Analyzes a recent sample copy of the publication; briefly describes selected articles, stories, departments, etc.

RIGHTS AND PAYMENT

Lists types of rights acquired, payment rate, and number of copies provided to freelance writers

All or second North American serial rights. Written material, $25+. Artwork, $500 per spread, $250 per page. Pays on publication. Provides 6 contributor's copies.

➥ EDITOR'S COMMENTS

While we always welcome submissions from new writers, please be aware that we have very high standards. Your material must be top quality to get our attention.

Offers advice from the editor about the publication's writing style, freelance needs, audience, etc.

Icon Key

 New Listing   E-publisher   Overseas Publisher

 Not currently accepting submissions

Ad Astra

1155 15th Street NW, Suite 500
Washington, DC 20005

Assignment Editor: Katherine Brick

DESCRIPTION AND INTERESTS
As the member publication of the National Space Society, *Ad Astra* features the latest news and research in space exploration and aerospace science. Its readership is made up of avid space enthusiasts as well as scientists and technologists. Circ: 20,000.

Audience: YA–Adult
Frequency: Quarterly
Website: www.nss.org

FREELANCE POTENTIAL
80% written by nonstaff writers. Publishes 40–50 freelance submissions yearly. Receives 200 queries, 100 unsolicited mss yearly.

SUBMISSIONS
Query or send complete ms with résumé. Accepts disk submissions and email to adastra@nss.org. SASE. Response time varies.

- Articles: Word lengths vary. Informational and factual articles; profiles; and interviews. Topics include science and technology related to space exploration; and issues related to the aerospace industry.
- Depts/columns: 600–750 words. Reviews and opinion pieces.
- Artwork: 8x10 color digital images at 300 dpi.

SAMPLE ISSUE
64 pages (14% advertising): 9 articles; 6 depts/columns. Sample copy, $11.25 with 9x12 SASE ($4 postage). Guidelines and editorial calendar available at website.

- "The President's Agenda for Space." Article examines President Obama's commitment to NASA's mission and the role of space in the future.
- "Finding Solutions in Thin Air." Article discusses problem-solving tactics for the International Space Station.
- Sample dept/column: "Books" offers a review of *How to Find a Habitable Planet*, by James Kasting.

RIGHTS AND PAYMENT
First North American serial rights. Written material, payment rates vary. Artwork, payment rates negotiable. Payment policy varies.

⦿EDITOR'S COMMENTS
Our writers should be every bit as passionate about their subject as our readers are.

ADDitude

39 West 37th Street, 15th Floor
New York, NY 10018

Editorial Assistant: Caitlin Ford

DESCRIPTION AND INTERESTS
ADDitude covers the news and issues surrounding Attention Deficit Disorder and related syndromes. It is written for families who are dealing with the ADD of one of their members. Circ: 40,000.

Audience: Adults
Frequency: 5 times each year
Website: www.additudemag.com

FREELANCE POTENTIAL
80% written by nonstaff writers. Publishes 15–20 freelance submissions yearly; 30% by unpublished writers, 30% by authors who are new to the magazine. Receives 96 queries each year.

SUBMISSIONS
Query. Prefers email to submissions@additudemag.com (file attached); will accept hard copy. SASE. Responds in 6–8 weeks.

- Articles: To 2,000 words. Informational articles and personal experience pieces. Topics include ADD and ADHD, education, medication, recreation, organization, parenting, and child development.
- Depts/columns: Word lengths vary. Profiles of students, teachers, and schools; first-person essays; healthy living; organization; product reviews; and ADD/ADHD news.

SAMPLE ISSUE
62 pages (33% advertising): 2 articles; 22 depts/columns. Sample copy, $6.95. Guidelines available at website.

- "Helping ADHD Kids Who Hit." Article outlines nine ways to help children with ADD/ADHD rein in their urge to get physically aggressive.
- "7 Quick Fixes for ADHD Meltdowns." Article provides parents with seven tips for dealing with ADHD meltdowns and the onlookers who may witness them.

RIGHTS AND PAYMENT
First rights. Written material, payment rates vary. Kill fee, $75. Pays on publication. Provides a 1-year subscription.

⦿EDITOR'S COMMENTS
Informational articles are written by journalists and mental health professionals. Parents and family members, however, are invited to write about their experiences.

Administrator

Scholastic, Inc.
557 Broadway
New York, NY 10012-3999

Editorial Director: Dana Truby

DESCRIPTION AND INTERESTS
Administrator seeks to provide "smart strategies and proven solutions" to education issues for kindergarten through grade 12. Leadership, staff development, curriculum and instruction, funding, and technology are some of the topics covered. Circ: 240,000.

Audience: School administrators, grades K–12
Frequency: 8 times each year
Website: www.scholastic.com/administrator

FREELANCE POTENTIAL
80% written by nonstaff writers. Publishes 25 freelance submissions yearly; 10% by unpublished writers.

SUBMISSIONS
Query with résumé. Accepts hard copy and email queries to dtruby@scholastic.com. SASE. Responds in 3–4 months.

- Articles: 1,200 words. Informational and how-to articles; profiles; and interviews. Topics include teacher recruitment and retention, salary negotiation, intervention programs, working with school boards, gifted education, school menus, grants and spending, crisis management, social issues, education trends and legislation, and technology.
- Depts/columns: Word lengths vary. News, opinions, technology, and book reviews.

SAMPLE ISSUE
64 pages: 4 articles; 7 depts/columns. Sample copy available at website. Writers' guidelines available.

- "Let's Be Clear." Article includes a book excerpt about two public school administrators who challenged the school district to open up its ledger books.
- "Who Makes What?" Article ranks the contract agreements of America's largest school districts.
- Sample dept/column: "Hands On Favorites" looks at three school districts and examines how they use video on demand.

RIGHTS AND PAYMENT
All rights. All material, payment rates vary. Pays on publication.

❖ EDITOR'S COMMENTS
We welcome submissions from school administrators and educators, as well as from freelance writers and journalists.

Adoptalk

North American Council on Adoptable Children
970 Raymond Street, Suite 106
St. Paul, MN 55114-1149

Editor: Diane Riggs

DESCRIPTION AND INTERESTS
This newsletter, read by members of the NACAC, covers a wide variety of issues related to adoption and foster care, with a focus on special-needs adoptions. Circ: 2,900.

Audience: Adults
Frequency: Quarterly
Website: www.nacac.org

FREELANCE POTENTIAL
25% written by nonstaff writers. Publishes 8 freelance submissions yearly; 5% by unpublished writers, 10% by authors who are new to the magazine. Receives 6 queries, 2 unsolicited mss yearly.

SUBMISSIONS
Query or send complete ms with brief author biography. Accepts hard copy and email to dianeriggs@nacac.org. SASE. Responds in 2–3 weeks.

- Articles: To 2,200 words. Informational articles; profiles; personal experience pieces; and interviews. Topics include adoptive and foster care, parenting, recruitment, adoption news, conference updates, and NACAC membership news and updates.
- Depts/columns: Word lengths vary. Book reviews and first-person essays.

SAMPLE ISSUE
16 pages (no advertising): 6 articles; 3 depts/columns. Sample copy, free with 9x12 SASE ($1.22 postage).

- "Reinvestment: Raising Permanency Rates During Fiscal Crises." Article discusses how California's Sacramento County proposed a strategy to successfully place older foster children in permanent families.
- "My Life: From Rage to Reason." Personal experience piece tells how a former foster child overcame attachment disorder to become a happy and productive woman.
- Sample dept/column: "Adoption and Foster Care Resources" reviews children's books about adoption.

RIGHTS AND PAYMENT
Rights vary. No payment. Provides 5 contributor's copies.

❖ EDITOR'S COMMENTS
Send your submission at least two months prior to the scheduled publication date.

Adoptive Families

39 West 37th Street, 15th Floor
New York, NY 10018

Editorial Assistant: Caitlin Ford

DESCRIPTION AND INTERESTS
This magazine addresses the issues, emotions, and decisions faced by families in all steps of the adoption process. Circ: 40,000.
Audience: Adoptive parents
Frequency: 6 times each year
Website: www.adoptivefamilies.com

FREELANCE POTENTIAL
75% written by nonstaff writers. Publishes 100 freelance submissions yearly; 20% by unpublished writers, 50% by authors who are new to the magazine. Receives 500–600 queries and unsolicited mss yearly.

SUBMISSIONS
Query with clips for articles. Send complete ms for personal essays. Prefers email to submissions@adoptivefamilies.com (Microsoft Word attachments); will accept hard copy. SASE. Responds in 6–8 weeks.

- Articles: 500–1,800 words. Informational, self-help, and how-to articles; and personal experience pieces. Topics include preparing for adoption; health; education; birth families; and parenting tips.
- Depts/columns: To 1,200 words. Pre-adoption issues, birthparents, advice, opinion pieces, personal essays, single parenting, cultural diversity, child development, legal issues, and book reviews.

SAMPLE ISSUE
66 pages (40% advertising): 4 articles; 10 depts/columns. Sample copy, $6.95. Guidelines available at website.

- "Adoption & The Economy." Article questions whether the economic crisis is affecting people's decision to adopt.
- Sample dept/column: "And So It Begins" shares a mother's thoughts and emotions as she meets her son for the first time.

RIGHTS AND PAYMENT
All rights. Written material, payment rates vary. Payment policy varies. Provides 2 contributor's copies.

➥EDITOR'S COMMENTS
If you are part of or work with an adoptive family, we'd like to hear your stories. We encourage you to share your insights and experiences with others. We'll consider any issue that pertains to adoption.

Alateen Talk

Al-Anon Family Group Headquarters
1600 Corporate Landing Parkway
Virginia Beach, VA 23454-5617

Editor: Mary Lou Mahlman

DESCRIPTION AND INTERESTS
Filled with teenagers' own stories and thoughts, *Alateen Talk* is written by and for members of Alateen and others who have been adversely affected by having an alcoholic or substance abuser in their lives. Circ: 4,000.
Audience: 6–18 years
Frequency: Quarterly
Website: www.al-anon.alateen.org

FREELANCE POTENTIAL
90% written by nonstaff writers. Publishes 85–120 freelance submissions yearly; 80% by unpublished writers, 75% by authors who are new to the magazine. Receives 100–150 unsolicited mss yearly.

SUBMISSIONS
Alateen members only. Send complete ms. Accepts hard copy. SASE. Responds in 2 weeks.

- Articles: Word lengths vary. Self-help and personal experience pieces. Topics include social issues, family life, and alcoholism and its effects on relationships.
- Depts/columns: Staff written.
- Artwork: B/W line art.
- Other: Poetry

SAMPLE ISSUE
8 pages (no advertising): 2 articles; 1 dept/column. Sample copy, free with #10 SASE ($.87 postage). Guidelines available to Alateen members only.

- "Sharings." Article lets Alateen members from Buffalo, Minn., share their thoughts about what alcoholism has done to their lives and how Alateen has helped them.
- "Younger Members." Article showcases the thoughts and experiences of members of the Caring Nu Life Alateen Group.

RIGHTS AND PAYMENT
All rights. No payment.

➥EDITOR'S COMMENTS
If you are a member of Alateen, we invite you to share an experience from the heart with the focus on yourself—not the alcoholic, the non-drinking parent, or anyone else. Tell us what has happened to you and what it was like. And tell us how Alateen has helped you and how your life has changed. We believe that all Alateen members benefit from hearing of other members' experiences.

Alfred Hitchcock's Mystery Magazine

267 Broadway, 4th Floor
New York, NY 10007

Editor: Linda Landrigan

DESCRIPTION AND INTERESTS

This mystery magazine publishes fresh, well-written, and entertaining stories of crime, either as an outright act or an insinuated one. New writers are welcome to submit their manuscripts. Circ: 75,000.

Audience: Adults
Frequency: 10 times each year
Website: www.themysteryplace.com

FREELANCE POTENTIAL

98% written by nonstaff writers. Publishes 90–100 freelance submissions yearly; 5–10% by unpublished writers, 25–50% by authors who are new to the magazine. Receives 600–1,200 unsolicited mss yearly.

SUBMISSIONS

Send complete ms. Accepts hard copy. No simultaneous submissions. SASE. Responds in 3–5 months.

- Fiction: To 12,000 words. Genres include classic crime mysteries, detective stories, suspense, private investigator tales, courtroom drama, and espionage.
- Depts/columns: Word lengths vary. Reviews, puzzles, and profiles of bookstores.

SAMPLE ISSUE

192 pages (2% advertising): 8 stories; 1 novella; 8 depts/columns. Sample copy, $7.99. Guidelines available at website.

- "The High House Writer." Story features a private investigator who uncovers a scam by a well-known writer after one of his clients is murdered.
- "Scavenger." Story tells of a man who stays in New Orleans during Hurricane Katrina and spends the time stealing from mansions.
- Sample dept/column: "Reel Crime" reviews three movie thrillers, and includes an interview with one of the screenwriters.

RIGHTS AND PAYMENT

First serial, anthology, and foreign rights. Written material, payment rates vary. Pays on acceptance. Provides 2 contributor's copies.

☛EDITOR'S COMMENTS

We are interested in nearly every kind of mystery: stories of detection of the classic kind, police procedurals, private eye tales, suspense, courtroom dramas, tales of espionage, and so on.

American Baby

375 Lexington Avenue, 10th Floor
New York, NY 10017

Editorial Assistant: Jessica Wohlgemuth

DESCRIPTION AND INTERESTS

This consumer magazine addresses the needs and fears of new parents. Topics related to pregnancy, childbirth, breastfeeding, infancy, and early childhood development are covered by articles designed to inform as well as support and encourage. Circ: 2.1 million.

Audience: Parents
Frequency: Monthly
Website: www.americanbaby.com

FREELANCE POTENTIAL

55% written by nonstaff writers. Publishes 24 freelance submissions yearly; 1% by unpublished writers, 1% by new authors. Receives 996 queries and unsolicited mss yearly.

SUBMISSIONS

Query with clips and writing samples; or send complete ms. Accepts hard copy and simultaneous submissions if identified. SASE. Responds in 2 months.

- Articles: 1,000–2,000 words. Informational and how-to articles; profiles; interviews; humor; and personal experience pieces. Topics include pregnancy, childbirth, parenting, child care and development, health, fitness, nutrition, and family travel.
- Depts/columns: 1,000 words. Health briefs, fitness tips, new products, and fashion.
- Other: Submit seasonal material 3 months in advance.

SAMPLE ISSUE

72 pages (50% advertising): 3 articles; 12 depts/columns. Sample copy, free with 9x12 SASE ($2 postage) or at newsstands. Guidelines available.

- "4 Routines For a Happy Baby." Article outlines the structure that will keep one's baby content and compliant.
- Sample dept/column: "Pregnancy" puts expectant moms' common delivery-day fears into perspective.

RIGHTS AND PAYMENT

First serial rights. Articles, to $2,000. Depts/columns, to $1,000. Kill fee, 25%. Pays on acceptance. Provides 5 contributor's copies.

☛EDITOR'S COMMENTS

We forgo the theoretical approach to offer quick-to-read, hands-on information that our readers can put to use immediately.

American Careers

6701 West 64th Street
Overland Park, KS 66202

Editor: Mary Pitchford

DESCRIPTION AND INTERESTS
Designed to promote career development and education for middle school and high school students, *American Careers* offers in-depth information on a variety of career choices. It also features how-to articles on career planning, life skills, and résumés. It is distributed through the school market. Circ: 350,000.

Audience: 12–18 years
Frequency: Annually
Website: www.carcom.com

FREELANCE POTENTIAL
5% written by nonstaff writers. Publishes 5 freelance submissions yearly; 1–2% by authors who are new to the magazine. Receives 100+ queries yearly.

SUBMISSIONS
Query with résumé and clips. Accepts hard copy. SASE. Responds in 1 month.

- Articles: 300–750 words. Informational and how-to articles; profiles; and personal experience pieces. Topics include types of careers, career planning, and education.
- Artwork: Color prints; high-resolution digital images.
- Other: Quizzes and self-assessments.

SAMPLE ISSUE
64 pages (no advertising): 16 articles; 3 self-assessments. Sample copy, $4 with 9x12 SASE (7 first-class stamps). Guidelines available.

- "Ensuring Drug Product Quality." Article profiles a regulatory research scientist for the U.S. Food and Drug Administration and discusses careers in health science.
- "A Brand New Look at Marketing Careers." Article provides details on different marketing careers, including sports and consumer products.
- "Employability and Life Skills." Article offers tips on honing a résumé.

RIGHTS AND PAYMENT
All rights. All material, payment rates vary. Pays on acceptance. Provides 2 contributor's copies.

➥EDITOR'S COMMENTS
Articles should be written at a seventh- to tenth-grade reading level for a national audience. When possible, please submit photography to complement your article.

American Cheerleader

110 William Street, 23rd Floor
New York, NY 10038

Editor-in-Chief: Marisa Walker

DESCRIPTION AND INTERESTS
Celebrating its 16th anniversary this year, *American Cheerleader* covers all things cheer-related—from profiling teams and athletes and providing training tips to fitness advice. It also reports on cheerleading competitions and trends. Circ: 150,000.

Audience: 13–18 years
Frequency: 6 times each year
Website: www.americancheerleader.com

FREELANCE POTENTIAL
40% written by nonstaff writers. Publishes 30 freelance submissions yearly; 20% by unpublished writers, 10% by authors who are new to the magazine. Receives hundreds of queries, few unsolicited mss yearly.

SUBMISSIONS
Query with clips; or send complete ms. Prefers email to mwalker@americancheerleader.com; will accept hard copy. SASE. Responds in 3 months.

- Articles: To 1,000 words. Informational and how-to articles; profiles; interviews; personal experience pieces; and photo-essays. Topics include cheerleading, cheerleaders and teams, workouts, competitions, scholarships, college, careers, and popular culture.
- Depts/columns: Word lengths vary. Safety issues, health, nutrition, beauty, fashion, fundraising, and new product information.
- Artwork: High-resolution digital images; 35mm color slides.

SAMPLE ISSUE
96 pages (40% advertising): 6 articles; 14 depts/columns. Sample copy, $3.99 with 9x12 SASE ($1.70 postage). Editorial calendar available.

- "Crazy About Camp!" Article reports on the many advantages of cheerleading camp.
- Sample dept/column: "Tumbling Tech" offers step-by-step instructions for a front handspring front tuck.

RIGHTS AND PAYMENT
All rights. All material, payment rates vary. Pays on publication. Provides 1 contributor's copy.

➥EDITOR'S COMMENTS
Writers should have some sort of background in cheerleading and know the kind of determination and passion this sport takes.

American Educator

555 New Jersey Avenue NW
Washington, DC 20001-2079

Editor: Lisa Hansel

DESCRIPTION AND INTERESTS
Published by the American Federation of Teachers, this professional magazine offers educators news of the field. It also publishes articles on policy, international affairs, trends, and labor issues of interest to AFT members. Circ: 900,000.

Audience: Teachers, professors, policymakers
Frequency: Quarterly
Website: www.aft.org/pubs-reports/
　　　　　　american-educator/index.htm

FREELANCE POTENTIAL
25% written by nonstaff writers. Publishes 5–6 freelance submissions yearly; 10% by unpublished writers, 20% by authors who are new to the magazine. Receives 360 queries yearly.

SUBMISSIONS
Query with contact information. Accepts hard copy and email queries to amered@aft.org. SASE. Responds in 2 months.

- Articles: 1,500–3,000 words. Informational articles; profiles; and opinion pieces. Topics include trends in education, politics, education law, professional ethics, social and labor issues, and international affairs.

SAMPLE ISSUE
40 pages (9% advertising): 7 articles. Writers' guidelines available.

- "The Most Daring Education Reform of All." Article posits that public school reforms must be made thoughtfully, by combining proven traditional methods with innovative 21st-century skillbuilders.
- "What Does—and What Should—P21 Advocate?" Article critiques the lessons proposed by the Partnership for 21st Century Skills (P21).

RIGHTS AND PAYMENT
All rights. Written material, payment rates vary. Pays on publication. Provides 10 contributor's copies.

❖EDITOR'S COMMENTS
While our readership is composed of professional educators, our articles are not laden with education and research jargon, nor do we publish research papers or doctoral theses as articles. Personal narratives are rarely published, but submissions based on informed opinion are always welcome.

American Girl

American Girl Publishing
8400 Fairway Place
Middleton, WI 53562

Editorial Assistant

DESCRIPTION AND INTERESTS
Building a young girl's confidence, curiosity, and self-esteem is the goal of this magazine. Each issue includes inspiring profiles, entertaining articles, and craft and cooking ideas. It is always in search of new twists on familiar topics. Circ: 700,000.

Audience: 8–12 years
Frequency: 6 times each year
Website: www.americangirl.com

FREELANCE POTENTIAL
4% written by nonstaff writers. Publishes 5 freelance submissions yearly; 2% by unpublished writers, 2% by authors who are new to the magazine. Receives 780 queries yearly.

SUBMISSIONS
Query. Accepts hard copy and simultaneous submissions if identified. Responds in 4 months.

- Articles: 500–1,000 words. Informational articles; profiles; and interviews. Topics include history, nature, food, hobbies, crafts, sports, and culture.
- Depts/columns: 175 words. Profiles, how-to pieces, and craft ideas.

SAMPLE ISSUE
72 pages (no advertising): 4 articles; 1 story; 8 depts/columns. Sample copy, $5.95 at newsstands. Guidelines available.

- "Splish, Splash, Sports." Article suggests several summer water activities for keeping both cool and active.
- "Are You E-nnoying?" Article includes a quiz to determine one's email and text etiquette, along with tech tips.
- Sample dept/column: "Girls Express" shares tips for packing a suitcase.

RIGHTS AND PAYMENT
Rights vary. All material purchased under work-for-hire agreement. Written material, payment rates vary. Pays on acceptance. Provides 3 contributor's copies.

❖EDITOR'S COMMENTS
Our "Girls Express" department offers the most opportunities for freelance writers. We're looking for short profiles of girls who are into sports, the arts, or interesting hobbies, as well as true stories about girls who have had unusual experiences.

American Libraries

American Library Association
50 East Huron Street
Chicago, IL 60611

Acquisitions Editor: Pamela Goodes

DESCRIPTION AND INTERESTS
This publication of the American Library Association features articles regarding the professional concerns of librarians everywhere. It also covers the news, regulations, and trends of the library industry. Circ: 56,000.
Audience: Librarians
Frequency: 10 times each year
Website: www.ala.org/alonline

FREELANCE POTENTIAL
60% written by nonstaff writers. Publishes 10 freelance submissions yearly; 50% by authors who are new to the magazine. Receives 492 unsolicited mss yearly.

SUBMISSIONS
Professional librarians only. Send complete ms. Accepts hard copy and email submissions to americanlibraries@ala.org. No simultaneous submissions. SASE. Responds in 8–10 weeks.

- Articles: 600–2,000 words. Informational articles; profiles; interviews; and personal experience pieces. Topics include modern libraries, library and ALA history, technology, leadership, advocacy, funding, and privacy.
- Depts/columns: Word lengths vary. News, opinions, profiles, media reviews, information technology, ALA events, career leads, and professional development.

SAMPLE ISSUE
72 pages (27% advertising): 5 articles; 15 depts/columns. Sample copy, $6. Writers' guidelines available.

- "A Greener Library, A Greener You." Article examines how several libraries across the country have become more eco-friendly in design and operation.
- Sample dept/column: "Youth Matters" discusses how librarians can use online gaming as a teaching tool.

RIGHTS AND PAYMENT
First North American serial rights. Written material, $50–$400. Pays on acceptance. Provides 1+ contributor's copies.

➡ EDITOR'S COMMENTS
We are a professional journal, and accept material from professionals in the library sciences only. All material must be well researched and culled from your experience in a library.

American School & University

9800 Metcalf Avenue
Overland Park, KS 66212-2215

Executive Editor: Susan Lustig

DESCRIPTION AND INTERESTS
This magazine is read by education facilities and business professionals, as well as architects. It offers how-to articles and reports on industry news and trends. Circ: 65,000.
Audience: School facilities managers
Frequency: Monthly
Website: www.asumag.com

FREELANCE POTENTIAL
35% written by nonstaff writers. Publishes 40 freelance submissions yearly; 30% by authors who are new to the magazine. Receives 180 queries yearly.

SUBMISSIONS
Query with outline. Prefers email queries to slustig@asumag.com; will accept hard copy. SASE. Responds in 2 weeks.

- Articles: 1,200 words. Informational and how-to articles. Topics include educational facilities management, maintenance, security, planning, design, construction, operations, and furnishings.
- Depts/columns: 250–350 words. Opinions, environmental practices, technology, planning issues, and new products.

SAMPLE ISSUE
58 pages (55% advertising): 5 articles; 7 depts/columns. Sample copy, $10. Guidelines and editorial calendar available.

- "Out with the Old." Article makes the case for replacing old classroom unit ventilators with displacement ventilation units, which use the natural buoyancy of warm air to improve ventilation and comfort.
- "Energy Demands." Article provides facilities managers with several energy-conservation tips that can save money for maintenance and operations.

RIGHTS AND PAYMENT
All rights. Written material, payment rates vary. Payment policy varies. Provides 2 contributor's copies.

➡ EDITOR'S COMMENTS
Articles should not promote a company or specific product; rather, they should offer the reader new insights into the general trends and market, provide tips about what to look for, and explain processes. Be sure all technical information is correct.

American Secondary Education

Ashland University
Dwight Schar COE, Room 231
401 College Avenue
Ashland, OH 44805

Editorial Assistant

DESCRIPTION AND INTERESTS

With a mix of practical and scholarly articles, this refereed journal examines current issues, theories, and practices of secondary education. It includes articles written by practitioners and researchers. Circ: 450.

Audience: Secondary school educators
Frequency: 3 times each year
Website: www.ashland.edu.ase

FREELANCE POTENTIAL

99% written by nonstaff writers. Publishes 20 freelance submissions yearly; 75% by authors who are new to the magazine. Receives 40–50 unsolicited mss yearly.

SUBMISSIONS

Send complete ms with 100-word abstract and credentials. Prefers email submissions to asejournal@ashland.edu; will accept hard copy. No simultaneous submissions. SASE. Response time varies.

- Articles: 10–25 double-spaced ms pages. Informational articles. Topics include secondary and middle school education research and practice.
- Depts/columns: Word lengths vary. Book reviews.

SAMPLE ISSUE

96 pages (no advertising): 6 articles; 1 book review. Sample copy, free. Guidelines available in each issue.

- "The Status of Special Education Teachers at the Secondary Level: Effects of the 'Highly Qualified Teacher' Standard." Article details the issues teachers are facing as a result of this legally mandated requirement.
- "Government Course Changes Will Affect Secondary Education." Article reviews the changes promised by President Obama that will affect secondary education.
- Sample dept/column: "Review" discusses *See Me After Class: Advice for Teachers By Teachers*, a humorous book of advice for new teachers.

RIGHTS AND PAYMENT

All rights. No payment. Provides 1 copy.

⚫➔EDITOR'S COMMENTS

We want our articles to reflect what educators in both the public and private sectors are discussing and thinking.

American String Teacher

4153 Chain Bridge Road
Fairfax, VA 22030

Editor: Mary Jane Dye

DESCRIPTION AND INTERESTS

The official publication of the American String Teachers Association and available exclusively to members, this magazine features articles regarding the teaching of stringed instruments and/or the performance of music for strings. Circ: 11,500.

Audience: String instrument teachers
Frequency: Quarterly
Website: www.astaweb.com

FREELANCE POTENTIAL

100% written by nonstaff writers. Publishes 30 freelance submissions yearly; 5% by unpublished writers, 50% by authors who are new to the magazine. Receives 50 queries and unsolicited mss yearly.

SUBMISSIONS

Query or send complete ms. Prefers email submissions to ASTarticles@astaweb.com (Microsoft Word attachments); will accept 5 hard copies. SASE. Responds in 3 months.

- Articles: 1,500–3,000 words. Informational and factual articles; profiles; and association news. Topics include teaching, methodology, techniques, competitions, and auditions.
- Depts/columns: Word lengths vary. Teaching tips, opinion pieces, and industry news.

SAMPLE ISSUE

80 pages (45% advertising): 5 articles; 9 depts/columns. Sample copy, free with 9x12 SASE ($3.25 postage). Guidelines available at website.

- "The String Teacher as Arranger: Meeting the Needs of Our Students." Article discusses the need for music teachers to constantly develop and reevaluate their curricula for teaching strings.
- Sample dept/column: "Teaching Tips" explains the four hand patterns used for violin, and how practice of each will prepare a student to play anything.

RIGHTS AND PAYMENT

All rights. No payment. Provides 5 copies.

⚫➔EDITOR'S COMMENTS

Topics should not be too broad, nor too narrow. All articles should provide useful information that will help our readers become better string teachers. All articles go through a peer review before acceptance.

Analog Science Fiction and Fact

Dell Magazine Group
475 Park Avenue South
New York, NY 10016

Editor: Stanley Schmidt

DESCRIPTION AND INTERESTS
Fiction exploring future science or technology is the mainstay of this magazine. Also published are factual articles, mostly on current and future scientific topics. Circ: 40,000.

Audience: YA–Adult
Frequency: 10 times each year
Website: www.analogsf.com

FREELANCE POTENTIAL
100% written by nonstaff writers. Publishes 80–90 freelance submissions yearly; 10% by unpublished writers, 10% by new authors. Receives 6,000 unsolicited mss yearly.

SUBMISSIONS
Send complete ms. Query for serials only. Accepts hard copy. SASE. Responds in 6 weeks.

- Articles: To 6,000 words. Informational articles. Topics include science and technology.
- Fiction: Serials, 40,000–80,000 words. Novellas and novelettes, 10,000–20,000 words. Short stories, 2,000–7,000 words. Physical, sociological, psychological, and technological science fiction.
- Depts/columns: Staff written.

SAMPLE ISSUE
240 pages (7% advertising): 2 articles; 1 serial; 1 novella; 3 novelettes; 5 short stories; 6 depts/columns. Sample copy, $5 with 9x12 SASE. Guidelines available at website.

- "The Exoanthropic Principle." Story follows two communications specialists who receive hard-to-decipher transmissions and conclude that the signals are from a universe with five dimensions.
- "Hook, Lure, and Narrative: The Art of Writing Story Leads." Article offers tips on how to draw readers into stories.

RIGHTS AND PAYMENT
First North American serial and non-exclusive rights. Serials, $.04 per word; other written material, $.05–$.08 per word. Pays on acceptance. Provides 2 contributor's copies.

➦EDITOR'S COMMENTS
Because we cover such a broad spectrum of science fiction subgenres, we welcome all well-crafted submissions. Keep in mind, however, that stories must be believable, no matter how fantastic the circumstances.

AppleSeeds

Cobblestone Publishing Company
30 Grove Street
Peterborough, NH 03458

Editor: Susan Buckley

DESCRIPTION AND INTERESTS
Written for kids in third through fifth grades, *AppleSeeds* explores world cultures and history. Each issue focuses on a particular place or country. Circ: 10,000.

Audience: 8–10 years
Frequency: 9 times each year
Website: www.cobblestonepub.com

FREELANCE POTENTIAL
80% written by nonstaff writers. Publishes 90–100 freelance submissions yearly; 33% by authors who are new to the magazine. Receives 600+ queries yearly.

SUBMISSIONS
Query with article description, source list, and proposed word count. Accepts email queries to susanbuckleynyc@gmail.com (no attachments). Responds in 2–3 months if interested.

- Articles: 150–600 words. Informational and how-to articles; profiles; and interviews. Topics include history, biography, biology, geology, technology, geography, literature, and the environment.
- Depts/columns: "Reading Corner" (folktales and public domain literature), "By the Numbers" (theme-related math activities), "Fun Stuff" (hands-on activities), "Your Turn," and "Experts in Action," 150 words. "From the Source," 150–300 words.
- Artwork: B/W and color prints.

SAMPLE ISSUE
34 pages (no advertising): 9 articles; 5 depts/columns. Sample copy available. Guidelines and theme list available at website.

- "Young Lincoln: Different From the Start." Article offers a glimpse into Abraham Lincoln's boyhood.
- "Words of Wisdom." Article discusses Lincoln's skill as a storyteller and shows how he used that skill to explain his policies and decisions, as well as to entertain.

RIGHTS AND PAYMENT
All rights. Written material, $50 per page. Artwork, payment rates vary. Pays after publication. Provides 2 contributor's copies.

➦EDITOR'S COMMENTS
We look for lively, age-appropriate articles that exhibit an original approach to the specified theme. Accuracy is essential.

Art Education

University of Cincinnati
6431C Aronoff
P.O. Box 210016
Cincinnati, OH 45221-0016

Editor: Flavio Bastos

DESCRIPTION AND INTERESTS
This journal of the National Art Education Association covers a diverse range of topics of interest to professional art educators, including lesson plans and successful model programs. Circ: 20,000.

Audience: Art educators
Frequency: 6 times each year
Website: www.arteducators.org/
publications.html

FREELANCE POTENTIAL
90% written by nonstaff writers. Publishes 42 freelance submissions yearly; 40% by unpublished writers, 40% by authors who are new to the magazine. Receives 150–200 unsolicited mss yearly.

SUBMISSIONS
Send complete ms with cover letter. Accepts hard copy with disk and simultaneous submissions if identified. SASE. Responds in 8–10 weeks.

- Articles: To 3,000 words. Researched-based informational articles; profiles; interviews; and personal experience pieces. Topics include the visual arts, curriculum planning, art history, and art criticism.
- Depts/columns: To 2,750 words. "Instructional Resources," lesson plan ideas.
- Artwork: 8x10 or 5x7 B/W prints or slides; digital images.

SAMPLE ISSUE
54 pages (7% advertising): 6 articles; 1 dept/column. Sample copy, $3 with 9x12 SASE ($1.85 postage). Guidelines available.

- "Art Lessons for a Young Artist with Asperger Syndrome." Article outlines how a teacher adapted an art lesson and used behavior modification techniques with a special education student.
- Sample dept/column: "Instructional Resources" shows how the history of a female pharaoh in ancient Egypt was used to study art, sculpture, and the power of an image.

RIGHTS AND PAYMENT
All rights. No payment. Provides 2 copies.

☛EDITOR'S COMMENTS
Each manuscript is peer-reviewed before a final decision is made on whether to accept or reject it.

Arts & Activities

12345 World Trade Drive
San Diego, CA 92128

Editor: Maryellen Bridge

DESCRIPTION AND INTERESTS
This art education magazine provides art teachers with the inspiration and information that can help them do their jobs better. It views its articles as conduits for the exchange of professional experiences, advice, lesson plans, and fresh ideas. Circ: 20,000.

Audience: Art educators, grades K–12
Frequency: 10 times each year
Website: www.artsandactivities.com

FREELANCE POTENTIAL
95% written by nonstaff writers. Publishes 100 freelance submissions yearly; 50% by unpublished writers, 50% by authors who are new to the magazine. Receives 240 unsolicited mss each year.

SUBMISSIONS
Send complete ms. Accepts disk submissions with hard copy. Availability of artwork improves chance of acceptance. No simultaneous submissions. SASE. Responds in 4–8 months.

- Articles: Word lengths vary. Informational, how-to, and practical application articles; and personal experience pieces. Topics include art education, program development, collage, printmaking, art appreciation, and composition.
- Depts/columns: Word lengths vary. New product information, news items, and media reviews.
- Artwork: High-resolution digital images.
- Other: Lesson plans for classroom projects.

SAMPLE ISSUE
66 pages (29% advertising): 11 articles; 5 depts/columns. Sample copy, $3 with 9x12 SASE ($2 postage). Writers' guidelines and theme list available.

- "Riding the Wave: A Self-Portrait Study." Article describes a lower-elementary project involving self-portraits.
- Sample dept/column: "Media Reviews" offers reviews of two books and a DVD.

RIGHTS AND PAYMENT
First North American serial rights. All material, payment rates vary. Pays on publication. Provides 2 contributor's copies.

☛EDITOR'S COMMENTS
Our readers want practical information about things they can do in their art classes.

Asimov's Science Fiction

Dell Magazine Group
267 Broadway, 4th Floor
New York, NY 10007

Editor: Sheila Williams

DESCRIPTION AND INTERESTS

Serving a readership of young adult and adult science fiction fans, this journal features stories in which the characters, rather than the science, provide the main focus. It also publishes poetry and book reviews. Circ: 60,000.

Audience: YA–Adult
Frequency: 10 times each year
Website: www.asimovs.com

FREELANCE POTENTIAL

97% written by nonstaff writers. Publishes 85 freelance submissions yearly; 10% by unpublished writers, 30% by authors who are new to the magazine. Receives 8,400 unsolicited mss each year.

SUBMISSIONS

Send complete ms. Accepts hard copy and electronic submissions via website (RTF or DOC formats). No simultaneous submissions. SASE. Responds in 5 weeks.

- Fiction: To 20,000 words. Genres include science fiction and fantasy.
- Depts/columns: Word lengths vary. Book and website reviews.
- Other: Poetry, to 40 lines.

SAMPLE ISSUE

112 pages (10% advertising): 2 novelettes; 5 stories; 5 poems; 6 depts/columns. Sample copy, $5 with 9x12 SASE. Guidelines available at website.

- "The Consciousness Problem." Story follows an American woman living in South Korea and dealing with a concussion-caused mental health issue and her boyfriend's clone.
- Sample dept/column: "On Books" offers reviews of five science fiction books.

RIGHTS AND PAYMENT

First worldwide English-language serial rights. Fiction, $.05–$.06 per word. Poetry, $1 per line. Depts/columns, payment rates vary. Pays on acceptance. Provides 2 contributor's copies.

➡ EDITOR'S COMMENTS

Please note that we now accept electronic submissions. Before submitting material online, check our manuscript guidelines. Submissions of stories and poetry should be sent to us via our online form. While we do accept fantasy, we like what we call "borderline" fantasy—no sword and sorcery, please.

Ask

Cricket Magazine Group
70 East Lake Street, Suite 300
Chicago, IL 60601

Submissions Editor

DESCRIPTION AND INTERESTS

Young children have lots of questions about the world. *Ask* magazine exists to give them answers in language they understand and in formats they enjoy. Though most of its articles deal with facts about nature and science, all subjects are fair game. Circ: 42,000.

Audience: 7–10 years
Frequency: 9 times each year
Website: www.cricketmag.com

FREELANCE POTENTIAL

80% written by nonstaff writers.

SUBMISSIONS

Send résumé and clips. All material is commissioned from experienced writers. Response time varies.

- Articles: To 1,500 words. Informational articles; interviews; and photo-essays. Topics include science, nature, technology, math, history, and the arts.
- Depts/columns: Word lengths vary. Science news and Q&As.
- Other: Activities, cartoons, and contests.

SAMPLE ISSUE

34 pages (no advertising): 4 articles; 2 depts/columns; 1 activity; 2 cartoons; 1 contest. Sample copy available at website.

- "Water: The Liquid of Life." Article provides theories on the origins of water, and explains how it is vital for all life.
- "Can We Be Too Clean?" Article explains the difference between good germs and bad germs in our bodies and environments.
- "Codes: Keeping Secrets Secret." Article explains how people throughout history used codes to transmit secret information, and provides some examples of simple codes that readers can replicate.

RIGHTS AND PAYMENT

Rights vary. Written material, payment rates vary. Payment policy varies.

➡ EDITOR'S COMMENTS

Please do not query us with a pitch for a specific article. We assign all of the material we publish. You must have experience in writing nonfiction articles for young children and demonstrate an ability to engage young readers with information that is presented in fun and entertaining ways.

Atlanta Parent

2346 Perimeter Park Drive
Atlanta, GA 30341

Managing Editor: Kate Parrott

DESCRIPTION AND INTERESTS
Parenting advice, educational topics, local recreational opportunities, and children's social and emotional development are all covered in this magazine for parents living in the greater Atlanta region. Circ: 120,000.
Audience: Parents
Frequency: Monthly
Website: www.atlantaparent.com

FREELANCE POTENTIAL
40% written by nonstaff writers.

SUBMISSIONS
Send complete ms. Prefers email submissions to editor@atlantaparent.com (Microsoft Word attachments); will accept hard copy and disk submissions. SASE. Response time varies.

- Articles: 800–1,200 words. Informational and how-to articles; and humor. Topics include education, child care, child development, health, and parenting.
- Depts/columns: Word lengths vary. Health, trends, medical advice, parenting tips, and humorous pieces.
- Other: Submit seasonal material 6 months in advance.

SAMPLE ISSUE
82 pages (55% advertising): 5 articles; 10 depts/columns; 1 special section; 2 calendars. Sample copy, $3 with 9x12 SASE. Writers' guidelines available.

- "Kid Collectors." Article examines why kids collect and trade things, and what this habit is teaching them.
- "In a Dinosaur Daze." Article reports on the toys, movies, exhibits, and books that are sure to please a dinosaur-obsessed child.
- Sample dept/column: "Humor" offers a funny take on one mother's attempt to keep her kids occupied all summer long.

RIGHTS AND PAYMENT
One-time and Internet rights. Written material, $35–$50. Pays on publication. Provides 1 contributor's copy.

❖EDITOR'S COMMENTS
All of our articles are down-to-earth in tone. We do not publish philosophical or theoretical pieces. Most articles are written in the third person; with the exception of humor essays, we rarely publish first-person pieces.

Autism Asperger's Digest

P.O. Box 1519
Waynesville, NC 28786

Managing Editor: Veronica Zysk

DESCRIPTION AND INTERESTS
This magazine on autism spectrum disorders presents real-life information for readers trying to meet the real-life challenges of ASD. Its articles feature practical, tested strategies and ideas addressing traditional, alternative, and emerging thought on ASD. Circ: 12,000.
Audience: Parents and ASD professionals
Frequency: 6 times each year
Website: www.autismdigest.com

FREELANCE POTENTIAL
75% written by nonstaff writers. Publishes 50–60 freelance submissions yearly; 60% by unpublished writers, 60% by authors who are new to the magazine. Receives 100 queries, 200–300 unsolicited mss yearly.

SUBMISSIONS
Query or send complete ms. Accepts hard copy and email submissions to editor@autismdigest.com (Microsoft Word attachments or pasted into body of text). SASE. Responds in 2–4 weeks.

- Articles: Personal experience pieces, 1,000–1,200 words. Informational and how-to articles, 1,200–2,000 words. Topics include living with autism, strategies for parents and educators, and current research.
- Depts/columns: Newsbites, 100–300 words.
- Artwork: Color prints; JPEGs at 300 dpi.

SAMPLE ISSUE
58 pages: 8 articles; 7 depts/columns. Guidelines available at website.

- "When Times Are Sad." Article outlines ways parents and therapists can help children on the autism spectrum manage grief.
- Sample dept/column: "Think Social!" discusses how to bring one's eyes into the communicative process and the role they play in relating to others.

RIGHTS AND PAYMENT
First rights. No payment. Provides contributor's copies and a 1-year subscription.

❖EDITOR'S COMMENTS
We prefer articles that have a strong hands-on approach to their subject matter, rather than those that simply provide a general overview of a topic. Personal accounts are acceptable as long as they are motivational and have "real life" application.

Babybug

Cricket Magazine Group
70 East Lake Street, Suite 300
Chicago, IL 60601

Associate Editor: Jenny Gillespie

DESCRIPTION AND INTERESTS
This magazine is designed in board book style
for the littlest readers. Its brightly colored
pages feature stories, poems, words, and concepts that help young children discover the
world around them. It is part of the Cricket
Magazine Group. Circ: 50,000.

Audience: 6 months–2 years
Frequency: 9 times each year
Website: www.babybugmagkids.com

FREELANCE POTENTIAL
100% written by nonstaff writers. Publishes
30–40 freelance submissions yearly; 50% by
authors who are new to the magazine.
Receives 2,400 unsolicited mss yearly.

SUBMISSIONS
Send complete ms. Accepts hard copy and
simultaneous submissions if identified. SASE.
Responds in 6 months.

- Articles: 10 words. Features material that
  conveys simple concepts and ideas.
- Fiction: 4–6 short sentences. Simple stories.
- Artwork: By assignment only. Send sample
  tearsheets, photoprints, or photocopies to
  be kept on file.
- Other: Parent-child activities, to 8 lines.
  Rhyming and rhythmic poetry, to 8 lines.
  Action rhymes, 4–8 lines.

SAMPLE ISSUE
24 pages (no advertising): 4 stories; 4 poems;
1 activity. Sample copy, $5. Guidelines avail-
able at website.

- "Kim and Carrots." Story features a little girl
  who likes to draw alongside her mother.
- "My Letter." Story tells of a young girl making
  and then sending Valentine's Day cards to
  her grandparents.
- "Play Dough." Poem looks at the fun of playing with play dough.

RIGHTS AND PAYMENT
All or second North American serial rights.
Written material, $25+. Artwork, $500 per
spread, $250 per page. Pays on publication.
Provides 6 contributor's copies.

•❖EDITOR'S COMMENTS
While we always welcome submissions from
new writers, please be aware that we have
very high standards. Your material must be
top quality to get our attention.

Babytalk

460 North Orlando Avenue, Suite 200
Winter Park, FL 32789

Editor-in-Chief: Ana Connery

DESCRIPTION AND INTERESTS
This magazine provides "straight talk for new
moms." It features informational and supportive articles on issues faced by parents of
babies. Circ: 2 million.

Audience: Parents
Frequency: 10 times each year
Website: www.babytalk.com

FREELANCE POTENTIAL
50% written by nonstaff writers. Publishes 40
freelance submissions yearly; 20% by authors
who are new to the magazine. Receives 500
queries yearly.

SUBMISSIONS
Query with clips or writing samples. Accepts
hard copy. No simultaneous submissions.
SASE. Responds in 2 months.

- Articles: 1,500–2,000 words. Informational,
  how-to, and self-help articles; and personal
  experience pieces. Topics include fertility,
  pregnancy, childbirth, new motherhood,
  breastfeeding, infant health and development, baby care, juvenile equipment and
  toys, day care, nutrition, and marital issues.
- Depts/columns: 500–1,200 words. Baby
  health, milestones, product information,
  postpartum issues, Q&As, home economics,
  and humor.

SAMPLE ISSUE
64 pages (50% advertising): 5 articles; 11
depts/columns. Sample copy, free with 9x12
SASE. Guidelines available. Editorial calendar
available at website.

- "Wanted: The Perfect Babysitter." Article
  examines what to look for in a babysitter
  and where to find him or her.
- Sample dept/column: "Laugh It Off" offers a
  humorous take on the birth announcement
  we'd all like to see, but likely never will.

RIGHTS AND PAYMENT
First rights. Articles, $1,000–$2,000. Depts/
columns, $300–$1,200. Pays on acceptance.
Provides 2–4 contributor's copies.

•❖EDITOR'S COMMENTS
Articles should be supportive and informative
without being preachy. We understand that
being a new mom is stressful enough without
know-it-all writers pushing their opinions.

Baltimore's Child

11 Dutton Court
Baltimore, MD 21228

Editor: Dianne R. McCann

DESCRIPTION AND INTERESTS

In addition to covering local activities, resources, and services for families in the Baltimore region, the articles here emphasize positive, constructive, and practical advice regarding parenting issues. Circ: 60,000.

Audience: Parents
Frequency: Monthly
Website: www.baltimoreschild.com

FREELANCE POTENTIAL

90% written by nonstaff writers. Publishes 250 freelance submissions yearly; 5% by unpublished writers, 10% by authors who are new to the magazine.

SUBMISSIONS

Prefers query; will accept complete ms. Accepts email submissions to dianne@baltimoreschild.com. Response time varies.

- Articles: 1,000–1,500 words. Informational articles. Topics include parenting, education, health, fitness, child care, social issues, and regional news.
- Depts/columns: Word lengths vary. Music, family cooking, pet care, baby and toddler issues, parenting children with special needs, parenting teens, and family finances.

SAMPLE ISSUE

92 pages: 4 articles; 14 depts/columns; 4 calendars; 1 party directory. Sample copy and guidelines available at website.

- "Poison Ivy: Nothing to Sing About." Article explains how the oil from the poison ivy plant causes rashes in humans, and provides tips for treating the itch.
- "Where Are All the Babysitters?" Article shares the frustration of trying to find the right babysitter for a family, and provides hints on where to find them.

RIGHTS AND PAYMENT

One-time rights. Written material, payment rates vary. Pays on publication.

⇥EDITOR'S COMMENTS

We prefer articles that are about living and raising children in the Baltimore region. We will accept general parenting topics, but the article must have local sources. Our typical reader is looking for suggestions on where to go or what to do with children, or how to solve a common parenting problem.

Baseball Youth

Dugout Media
P.O. Box 983
Morehead, KY 40351

Managing Editor: Nathan Clinkenbeard

DESCRIPTION AND INTERESTS

This magazine allows kids to get lost in the world of baseball. Covering everything from youth leagues to the major leagues, *Baseball Youth* features profiles, interviews, advice, and tips. Circ: 100,000.

Audience: Boys, 7–14 years
Frequency: 6 times each year
Website: www.baseballyouth.com

FREELANCE POTENTIAL

10% written by nonstaff writers. Publishes 10–20 freelance submissions yearly. Receives 96 queries yearly.

SUBMISSIONS

Query with word length and availability of artwork. Prefers email queries to nathanc@dugoutmedia.com (Microsoft Word attachments); will accept hard copy. Availability of artwork improves chance of acceptance. SASE. Response time varies.

- Articles: Word lengths vary. Informational and how-to articles; profiles; interviews; photo-essays; and personal experience pieces. Topics include youth baseball, major and minor league baseball, players, coaches, training, ballparks, baseball equipment, and baseball cards.
- Depts/columns: Word lengths vary. Baseball news, card collections, mascot interviews, fan club information, first-person essays, and video game reviews.
- Artwork: Color digital images or prints.
- Other: Puzzles, quizzes, and comics.

SAMPLE ISSUE

46 pages: 4 articles; 9 depts/columns. Sample copy available at website. Guidelines available.

- "Nate the Great." Article is an interview with Atlanta Braves center fielder Nate McLouth.
- Sample dept/column: "The Clubhouse" reveals the top 10 baseball cards most sought after by kids.

RIGHTS AND PAYMENT

All rights. Written material, payment rates vary. Payment policy varies.

⇥EDITOR'S COMMENTS

We are always looking for cool and interesting facts about our national pastime. Young writers-to-be are welcome to query us on ideas for personality profiles.

Bay State Parent

117 Elm Street
Millbury, MA 01527

Editor: Carrie Wattu

DESCRIPTION AND INTERESTS
Bay State Parent is dedicated to providing up-to-date parenting information and activity guides to families living in eastern and central Massachusetts. Its features and regular departments cover health, education, entertainment, and travel. Circ: 42,000.

Audience: Parents
Frequency: Monthly
Website: www.baystateparent.com

FREELANCE POTENTIAL
95% written by nonstaff writers. Publishes 72–144 freelance submissions yearly; 5% by unpublished writers, 30% by authors who are new to the magazine. Receives 120 queries each year.

SUBMISSIONS
Query. Accepts email queries to editor@baystateparent.com (Microsoft Word attachments). Availability of artwork improves chance of acceptance. Responds in 1 month.

- Articles: To 2,000 words. Informational and how-to articles; and humor. Topics include parenting and family issues, regional and local events, health, travel, books, arts and crafts, family finance, and computers.
- Depts/columns: To 1,500 words. Family health, profiles of fathers, travel pieces.
- Artwork: B/W or color prints; JPEG images at 200 dpi.
- Other: Submit seasonal material 4 months in advance.

SAMPLE ISSUE
60 pages (15% advertising): 3 articles; 6 depts/columns; 3 event calendars. Sample copy, free. Guidelines available.

- "Colorful Food, Crazy Kids!" Article considers whether food dyes could cause behavioral problems in children.
- Sample dept/column: "Take Good Care" tells how to treat "nursemaid's elbow."

RIGHTS AND PAYMENT
First Massachusetts exclusive and electronic rights. Articles, $50–$85. Depts/columns, no payment. Kill fee varies. Pays on publication.

◆ EDITOR'S COMMENTS
We're much more likely to respond to a query if it comes from a local writer and if it cites local sources.

BC Parent News Magazine

Sasamat RPO 72086
Vancouver, British Columbia V6R 4P2
Canada

Editor: Elizabeth Shaffer

DESCRIPTION AND INTERESTS
This magazine gives parents in British Columbia the information they want on family health care, education, birthing, the arts, and issues of interest to parents. It also serves as a resource for parents looking for local events, organizations, and services. Circ: 45,000.

Audience: Parents
Frequency: 9 times each year
Website: www.bcparent.ca

FREELANCE POTENTIAL
80% written by nonstaff writers. Publishes 25 freelance submissions yearly; 10–30% by authors who are new to the magazine.

SUBMISSIONS
Send complete ms. Prefers email submissions to eshaffer@telus.net (RTF attachments); will accept disk submissions. No simultaneous submissions. SAE/IRC. Responds in 2 months.

- Articles: 500–1,000 words. Informational articles. Topics include pregnancy, childbirth, adoption, baby and child care, teen issues, family issues, health care, education, computers, sports, money matters, the arts, and community events.
- Depts/columns: Word lengths vary. Parent health, family news, and media reviews.

SAMPLE ISSUE
26 pages: 3 articles; 3 depts/columns. Sample copy available at website. Guidelines and editorial calendar available.

- "Involved Dads Make a Difference." Article extols the more hands-on roles that many fathers are playing in their children's lives.
- "Are Parents Contributing to the End of Modesty?" Article examines the role that parents play in promoting or destroying a child's sense of modesty.
- Sample dept/column: "Family Health" explains the effect of sun exposure on skin, and provides tips for protecting children's skin while outside.

RIGHTS AND PAYMENT
First rights. Articles, $85. Reprints, $50. Depts/columns, payment rates vary. Pays on acceptance.

◆ EDITOR'S COMMENTS
Any topic that will be of interest or help to a parent will be of interest to us.

Better Homes and Gardens

1716 Locust Street
Des Moines, IA 50309-3023

Department Editor

DESCRIPTION AND INTERESTS
This well-known lifestyle magazine includes practical and inspirational material relating to home life. *Better Homes and Gardens* covers everything from fashion, beauty, and cooking to family finances, parenting, and child development. Circ: 7.6 million.
Audience: Adults
Frequency: Monthly
Website: www.bhg.com

FREELANCE POTENTIAL
10% written by nonstaff writers. Publishes 25–30 freelance submissions yearly; 25% by authors who are new to the magazine. Receives 240 queries yearly.

SUBMISSIONS
Query with résumé and clips or writing samples. Accepts hard copy. SASE. Responds in 1 month.

- Articles: Word lengths vary. Informational and how-to articles; profiles; and personal experience pieces. Topics include food and nutrition, home design, gardening, outdoor living, travel, the environment, health and fitness, holidays, education, parenting, and child development.
- Depts/columns: Staff written.

SAMPLE ISSUE
260 pages (48% advertising): 31 articles; 3 depts/columns. Sample copy, $3.99 at newsstands. Guidelines available.

- "On-Screen Talent." Article provides an overview of video games that the whole family can enjoy together.
- "Sweet Tradition." Article shows how a young mother brings family and friends together for a yearly gingerbread-house-making party.

RIGHTS AND PAYMENT
All rights. Written material, payment rates vary. Kill fee, 25%. Pays on acceptance. Provides 1 contributor's copy.

✎EDITOR'S COMMENTS
We'll consider parenting pieces that have a personal angle—as long as they share information that is helpful to other parents. For informational articles, you must be able to show us that you have expertise in the subject you are tackling.

Beyond Centauri

P.O. Box 782
Cedar Rapids, IA 52406

Managing Editor: Tyree Campbell

DESCRIPTION AND INTERESTS
Beyond Centauri is a magazine of fantasy and science fiction designed specifically for tweens through young adults. It features short stories, informational articles, and reviews. Circ: 150.
Audience: 9–18 years
Frequency: Quarterly
Website: www.samsdotpublishing.com

FREELANCE POTENTIAL
95% written by nonstaff writers. Publishes 80 freelance submissions yearly; 15% by unpublished writers, 25% by authors who are new to the magazine. Receives 36–60 queries, 1,200 unsolicited mss yearly.

SUBMISSIONS
Query or send complete ms. Accepts hard copy and email to beyondcentauri@yahoo.com (RTF attachments). SASE. Responds to queries in 2 weeks, to mss in 2–3 months.

- Articles: To 500 words. Informational articles; opinion pieces; and media reviews. Topics include space exploration, science, and technology.
- Fiction: To 2,500 words. Genres include science fiction, fantasy, and adventure.
- Artwork: B/W illustrations.
- Other: Poetry, to 50 lines. Science fiction, fantasy, and insect themes.

SAMPLE ISSUE
50 pages (no advertising): 4 articles; 8 stories; 10 poems. Sample copy, $7 with 9x12 SASE. Guidelines available.

- "The Wendigo." Article explains a mythical, cannibalistic creature from the Cree and Ojibwa peoples.
- "A Piece of the Wind." Story follows a dragon from his youngest days with his mother through his first battle and, ultimately, his first kill.

RIGHTS AND PAYMENT
First North American serial rights. Articles, $3. Fiction, $5. Poetry, $2. Artwork, $5. Pays on publication. Provides 1 contributor's copy.

✎EDITOR'S COMMENTS
We are always in need of well-crafted science fiction adventures. We are happy to work with new authors, and often publish the work of teenage writers.

Birmingham Christian Family

P.O. Box 382724
Birmingham, AL 35238

Editor: Laurie Stroud

DESCRIPTION AND INTERESTS
Birmingham Christian Family is read by parents for its uplifting articles and stories, with all content originating from a Christian perspective. It specifically addresses families living in and around Birmingham. Circ: 35,000.

Audience: Families
Frequency: Monthly
Website:
  www.christianfamilypublications.com

FREELANCE POTENTIAL
72% written by nonstaff writers. Publishes 15 freelance submissions yearly; 5% by unpublished writers, 3% by authors who are new to the magazine. Receives 240 queries yearly.

SUBMISSIONS
Query with artwork, if applicable. Accepts email to laurie@christianfamilypublications.com. Availability of artwork improves chance of acceptance. Responds in 1 month.

- Articles: To 500 words. Informational, self-help, and how-to articles; profiles; and personal experience pieces. Topics include love, family life, parenting, Christianity, churches, philanthropy, education, recreation, the arts, travel, and sports.
- Fiction: To 500 words. Inspirational and humorous stories.
- Depts/columns: To 500 words. Media and restaurant reviews; faith in the workplace; financial, health, home improvement, and business tips; recipes; and family travel.
- Artwork: B/W and color prints.

SAMPLE ISSUE
32 pages (25% advertising): 7 articles; 20 depts/columns. Sample copy, free with 9x12 SASE ($3 postage). Editorial calendar available.

- "*The Blind Side* Mom, Leigh Anne Tuohy." Article profiles the real-life woman who inspired the popular Oscar-winning film.
- Sample dept/column: "Hassle Free Zone" explains the many benefits of being organized in business and the office.

RIGHTS AND PAYMENT
Rights vary. No payment.

➥EDITOR'S COMMENTS
While submissions on a wide variety of topics are welcome, a local angle is mandatory, as is a Christian perspective.

The Black Collegian

140 Carondelet Street
New Orleans, LA 70130

Chief Executive Officer: Preston J. Edwards, Sr.

DESCRIPTION AND INTERESTS
Launched in 1970, this career and self-development magazine targeting African American college students provides information about careers, job opportunities, and employment trends. Profiles of corporations and graduate programs are other regular features. Circ: 121,000.

Audience: 18–30 years
Frequency: Twice each year
Website: www.blackcollegian.com

FREELANCE POTENTIAL
95% written by nonstaff writers. Publishes 20 freelance submissions yearly; 33% by authors who are new to the magazine. Receives 24 queries yearly.

SUBMISSIONS
Query. Prefers email queries to preston@ imdiversity.com; will accept hard copy. SASE. Responds in 3 months.

- Articles: 1,500–2,000 words. Informational, self-help, and how-to articles; profiles; and personal experience pieces. Topics include careers, job opportunities, graduate and professional school, internships, study-abroad programs, personal development, financial aid, history, technology, and multicultural and ethnic issues.
- Depts/columns: Word lengths vary. Health issues and media reviews.
- Artwork: 5x7 and 11x14 B/W and color transparencies. B/W and color line art.

SAMPLE ISSUE
72 pages: 16 articles. Sample copy and guidelines available at website.

- "Fostering A New Generation of Researchers and Graduate Scholars." Article profiles the Ronald E. McNair Baccalaureate Achievement Program, which supports the studies of first-generation students across the country.
- "Career and Life Management Plan: Why Include Graduate School?" Article touts the advantages of post-graduate education.

RIGHTS AND PAYMENT
One-time rights. All material, payment rates vary. Pays after publication. Provides 1 copy.

➥EDITOR'S COMMENTS
Articles should provide useful information for black college students planning their futures.

Blaze Magazine

P.O. Box 2660
Niagara Falls, NY 14302

Editor: Brenda McCarthy

DESCRIPTION AND INTERESTS

Blaze gives children a ride into the wonderful world of horses. It is filled with articles about horses and the natural world, and horse-based activities and games. Circ: 4,000.

Audience: 8–14 years
Frequency: Quarterly
Website: www.blazekids.com

FREELANCE POTENTIAL

50% written by nonstaff writers. Publishes 25–30 freelance submissions yearly.

SUBMISSIONS

Query. Accepts email queries to brenda@ blazekids.com. Availability of artwork improves chance of acceptance. Response time varies.

- Articles: 200–500 words. Informational and how-to articles; and profiles. Topics include horseback riding, training, and breeds.
- Fiction: Word lengths vary. Stories featuring horses.
- Depts/columns: Word lengths vary. Short news items, arts and crafts.
- Artwork: B/W and color prints and transparencies.
- Other: Puzzles and games.

SAMPLE ISSUE

40 pages (15% advertising): 4 articles; 1 story; 5 depts/columns; 5 puzzles and games. Sample copy, $3.75.

- "Fairy Tale Horses: The Andalusian." Article profiles the Andalusian breed, known for its beauty and athleticism.
- "Pepito's Adventure." Story brings readers into a young horse's daydream of participating in a trail ride in the Andes.
- Sample dept/column: "Friend or Foe" offers interesting facts about the dragonfly.

RIGHTS AND PAYMENT

Rights vary. Written material, $.25 per word. Payment policy varies.

☛EDITOR'S COMMENTS

We never forget that our readers are horse-crazy kids who love to ride and learn about horses. We like articles that employ a mix of entertainment and education. Yes, we are a magazine about horses, but we are also a magazine of discovery for children, and are happy to receive articles about other animals and the environment.

bNetS@vvy

1201 16th Street NW, Suite 216
Washington, DC 20036

Editor: Mary Esselman

DESCRIPTION AND INTERESTS

This e-newsletter is dedicated to promoting Internet safety for children and teens. Read by parents, teachers, and others who work with youth, it puts a particular focus on social networking sites. It is published by the National Education Association Health Information Network. Hits per month: Unavailable.

Audience: Parents and teachers
Frequency: 6 times each year
Website: www.bnetsavvy.org

FREELANCE POTENTIAL

90% written by nonstaff writers. Publishes 20 freelance submissions yearly; 80% by unpublished writers, 90% by authors who are new to the magazine.

SUBMISSIONS

Query. Accepts email queries with clips (or links to published work) to internetsafety@ nea.org. Responds in 2 weeks.

- Articles: 600–950 words. Informational and how-to articles; and reviews. Topics include the Internet and Internet safety, and social networking sites.
- Depts/columns: 600–950 words. Expert advice and ideas from parents and teens.

SAMPLE ISSUE

1 article; 3 depts/columns. Sample copy and guidelines available at website.

- "Learning to Model and Monitor Responsible Online Behavior." Article features perspectives from several parents on helping kids understand the future consequences of current online activity.
- "A Smart Girl's Guide to the Internet." Article presents two reviews, written by middle school girls, of a new book on the Internet.
- Sample dept/column: "Cyberbullying" offers advice on what to do if your child is threatening other children via text messaging.

RIGHTS AND PAYMENT

All rights. Written material, payment rates vary. Payment policy varies.

☛EDITOR'S COMMENTS

We welcome contributions by parents, teachers, school staff, and tweens who want to share their advice, stories, ideas, and lessons. Remember, everything must be related to the responsible use of technology.

Bonbon

2123 Preston Square Court, Suite 300
Falls Church, VA 22043

Publisher: Sitki Kazanci

DESCRIPTION AND INTERESTS

This bilingual magazine for Turkish children features articles that reflect Turkey's culture, traditions, and values while conveying a message of tolerance and understanding. It is read by Turkish children living in America as well as by children living in Turkey. Circ: 6,000.

Audience: 6–14 years
Frequency: 6 times each year
Website: www.bonbonkids.com

FREELANCE POTENTIAL

60% written by nonstaff writers. Publishes 30 freelance submissions yearly; 25% by unpublished writers, 10% by authors who are new to the magazine.

SUBMISSIONS

Query with brief author biography. Accepts email queries to info@bonbonkids.com (include "Bonbon query" in subject field). Responds in 2 weeks.

- Articles: 250 words. Informational articles; profiles; and interviews. Topics include the Turkish language, culture, and traditions; news; animals; nature; and history.
- Fiction: 500 words. Stories that feature Turkish traditions, culture, and values.
- Other: Comics, puzzles, games, jokes, and activities. Poetry.

SAMPLE ISSUE

26 pages: 4 articles; 2 stories; 5 comics; 2 games and activities.

- "Turkish Ceramic Artist Sitki Usta." Article presents an interview with the artist about his work and his reverence for the ancient Turkish art.
- "10 Tips for Improving Your Test Scores." Article offers tips for developing good study habits.
- Sample dept/column: "Test Your Brain" offers brain-teaser puzzles and activities.

RIGHTS AND PAYMENT

One-time rights. No payment.

➡ EDITOR'S COMMENTS

As a nonprofit magazine, we cannot compensate contributors at this time. We're always looking for talented writers and artists, though —especially those interested in enhancing awareness of Turkish culture, and in helping kids learn to read and speak Turkish.

Book Links

American Library Association
50 East Huron Street
Chicago, IL 60611

Editor: Laura Tillotson

DESCRIPTION AND INTERESTS

This publication of the American Library Association aims to be a source of ideas and strategies for encouraging a love of reading. Articles feature techniques for integrating books in the classroom, bibliographies, and author and illustrator profiles. Circ: 20,577.

Audience: Teachers and librarians
Frequency: Quarterly
Website: www.ala.org/booklinks

FREELANCE POTENTIAL

90% written by nonstaff writers. Publishes 60 freelance submissions yearly; 20% by unpublished writers, 30% by authors who are new to the magazine. Receives 96 queries and unsolicited mss yearly.

SUBMISSIONS

Query or send complete ms. Accepts email to ltillotson@ala.org. Response time varies.

- Articles: Word lengths vary. Informational and how-to articles; profiles; interviews; and annotated bibliographies. Topics include multicultural literature, literacy, language arts, core curriculum subjects, education, the arts, authors, illustrators, and teaching techniques.
- Depts/columns: Word lengths vary. Curriculum ideas, personal essays, and themed book lists.

SAMPLE ISSUE

64 pages (28% advertising): 12 articles; 10 depts/columns. Sample copy, $6. Guidelines and editorial calendar available at website.

- "Casting the Spell: Fairy Tales in Novel Form." Article recommends recent novelized versions of classic fairy tales that are appropriate for tweens and teens.
- Sample dept/column: "Making Every Book Count" recommends books for each grade level that will encourage shared learning.

RIGHTS AND PAYMENT

All rights. Articles, $100. Pays on publication. Provides 2 contributor's copies.

➡ EDITOR'S COMMENTS

Each issue focuses on a core curriculum area, such as social studies, science, or history. While not every piece published is theme-related, the bulk of the articles do have relevance to one of the subjects.

Boys' Life

Boy Scouts of America
1325 West Walnut Hill Lane
P.O. Box 152079
Irving, TX 75015-2079

Senior Writer: Aaron Derr

DESCRIPTION AND INTERESTS
If it is of interest to boys, it will be covered here. Published by the Boy Scouts of America since 1911, *Boys' Life* publishes articles that entertain and inform boys. Topics include outdoor adventure, scouting news, sports, video games, television, and films. Circ: 1.1 million.
Audience: 6–18 years
Frequency: Monthly
Website: www.boyslife.org

FREELANCE POTENTIAL
80% written by nonstaff writers. Publishes 50 freelance submissions yearly; 1% by unpublished writers, 2% by authors who are new to the magazine.

SUBMISSIONS
Query. Accepts hard copy. SASE. Responds in 4–6 weeks.

- Articles: 500–1,500 words. Informational and how-to articles; profiles; and humor. Topics include sports, science, American history, geography, nature, and the environment.
- Fiction: By assignment only.
- Depts/columns: To 600 words. Advice, humor, collecting, computers, and pets.
- Other: Puzzles and cartoons.

SAMPLE ISSUE
52 pages (18% advertising): 5 articles; 7 depts/columns; 6 comics. Sample copy, $3.60 with 9x12 SASE. Guidelines available.

- "This Job's a Hit!" Article interviews Phillies' play-by-play radio announcer Scott Franzke.
- "Hiking Half Dome." Article presents a Scout troop from California that drew on months of preparation and determination to reach the summit of this famous Yosemite landmark.
- Sample dept/column: "BL Headliners" offers a short profile about a young skateboarder.

RIGHTS AND PAYMENT
First rights. Articles, $400–$1,500. Fiction, $750+. Depts/columns, $100–$400. Pays on acceptance. Provides 2 contributor's copies.

➥EDITOR'S COMMENTS
Because of our high standards, all of our articles are commissioned. Though we accept article queries, unsolicited manuscripts will be returned unread. Our articles emphasize good character, kindness, adventure, and an appreciation of the world around us.

Boys' Quest

P.O. Box 227
Bluffton, OH 45817-0227

Editor: Marilyn Edwards

DESCRIPTION AND INTERESTS
A magazine for boys that can be used in the classroom or for pleasure reading at home, *Boys' Quest* is filled with articles offering information, adventure, and fun. Circ: 12,000.
Audience: 6–13 years
Frequency: 6 times each year
Website: www.boysquest.com

FREELANCE POTENTIAL
70% written by nonstaff writers. Publishes 100–150 freelance submissions yearly; 30% by unpublished writers, 40% by new authors. Receives 120 queries, 2,400 mss yearly.

SUBMISSIONS
Prefers complete ms; will accept query. Accepts hard copy and simultaneous submissions if identified. Availability of artwork improves chance of acceptance. SASE. Responds to queries in 1–2 weeks, to mss in 2–3 months.

- Articles: 500 words. Informational and how-to articles; profiles; personal experience pieces; and humor. Topics include nature, pets, hobbies, sports, family, and careers.
- Fiction: 500 words. Genres include adventure, mystery, and multicultural fiction.
- Depts/columns: 300–500 words. Science experiments and carpentry projects.
- Artwork: B/W and color prints.
- Other: Poetry. Puzzles and games.

SAMPLE ISSUE
48 pages (no advertising): 12 articles; 8 depts/columns; 8 puzzles. Sample copy, $6. Guidelines and theme list available at website.

- "The Horse Fell on the Camera." Article tells about the challenges faced by the photographers who captured images of the American West in the nineteenth century.
- Sample dept/column: "Computer Quest" explains how to program and play a game with your computer.

RIGHTS AND PAYMENT
First North American serial rights. Articles and fiction, $.05+ per word. Depts/columns, $35. Poetry and puzzles, $10+. Artwork, $5 per photo. Pays on publication. Provides 1 copy.

➥EDITOR'S COMMENTS
We continue to update our theme lists and deadlines, so check our website regularly.

Brass

P.O. Box 1220
Corvallis, OR 97339

Editorial Content Manager: Jennie Bartlemay

DESCRIPTION AND INTERESTS
Brass magazine has a mission to make money matters interesting, simple, and relevant for young adults. It provides entertaining yet educational articles about financial issues, and profiles up-and-coming young adults who are making a difference. Circ: Unavailable.

Audience: 16–25 years
Frequency: Monthly
Website: www.brassmagazine.com

FREELANCE POTENTIAL
50% written by nonstaff writers. Publishes 20–30 freelance submissions yearly; 40% by unpublished writers, 40% by authors who are new to the magazine. Receives 24 queries and unsolicited mss yearly.

SUBMISSIONS
Prefers query; will accept complete ms. Accepts email to editor@brassmagazine.com. Response time varies.

- Articles: 500–700 words. Informational, self-help, and how-to articles; and profiles. Topics include personal improvement, professional advancement, education, fashion, sports, entertainment, health, travel, investments, saving strategies, banking, and portfolio management.
- Depts/columns: Word lengths vary. Starting a business, finance fundamentals, and trends.
- Other: Crossword puzzles.

SAMPLE ISSUE
28 pages: 3 articles; 6 depts/columns; 1 puzzle. Sample copy and writers' guidelines available at website.

- "Systematic Savings: Start Early and Stay Rich." Article explains how to set up a system of saving and investing that will earn big bucks in the long run.
- Sample dept/column: "Brass Ten" outlines 10 questions to ask at a job interview, and explains why they are so important.

RIGHTS AND PAYMENT
All rights. Written material, payment rates vary. Pays on publication. Provides up to 5 contributor's copies.

➡️ EDITOR'S COMMENTS
Please log in at our website to receive the latest update on our current editorial needs, and to register your areas of expertise.

Brilliant Star

1233 Central Street
Evanston, IL 60201

Associate Editor: Susan Engle

DESCRIPTION AND INTERESTS
Designed for children of middle-school age, *Brilliant Star* presents the history and spirituality of the Bahá'í faith through stories, articles, and activities. Circ: 7,000.

Audience: 8–12 years
Frequency: 6 times each year
Website: www.brilliantstarmagazine.org

FREELANCE POTENTIAL
35% written by nonstaff writers. Publishes 5 freelance submissions yearly; 5% by unpublished writers, 80% by authors who are new to the magazine. Receives 24 queries, 120 unsolicited mss yearly.

SUBMISSIONS
Query with clips for articles. Send complete ms for fiction. Accepts hard copy, email queries to brilliant@usbnc.org, and simultaneous submissions if identified. SASE. Responds in 6–8 months.

- Articles: To 350 words. Informational and how-to articles; personal experience pieces; interviews; profiles; and biographies. Topics include historical Bahá'í figures, religion, history, ethnic and social issues, travel, music, and nature.
- Fiction: To 700 words. Early reader fiction. Genres include ethnic, historical, contemporary, and problem-solving fiction.
- Depts/columns: To 600 words. Religion, ethics, and profiles of kids.
- Other: Puzzles, activities, and games.

SAMPLE ISSUE
30 pages: 9 articles; 1 story; 9 depts/columns; 1 song. Sample copy, $3.50 with 9x12 SASE (5 first-class stamps). Guidelines and theme list/editorial calendar available.

- "Now Showing: Your Life." Article helps readers determine what their future professions might be.
- Sample dept/column: "Maya's Mysteries" lets readers create their own personal statement about their character.

RIGHTS AND PAYMENT
All or one-time rights. No payment. Provides 2 contributor's copies.

➡️ EDITOR'S COMMENTS
Everything we print supports the Bahá'í philosophy of humanity, love, and harmony.

Broomstix

P.O. Box 8139
Bridgewater, NJ 08807

Submissions: Katharine Clark

DESCRIPTION AND INTERESTS
Broomstix is an online children's magazine that embraces the pagan perspective. It features articles, creative writing, poetry, rituals, and activities that relate to the seasons, Mother Earth, and New Age topics. *Broomstix* also accepts writing and artwork from children. Hits per month: 6,000.

Audience: Children
Frequency: Quarterly
Website: www.broomstix.com

FREELANCE POTENTIAL
30% written by nonstaff writers. Publishes 10 freelance submissions yearly; 75% by unpublished writers, 50% by authors who are new to the magazine. Receives 60 unsolicited mss each year.

SUBMISSIONS
Send complete ms. Accepts hard copy. SASE for artwork only; mss are not returned. Responds in 2 weeks.

- Articles: To 750 words. Informational articles. Topics include nature-based spirituality, pagan rituals and Sabbats, the environment, social and multicultural issues, and the arts.
- Fiction: To 750 words. "Pagan Parables," including folktales and myths.
- Depts/columns: 500 words. "Hearth and Home," "Pruitt the Druid," "Wicc'ed Ways," and craft projects.
- Artwork: B/W and color prints. Line art.
- Other: Theme-related and seasonal poetry.

SAMPLE ISSUE
Sample copy, guidelines, and theme list available at website.

- "Familiarity Lesson Number 10: Spring Chickens." Article explains the importance of the chicken or rooster symbol in several cultures.
- Sample dept/column: "Hearth and Home" suggests that readers celebrate an "Un-Birthday" by giving presents to organizations in need.

RIGHTS AND PAYMENT
One-time electronic rights. Written material, $.01 per word, $5.00 maximum. Artwork, $1–$5. Pays 1 month after publication.

➥EDITOR'S COMMENTS
We want to use more freelance writers! We're trying to cover a variety of New Age topics, as well as feng shui, Reiki, and meditation.

Cadet Quest

Calvinist Cadet Corps
1333 Alger Street SE
P.O. Box 7259
Grand Rapids, MI 49510

Editor: G. Richard Broene

DESCRIPTION AND INTERESTS
This Christian magazine for boys is filled with articles, stories, projects, cartoons, and Bible lessons. Each issue of the magazine revolves around a single theme. Circ: 8,000.

Audience: Boys, 9–14 years
Frequency: 7 times each year
Website: www.calvinistcadets.org

FREELANCE POTENTIAL
58% written by nonstaff writers. Publishes 35 freelance submissions yearly; 3% by unpublished writers, 10% by authors who are new to the magazine. Receives 360–600 unsolicited mss yearly.

SUBMISSIONS
Send complete ms. Accepts hard copy, email to submissions@calvinistcadets.org (no attachments), and simultaneous submissions if identified. SASE. Responds in 1 month.

- Articles: 400–1,000 words. Informational and factual articles; profiles; and interviews. Topics include religion, spirituality, stewardship, camping, crafts and hobbies, sports, the environment, and serving God.
- Fiction: 1,000–3,000 words. Stories that appeal to boys' sense of adventure and humor; must fit one of the planned themes.
- Depts/columns: Word lengths vary. Cadet Corps news items, Bible lessons.
- Other: Puzzles and cartoons.

SAMPLE ISSUE
24 pages (2% advertising): 1 article; 3 stories; 4 depts/columns. Sample copy, free with 9x12 SASE ($1.17 postage). Guidelines and theme list available at website.

- "Geocaching." Article explains the who, what, where, when, and how of this popular outdoor activity.
- Sample dept/column: "Project" describes how to make a glow-in-the-dark comet.

RIGHTS AND PAYMENT
First and second serial rights. Written material, $.04–$.05 per word. Other material, payment rates vary. Pays on acceptance. Provides 1 contributor's copy.

➥EDITOR'S COMMENTS
Submissions that are unrealistic, too predictable, or preachy are likely to get rejected. Your best bet is to follow our theme list.

Calliope

Cobblestone Publishing
30 Grove Street, Suite C
Peterborough, NH 03458

Editor: Rosalie F. Baker

DESCRIPTION AND INTERESTS
Keeping its focus on helping readers explore world history, *Calliope* publishes articles and fiction on the history makers and cultures of the world. Circ: 13,000.

Audience: 8–14 years
Frequency: 9 times each year
Website:
www.cobblestonepub.com/magazine/CAL

FREELANCE POTENTIAL
85% written by nonstaff writers. Publishes 75 freelance submissions yearly; 15–20% by unpublished writers, 60–70% by new authors. Receives 240 queries yearly.

SUBMISSIONS
Query with outline, bibliography, and writing sample. All material must relate to upcoming themes. Accepts hard copy. SASE. Responds 5 months prior to theme issue publication.

- Articles: Features, 700–800 words. Sidebars, 300–600 words. Informational articles and profiles. Topics include world history.
- Fiction: To 800 words. Genres include historical and multicultural fiction, adventure, and historical plays.
- Depts/columns: 300–600 words. Current events, archaeology, languages, book reviews.
- Artwork: B/W and color prints. Line art.
- Other: To 700 words. Activities, word puzzles, games, crafts, and recipes.

SAMPLE ISSUE
48 pages (no advertising): 16 articles; 7 depts/columns; 3 activities. Sample copy, $6.95 with 9x12 SASE ($2 postage). Guidelines and theme list available at website.

- "The Jewel of the World." Article profiles the history and culture of Cordoba, which was for centuries the capital of Islamic Spain.
- Sample dept/column: "Fun With Words" discusses several common words that have their origins in the Middle East.

RIGHTS AND PAYMENT
All rights. Articles and fiction, $.20–$.25 per word. Artwork, $15–$100. Other material, payment rates vary. Pays on publication. Provides 2 contributor's copies.

⇒EDITOR'S COMMENTS
Please be sure your query relates to one of our upcoming themes.

Camping Magazine

American Camp Association
5000 State Road 67 North
Martinsville, IN 46151-7902

Editor-in-Chief: Harriet Lowe

DESCRIPTION AND INTERESTS
Read by camp owners and administrators, this magazine covers the news and trends of the recreational and educational camp industry. Articles on innovative programming, safety issues, and management are also featured. Circ: 7,500.

Audience: Camp managers and educators
Frequency: 6 times each year
Website: www.acacamps.org/campmag

FREELANCE POTENTIAL
90% written by nonstaff writers. Publishes 30–35 freelance submissions yearly; 50% by unpublished writers, 30% by authors who are new to the magazine. Receives 96 unsolicited mss yearly.

SUBMISSIONS
Send complete ms. Accepts disk submissions with hard copy and email submissions to magazine@acacamps.org (Microsoft Word attachments). SASE. Response time varies.

- Articles: 1,500–3,000 words. Informational and how-to articles. Topics include camp management, special education, social issues, careers, health, recreation, crafts, and hobbies.
- Depts/columns: 800–1,000 words. News, opinion pieces, risk management, and building and construction information.
- Artwork: Color prints; high-resolution JPEG or TIFF images at 300 dpi.

SAMPLE ISSUE
72 pages (20% advertising): 5 articles; 11 depts/columns. Sample copy, $4.50 with 9x12 SASE. Guidelines and editorial calendar available at website.

- "To Climb a Mountain." Article profiles a world-class mountain climber who also leads climbing expeditions for camps.
- Sample dept/column: "A Place to Share" reveals the author's emotions upon visiting the camp he attended in his youth.

RIGHTS AND PAYMENT
All rights. No payment. Provides 3 copies.

⇒EDITOR'S COMMENTS
Many of our articles are written by camp directors and other camp professionals—people in the field who have firsthand knowledge and experience with the subject matter.

Canadian Guider

Girl Guides of Canada
50 Merton Street
Toronto, Ontario M4S 1A3
Canada

Submissions: Veveen Gregory

DESCRIPTION AND INTERESTS
Canadian Guider is the magazine for busy Girl Guide leaders and Rangers who are looking for ideas and inspiring stories that will help them offer dynamic programs to girls. Circ: 40,000.
Audience: Girl Guide leaders
Frequency: 3 times each year
Website: www.girlguides.ca

FREELANCE POTENTIAL
75% written by nonstaff writers. Receives 12 queries and unsolicited mss yearly.

SUBMISSIONS
Girl Guide leaders only. Query with résumé for articles; send complete ms for depts/columns. Accepts hard copy. Availability of artwork improves chance of acceptance. SASE. Responds in 1 month.

- Articles: To 200 words. Informational and how-to articles; profiles; interviews; and personal experience pieces. Topics include leadership, life skills, crafts, activities, community service, camping, outdoor adventure, nature, the arts, social issues, and international travel.
- Depts/columns: 50–100 words. Leadership profiles, program ideas, personal experience pieces, contests, and organizational business.
- Artwork: B/W and color prints. Digital images at 300 dpi.

SAMPLE ISSUE
46 pages (12% advertising): 6 articles; 15 depts/columns. Sample copy, $3 with 9x12 SASE. Guidelines available.

- "Creative Computing." Article explains the many ways girls can express their creativity digitally.
- "Creating Memories: The Art of Scrapbooking." Article explains how the popular scrapbooking hobby can be used by girls to preserve their Girl Guides memories.
- Sample dept/column: "Innovators" reports on a successful sewing project.

RIGHTS AND PAYMENT
All rights. No payment. Provides 2 contributor's copies.

↝EDITOR'S COMMENTS
We love to hear from Guiders throughout the country who have spearheaded a successful project or have some inspiration to share.

Capper's

1503 SW 42nd Street
Topeka, KS 66609-1265

Editor-in-Chief: Katherine Compton

DESCRIPTION AND INTERESTS
Recently redesigned and now published in full-color, glossy format, *Capper's* celebrates rural life. It focuses on family gardening and farming, while also offering nostalgia pieces and reflections on the joys of country life. Circ: 15,000.
Audience: Families
Frequency: Monthly
Website: www.cappers.com

FREELANCE POTENTIAL
90% written by nonstaff writers. Publishes 40–50 freelance submissions yearly; 50% by unpublished writers, 70% by authors who are new to the magazine. Receives 480 queries and unsolicited mss yearly.

SUBMISSIONS
Send complete ms with artwork for articles. Query for fiction. Accepts hard copy. SASE. Responds to queries in 1 month, to mss in 3–4 months.

- Articles: 700 words. Informational, general interest, historical, inspirational, and nostalgic articles. Topics include family life, travel, hobbies, and occupations.
- Fiction: To 25,000 words. Serialized novels.
- Depts/columns: 300 words. Personal experience pieces, humor, and essays.
- Artwork: 35mm color slides, transparencies, or prints.
- Other: Jokes, 5–6 per submission.

SAMPLE ISSUE
108 pages (3% advertising): 14 articles; 9 depts/columns. Sample copy, $1.95. Guidelines available.

- "The Appeal of Diminutive Donkeys." Article discusses why miniature donkeys can be a welcome addition to any homestead.
- Sample dept/column: "Looking Back" is a nostalgia piece about the author's attachment to the red tractor of her childhood.

RIGHTS AND PAYMENT
Standard rights. Articles, $2.50 per column inch. Serialized novels, $75–$300. Pays on publication for nonfiction; on acceptance for fiction. Provides up to 5 contributor's copies.

↝EDITOR'S COMMENTS
We're always interested in family-oriented material about rural living. Submissions can be practical or inspirational.

Careers and Colleges

2 LAN Drive, Suite 100
Westford, MA 01886

Editor: Anne Kandra

DESCRIPTION AND INTERESTS
Careers and Colleges serves as a guide for high school students as they start making decisions about their futures. Its articles cover career choices and everything teens will need to know about college—from financing it to making the best of dorm life. Circ: 752,000.

Audience: 15–18 years
Frequency: 3 times each year
Website: www.careersandcolleges.com

FREELANCE POTENTIAL
80% written by nonstaff writers. Publishes 6 freelance submissions yearly; 10% by authors who are new to the magazine. Receives 50 queries yearly.

SUBMISSIONS
Query with clips; or send complete ms. Accepts email to editor@careersandcolleges.com. Responds in 2 months.

- Articles: 800–2,400 words. Informational and how-to articles; profiles; interviews; and personal experience pieces. Topics include post-secondary education, independent living, campus life, career choices, social issues, and personal growth.
- Depts/columns: Staff written.

SAMPLE ISSUE
32 pages (29% advertising): 8 articles; 2 depts/columns. Sample copy available at website. Guidelines available.

- "Mixed-Gender Dorm Rooms Gaining Acceptance." Article reports on the growing trend of colleges allowing students to choose their roommates, even if they are the opposite sex.
- "The Future Begins Now: Starting Your College Search." Article offers advice on finding the "right" college for one's needs.

RIGHTS AND PAYMENT
First North American serial and electronic rights. Written material, payment rates vary. Pays 2 months after acceptance. Provides 2 contributor's copies.

➡ EDITOR'S COMMENTS
We want practical information that helps our readers achieve their goals: to have a satisfying college experience and to lay the foundation for the career of their choice. New topics and subject matter are welcome here.

Carolina Parent

5716 Fayetteville Road, Suite 201
Durham, NC 27713

Editor: Cricket Gibbons

DESCRIPTION AND INTERESTS
Issues and information relating to the care and education of children from birth through the teen years are presented in this magazine for parents and caregivers. Preference is given to localized articles. Circ: 54,000.

Audience: Parents
Frequency: Monthly
Website: www.carolinaparent.com

FREELANCE POTENTIAL
60% written by nonstaff writers. Publishes 156 freelance submissions yearly; 2% by unpublished writers, 5% by authors who are new to the magazine. Receives 600 queries, 480 unsolicited mss yearly.

SUBMISSIONS
Query with outline and writing samples. New writers, send complete ms. Accepts hard copy and email submissions to editorial@carolinaparent.com (Microsoft Word attachments). SASE. Response time varies.

- Articles: 500–1,600 words. Informational, self-help, and how-to articles; and profiles. Topics include college planning, technology, crafts, hobbies, education, health, fitness, humor, music, nature, the environment, parenting, children's issues, recreation, regional news, sports, and travel.
- Depts/columns: Word lengths vary. "Ages and Stages," family finances, family issues, home and garden, child development, pregnancy, health, news, and events.

SAMPLE ISSUE
96 pages: 10 articles; 17 depts/columns. Sample copy, guidelines, and editorial calendar available at website.

- "Perspectives on Fatherhood." Article presents the thoughts of several men regarding their approach to fatherhood.
- "Which Carolina Beach is Best for Your Family?" Article reviews local beaches with an eye toward family-friendliness.

RIGHTS AND PAYMENT
First and electronic rights. Written material, payment rates vary. Pays on publication.

➡ EDITOR'S COMMENTS
Though general information articles are accepted, we prefer pieces that use local references and subjects.

Catholic Digest

1 Montauk Avenue, Suite 200
P.O. Box 6015
New London, CT 06320

Articles Editor: Kerry Weber

DESCRIPTION AND INTERESTS
Since its beginning in 1936, *Catholic Digest* has used stories of real people to demonstrate that a life guided by faith can be exciting, enlivening, and joyous. Informational articles and personal stories of faith—with an emphasis on the family experience—fill its pages. Circ: 285,000.

Audience: Families
Frequency: 11 times each year
Website: www.catholicdigest.com

FREELANCE POTENTIAL
44% written by nonstaff writers. Publishes 100–200 freelance submissions yearly; 12% by authors who are new to the magazine. Receives 4,800 unsolicited mss yearly.

SUBMISSIONS
Send complete ms. Accepts hard copy and email submissions to cdfillers@bayard-us.com. No simultaneous submissions. SASE. Responds in 6–8 weeks.

- Articles: 1,000–2,000 words. Informational articles; profiles; and personal experience pieces. Topics include religion, prayer, spirituality, relationships, family issues, history, and nostalgia.
- Depts/columns: 50–500 words. True stories about faith, and profiles of volunteers.
- Artwork: JPEG files at 300 dpi.
- Other: Filler, to 1,000 words. Submit seasonal material 3–4 months in advance.

SAMPLE ISSUE
128 pages (13% advertising): 9 articles; 18 depts/columns. Sample copy, free with 6x9 SASE ($1 postage). Guidelines available.

- "The Easiest Way to Pray." Article examines the many ways to find God through prayer.
- "You're More Spiritual Than You Think." Article depicts six scenarios when God is present in our lives.

RIGHTS AND PAYMENT
First rights. Articles, $100–$300. Depts/columns and filler, $2 per published line. Pays on publication. Provides 2 contributor's copies.

☛EDITOR'S COMMENTS
We do not consider material that is overtly political or demeaning to others. We look for original ideas or inspirational stories that will help our readers feel closer to God.

Catholic Forester

P.O. Box 3012
335 Shuman Boulevard
Naperville, IL 60566-7012

Associate Editor: Patricia Baron

DESCRIPTION AND INTERESTS
The Catholic Order of Foresters, a century-old Catholic fraternal life insurance society, publishes this magazine for its members. It features industry news, general interest articles, articles pertaining to family life, and inspirational articles. Circ: 87,000.

Audience: Catholic Forester members
Frequency: Quarterly
Website: www.catholicforester.org

FREELANCE POTENTIAL
20% written by nonstaff writers. Publishes 4–8 freelance submissions yearly; 20% by authors who are new to the magazine. Receives 240 unsolicited mss yearly.

SUBMISSIONS
Send complete ms. Accepts hard copy and email to pbaron@catholicforester.org. SASE. Responds in 3–4 months.

- Articles: 1,000 words. Informational and inspirational articles. Topics include money management, fitness, health, family life, investing, senior issues, parenting, and nostalgia.
- Fiction: 500–1,000 words. Genres include inspirational, humorous, and light fiction.
- Depts/columns: Staff written.

SAMPLE ISSUE
40 pages (no advertising): 6 articles; 1 story; 4 depts/columns. Sample copy, free with 9x12 SASE (3 first-class stamps). Guidelines available at website.

- "Be a More Positive Person." Article outlines seven ways to incorporate a more positive outlook into one's life.
- "Enchanted Highway." Article showcases the massive sculptures that sit along a winding road in North Dakota.

RIGHTS AND PAYMENT
First North American serial rights. Written material, $.50 per word. Reprints, $50. Pays on acceptance. Provides 3 contributor's copies.

☛EDITOR'S COMMENTS
Topics that appeal to our members include health and wellness, money management and investing, parenting and family life, inspiration, and nostalgia. Although we are primarily interested in informational articles, we do entertain the occasional light fiction, children's story, or humor piece.

Catholic Library World

Catholic Library Association
100 North Street, Suite 224
Pittsfield, MA 01201-5178

Editor

DESCRIPTION AND INTERESTS
Library professionals turn to this journal for in-depth reviews of religious and secular books and media, as well as informative articles on professional development. It is the member publication of the Catholic Library Association. Circ: 1,100.
Audience: Library professionals
Frequency: Quarterly
Website: www.cathla.org

FREELANCE POTENTIAL
90% written by nonstaff writers. Publishes 12–16 freelance submissions yearly. Receives 24–36 queries and unsolicited mss yearly.

SUBMISSIONS
Query or send complete ms. Accepts hard copy and email submissions to cla@cathla.org (Microsoft Word attachments). SASE. Response time varies.

- Articles: Word lengths vary. Informational articles and reviews. Topics include books, reading, library science, and Catholic Library Association news.
- Depts/columns: 150–300 words. Media and book reviews. Topics include biography, fiction, multicultural issues, picture books, reference materials, science, social studies, and Catholic values.
- Artwork: B/W or color prints or transparencies. Line art.

SAMPLE ISSUE
80 pages (2% advertising): 3 articles; 2 depts/columns; 160 book reviews. Sample copy, $15. Guidelines available.

- "The Road Ahead for Catholic Libraries." Article discusses the transformations libraries need to undertake in order to stay current, and offers a case study on the Saint Xavier University Library.
- Sample dept/column: "News Notes" offers updates on new product lines from ProQuest.

RIGHTS AND PAYMENT
All rights. No payment. Provides 1 contributor's copy.

➻EDITOR'S COMMENTS
We welcome submissions from writers who are new to us. Feature articles should be relevant to librarians, library science students, and others interested in librarianship.

Celebrate

2923 Troost Avenue
Kansas City, MO 64109

Senior Editor: Melissa K. Hammer

DESCRIPTION AND INTERESTS
Celebrate is a weekly take-home paper for use in religious education programs. It is filled with stories and Bible-based activities and games that help young children understand the glory of God and the role He can play in their lives. Circ: 40,000.
Audience: 3–6 years
Frequency: Weekly
Website: www.wordaction.com

FREELANCE POTENTIAL
90% written by nonstaff writers. Publishes 100 freelance submissions yearly; 30% by unpublished writers, 35% by authors who are new to the magazine. Receives 200 queries yearly.

SUBMISSIONS
Query. Accepts hard copy. SASE. Responds in 2–4 weeks.

- Fiction: Word lengths vary. Stories that show children dealing with issues related to a Bible story or lesson.
- Other: Bible stories, songs, finger plays, action rhymes, crafts, activities. Poetry, 4–8 lines.

SAMPLE ISSUE
4 pages (no advertising): 1 story; 1 dept/column; 4 activities. Sample copy, free with #10 SASE (1 first-class stamp). Guidelines and theme list available.

- "Church Friends Are Family Too." Bible story tells how Jesus considered his disciples his family, and explains how the people who worship with us are members of the family of God.
- Sample activity: "Links of Love" describes an activity involving a paper chain and the names of church family members.

RIGHTS AND PAYMENT
Rights vary. Written material, payment rates vary. Payment policy varies.

➻EDITOR'S COMMENTS
The stories and activities we choose are designed to help children keep the lessons they learned in Sunday school with them all week long, and to share them with Mom and Dad. Please contact us to get a list of upcoming themes, as all material revolves around them. We welcome new ideas regarding themes and related activities.

Central Penn Parent

1500 Paxton Street
Harrisburg, PA 17104

Editor: Nikki M. Murry

DESCRIPTION AND INTERESTS
Accessible, informative writing about regional parenting topics appears in *Central Penn Parent*. Targeting families in Pennsylvania's Dauphin, Lancaster, Cumberland, and York Counties, it includes regional updates, travel tips, and event calendars. Circ: 35,000.

Audience: Parents
Frequency: Monthly
Website: www.centralpennparent.com

FREELANCE POTENTIAL
75% written by nonstaff writers. Publishes 60 freelance submissions yearly; 20% by unpublished writers, 10% by authors who are new to the magazine. Receives 1,300 queries yearly.

SUBMISSIONS
All articles are assigned to local writers. Query for reprints only. Accepts email queries to nikkim@journalpub.com. Availability of artwork improves chance of acceptance. Responds in 2 weeks.

- Articles: 1,200–1,500 words. Informational articles and reviews. Topics include local family events and activities, health, nutrition, discipline, education, home life, technology, literature, parenting, and travel.
- Depts/columns: 700 words. Family finances, health, infant issues, news, and education.
- Artwork: Color prints and transparencies. Line art.
- Other: Submit seasonal material at least 2 months in advance.

SAMPLE ISSUE
54 pages (50% advertising): 3 articles; 9 depts/columns; 1 calendar of events. Sample copy, free. Guidelines available.

- "Sweet Success." Article offers ideas for decorating cakes like a professional.
- Sample dept/column: "Ages & Stages" examines the unique challenges faced by gifted teens.

RIGHTS AND PAYMENT
All rights. Reprints, $35–$50. Pays on publication. Provides author's copies upon request.

➥EDITOR'S COMMENTS
We're interested in topics that relate to parenting children of all ages—from infants to teens. Please note that we strongly prefer to work with local writers.

Charlotte Parent

2125 Southend Drive, Suite 253
Charlotte, NC 28230

Editor: Eve C. White

DESCRIPTION AND INTERESTS
This magazine for families living in the Charlotte area of North Carolina offers articles on parenting and local events. Circ: 123,000.

Audience: Parents
Frequency: Monthly
Website: www.charlotteparent.com

FREELANCE POTENTIAL
50% written by nonstaff writers. Publishes 45 freelance submissions yearly; 15% by unpublished writers, 25% by authors who are new to the magazine. Receives 1,000 queries, 800 unsolicited mss yearly.

SUBMISSIONS
Query or send complete ms with résumé and bibliography. Prefers email to editorial@charlotteparent.com; will accept hard copy, Macintosh disk submissions, and simultaneous submissions. SASE. Responds if interested.

- Articles: 500–1,000 words. Informational and how-to articles; profiles; and personal experience pieces. Topics include parenting, family life, finances, education, health, fitness, vacations, entertainment, regional activities, and the environment.
- Depts/columns: Word lengths vary. Child development, restaurant and media reviews, and children's health.
- Artwork: High-density Macintosh images.
- Other: Activities. Submit seasonal material 2–3 months in advance.

SAMPLE ISSUE
72 pages (50% advertising): 7 articles; 11 depts/columns; 1 calendar. Sample copy, free with 9x12 SASE (5 first-class stamps). Guidelines and editorial calendar available.

- "Catching Up with a Terrific Teen." Article profiles a high school baseball player who has a bright future.
- "Pet Sitting Business for Kids." Article offers tips for kids who want to work as pet sitters.

RIGHTS AND PAYMENT
First and Internet rights. Written material, payment rates vary. Pays on publication. Provides 1 contributor's copy.

➥EDITOR'S COMMENTS
Our readers—and therefore we—are most interested in articles with a regional slant. Writers from the area are encouraged to submit.

ChemMatters

American Chemical Society
1155 16th Street NW
Washington, DC 20036

Editor: Patrice Pages

DESCRIPTION AND INTERESTS
ChemMatters seeks to "demystify everyday chemistry." Targeting teachers as well as students, it presents articles that make chemistry interesting and fun. Circ: 40,000.

Audience: YA–Adult
Frequency: Quarterly
Website: www.acs.org/chemmatters

FREELANCE POTENTIAL
90% written by nonstaff writers. Publishes 21 freelance submissions yearly; 50% by authors who are new to the magazine. Receives 36 queries yearly.

SUBMISSIONS
Query with abstract, outline, source list, possible artwork, estimated word count, writing samples, and résumé. Prefers email queries to chemmatters@acs.org; will accept hard copy. Availability of artwork improves chance of acceptance. SASE. Responds in 2 weeks.

- Articles: 1,400–2,100 words. Informational articles. Topics include the chemical aspects of everyday things, such as food, beverages, and biological functions; and hot topics.
- Depts/columns: 100 words. News, chemistry of common products used by teens.
- Artwork: JPEG or GIF images.

SAMPLE ISSUE
20 pages (no advertising): 7 articles; 1 dept/column. Sample copy available at website. Guidelines and theme list available via email request to chemmatters@acs.org.

- "Letting Off Steam." Article examines the chemical composition of geyser water.
- "Those Blooming Algae!" Article explains why coastal algae blooms happen, and how they change the makeup of the water.

RIGHTS AND PAYMENT
All rights. Articles, $500–$1,000. Depts/columns, $.50 per word. Pays on acceptance. Provides 5 contributor's copies.

➡️EDITOR'S COMMENTS
We will notice your article idea if it takes a subject that students are familiar with and explains the chemistry behind it. The best topics are ones that interest teens, and the best articles are the ones that make chemistry fun. We strive for a "Wow! I didn't know that" reaction from the reader.

Chesapeake Family

929 West Street, Suite 210
Annapolis, MD 21401

Editor: Kristen Page-Kirby

DESCRIPTION AND INTERESTS
Family activities, travel, and resources are the focus of this magazine for parents living in Maryland's Chesapeake Bay region. It also publishes feature articles on health, education, and child development. Circ: 40,000.

Audience: Parents
Frequency: Monthly
Website: www.chesapeakefamily.com

FREELANCE POTENTIAL
80% written by nonstaff writers. Publishes 40 freelance submissions yearly; 10% by unpublished writers, 40% by authors who are new to the magazine. Receives 1,200 queries, 480 unsolicited mss yearly.

SUBMISSIONS
Prefers query; will accept complete ms. Accepts email to editor@chesapeakefamily.com. Response time varies.

- Articles: 1,000–1,200 words. Informational and how-to articles. Topics include parenting, education, the environment, entertainment, regional news and events, family health, and family travel.
- Fiction: Word lengths vary. Stories by local children, ages 4–12.
- Depts/columns: Staff written.
- Other: Poetry by children ages 4–12. Submit seasonal material 6 months in advance.

SAMPLE ISSUE
60 pages (45% advertising): 4 articles; 6 depts/columns; 1 calendar; 1 camp directory. Sample copy, writers' guidelines, and editorial calendar available.

- "Who Cares for the Caregiver?" Article offers suggestions for dealing with stress when caring for a disabled or aged family member.
- Sample dept/column: "Family Fun" plots out a driving tour of Underground Railroad landmarks in Maryland.

RIGHTS AND PAYMENT
One-time print and electronic rights. Articles, $75–$150. Depts/columns, $50. Reprints, $35. Kill fee, $25. Pays on publication.

➡️EDITOR'S COMMENTS
Our articles are written in an easy-to-read, accessible tone—but they pack plenty of information into a few words.

Chess Life

P.O. Box 3967
Crossville, TN 38557-3967

Editor: Daniel Lucas

DESCRIPTION AND INTERESTS
For more than 20 years, the U.S. Chess Federation has been publishing this magazine for players of all ages. Each issue includes information on playing strategies for novices through experts, as well as reports on tournaments around the globe. Circ: 80,000.

Audience: YA–Adult
Frequency: Monthly
Website: www.uschess.org

FREELANCE POTENTIAL
75% written by nonstaff writers. Publishes 30 freelance submissions yearly; 30% by unpublished writers. Receives 180–420 queries yearly.

SUBMISSIONS
Query with clips or writing samples. Accepts hard copy and email queries to dlucas@uschess.org. SASE. Responds in 1–3 months.

- Articles: 800–3,000 words. Informational, how-to, and historical articles; profiles; humor; and personal experience and opinion pieces. Topics include chess games and strategies, tournaments and events, and personalities in the game.
- Depts/columns: To 1,000 words. Book and product reviews, short how-to's, and brief player profiles.
- Artwork: B/W or color prints.
- Other: Chess-oriented cartoons, contests, and games.

SAMPLE ISSUE
72 pages (16% advertising): 4 articles; 11 depts/columns. Sample copy, free with 9x12 SASE. Guidelines available at website.

- "Karpov on Fischer." Article interviews seven-time World Champion Anatoly Karpov about the 1972 Fischer-Spassky match.
- Sample dept/column: "Looks at Books" examines one of the game's most fascinating sidelines, Blindfold Chess.

RIGHTS AND PAYMENT
All rights. Written material, $100 per page. Artwork, $15–$100. Kill fee, 30%. Pays on publication. Provides 2 contributor's copies.

➦EDITOR'S COMMENTS
Send us articles about chess in everyday life or a profile of a relatively unknown player. Your writing must reflect your knowledge of the game.

Chess Life for Kids

P.O. Box 3967
Crossville, TN 38577

Editor: Glenn Petersen

DESCRIPTION AND INTERESTS
Published by the United States Chess Federation, this magazine is the junior version of *Chess Life* magazine. It features articles on the art of chess, tips from the masters, profiles of young chess players, and news of junior chess competitions. Circ: 22,700.

Audience: To 12 years
Frequency: 6 times each year
Website: www.uschess.org

FREELANCE POTENTIAL
30% written by nonstaff writers. Publishes 12–18 freelance submissions yearly; 10% by unpublished writers. Receives 36 queries, 12 unsolicited mss yearly.

SUBMISSIONS
Query or send complete ms. Accepts email submissions to gpetersen@uschess.org and simultaneous submissions if identified. Responds in 2 weeks.

- Articles: To 1,000 words. Informational and instructional articles; and profiles. Topics include chess strategies, tournaments, masters, camps, and lessons.
- Depts/columns: Staff written.

SAMPLE ISSUE
24 pages: 10 articles; 4 depts/columns.

- "Pin It and Win It." Article explains strategy and tactics—that is, creating a plan and then deciding how to carry out that plan.
- "Tales of the Arabian Knights." Article uses a story to set up a chess problem to solve.
- Sample dept/column: "Spotlight On . . ." profiles a 12-year-old chess champ.

RIGHTS AND PAYMENT
First North American serial rights. Written material, $75 per page. Pays on publication.

➦EDITOR'S COMMENTS
If you don't know your way around a chess board, we'll be able to tell—and we will not accept your work. We choose authors who can write for and about young people, and who can capture the essence of chess competition. Instructional articles should include step-by-step instructions and explanations of strategy. Our goal as a magazine is to inspire young chess players to continue in competition.

Chicago Parent

141 South Oak Park Avenue
Oak Park, IL 60302

Editor: Tamara O'Shaughnessy

DESCRIPTION AND INTERESTS
Each issue of *Chicago Parent* features a family event calendar, feature articles on parenting issues, and columns on health, nutrition, and travel. Everything it publishes has a regional slant. Circ: 138,000.

Audience: Parents
Frequency: Monthly
Website: www.chicagoparent.com

FREELANCE POTENTIAL
85% written by nonstaff writers. Publishes 50+ freelance submissions yearly; 30% by unpublished writers, 45% by authors who are new to the magazine. Receives 1,560 queries yearly.

SUBMISSIONS
Query with résumé and clips. Accepts email queries to chiparent@chicagoparent.com. Responds in 6 weeks.

- Articles: 1,500–2,500 words. Informational articles; profiles; personal experience pieces; and humor. Topics include pregnancy, childbirth, parenting, grandparenting, foster care, adoption, day care, child development, health, education, recreation, and family issues.
- Depts/columns: 850 words. Crafts, activities, media reviews, health, travel, family finances, and regional events.
- Other: Cartoons for parents. Submit seasonal material at least 2 months in advance.

SAMPLE ISSUE
100 pages (60% advertising): 5 articles; 14 depts/columns; 1 calendar of events. Sample copy, $3.95. Writers' guidelines and editorial calendar available.

- "Mama Kellie." Article profiles a grandmother who built a school in a village in Tanzania.
- Sample dept/column: "Kid Culture" reviews two new children's music CDs.

RIGHTS AND PAYMENT
One-time northwest Indiana and Illinois exclusive rights. Articles, $125–$350. Depts/columns, $25–$100. Kill fee, 10%. Pays on publication. Provides contributor's copies upon request.

➡️ EDITOR'S COMMENTS
Our pages are filled with articles and columns written by Chicago-area writers. All submissions must have a local angle.

Child Care Information Exchange

P.O. Box 3249
Redmond, WA 98073-3249

Associate Editor: Donna Rafanello

DESCRIPTION AND INTERESTS
Early childhood professionals read this magazine for informative articles about trends in the field, as well as strategies that work in real-life settings. Circ: 30,000.

Audience: Child-care professionals
Frequency: 6 times each year
Website: www.childcareexchange.com

FREELANCE POTENTIAL
75% written by nonstaff writers. Publishes 60 freelance submissions yearly; 50% by unpublished writers, 60% by authors who are new to the magazine. Receives 75 unsolicited mss each year.

SUBMISSIONS
Send complete ms with brief author biography and list of article references. Accepts email submissions to donna@childcareexchange.com (Microsoft Word attachments) plus hard copy. Availability of artwork improves chance of acceptance. SASE. Response time varies.

- Articles: 1,800 words. Informational, how-to, and self-help articles. Topics include child development; education; and social, multicultural, and ethnic issues.
- Depts/columns: Word lengths vary. Staff development and training, parent perspectives, child nutrition, program profiles, and product reviews.
- Artwork: Color prints. Line art.

SAMPLE ISSUE
104 pages: 14 articles; 15 depts/columns. Sample copy, $8. Guidelines and theme list available at website.

- "The Role of Music in Your Classroom." Article explains the dynamic relationship between music and play in children's early development.
- Sample dept/column: "From a Parent's Perspective" tells why doing what you say you'll do teaches children about consequences.

RIGHTS AND PAYMENT
All rights. Articles, $300. Pays on publication. Provides 2 contributor's copies.

➡️ EDITOR'S COMMENTS
We're always looking for information that supports early childhood professionals, including articles that provide practical, field-tested methods.

Childhood Education

Association for Childhood Education
International
17904 Georgia Avenue, Suite 215
Olney, MA 20832

Editor: Anne W. Bauer

DESCRIPTION AND INTERESTS
Childhood Education is a magazine for professionals involved in the care and education of children from birth through the early teen years. It presents emerging ideas in the field and serves as a forum for opinions backed by research. Circ: 10,000.

Audience: Educators; child-care professionals
Frequency: 6 times each year
Website: www.acei.org

FREELANCE POTENTIAL
98% written by nonstaff writers. Publishes 40 freelance submissions yearly; 75% by authors who are new to the magazine. Receives 120 unsolicited mss yearly.

SUBMISSIONS
Send 4 copies of complete ms. Accepts hard copy, Macintosh disk submissions, and email submissions to abauer@acei.org. SASE. Responds in 3 months.

- Articles: 1,400–3,500 words. Informational articles. Topics include innovative teaching strategies, the teaching profession, research findings, parenting and family issues, communities, drug education, and safe environments for children.
- Depts/columns: 1,000 words. Research news, education issues, parenting, and book and media reviews.

SAMPLE ISSUE
62 pages: 5 articles; 8 depts/columns. Sample copy, free with 9x12 SASE (3 first-class stamps). Writers' guidelines and editorial calendar available.

- "The Argument for Recess." Article stresses the need for more research about the benefits of free play during the school day.
- "The Care and Education of Orphan Children With Disabilities in China." Article outlines programs and strategies that can help China address this problem.

RIGHTS AND PAYMENT
All rights. No payment. Provides 5 copies.

➙EDITOR'S COMMENTS
The mission of our organization is to promote children's education and development, and influence educators' professional growth. All manuscripts are judged according to how well they reflect that mission.

Children and Families

1651 Prince Street
Alexandria, VA 22314

Editor: Julie Antoniou

DESCRIPTION AND INTERESTS
Best practices and the latest developments in the field of early childhood education are discussed in this magazine from the National Head Start Association. It primarily targets early childhood directors, administrators, educators, and support staff. Circ: 50,000.

Audience: Early childhood professionals
Frequency: 3 times each year
Website: www.nhsa.org

FREELANCE POTENTIAL
90% written by nonstaff writers. Publishes 25 freelance submissions yearly; 30% by unpublished writers, 70% by authors who are new to the magazine. Receives 24 queries yearly.

SUBMISSIONS
Query with biography, outline, and possible sidebar information. Accepts email queries to julie@nhsa.org. Responds in 1–3 months.

- Articles: 1,800–3,800 words. Informational and how-to articles. Topics include teaching skills, advocacy strategies, problem-solving, administrative issues, school readiness, professional development, special needs and inclusion, parental involvement and partnerships, and child development research.
- Depts/columns: Word lengths vary. News, tips for home visits, teaching tactics, leadership advice, lesson plans, literacy projects, and baby-care issues.

SAMPLE ISSUE
60 pages (20% advertising): 5 articles; 8 depts/columns. Sample copy and guidelines available at website.

- "The Benefits of Learning with Nature." Article presents ideas for connecting young children with the outdoors.
- Sample dept/column: "Tactics for Teaching" tells how to make families of all economic classes and ethnic backgrounds feel welcome in an early childhood program.

RIGHTS AND PAYMENT
First rights. No payment. Provides 2+ contributor's copies.

➙EDITOR'S COMMENTS
We help our readers provide exceptional services to children and their families. Be concise and tell readers how they can apply what they learn from your article in the classroom.

Children's Ministry

1515 Cascade Avenue
Loveland, CO 80539

Associate Editor: Carmen Kamrath

DESCRIPTION AND INTERESTS
Children's Ministry publishes practical ideas for running successful religious education classes for kids. It features articles on Christian education, emerging church/ministry trends, motivating volunteers, and developmental trends and insights. Circ: 65,000.
Audience: Children's ministry leaders
Frequency: 6 times each year
Website: www.childrensministry.com

FREELANCE POTENTIAL
90% written by nonstaff writers. Publishes 180 freelance submissions yearly; 60% by unpublished writers, 60% by authors who are new to the magazine. Receives 100+ unsolicited mss each year.

SUBMISSIONS
Send complete ms. Prefers email submissions to ckamrath@cmmag.com; will accept hard copy. SASE. Responds in 2–3 months.

- Articles: 500–1,700 words. Informational and how-to articles and personal experience pieces. Topics include Christian education, family issues, child development, and faith.
- Depts/columns: 50–300 words. Educational issues, activities, devotionals, family ministry, parenting, crafts, and resources.
- Other: Activities, games, and tips. Submit seasonal material 6–8 months in advance.

SAMPLE ISSUE
122 pages (50% advertising): 6 articles; 12 depts/columns. Sample copy, $2 with 9x12 SASE. Guidelines available at website.

- "Pray without Ceasing." Article outlines ways to teach kids to make prayer a natural and constant part of life.
- Sample dept/column: "Age-Level Insights: 0–2" offers ways to introduce young children to Jesus.

RIGHTS AND PAYMENT
All rights. Articles, $40–$400. Depts/columns, $40–$75. Pays on acceptance. Provides 1 contributor's copy.

➠EDITOR'S COMMENTS
Writers who are new to us stand a good chance at publication with an article that describes a teaching technique that has worked for them. Our readers learn from the experiences of other successful teachers.

Children's Voice

Child Welfare League of America
2345 Crystal Drive, Suite 250
Arlington, VA 22202

Managing Editor: Emily Shenk

DESCRIPTION AND INTERESTS
A publication of the Child Welfare League of America, *Children's Voice* covers the issues that affect children and families, as well as the organizational and bureaucratic challenges that face advocates and other professionals working within the child welfare system. Circ: 15,000.
Audience: Child welfare advocates
Frequency: 6 times each year
Website: www.cwla.org/voice

FREELANCE POTENTIAL
20% written by nonstaff writers. Publishes 12 freelance submissions yearly; 50% by unpublished writers, 50% by authors who are new to the magazine. Receives 60 queries yearly.

SUBMISSIONS
Query. Accepts email queries to voice@cwla.org (text only). Responds in 1 month.

- Articles: 2,000–2,500 words. Informational and how-to articles; profiles; interviews; and personal experience pieces. Topics include child welfare issues, nonprofit management and leadership, legal issues, and agency problems and practices.
- Depts/columns: 700 words. Agency news, public policy alerts, state-level child welfare news, staff Q&As, and reports on special education.

SAMPLE ISSUE
38 pages (20% advertising): 4 articles; 7 depts/columns. Sample copy, $10. Guidelines available at website.

- "What Early Education Can Teach Child Welfare." Article explains the four key goals that early education and child welfare have in common, and the common lessons their advocates have learned.
- "Board Pitfalls: How to Avoid Common Mistakes." Article discusses the pragmatic concerns of a responsible nonprofit organization.
- Sample dept/column: "Exceptional Children" discusses the importance of teaching students to ask for help.

RIGHTS AND PAYMENT
All rights. No payment. Provides contributor's copies and a 1-year subscription.

➠EDITOR'S COMMENTS
We are currently interested in articles about management issues in nonprofit organizations.

Children's Writer

Institute of Children's Literature
93 Long Ridge Road
West Redding, CT 06896-1124

Editor-in-Chief: Susan Tierney

DESCRIPTION AND INTERESTS
Children's Writer is a monthly newsletter for writers that reports on and analyzes trends in children's book and magazine publishing. It covers all categories, from picture books through YA, and magazines for all ages. The Marketplace section highlights specific publishers' needs. Circ: 14,000.

Audience: Adults
Frequency: Monthly
Website: www.childrenswriter.com

FREELANCE POTENTIAL
90% written by nonstaff writers. Publishes 75 freelance submissions yearly; 10% by unpublished writers, 15% by authors who are new to the magazine. Receives 60+ queries yearly.

SUBMISSIONS
Query with outline and brief résumé via email. Prefers submissions via website; will accept hard copy. SASE. Responds in 2 months.

- Articles: 1,700 words. Informational, analytical, and how-to articles that include interviews with editors and writers. Topics include children's book and magazine publishing trends, new markets, genres, writing techniques, research, motivation, and business issues.
- Depts/columns: To 750 words, plus 125-word sidebar. Writing and career tips, commentary, technology, practical motivational pieces, and editor or publisher profiles.

SAMPLE ISSUE
12 pages (no advertising): 3 articles; 7 depts/columns. Sample copy, free with #10 SASE (1 first-class stamp). Guidelines available at website or with SASE.

- "Who Can Write Just One? Series Fiction." Article explains how to break into the field of series fiction.
- Sample dept/column: "Editor Profile" talks to longtime children's editor Melanie Kroupa.

RIGHTS AND PAYMENT
First North American serial rights. Features, $300; columns $200. Pays on publication.

➥EDITOR'S COMMENTS
We report on publishing today with the goal of helping all our readers, beginners and experienced writers, gain insight into current markets, strengthen their skills, and remain inspired to write for children.

Christian Home & School

3350 East Paris Avenue SE
Grand Rapids, MI 48512-3054

Managing Editor: Rachael Heyboer

DESCRIPTION AND INTERESTS
Christian parents read this magazine for articles on education, parenting, health, family travel and recreation, and matters related to Christian schooling. Circ: 66,000.

Audience: Parents
Frequency: Twice each year
Website: www.csionline.org/chs

FREELANCE POTENTIAL
95% written by nonstaff writers. Publishes 25–30 freelance submissions yearly; 25% by unpublished writers, 30% by authors who are new to the magazine. Receives 36–60 queries, 120 unsolicited mss yearly.

SUBMISSIONS
Query or send complete ms. Accepts hard copy, email to rheyboer@csionline.org, and simultaneous submissions if identified. SASE. Responds in 7–10 days.

- Articles: 1,000–2,000 words. Informational, how-to, and self-help articles; and personal experience pieces. Topics include education, parenting, life skills, decision-making, self-control, discipline, family travel, faith, marriage, and social customs.
- Fiction: Word lengths vary. Stories with Christian themes, and stories about Christmas.
- Depts/columns: "Parentstuff," 100–250 words. Reviews and parenting tips; word lengths vary.

SAMPLE ISSUE
34 pages (15% advertising): 4 articles; 9 depts/columns. Sample copy, free with 9x12 SASE ($1.11 postage). Guidelines available. Theme list available at website.

- "Job Loss." Article posits that children suffer more than bank accounts when a parent loses his or her job.
- Sample dept/column: "Profile" highlights the Sandhills Classical Christian School in Southern Pines, North Carolina.

RIGHTS AND PAYMENT
First rights. Written material, $50–$250. Pays on publication. Provides 3 contributor's copies.

➥EDITOR'S COMMENTS
We receive too many articles that have nothing to do with education or schooling. Articles must have real-world applications and offer a mature, biblical perspective.

The Christian Science Monitor

210 Massachusetts Avenue
Boston, MA 02115

Home Forum Editors:
Susan Leach & Marjorie Kehe

DESCRIPTION AND INTERESTS
This popular news and opinion magazine also features a regular section of articles dedicated to family issues and parenting. The "Home Forum" features essays, poems, and personal experience pieces, many with a humorous tone. Circ: 80,000.
Audience: Adults
Frequency: Weekly
Website: www.csmonitor.com

FREELANCE POTENTIAL
95% written by nonstaff writers. Publishes 150 freelance submissions yearly; 10% by unpublished writers, 40% by authors who are new to the magazine. Receives 6,000 unsolicited mss each year.

SUBMISSIONS
Send complete ms. Accepts email submissions to homeforum@csmonitor.com. Responds in 3 weeks.
- Articles: 300–1,000 words. Personal experience pieces and humor. Topics include home life, family, and parenting.
- Other: Short informational bits, 150–400 words. Poetry, to 20 lines. Submit seasonal material 6 weeks in advance.

SAMPLE ISSUE
48 pages (15% advertising): 27 articles; 3 "Home Forum" essays. Sample copy, $3.50. Guidelines available at website.
- "Filling in the Blanks." Essay reveals a mother's fondness for displaying sentences on a wall to communicate the emotions she cannot bring herself to speak.
- "Mrs. Mugabe, I Presume." Essay explains the author's confusion at being misidentified as the wife of the president of Zimbabwe.

RIGHTS AND PAYMENT
Exclusive rights. Essays, $75–$160. Poetry, $20–$40 per poem. Short bits, $70. Pays on publication. Provides 1 contributor's copy.

⌖EDITOR'S COMMENTS
Our "Home Forum" essays are first-person explorations of or responses to a situation, place, or person one has faced. Humor, if present, should be gentle. We accept essays on a variety of topics, and we're always looking for pieces on parenting, travel, home, family, and gardening.

Christian Work at Home Moms

P.O. Box 974
Bellevue, NE 68123

Editor: Jill Hart

DESCRIPTION AND INTERESTS
Support, information, and advice for mothers who are establishing work-at-home careers are found in this online resource, which includes a website, newsletter, and blogging center. It also offers inspirational pieces and devotionals. Hits per month: 1.5 million.
Audience: Parents
Frequency: Weekly
Website: www.cwahm.com

FREELANCE POTENTIAL
75% written by nonstaff writers. Publishes 50–100 freelance submissions yearly; 20% by unpublished writers, 20% by authors who are new to the magazine. Receives 120 unsolicited mss yearly.

SUBMISSIONS
Send complete ms. Accepts submissions through website only. Response time varies.
- Articles: 600–800 words. Informational and how-to articles; profiles; and personal experience pieces. Topics include telecommuting, home businesses, technology for business, website management and design, search engine optimization, copywriting, money management, marriage, parenting, spiritual growth, and homeschooling.
- Depts/columns: Word lengths vary. Book and media reviews, career information, blogs, and devotionals.

SAMPLE ISSUE
Sample copy and writers' guidelines available at website.
- "It's Always the Season." Article examines the Scripture verse that emphasizes putting the needs of others before our own needs.
- "Celebrating Accomplishments." Article stresses the importance of marking the milestones in family life.

RIGHTS AND PAYMENT
Electronic rights. No payment.

⌖EDITOR'S COMMENTS
We're always happy to receive contributions to our website and weekly newsletter. While we don't offer compensation, we include an "About the Author" section at the end of the article with a link back to your website. Practical at-home business information is needed, as well as inspirational reflections.

Cicada

Cricket Magazine Group
70 East Lake Street, Suite 300
Chicago, IL 60601

Executive Editor: Deborah Vetter

DESCRIPTION AND INTERESTS

Cicada celebrates ideas, reasonings, expressions, and creative endeavors by and for teens and young adults. It is a magazine of creative nonfiction and fiction by both young and adult writers. Circ: 10,000.

Audience: 14–21 years
Frequency: 6 times each year
Website: www.cicadamag.com

FREELANCE POTENTIAL

95% written by nonstaff writers. Publishes 50 freelance submissions yearly; 40% by unpublished writers, 50% by authors who are new to the magazine. Receives 1,000 unsolicited mss each year.

SUBMISSIONS

Authors aged 14–23 only, or adult writers previously published here. Send ms with word count; line count for poetry. Accepts hard copy and email to mail@cicadamag.com (with "General Submissions" in subject line). SASE. Responds in 4 months.

- Articles: To 5,000 words. Creative nonfiction and personal experience pieces.
- Fiction: To 5,000 words. Genres include adventure; fantasy; humor; romance; and historical, contemporary, and science fiction. Plays and stories presented in sophisticated cartoon format. Novellas, to 15,000 words.
- Depts/columns: "Expressions," 350–2,000 words.
- Other: Poetry, to 25 lines.

SAMPLE ISSUE

48 pages (no advertising): 4 stories; 1 dept/column; 19 poems. Sample copy, $8.50. Guidelines available at www.cricketmag.com.

- "Waltzing by Moonlight." Story tells of a surprise family reunion just after the Civil War.
- Sample dept/column: "Expressions" explores how the author came to terms with her non-goddess-like appearance, but very goddess-like attitude.

RIGHTS AND PAYMENT

Rights vary. Written material, payment rates vary. Pays on publication.

◆EDITOR'S COMMENTS

Writers ages 14 to 23 should visit the "Call for Critical Endeavors" portion of our website to view our current needs.

City Parent

447 Speers Road, Suite 4
Oakville, Ontario L6K 3S7
Canada

Editor: Diane Tierney

DESCRIPTION AND INTERESTS

Parenting issues that relate to raising children in the Toronto area are covered in this magazine. It puts a premium on local information and resources. Circ: 70,000.

Audience: Parents
Frequency: Monthly
Website: www.cityparent.com

FREELANCE POTENTIAL

60% written by nonstaff writers. Publishes 24–30 freelance submissions yearly; 10% by authors who are new to the magazine. Receives 300+ unsolicited mss yearly.

SUBMISSIONS

Send complete ms. Accepts email submissions to cityparent@haltonsearch.com. Availability of artwork improves chance of acceptance. Responds immediately if interested.

- Articles: 500–1,000 words. Informational articles. Topics include parenting issues, arts and entertainment, health, fitness, multicultural and ethnic issues, recreation, self-help, social issues, travel, and crafts for children.
- Depts/columns: Word lengths vary. Child development stages, education tips, environmental issues, teen issues, and reviews of parenting and children's books.
- Artwork: Color prints or transparencies.

SAMPLE ISSUE

48 pages (65% advertising): 8 articles; 7 depts/columns. Sample copy available at website. Editorial calendar available.

- "Protect Your Child's Skin." Article reports on the damaging effects of the sun's rays on young skin, and what parents can do to protect it.
- "The Importance of Daddy-time." Article lauds the good things fathers do for their children and the importance of their role.

RIGHTS AND PAYMENT

First rights. Written material, $50–$100. Pays on publication. Provides 1 contributor's copy.

◆EDITOR'S COMMENTS

We welcome the common topics that are of interest to parents, but we love articles that go beyond the usual parenting magazine content. We look for unique insights and information that parents can use. Local sources will always put you ahead of the rest.

CKI Magazine

Circle K International
3636 Woodview Trace
Indianapolis, IN 46268-3196

Executive Editor: Amberly Peterson

DESCRIPTION AND INTERESTS
Targeting members of Circle K International, a collegiate service organization affiliated with the Kiwanis Club, this magazine reports on chapter events and activities, while also offering advice on college life and job hunting. Circ: 10,000.

Audience: YA–Adult
Frequency: Annually
Website: www.circlek.org

FREELANCE POTENTIAL
20% written by nonstaff writers. Publishes 2–4 freelance submissions yearly; 5% by authors who are new to the magazine. Receives 24–48 queries yearly.

SUBMISSIONS
Query. Accepts hard copy, email queries to ckimagazine@kiwanis.org, and faxes to 317-879-0204. SASE. Responds in 2 weeks.

- Articles: 1,500–2,000 words. Informational and self-help articles. Topics include social issues, collegiate trends, community service, leadership, fundraising, and career planning and development.
- Depts/columns: Word lengths vary. News and information about Circle K activities.
- Artwork: 5x7 or 8x10 glossy prints. TIFF or JPEG images at 300 dpi or higher.

SAMPLE ISSUE
16 pages (no advertising): 2 articles; 2 depts/columns. Sample copy available at website. Guidelines available.

- "Parlez-vous Kiwanis?" Article profiles a college student who connected with Kiwanis Clubs in Strasbourg, France, while studying abroad.
- Sample dept/column: "Job Market" focuses on the importance of writing thank-you notes, and offers job searching tips.

RIGHTS AND PAYMENT
First North American serial rights. Written material, $150–$400. Artwork, payment rates vary. Pays on acceptance. Provides 3 copies.

➡EDITOR'S COMMENTS
We publish articles on broad areas of interest to all college students, with a focus on community service. The print edition is published once each year, but we update our website more frequently.

The Claremont Review

4980 Wesley Road
Victoria, British Columbia V8Y 1Y9
Canada

The Editors

DESCRIPTION AND INTERESTS
Young adult writers have their voices heard in this literary magazine that features poetry, short fiction, and plays. Circ: 500.

Audience: 13–19 years
Frequency: Twice each year
Website: www.theclaremontreview.ca

FREELANCE POTENTIAL
100% written by nonstaff writers. Publishes 300 freelance submissions yearly; 90% by unpublished writers, 90% by authors who are new to the magazine. Receives 300 unsolicited mss yearly.

SUBMISSIONS
Send complete ms with author biography. Accepts hard copy. SAE/IRC. Responds in 4–6 weeks.

- Articles: Word lengths vary. Interviews with contemporary authors and editors.
- Fiction: To 5,000 words. Genres include traditional, literary, experimental, and contemporary fiction.
- Artwork: B/W or color prints or transparencies.
- Other: Poetry, no line limit. Plays.

SAMPLE ISSUE
134 pages (15% advertising): 12 stories; 53 poems; 4 visual art submissions. Sample copy, $10 with 9x12 SAE/IRC. Guidelines available at website.

- "Tell Me I Want to Know." Story is a touching account of a daughter who wants to hear about her father's most memorable life moments as he battles cancer.
- "Eighteen Years in a Suitcase." Story reveals a young woman's thoughts on the things that have been most important to her so far.
- "Maps." Story describes a family's visit to its dying matriarch, whose failing body reflects the many places, all over the world, where she has lived.

RIGHTS AND PAYMENT
Rights vary. No payment. Provides 1 copy.

➡EDITOR'S COMMENTS
We seek finely crafted works that reveal something of the human condition. We're not interested in fantasies or soap opera–style romances. While we publish mostly Canadian writers, we welcome submissions from all over the English-speaking world.

Cleveland Family

11630 Chillicothe Road
Chesterland, OH 44026

Editor: Terri Nighswonger

DESCRIPTION AND INTERESTS
Parents of tots through teens pick up this publication to learn about local family events and to get up-to-date information about Cleveland-area educational opportunities and family resources. It is distributed through schools, child care centers, libraries, retail outlets, and grocery stores. Circ: 7,500.

Audience: Parents
Frequency: Monthly
Website: www.neohiofamily.com

FREELANCE POTENTIAL
50% written by nonstaff writers. Publishes 40–50 freelance submissions yearly; 33% by authors who are new to the magazine. Receives 9,000+ queries yearly.

SUBMISSIONS
Query. Accepts email queries to editor@ tntpublications.com. Responds if interested.

- Articles: 500+ words. Informational, self-help, and how-to articles; profiles; and reviews. Topics include the arts, animals, computers, crafts, health, fitness, education, popular culture, sports, the environment, religion, family travel, and regional issues.
- Depts/columns: Word lengths vary. News, advice, education, teen issues, humor, and stepfamilies.
- Artwork: High-resolution JPEG and TIFF files.

SAMPLE ISSUE
42 pages (50% advertising): 5 articles; 8 depts/columns. Editorial calendar available.

- "Backyard Safari." Article explains how bird-watching with children can be a great way to connect them with the outdoors.
- "Lawrence School Teaches, Ignites, Inspires." Article profiles a school that provides a quality education to students who have learning differences.

RIGHTS AND PAYMENT
Exclusive rights. Written material, payment rates vary. Pays on publication. Provides 1 contributor's copy.

➡EDITOR'S COMMENTS
We're looking for local contributors who write well and can provide us with articles filled with practical information for parents living in northeastern Ohio. We prefer factual pieces to first-person essays.

Click

Cricket Magazine Group
70 East Lake Street, Suite 300
Chicago, IL 60601

Editor: Amy Tao

DESCRIPTION AND INTERESTS
Click is a themed magazine of science and discovery. Led by Click the Mouse and his pals, young children are brought along on a journey through science, art, nature, and the environment. Circ: 62,000.

Audience: 3–7 years
Frequency: 9 times each year
Website: www.cricketmag.com

FREELANCE POTENTIAL
70% written by nonstaff writers. Of the freelance submissions published yearly, 10% are by authors who are new to the magazine. Receives 48–60 queries yearly.

SUBMISSIONS
All material is commissioned from experienced writers. Send résumé and clips. Accepts hard copy. SASE. Response time varies.

- Articles: To 1,000 words. Informational articles; interviews; and photo-essays. Topics include the natural, physical, and social sciences; the arts; technology and science; math; and history.
- Fiction: Word lengths vary. Stories that relate to the issue's theme.
- Other: Poetry, cartoons, and activities.

SAMPLE ISSUE
40 pages (no advertising): 3 articles; 2 stories; 2 cartoons; 2 activities. Sample copy available at website.

- "Why Is Summer Hot?" Article explains why the weather is warmer and the days are longer during the summer months.
- "Animal Ears." Article presents the various types of ears in the animal world, and explains why some are so big while others are small.

RIGHTS AND PAYMENT
Rights vary. Written material, payment rates vary. Payment policy varies.

➡EDITOR'S COMMENTS
We are a specialty magazine with a focused theme and presentation. Therefore, we choose the content and commission writers to create it to our specifications. We are not a publication for beginners. If you have experience in writing for young children, send us your résumé and clips and we will be happy to consider you for assignments.

Cobblestone

Cobblestone Publishing
30 Grove Street, Suite C
Peterborough, NH 03458

Editor: Meg Chorlian

DESCRIPTION AND INTERESTS

Each theme-based issue of *Cobblestone* delves deep into a place, era, or event from American history. Its content is designed to meet curriculum standards while offering a lively and entertaining reading experience. Circ: 27,000.

Audience: 8–14 years
Frequency: 9 times each year
Website: www.cobblestonepub.com

FREELANCE POTENTIAL

85% written by nonstaff writers. Publishes 180 freelance submissions yearly; 20% by unpublished writers, 25% by new authors. Receives 600 queries yearly.

SUBMISSIONS

Query with outline, bibliography, and clips or writing samples. All queries must relate to an upcoming theme. No unsolicited mss. Accepts hard copy. SASE. Responds 5 months prior to theme issue publication.

- Articles: Features, 700–800 words. Sidebars, 300–600 words. Informational articles; profiles; and interviews. Topics include American history and historical figures.
- Fiction: To 800 words. Genres include historical, multicultural, and biographical fiction; adventure; and retold legends.
- Depts/columns: Word lengths vary. Interviews, short profiles, fun facts.
- Artwork: Color prints and slides. Line art.
- Other: Activities, to 700 words. Puzzles and games. Poetry, to 100 lines.

SAMPLE ISSUE

52 pages (no advertising): 15 articles; 2 activities; 1 cartoon; 7 depts/columns. Sample copy, $6.95 with 10x13 SASE ($2 postage). Guidelines and theme list available at website.

- "Walt Disney: Animation Pioneer." Article profiles the creator of Mickey Mouse.
- "Vaudeville: Forerunner to the Movies." Article explains the impact vaudeville had on American entertainment.

RIGHTS AND PAYMENT

All rights. Written material, $.20–$.25 per word. Artwork, $15–$100. Pays on publication. Provides 2 contributor's copies.

➥EDITOR'S COMMENTS

Articles should be historically accurate and have a lively, original approach to the subject.

College Outlook

20 East Gregory Boulevard
Kansas City, MO 64114-1145

Editor: Kellie Houx

DESCRIPTION AND INTERESTS

College Outlook publishes articles that speak to the concerns of high school seniors and their parents. Topics covered include choosing a college, financing an education, preparing for college life, and selecting a major. Circ: 440,000 (spring); 710,000 (fall).

Audience: College-bound students
Frequency: Twice each year
Website: www.collegeoutlook.net

FREELANCE POTENTIAL

10% written by nonstaff writers. Publishes 4 freelance submissions yearly; 10% by unpublished writers, 20% by authors who are new to the magazine. Receives 2–3 queries yearly.

SUBMISSIONS

Query with clips or writing samples. Accepts hard copy. Availability of artwork improves chance of acceptance. SASE. Responds in 1 month.

- Articles: To 1,500 words. Informational and how-to articles; personal experience pieces; and humor. Topics include school selection, financial aid, scholarships, money management, and college admissions procedures.
- Artwork: 5x7 B/W and color transparencies.
- Other: Gazette items on campus subjects, including fads, politics, classroom news, current events, leisure activities, and careers.

SAMPLE ISSUE

40 pages (15% advertising): 11 articles. Sample copy, free. Guidelines available.

- "Campus Tours." Article explains how to get the most out of a campus tour, and lists important questions to ask.
- "Summer Could Be the Best Time to Prepare for College." Article states that college-bound students should use their down time in the summer to research colleges, visit campuses, and prepare for financing their tuition.

RIGHTS AND PAYMENT

All rights. All material, payment rates vary. Payment policy varies. Provides author's copies.

➥EDITOR'S COMMENTS

We seek student-centered articles that can be true resources to our readers. We're open to all subjects that relate to that stressful, pre-college experience. Many of our authors are college administrators or counselors.

Columbus Parent

7801 North Central Drive
Lewis Center, OH 43035

Editor: Staci Perkins

DESCRIPTION AND INTERESTS
Practical and locally relevant information fills the pages of this parenting magazine that is distributed in the greater Columbus area of Ohio. Its focus is on raising happy, healthy children and on the needs and concerns of their parents. Circ: 58,500.

Audience: Parents
Frequency: Monthly
Website: www.columbusparent.com

FREELANCE POTENTIAL
75% written by nonstaff writers. Publishes 50 freelance submissions yearly; 25% by authors who are new to the magazine. Receives 900–1,200 queries yearly.

SUBMISSIONS
Query. Accepts email to columbusparent@ thisweeknews.com. Response time varies.

- Articles: 700 words. Informational, self-help, and how-to articles; profiles; interviews; and reviews. Topics include current events, family health, child development, education, humor, music, recreation, and travel.
- Depts/columns: 300 words. Recipes, travel, health, nutrition, education, news, events, sports, family humor, behavioral develop-ment, and media and product reviews.
- Other: Submit seasonal material at least 2 months in advance.

SAMPLE ISSUE
56 pages (50% advertising): 5 articles; 16 depts/columns. Sample copy, free. Guidelines and editorial calendar available.

- "The Morning Zoo's Dave Kaelin: Laughter and Limits." Article profiles a local DJ, who shares his thoughts about fatherhood and the experiences that impact his radio show.
- Sample dept/column: "Family Getaways" spotlights Pennsylvania's Laurel Highlands as an ideal family trip.

RIGHTS AND PAYMENT
Rights vary. Written material, $.10–$.20 per word. Pays on publication.

➛EDITOR'S COMMENTS
We rarely accept material that does not have a local slant and uses local sources. Fiction, poetry, or children's stories almost never make it onto our pages. Please do not call to follow up on a submission.

Community Education Journal

3929 Old Lee Highway, Suite 91A
Fairfax, VA 22030

Executive Director: Beth Robertson

DESCRIPTION AND INTERESTS
This journal is published by the National Community Education Association, a group that advocates the creation of lifelong learning opportunities for all community members. It publishes research reports and articles that explore the ways in which schools and commu-nities can better provide educational resources for young children, professionals, and at-risk students. Circ: Unavailable.

Audience: Community educators
Frequency: Quarterly
Website: www.ncea.com

FREELANCE POTENTIAL
85% written by nonstaff writers. Publishes 24 freelance submissions yearly; 20% by unpub-lished writers, 45% by authors who are new to the magazine. Receives 12–24 unsolicited mss each year.

SUBMISSIONS
Send complete ms. Accepts email submissions to ncea@ncea.com (Microsoft Word or PDF attachments). Responds in 2 months.

- Articles: 1,500–2,000 words. Informational articles and opinion pieces. Topics include community education programs, research projects, and trends.

SAMPLE ISSUE
36 pages (no advertising): 6 articles. Sample copy, guidelines, and theme list, $5.

- "Authentic Partnerships in the Preparation of Community Education Professionals." Article examines the role of a director of communi-ty education, and identifies ways to prepare for such a role.
- "Lessons Learned from Providing University Support for Community Organizations and Public Schools." Article reports on the efforts of one professor to create a university/com-munity partnership to enhance the resources that aid poor children to do better in school.

RIGHTS AND PAYMENT
All rights. No payment. Provides up to 5 con-tributor's copies.

➛EDITOR'S COMMENTS
Our articles are written by professional edu-cators and/or administrators with direct expe-rience in community education.

Complete Woman

875 North Michigan Avenue, Suite 3434
Chicago, IL 60611-1901

Executive Editor: Lora Wintz

DESCRIPTION AND INTERESTS

This women's magazine covers a range of topics from a woman's perspective, including parenting, careers, money, relationships, entertainment, pop culture, and leading a healthy lifestyle. Circ: 875,000.

Audience: Women
Frequency: Quarterly
Website:
   www.thecompletewomanmagazine.com

FREELANCE POTENTIAL

90% written by nonstaff writers. Publishes 75 freelance submissions yearly; 20% by unpublished writers, 30% by authors who are new to the magazine. Receives 720 queries yearly.

SUBMISSIONS

Query with clips; or send complete ms. Accepts hard copy and simultaneous submissions if identified. SASE. Responds in 3 months.

- Articles: 800–1,200 words. Self-help articles; profiles; humor; confession and personal experience pieces; and interviews. Topics include health, fitness, beauty, skin care, fashion, dining, relationships, romance, business, self-improvement, and celebrities.
- Depts/columns: Word lengths vary. Careers, new products, beauty tips, and news briefs.

SAMPLE ISSUE

106 pages (15% advertising): 15 articles; 28 depts/columns. Sample copy, $4.50 at newsstands.

- "Confessions of a Celebrity DJ." Article presents an interview with Colleen Shannon about working celebrity parties and posing for *Playboy.*
- "10 Things That Really Do Change After Marriage." Article discusses how couples behaved while dating versus after marriage.
- Sample dept/column: "Guy Talk" offers insight into what men really think of their girlfriends' friends.

RIGHTS AND PAYMENT

Rights vary. Written material, payment rates vary. Pays on publication. Provides 1 contributor's copy.

⇢ EDITOR'S COMMENTS

We fit a lot of material into each issue, which translates into good opportunities for freelance writers.

Conceive Magazine

Editorial Department
460 North Orlando Avenue, Suite 200
Winter Park, FL 32789

Editorial Director: Beth Weinhouse

DESCRIPTION AND INTERESTS

Comprehensive information about women's health and fertility, and about the many methods of conception, appears in this publication. *Conceive Magazine* also publishes articles designed to support, inspire, and empower women contemplating starting or expanding their families. Circ: 200,000.

Audience: Women
Frequency: 5 times each year
Website: www.conceiveonline.com

FREELANCE POTENTIAL

75% written by nonstaff writers. Publishes 60 freelance submissions yearly; 5% by unpublished writers, 10% by authors who are new to the magazine. Receives 1,200 queries yearly.

SUBMISSIONS

Query with résumé and clips. Accepts hard copy and email queries to beth.weinhouse@ bonniercorp.com. SASE. Response time varies,

- Articles: Word lengths vary. Informational articles; profiles; and interviews. Topics include family planning, infertility issues, adoption, and baby products.
- Depts/columns: Word lengths vary. News, reproductive health notes, fitness tips, medical updates, relationship issues, expert advice, and personal experience pieces.

SAMPLE ISSUE

72 pages: 2 articles; 11 depts/columns. Sample copy, $4.99 at newsstands. Guidelines available at website.

- "Stopping the Fertility Clock." Article reports on new techniques that are giving women more opportunities to preserve their fertility as they age.
- Sample dept/column: "Success" profiles a couple who adopted seven boys when their own biological children were grown and ready to leave the nest.

RIGHTS AND PAYMENT

All or first rights. Written material, $.50–$1 per word. Kill fee varies. Pays on publication.

⇢ EDITOR'S COMMENTS

Many of our articles are written by professionals in the field, but we still have plenty of room for you to tell your personal journey or to profile someone who found a way to start a family.

Connecticut Parent

420 East Main Street, Suite 18
Branford, CT 06405

Editor & Publisher: Joel MacClaren

DESCRIPTION AND INTERESTS
This magazine offers Connecticut families a complete guide to regional attractions, events, and news. In addition, it features practical information and tips on everything from health and nutrition to travel and children's books. Circ: 60,000.

Audience: Parents
Frequency: Monthly
Website: www.ctparent.com

FREELANCE POTENTIAL
20% written by nonstaff writers. Publishes 50 freelance submissions yearly; 10% by authors who are new to the magazine. Receives 1,000+ unsolicited mss yearly.

SUBMISSIONS
Send complete ms. Prefers email submissions to ctparent@aol.com; will accept hard copy. SASE. Response time varies.

- Articles: 500–1,000 words. Informational, self-help, and how-to articles; profiles; and interviews. Topics include maternity and childbirth issues, parenting, regional news, family relationships, social issues, education, special education, health, fitness, nutrition, safety, entertainment, and travel.
- Depts/columns: 600 words. Family news, new product information, and reviews.

SAMPLE ISSUE
100 pages (60% advertising): 6 articles; 1 guide; 3 depts/columns. Sample copy, $5 with 9x12 SASE. Guidelines available.

- "Here's to a Peaceful Night's Sleep." Article offers new parents tips for establishing good bedtime routines.
- "Swing into Spring the Safe Way." Article explains how to avoid injuries on playground equipment.
- Sample dept/column: "Smalltalk" reviews a local performance of *Sesame Street*.

RIGHTS AND PAYMENT
One-time rights. Written material, payment rates vary. Pays on publication. Provides 1 contributor's tearsheet.

❖EDITOR'S COMMENTS
Our readers are parents of children up to age 12, so your article's focus must be age appropriate. Photography should accompany your submission whenever possible.

Countdown for Kids

Juvenile Diabetes Research Foundation
120 Wall Street, 19th Floor
New York, NY 10005

Submissions Editor: Marieke Gartner

DESCRIPTION AND INTERESTS
This magazine for children with diabetes provides information about the condition in age-appropriate language. Its articles explore ways to manage diabetes and still enjoy being a kid. Circ: Unavailable.

Audience: 10+ years
Frequency: Twice each year
Website: www.jdrf.org

FREELANCE POTENTIAL
50% written by nonstaff writers. Publishes 6–8 freelance submissions yearly; 10% by unpublished writers. Receives 120 queries and unsolicited mss yearly.

SUBMISSIONS
Query or send complete ms. Accepts hard copy. SASE. Response time varies.

- Articles: Word lengths vary. Informational, factual, and self-help articles; profiles; interviews; and personal experience pieces. Topics include coping with Type 1 diabetes, health, fitness, careers, college, popular culture, social issues, and diabetes research.
- Depts/columns: Word lengths vary. Diabetes news and information, career profiles, and health advice.

SAMPLE ISSUE
16 pages (1% advertising): 3 articles; 2 depts/columns. Sample copy available.

- "Help Researchers Help You." Article reports on some current treatment trials and studies, and explains how readers can participate and aid in the research.
- "Success at Sports." Article provides advice on successfully balancing diabetes with an active sports life.
- Sample dept/column: "Let It Snow!" offers instructions for making snow globes.

RIGHTS AND PAYMENT
First North American serial rights. Written material, payment rates vary. Pays on publication. Provides 1 contributor's copy.

❖EDITOR'S COMMENTS
We welcome published writers and new authors equally—as long as they can share their knowledge of juvenile diabetes with our readers without being boring or preachy. We like articles about topics that our readers care about, such as school and sports.

Creative Kids

Prufrock Press
P.O. Box 8813
Waco, TX 76714-8813

Editor: Lacy Compton

DESCRIPTION AND INTERESTS
Creative kids create all the content of this magazine. Circ: 3,600.
Audience: 8–16 years
Frequency: Quarterly
Website: www.prufrock.com

FREELANCE POTENTIAL
95% written by nonstaff writers. Publishes 150 freelance submissions yearly; 75% by unpublished writers, 75% by new authors. Receives 1,800 unsolicited mss each year.

SUBMISSIONS
Child authors only. Send complete ms. Accepts hard copy with author's birthday, grade, and school. SASE. Responds in 4–6 weeks.

- Articles: 500–1,200 words. Informational, self-help, and how-to articles; profiles; essays; photo-essays; humor; and personal experience pieces. Topics include animals and pets, sports, travel, social issues, and gifted education.
- Fiction: 500–1,200 words. Genres include realistic, inspirational, historical, and multicultural fiction; mystery; suspense; folktales; humor; and problem-solving stories. Also publishes plays.
- Depts/columns: Word lengths vary. Short opinion pieces and book reviews.
- Artwork: B/W and color prints. Line art.
- Other: Poetry and songs. Puzzles, games, and cartoons. Submit seasonal material 1 year in advance.

SAMPLE ISSUE
34 pages (no advertising): 4 articles; 6 stories; 1 dept/column; 11 poems; 2 cartoons; 7 activities. Sample copy and guidelines available at website.

- "Space Tragedy." Story tells of a brief but eventful space flight that involved an alien encounter.
- Sample dept/column: "Under Review" recommends a book about how prejudice affects the characters in the story.

RIGHTS AND PAYMENT
Rights vary. No payment. Provides 1 copy.

•❖EDITOR'S COMMENTS
We consider child-authored submissions only, with age indicated. Send us your best work.

Cricket

Cricket Magazine Group
70 East Lake Street, Suite 300
Chicago, IL 60601

Submissions Editor

DESCRIPTION AND INTERESTS
Entertaining the imaginations of tweens and early teens for almost four decades, *Cricket* is known for its high-quality fiction. It also features biographies, profiles, poetry, and activities. Circ: 55,000.
Audience: 9–14 years
Frequency: 9 times each year
Website: www.cricketmag.com

FREELANCE POTENTIAL
100% written by nonstaff writers. Publishes 100 freelance submissions yearly; 30% by unpublished writers, 50% by authors who are new to the magazine. Receives 12,000 unsolicited mss yearly.

SUBMISSIONS
Send complete ms; include bibliography for nonfiction. Accepts hard copy and simultaneous submissions if identified. SASE. Responds in 4–6 months.

- Articles: 200–1,500 words. Informational and how-to articles; biographies; and profiles. Topics include science, art, technology, history, architecture, geography, foreign culture, adventure, and sports.
- Fiction: 200–2,000 words. Genres include humor, mystery, fantasy, science fiction, folktales, fairy tales, mythology, and historical and contemporary fiction.
- Depts/columns: Staff written.
- Other: Poetry, to 50 lines. Puzzles, games, crafts, recipes, and science experiments; word lengths vary.

SAMPLE ISSUE
48 pages (no advertising): 3 articles; 4 stories; 6 depts/columns; 2 poems. Sample copy, $5 with 9x12 SASE. Guidelines available at website.

- "Judgment Day." Story features a girl whose passion is entering spelling bees.
- "The Story of Peg Leg Bates." Article profiles an African American dancer who overcame a disability to become a professional.

RIGHTS AND PAYMENT
Rights vary. Articles and fiction, to $.25 per word. Poetry, to $3 per line. Pays on publication. Provides 2 contributor's copies.

•❖EDITOR'S COMMENTS
Submissions on all appropriate topics will be considered at any time during the year.

Curious Parents

Current Health Kids

2345 Bethel Avenue
Merchantville, NJ 08109

Submissions: Jackie Piccone

Weekly Reader Publishing
1 Reader's Digest Road
Pleasantville, NY 10570

Senior Editor: Meredith Matthews

DESCRIPTION AND INTERESTS
Parenting issues as well as general topics that are of interest to parents are covered in this family-oriented magazine for moms and dads in the Pennsylvania, New Jersey, and Delaware triangle. Circ: 120,000.
Audience: Parents
Frequency: Monthly
Website: www.curiousparents.com

FREELANCE POTENTIAL
80% written by nonstaff writers. Publishes 45 freelance submissions yearly; 60% by unpublished writers, 40% by authors who are new to the magazine. Receives 120 unsolicited mss each year.

SUBMISSIONS
Send complete ms with brief description and brief author biography. Accepts email submissions to editor@curiousparents.com. Response time varies.

- Articles: Word lengths vary. Informational, how-to, and self-help articles. Topics include crafts, hobbies, current events, recreation, education, safety, health, family entertainment, networking, parenting, and travel.
- Depts/columns: Word lengths vary. Health issues and automobile safety; and book reviews.

SAMPLE ISSUE
30 pages: 5 articles; 3 depts/columns. Sample copy, free with 9x12 SASE. Guidelines available at website.

- "10 Tips for Parents of an ADD Child." Article provides ways for parents to cope with their special child.
- Sample dept/column: "Family Health" explains the benefits of a gluten-free diet, and offers cooking and food shopping tips.

RIGHTS AND PAYMENT
All rights. No payment.

↠EDITOR'S COMMENTS
We're in the process of expanding our editorial subject base, and are now accepting articles on camps, education, going green, college prep, summer fun, and family gardening. We would like to see more articles dealing with how the economy has changed family life, and ways that families can adapt to a different financial situation.

DESCRIPTION AND INTERESTS
Formerly called *Current Health 1*, *Current Health Kids* is geared toward middle-grade students. Distributed through schools, the magazine contains articles on health, fitness, nutrition, and emotional well-being. A teacher's guide is included. Circ: 163,973.
Audience: Grades 4–7
Frequency: 8 times each year
Website: www.weeklyreader.com/ch1

FREELANCE POTENTIAL
60% written by nonstaff writers. Publishes 20 freelance submissions yearly; 5% by authors who are new to the magazine. Receives 12 queries yearly.

SUBMISSIONS
Query with letter of introduction outlining areas of expertise, list of publishing credits, and clips. Accepts email queries to currenthealth@weeklyreader.com. Responds in 1–4 months.

- Articles: 800–1,000 words. Informational articles. Topics include personal and public health, fitness, nutrition, sexuality, disease, psychology, first aid, safety, drug education, risky behavior, and relationships.
- Depts/columns: Word lengths vary. Health news, safety issues, Q&As, fitness tips, and careers in the healthcare field.

SAMPLE ISSUE
32 pages (1% advertising): 6 articles; 6 depts/columns. Sample copy, guidelines, and editorial calendar available.

- "Lunch Around the World" is a "Your Food" feature article that looks at children's school lunches internationally.
- "Are Americans Getting Too Heavy?" looks at the obesity epidemic and why people are concerned about its consequences.
- Sample dept/column: "Get Fit!" tests students' knowledge of exercise.

RIGHTS AND PAYMENT
All rights. Articles, $.50 per word. Depts/columns, payment rates vary. Kill fee, 25%. Pays on publication. Provides 2 copies.

↠EDITOR'S COMMENTS
We think the new name better describes our mission: To provide timely, smart, and straightforward health information.

Current Health Teens

Weekly Reader Publishing
1 Reader's Digest Road
Pleasantville, NY 10570

Senior Editor: Meredith Matthews

DESCRIPTION AND INTERESTS
General health issues of interest to tweens and teens are tackled in this classroom supplement, formerly *Current Health 2*. It seeks relevant, current, and engaging articles on nutrition, fitness, relationships, and sexuality. Circ: 101,000.

Audience: Grades 7–12
Frequency: 8 times each year
Website: www.weeklyreader.com/ch2

FREELANCE POTENTIAL
67% written by nonstaff writers. Publishes 36 freelance submissions yearly; 10% by unpublished writers, 15% by authors who are new to the magazine. Receives 12–24 queries yearly.

SUBMISSIONS
Query with outline and sources. Accepts email queries to currenthealth@weeklyreader.com (Microsoft Word attachments). Responds in 1–4 months.

- Articles: 800–1,000 words. Informational articles. Topics include personal and public health, fitness, nutrition, sexuality, disease, psychology, first aid, safety, drug education, risky behavior, and relationships.
- Depts/columns: Word lengths vary. Health news, safety issues, Q&As, fitness tips, and careers in the healthcare field.

SAMPLE ISSUE
32 pages (1% advertising): 6 articles; 6 depts/columns. Sample copy, guidelines, and editorial calendar available.

- "An Equal Opportunity Destroyer." Article explains how eating disorders, such as anorexia and bulimia, can also affect boys.
- "Healthy People 2010." Article reports on the nation's overall health and includes statistics on obesity, tobacco use, and physical activity.
- Sample dept/column: "Safety Zone" offers tips on preserving one's hearing.

RIGHTS AND PAYMENT
All rights. Articles, $.50 per word. Depts/columns, payment rates vary. Kill fee, 25%. Pays on publication. Provides 2 copies.

➡ EDITOR'S COMMENTS
We will be moving sometime within the year, so check our website for our current address. Because of budget pressures, we will be more selective when evaluating new writers.

The Dabbling Mum

508 West Main Street
Beresford, SD 57004

Editor: Alyice Edrich

DESCRIPTION AND INTERESTS
The articles and essays found in this online magazine are geared to busy parents, many of whom work from home or run small businesses. It covers everything from learning to write for the Web to general parenting topics. New this year is an art section that features art tutorials geared to those dealing with loss. Hits per month: 40,000.

Audience: Parents
Frequency: Weekly
Website: www.thedabblingmum.com

FREELANCE POTENTIAL
99% written by nonstaff writers. Publishes 24 freelance submissions yearly; 25% by unpublished writers, 70% by authors who are new to the magazine. Receives 300 queries yearly.

SUBMISSIONS
Query with writing samples. Accepts queries via website only. Responds in 2–4 months.

- Articles: 500–1,500 words. Informational and how-to articles; and personal experience pieces. Topics include family life, parenting, women's issues, home businesses, sales and marketing, and simple/ecofriendly living.

SAMPLE ISSUE
Sample copy, editorial calendar, and guidelines available at website.

- "Play with Your Kids." Personal experience piece discusses ways to maximize time and fun while playing with the kids.
- "14 Questions to Ask Before You Choose a Business Idea." Article guides readers through the process of choosing an idea for a new business.
- "Care Package Received." Essay recounts the many acts of kindness the author received from friends and strangers after the loss of her daughter.

RIGHTS AND PAYMENT
One-month exclusive online rights; indefinite archival rights. Written material, $20–$40; reprints, $5. Pays on acceptance.

➡ EDITOR'S COMMENTS
Among our current needs are articles on how to run a successful business, including social networking, marketing, advertising, and niche markets. We're always interested in hearing from new writers.

Dallas Child

Lauren Publications
4275 Kellway Circle, Suite 146
Addison, TX 75001

Editorial Content: Joylyn Niebes

DESCRIPTION AND INTERESTS
Dallas Child features a local and relevant perspective on issues affecting families in the region, with a special emphasis on children from prenatal through adolescence. It covers everything from education and health to entertainment and recreation. Circ: 80,000.
Audience: Parents
Frequency: Monthly
Website: www.dallaschild.com

FREELANCE POTENTIAL
30% written by nonstaff writers. Publishes 25 freelance submissions yearly; 5–10% by authors who are new to the magazine. Receives 396 queries yearly.

SUBMISSIONS
Query with résumé. Accepts hard copy, email queries to editorial@dallaschild.com, faxed queries to 972-447-0633, and simultaneous submissions if identified. SASE. Responds in 2–3 months.

- Articles: 1,000–2,000 words. Informational, self-help, and how-to articles; profiles; interviews; humor; and personal experience pieces. Topics include parenting, education, child development, family travel, regional news, recreation, entertainment, current events, social issues, multicultural and ethnic subjects, health, fitness, and crafts.
- Depts/columns: 800 words. Local events, travel tips, and health news.

SAMPLE ISSUE
74 pages (15% advertising): 2 articles; 15 depts/columns. Sample copy and guidelines available at website.

- "A New Order." Article offers several strategies for organizing and taking charge of the family's schedule.
- Sample dept/column: "Mommy Diary" details a day in the life of a mother of quadruplet toddlers.

RIGHTS AND PAYMENT
First rights. Written material, payment rates vary. Pays on publication. Provides contributor's copies upon request.

❧ EDITOR'S COMMENTS
We prefer to work with writers living in our region. Articles should inspire, inform, and entertain our readers.

Dance International

677 Davie Street
Vancouver, British Columbia V6B 2G6
Canada

Managing Editor: Maureen Riches

DESCRIPTION AND INTERESTS
Dance International brings global coverage of both classical and contemporary dance to its readers. It offers reviews, criticism, profiles, and interviews. Circ: 4,000.
Audience: YA–Adult
Frequency: Quarterly
Website: www.danceinternational.org

FREELANCE POTENTIAL
85% written by nonstaff writers. Publishes 95 freelance submissions yearly; 9% by authors who are new to the magazine.

SUBMISSIONS
Send complete ms. Accepts email submissions to danceint@direct.ca (attach file) and disk submissions (RTF files). SASE. Responds in 2 months.

- Articles: 1,500 words. Informational articles; profiles; interviews; opinion pieces; and media reviews—all related to dance.
- Depts/columns: 1,000 words. Commentaries, and book and performance reviews.

SAMPLE ISSUE
62 pages (10% advertising): 7 articles; 23 depts/columns. Guidelines available at website.

- "In Character." Article profiles Kevin Bowles of National Ballet of Canada, who has moved up the ranks to principal character artist.
- "The 21st International Ballet Festival of Havana." Article reports on the Cuban festival, staged by the country's uncrowned queen of ballet, Alicia Alonso.
- Sample dept/column: "Russian Profile" discusses the resignation of the Maryinsky Ballet's manager and the former company dancer who succeeded him.

RIGHTS AND PAYMENT
First rights. Articles, $100–$150. Depts/columns, $100. Kill fee, 50%. Pays on publication. Provides 2 contributor's copies.

❧ EDITOR'S COMMENTS
Our writers are often dancers themselves, or they have extensive professional experience within (or covering) the dance world. We cover contemporary dance and ballet companies from around the globe, and we're always in need of reviews of productions on foreign soil. We welcome the chance to work with new freelancers.

Dance Magazine

110 William Street, 23rd Floor
New York, NY 10038

Editor-in-Chief: Wendy Perron

DESCRIPTION AND INTERESTS
Dance students, teachers, and professionals read this magazine for articles that keep them abreast of what is going on in all disciplines of dance. It features techniques; training strategies; and profiles of dancers, companies, and productions. Circ: 50,000.
Audience: YA–Adult
Frequency: Monthly
Website: www.dancemagazine.com

FREELANCE POTENTIAL
80% written by nonstaff writers. Publishes 200 freelance submissions yearly; 5% by unpublished writers, 25% by authors who are new to the magazine. Receives many queries yearly.

SUBMISSIONS
Query. Accepts hard copy and email queries to wperron@dancemedia.com. SASE. Response time varies.

- Articles: To 1,500 words. Informational articles; profiles; and interviews. Topics include dance, dance instruction, choreography, the arts, family, and health concerns.
- Depts/columns: Word lengths vary. New product information, reviews, dance news, and instruction.

SAMPLE ISSUE
138 pages (33% advertising): 5 articles; 15 depts/columns. Sample copy available at website.

- "Your Body: Memory Builders." Article reports on brain research that has revealed how dancers learn new movement.
- "Exotic or Offensive?" Article examines the characters from some of ballet's classic pieces, and posits that perhaps it's time for updates that rid them of stereotypes.
- Sample dept/column: "On the Rise" offers a profile of up-and-coming dancer Arolyn Williams.

RIGHTS AND PAYMENT
Rights vary. Written material, payment rates vary. Pays on publication.

⟶EDITOR'S COMMENTS
We look for writers who have a history with dance, either in performance, teaching, or critiquing. Though most of our coverage leans toward ballet and contemporary, we are open to pieces about any style.

Davey and Goliath's Devotions

Augsburg Fortress Publishers
P.O. Box 1209
Minneapolis, MN 55440-1209

Lead Editor: Becky Weaver Carlson

DESCRIPTION AND INTERESTS
Based on the characters of the popular 1960s television series, this magazine features a mix of Bible stories, activities, and games that help children experience faith lessons in a fun way. It is geared to children in preschool through grade four. Circ: 50,000.
Audience: 3–9 years
Frequency: Quarterly
Website: www.augsburgfortress.org/dg/
　　　　devotions

FREELANCE POTENTIAL
100% written by nonstaff writers. Publishes 40 freelance submissions yearly; 25% by unpublished writers, 50% by authors who are new to the magazine. Receives 40 queries yearly.

SUBMISSIONS
Query with sample content per writers' guidelines. Accepts email queries to cllsub@ augsburgfortress.org (with "Family Devotions" in subject line). All work is assigned. Response time varies.

- Articles: Bible stories, 100–170 words.
- Depts/columns: Questions and prayers, 15–20 words. Bible facts and parenting tips, 30–50 words. Family discussion topics, 100–125 words.
- Other: Puzzles, mazes, activities, and games.

SAMPLE ISSUE
64 pages (no advertising): 44 depts/columns. Sample copy available at website. Guidelines available at www.augsburgfortress.org/ company/submitcongregational.jsp.

- "From Abram to Abraham." Bible story relates how God promised Abraham and Sarah a son.
- "Lessons in Love." Bible story reminds readers of the strong love Jesus has for His followers.
- Sample dept/column: "Bible Activity" recommends making a family fruit tree that each member decorates with their promises.

RIGHTS AND PAYMENT
All rights. Written material, payment rates vary. Pays on acceptance. Provides 2 copies.

⟶EDITOR'S COMMENTS
Please consult our guidelines for detailed information on how to submit a query.

Delmarva Youth Magazine

1226 North Division Street
Salisbury, MD 21801

Editor: Marla Cook

DESCRIPTION AND INTERESTS
This magazine targets parents in the Delmarva Peninsula of Maryland and provides them with articles on activities for young people, parenting, and family life. Circ: 15,000.

Audience: Parents
Frequency: 10 times each year
Website: www.delmarvayouth.com

FREELANCE POTENTIAL
80% written by nonstaff writers. Publishes 60 freelance submissions yearly; 15% by unpublished writers, 20% by authors who are new to the magazine.

SUBMISSIONS
Query or send complete ms. Accepts email to delmarvayouth@hotmail.com (Microsoft Word attachments). Response time varies.

- Articles: 500–3,000 words. Informational and how-to articles; and interviews. Topics include parenting, family life, family events and activities, travel, education, health, music, sports, and family finance.
- Depts/columns: Word lengths vary. School and camp news, family health and fitness, and the arts.

SAMPLE ISSUE
40 pages (15% advertising): 6 articles; 5 depts/columns; 1 calendar. Sample copy, $2.50. Guidelines available at website.

- "Children Achieve More Through the Dramatic Arts." Article examines the social and developmental benefits for children participating in theater programs.
- "Get Your Child to Listen the First Time!" Article discusses reasons why children may have a hard time responding to requests, and explains how parents can help.
- Sample dept/column: "Youth Excellence" reports on the activities of two youngsters, one a champion sport stacker and one an avid roller skater.

RIGHTS AND PAYMENT
First print and electronic rights. Articles, $25–$150. Pays on publication. Provides 1 contributor's copy.

☛EDITOR'S COMMENTS
We welcome all material that will be informational or of interest to parents. All articles should contain local information.

Devozine

1908 Grand Avenue
P.O. Box 340004
Nashville, TN 37203-0004

Editor: Sandy Miller

DESCRIPTION AND INTERESTS
Described as a devotional lifestyle magazine, *Devozine* targets Christian teens. It helps readers grow in their faith and discover how Christianity relates to the issues they face in their daily lives. In addition to feature articles, it includes daily meditations and stories about faith. Circ: 90,000.

Audience: 15–19 years
Frequency: 6 times each year
Website: www.devozine.org

FREELANCE POTENTIAL
100% written by nonstaff writers. Publishes 400 freelance submissions yearly; 50% by authors who are new to the magazine. Receives 150+ queries, 1,000+ unsolicited mss yearly.

SUBMISSIONS
Query for feature articles. Send complete ms for daily meditations. Accepts hard copy and email submissions to devozine@upperroom.org. SASE. Responds in 4 months.

- Articles: 150–500 words. Informational articles; profiles; personal experience pieces; and reviews. Topics include faith, mentoring, independence, courage, teen parenting, creativity, social issues, and relationships.
- Fiction: 150–250 words. Genres include adventure, and historical and multicultural fiction.
- Depts/columns: 75–100 words. Reviews, new product information.
- Other: Daily meditations, 150–250 words. Prayers and poetry, 10–20 lines. Submit seasonal material 6–8 months in advance.

SAMPLE ISSUE
80 pages (no advertising): 8 articles; 2 depts/columns; 50 devotionals. Guidelines and theme list available at website.

- "Rebuilding Ruins." Article reports on teens who are rebuilding houses in Durham.
- "Is Cyberspace a Spirit Place?" Article explores myths about teens and technology.

RIGHTS AND PAYMENT
First and second rights. Features, $100. Meditations, $25. Pays on acceptance.

☛EDITOR'S COMMENTS
We urge writers to check the theme list and guidelines at our website before submitting.

Dig

Cobblestone Publishing
30 Grove Street, Suite C
Peterborough, NH 03458

Editor: Rosalie F. Baker

DESCRIPTION AND INTERESTS

Dig publishes informative articles and fun activities designed to introduce children to the wonders of archaeology. Circ: 18,000.

Audience: 8–14 years
Frequency: 9 times each year
Website: www.digonsite.com

FREELANCE POTENTIAL

85% written by nonstaff writers. Publishes 50–70 freelance submissions yearly; 10% by unpublished writers, 50% by authors who are new to the magazine. Receives 300 queries each year.

SUBMISSIONS

Query with outline, bibliography, and writing sample. All material must relate to upcoming themes. Accepts hard copy. SASE. Responds 5 months prior to theme publication date.

- Articles: Features, 700–800 words. Sidebars, 300–600 words. Informational articles and photo-essays. Topics include archaeology, history, nature, science, and technology.
- Fiction: To 800 words. Genres include historical fiction, adventure, and folklore.
- Depts/columns: 300–600 words. Art, archaeology facts and discoveries, and archaeology-related projects.
- Artwork: B/W and color prints. Line art.
- Other: To 700 words. Activities, word puzzles, mazes, games, and crafts.

SAMPLE ISSUE

32 pages (no advertising): 9 articles; 4 depts/columns; 3 activities. Sample copy, $6.95 with 9x12 SASE ($2 postage). Guidelines and theme list available at website.

- "Rome Lives Again!" Article discusses a digital reconstruction of the ancient Roman Forum.
- Sample dept/column: "Stones & Bones" covers the recent discovery of two sauropods.

RIGHTS AND PAYMENT

All rights. Articles and fiction, $.20–$.25 per word. Artwork, $15–$100. Other material, payment rates vary. Pays on publication. Provides 2 contributor's copies.

⌖EDITOR'S COMMENTS

Please refer to our detailed theme list before submitting your query. Note that all material must relate to one of our upcoming themes.

Dimensions

DECA, Inc.
1908 Association Drive
Reston, VA 20191-1594

Editor: Christopher Young

DESCRIPTION AND INTERESTS

Targeting an international group of marketing students, *Dimensions* is a classroom tool used to prepare readers for the business world. It provides information and advice on entrepreneurship, leadership, college admissions, job skills, and volunteerism. Circ: 176,000.

Audience: 14–18 years
Frequency: Quarterly
Website: www.deca.org

FREELANCE POTENTIAL

25% written by nonstaff writers. Publishes 6–8 freelance submissions yearly; 50–75% by authors who are new to the magazine.

SUBMISSIONS

Query or send complete ms with author bio. Accepts hard copy, email submissions to deca_dimensions@deca.org, Macintosh disk submissions (RTF files), and simultaneous submissions if identified. SASE. Response time varies.

- Articles: 800–1,200 words. Informational and how-to articles; profiles; interviews; and personal experience pieces. Topics include general business, management, marketing, sales, leadership development, entrepreneurship, franchising, personal finance, advertising, e-commerce, business technology, and career opportunities.
- Depts/columns: 400–600 words. DECA chapter news briefs, and opinions.

SAMPLE ISSUE

24 pages (45% advertising): 10 articles; 5 depts/columns. Sample copy, free with 9x12 SASE. Guidelines available.

- "Supporting Entrepreneurial Dreams." Article profiles a foundation that offers college scholarships to young business owners.
- Sample dept/column: "Short Stuff" offers five tips for finding a job in a tight economy.

RIGHTS AND PAYMENT

First serial rights. Written material, payment rates vary. Pays on publication. Provides 2 contributor's copies.

⌖EDITOR'S COMMENTS

We have a young yet sophisticated audience that expects valuable, timely information that they can learn from and refer back to as they move into the business world.

Dimensions of Early Childhood

Southern Early Childhood Association
P.O. Box 55930
Little Rock, AR 72215-5930

Editor: Janet B. Stivers

DESCRIPTION AND INTERESTS
This publication supports high-quality experiences for young children, their families, and educators by advancing the best practices in, and knowledge base of, early childhood education. Its readership includes teachers of young children, family and group child care providers, administrators, and researchers. Circ: 19,000.

Audience: Early childhood professionals
Frequency: 3 times each year
Website: www.southernearlychildhood.org

FREELANCE POTENTIAL
99% written by nonstaff writers. Publishes 40 freelance submissions yearly; 10% by unpublished writers, 80% by authors who are new to the magazine. Receives 50 unsolicited mss each year.

SUBMISSIONS
Send complete ms. Accepts email submissions to editor@southernearlychildhood.org. Responds in 3–4 months.

- Articles: Word lengths vary. Informational articles. Topics include emergent curricula for children, effective classroom practices, theory, research, program administration, family relationships, and resource systems.
- Depts/columns: Word lengths vary. Reviews.

SAMPLE ISSUE
40 pages (5% advertising): 5 articles; 2 book reviews. Sample copy, $5. Writers' guidelines available.

- "Blue Eyes, Brown Eyes, Cornrows, and Curls: Building on Books to Explore Physical Diversity with Preschool Children." Article discusses early experiences that can help children develop positive attitudes about diversity.
- "Addressing the 'Epidemic' of Overweight Children by Using the Internet." Article explores online resources that can assist teachers with educational activities about fitness.
- Sample dept/column: "Reviews" discusses the book *Increasing the Power of Instruction*.

RIGHTS AND PAYMENT
All rights. No payment. Provides 2 copies.

➬EDITOR'S COMMENTS
We're always interested in hearing about emergent curricula, adult education strategies, and effective classroom strategies.

Discovery Girls

4300 Stevens Creek Boulevard, Suite 190
San Jose, CA 95129

Editorial Director: Sarah Verney

DESCRIPTION AND INTERESTS
Discovery Girls features articles written by girls for girls—with some articles written by adults. This means its content touches on topics that really matter to tween girls. Its mission is to help girls grow and develop with a positive sense of self, confidence, and independence. Circ: 220,000.

Audience: Ages 8 and up
Frequency: 6 times each year
Website: www.discoverygirls.com

FREELANCE POTENTIAL
25% written by nonstaff writers. Publishes 10–18 freelance submissions yearly; 50% by authors who are new to the magazine.

SUBMISSIONS
Query with sample paragraph; or send complete ms. Accepts hard copy and submissions through the website. SASE. Response time varies.

- Articles: Word lengths vary. Informational and how-to articles; and personal experience pieces. Topics include friendship, family relationships, self-esteem, peer pressure, fitness, health and beauty, entertainment, recreation, crafts, and social issues.
- Depts/columns: Word lengths vary. Celebrity news, relationship advice, embarrassing moments, opinions, health and beauty, and book reviews.
- Other: Quizzes and contests.

SAMPLE ISSUE
58 pages: 7 articles; 14 depts/columns. Sample copy, $4.50. Editorial calendar available at website.

- "What To Do When You're Losing Your BFF." Article explains the natural changes that friendships go through, and offers advice on how to cope with them.
- Sample dept/column: "Celebrities" presents teen celebrities' embarrassing moments on the sets of their TV shows.

RIGHTS AND PAYMENT
All rights. Written material, payment rates vary. Payment policy varies.

➬EDITOR'S COMMENTS
From our adult contributors, we look for an ability to channel their inner "tween" and write about issues that are important to young girls.

Dramatics

Educational Theatre Association
2343 Auburn Avenue
Cincinnati, OH 45219

Editor: Donald Corathers

DESCRIPTION AND INTERESTS
Written for theater students and teachers, *Dramatics* features informational articles on acting, directing, and set design. It also publishes profiles of theater professionals, reviews, and theater news. Circ: 37,000.

Audience: High school students and teachers
Frequency: 9 times each year
Website: www.edta.org

FREELANCE POTENTIAL
80% written by nonstaff writers. Publishes 41 freelance submissions yearly; 25% by unpublished writers, 50% by authors who are new to the magazine. Receives 480 unsolicited mss each year.

SUBMISSIONS
Send complete ms. Accepts hard copy and email submissions to dcorathers@edta.org. SASE. Responds in 2–4 months.

- Articles: 750–4,000 words. Informational articles; interviews; and book reviews. Topics include playwriting, musical theater, acting, auditions, stage makeup, set design, and theater production.
- Fiction: Word lengths vary. Full-length and one-act plays for high school audiences.
- Depts/columns: Word lengths vary. Industry news, acting techniques.
- Artwork: 5x7 or larger B/W prints; 35mm or larger color transparencies; high-resolution JPEGs or TIFFs. Line art.

SAMPLE ISSUE
56 pages (40% advertising): 1 article; 4 depts/columns; 1 play. Sample copy, $3 with 9x12 SASE. Guidelines available at website.

- "Backstage Kitchen Confidential." Article provides inside information about how professionals prepare—and act with—stage food.
- Sample dept/column: "Journal" features an interview with actress Gabourey Sidibe.

RIGHTS AND PAYMENT
First rights. Written material, $100–$500. Pays on publication. Provides 5 author's copies.

➦ EDITOR'S COMMENTS
The test we apply to a submission is whether it would engage an above-average high-school theater student and deepen his or her understanding and appreciation of the performing arts.

Earlychildhood News

2 Lower Ragsdale, Suite 200
Monterey, CA 93940

Assistant Editor: Susan Swanson

DESCRIPTION AND INTERESTS
This e-zine is written for teachers, childcare workers, and homeschooling parents. Designed as a source of information regarding the education and development of children up to age eight, it features articles on children's behavior and guidance, appropriate practices, health and fitness, assessment, teaching strategies, and classroom ideas. Hits per month: 50,000.

Audience: Early childhood professionals, teachers, and parents
Frequency: Monthly
Website: www.earlychildhoodnews.com

FREELANCE POTENTIAL
99% written by nonstaff writers. Publishes 10+ freelance submissions yearly; 5% by unpublished writers, 15% by authors who are new to the magazine. Receives 96 queries yearly.

SUBMISSIONS
Query with author biography. Accepts email queries to sswanson@excelligence.com. No simultaneous submissions. Responds in 2 months.

- Articles: 800–1,200 words. Informational, how-to, and research-based articles; and personal experience pieces. Topics include child development, curricula, family relationships, health and safety, nutrition, behavior management, and professional development.
- Other: Classroom activities and crafts.

SAMPLE ISSUE
Sample copy, writers' guidelines, and editorial calendar available.

- "10 Ways to Create Self-Reliant Learners." Article provides tips for promoting independent learning in the classroom.
- "Bullying: The Problem and How to Deal With It." Article addresses the issue of bullying, including how to recognize it and put an end to it.

RIGHTS AND PAYMENT
All rights. Written material, $75–$300. Pays on acceptance.

➦ EDITOR'S COMMENTS
The majority of our writers are education or child development professionals. We consider ourselves a resource for professionals, so all articles should have a practical application in the classroom or at home.

Educational Horizons

Pi Lambda Theta
P.O. Box 6626
4101 East Third Street
Bloomington, IN 47407-6626

Managing Editor

DESCRIPTION AND INTERESTS
Scholarly essays and research articles about education and learning are the mainstay of this publication, written for members of Pi Lambda Theta. Circ: 14,000.

Audience: Pi Lambda Theta members
Frequency: Quarterly
Website: www.pilambda.org

FREELANCE POTENTIAL
100% written by nonstaff writers. Publishes 10–15 freelance submissions yearly; few by unpublished writers; 65–75% by authors who are new to the magazine. Receives 48–60 queries, 24–36 unsolicited mss yearly.

SUBMISSIONS
Prefers query with proposed word count; will accept complete ms. Accepts hard copy, disk submissions (.txt files), email to publications@pilambda.org, and simultaneous submissions if identified. SASE. Responds to queries in 1 month, to mss in 3–4 months.

- Articles: Research articles, 2,500–4,000 words. Scholarly essays, 1,000–2,000 words. Topics include educational, social, and cultural topics of significance.
- Depts/columns: 500–750 words. Education topics in the news, multicultural education, legal issues, and book reviews.
- Artwork: Graphs and charts created in Microsoft Excel and saved as separate files.

SAMPLE ISSUE
64 pages (4% advertising): 4 articles; 4 depts/columns; 2 book reviews. Sample copy, $5 with 9x12 SASE. Writers' guidelines available at website.

- "Gen Y: Who They Are and How They Learn." Article explains how our increasingly global-oriented society has impacted education.
- Sample dept/column: "From the Trenches" is a report from an educator on how policies may or may not change behavior.

RIGHTS AND PAYMENT
First rights. No payment. Provides 5 contributor's copies.

➾EDITOR'S COMMENTS
Education must be the focus of every submission; thorough research and quality of writing must be evident. A preliminary query is strongly recommended.

Educational Leadership

ASCD
1703 North Beauregard Street
Alexandria, VA 22311-1714

Assistant Editor: Lucy Robertson

DESCRIPTION AND INTERESTS
This publication of the Association for supervision and Curriculum Development is read by teachers, school administrators, and other education professionals for timely articles and opinion pieces. Circ: 105,000.

Audience: Educators
Frequency: 8 times each year
Website: www.ascd.org/el

FREELANCE POTENTIAL
95% written by nonstaff writers. Publishes 130 freelance submissions yearly; 50% by unpublished writers, 50% by authors who are new to the magazine. Receives 900 unsolicited mss each year.

SUBMISSIONS
Send 2 copies of complete ms. Prefers email to elsubmissions@ascd.org; will accept hard copy. SASE. Responds in 2 months.

- Articles: 1,500–2,500 words. Informational, how-to, and research-based articles; program descriptions; and personal experience and opinion pieces. Topics include reading, assessment, instructional strategies, student achievement, gifted and special education, science, technology, and multicultural issues.
- Depts/columns: Word lengths vary. Opinions, accountability issues, research findings, leadership challenges, principals' perspectives, ASCD news, and policy reviews.
- Artwork: B/W or color prints or slides; digital images at 300 dpi. Line art.

SAMPLE ISSUE
96 pages (25% advertising): 15 articles; 9 depts/columns. Sample copy, $7. Guidelines and theme list available at website.

- "Holding on to Gen Y." Article describes ways to motivate young teachers to continue their careers in the classroom.
- "Who's Teaching Our Children?" Article reveals changes in the demographics of teachers in the last 20 years.

RIGHTS AND PAYMENT
All or first rights. No payment. Provides 5 contributor's copies.

➾EDITOR'S COMMENTS
We're always interested in submissions that describe successful classroom-tested methods and real-life experiences.

Education Forum

60 Mobile Drive
Toronto, Ontario M4A 2P3
Canada

Managing Editor: Rhonda Allan

DESCRIPTION AND INTERESTS
Education issues, trends, and strategies are covered in this bilingual journal for Ontario-based teachers and administrators. It also features the success stories of workers in public education. Circ: 50,000.

Audience: Educators
Frequency: 3 times each year
Website: www.osstf.on.ca

FREELANCE POTENTIAL
90% written by nonstaff writers. Publishes 35 freelance submissions yearly; 20% by unpublished writers, 80% by authors who are new to the magazine. Receives 48 queries and unsolicited mss yearly.

SUBMISSIONS
Query with clips or writing samples; or send ms. Accepts hard copy. No simultaneous submissions. SAE/IRC. Responds in 1–2 months.

- Articles: To 2,500 words. How-to and practical application articles; essays; and opinion pieces. Topics include education trends, teaching techniques, and controversial issues relating to education.
- Depts/columns: "Openers," to 300 words; news and opinion pieces. "Forum Picks," word lengths vary; media and software reviews.
- Artwork: B/W or color prints or color transparencies. Line art.
- Other: Classroom activities, puzzles, and games. Submit seasonal material 8 months in advance.

SAMPLE ISSUE
46 pages (18% advertising): 4 articles; 8 depts/columns. Sample copy, free with 9x12 SAE/IRC. Guidelines available.

- "From Me to We." Article profiles two brothers who are creating a program to help schools take action on social justice issues.
- Sample dept/column: "Forum Picks" highlights the tours and walks offered by the Royal Ontario Museum.

RIGHTS AND PAYMENT
First North American serial rights. No payment. Provides 5 contributor's copies.

➡EDITOR'S COMMENTS
We are eager to work with new writers. All work should be clear and focused.

Education Week

6935 Arlington Road, Suite 100
Bethesda, MD 20814-5233

Executive Editor: Greg Chronister

DESCRIPTION AND INTERESTS
As "American Education's Newspaper of Record," this publication of the nonprofit Editorial Projects in Education covers critical issues facing American schools. Its articles cover education news, politics, government programs, and trends in education. Circ: 50,000.

Audience: Educators
Frequency: 45 times each year
Website: www.edweek.org

FREELANCE POTENTIAL
20% written by nonstaff writers. Publishes 135 freelance submissions yearly; 80% by unpublished writers, 75% by authors who are new to the magazine. Receives 500 unsolicited mss each year.

SUBMISSIONS
Send complete ms. Accepts disk submissions. SASE. Responds in 6–8 weeks.

- Articles: Staff written.
- Depts/columns: To 1,200 words. "Commentary," essays about child development and education related to grades K–12.

SAMPLE ISSUE
40 pages (25% advertising): 15 articles; 8 depts/columns. Sample copy, $3 with 9x12 SASE ($1 postage). Guidelines available.

- Sample dept/column: "Commentary" offers an essay about the economic realities facing school budgets, and posits that merely threatening to cut teachers will no longer work.
- Sample dept/column: "Commentary" explains why changing the way school districts approach professional development may benefit all teachers.

RIGHTS AND PAYMENT
First rights. "Commentary" essays, $200. Pays on publication. Provides 2 contributor's copies.

➡EDITOR'S COMMENTS
Please note that the vast majority of our publication is written by our staff journalists. We invite educators, administrators, economists, and other professionals knowledgeable about the education field to submit their opinions in an essay. Submissions should be opinion essays, not scholarly reviews. They will be edited for clarity and length and to conform to our editorial style, but your opinion will be left intact.

EduGuide

Partnership for Learning
321 North Pine
Lansing, MI 48933

Editor: Mary Kat Parks-Workinger

DESCRIPTION AND INTERESTS

Published by Partnership for Learning, *EduGuide* offers a "roadmap for student success." As such, it is packed with advice, resources, and strategies for educating children from kindergarten through college. Circ: 600,000.

Audience: Parents and students
Frequency: Annually
Website: www.eduguide.org

FREELANCE POTENTIAL

40% written by nonstaff writers. Publishes 25–30 freelance submissions yearly; 10% by unpublished writers, 40% by authors who are new to the magazine.

SUBMISSIONS

Query. Accepts hard copy. SASE. Responds in 4–6 weeks.

- Articles: 500–1,000 words. Informational and how-to articles; profiles; interviews; and personal experience pieces. Topics include the arts, college, careers, computers, gifted education, health, fitness, history, humor, mathematics, music, science, technology, special education, and issues related to elementary and secondary education.
- Depts/columns: Staff written.
- Artwork: Color prints and transparencies. Line art.
- Other: Submit seasonal material 3 months in advance.

SAMPLE ISSUE

12 pages: 4 articles; 3 depts/columns. Sample copy, $3 with 9x12 SASE ($1 postage). Guidelines and editorial calendar available.

- "Beating Middle School Homework Hassles." Article explains that instilling good work habits in middle school children will benefit them for the rest of their lives.
- "What Teachers Wish Parents Knew." Article discusses ways parents can partner with teachers to help their children succeed.

RIGHTS AND PAYMENT

First or second rights. All material, payment rates vary. Pays on acceptance. Provides 5 contributor's copies.

↔EDITOR'S COMMENTS

We offer four editions that serve the needs of students in the elementary, middle school, high school, and college years.

Edutopia

The George Lucas Educational Foundation
P.O. Box 3494
San Rafael, CA 94912

Executive Editor: Jennifer Sweeney

DESCRIPTION AND INTERESTS

This magazine, published by the George Lucas Educational Foundation, has a mission to share ideas about interactive educational environments. It is filled with articles that address the issues of our current education system and provide innovative ideas on integrated studies, learning, teacher development, and using technology in education. Circ: 100,000.

Audience: Teachers, parents, policy makers
Frequency: 8 times each year
Website: www.edutopia.org

FREELANCE POTENTIAL

70% written by nonstaff writers. Publishes 20 freelance submissions yearly; 30% by authors who are new to the magazine. Receives 36–60 queries yearly.

SUBMISSIONS

Query with résumé and clips. Accepts email to edit@edutopia.org. Response time varies.

- Articles: 300–2,500 words. Informational and how-to articles; and personal experience pieces. Topics include education, computers, science, technology, social issues, current events, health and fitness, nature and the environment, popular culture, recreation, and travel.
- Depts/columns: 700 words. Health, education, and ethnic and multicultural issues.

SAMPLE ISSUE

56 pages (35% advertising): 10 articles; 10 depts/columns. Sample copy, $4.95.

- "Global Language Education: Learning the Lingo." Article explores the many ways new technology allows us to teach and learn a foreign language.
- "Teaching Tolerance: Meet the Teacher Who Started Gay-Straight Alliances." Article profiles teacher Bob Parlin and his work with gay and straight students.

RIGHTS AND PAYMENT

First North American serial rights. Written material, payment rates vary. Pays on acceptance. Provides 2 contributor's copies.

↔EDITOR'S COMMENTS

We are interested in articles on best practices, ideal learning environments, and new approaches to education. Most of our writers are experienced educators.

Elementary School Writer

Writer Publications
P.O. Box 718
Grand Rapids, MI 55744-0718

Editor: Emily Benes

DESCRIPTION AND INTERESTS
For more than 25 years, *Elementary School Writer* has been showcasing the stories, poems, essays, and articles of young authors. It was founded by an English teacher to foster creativity and enable students to learn from the writing of their peers. Circ: Unavailable.

Audience: Elementary and middle school students and their teachers
Frequency: 6 times each year
Website: www.writerpublications.com

FREELANCE POTENTIAL
100% written by nonstaff writers. Publishes 300 freelance submissions yearly; 95% by unpublished writers, 75% by authors who are new to the magazine. Receives 100 unsolicited mss yearly.

SUBMISSIONS
Accepts complete ms from subscribing teachers only. Accepts hard copy, email submissions to writer@mx3.com (ASCII text only), and simultaneous submissions if identified. SASE. Response time varies.

- Articles: To 1,000 words. Informational and how-to articles; profiles; humor; opinion; and personal experience pieces. Topics include current events, multicultural and ethnic issues, nature, the environment, popular culture, sports, and travel.
- Fiction: To 1,000 words. Genres include humor, science fiction, and stories about nature and sports.
- Other: Poetry, no line limits. Seasonal material.

SAMPLE ISSUE
8 pages (no advertising): 15 articles; 3 stories; 9 poems. Guidelines available in each issue and at website.

- "The Dog Who Dug Lake Superior." Story offers an explanation for the creation of this Great Lake.
- "First Class Luxury." Article recounts the author's experiences traveling from Beirut to Minneapolis, Minnesota.

RIGHTS AND PAYMENT
One-time rights. No payment.

➥EDITOR'S COMMENTS
We accept submissions from young writers and from teachers who are subscribers.

Ellery Queen's Mystery Magazine

475 Park Avenue South, 11th Floor
New York, NY 10016

Editor: Janet Hutchings

DESCRIPTION AND INTERESTS
Since 1941 *Ellery Queen* has been entertaining its audience with every type of mystery short story—from the psychological suspense tale and detective puzzle to the private eye case. It accepts work from both new and established writers. Circ: 120,000.

Audience: Adult
Frequency: 10 times each year
Website: www.themysteryplace.com/eqmm

FREELANCE POTENTIAL
100% written by nonstaff writers. Publishes 120 freelance submissions yearly; 7% by unpublished writers, 25% by authors who are new to the magazine. Receives 2,600 unsolicited mss yearly.

SUBMISSIONS
Send complete ms. Accepts hard copy and simultaneous submissions if identified. SASE. Responds in 3 months.

- Fiction: Feature stories, 2,500–8,000 words. Minute Mysteries, 250 words. Novellas by established authors, to 20,000 words. Genres include contemporary and historical crime fiction, psychological thrillers, mystery, suspense, and detective/private eye stories.
- Depts/columns: Book reviews.
- Other: Poetry.

SAMPLE ISSUE
112 pages (6% advertising): 11 stories; 2 book reviews. Sample copy, $5.50. Writers' guidelines available.

- "Between Sins." Story tells of a cop who is hired to protect a judge from a killer who was set free, and the sexual relationship that commences.
- "Material Evidence." Story relates the experience of a policeman who is searching an elderly widower's apartment to find evidence connected with his murder.

RIGHTS AND PAYMENT
First and anthology rights. Written material, $.05–$.08 per word. Pays on acceptance. Provides 3 contributor's copies.

➥EDITOR'S COMMENTS
Occasionally we use stories of up to 12,000 words and we feature one or two short novels each year, though these spaces are usually reserved for established writers.

Equine Journal

102 Roxbury Street
Keene, NH 03431

Editor: Kelly Ballou

DESCRIPTION AND INTERESTS
Horse enthusiasts and amateur and professional equestrians read this journal to stay on top of all horse-related news and activities. It covers breeds, riding styles, equine health, and competitions. Circ: 30,000.
Audience: 14 years–Adult
Frequency: Monthly
Website: www.equinejournal.com

FREELANCE POTENTIAL
95% written by nonstaff writers. Publishes 100 freelance submissions yearly; 3% by authors who are new to the magazine. Receives 36–60 queries, 5 unsolicited mss yearly.

SUBMISSIONS
Prefers query with résumé and clips; will accept complete ms with clips. Accepts hard copy and email submissions to editorial@equinejournal.com. Responds in 2 months.

- Articles: 1,800–2,000 words. Informational and how-to articles. Topics include horse breeds; riding; carriage driving; horse training, housing, transportation, and care; ranch management; and equine insurance.
- Depts/columns: Word lengths vary. "Horse Health" and "Last Laugh."

SAMPLE ISSUE
146 pages (66% advertising): 11 articles; 5 depts/columns. Sample copy, $6. Guidelines and editorial calendar available at website.

- "Team Hannigan." Article profiles a dressage competitor who runs her own dressage business on the side, offering training, sales, boarding, and clinics.
- "A Mustang Must Read." Article reports on several rehabilitation programs using wild mustangs that have been captured to control their numbers.
- Sample dept/column: "Last Laugh" offers a humorous essay on how *not* to get ready for a show.

RIGHTS AND PAYMENT
First North American serial rights. Articles, $150–$175. Depts/columns, $25–$125. Pays on acceptance. Provides 1 contributor's copy.

➥EDITOR'S COMMENTS
We're open to just about any horse-related topic that would be of interest to riders, owners, breeders, trainers—or anyone who simply loves horses.

Exceptional Parent

416 Main Street
Johnstown, PA 15901

Managing Editor: Laura Apel

DESCRIPTION AND INTERESTS
This magazine examines the social, psychological, legal, financial, and educational issues faced by individuals with disabilities. It is filled with practical information and valuable advice to make life easier and happier. Its articles are written by lay persons as well as doctors and healthcare practitioners. Circ: 70,000.
Audience: Parents and professionals
Frequency: Monthly
Website: www.eparent.com

FREELANCE POTENTIAL
90% written by nonstaff writers. Publishes 250 freelance submissions yearly; 30% by unpublished writers, 30% by authors who are new to the magazine. Receives 840 queries yearly.

SUBMISSIONS
Query. Accepts email queries to lapel@eparent.com. Responds in 3–4 weeks.

- Articles: To 2,500 words. Informational articles; profiles; interviews; and personal experience pieces. Topics include the social, psychological, legal, political, technological, financial, and educational concerns of individuals with disabilities and their caregivers.
- Depts/columns: Word lengths vary. Opinions, personal essays, news, new product information, and media reviews.

SAMPLE ISSUE
98 pages (50% advertising): 19 articles; 13 depts/columns. Sample copy, $4.99 with 9x12 SASE ($2 postage). Guidelines and editorial calendar available at website.

- "Therapeutic Play at Inflatable Playgrounds." Article discusses the benefits of indoor bounce houses and slides for children with autism.
- Sample dept/column: "Organizational Spotlight" profiles Bright Futures, a national health promotion and disease prevention program aimed at families.

RIGHTS AND PAYMENT
All rights. No payment. Provides 6 copies.

➥EDITOR'S COMMENTS
Our tone is generally upbeat, but we also recognize that our audience is no stranger to difficulty and reality. We avoid discussion of what could have been done to prevent a disability, and focus on what can be done now.

Faces

Cobblestone Publishing
30 Grove Street, Suite C
Peterborough, NH 03458

Editor: Elizabeth Carpentiere

DESCRIPTION AND INTERESTS
This children's magazine takes its readers on a journey around the world, sharing engaging and fun stories about people, places, and cultures near and far. Circ: 15,000.

Audience: 9–14 years
Frequency: 9 times each year
Website: www.cobblestonepub.com

FREELANCE POTENTIAL
50% written by nonstaff writers. Publishes 45–45 freelance submissions yearly; 10% by unpublished writers, 30% by authors who are new to the magazine. Receives 600 queries each year.

SUBMISSIONS
Query with outline, bibliography, and clips or writing samples. Accepts email queries to facesmag@yahoo.com. Responds in 5 months.

- Articles: 800 words. Sidebars, 300–600 words. Informational articles and personal experience pieces. Topics include culture, geography, the environment, cuisine, special events, travel, history, and social issues.
- Fiction: To 800 words. Stories, legends, and folktales from around the world.
- Depts/columns: Staff written.
- Artwork: Color prints or transparencies.
- Other: Games, crafts, puzzles, and activities, to 700 words.

SAMPLE ISSUE
50 pages (no advertising): 13 articles; 1 story; 1 activity; 9 depts/columns. Sample copy, $6.95 with 9x12 SASE ($2 postage). Guidelines and theme list available at website.

- "A Day in the Life of a Ugandan Family." Article portrays a day's events for children living in a small Ugandan town.
- "Growing Up Amish." Article relates the experiences of children growing up in Amish communities.

RIGHTS AND PAYMENT
All rights. Articles and fiction, $.20–$.25 per word. Activities and puzzles, payment rates vary. Pays on publication. Provides 2 copies.

➹EDITOR'S COMMENTS
For your best chance of acceptance, send us a query that follows our theme list. We like lively stories of people living within the culture we are covering.

Face Up

Redemptorist Communications
75 Orwell Road
Rathgar, Dublin 6
Ireland

Editor: Gerard Moloney

DESCRIPTION AND INTERESTS
This magazine offers teens lively and thoughtful articles and personal experience pieces on the social and spiritual issues most important to them. Circ: 12,000.

Audience: 14–17 years
Frequency: 10 times each year
Website: www.faceup.ie

FREELANCE POTENTIAL
80% written by nonstaff writers. Publishes 60 freelance submissions yearly; 25% by unpublished writers, 25% by authors who are new to the magazine. Receives 100+ unsolicited mss each year.

SUBMISSIONS
Send complete ms. Accepts email submissions to info@faceup.ie. Responds in 1 month.

- Articles: 900 words. Informational and how-to articles; profiles; and personal experience pieces. Topics include college; careers; current events; relationships; health; fitness; music; popular culture; celebrities; sports; and multicultural, ethnic, and social issues.
- Depts/columns: 500 words. Opinions, essays, reviews, advice, self-help, profiles, interviews, and "Words of Wisdom."
- Other: Quizzes and crossword puzzles.

SAMPLE ISSUE
48 pages (5% advertising): 6 articles; 13 depts/columns. Sample copy, guidelines, and editorial calendar available at website.

- "Get Happy!" Article offers ten instant mood boosters to chase away the blues.
- "More Than Just Friends." Article provides advice about how to respond when a friend of the opposite sex declares romantic feelings.
- "Hearing the Cries for Help." Article explains how to read the signs of depression and potential suicidal tendencies in others.

RIGHTS AND PAYMENT
Rights vary. Written material, payment rates vary. Pays on publication. Provides 2 contributor's copies.

➹EDITOR'S COMMENTS
While we are an official ministry of the Irish Redemptorists, and a Catholic publication, our aim is not to preach religion but to tackle real issues facing today's Christian teens. We seek intelligent and compassionate writers.

Faith & Family

432 Washington Avenue
North Haven, CT 06473

Assistant Editor: Robyn Lee

DESCRIPTION AND INTERESTS
Written for educated, professional, "real-world" Catholic moms, *Faith & Family* focuses on spirituality, raising children, homekeeping, and finances. It is read by parents from diverse Catholic traditions. Circ: 35,000.

Audience: Catholic mothers
Frequency: 6 times each year
Website: www.faithandfamilylive.com

FREELANCE POTENTIAL
75% written by nonstaff writers. Publishes 35 freelance submissions yearly; 15% by unpublished writers, 10% by authors who are new to the magazine. Receives 300 queries yearly.

SUBMISSIONS
Query. Accepts email queries to editor@faithandfamilylive.com. Responds in 2–3 months.

- Articles: 600–2,000 words. Informational, inspirational, how-to, and self-help articles; profiles; interviews; and personal experience pieces. Topics include home, family, parenting, marriage, relationships, spirituality, personal development, virtues, children's books, and current events and issues—all from a broad Catholic perspective.
- Depts/columns: Word lengths vary. Home, self-improvement, finance, health, fitness, marriage, Catholic holidays, food, entertainment, spiritual guidance, crafts, activities, and personal experience pieces.
- Artwork: Color prints or slides.

SAMPLE ISSUE
96 pages (30% advertising): 5 articles; 15 depts/columns. Sample copy, $6. Writers' guidelines available.

- "Know Thy Spouse." Article interviews the authors of a new book about marriage.
- Sample dept/column: "Spiritual Directions" discusses dealing with rage after the death of a child.

RIGHTS AND PAYMENT
First North American serial rights. Written material, $.33 per word. Pays on publication.

➥EDITOR'S COMMENTS
We want to work with authors who can provide high-quality magazine writing that is accessible, creative, and concise. Use an honest, non-preachy tone.

Faith Today

M.I.P. Box 3745
Markham, Ontario L3R 0Y4
Canada

Senior Editor: Bill Fledderus

DESCRIPTION AND INTERESTS
Founded in 1983 by the Evangelical Fellowship of Canada, *Faith Today* is a general interest magazine featuring articles aimed at Canadian Evangelicals. It includes news and profiles of Canadian ministries and people of faith. Circ: 20,000.

Audience: Canadian Evangelical Christians
Frequency: 6 times each year
Website: www.faithtoday.ca

FREELANCE POTENTIAL
60% written by nonstaff writers. Publishes 120 freelance submissions yearly; 1% by unpublished writers, 10% by authors who are new to the magazine. Receives 120 queries yearly.

SUBMISSIONS
Query. Prefers email to editor@faithtoday.ca (Microsoft Word attachments); will accept hard copy. SAE/IRC. Responds in 3 weeks.

- Articles: 800–1,800 words. Cover articles, 2,000 words. Essays, 650–1,200 words. Informational and how-to articles; profiles; interviews; and opinion pieces. Topics include Christianity in Canada, ministry initiatives, prayer, the Bible, and issues of concern to Evangelical Christians.
- Depts/columns: "Kingdom Matters," 50–350 words. News, 300–700 words. Media reviews, to 300 words.

SAMPLE ISSUE
54 pages (20% advertising): 5 articles; 11 depts/columns. Sample copy and guidelines available at website.

- "Active Faith." Article profiles five Canadians who are using their faith and actions to make the world a better place.
- Sample dept/column: "A Church You Should Know" profiles a Toronto church that is reaching out to immigrants from Myanmar, Vietnam, Laos, and Thailand.

RIGHTS AND PAYMENT
First North American serial and perpetual electronic rights. Articles, $.25 Canadian per word. Essays, $.15 per word. Depts/columns, $.20 per word. Kill fee, 30–50%. Pays within 6 weeks of acceptance. Provides 2 copies.

➥EDITOR'S COMMENTS
Please remember that all material must have a Canadian connection.

Families on the Go

Life Media
P.O. Box 55445
St. Petersburg, FL 33732

Editor: Barbara Doyle

DESCRIPTION AND INTERESTS

With separate print and online versions, *Families on the Go* offers a mix of parenting-related articles and travel and destination pieces for families looking to enjoy some vacation or adventure time. It has four editions, each of which focuses on a particular region of Florida. Circ: 120,000.

Audience: Parents
Frequency: 6 times each year
Website: www.familiesonthego.com

FREELANCE POTENTIAL

80% written by nonstaff writers. Publishes 50 freelance submissions yearly; 25% by unpublished writers, 20% by authors who are new to the magazine.

SUBMISSIONS

Query or send complete ms. Accepts hard copy and email submissions to editor@ familiesonthego.org (Microsoft Word attachments). SASE. Responds if interested.

- Articles: 350–750 words. Informational articles. Topics include health, wellness, fitness, parenting issues, education, family relationships, home and garden, the arts, travel, and entertainment.
- Depts/columns: Word lengths vary. Community news.

SAMPLE ISSUE

48 pages: 3 articles; 13 depts/columns. Sample copy, free with 9x12 SASE (4 first-class stamps) or available at website. Guidelines available at website.

- "Making Time-Out Work." Article provides insight into the "time-out" form of discipline and explains how to make it work.
- "Florida Critters: Poisonous or Not." Article explains the common bites and stings that come with summer in Florida, and provides tips for treating them.

RIGHTS AND PAYMENT

Exclusive regional rights. Written material, payment rates vary. Pays on publication. Provides 2 contributor's copies.

➡ EDITOR'S COMMENTS

All articles should include at least one sidebar and a list of local resources. Once accepted, your article may be used for one or several of our editions, or our website.

Family Circle

Meredith Corporation
375 Lexington Avenue, 9th Floor
New York, NY 10017

Executive Editor: Darcy Jacobs

DESCRIPTION AND INTERESTS

Family Circle offers advice on parenting issues, provides suggestions for fun family activities, delivers the latest health news, and showcases projects to create a comfortable home in every issue. Circ: 3.8 million.

Audience: Families
Frequency: 15 times each year
Website: www.familycircle.com

FREELANCE POTENTIAL

80% written by nonstaff writers. Publishes many freelance submissions yearly. Receives hundreds of queries yearly.

SUBMISSIONS

Query with clips (including 1 from a national magazine) and author bio. Accepts hard copy. No simultaneous submissions. SASE. Responds in 6–8 weeks if interested.

- Articles: 1,000–2,000 words. Informational and how-to articles; profiles; and personal experience pieces. Topics include parenting, relationships, health, safety, fitness, home decor, travel, fashion, and cooking.
- Depts/columns: 750 words. "My Hometown," "My Family Life," "Good Works," recipes, beauty tips, shopping tips, fitness routines, and advice.

SAMPLE ISSUE

210 pages (48% advertising); 18 articles; 1 story; 20 depts/columns. Sample copy, $1.99 at newsstands. Guidelines available.

- "Special Delivery." Article tells the inspiring story of a mother and daughter who collect books for donation to children in poor Kenyan villages.
- "Decode Your Headaches." Article describes seven top causes of headaches.
- Sample dept/column: "Family" discusses common ailments that affect aging pets.

RIGHTS AND PAYMENT

All rights. Written material, payment rates vary. Kill fee, 25%. Pays on acceptance. Provides 1 contributor's copy.

➡ EDITOR'S COMMENTS

True stories about women making a difference in the community, and newsworthy reports on social issues that affect American families are always of interest. We welcome new writers with national magazine experience.

The Family Digest

P.O. Box 40137
Fort Wayne, IN 46804

Manuscript Editor: Corine B. Erlandson

DESCRIPTION AND INTERESTS

This magazine seeks to enrich the lives of Catholic families through enlightening articles and inspirational personal experience pieces. Circ: 150,000.

Audience: Families
Frequency: Quarterly

FREELANCE POTENTIAL

95% written by nonstaff writers. Publishes 44 freelance submissions yearly; 25% by authors who are new to the magazine. Receives 500 unsolicited mss yearly.

SUBMISSIONS

Send complete ms. Accepts hard copy. No simultaneous submissions. Previously published material will be considered. SASE. Responds in 1–2 months.

- Articles: 700–1,200 words. Informational, self-help, how-to, and inspirational articles; and personal experience pieces. Topics include Catholic traditions, parish and family life, spirituality, the saints, prayer life, and seasonal material.
- Depts/columns: Staff written.
- Other: Humorous anecdotes, 15–100 words. Cartoons. Submit seasonal material 7 months in advance.

SAMPLE ISSUE

48 pages (no advertising): 10 articles; 5 depts/columns. Sample copy, free with 6x9 SASE (2 first-class stamps). Guidelines and theme list available.

- "One Man's Invention." Article tells of a man who, at the end of his life, came to understand how his invention made a positive difference in someone else's life.
- "Praying the Liturgy of the Hours." Article explains how this form of meditative prayer can enrich one's prayer life.

RIGHTS AND PAYMENT

First North American serial rights. Articles, $50–$60. Anecdotes, $25. Cartoons, $40. Pays 1–2 months after acceptance. Provides 2 contributor's copies.

☛EDITOR'S COMMENTS

We're always interested in new material, but will consider previously published articles that fit an issue's theme. Please do not send poetry or fiction.

FamilyFun

47 Pleasant Street
Northampton, MA 01060

Department Editor: Jonathan Adolph

DESCRIPTION AND INTERESTS

For the past 20 years, *FamilyFun* has been providing parents with ideas for having fun with their children. It features creative and unique party plans, craft projects, cooking ideas, and travel destinations. Circ: 2 million.

Audience: Parents
Frequency: 10 times each year
Website: www.familyfun.com

FREELANCE POTENTIAL

80% written by nonstaff writers. Publishes 100+ freelance submissions yearly; 1% by unpublished writers, 2% by authors who are new to the magazine. Receives thousands of queries and unsolicited mss yearly.

SUBMISSIONS

Query for features. Send complete ms for depts/columns. Accepts hard copy and email queries to queries.familyfun@disney.com. SASE. Responds in 4–6 weeks.

- Articles: 850–3,000 words. Informational and how-to articles. Topics include food, crafts, parties, holidays, sports, and games.
- Depts/columns: 50–1,200 words. See guidelines for details. Crafts, nature activities, recipes, family getaways and traditions, household hints, healthy fun, home decorating and gardening tips, and product reviews.
- Other: Submit seasonal material 6 months in advance.

SAMPLE ISSUE

116 pages (47% advertising): 5 articles; 10 depts/columns. Sample copy, $3.95 at newsstands. Guidelines available at website.

- "Adventure Awaits on the Freedom Trail." Article tells how a trip to Boston can turn into a fun family history lesson.
- Sample dept/column: "Creative Solutions" explains how one family entertains company with games inspired by TV reality shows.

RIGHTS AND PAYMENT

First serial rights. Written material, payment rates vary. Pays on acceptance.

☛EDITOR'S COMMENTS

Good, original ideas for family projects and family-friendly travel destinations are always welcome. We ask potential writers to please check our website for guidelines before contacting us.

FamilyWorks Magazine

4 Joseph Court
San Rafael, CA 94903

Editor: Lew Tremaine

DESCRIPTION AND INTERESTS
FamilyWorks Magazine covers parenting, education, recreation, and family finances, and also offers regional event coverage. Its readership resides in Marin and Sonoma counties in California. Circ: 20,000.
Audience: Parents
Frequency: 6 times each year
Website: www.familyworks.org

FREELANCE POTENTIAL
80% written by nonstaff writers. Publishes 75 freelance submissions yearly; 25% by authors who are new to the magazine. Receives 100+ unsolicited mss yearly.

SUBMISSIONS
Send complete ms. Accepts hard copy, disk submissions, and email submissions to familynews@familyworks.org. Availability of artwork improves chance of acceptance. SASE. Responds in 1 month.

- Articles: 1,000 words. Informational articles; profiles; and interviews. Topics include parenting, family issues, recreation, education, finance, crafts, hobbies, sports, health, fitness, nature, and the environment.
- Depts/columns: Word lengths vary. Community news, reviews, and recipes.
- Artwork: B/W and color prints.

SAMPLE ISSUE
24 pages (46% advertising): 10 articles. Sample copy available at website. Writers' guidelines available.

- "New Math for a New Economy." Article shows how a mom has cut her spending by reassessing her wants versus her needs.
- "Teaching Gratitude." Article reflects on why it's important to be grateful, and how to instill this attitude in children.
- "Preparing Your Kids Emotionally for College." Article explains why parents need to foster independence and autonomy in their high school-aged kids.

RIGHTS AND PAYMENT
One-time rights. No payment. Provides 3 contributor's copies.

➥ EDITOR'S COMMENTS
Keep in mind that we strive to help our readers improve communication skills, build compassion, and increase self-awareness.

Faze

4936 Yonge Street, Suite 2400
North York, Ontario M2N 6S3
Canada

Managing Editor: Dana Marie Krook

DESCRIPTION AND INTERESTS
Pets, hobbies, and sports are covered in this magazine for girls. Its philosophy is that every girl deserves the right to be young before becoming an adult. Circ: 120,000.
Audience: Girls, 13–24
Frequency: 5 times each year
Website: www.faze.ca

FREELANCE POTENTIAL
35–40% written by nonstaff writers. Publishes 50–60 freelance submissions yearly; 10% by unpublished writers, 10% by authors who are new to the magazine. Receives 150 queries each year.

SUBMISSIONS
Query with résumé and writing samples. Accepts email queries to editor@faze.ca. Responds if interested.

- Articles: Word lengths vary. Informational and factual articles; profiles; interviews; and personal experience pieces. Topics include current affairs, real-life and social issues, celebrities, entertainment, sports, science, travel, business, technology, and health.
- Depts/columns: Word lengths vary. Short profiles, career descriptions, new products.

SAMPLE ISSUE
66 pages (30% advertising): 7 articles; 7 depts/columns. Sample copy, $3.50 Canadian. Guidelines available at website.

- "Hate to Hope." Article tells the story of a skinhead who, after many years of violence toward gays, learns tolerance.
- "Smokin' Hot Yoga." Article describes Bikram yoga, which is becoming a popular new workout trend across North America.
- Sample dept/column: "Just Be" offers a recipe for a strawberry facial mask.

RIGHTS AND PAYMENT
All rights. Written material, $50–$250. Payment policy varies. Provides 1 contributor's copy.

➥ EDITOR'S COMMENTS
We need more crafts and cooking pieces that relate to upcoming themes. We also welcome theme-related nonfiction with photos.

Fertility Today

P.O. Box 117
Laurel, MD 20725-0177

Editor: Diana Broomfield, M.D.

DESCRIPTION AND INTERESTS
Fertility Today serves as a comprehensive and up-to-date resource for all aspects of fertility and infertility. Articles written by experts cover medical and legal issues, and the spiritual, emotional, and physical aspects of infertility. Circ: 175,000.
Audience: Adults
Frequency: Quarterly
Website: www.fertilitytoday.org

FREELANCE POTENTIAL
75% written by nonstaff writers. Publishes 150 freelance submissions yearly; 15% by authors who are new to the magazine. Receives 144 queries yearly.

SUBMISSIONS
Query with author biography; physicians should also include address of practice. Accepts email queries to articles@ fertilitytoday.org. Responds in 2 months.

- Articles: 800–1,500 words. Informational articles; profiles; interviews; and opinion and personal experience pieces. Topics include fertility issues and treatments, and male and female reproductive health.
- Depts/columns: 1,500 words. "Exercise and Nutrition," "Adoption/Child-Free Living," "Mind, Body & Soul," "My Story." Reviews of books on fertility topics. "Health Forum," written by physicians.

SAMPLE ISSUE
96 pages (25% advertising): 2 articles; 11 depts/columns. Sample copy, $6.95. Writers' guidelines and editorial calendar available at website.

- "Questions for Carly." Article features an interview with a Hollywood star about her future plans for a family and her steps to protect her fertility.
- Sample dept/column: "Exercise and Nutrition" discusses factors to consider when doing a nutrient-dense cleanse to increase fertility chances.

RIGHTS AND PAYMENT
All rights. Written material, $.50 per word. Pays on acceptance. Provides 3 author's copies.

⟐EDITOR'S COMMENTS
Our goal is to become the nation's leader in educating the public on reproductive health.

FitPregnancy

21100 Erwin Street
Woodland Hills, CA 91367

Executive Editor: Sharon Cohen

DESCRIPTION AND INTERESTS
This magazine is a pregnant woman's guide to health, nutrition, exercise, and beauty. It also offers editorial on infant and baby care, as well as postpartum issues. Circ: 500,000.
Audience: Women
Frequency: 6 times each year
Website: www.fitpregnancy.com

FREELANCE POTENTIAL
40% written by nonstaff writers. Publishes 50 freelance submissions yearly; 30% by authors who are new to the magazine. Receives 360 queries yearly.

SUBMISSIONS
Query with clips. Accepts email to scohen@ fitpregnancy.com. Responds in 1 month.

- Articles: 1,000–1,800 words. Informational articles; profiles; and personal experience pieces. Topics include prenatal fitness and nutrition, postpartum issues, breastfeeding, baby care, psychology, and health.
- Depts/columns: 550–1,000 words. Essays by fathers, family issues, prenatal health, newborn health, psychology, childbirth, prenatal nutrition, and relevant news briefs. "Time Out," 550 words.
- Other: Recipes and meal plans.

SAMPLE ISSUE
128 pages (42% advertising): 5 articles; 12 depts/columns. Sample copy, $5.95 at newsstands. Guidelines available at website.

- "Be Prepared." Article discusses choosing a childbirth class, creating a birth plan, and learning about pain-relief options.
- "Miss Molly's a Mom." Article features an interview with Molly Ringwald about the impending birth of her twins.
- Sample dept/column: "Healthy Baby" reports on the factors that affect a baby's risk for allergies and asthma.

RIGHTS AND PAYMENT
Rights vary. Written material, payment rates vary. Pays on publication. Provides 2 contributor's copies.

⟐EDITOR'S COMMENTS
Be clear in your query whether you are presenting an idea for a feature or a specific column. Tell us why your idea is new or particularly important to our audience.

FLW Outdoors

30 Gamble Lane
Benton, KY 42054

Editor: Jason Sealock

DESCRIPTION AND INTERESTS

This magazine for avid anglers covers all aspects of sport fishing, including techniques and tips, destinations, and tournaments. Each issue includes a pull-out section that is written specifically for children who are interested in fishing. Circ: 100,000.

Audience: 5–12 years; Adults
Frequency: 8 times each year
Website: www.flwoutdoors.com

FREELANCE POTENTIAL

50% written by nonstaff writers. Of the freelance submissions published yearly, 10% are by authors who are new to the magazine. Receives 300 queries yearly.

SUBMISSIONS

Query with writing sample. Accepts email queries to info@flwoutdoors.com. Responds in 1 week.

- Articles: 200 words. Informational and how-to articles; profiles; and humor. Topics include fish, fishing techniques, fishing gear, nature, and the environment.
- Fiction: To 500 words. Genres include adventure. Also publishes nature stories.
- Depts/columns: Word lengths vary. Tournaments, boat technology, fishing destinations, product reviews, and environmental issues.
- Other: Puzzles.

SAMPLE ISSUE

88 pages: 5 articles; 13 depts/columns. Sample copy, $3.95 at newsstands. Writers' guidelines available.

- "Rising Water Worsens Winnebago Bite." Article reports on how Mother Nature has affected fishing conditions in one of the most diverse walleye fisheries in the country.
- Sample dept/column: "Reel Chat" interviews a recent Lake Guntersville champion.

RIGHTS AND PAYMENT

First North American serial rights. Written material, $200–$500. Payment policy varies.

◆ EDITOR'S COMMENTS

We continue to welcome material about fishing with children and articles that will involve youngsters in the sport. While many of our readers are experienced anglers who participate in tournaments, many are beginning fishermen.

Focus on the Family Clubhouse

Focus on the Family
8605 Explorer Drive
Colorado Springs, CO 80920

Editorial Assistant: Ashley Eiman

DESCRIPTION AND INTERESTS

Written for middle-grade readers, this Christian magazine features a mix of wholesome stories, articles, and activities that both educate and entertain. Circ: 85,000.

Audience: 8–14 years
Frequency: Monthly
Website: www.clubhousemagazine.com

FREELANCE POTENTIAL

75% written by nonstaff writers. Publishes 120 freelance submissions yearly; 10% by unpublished writers, 30% by authors who are new to the magazine. Receives 960 unsolicited mss each year.

SUBMISSIONS

Send complete ms. Accepts hard copy. SASE. Responds in 6–8 weeks.

- Articles: 800–1,000 words. Informational, how-to, and factual articles; interviews; personal experience pieces; and humor. Topics include sports, nature, travel, history, religion, current events, multicultural issues, and noteworthy Christians.
- Fiction: Humor, 500 words. Historical Christian fiction, 900–1,600 words. Choose-your-own-adventure stories, 1,600–1,800 words. Mysteries and contemporary, multicultural, fantasy, and science fiction, 1,600 words.
- Depts/columns: 300 words. Short, humorous news articles emphasizing biblical lessons.
- Other: Activities, quizzes, jokes, and recipes.

SAMPLE ISSUE

32 pages (5% advertising): 1 article; 6 stories; 8 depts/columns; 2 puzzles; 1 cartoon. Sample copy, $2.50 with 9x12 SASE (2 first-class stamps). Guidelines available.

- "Finding Festo." Story tells of a boy living through genocide in Uganda.
- Sample dept/column: "Truth Pursuer" profiles some of the Bible's positive role models.

RIGHTS AND PAYMENT

First rights. Written material, to $250. Pays on acceptance. Provides 5 contributor's copies.

◆ EDITOR'S COMMENTS

We're looking for short fiction with strong character-based takeaways, and stories based outside of the U.S. that teach young readers something about the world.

Focus on the Family Clubhouse Jr.

Focus on the Family
8605 Explorer Drive
Colorado Springs, CO 80920

Editor: Suzanne Hadley

DESCRIPTION AND INTERESTS
This magazine targets young children with Christian-based fiction, nonfiction, and rebus stories. Each issue also features crafts and activities, puzzles, and poetry. Circ: 65,000.

Audience: 4–8 years
Frequency: Monthly
Website: www.clubhousejr.com

FREELANCE POTENTIAL
45% written by nonstaff writers. Publishes 10–15 freelance submissions yearly; 5% by unpublished writers, 10% by authors who are new to the magazine. Receives 720 unsolicited mss yearly.

SUBMISSIONS
Send complete ms. Accepts hard copy. No simultaneous submissions. SASE. Responds in 4–6 weeks.

- Articles: To 600 words. Informational articles. Topics include entertainment, sports, recreation, fitness, health, nature, the environment, hobbies, and multicultural issues.
- Fiction: 250–1,000 words. Genres include Bible stories; humor; folktales; and religious, contemporary, and historical fiction. Also publishes rebuses.
- Depts/columns: Word lengths vary. Personal anecdotes, humor, recipes, and crafts.
- Other: Games, jokes, and comic strips.

SAMPLE ISSUE
24 pages (no advertising): 2 articles; 1 rebus; 6 depts/columns; 2 comic strips; 1 poem; 1 game. Sample copy, $1.50 with 9x12 SASE (2 first-class stamps). Guidelines available.

- "Living Sticks." Article describes the walking stick insect and its anatomy, food choices, and life span.
- Sample dept/column: "You Said It" includes readers' drawings showing the activities they can do in place of watching television.

RIGHTS AND PAYMENT
First North American serial rights. Written material, to $150. Pays on acceptance. Provides 2 contributor's copies.

➽EDITOR'S COMMENTS
The most published authors in our magazine are those who understand the needs of our audience. Read past issues and model your work after our style.

The Forensic Teacher

P.O. Box 5263
Wilmington, DE 19808

Editor: Mark Feil

DESCRIPTION AND INTERESTS
Teaching forensic topics, such as decomposition, fibers, and toxicology, is the focus of this magazine by and for teachers. Circ: 30,000.

Audience: Middle school and college teachers
Frequency: Quarterly
Website: www.theforensicteacher.com

FREELANCE POTENTIAL
50% written by nonstaff writers. Publishes 18 freelance submissions yearly. Receives 24–60 queries, 24–36 unsolicited mss yearly.

SUBMISSIONS
Query with clips or writing samples; or send complete ms. Accepts email submissions to admin@theforensicteacher.com (Microsoft Word attachments; attach photos separately). Availability of artwork improves chance of acceptance. Responds to queries in 2 weeks, to mss in 2 months.

- Articles: 400–2,000 words. Informational and how-to articles; lesson plans; photo-essays; and personal experience pieces. Topics include forensics, industry news, science, technology, and forensic law.
- Depts/columns: Word lengths vary. Classroom mystery projects, forensic history and trivia, book reviews.
- Artwork: Color prints.
- Other: Submit seasonal information 6 months in advance.

SAMPLE ISSUE
32 pages: 8 articles; 6 depts/columns. Sample copy, $5. Guidelines available at website.

- "With Forensic Mentoring Everybody Wins." Article explains how letting high school students teach forensics to middle schoolers helped both groups learn better.
- Sample dept/column: "Mini Mystery" challenges the reader to solve the mystery of a murdered retired army colonel.

RIGHTS AND PAYMENT
First, second, and electronic rights. Articles and depts/columns, $.02 per word. News items, $10 each. Pays 60 days after publication.

➽EDITOR'S COMMENTS
Remember to keep lab units simple, and offer practical tips for success. If you are not a teacher, please explain how teachers can use the information in the classroom.

For Every Woman

Fort Myers & Southwest Florida

General Council of the Assemblies of God
1445 North Boonville Avenue
Springfield, MO 65802

Administrative Coordinator: Deborah Hampton

15880 Summerlin Road, Suite 189
Fort Myers, FL 33908

Publisher: Andrew Elias

DESCRIPTION AND INTERESTS
This e-zine is hosted by the National Women's Ministries Department of the Assemblies of God. It features inspirational writing on relationships, family, careers, and ministering to others. Hits per month: 83,000.

Audience: Women
Frequency: Ongoing
Website: www.women-ag.org

FREELANCE POTENTIAL
50% written by nonstaff writers. Of the freelance submissions published yearly, 80% are by unpublished writers, 10% are by authors who are new to the magazine. Receives 240–360 unsolicited mss yearly.

SUBMISSIONS
Send complete ms. Accepts email submissions to dhampton@ag.org (Microsoft Word attachments). Response time varies.

- Articles: 500–800 words. Informational, inspirational, and self-help articles; and personal experience pieces. Topics include blended families, marriage, family life, special education, health, crafts, hobbies, multicultural and ethnic issues, music, popular culture, religion, faith, and social issues.
- Other: Submit seasonal material 4–6 months in advance.

SAMPLE ISSUE
Sample copy, guidelines, and theme list available at website.

- "Be a Mom of Integrity." Article emphasizes the importance of teaching children by example.
- "How Can I Create Healthy Boundaries with My Troubled Adult Children?" Article provides a four-step solution for creating sanity in your life when you have adult children who are engaged in negative behavior.

RIGHTS AND PAYMENT
One-time and electronic rights. No payment.

➡️EDITOR'S COMMENTS
We target Christian women in all stages of life, and we're always interested in inspirational stories that have basis in Scripture. Topics of interest include blended families, dealing with divorce, forgiveness, character, compassion, and loving our neighbors.

DESCRIPTION AND INTERESTS
This regional magazine covers the various "scenes" of southwestern Florida—the arts scene, the cultural scene, and the entertainment scene. It also publishes parenting articles and regional lifestyle pieces. Circ: 20,000.

Audience: Adults
Frequency: 6 times each year
Website: www.ftmyersmagazine.com

FREELANCE POTENTIAL
90% written by nonstaff writers. Publishes 10–20 freelance submissions yearly; 25% by unpublished writers, 25% by authors who are new to the magazine. Receives 60 unsolicited mss yearly.

SUBMISSIONS
Send complete ms. Accepts email submissions to ftmyers@optonline.net (Microsoft Word attachments or pasted into body of email). Responds in 1–6 weeks.

- Articles: 500–2,000 words. Informational articles; profiles; interviews; reviews; and local news. Topics include the arts, media, entertainment, travel, computers, crafts, current events, health and fitness, history, popular culture, recreation, social and environmental issues, and parenting.
- Depts/columns: Word lengths vary. Sports, recreation, and book reviews.
- Artwork: JPEG, TIFF, or PDF images.

SAMPLE ISSUE
40 pages (40% advertising): 3 articles; 3 depts/columns; 1 calendar. Sample copy, $3 with 9x12 SASE. Guidelines and editorial calendar available at website.

- "Great Gardens." Article profiles the newly expanded Naples Botanical Garden.
- Sample dept/column: "Books" offers a review of Karna Small Bodman's latest thriller.

RIGHTS AND PAYMENT
One-time rights. Written material, $.10 per word. Artwork, $20–$50. Pays 30 days from publication. Provides 2 contributor's copies.

➡️EDITOR'S COMMENTS
Our magazine caters to sophisticated adults who have a strong interest in the arts. All submissions must focus on a local subject, be impeccably researched, and present a high caliber of writing.

Fort Worth Child

Lauren Publications
4275 Kellway Circle, Suite 146
Addison, TX 75001

Editorial Director: Tanya Anne Crosby

DESCRIPTION AND INTERESTS
A mix of entertaining information, valuable advice, and helpful resources are packed into this publication for parents living in Texas' Tarrant County. Circ: 45,000.
Audience: Parents
Frequency: Monthly
Website: www.fortworthchild.com

FREELANCE POTENTIAL
25% written by nonstaff writers. Publishes 12–15 freelance submissions yearly; 20% by authors who are new to the magazine. Receives 240 queries yearly.

SUBMISSIONS
Query with résumé. Accepts hard copy, email queries to editorial@fortworthchild.com, faxes to 972-447-0633, and simultaneous submissions if identified. SASE. Response time varies.

- Articles: 1,000–2,500 words. Informational, self-help, and how-to articles; humor; profiles; and personal experience pieces. Topics include parenting, education, child development, family travel, regional news, recreation, entertainment, current events, social issues, multicultural and ethnic subjects, health, fitness, and crafts.
- Depts/columns: 800 words. Family activities, health, safety, news briefs, education, child development, humor, fathers' perspectives, and reviews.

SAMPLE ISSUE
74 pages (14% advertising): 2 articles; 12 depts/columns. Sample copy, free with 9x12 SASE. Guidelines available at website.

- "Mommy Wants Her Body Back." Article examines the increase in women seeking plastic surgery after childbirth.
- Sample dept/column: "The Manifesto" is an essay about why the author is living and raising his family in Texas.

RIGHTS AND PAYMENT
First rights. Written material, payment rates vary. Pays on publication. Provides contributor's copies upon request.

➥EDITOR'S COMMENTS
Fresh voices, ideas, and perspectives are always considered. We welcome your query as long as it has a local focus, and we prefer that you live in our region.

Fostering Families Today

541 East Garden Drive, Unit N
Windsor, CO 80550

Editor: Richard Fischer

DESCRIPTION AND INTERESTS
Practical information and personal experiences that help foster parents and adoptive parents deal with the challenges and joys of raising children are found in this magazine. It also offers articles of interest to professionals working in the field of child welfare. Circ: 26,000.
Audience: Adoptive and foster parents
Frequency: 6 times each year
Website: www.fosteringfamiliestoday.com

FREELANCE POTENTIAL
85% written by nonstaff writers. Publishes 40–45 freelance submissions yearly; 30% by unpublished writers, 30% by new authors. Receives 72–120 unsolicited mss yearly.

SUBMISSIONS
Send complete ms with permission agreement form (available at website). Accepts hard copy and email submissions to louis@adoptinfo.net (attach file). SASE. Response time varies.

- Articles: 500–1,200 words. Informational and how-to articles; profiles; and personal experience pieces. Topics include adoption, foster parenting, child development, relevant research, health, education, and legal issues.
- Depts/columns: Word lengths vary. News, opinions, advice, profiles, legislation, book reviews, and child advocacy.
- Other: Poetry.

SAMPLE ISSUE
62 pages (no advertising): 14 articles; 8 depts/columns. Sample copy and guidelines available at website.

- "Laughter, Bonding, and Adopting Older Children." Article explains why laughter, playfulness, and silliness can be keys to cementing the parent/youth relationship.
- "Making the Relationship Work for Children." Article emphasizes the importance of court-appointed advocates and parents working together to benefit children.

RIGHTS AND PAYMENT
Non-exclusive print and electronic rights. No payment. Provides 3 contributor's copies and a 1-year subscription.

➥EDITOR'S COMMENTS
We use pieces of interest to all members of the child welfare community. Personal stories that benefit other parents are also welcome.

The Friend

The Church of Jesus Christ of Latter-day Saints
50 East North Temple, 24th Floor
Salt Lake City, UT 84150

Managing Editor: Julie Wardell

DESCRIPTION AND INTERESTS
The Friend features short, informational articles and true stories that teach children about the Gospel—and the Mormon faith in particular. Circ: 285,000.
Audience: 3–12 years
Frequency: Monthly
Website: www.lds.org

FREELANCE POTENTIAL
60% written by nonstaff writers.

SUBMISSIONS
Send complete ms. Accepts hard copy and email submissions to friend@ldschurch.org. No simultaneous submissions. SASE. Responds in 2 months.

- Articles: To 900 words. Informational articles; profiles; true stories; photo-essays; and personal experience pieces. True stories for young readers and preschool children, 250 words. Topics include spirituality, the Mormon church, personal faith, and conflict resolution.
- Depts/columns: Word lengths vary. Profiles of children from different countries.
- Artwork: B/W or color prints.
- Other: Poetry, line lengths vary. Puzzles, activities, crafts, and cartoons. Submit seasonal material 8 months in advance.

SAMPLE ISSUE
48 pages (no advertising): 15 articles; 2 depts/columns, 6 puzzles and activities. Sample copy, $1.50 with 9x12 SASE (4 first-class stamps). Guidelines available at website.

- "The Christmas Basket." True story tells how two young siblings gave of themselves to help a family in need.
- Sample dept/column: "Trying to Be Like Jesus" features stories from young readers about the little things they have done to imitate Jesus.

RIGHTS AND PAYMENT
First rights. Written material, $100–$250. Poetry, $25. Activities, $20. Pays on acceptance. Provides 2 contributor's copies.

⟡EDITOR'S COMMENTS
Everything we publish is designed to encourage children to live according to the philosophy of the Mormon church. We appreciate your desire to share your talents and experiences with our young readers.

Fun For Kidz

P.O. Box 227
Bluffton, OH 45817-0227

Editor: Marilyn Edwards

DESCRIPTION AND INTERESTS
Filled with engaging articles that make reading and learning fun, *Fun For Kidz* promotes family values and age-appropriate material. Circ: 7,000.
Audience: 6–13 years
Frequency: 6 times each year
Website: www.funforkidz.com

FREELANCE POTENTIAL
70% written by nonstaff writers. Publishes 100–150 freelance submissions yearly; 40% by unpublished writers, 40% by authors who are new to the magazine. Receives 120 queries, 1,200 unsolicited mss yearly.

SUBMISSIONS
Prefers complete ms; will accept query. Accepts hard copy and simultaneous submissions if identified. Availability of artwork improves chance of acceptance. SASE. Responds in 4–6 months.

- Articles: 500 words. Informational and how-to articles. Topics include nature, science, pets, hobbies, cooking, sports, and careers.
- Fiction: 500 words. Genres include adventure, mystery, and humor.
- Depts/columns: Word lengths vary. Activities and science experiments.
- Artwork: B/W and color prints. Line art.
- Other: Poetry. Puzzles, games, and cartoons. Submit seasonal material 6–12 months in advance.

SAMPLE ISSUE
48 pages (no advertising): 8 articles; 6 depts/columns; 3 poems; 7 puzzles; 4 cartoons. Sample copy, $6. Guidelines and theme list available at website.

- "Ready, Set, Sun!" Article explains why the sky turns such amazing colors at sunset.
- Sample dept/column: "Science" explains how to accurately measure rainfall in different regions.

RIGHTS AND PAYMENT
First North American serial rights. Articles and fiction, $.05+ per word. Poetry and puzzles, $10+. Artwork, $5–$35. Pays on publication. Provides 1 contributor's copy.

⟡EDITOR'S COMMENTS
Our editorial theme list will tell you exactly the kinds of topics we are accepting and the deadlines for them.

Games

Kappa Publishing Group, Inc.
6198 Butler Pike, Suite 200
Blue Bell, PA 19422-2600

Editor-in-Chief: R. Wayne Schmittberger

DESCRIPTION AND INTERESTS
Teens and adults who are fascinated by games and puzzles read this magazine to challenge their minds. Each issue offers inventive games and puzzles, while also presenting articles on the history of, and creative processes behind, game and puzzle development. Circ: 75,000.
Audience: YA–Adult
Frequency: 10 times each year
Website: www.gamesmagazine-online.com

FREELANCE POTENTIAL
86% written by nonstaff writers. Publishes 200+ freelance submissions yearly; 10% by unpublished writers, 20% by authors who are new to the magazine. Receives 960 queries and unsolicited mss yearly.

SUBMISSIONS
Query with outline; or send complete ms. Accepts hard copy and email to games@kappapublishing.com. SASE. Responds in 6–8 weeks.

- Articles: 1,500–3,000 words. Informational articles; profiles; and humor. Topics include game-related events and people, wordplay, and human ingenuity. Game reviews by assignment only.
- Depts/columns: Staff written, except for "Gambits."
- Other: Visual and verbal puzzles, quizzes, contests, two-play games, and adventures.

SAMPLE ISSUE
80 pages (8% advertising): 5 articles; 6 depts/columns; 16 puzzles and activities. Sample copy, $4.50 with 9x12 SASE ($1.24 postage). Guidelines available.

- "Mental Bowling Anyone?" Article discusses Kayles, a simple two-player game invented by an English mathematician.
- "Botanical Bedlam." Article presents an original paper-and-pencil game for two or more players.

RIGHTS AND PAYMENT
All North American serial rights. Articles, $500–$1,200. "Gamebits," $100–$250. Pays on publication. Provides 1 contributor's copy.

➪ EDITOR'S COMMENTS
We welcome ideas for feature articles about games, puzzles, wordplays, and the people who create them.

Genesee Valley Parent

266 Alexander Street
Rochester, NY 14607

Managing Editor: Jillian Melnyk

DESCRIPTION AND INTERESTS
This regional magazine offers parents in the greater Rochester, New York, area coverage of local events, as well as articles on family and child-rearing issues. It also features profiles and personal experience pieces. Circ: 30,000.
Audience: Parents
Frequency: Monthly
Website: www.gvparent.com

FREELANCE POTENTIAL
75% written by nonstaff writers. Publishes 50 freelance submissions yearly; 5% by authors who are new to the magazine. Receives 240 queries yearly.

SUBMISSIONS
Query with clips or writing samples. Accepts hard copy and simultaneous submissions if identified. SASE. Responds in 1–3 months.

- Articles: 700–1,200 words. Informational and how-to articles; profiles; reviews; humor; and personal experience pieces. Topics include regional family events, local goods and services, special and gifted education, social issues, family problems, health and fitness, and parenting.
- Depts/columns: 500–600 words. Family health, teen issues, toddler issues, and short news items.
- Other: Submit seasonal material 4 months in advance.

SAMPLE ISSUE
68 pages (50% advertising): 5 articles; 9 depts/columns; 1 calendar. Guidelines and editorial calendar available.

- "Music to My Ears." Article explains how the benefits of music extend far beyond the simple joy of making sound.
- Sample dept/column: "Teens & Tweens" discusses the necessity, logistics, and meaning of setting curfews for this age group.

RIGHTS AND PAYMENT
Second rights. Articles, $30–$45. Depts/columns, $25–$30. Pays on publication. Provides 1 tearsheet.

➪ EDITOR'S COMMENTS
The emphasis is on local information and resources, but any submission that will help our readers parent more wisely and joyfully would be welcome.

GeoParent

16101 North 82nd Street, Suite A-9
Scottsdale, AZ 85260

Editors: Betsy Bailey & Nancy Price

DESCRIPTION AND INTERESTS
GeoParent seeks to foster successful parenting and the healthy growth and development of children from birth through adolescence and beyond. Published online, it features practical pieces on education, nutrition, and wellness, while also offering perspectives on building positive relationships with your children. Hits per month: Unavailable.

Audience: Parents
Frequency: Weekly
Website: www.geoparent.com

FREELANCE POTENTIAL
90% written by nonstaff writers. Publishes 50 freelance submissions yearly. Receives 50 queries and unsolicited mss yearly.

SUBMISSIONS
Prefers query; will accept complete ms. Accepts hard copy, email submissions to content@coincide.com, and submissions via the website. SASE. Response time varies.

- Articles: 500–2,500 words. Informational articles; and advice. Topics include parenting, child development, family issues, pregnancy and childbirth, infancy, child care, nutrition, health, education, and gifted and special education.
- Depts/columns: Word lengths vary. Parenting tips and advice.

SAMPLE ISSUE
Sample copy and writers' guidelines available at website.

- "Teen Depression or Normal Mood Swings?" Article advises parents about whether to seek professional help for teens who seem depressed.
- "*Biggest Loser*: Where Are They?" Article offers tips from stars of the *Biggest Loser* television series.

RIGHTS AND PAYMENT
Rights vary. Written material, $25–$50; $10 for reprints. Pays on publication.

➡️EDITOR'S COMMENTS
Freelance writers should remember that we have a national audience, and we look for well-researched pieces that have broad appeal. While we value your experience with children, you should include interviews with experts. Write in a personal, friendly style.

Gifted Education Press Quarterly

10201 Yuma Court
P.O. Box 1586
Manassas, VA 20108

Editor & Publisher: Maurice D. Fisher

DESCRIPTION AND INTERESTS
This newsletter, available online as well as in print, addresses issues related to educating gifted students. Written by leaders in the field, the articles and research studies target administrators, program coordinators, academics, and parents. Circ: 15,000.

Audience: Educators and parents
Frequency: Quarterly
Website: www.giftedpress.com

FREELANCE POTENTIAL
75% written by nonstaff writers. Publishes 14 freelance submissions yearly; 67% by authors who are new to the magazine. Receives 30 queries yearly.

SUBMISSIONS
Query with writing sample. Accepts email queries to mfisher345@comcast.net. Responds in 1 week.

- Articles: 2,500–4,000 words. Informational, how-to, and research articles; personal experience pieces; profiles; interviews; and scholarly essays. Topics include gifted education; multicultural, ethnic, and social issues; homeschooling; multiple intelligence; parent advocates; academic subjects; the environment; and popular culture.

SAMPLE ISSUE
14 pages (no advertising): 4 articles. Sample copy available at website.

- "Screening and Identifying Gifted Children: What All Educators and Parents Should Know." Article examines the pros and cons of the traditional methods of identifying gifted students.
- "Varsity Academics." Essay suggests that educators in the gifted field find ways to challenge—but also reward—students for extra effort.

RIGHTS AND PAYMENT
All rights. No payment. Provides a 1-year subscription.

➡️EDITOR'S COMMENTS
Before querying, please read a few issues of our magazine. You will find that we have a specific audience and a scholarly tone, and that we demand extensive research and references. You will also find that we are open to multiple viewpoints.

Girls' Life

4529 Harford Road
Baltimore, MD 21214

Editor: Katie Abbondanza

DESCRIPTION AND INTERESTS
This magazine is like a girl's best friend—it offers guidance and support on everyday issues such as relationships, school, fashion, and beauty. Profiles of girls who are making a difference are also featured. Circ: 400,000.

Audience: Girls, 10–15 years
Frequency: 6 times each year
Website: www.girlslife.com

FREELANCE POTENTIAL
25% written by nonstaff writers. Publishes 40 freelance submissions yearly; 10% by unpublished writers, 20% by authors who are new to the magazine. Receives 1,200 queries yearly.

SUBMISSIONS
Query with outline. Accepts hard copy and email queries to katiea@girlslife.com. SASE. Responds in 3 months.

- Articles: 1,200–2,500 words. Informational, service-oriented articles. Topics include self-esteem, health, friendship, relationships, sibling rivalry, school issues, facing challenges, and setting goals.
- Fiction: 2,000–2,500 words. Stories featuring girls.
- Depts/columns: 300–800 words. Celebrity spotlights; profiles of real girls; advice about friendship, beauty, and dating; fashion trends; decorating tips; cooking; crafts; and media reviews.
- Other: Quizzes; fashion spreads.

SAMPLE ISSUE
80 pages (30% advertising): 6 articles; 24 depts/columns. Sample copy, $5. Guidelines and editorial calendar available at website.

- "Taylor's Love Lessons." Article profiles singer Taylor Swift and her lessons learned from past dating relationships.
- Sample dept/column: "GL Beauty: Your Perfect Skin" offers tips for smooth skin.

RIGHTS AND PAYMENT
All or first rights. Written material, payment rates vary. Pays on publication. Provides 1 contributor's copy.

☛EDITOR'S COMMENTS
Keep in mind that articles should be written using an appealing voice that speaks to our readers. Our website welcomes submissions from writers under the age of 18.

Girlworks

4 Wesleyan Street
Georgetown, Ontario L7G 2E1
Canada

Publisher: Janet Kim

DESCRIPTION AND INTERESTS
This "magazine for smart girls" features articles about the complexity and diversity of girls and young women. Its articles tackle subjects from style, beauty, and trends to issues such as self-esteem, body image, sexuality, loneliness, and depression. Circ: 10,000.

Audience: Girls, 11–16 years
Frequency: 6 times each year
Website: www.girlworks.ca

FREELANCE POTENTIAL
20% written by nonstaff writers. Publishes 24 freelance submissions yearly; 5% by unpublished writers, 100% by authors who are new to the magazine.

SUBMISSIONS
Query or send complete ms. Accepts hard copy and email submissions to publisher@girlworks.ca. SASE. Responds in 1–2 months.

- Articles: 400–800 words. Informational and how-to articles; profiles; and interviews. Topics include money, careers, health, beauty, fashion, style, entertainment, art and design, sports, fitness, technology, and girl-centered issues.
- Depts/columns: Word lengths vary. Beauty, crafts, media reviews.
- Other: Puzzles, quizzes, and games.

SAMPLE ISSUE
64 pages: 6 articles; 7 depts/columns; 5 quizzes and games. Sample copy, $6.50 Canadian, $6.25 U.S. with SAE/IRC. Guidelines available at website.

- "The Technogirl Guide to Eco-Friendly Technology." Article examines a variety of gear and gadgets that use clean energy.
- Sample dept/column: "The Book Stops Here" offers reviews of four age-appropriate books for girls.

RIGHTS AND PAYMENT
First, second, or licensing rights. Written material, $50 per printed page. Pays on acceptance.

☛EDITOR'S COMMENTS
We are only interested in articles that are age-appropriate and written in a style that neither talks down nor preaches to our readers. As a new publication, we're open to ideas. If a girl would be interested in it, we are likely to be interested in it, too.

Green Teacher

95 Robert Street
Toronto, Ontario M5S 2K5
Canada

Co-Editor: Tim Grant

DESCRIPTION AND INTERESTS
Promoting environmental and global awareness in students in kindergarten through high school is the purpose of *Green Teacher*. It includes classroom-ready activities and general informational articles. Circ: 7,500.

Audience: Teachers, grades K–12
Frequency: Quarterly
Website: www.greenteacher.com

FREELANCE POTENTIAL
100% written by nonstaff writers. Publishes 120 freelance submissions yearly; 80% by unpublished writers. Receives 500 queries and unsolicited mss yearly.

SUBMISSIONS
Prefers query with outline; will accept complete ms with 8–10 photos. Prefers email submissions to tim@greenteacher.com (Microsoft Word, RTF, or TXT attachments); will accept disk submissions with hard copy. Availability of artwork improves chance of acceptance. SAE/IRC. Responds in 2 months.

- Articles: 1,500–3,000 words. Informational and how-to articles; opinion pieces; and lesson plans. Topics include environmental and global education.
- Depts/columns: Word lengths vary. Reviews, resources, and announcements.
- Artwork: JPEG and TIFF images at 300 dpi; B/W and color prints or slides. Line art.
- Other: Submit Earth Day material 6 months in advance.

SAMPLE ISSUE
48 pages (12% advertising): 12 articles; 2 depts/columns. Sample copy and guidelines available at website.

- "First Person Singular: Documenting Climate Change." Article reports on an environmental project conducted by Alaskan students.
- "Bringing Children Back to Nature." Article features five activities for children that follow the principles of "Flow Learning."

RIGHTS AND PAYMENT
Rights negotiable. No payment. Provides 5 contributor's copies and a free subscription.

➥EDITOR'S COMMENTS
We need more crafts and cooking pieces that relate to upcoming themes. We also welcome theme-related nonfiction with photos.

Group

Group Publishing, Inc.
P.O. Box 481
Loveland, CO 80539-0481

Associate Editor: Scott Firestone

DESCRIPTION AND INTERESTS
Group provides practical resources and inspiration for leaders of Christian youth groups. It focuses on strategies and ideas for effectively working with teens to encourage their spiritual development. It is an interdenominational publication. Circ: 40,000.

Audience: Youth ministry leaders
Frequency: 6 times each year
Website: www.youthministry.com

FREELANCE POTENTIAL
60% written by nonstaff writers. Publishes 200 freelance submissions yearly; 50% by unpublished writers, 80% by authors who are new to the magazine. Receives 300 queries yearly.

SUBMISSIONS
Query with outline and clips or writing samples; state availability of artwork. Accepts hard copy. SASE. Responds in 2–3 months.

- Articles: 500–1,700 words. Informational and how-to articles. Topics include youth ministry strategies, recruiting and training adult leaders, understanding youth culture, professionalism, time management, leadership skills, and the professional and spiritual growth of youth ministers.
- Depts/columns: "Try This One," to 300 words. "Hands-On Help," to 175 words.
- Artwork: B/W or color illustration samples. No prints.

SAMPLE ISSUE
82 pages (30% advertising): 3 articles; 23 depts/columns. Sample copy, $2 with 9x12 SASE. Guidelines available.

- "Exclusive Survey Report: Teenagers' Top Needs." Article reports that most teens need help building positive relationships with God and with their parents.
- "Business or Botany?" Article tells why strategies that work for business leaders can't always be applied to youth ministry.

RIGHTS AND PAYMENT
All rights. Articles, $125–$225. Depts/columns, $50. Pays on acceptance.

➥EDITOR'S COMMENTS
We're always interested in descriptions of successful youth ministry strategies, as well as articles about understanding kids and youth culture.

Guide

Review and Herald Publishing Association
55 West Oak Ridge Drive
Hagerstown, MD 21740

Associate Editor: Rachel Whitaker

DESCRIPTION AND INTERESTS
Geared to middle school-aged children, *Guide* is a Christian magazine of true stories that apply biblical principles to daily challenges, such as friendship, school, entertainment, and family issues. Circ: 26,000.
Audience: 10–14 years
Frequency: Weekly
Website: www.guidemagazine.org

FREELANCE POTENTIAL
97% written by nonstaff writers. Publishes 250 freelance submissions yearly; 10% by unpublished writers, 20% by authors who are new to the magazine. Receives 600 unsolicited mss each year.

SUBMISSIONS
Send complete ms. Prefers email submissions to guide@rhpa.org; will accept hard copy and simultaneous submissions if identified. SASE. Responds in 4–6 weeks.

- Articles: 450–1,200 words. Personal experience pieces; Christian humor; and profiles. Topics include adventure, angels, Bible doctrine, compassion, integrity, faith, family, health, media choices, personal growth, social issues, and Seventh-day Adventist history.
- Other: Puzzles, activities, and games. Submit seasonal material about Thanksgiving, Christmas, Mother's Day, and Father's Day 8 months in advance.

SAMPLE ISSUE
32 pages: 6 articles; 2 activities. Sample copy, free with 9x12 SASE (2 first-class stamps). Guidelines available.

- "Worm Against the World." Article tells of a boy who learns to stand up to a bully in his band class.
- "Broken Promises." Article focuses on a girl who learns to forgive her absentee father.

RIGHTS AND PAYMENT
First serial and reprint rights. Articles, $.07–$.10 per word. Games and puzzles, $20–$40. Pays on acceptance. Provides 3 copies.

➼EDITOR'S COMMENTS
New authors are always welcome and encouraged to submit material. We would like to see more stories that reflect the experiences of diverse ethnicities. Please do not send fiction or poetry.

Gwinnett Parents Magazine

3651 Peachtree Parkway, Suite 325
Suwanee, GA 30024

Editor: Terrie Carter

DESCRIPTION AND INTERESTS
This publication gives advice and information to parents living in Gwinnett County, Georgia. It focuses on education, child care, health, and after-school activities. Ideas for spending quality recreational time with children are also featured. Circ: Unavailable.
Audience: Parents
Frequency: Monthly
Website: www.gwinnettparents.com

FREELANCE POTENTIAL
75% written by nonstaff writers. Publishes several freelance submissions yearly; 5% by unpublished writers, 14% by authors who are new to the magazine.

SUBMISSIONS
Query or send complete ms. Accepts email submissions to editor@gwinnettparents.com (include "Editorial Submission" in subject line). Responds in 3–4 weeks.

- Articles: 500–1,000 words. Profiles, 350–450 words. Informational and self-help articles; profiles; and personal experience pieces. Topics include education, recreation, sports, health, working parents, and family finances.
- Depts/columns: Word lengths vary. Parenting advice, health, education, community news, recipes, home improvement, and reviews.

SAMPLE ISSUE
60 pages (50% advertising): 5 articles; 15 depts/columns. Sample copy, $4 with 9x12 SASE ($.77 postage). Guidelines available.

- "Ten Tips for Traveling with Children." Article tells parents to pack light, expect the unexpected, and be flexible when taking trips with kids.
- "Choosing the Right Summer Camp." Article stresses the importance of doing research before sending children to camp.

RIGHTS AND PAYMENT
First and non-exclusive online archival rights. Written material, $25–$75. Profiles, $25–$50. Pays on publication.

➼EDITOR'S COMMENTS
We try to help parents in their everyday decision making. We want pieces that entertain and educate while focusing on the local community here in Gwinnett . . . where we live, work, play, and raise our children.

Happiness

P.O. Box 2379
Midland, MI 48641

Editor: Diane Lynn Nolan

DESCRIPTION AND INTERESTS
Happiness is a television guide that also features uplifting articles about self-improvement, good health, and family relationships. Poems, activities, and children's stories are also included. Circ: 150,000.
Audience: Families
Frequency: Weekly
Website: www.happiness.com

FREELANCE POTENTIAL
75% written by nonstaff writers. Of the freelance submissions published yearly, 25% are by unpublished writers, 25% are by authors who are new to the magazine.

SUBMISSIONS
Send complete ms. Accepts hard copy. Availability of artwork improves chance of acceptance. SASE. Responds in 3 months.

- Articles: 500 words. Informational, self-help, and how-to articles; humor; and personal experience pieces. Topics include careers, education, health, fitness, hobbies, animals, pets, nature, the environment, recreation, and travel.
- Depts/columns: 25–75 words. Cooking, health, humor, and tips from readers.
- Artwork: Color prints.
- Other: Puzzles and games. Poetry. Submit seasonal material 4 months in advance.

SAMPLE ISSUE
16 pages (no advertising): 2 articles; 8 depts/columns; 10 activities. Guidelines available.

- "How to Stop Worrying and Start Living." Article offers six tips for reducing everyday stress.
- Sample dept/column: "Happiness Within" reminds readers not to let unresolved anger take control of their lives.

RIGHTS AND PAYMENT
First rights. All material, payment rates vary. Pays on publication.

❖ EDITOR'S COMMENTS
Please note that articles submitted should be based on incidents that are true, or true-to-life. They should build character and emphasize a more fulfilling or happier life in health, personality, or behavior. We do not want religious material with a specific doctrinal slant.

Higher Things
Dare To Be Lutheran

Good Shepherd Lutheran Church
5009 Cassia Street
Boise, ID 83705

Managing Editor: Adriane Dorr

DESCRIPTION AND INTERESTS
The mission of *Higher Things* is to show teens how the Gospel message can be applied to their lives. Its articles contain messages of the importance of service, prayer, and living with God in one's life, as well as information on religion and faith. Circ: Unavailable.
Audience: 13–19 years
Frequency: Quarterly
Website: www.higherthings.org

FREELANCE POTENTIAL
60% written by nonstaff writers. Publishes 36 freelance submissions yearly; 40% by unpublished writers, 30% by authors who are new to the magazine. Receives 12 queries, 24 unsolicited mss yearly.

SUBMISSIONS
Query or send complete ms. Accepts hard copy and email submissions to submissions@ higherthings.org. SASE. Response time varies.

- Articles: 500–800 words. Informational and how-to articles; profiles; interviews; and personal experience pieces. Topics include religion, current events, recreation, social issues, and travel.
- Depts/columns: Staff written.

SAMPLE ISSUE
32 pages (10% advertising): 10 articles; 2 depts/columns. Sample copy, $3. Guidelines and theme list available at website.

- "Purgatory, Parousia, and Getting Lost." Article examines the message of purgatory in the television show *Lost,* and what theologians say about faith and purgatory.
- "Father Knows Best: The Power of Prayer." Article explains the purpose of prayer, and discusses the kinds of things for which there is no use praying.
- "Happy Lent." Article discusses the real purpose of Lent, and encourages readers to focus on the meaning of repentance for the love of God.

RIGHTS AND PAYMENT
Rights vary. No payment. Provides several contributor's copies.

❖ EDITOR'S COMMENTS
Articles should tackle serious topics, but should also be written in a style that will appeal to teen readers.

Highlights for Children

803 Church Street
Honesdale, PA 18431

Manuscript Coordinator

DESCRIPTION AND INTERESTS
This magazine has been entertaining children for 65 years with its informative articles, engaging stories, and plenty of crafts and activities. Circ: Unavailable.
Audience: Up to 12 years
Frequency: Monthly
Website: www.highlights.com

FREELANCE POTENTIAL
99% written by nonstaff writers. Publishes 200 freelance submissions yearly; 40% by unpublished writers, 60% by authors who are new to the magazine. Receives 6,500 unsolicited mss each year.

SUBMISSIONS
Send complete ms for fiction. Query or send complete ms for nonfiction. Accepts hard copy. SASE. Responds to queries in 2–4 weeks, to mss in 4–6 months.

- Articles: To 500 words for 3–7 years; to 800 words for 8–12 years. Informational articles; interviews; profiles; and personal experience pieces. Topics include nature, animals, science, crafts, games, activities, world cultures, history, arts, and sports.
- Fiction: To 500 words for 3–7 years; to 800 words for 8–12 years. Genres include adventure, mystery, sports stories, multicultural fiction, and retellings of traditional stories.
- Depts/columns: Word lengths vary. Science experiments and crafts.
- Other: Puzzles, games. Poetry, to 10 lines.

SAMPLE ISSUE
42 pages (no advertising): 4 articles; 3 stories; 1 rebus; 2 poems; 8 activities; 5 depts/columns. Sample copy, free with 9x12 SASE (4 first-class stamps). Guidelines available at website.

- "Musical Plumbing." Article profiles a musician who uses PVC pipes to make his own instruments.
- "Finding 42." Article explains how baseball player Jackie Robinson changed the game.

RIGHTS AND PAYMENT
All rights. Written material, payment rates vary. Pays on acceptance. Provides 2 copies.

✎ EDITOR'S COMMENTS
Stories should avoid preaching, be free of crime and violence, and feature characters that set a positive example.

Home Education Magazine

P.O. Box 1083
Tonasket, WA 98855

Articles Editor: Jeanne Faulconer

DESCRIPTION AND INTERESTS
Since 1984, this magazine has brought homeschooling parents timely articles and columns about the issues homeschoolers deal with, and how homeschooling can enhance the joy of family life. Circ: 110,000.
Audience: Parents
Frequency: 6 times each year
Website: www.homeedmag.com

FREELANCE POTENTIAL
90% written by nonstaff writers. Publishes 35–40 freelance submissions yearly; 25% by unpublished writers, 40% by new authors. Receives 240 queries, 240 mss yearly.

SUBMISSIONS
Prefers complete ms; will accept query. Prefers email to articles@homeedmag.com (Microsoft Word attachments); will accept hard copy. SASE. Responds in 1–2 months.

- Articles: 900–1,700 words. Informational and how-to articles; profiles; interviews; and personal experience pieces. Topics include homeschooling, activism, lessons, and parenting issues.
- Depts/columns: Staff written.
- Artwork: B/W and color prints; digital images at 200 dpi, 300 dpi for cover images.

SAMPLE ISSUE
42 pages (13% advertising): 7 articles; 9 depts/columns. Sample copy, $6.50. Guidelines available at website.

- "Get Out of the Way and Let the Kids Write!" Article reports that releasing kids from traditional writing restrictions can lead to a writing momentum that will continue to build.
- "Fight!" Personal experience piece tells of the author's sons' innate tendency toward fighting and competing against each other—just like regular school kids.

RIGHTS AND PAYMENT
First North American serial and electronic rights. Articles, $50–$100. Artwork, $12.50; $100 for cover art. Kill fee, 25%. Pays on acceptance. Provides 1+ contributor's copies.

✎ EDITOR'S COMMENTS
We look for articles that offer practical lesson ideas, support, and inspiration for homeschoolers, or information on getting started for those considering homeschooling their kids.

Home Educator's Family Times

P.O. Box 6442
Brunswick, ME 04011

Editor: Jane R. Boswell

DESCRIPTION AND INTERESTS

Appearing in both print and online, *Home Educator's Family Times* covers relevant trends and issues in homeschooling. It also offers curriculum ideas and teaching strategies. Circ: 25,000. Hits per month: 400,000.

Audience: Parents
Frequency: 6 times each year
Website: www.homeeducator.com/
      familytimes

FREELANCE POTENTIAL

90% written by nonstaff writers. Publishes 50 freelance submissions yearly; 25% by authors who are new to the magazine.

SUBMISSIONS

Send complete ms with author biography and permission statement from website. Accepts CD submissions and email submissions to famtimes@blazenetme.net (Microsoft Word or text attachments). SASE. Response time varies.

- Articles: 1,000–1,500 words. Informational and how-to articles; opinion pieces; and personal experience pieces. Topics include homeschooling methods and lessons, family life, parenting, pets, reading, art, science, and creative writing.
- Depts/columns: Staff written.

SAMPLE ISSUE

24 pages (41% advertising): 11 articles; 2 depts/columns. Sample copy and guidelines available at website.

- "How Do You Know Your Children Are Learning?" Article describes the author's frustrations with the requirements for outside evaluations to determine her child's learning progress.
- "Private Schools and Homeschools—From NHELD." Article explains the state and federal regulations that prohibit homeschools from acting as private schools.

RIGHTS AND PAYMENT

One-time and electronic reprint rights. No payment.

➡ EDITOR'S COMMENTS

Since we do not pay for articles, we ask that writers provide us with a brief bio and short byline to appear at the end of their article. This is intended to promote the writer's product or service.

Homeschooling Today

P.O. Box 244
Abingdon, VA 24212

Editor-in-Chief: Jim Bob Howard

DESCRIPTION AND INTERESTS

Presenting a mix of practical ideas and inspirational articles, this magazine is read by parents who seek information and support for their homeschooling activities. Its editorial reflects a Christian perspective. Circ: 11,500.

Audience: Parents
Frequency: 6 times each year
Website: www.homeschooltoday.com

FREELANCE POTENTIAL

85% written by nonstaff writers. Publishes 60–70 freelance submissions yearly; 6% by unpublished writers, 14% by authors who are new to the magazine. Receives 60–120 unsolicited mss yearly.

SUBMISSIONS

Send ms. Accepts email to management@ homeschooltoday.com (Microsoft Word attachments; include "Article Submission" in subject line). Responds in 3–6 months.

- Articles: 1,400–2,000 words. Informational, self-help, and how-to articles; profiles; and personal experience pieces. Topics include education, religion, music, technology, special education, the arts, history, mathematics, and science.
- Columns: Staff written.
- Departments: 875 words. Time management, history, music, religion, the arts, and homeschooling tips. Books and media reviews, 250–500 words.

SAMPLE ISSUE

68 pages: 4 articles; 18 depts/columns. Sample copy, $5.95. Guidelines and theme list available at website.

- "The Power of Play." Article reports on how a child's playtime serves as a foundation for later learning.
- Sample dept/column: "Faces of Homeschooling" offers a profile of a Virginia family that homeschools and runs a farm.

RIGHTS AND PAYMENT

All rights. Written material, $.08 per word. Pays on publication. Provides 1 contributor's copy.

➡ EDITOR'S COMMENTS

Our commitment to bringing the homeschool community useful information and resources is supported by a biblical conviction that God uses families to change the world.

Hopscotch

P.O. Box 164
Bluffton, OH 45817-0164

Editor: Marilyn Edwards

DESCRIPTION AND INTERESTS

Wholesome information and entertainment is the focus of this magazine. Free of teen material, each themed issue aims to help young girls enjoy and make the most of their childhood. Circ: 16,000.

Audience: Girls, 6–13 years
Frequency: 6 times each year
Website: www.hopscotchmagazine.com

FREELANCE POTENTIAL

80% written by nonstaff writers. Publishes 80–100 freelance submissions yearly; 30% by unpublished writers, 40% by new authors. Receives 240 queries, 2,400 mss yearly.

SUBMISSIONS

Prefers complete ms; will accept query. Accepts hard copy and simultaneous submissions if identified. Availability of artwork improves chance of acceptance. SASE. Responds to queries in 1–2 weeks, to mss in 2–3 months.

- Articles: 500 words. Informational and how-to articles; profiles; humor; and personal experience pieces. Topics include nature, pets, hobbies, sports, cooking, and careers.
- Fiction: To 1,000 words. Genres include adventure, mystery, historical, and multicultural fiction.
- Depts/columns: 500 words. Crafts, cooking.
- Artwork: B/W and color prints. Line art.
- Other: Poetry. Puzzles and games.

SAMPLE ISSUE

48 pages (no advertising): 10 articles; 2 stories; 5 depts/columns; 1 poem; 5 puzzles; 1 cartoon. Sample copy, $6 with 9x12 SASE. Guidelines and theme list available at website.

- "Singer of Courage." Article tells of Marian Anderson's efforts to break the color barrier at her concerts.
- Sample dept/column: "Crafts" explains how to make a creative zipper pull.

RIGHTS AND PAYMENT

First North American serial rights. Articles and fiction, $.05+ per word. Poetry and puzzles, $10+. Artwork, $5 per photo. Pays on publication. Provides 1 contributor's copy.

⇒EDITOR'S COMMENTS

We look for lively writing, usually about a girl or from a girl's perspective.

The Horn Book Magazine

56 Roland Street, Suite 200
Boston, MA 02129

Editor-in-Chief: Roger Sutton

DESCRIPTION AND INTERESTS

Individuals interested in children's literature turn to *The Horn Book Magazine* for informative articles on the industry. Book reviews, interviews, and essays are also regularly featured. Circ: 8,500.

Audience: Parents, teachers, librarians
Frequency: 6 times each year
Website: www.hbook.com

FREELANCE POTENTIAL

70% written by nonstaff writers. Publishes 12–15 freelance submissions yearly; 10% by unpublished writers, 30% by authors who are new to the magazine. Receives 120 queries, 60 unsolicited mss yearly.

SUBMISSIONS

Query or send complete ms. Accepts email to info@hbook.com (Microsoft Word attachments, include "Horn Book Article Submission" in the subject line); will accept hard copy. SASE. Responds in 4 months.

- Articles: To 2,800 words. Informational articles; interviews; essays; criticism; and book reviews. Topics include children's and young adult literature, authors, illustrators, and editors.
- Depts/columns: Word lengths vary. Perspectives from illustrators, children's publishing updates, and special columns.

SAMPLE ISSUE

104 pages (20% advertising): 3 articles; 46 reviews; 6 depts/columns. Sample copy, free with 9x12 SASE. Guidelines and editorial calendar available at website.

- "An Interview with Katherine Paterson." interview is a conversation with the new National Ambassador for Young People's Literature.
- Sample dept/column: "Sight Reading" relates that photography is gaining more respect in picture book publishing.

RIGHTS AND PAYMENT

All rights. Written material, payment rates vary. Pays on publication. Provides 3 author's copies.

⇒EDITOR'S COMMENTS

We're always interested in submissions of articles about fiction, but never in submissions of actual fiction. And while we publish reviews of children's literature, we will not publish works written by children.

Horsemen's Yankee Pedlar

83 Leicester Street
North Oxford, MA 01537

Editor: Elisabeth Gilbride

DESCRIPTION AND INTERESTS
This magazine serves as a resource for horse owners, breeders, riders, and trainers in the northeastern U.S., offering show and tournament coverage in addition to informative articles on all things equine. Circ: 50,000.

Audience: YA–Adult
Frequency: Monthly
Website: www.pedlar.com

FREELANCE POTENTIAL
85% written by nonstaff writers. Publishes 40 freelance submissions yearly; 5% by authors who are new to the magazine. Receives 360 queries, 240 unsolicited mss yearly.

SUBMISSIONS
Query or send complete ms. Accepts hard copy and simultaneous submissions if identified. SASE. Responds to queries in 1–2 weeks, to mss in 2–3 months.

- Articles: 500–800 words. Informational and how-to articles; interviews; reviews; and personal experience pieces. Topics include horse breeds, disciplines, training, health care, and equestrian management.
- Depts/columns: Word lengths vary. News, book reviews, business and legal issues, and equine nutrition.
- Artwork: B/W and color prints.

SAMPLE ISSUE
226 pages (75% advertising): 39 articles; 15 depts/columns. Sample copy, $3.99 with 9x12 SASE (7 first-class stamps). Writers' guidelines available.

- "Get the Canter You Want." Article explains how to get your horse to transition smoothly into the three-beat gait.
- Sample dept/column: "Stable Solutions" provides detailed information on equine allergies and their treatment in a Q&A format.

RIGHTS AND PAYMENT
First North American serial rights. Written material, $2 per published column inch. Show coverage, $75 per day. Pays 30 days after publication. Provides 1 tearsheet.

➡EDITOR'S COMMENTS
We encourage new writers who are familiar with the region's horse show circuit to submit their well-written coverage of events, personal experience pieces, or interviews.

Horsepower

P.O. Box 670
Aurora, Ontario L4G 4J9
Canada

Managing Editor: Susan Stafford

DESCRIPTION AND INTERESTS
Canadian children who love horses are the audience for this publication. Provided as a pull-out in *Horse Canada*, it features breed profiles and information on horseback riding, and equine care and training. Circ: 10,000.

Audience: 8–15 years
Frequency: 6 times each year
Website: www.horse-canada.com

FREELANCE POTENTIAL
75% written by nonstaff writers. Publishes 50 freelance submissions yearly. Receives 50 queries, 20 unsolicited mss yearly.

SUBMISSIONS
Query or send complete ms with résumé. Accepts hard copy, disk submissions, and email submissions to fearless.editor@ gmail.com. SAE/IRC. Responds to queries in 1–2 weeks, to mss in 2–3 months.

- Articles: 500–1,000 words. Informational and how-to articles; profiles; and humor. Topics include riding and stable skills, equine health, horse breeds, training issues, equine celebrities, and equestrian careers.
- Depts/columns: Staff written.
- Artwork: B/W and color prints.
- Other: Activities, games, and puzzles.

SAMPLE ISSUE
16 pages (20% advertising): 3 articles; 2 depts/columns; 2 puzzles; 2 contests. Sample copy, $3.95 Canadian. Guidelines and editorial calendar available.

- "How to Pack for Riding Camp." Article provides practical information for both day and overnight campers.
- Sample dept/column: "Spotlight" profiles a Canadian bred, trained, and owned harness racing horse.

RIGHTS AND PAYMENT
First North American serial rights. Written material, $50–$90 Canadian. Artwork, $15–$75 Canadian. Pays on publication. Provides 1 contributor's copy.

➡EDITOR'S COMMENTS
Because of grant guidelines, we have to give preference to Canadian authors. Writers should understand that the underlying emphasis of our publication is always safety, especially with regard to instructional pieces.

Hudson Valley Parent

174 South Street
Newburgh, NY 12550

Editor: Mark Roland

DESCRIPTION AND INTERESTS
Targeting families in New York State's Mid-Hudson Valley, this magazine focuses on resources for raising children, practical health and education information, and family-oriented, regional events and activities. Circ: 50,000.

Audience: Parents
Frequency: Monthly
Website: www.hvparent.com

FREELANCE POTENTIAL
60% written by nonstaff writers. Publishes 52 freelance submissions yearly; 5% by unpublished writers, 20% by authors who are new to the magazine. Receives 240 queries, 120 unsolicited mss yearly.

SUBMISSIONS
Query with writing samples; or send complete ms with sidebar and author bio. Accepts email submissions to editor@excitingread.com. Responds in 3–6 weeks.

- Articles: 700–1,200 words. Informational and how-to articles. Topics include child care and development, discipline, education, learning disabilities, family health, recreation, travel, and entertainment.
- Depts/columns: 700 words. Health, education, behavior, and kid-friendly recipes.
- Artwork: 8x10 B/W and color prints.
- Other: Submit seasonal material 6 months in advance.

SAMPLE ISSUE
58 pages (50% advertising): 5 articles; 2 depts/columns; 1 resource guide; 1 calendar. Sample copy, free with 9x12 SASE. Guidelines and editorial calendar available.

- "Keep Your Preschooler Happy All Summer Long." Article looks at educational summer activities for the under-five set.
- "To Delay or Not Delay?" Article discusses whether parents should delay giving solid foods to infants to prevent food allergies.

RIGHTS AND PAYMENT
One-time rights. Articles, $50–$120. Reprints, $25–$55. Pays on publication. Provides 2 contributor's copies.

❖EDITOR'S COMMENTS
We like first-person accounts, as our research has shown that our readers want to learn from other people and their experiences.

Humpty Dumpty

U.S. Kids Magazines
1100 Waterway Boulevard
P.O. Box 567
Indianapolis, IN 46206-0567

Editor: Terry Harshman

DESCRIPTION AND INTERESTS
Keeping young minds active is the mission of *Humpty Dumpty Magazine*, which publishes a mix of simple stories, puzzles, cartoons, and activities for young readers. Healthy living and protecting the environment are frequent messages. Circ: 236,000.

Audience: 4–6 years
Frequency: 6 times each year
Website: www.uskidsmags.com/
magazines/humptydumpty

FREELANCE POTENTIAL
50% written by nonstaff writers. Publishes 45 freelance submissions yearly; 5% by unpublished writers, 12% by authors who are new to the magazine.

SUBMISSIONS
Send complete ms. Accepts hard copy. SASE. Responds in 2–3 months.

- Articles: To 350 words. Informational and how-to articles. Topics include health, fitness, sports, science, nature, animals, crafts, and hobbies.
- Fiction: To 350 words. Genres include early reader contemporary and multicultural fiction, fantasy, folktales, humor, and mystery.
- Depts/columns: Word lengths vary. Recipes, health advice, and book excerpts.
- Other: Puzzles, activities, and games. Poetry, lengths vary. Submit seasonal material 8 months in advance.

SAMPLE ISSUE
36 pages (2% advertising): 1 article; 2 stories; 3 depts/columns; 9 activities; 1 poem. Sample copy, $1.25. Guidelines available at website.

- "Too Big To Be Scared." Rebus story features a bedtime conversation between a father and daughter as she is trying to overcome her fear of the dark.
- Sample dept/column: "Mix & Fix" offers a recipe for pineapple moon balls.

RIGHTS AND PAYMENT
All rights. Written material, to $.35 per word. Pays on publication. Provides 10 copies.

❖EDITOR'S COMMENTS
Material submitted should reflect good values and healthy living. We're currently seeking poetry, crafts, recipes, rebuses, and simple, age-appropriate fiction and nonfiction.

The Illuminata

5486 Fairway Drive
Zachary, LA 70791

Editor-in-Chief: Bret Funk

DESCRIPTION AND INTERESTS
This electronic journal is written and read by avid fans of fantasy and science fiction. It accepts fiction, essays, critiques, and reviews. Hits per month: 600.
Audience: YA–Adult
Frequency: Quarterly
Website: www.tyrannosauruspress.com

FREELANCE POTENTIAL
25% written by nonstaff writers. Publishes 5–10 freelance submissions yearly; 95% by unpublished writers, 50% by authors who are new to the magazine. Receives 10 queries each year.

SUBMISSIONS
Query. Accepts email queries to info@ tyrannosauruspress.com (no attachments). Responds in 1–3 months.

- Articles: 1–2 pages. Informational articles. Topics include writing science fiction, fantasy, and horror.
- Fiction: Word lengths vary. Genres include science fiction, fantasy, and horror.
- Depts/columns: "Reviews," 500–1,000 words. Reviews of science fiction and fantasy books and stories.

SAMPLE ISSUE
26 pages (no advertising): 5 articles; 1 story; 5 depts/columns. Sample copy and guidelines available at website.

- "Changing Roles of Television's Women in Space." Article examines the dress, function, and amount of respect given to female roles in science fiction television programs throughout the decades.
- "Slaves of the Machines." Article examines how real life mirrors science fiction regarding man's dependence on machines.
- Sample dept/column: "Reviews" offers a review of Harry Connolly's *Child of Fire*, and his depiction of romance in fantasy fiction.

RIGHTS AND PAYMENT
Rights vary. No payment.

➼ EDITOR'S COMMENTS
We are actively seeking regular as well as occasional contributors. At this time, our current needs are for reviews and original fiction. Reviews may be negative, but they may not be cruel.

Imagination-Café

P.O. Box 1536
Valparaiso, IN 46384

Editor: Rosanne Tolin

DESCRIPTION AND INTERESTS
Imagination-Café encourages kids to dream about their futures through its engaging presentation of career information. Appearing in e-zine format, it also offers regular updates on sports, science, history, and health. Hits per month: Unavailable.
Audience: 7–12 years
Frequency: Updated daily
Website: www.imagination-cafe.com

FREELANCE POTENTIAL
75% written by nonstaff writers. Publishes 40–50 freelance submissions yearly. Receives 1,800 queries, 1,560 unsolicited mss yearly.

SUBMISSIONS
Prefers complete ms; will accept query. Accepts email to submissions@imagination-café.com (no attachments). Response time varies.

- Articles: Word lengths vary. Informational and how-to articles; profiles; interviews; and reviews. Topics include animals, careers, crafts, hobbies, history, science, technology, sports, and celebrities.
- Fiction: To 1,000 words. Contemporary stories with young protagonists.
- Depts/columns: Word lengths vary. "Cool Careers," "Before They Were Famous," "Celebrity Screw-Ups," and "School Strategies."
- Other: Puzzles, mazes, word games, quizzes, and recipes.

SAMPLE ISSUE
Sample copy and writers' guidelines available at website.

- "What's Up with the Hiccups?" Article explains the science behind the hiccups and lists lesser-known remedies.
- Sample dept/column: "Before They Were Famous" spotlights Matt Damon, who dropped out of Harvard just 12 credits shy of a degree.

RIGHTS AND PAYMENT
Non-exclusive print and electronic rights. Written material, $20–$100. Pays on acceptance.

➼ EDITOR'S COMMENTS
Our e-zine is dedicated to empowering kids and tweens by encouraging curiosity in the world around them, as well as exploration of their talents and aspirations.

Indy's Child

1901 Broad Ripple Avenue
Indianapolis, IN 46220

Executive Editor: Lynette Rowland

DESCRIPTION AND INTERESTS

Articles on parenting topics, with a focus on Indianapolis, are the mainstay of this magazine. Circ: 120,000.
Audience: Parents
Frequency: Monthly
Website: www.indyschild.com

FREELANCE POTENTIAL

95% written by nonstaff writers. Publishes 240+ freelance submissions yearly; 35% by unpublished writers, 60% by authors who are new to the magazine. Receives thousands of queries, 600 unsolicited mss yearly.

SUBMISSIONS

Query with writing samples, list of sources, and clips (one topic per query); or send complete ms with author bio. Accepts email to editor@indyschild.com (Microsoft Word attachments). Responds if interested.

- Articles: 1,500–2,000 words. Informational and how-to articles; profiles; and humor. Topics include parenting, child development, family-oriented events and activities, sports, travel, health, balancing career and family, and fatherhood.
- Depts/columns: 800–1,000 words. "Ages & Stages," "One Chic Mama," "My Parent, My Mentor," "Growing Up Online," and "Tweens & Teens." News, education, pediatric health, special needs, local profiles, and reviews.
- Artwork: Color digital images at 200 dpi.
- Other: Submit seasonal material 2 months in advance.

SAMPLE ISSUE

54 pages (50% advertising): 3 articles; 18 depts/columns. Sample copy, guidelines, and editorial calendar available at website.

- "Birthday Party Bonanza." Article tells how to throw a party without breaking the bank.
- "What You (and Baby) Can Expect Upon Arrival." Article provides an overview of the many changes a new baby brings.

RIGHTS AND PAYMENT

First rights. Written material, payment rates vary. Pays within 30 days of publication.

❖EDITOR'S COMMENTS

We expect well-researched articles that will offer our readers information they can use in real life. Humor is always welcome.

Inland Empire Family

11731 Stearling, Suite H
Riverside, CA 92503

Editor: Lynn Armitage

DESCRIPTION AND INTERESTS

This magazine is for families living in Riverside and San Bernadino counties in California. It covers a range of parenting topics specific to the region. Circ: 55,000.
Audience: Parents
Frequency: Monthly
Website: www.inlandempirefamily.com

FREELANCE POTENTIAL

95% written by nonstaff writers. Publishes several freelance submissions yearly.

SUBMISSIONS

Query. Accepts hard copy. SASE. Response time varies.

- Articles: Word lengths vary. Informational and how-to articles. Topics include parenting, child care and development, education, entertainment, sports, recreation, travel, health, nutrition, summer camp, and pets.
- Depts/columns: Word lengths vary. Parenting advice by age group, self-help for parents and couples, children's health, fashion, food and dining, and education; also publishes essays and media reviews.

SAMPLE ISSUE

106 pages: 1 article; 15 depts/columns. Sample copy, writers' guidelines, and editorial calendar available.

- "50 Ways to Rock Your Summer." Article offers extensive coverage of summer recreation venues throughout the region, with links to websites.
- Sample dept/column: "First Years" looks at recent research into the question of whether parents can help make their baby a genius.
- Sample dept/column: "Education" explains how a program called Destination Imagi-Nation fosters learning in local schools.

RIGHTS AND PAYMENT

All rights. Articles, $100–$500. Depts/columns, payment rates vary. Kill fee, $50. Pays within 45 days of publication.

❖EDITOR'S COMMENTS

No matter the topic, and no matter how well written, your submission must have a local connection before we will consider publishing it. Be sure to include online sources and updated information for all places referenced.

Insight

55 West Oak Ridge Drive
Hagerstown, MD 21740

Editor: Dwain Neilson Esmond

DESCRIPTION AND INTERESTS
Insight's mission is to reach Seventh-day Adventist teens with articles that help them grow in friendship with God. It addresses topics such as friendship, social issues, faith, and serving one's community. Circ: 12,000.

Audience: 13–19 years
Frequency: Weekly
Website: www.insightmagazine.org

FREELANCE POTENTIAL
50% written by nonstaff writers. Publishes 200–300 freelance submissions yearly; 50% by unpublished writers, 70% by authors who are new to the magazine. Receives 700 unsolicited mss yearly.

SUBMISSIONS
Send complete ms. Accepts hard copy and email submissions to insight@rhpa.org (Microsoft Word attachments). SASE. Responds in 1–3 months.

- Articles: 500–1,500 words. Informational articles; profiles; biographies; personal experience pieces; and humor. Topics include religion, social issues, and careers.
- Depts/columns: Word lengths vary. Bible lessons, relationship advice, true stories, and personal experience pieces.
- Other: Submit seasonal material 6 months in advance.

SAMPLE ISSUE
16 pages (2% advertising): 3 articles; 3 depts/columns. Sample copy, $2 with 9x12 SASE (2 first-class stamps). Writers' guidelines available at website.

- "My Two Blessings." Personal experience piece tells how the author learned that dressing to worship God is more important than dressing for others, and one's wardrobe should be a sign of reverence.
- Sample dept/column: "Unplugged" offers advice to a teen whose father is losing his Christian focus.

RIGHTS AND PAYMENT
First rights. Written material, $50–$125. Pays on acceptance. Provides 3 contributor's copies.

➮EDITOR'S COMMENTS
Articles should address topics of interest to today's teens from a Christian perspective. Each should have a biblical reference.

InSite

405 West Rockrimmon Boulevard
Colorado Springs, CO 80919

Editor: Martha Krienke

DESCRIPTION AND INTERESTS
Both practical and inspirational articles about Christian camp and conference management are found in *InSite*. It is written for members of the Christian Camp and Conference Association. Circ: 8,500.

Audience: Adults
Frequency: 6 times each year
Website: www.ccca.org

FREELANCE POTENTIAL
90% written by nonstaff writers. Publishes 40 freelance submissions yearly; 15% by unpublished writers, 22% by authors who are new to the magazine. Receives 10 queries yearly.

SUBMISSIONS
Query with résumé and writing samples. Accepts email queries to editor@ccca.org. Availability of artwork improves chance of acceptance. Responds in 1 month.

- Articles: 800–1,500 words. Informational and how-to articles; profiles; and interviews. Topics include Christian camp and conference operations, programs, fundraising, leadership, personnel, recreation, religion, social issues, crafts, hobbies, health, fitness, multicultural and ethnic issues, nature, popular culture, and sports.
- Depts/columns: Staff written.
- Artwork: Color prints and digital images.
- Other: Submit seasonal material 6 months in advance.

SAMPLE ISSUE
50 pages (25% advertising): 8 articles; 10 depts/columns. Sample copy, $4.95 with 9x12 SASE ($1.40 postage). Guidelines and editorial calendar available at website.

- "Sending Success." Article explains the critical role of email marketing in fundraising.
- "Dirty Jobs." Article provides practical information for handling unexpected maintenance tasks.

RIGHTS AND PAYMENT
First rights. Articles, $.20 per word. Artwork, $25–$250. Pays on publication. Provides 1 contributor's copy.

➮EDITOR'S COMMENTS
Send us practical articles that show what God is doing in and through Christian camp and conference ministries.

Instructor

Scholastic Inc.
557 Broadway
New York, NY 10012-39999

Editorial Assistant: Megan Kaesshaefer

DESCRIPTION AND INTERESTS
This magazine is dedicated to helping teachers in kindergarten though eighth grade be as effective as they possibly can. Published by Scholastic, *Instructor* includes articles on facing the everyday challenges of teaching, as well as lesson plans and reviews of teacher resources. Circ: 200,000+.

Audience: Teachers, grades K–8
Frequency: 6 times each year
Website: www.scholastic.com/instructor

FREELANCE POTENTIAL
90% written by nonstaff writers. Publishes 55 freelance submissions yearly; 10% by unpublished writers. Receives 100 queries yearly.

SUBMISSIONS
Query. Accepts email queries to instructor@scholastic.com. Availability of artwork improves chance of acceptance. Responds in 3–4 months.

- Articles: 1,200 words. Informational and how-to articles; and personal experience pieces. Topics include lesson planning, classroom management, career development, workplace issues, learning and literacy issues, and technology.
- Depts/columns: News, Q&A's, technology briefs, book reviews, and "Teachers' Picks," word lengths vary. Classroom activities, to 250 words. Humorous or poignant personal essays, to 400 words.
- Artwork: Color prints or transparencies.

SAMPLE ISSUE
64 pages (40% advertising): 4 articles; 12 depts/columns. Sample copy, $3 with 9x12 SASE. Guidelines available.

- "Icky, Creepy, Smelly, and Just Plain Gross Science Projects." Article details experiments that will appeal to kids who love hands-on, dirty projects.
- Sample dept/column: "Teachers' Picks" notes favorite science and math games.

RIGHTS AND PAYMENT
All rights. Written material, $.80 per word. Pays on publication. Provides 2 author's copies.

❖EDITOR'S COMMENTS
We like to receive classroom-tested ideas that have been developed by creative elementary and middle school teachers.

InTeen

1551 Regency Court
Calumet City, IL 60409

Editor: LaTonya Taylor

DESCRIPTION AND INTERESTS
Each issue of this Christian teen magazine features thought-provoking Bible studies, inspiring articles, and Scripture passages that link Bible verses to problems facing today's urban teens. Circ: 75,000.

Audience: 15–17 years
Frequency: Quarterly
Website: www.urbanministries.com

FREELANCE POTENTIAL
90% written by nonstaff writers. Publishes 52 freelance submissions yearly.

SUBMISSIONS
All material is written on assignment. Send résumé with writing samples. SASE. Responds in 3–6 months.

- Articles: Word lengths vary. Bible study guides and lessons; how-to articles; profiles; interviews; and reviews. Topics include religion, college and careers, black history, music, social issues, and multicultural and ethnic issues. Also publishes biographies.
- Fiction: Word lengths vary. Stories may be included in Bible lessons. Genres include inspirational, multicultural, and ethnic fiction.
- Other: Puzzles, activities, and poetry. Submit seasonal material 1 year in advance.

SAMPLE ISSUE
48 pages (no advertising): 7 articles; 2 poems; 14 Bible studies. Guidelines available.

- "Five Ways To Look Like Jesus." Article offers suggestions for handling disappointment, anger, and forgiveness by acting as Jesus would.
- "That Boy Is Bad!" Bible study is a reminder to face challenges with the strength that God gives us.

RIGHTS AND PAYMENT
All rights. All material, payment rates vary. Pays 2 months after acceptance. Provides 2 contributor's copies.

❖EDITOR'S COMMENTS
We specifically target African American teens, and our goal is to help them develop and nurture their relationships with Jesus Christ and others. We are open to working with new writers as long as they take the time to read a few of our issues and familiarize themselves with our format.

InTeen Teacher

1551 Regency Court
Calumet City, IL 60409

Editor: LaTonya Taylor

DESCRIPTION AND INTERESTS
Each issue of *InTeen Teacher* features comprehensive teaching plans and Bible study guides
that are used in conjunction with the student
magazine, *InTeen*. Its content specifically
addresses the needs and concerns of urban
teens. Circ: 75,000.

Audience: Religious educators
Frequency: Quarterly
Website: www.urbanministries.com

FREELANCE POTENTIAL
90% written by nonstaff writers. Publishes 52
freelance submissions yearly.

SUBMISSIONS
All material is written on assignment. Send
résumé with writing samples. SASE. Responds
in 3–6 months.

- Articles: Word lengths vary. Bible study plans
  and guides for teaching Christian values to
  African American teens; and how-to articles.
- Fiction: Word lengths vary. Stories may be
  included as part of study plans. Genres
  include inspirational, multicultural, and
  ethnic fiction; and real-life and problem-
  solving stories.
- Other: Puzzles, activities, and poetry. Submit
  seasonal material 1 year in advance.

SAMPLE ISSUE
96 pages (no advertising): 2 articles; 14 teaching plans; 14 Bible study guides. Writers'
guidelines available.

- "The Two Sides of Justice." Article explains
  how to instruct urban youth to do less
  protesting about injustices, and more investing in their future.
- "Doers of the World." Bible study guide uses
  Scripture from James to stress the importance of becoming a doer of God's work.
- "Put a Sock in It!" Teaching plan reminds
  students that one's words can either hurt or
  bring joy to someone.

RIGHTS AND PAYMENT
All rights. Written material, payment rates vary.
Pays 2 months after acceptance. Provides 2
contributor's copies.

➥EDITOR'S COMMENTS
New writers are welcome to contact us. We
are looking for material that will educate and
stimulate teens.

International Gymnast

3214 Bart Conner Drive
Norman, OK 73072

Editor: Dwight Normile

DESCRIPTION AND INTERESTS
Pre-teen and teen gymnastics—and those
involved in the sport—are the focus of this
magazine. Competition reports, athlete profiles, and training techniques are some of its
regular features. Circ: 14,000.

Audience: Gymnasts, 10–16 years
Frequency: 10 times each year
Website: www.intlgymnast.com

FREELANCE POTENTIAL
10% written by nonstaff writers. Publishes 5
freelance submissions yearly; 50% by authors
who are new to the magazine. Receives 12
unsolicited mss yearly.

SUBMISSIONS
Send complete ms. Accepts hard copy and
simultaneous submissions if identified. SASE.
Responds in 1 month.

- Articles: 1,000–2,250 words. Informational
  articles; profiles; and interviews. Topics
  include gymnastics competitions, coaching,
  and personalities involved in the sport.
- Fiction: To 1,500 words. Gymnastics stories.
- Depts/columns: 700–1,000 words. News,
  training tips, and opinion pieces.
- Artwork: B/W prints, 35mm color slides for
  cover art.

SAMPLE ISSUE
46 pages (14% advertising): 4 articles; 12
depts/columns. Sample copy, $5 with 9x12
SASE. Guidelines available.

- "U.S. Olympic Trials." Article provides an
  overview of the results of the four-day
  Olympic Trials.
- "Sudden Impact." Article describes the
  mishaps that ended Paul Hamm's reign as
  Olympic all-around champion.
- Sample dept/column: "Stretching Out" outlines proposed technical regulations and
  their impact on gymnastics.

RIGHTS AND PAYMENT
All rights. Written material, $15–$25. Artwork,
$5–$50. Pays on publication. Provides 1 contributor's copy.

➥EDITOR'S COMMENTS
Writers should be well-versed in gymnastics
and be able to provide us with interesting
facts that we don't already know. Interviews
and profiles are always of interest.

Jack and Jill

U.S. Kids Magazines
1100 Waterway Boulevard
P.O. Box 567
Indianapolis, IN 46206-0567

Editor: Terry Harshman

DESCRIPTION AND INTERESTS
A mix of articles, stories, puzzles, and poetry—all designed to encourage children to be happy, healthy, and fit—are found in each issue of this magazine. Circ: 200,000.

Audience: 7–10 years
Frequency: 6 times each year
Website: www.jackandjillmag.org

FREELANCE POTENTIAL
50% written by nonstaff writers. Publishes 24 freelance submissions yearly; 70% by authors who are new to the magazine. Receives 1,200 unsolicited mss yearly.

SUBMISSIONS
Send complete ms. Accepts hard copy. SASE. Responds in 3 months.

- Articles: 500–600 words. Informational and how-to articles; humor; profiles; and biographies. Topics include sports, health, exercise, safety, nutrition, and hygiene.
- Fiction: 500–900 words. Genres include mystery, fantasy, folktales, humor, science fiction, and stories about sports and animals.
- Artwork: Submit sketches to Jennifer Saulovic, art director; submit photos to Terry Harshman, editor.
- Other: Poetry. Games, puzzles, activities, and cartoons. Submit seasonal material 8 months in advance.

SAMPLE ISSUE
36 pages (4% advertising): 2 articles; 2 stories; 3 depts/columns; 3 activities; 1 cartoon; 3 poems. Sample copy, $3.95 ($2 postage). Guidelines available.

- "Speedy Splinters." Article describes the Boy Scouts' Pinewood Derby event that took place at the Indiana State Museum.
- "Adventures of the Puzzle Squad." Story features two friends who travel back to the 1840s to search for gold in California.

RIGHTS AND PAYMENT
All rights. Written material, $.17 per word. Artwork, payment rates vary. Pays on publication. Provides 10 contributor's copies.

⇢EDITOR'S COMMENTS
Reading our editorial guidelines is not enough. Careful study of past issues will acquaint you with the magazine's personality, as well as its regular features and departments.

JAKES Magazine

P.O. Box 530
Edgefield, SC 29824

Editor

DESCRIPTION AND INTERESTS
A publication of the National Wild Turkey Federation, *JAKES* teaches boys and girls about the importance of wildlife preservation. It also features articles on responsible hunting and fishing, and includes articles on fascinating animals. Circ: 170,000.

Audience: To 12 years
Frequency: Quarterly
Website: www.nwtf.org/jakes

FREELANCE POTENTIAL
50% written by nonstaff writers. Publishes 30 freelance submissions yearly; 10% by unpublished writers, 30% by authors who are new to the magazine. Receives 150–200 queries and unsolicited mss yearly.

SUBMISSIONS
Query or send complete ms. Accepts hard copy, email to dearjake@nwtf.net, and simultaneous submissions between May and December only. SASE. Response time varies.

- Articles: 1,000–1,200 words. Informational articles; profiles; and personal experience pieces. Topics include nature, the environment, animals, pets, hunting, fishing, and other outdoor and extreme sports.
- Fiction: 800–1,200 words. Historical fiction.
- Depts/columns: Word lengths vary. Association news, new products and gear, essays.
- Artwork: Color slides, transparencies, or prints; high-resolution digital images.

SAMPLE ISSUE
18 pages: 2 articles; 8 depts/columns. Guidelines available at website.

- "How a Fish Is Like a Tree." Article explains that "fish aging" is done by counting the rings on the small ear bones.
- Sample dept/column: "Backyard Ecology" gives the lowdown on ladybugs.

RIGHTS AND PAYMENT
First North American serial and Web rights. Written material, $.05 per word. Artwork, payment rates vary. Kill fee, 25%. Pays on publication. Provides 2 contributor's copies.

⇢EDITOR'S COMMENTS
We believe in involving kids in wildlife conservation and the wise use of our natural resources. All material must be tailored to the young outdoorsman.

Jeunesse
Young People, Text, Cultures

Department of English, University of Winnipeg
515 Portage Avenue
Winnipeg, Manitoba R3B 2E9
Canada

General Editor: Mavis Reimer

DESCRIPTION AND INTERESTS
This interdisciplinary academic journal publishes research and opinion on literature and other media for, by, and about children. It focuses on the cultural functions and representations of "the child." Though international in scope, it has a special interest in Canada. Circ: 400.

Audience: Educators, scholars, librarians
Frequency: Twice each year
Website: www.jeunessejournal.ca

FREELANCE POTENTIAL
95% written by nonstaff writers. Publishes 25 freelance submissions yearly; 10% by unpublished writers, 40% by authors who are new to the magazine. Receives 40 unsolicited mss each year.

SUBMISSIONS
Send complete ms. Prefers email submissions to jeunesse@uwinnipeg.ca (Microsoft Word or RTF attachments); will accept 3 hard copies. SAE/IRC. Responds in 3 months.

- Articles: 2,000–6,000 words. Informational articles; reviews; essays; profiles; and interviews. Topics include children's literature; film, video, and drama for children; and children's authors.

SAMPLE ISSUE
222 pages (2% advertising): 12 articles. Sample copy, $10. Guidelines and theme list available at website.

- "Little Red Riding Hood and the Pedophile in Film." Article examines how three films have eroticized the traditional folktale.
- "On the Function of Money, Spending, and Saving in Recent Canadian Children's Texts Dealing with Poverty and Homelessness." Essay explores the function of money in four Canadian children's books.

RIGHTS AND PAYMENT
First serial rights. No payment. Provides 1 contributor's copy.

⏥EDITOR'S COMMENTS
We welcome articles in both English and French. Your name and contact information should not appear on the submission itself, but on a separate file or piece of paper (along with a 100-word abstract) so it may undergo a blind review by peers.

Journal of Adolescent & Adult Literacy

International Reading Association
800 Barksdale Road
P.O. Box 8139
Newark, DE 19714-8139

Managing Editor: James Henderson

DESCRIPTION AND INTERESTS
This peer-reviewed journal targets those who work with new, struggling, and skilled readers alike. Read by literacy teachers and administrators, it highlights research-based practices aimed at improving literacy achievement in students age 12 and older. Circ: 16,000.

Audience: Reading education professionals
Frequency: 8 times each year
Website: www.reading.org

FREELANCE POTENTIAL
95% written by nonstaff writers. Publishes 50 freelance submissions yearly; 30% by unpublished writers, 50% by authors who are new to the magazine. Receives 300 unsolicited mss each year.

SUBMISSIONS
Send complete ms. Accepts electronic submissions via http://mc.manuscriptcentral.com/jaal. Responds in 2–3 months.

- Articles: 5,000–6,000 words. Informational and how-to articles; and personal experience pieces. Topics include reading theory, research, and practice; and trends in teaching literacy.
- Depts/columns: Word lengths vary. Opinion pieces, reviews, and technology information.

SAMPLE ISSUE
88 pages (7% advertising): 6 articles; 4 depts/columns. Sample copy, $10. Guidelines available at website.

- "English-Language Learners, Fan Communities, and 21st-Century Skills." Article explores how learning in technology-mediated places—such as online fan fiction communities—can provide a basis for valuable print literacy.
- Sample dept/column: "Commentary" is an opinion piece about censorship that discusses the ramifications of a book that was banned in 1994.

RIGHTS AND PAYMENT
All rights. No payment. Provides 5 contributor's copies for articles, 2 for depts/columns.

⏥EDITOR'S COMMENTS
We seek articles that make a significant contribution to advancing and integrating theory and practice. Your submission will be judged on originality, significance, scholarship, audience appropriateness, and writing style.

Journal of School Health

American School Health Association
7263 State Road 43
P.O. Box 708
Kent, OH 44240-0708

Editor: James H. Price

DESCRIPTION AND INTERESTS
Health educators, school nurses, and school administrators subscribe to this professional journal from the American School Health Association. It covers everything from fetal alcohol syndrome to teen pregnancy and depression. Circ: 5,000.

Audience: School health professionals
Frequency: 10 times each year
Website: www.ashaweb.org

FREELANCE POTENTIAL
95% written by nonstaff writers. Publishes 60 freelance submissions yearly; 90% by authors who are new to the magazine. Receives 120 queries and unsolicited mss yearly.

SUBMISSIONS
Query or send complete ms. Accepts email submissions via www.manuscriptcentral.com/josh. Responds to queries in 2 weeks, to mss in 3–4 months.

- Articles: 2,500 words. Informational articles; research papers; commentaries; and practical application pieces. Topics include teaching techniques, health services in the school system, nursing, medicine, substance abuse, nutrition, counseling, and ADD/AHD.

SAMPLE ISSUE
58 pages (no advertising): 3 articles; 4 research papers; 1 commentary. Sample copy, $8.50 with 9x12 SASE. Writers' guidelines available at website.

- "Obesity Prevention in Early Adolescence: Student, Parent, and Teacher Views." Article reports on a focus group study with seventh graders, their parents, and their teachers, which found that many teens have a limited understanding of healthy eating.
- "Physical Activity and Sports Team Participation: Associations with Academic Outcomes in Middle School and High School Students." Article explores the relationship between sports participation and GPA.

RIGHTS AND PAYMENT
All rights. No payment. Provides 2 copies.

➥EDITOR'S COMMENTS
We're interested in all health-related topics affecting preschoolers through high school students. All submissions must be factually accurate and based on rigorous research.

Junior Baseball

14 Woodway Lane
Wilton, CT 06897

Editor/Publisher: Jim Beecher

DESCRIPTION AND INTERESTS
Launched in 1996, this independent magazine focuses on all aspects of youth baseball and aims to connect families to American's favorite pastime. Its articles instruct, inform, and entertain readers with topics ranging from coaching techniques to the secret behind a good knuckleball. Circ: 50,000.

Audience: 7–17 years; parents; coaches
Frequency: 6 times each year
Website: www.juniorbaseball.com

FREELANCE POTENTIAL
50% written by nonstaff writers. Publishes 20 freelance submissions yearly; 10% by unpublished writers, 20% by new authors. Receives 50 queries and unsolicited mss yearly.

SUBMISSIONS
Query with writing samples; or send complete ms with artwork. Accepts email submissions to jim@juniorbaseball.com (Microsoft Word or text file attachments). Availability of artwork improves chance of acceptance. SASE. Responds in 1–2 weeks.

- Articles: 750–1,500 words. Informational and how-to articles; profiles; and interviews. Topics include playing tips, teams and leagues, and player safety.
- Depts/columns: "Player's Story," 500 words. "In the Spotlight," news and reviews, 50–100 words. "Hot Prospects," 500–1,000 words. "Coaches Clinic," 100–1,000 words.
- Artwork: 4x5, 5x7, and 8x10 color prints. Color digital images at 300 dpi.

SAMPLE ISSUE
40 pages (30% advertising): 11 articles; 6 depts/columns. Sample copy, $3.95 with 9x12 SASE ($1.35 postage). Guidelines available.

- "Where's Your Focus?" Article explains the importance of focusing on the pitcher's glove before the pitch.
- Sample dept/column: "In the Stands" discusses respecting the opponent.

RIGHTS AND PAYMENT
All rights. Articles, $.20 per word. Depts/columns, $25–$100. Artwork, $50–$100. Pays on publication. Provides 1 contributor's copy.

➥EDITOR'S COMMENTS
If you don't live and breathe baseball, you're most likely not a match for our magazine.

Junior Shooters

7154 West State Street
Boise, ID 83714

Editor: Andrew Fink

DESCRIPTION AND INTERESTS

With a mission to get youngsters (and their parents) interested and involved in all types of shooting sports, this magazine covers the shooting disciplines, organizations, events, techniques, and safety issues. Circ: 30,000.

Audience: 8–21 years
Frequency: Twice each year
Website: www.juniorshooters.net

FREELANCE POTENTIAL

80% written by nonstaff writers. Publishes several freelance submissions yearly; 60% by unpublished writers, 40% by authors who are new to the magazine. Receives 200 unsolicited mss yearly.

SUBMISSIONS

Send complete ms. Accepts email submissions to articles@juniorshooters.net and CD submissions (PC format) in Microsoft Word, accompanied by form found at website. Materials not returned. Response time varies.

- Articles: Word lengths vary. Informational articles; profiles; and personal experience pieces. Topics include all disciplines of shooting sports, techniques, training, coaching, products, and gear.
- Depts/columns: Word lengths vary. Shooting tips, gun safety, new products and gear.
- Artwork: High-resolution digital images.

SAMPLE ISSUE

68 pages: 14 articles; 5 depts/columns. Sample copy and guidelines available at website.

- "Spud: Cowboy Fast Draw Artist at 11." Article profiles a boy who competes in fast draw contests under his cowboy alias, "Spud."
- Sample dept/column: "Gunsmithing" offers an introduction to the shotgun and explains how to perform routine maintenance on it.

RIGHTS AND PAYMENT

Non-exclusive rights. No payment.

➡ EDITOR'S COMMENTS

We try to have about half of the articles in our print edition written by juniors about their experiences with shooting. We are actively encouraging more people to become involved in the shooting sports, and would welcome any article that speaks to that mission. Safety is a huge topic for us, and we can't get enough safety-themed articles.

JuniorWay

P.O. Box 436987
Chicago, IL 60643

Editor: Katherine Steward

DESCRIPTION AND INTERESTS

A publication of Urban Ministries, Inc., *JuniorWay* is a "student magazine for urban juniors" that complements religious education programs. It presents stories, Bible lessons, and activities designed to help children live their lives with Christ in mind. Circ: 75,000.

Audience: 9–11 years
Frequency: Quarterly
Website: www.urbanministries.com

FREELANCE POTENTIAL

95% written by nonstaff writers. Publishes 52 freelance submissions yearly. Receives 240 queries yearly.

SUBMISSIONS

All material is written on assignment. Query with résumé and writing samples. Accepts hard copy. SASE. Response time varies.

- Articles: Word lengths vary. Bible lessons; personal experience pieces; and humor. Topics include religion, relationships, social issues, hobbies, crafts, sports, recreation, and multicultural subjects.
- Fiction: Word lengths vary. Inspirational stories with multicultural subjects.
- Artwork: B/W or color prints or transparencies.
- Other: Puzzles, activities, games, and jokes. Poetry. Seasonal material about Vacation Bible School.

SAMPLE ISSUE

32 pages (no advertising): 13 Bible lessons; 6 activities; 1 poem; 1 comic. Sample copy, free. Guidelines and theme list available.

- "She Wasn't Talking to Me." Bible lesson teaches the value of respecting authority and what can happen when we don't obey.
- "I've Got Your Back." Bible lesson teaches us to have faith in God's protection.

RIGHTS AND PAYMENT

All rights. All material, payment rates vary. Pays on publication.

➡ EDITOR'S COMMENTS

Our mission is to present culturally relevant curricula materials for the African American church. Your writing samples should demonstrate cultural sensitivity. Lessons based on Bible stories must be relevant to the everyday lives of our urban, African American readers and feature a Christ-centered perspective.

Kaleidoscope

Exploring the Experience of Disability Through Literature & Fine Arts

701 South Main Street
Akron, OH 44311-1019

Editorial Coordinator: Mickey Shiplett

DESCRIPTION AND INTERESTS

Celebrating its 30th anniversary, *Kaleidoscope* expresses the experiences of disability from the perspective of individuals, families, health-care professionals, and society as a whole. Thought-provoking essays, stories, and poems fill its pages. Circ: 1,000.

Audience: YA–Adult
Frequency: Twice each year
Website: www.udsakron.org

FREELANCE POTENTIAL

90% written by nonstaff writers. Publishes 40 freelance submissions yearly; 10% by unpublished writers, 75% by authors who are new to the magazine. Receives 240 queries, 650 unsolicited mss yearly.

SUBMISSIONS

Query or send complete ms with author bio. Accepts hard copy and email submissions to mshiplett@udsakron.org (Microsoft Word attachments). SASE. Responds to queries in 2 weeks, to mss in 6 months.

- Articles: To 5,000 words. Informational articles; profiles; interviews; reviews; humor; and personal experience pieces. Topics include art, literature, biography, multicultural and social issues, and disabilities.
- Fiction: 5,000 words. Genres include folktales, humor, and multicultural and problem-solving fiction.
- Other: Poetry.

SAMPLE ISSUE

64 pages (no advertising): 5 articles; 4 stories; 9 poems. Sample copy, $6 with 9x12 SASE. Guidelines and editorial calendar available.

- "Learning Vision." Personal essay shares a mother's reflections on accepting her son's diagnosis of vision loss.
- "So Gifted, So Young." Story tells of a woman's troubled relationship with her handicapped artist friend who struggles with a drug addiction.

RIGHTS AND PAYMENT

First rights. Written material, $25–$100. Poetry, $10. Pays on publication. Provides 2 contributor's copies.

⇢EDITOR'S COMMENTS

We're interested in reviewing humor pieces from writers with or without disabilities.

Key Club

Key Club International
3636 Woodview Trace
Indianapolis, IN 46268-3196

Executive Editor

DESCRIPTION AND INTERESTS

This magazine is read by service-minded students who want to make a difference in their communities. It features academic, self-help, service, and leadership-related articles in each issue. Circ: 240,000.

Audience: 14–18 years
Frequency: Twice each year
Website: www.keyclub.org/magazine

FREELANCE POTENTIAL

20% written by nonstaff writers. Publishes 4 freelance submissions yearly; 5% by unpublished writers, 15% by authors who are new to the magazine. Receives 100 queries yearly.

SUBMISSIONS

Query with outline/synopsis and clips or writing samples. Accepts hard copy, email queries to keyclubnews@kiwanis.org, and simultaneous submissions if identified. SASE. Responds in 1 month.

- Articles: 250–1,500 words. Informational, self-help, and service-related articles. Topics include education, teen concerns, community service, leadership, school activities, social issues, and careers.
- Depts/columns: Staff written.
- Artwork: Color prints and illustrations.
- Other: Submit seasonal material about back to school, college, and summer activities 3–7 months in advance.

SAMPLE ISSUE

24 pages (5% advertising): 4 articles; 3 depts/columns. Sample copy, free with 9x12 SASE ($.83 postage). Guidelines available.

- "Swaziland: Those Kids Need Us." Article discusses fund-raising efforts to benefit African children affected by AIDS.
- "Building Uganda's Tomorrow." Article gives a first-person account of eight Key Club members' experiences helping to build a school in Uganda.

RIGHTS AND PAYMENT

First North American serial rights. All material, $100–$800. Pays on acceptance. Provides 3 contributor's copies.

⇢EDITOR'S COMMENTS

We like articles that have anecdotes and include Key Club members as sources. We're not looking for single-source stories.

Keys for Kids

P.O. Box 1001
Grand Rapids, MI 49501-1001

Editor: Hazel Marett

DESCRIPTION AND INTERESTS

CBH Ministries publishes *Keys for Kids* to provide young readers with daily devotionals and Gospel-based stories that will help them develop a closeness with Jesus Christ. Each devotional also includes a "key thought" that readers can bring with them throughout their day. Circ: 70,000.

Audience: 6–14 years
Frequency: 6 times each year
Website: www.keysforkids.org

FREELANCE POTENTIAL

100% written by nonstaff writers. Publishes 25 freelance submissions yearly; 50% by unpublished writers, 90% by authors who are new to the magazine. Receives 120 unsolicited mss each year.

SUBMISSIONS

Send complete ms. Accepts hard copy and email submissions to hazel@cbhministries.org. SASE. Responds in 2 months.

- Articles: 400 words. Devotionals with related Scripture passages and a key thought. Topics include contemporary social issues, family life, trust, friendship, salvation, witnessing, prayer, marriage, and faith.

SAMPLE ISSUE

80 pages: 61 devotionals. Sample copy, free with 9x6 SASE. Guidelines available at website.

- "Danger! Stay Away!" Devotional illustrates that, just as it's wise to stay away from physically dangerous environments, it's wise to avoid morally tempting situations.
- "Teaching Patience." Devotional teaches that God's patience with us knows no boundaries or time limits.

RIGHTS AND PAYMENT

First, second, and reprint rights. Written material, $25. Pays on acceptance. Provides 1 contributor's copy.

➥EDITOR'S COMMENTS

Every submission should include a Scripture passage, a story, a practical application, a key verse, and a key thought. Here are some tips to give your submission the best chance of acceptance: teach one lesson only; avoid fairy tale endings; and don't be afraid to deal with the very real social issues facing today's young people.

The Kids' Ark

P.O. Box 3160
Victoria, TX 77903

Editor: Joy Mygrants

DESCRIPTION AND INTERESTS

The Kids' Ark is a nondenominational Christian magazine. It appears in themed issues that teach biblical principles through enlightening and entertaining articles and stories. It also publishes activities and games. Circ: 8,000+.

Audience: 6–12 years
Frequency: Quarterly
Website: www.thekidsark.com

FREELANCE POTENTIAL

60% written by nonstaff writers. Publishes 12 freelance submissions yearly; 80–100% by authors who are new to the magazine. Receives 25 unsolicited mss yearly.

SUBMISSIONS

Send complete ms. Accepts email submissions to thekidsarksubmissions@yahoo.com (Microsoft Word attachments; indicate theme to which you are submitting in subject line). Responds in 2 months.

- Articles: To 650 words. Informational articles and personal experience pieces. Topics include religion, faith, and God's love.
- Fiction: To 650 words. Genres include contemporary, historical, and science fiction—all with Christian themes.
- Other: Puzzles, games, and comics.

SAMPLE ISSUE

32 pages: 9 articles; 3 stories; 7 activities. Sample copy, guidelines, and theme list available at website.

- "Learning to Listen." Story tells of a frustrated and stubborn young baseball player who finally succeeds when he learns to listen to his coaches.
- "Horsegate-Stubbornness." Personal experience piece relates how, with patience and trust, a horseman built a relationship with a stubborn mustang.

RIGHTS AND PAYMENT

First North American serial, second, worldwide, and electronic rights. Written material, $100. Reprints, $25. Pays on publication.

➥EDITOR'S COMMENTS

Stories featuring ethnic and multicultural characters are always welcome. And while a biblical lesson should be the underlying foundation of the story, we are not interested in heavy-handed preaching.

Kids Life

1426 22nd Avenue
Tuscaloosa, AL 35401

Publisher: Mary Jane Turner

DESCRIPTION AND INTERESTS

Kids Life is dedicated to providing information that is relevant to families in western Alabama. It publishes articles on parenting, child development, local recreation, family time, and education—all written from a local perspective. Circ: 30,000.

Audience: Parents
Frequency: 6 times each year
Website: www.kidslifemagazine.com

FREELANCE POTENTIAL

75% written by nonstaff writers. Publishes 12 freelance submissions yearly; 50% by unpublished writers, 10% by authors who are new to the magazine. Receives 240 queries, 240 unsolicited mss yearly.

SUBMISSIONS

Query or send complete ms. Accepts email submissions to kidslife@comcast.net. Availability of artwork improves chance of acceptance. Responds in 2 weeks.

- Articles: 1,000 words. Informational articles and personal experience pieces. Topics include parenting, education, sports, child care, religion, cooking, crafts, health, travel, and current events.
- Depts/columns: Staff written.
- Artwork: Color prints; JPEG files. Line art.
- Other: Filler.

SAMPLE ISSUE

50 pages (60% advertising): 5 articles; 4 depts/columns. Sample copy, free with SASE. Editorial calendar available.

- "How To Get Your Tween Ready for Home Alone." Article provides tips for preparing a child to spend time at home without adult supervision.
- "Lollipops & Fairytales." Article profiles the unique offerings of a baby and children's clothing boutique.

RIGHTS AND PAYMENT

Rights vary. Written material, to $30. Pays on publication. Provides 1 contributor's copy.

➡ EDITOR'S COMMENTS

Although we welcome material from writers everywhere, we give preference to local freelancers. All articles, regardless of the author's home base, must have a local angle and relate to families living in our region.

Kids' Ministry Ideas

55 West Oak Ridge Drive
Hagerstown, MD 21740

Editor: Candy DeVore

DESCRIPTION AND INTERESTS

This magazine, written for youth ministry leaders within the Seventh-day Adventist faith, aims to be a practical resource of helpful how-to's, inspiring true stories, and project ideas. Circ: 4,500.

Audience: Adventist youth ministry leaders
Frequency: Quarterly
Website: www.kidsministryideas.com

FREELANCE POTENTIAL

100% written by nonstaff writers. Publishes 60 freelance submissions yearly.

SUBMISSIONS

Query or send complete ms. Accepts hard copy and email submissions to cdevore@rhpa.org. SASE. Response time varies.

- Articles: 300–800 words. Informational and how-to articles; and essays. Topics include religious education, youth ministry, family issues, working with volunteers, lesson plans and props, faith, and prayer.
- Depts/columns: Word lengths vary. Leadership training, teaching tips, and crafts.
- Other: Submit seasonal material 6–12 months in advance.

SAMPLE ISSUE

32 pages: 3 articles; 7 depts/columns. Sample copy available. Guidelines available at website.

- "The Best Gift of All." Article explains how to prepare a sermon that will appeal to children as well as adults.
- "Teach 'Em Again for the First Time." Article explains how to successfully minister to unchurched children.
- Sample dept/column: "Leader Training" tells how to avoid misconceptions when teaching children.

RIGHTS AND PAYMENT

First North American serial rights. Written material, $20–$100. Pays 5–6 weeks after acceptance. Provides 2 contributor's copies.

➡ EDITOR'S COMMENTS

When submitting an article to us, keep in mind that first-person experiences are always best. Articles should be clear, concise, practical, relevant, and current. We welcome new writers who can share new ways to bring children to Jesus and inspire our faithful leaders and teachers.

Kids VT

P.O. Box 1089
Shelburne, VT 05482

Editor: Susan Holson

DESCRIPTION AND INTERESTS
Vermont's young families find information about events, activities, health, and education in this free regional tabloid. The tone is positive and practical. Circ: 25,000.

Audience: Parents
Frequency: 10 times each year
Website: www.kidsvt.com

FREELANCE POTENTIAL
80% written by nonstaff writers. Publishes 40–50 freelance submissions yearly; 20% by authors who are new to the magazine. Receives hundreds of unsolicited mss yearly.

SUBMISSIONS
Send complete ms. Accepts email submissions to editorial@kidsvt.com (no attachments) and simultaneous submissions if identified. Responds if interested.

- Articles: 500–1,500 words. Informational articles; profiles; interviews; and humor. Topics include the arts, education, recreation, nature, the environment, music, camps, pregnancy, infancy, and parenting.
- Depts/columns: Word lengths vary. News and media reviews.
- Other: Activities and games. Submit seasonal material 2 months in advance.

SAMPLE ISSUE
32 pages (50% advertising): 10 articles; 5 depts/columns. Guidelines and editorial calendar available at website.

- "Snakes, Snails, and Little Boy Tales: Unique Joys in Raising Sons." First-person piece explores the adventure of being a mother of four boys.
- Sample dept/column: "Science Watch" covers various aspects of wind power and provides instructions for making a wind sock.

RIGHTS AND PAYMENT
One-time and reprint rights. Written material, payment rates vary. Pays 30 days after publication. Provides 1–2 contributor's copies.

⇢EDITOR'S COMMENTS
We're always interested in upbeat material that makes parenting easier and life more fun for families living in the state of Vermont. Most of our pieces have a distinct regional angle, so submissions from authors living in Vermont are preferred.

Know
The Science Magazine for Curious Kids

501-3960 Quadra Street
Victoria, British Columbia V8X 4A3
Canada

Managing Editor: Adrienne Mason

DESCRIPTION AND INTERESTS
Launched in 2006, this magazine engages children in the study of science through fun, interactive articles and activities. It includes news briefs, short fiction, interviews, and hands-on fun. Circ: 13,000.

Audience: 6–9 years
Frequency: 6 times each year
Website: www.knowmag.ca

FREELANCE POTENTIAL
50% written by nonstaff writers. Publishes 150 freelance submissions yearly; 5% by unpublished writers, 30% by authors who are new to the magazine. Receives 300 queries, 180 unsolicited mss yearly.

SUBMISSIONS
Query with résumé and clips for nonfiction. Send complete ms for fiction and poetry. Accepts hard copy and email submissions to adrienne@knowmag.ca. SAE/IRC. Responds to queries in 1 month, to mss in 3 months.

- Articles: 250 words. Informational and how-to articles; science experiments; and interviews. Topics include chemistry, physics, biology, ecology, zoology, geology, technology, and mathematics.
- Fiction: To 500 words. Theme-related stories.
- Depts/columns: 200–250 words. Science news and discoveries, scientist profiles, astronomy, paleontology, and random facts.
- Other: Poetry. Puzzles, games, and activities.

SAMPLE ISSUE
32 pages (6% advertising): 5 articles; 8 depts/columns; 3 activities; 1 comic. Sample copy, writers' guidelines, and theme list available at website.

- "Eureka! The Science of Gold." Article presents fun facts about gold and how it has been used throughout the centuries.
- Sample dept/column: "Science in Action" profiles a geologist from British Columbia.

RIGHTS AND PAYMENT
First serial rights. Written material, $.40–$.50 Canadian per word. Pays on publication. Provides 2 contributor's copies.

⇢EDITOR'S COMMENTS
We are currently accepting theme-related fiction and poetry only, so please check our website to see the current theme list.

Lad

Ladies' Home Journal

4200 North Point Parkway
Alpharetta, GA 30022

Content Coordinator: David Nelms

Meredith Corporation
375 Lexington Avenue, 9th Floor
New York, NY 10017

Deputy Editor: Margot Gilman

DESCRIPTION AND INTERESTS

This children's magazine targets young boys of the Southern Baptist faith. It is filled with inspirational articles, short stories, and fun activities that are designed to foster personal growth and highlight the importance of mission work. It is published by the North American Mission Board. Circ: 13,000.

Audience: Boys, 6–9 years
Frequency: Monthly
Website: www.nambstore.com

FREELANCE POTENTIAL

90% written by nonstaff writers. Publishes 12 freelance submissions yearly; 5% by unpublished writers, 15% by authors who are new to the magazine.

SUBMISSIONS

Contract writers only. Send résumé. Accepts hard copy. Response time varies.

- Articles: Word lengths vary. Informational articles and personal experience pieces. Topics include biography, crafts, current events, religion, and humor.
- Fiction: Word lengths vary. Genres include adventure, mystery, nature, sports, and science fiction.
- Other: Puzzles, games, and jokes.

SAMPLE ISSUE

22 pages (10% advertising): 5 articles; 1 story. Sample copy available.

- "No Bible for Me?" Article reports on a mission trip to rural Georgia in which Bibles were donated to children who couldn't afford to buy them.
- "The One That Nearly Got Away." Story features a boy who learns a valuable lesson about being kind during a fishing trip with his dad.
- "Making Tracks to Meet Jesus." Article describes a mission trip to Peru in which a medical clinic was set up.

RIGHTS AND PAYMENT

All rights. Written material, payment rates vary. Pays on acceptance. Provides 1 author's copy.

➡EDITOR'S COMMENTS

We do not accept unsolicited submissions. If you think you would like to write for us, send along your résumé for us to review. Our writers must be of the Southern Baptist faith.

DESCRIPTION AND INTERESTS

This popular consumer magazine is dedicated to American women who want to look good, be healthy, and do well in life. Included in its editorial mix are pieces on marriage, relationships, parenting, healthy lifestyles, fashion, fitness, and home decor. Circ: 4.1 million.

Audience: Women
Frequency: Monthly
Website: www.lhj.com

FREELANCE POTENTIAL

85% written by nonstaff writers. Publishes 25 freelance submissions yearly; 1% by unpublished writers, 5% by authors who are new to the magazine. Receives 2,400 queries yearly.

SUBMISSIONS

Query with résumé, outline, and clips or writing samples for nonfiction. Accepts fiction through literary agents only. Accepts hard copy. SASE. Responds in 1–3 months.

- Articles: 1,500–2,000 words. Informational and how-to articles; profiles; interviews; and personal experience pieces. Topics include family issues, parenting, social concerns, fashion, beauty, and women's health.
- Fiction: Word lengths vary. Genres vary.
- Depts/columns: Word lengths vary. Motherhood, marriage, self-help, beauty, home, health, food, news, and lifestyle features.

SAMPLE ISSUE

166 pages (15% advertising): 7 articles; 14 depts/columns. Sample copy, $2.49 at newsstands.

- "Red Light Running." Article reports on the number of fatalities caused by drivers running red lights, and what is being done to curtail the problem.
- Sample dept/column: "Mind Over Matters" ponders why our high-profile sex scandals all have men at the helm.

RIGHTS AND PAYMENT

All rights. All material, payment rates vary. Pays on publication. Provides 2 contributor's copies.

➡EDITOR'S COMMENTS

We are about empowering women to lead the kinds of lives they *want* to have. We look for articles that inspire as well as inform. We are a high-profile magazine and accept only the highest quality writing.

Ladybug

Cricket Magazine Group
70 East Lake Street, Suite 300
Chicago, IL 60601

Submissions Editor: Jenny Gillespie

DESCRIPTION AND INTERESTS
Filled with lively stories that retain a sense of joy and wonder, this magazine is designed to be read aloud to preschoolers. Poems, activities, nonfiction, and rebus stories round out the editorial mix. Circ: 125,000.

Audience: 3–6 years
Frequency: 9 times each year
Website: www.ladybugmagkids.com

FREELANCE POTENTIAL
100% written by nonstaff writers. Publishes 100 freelance submissions yearly. Receives 2,400 unsolicited mss yearly.

SUBMISSIONS
Send complete ms with word count. Accepts hard copy and simultaneous submissions if identified. SASE. Responds in 6 months.

- Articles: To 400 words. Informational and how-to articles; and humor. Topics include nature, animals, family, the environment, and other age-appropriate topics.
- Fiction: To 800 words. Read-aloud, early reader, picture, and rebus stories. Genres include adventure, humor, fantasy, folktales, and contemporary and multicultural fiction.
- Other: Puzzles, learning activities, games, crafts, finger plays, action rhymes, cartoons, and songs. Poetry, to 20 lines.

SAMPLE ISSUE
36 pages (no advertising): 6 stories; 6 poems; 1 song; 1 finger play; 1 four-page activity section; 1 cartoon. Sample copy, $5. Guidelines available at website.

- "The Halloween Costume Countdown." Story features animal friends who are busy preparing Halloween costumes.
- "Max and Kate." Story tells of a boy and girl who spend the day apple-picking at a nearby orchard.

RIGHTS AND PAYMENT
Rights vary. Stories and articles, $.25 per word; $25 minimum. Poems, $3 per line; $25 minimum. Other material, payment rates vary. Pays on publication. Provides 6 copies.

☙EDITOR'S COMMENTS
We do not distribute theme lists for upcoming issues. Your best bet is to read several of our past issues and familiarize yourself with this age group.

L.A. Parent

443 East Irving Drive
Burbank, CA 91504

Editor: Carolyn Graham

DESCRIPTION AND INTERESTS
This regional parenting magazine is dedicated to all aspects of raising children in the Los Angeles area. Its articles cover parenting, education, and activities and outings in the region. Circ: 120,000.

Audience: Parents
Frequency: Monthly
Website: www.laparent.com

FREELANCE POTENTIAL
50% written by nonstaff writers. Publishes 20 freelance submissions yearly; 5% by unpublished writers, 10% by authors who are new to the magazine. Receives 120 queries yearly.

SUBMISSIONS
Query with clips. Prefers email queries to carolyn.graham@parenthood.com; will accept hard copy. SASE. Responds in 6 months.

- Articles: 400–1,500 words. Informational, practical application, and how-to articles; profiles; and interviews. Topics include parenting, health, fitness, social issues, travel, and gifted and special education.
- Depts/columns: 1,000 words. Family life, technology, travel destinations, and crafts.
- Artwork: B/W or color prints or transparencies.

SAMPLE ISSUE
58 pages (60% advertising): 2 articles; 8 depts/columns. Sample copy, $3. Guidelines and theme list available.

- "Beyond Time-Out." Article examines unruly child behavior and provides tips for restoring the balance of power in the household.
- Sample dept/column: "Kids Off the Couch!" offers several regional opportunities to introduce children to puppet theater.

RIGHTS AND PAYMENT
First serial rights. Written material, payment rates vary. Pays on publication. Provides contributor's copies.

☙EDITOR'S COMMENTS
While we will work with authors who do not live in the Los Angeles area, we insist that all material have a local angle or perspective. Any topic of interest to parents will most likely interest us, but articles must include information that readers can use in their own communities. Local resources should be highlighted whenever possible.

Leadership for Student Activities

1904 Association Drive
Reston, VA 20191-1537

Editor: James Paterson

DESCRIPTION AND INTERESTS
Read by student council members in middle school and high school and their advisors, this magazine is filled with articles about program ideas, motivational techniques, and nurturing leadership skills. Circ: 30,000.

Audience: YA
Frequency: 9 times each year
Website: www.nasc.us

FREELANCE POTENTIAL
67% written by nonstaff writers. Publishes 18–25 freelance submissions yearly; 75% by unpublished writers, 50% by new authors. Receives 12–24 queries, 48 mss yearly.

SUBMISSIONS
Query with clips; or send complete ms. Accepts hard copy and email submissions to jamespaterson7@gmail.com. SASE. Responds to queries in 2 weeks, to mss in 1 month.

- Articles: 1,200–1,700 words. Informational and how-to articles; profiles; and interviews. Topics include student activities, leadership development, and careers.
- Depts/columns: Reports on special events, 100–350 words. Advice for and by activity advisors, 1,000–1,500 words. National and regional news, leadership plans, and opinion pieces, word lengths vary.
- Artwork: B/W or color prints or slides.
- Other: Submit seasonal material 4 months in advance.

SAMPLE ISSUE
44 pages (21% advertising): 10 articles; 7 depts/columns. Sample copy, free with 9x12 SASE ($1.24 postage). Guidelines and theme list available.

- "Yeah, That's the Ticket!" Article explains how even small bits of student recognition can go far in motivating volunteers.
- Sample dept/column: "Civics in Action" profiles a program that puts students on a city's advisory panel.

RIGHTS AND PAYMENT
All rights. Written material, payment rates vary. Payment policy varies. Provides 5 contributor's copies.

❧EDITOR'S COMMENTS
Students, advisors, and freelance writers are all encouraged to write for us.

Learning & Leading with Technology

180 West Eighth Avenue
Eugene, OR 97401-2916

Managing Editor: Paul Wurster

DESCRIPTION AND INTERESTS
Featuring practical ideas for using today's technology tools to improve teaching and learning, this magazine is targeted to primary and secondary educators. The membership magazine of the International Society of Technology in Education, it offers articles, reviews, and case studies. Circ: 25,000.

Audience: Educators, grades K–12
Frequency: 8 times each year
Website: www.iste.org/LL

FREELANCE POTENTIAL
70% written by nonstaff writers. Publishes 70 freelance submissions yearly; 60% by unpublished writers, 75% by authors who are new to the magazine. Receives 144 queries yearly.

SUBMISSIONS
Query. Accepts email queries to submissions@iste.org and simultaneous submissions if identified. Response time varies.

- Articles: 300–2,000 words. Informational and how-to articles; and personal experience pieces. Topics include computers and computer science, software, technology, media applications, teaching methods, and telecommunications.
- Depts/columns: Word lengths vary. Research, software reviews, and curriculum ideas.
- Artwork: Color prints. Line art.

SAMPLE ISSUE
48 pages (20% advertising): 4 articles; 1 story; 15 depts/columns. Sample copy, free with 9x12 SASE (3 first-class stamps). Guidelines and editorial calendar available at website.

- "Computing in the Clouds." Article explains how free Web-based applications can help teachers, students, and school districts.
- Sample dept/column: "Point/Counterpoint" presents the differing viewpoints of two students concerning the effectiveness of Facebook as a communication tool.

RIGHTS AND PAYMENT
All rights; returns limited rights to author upon request. No payment. Provides 3 contributor's copies.

❧EDITOR'S COMMENTS
Our writers are typically education practitioners. One of our particular needs is for articles pertaining to Web 3.0.

Lexington Family Magazine

138 East Reynolds Road, Suite 201
Lexington, KY 40517

Publisher: Dana Tackett

DESCRIPTION AND INTERESTS
This regional publication offers parents in central Kentucky the most up-to-date information on activities and events in the area, as well as articles on parenting topics. Circ: 30,000.
Audience: Parents
Frequency: Monthly
Website: www.lexingtonfamily.com

FREELANCE POTENTIAL
50% written by nonstaff writers. Publishes 36 freelance submissions yearly; 40% by authors who are new to the magazine. Receives 250 unsolicited mss yearly.

SUBMISSIONS
Query or send complete ms. Accepts hard copy and email to info@lexingtonfamily.com. SASE. Response time varies.

- Articles: 500–1,500 words. Informational and how-to articles. Topics include parenting, the arts, hobbies, current events, education, health, fitness, recreation, regional history, multicultural issues, popular culture, science, technology, family travel, and women's issues.
- Depts/columns: 800 words. News briefs and family health tips.
- Artwork: B/W and color prints. Line art.
- Other: Puzzles, activities, and poetry.

SAMPLE ISSUE
32 pages (50% advertising): 5 articles; 4 depts/columns. Sample copy, free with 9x12 SASE ($1.50 postage). Guidelines and theme list available.

- "Birthdays." Article provides ideas for hosting parties that help others, and includes an extensive list of party venues and suppliers.
- "Sunproofing Summer Camp." Article lists ways parents can protect children from the damaging effects of the summer sun.
- Sample dept/column: "After School" offers tips for providing children with a safe horseback riding experience.

RIGHTS AND PAYMENT
All rights. Written material, payment rates vary. Pays on publication. Provides 2 copies.

➡️EDITOR'S COMMENTS
Useful information, sound advice, and a parent perspective are always sought. Please keep the focus local.

LibrarySparks

401 South Wright Road
P.O. Box 5207
Janesville, WI 53547

Submissions

DESCRIPTION AND INTERESTS
Bursting with exciting, hands-on program ideas and activities, *LibrarySparks* serves as a resource for children's and elementary school librarians. It also features articles on building reading skills, making curriculum connections, and promoting the library. Circ: Unavailable.
Audience: Librarians and teachers, grades K–6
Frequency: 9 times each year
Website: www.librarysparks.com

FREELANCE POTENTIAL
100% written by nonstaff writers. Publishes 15 freelance submissions yearly; 25% by authors who are new to the magazine. Receives 20 queries yearly.

SUBMISSIONS
Query. Accepts hard copy and email queries to librarysparks@sfsdayton.com. SASE. Response time varies.

- Articles: Word lengths vary. Informational articles and profiles. Topics include connecting literature to curricula, lesson plans for librarians, teaching library skills, children's authors and illustrators, and ideas for motivating children to read.
- Depts/columns: Word lengths vary. New resources, author profiles, storytelling activities, lesson plans, and helpful hints.
- Other: Reproducible activities and crafts.

SAMPLE ISSUE
56 pages (no advertising): 1 article; 14 depts/columns. Sample copy available at website. Guidelines and editorial calendar available.

- "Sports and Good Sports." Article explores how the themes of fair-mindedness, respect, and effort to learn can permeate library programs across the curriculum.
- Sample dept/column: "Storytime" offers ideas for hosting a storytime with an "I'm Mad!" theme.

RIGHTS AND PAYMENT
Rights vary. Written material, payment rates vary. Pays on publication. Provides 1 contributor's copy.

➡️EDITOR'S COMMENTS
We're open to all sorts of ideas that can bring library programs to life. Be sure you are prepared to offer hands-on programming ideas that can be replicated.

The Lion

Lions Clubs International
300 West 22nd Street
Oak Brook, IL 60523-8842

Senior Editor: Jay Copp

DESCRIPTION AND INTERESTS

This publication of the world's largest service organization covers the community-oriented activities—many of them benefitting children and families—of its clubs on the local, national, and international levels. Circ: 425,000.

Audience: Lions Clubs members
Frequency: 11 times each year
Website: www.lionsclubs.org

FREELANCE POTENTIAL

50% written by nonstaff writers. Publishes 30 freelance submissions yearly; 20% by authors who are new to the magazine. Receives 120 queries, 60 unsolicited mss yearly.

SUBMISSIONS

Prefers query; will accept complete ms. Accepts hard copy and email submissions to jay.copp@lionsclubs.org. SASE. Responds to queries in 10 days, to mss in 2 months.

- Articles: To 1,500 words. Informational articles; profiles; humor; and photo-essays. Topics include Lions Clubs service projects, disabilities, social issues, and special education.
- Depts/columns: Staff written.
- Artwork: 5x7 or larger color prints; JPEG files.

SAMPLE ISSUE

56 pages (6% advertising): 4 articles; 14 depts/columns. Sample copy, free. Writers' guidelines available.

- "Why Lions Matter in Small-Town America." Article explains the impact Lions Clubs' projects can have on small towns.
- "Second Tour of Duty." Article reports on a Lions member who returned to Vietnam, where he once was severely wounded as a soldier, with 2,400 pairs of eyeglasses to donate to villagers.
- "The Day I Became a Lion." Article profiles several members on their most meaningful experiences as a Lion.

RIGHTS AND PAYMENT

All rights. Written material, $100–$1,000. Pays on acceptance. Provides 4–10 author's copies.

➥EDITOR'S COMMENTS

We don't receive enough quality queries from established writers. You need not be a Lions Clubs member yourself to write about one of our members or projects. We are always in need of high-quality photographs.

Listen Magazine

35 West Oak Ridge Drive
Hagerstown, MD 21740

Editor: Céleste Perrino-Walker

DESCRIPTION AND INTERESTS

Listen Magazine promotes the development of good habits and high ideals of physical, social, and mental health. Written primarily for teens, it focuses on drug-abuse prevention and advocates for total abstinence from tobacco, alcohol, and other drugs. Circ: 40,000.

Audience: Students, grades 7–12
Frequency: 9 times each year
Website: www.listenmagazine.org

FREELANCE POTENTIAL

100% written by nonstaff writers. Publishes 90+ freelance submissions yearly; 15% by unpublished writers, 20% by authors who are new to the magazine. Receives 500–600 queries, 25–50 unsolicited mss yearly.

SUBMISSIONS

Query or send complete ms. Accepts hard copy, email to editor@listenmagazine.org, and simultaneous submissions if identified. SASE. Response time varies.

- Articles: 350–750 words. Informational articles; profiles; and self-help pieces. Topics include peer pressure, decision making, self-esteem, self-discipline, family conflict, sports, hobbies, friendship, and healthy choices.
- Depts/columns: Word lengths vary. Opinion pieces, social issues, and trends.

SAMPLE ISSUE

16 pages (no advertising): 7 articles; 2 depts/columns. Sample copy, $2 with 9x12 SASE (2 first-class stamps). Guidelines and editorial calendar available at website.

- "Open Hearts, Open Minds: The Keys to Tolerance." Article stresses the need to show respect and appreciation to all individuals.
- "Meth 101." Article details the destructiveness of methamphetamine addiction.

RIGHTS AND PAYMENT

All rights. Written material, $.05–$.10 per word. Pays on acceptance. Provides 3 contributor's copies.

➥EDITOR'S COMMENTS

Because our magazine is used extensively in public high school classes, we do not accept articles that have an overt religious emphasis. It's important to stick to the word counts. Many submissions are simply too long.

Live

General Council of the Assemblies of God
1445 North Boonville Avenue
Springfield, MO 65802-1894

Editor: Richard Bennett

DESCRIPTION AND INTERESTS
This take-home paper for adult religious education classes publishes upbeat informational articles, true stories, and fiction that encourage Christian readers to apply biblical principles to everyday problems, including parenting issues and family relationships. Circ: 38,000.

Audience: Adults
Frequency: Quarterly, in weekly sections

FREELANCE POTENTIAL
100% written by nonstaff writers. Publishes 110 freelance submissions yearly; 20% by unpublished writers, 20% by authors who are new to the magazine. Receives 96 queries, 1,320 unsolicited mss yearly.

SUBMISSIONS
Query or send complete ms. Accepts hard copy, email submissions to rl-live@gph.org, and simultaneous submissions if identified. SASE. Responds in 6 weeks.

- Articles: 400–1,100 words. Informational and how-to articles; humor; and personal experience pieces. Topics include family issues, parenting, and general Christian living issues.
- Fiction: 400–1,100 words. Genres include inspirational fiction, adventure, and stories about family celebrations and traditions.
- Other: Poetry, 12–25 lines. Submit seasonal material 18 months in advance.

SAMPLE ISSUE
8 pages (no advertising): 2 articles; 1 dept/column. Sample copy, free with #10 SASE (1 first-class stamp). Guidelines available.

- "That Wife of Mine." Article explains how a husband came to understand what his wife had found by turning to Jesus Christ.
- "What a Nice Young Man." True story relates the effect one act of kindness can have.

RIGHTS AND PAYMENT
First and second rights. Written material, $.10 per word for first rights; $.07 per word for second rights. Pays on acceptance. Provides 2 contributor's copies.

⟿EDITOR'S COMMENTS
We are especially searching for articles relating to holidays other than Thanksgiving and Christmas, as well as articles on spirit-filled living.

Living Safety

Canada Safety Council
1020 Thomas Spratt Place
Ottawa, Ontario K1G 5L5
Canada

President: Jack Smith

DESCRIPTION AND INTERESTS
The Canada Safety Council publishes this magazine as a tool for employers to use in their safety programs. Its goal is to raise safety awareness to the point where safety becomes a personal value and a conscious lifestyle choice. Circ: 80,000.

Audience: All ages
Frequency: Quarterly
Website: www.safety-council.org

FREELANCE POTENTIAL
75% written by nonstaff writers. Publishes 25 freelance submissions yearly; 65% by unpublished writers, 10% by authors who are new to the magazine. Receives 25 queries yearly.

SUBMISSIONS
Query with résumé and clips or writing samples. Accepts hard copy. SAE/IRC. Responds in 2 weeks.

- Articles: 1,500–2,500 words. Informational articles. Topics include recreational, home, and traffic safety; family health and safety; and environmental concerns.
- Depts/columns: Word lengths vary. Safety news, research findings, opinions, and product recalls.
- Other: Children's activities.

SAMPLE ISSUE
30 pages (no advertising): 4 articles; 4 depts/columns; 1 kids' page. Sample copy, free with 9x12 SAE/IRC. Guidelines available.

- "Falls: A Childhood Concern." Article reports that too many children are still falling from windows and balconies, despite news alerts and safety campaigns.
- "Effects of Lead on Human Health." Article outlines the health risks associated with lead exposure.
- Sample dept/column: "Kids' Page" offers an activity that teaches about campfire safety.

RIGHTS AND PAYMENT
All rights. Articles, to $500. Depts/columns, payment rates vary. Pays on acceptance. Provides 1–5 contributor's copies.

⟿EDITOR'S COMMENTS
Our magazine serves as a credible, reliable source of safety information, education, and awareness in all aspects of Canadian life—in traffic, at home, at work, and at leisure.

Long Island Woman

P.O. Box 176
Malverne, NY 11565

Publisher: Arie Nadboy

DESCRIPTION AND INTERESTS

With a readership consisting of upscale, educated women, this regional magazine features general interest articles on topics of interest to its audience. It also spotlights local entertainment venues, and provides a comprehensive list of area support groups. Circ: 40,000.

Audience: Women, 35–65 years
Frequency: Monthly
Website: www.liwomanonline.com

FREELANCE POTENTIAL

50% written by nonstaff writers. Publishes 25 freelance submissions yearly. Receives 500 queries, 350 unsolicited mss yearly.

SUBMISSIONS

Query or send complete ms. Accepts email submissions to editor@liwomanonline.com. Availability of artwork improves chance of acceptance. Responds in 8–10 weeks.

- Articles: 350–2,000 words. Informational and how-to articles; profiles; and interviews. Topics include regional news, family, health, lifestyles, sports, fitness, nutrition, fashion, beauty, business, finance, decorating, gardening, entertainment, media, travel, and celebrities.
- Depts/columns: 500–1,000 words. Book reviews, health advice, personal essays, and profiles.
- Artwork: Electronic B/W and color prints. Line art.
- Other: Submit seasonal material 3 months in advance.

SAMPLE ISSUE

40 pages (60% advertising): 1 article; 6 depts/columns; 1 calendar. Sample copy, $5. Guidelines available at website.

- "Two Rivers Run Through It." Article profiles entertainers Joan and Melissa Rivers.
- Sample dept/column: "Sustenance" offers cooking tips from professional chefs.

RIGHTS AND PAYMENT

One-time and electronic rights. Written material, $70–$200. Kill fee, 20%. Pays on publication. Provides 1 tearsheet.

➛EDITOR'S COMMENTS

Any topic that would be of interest to women age 35 and over will be of interest to us. Locally-focused articles are always best.

The Magazine

643 Queen Street East
Toronto, Ontario M4M 1G4
Canada

Editor: Karen Wong

DESCRIPTION AND INTERESTS

The Magazine is strictly for older children and young teens—no adults allowed! The digest-sized publication is filled with reviews of movies, music, and television; comics; games; celebrity information; and articles on healthy lifestyles and the environment. Circ: 15,000.

Audience: 8–14 years
Frequency: Monthly
Website: www.themagazine.ca

FREELANCE POTENTIAL

60% written by nonstaff writers. Publishes 20 freelance submissions yearly; 60% by unpublished writers, 30% by new authors. Receives 240 queries and unsolicited mss yearly.

SUBMISSIONS

Query or send complete ms. Accepts hard copy. SAE/IRC. Response time varies.

- Articles: To 1,000 words. Informational articles; profiles; interviews; and humor. Topics include popular culture, movies, music, video games, books, and lifestyle subjects.
- Depts/columns: Media reviews, to 4 sentences. News, entertainment, and health briefs, word lengths vary.
- Other: Contests, quizzes, surveys, posters, and horoscopes.

SAMPLE ISSUE

112 pages: 8 articles; 1 story; 24 depts/columns; 10 contests; 3 posters; 1 quiz. Sample copy, $3.95.

- "Online Gaming." Article outlines the dangers of playing too many online games, and provides warning signs that might indicate a habit that's out of control.
- "Get Stoked This Summer." Article examines a new television cartoon that takes place in a British Columbia beach town.
- Sample dept/column: "Booky" offers previews of new books for teens.

RIGHTS AND PAYMENT

All rights. Written material, $10–$60 Canadian. Payment policy varies.

➛EDITOR'S COMMENTS

Most of our editorial material comes from writers under age 25. We welcome submissions from youngsters about what they're interested in—because that's what our readers will be interested in.

The Magazine of Fantasy & Science Fiction

P.O. Box 3447
Hoboken, NJ 07030

Editor: Gordon Van Gelder

DESCRIPTION AND INTERESTS
Founded in 1949, *The Magazine of Fantasy & Science Fiction* publishes stories in these genres from writers at all stages of their careers. Although fiction is the only avenue open to freelancers, the magazine is also home to profiles, reviews, and critiques. Circ: 45,000.

Audience: YA–Adult
Frequency: 6 times each year
Website: www.sfsite.com/fsf

FREELANCE POTENTIAL
98% written by nonstaff writers. Publishes 60–90 freelance submissions yearly; 10% by unpublished writers, 20% by authors who are new to the magazine. Receives 6,000–8,400 unsolicited mss yearly.

SUBMISSIONS
Send complete ms. Accepts hard copy. No electronic or simultaneous submissions. SASE. Responds in 2 months.

- Fiction: To 25,000 words. Short stories and novellas. Genres include science fiction, fantasy, and humor.
- Depts/columns: Staff written.

SAMPLE ISSUE
258 pages (1% advertising): 7 novellas; 3 short stories; 1 poem; 2 classic reprints; 4 depts/columns. Sample copy, $6. Guidelines available at website.

- "You Are Such a One." Short story follows a middle-aged woman as she struggles with the discovery that she is the ghost that has been haunting a house.
- "Hunchster." Short story tells of a young man with Asperger's Syndrome who, relying on his uncannily accurate hunches, creates a video time machine.

RIGHTS AND PAYMENT
First world rights with option of anthology rights. Written material, $.06–$.09 per word. Pays on acceptance. Provides 2 contributor's copies.

➥EDITOR'S COMMENTS
We have been receiving a lot of science fiction, but would like to see more fantasy stories come our way. We prefer character-oriented stories. Not all stories accepted are science fiction or fantasy through-and-through. Some may have just a slight sci-fi or fantasy element, but it must be present.

Mahoning Valley Parent

100 DeBartolo Place, Suite 210
Youngstown, OH 44512

Editor & Publisher: Amy Leigh Wilson

DESCRIPTION AND INTERESTS
Parents in Ohio's Mahoning Valley turn to this magazine for the latest information regarding parenting, child development, education, and family relationships. It also features information on where to go and what to do in the area. Circ: 50,000.

Audience: Parents
Frequency: Monthly
Website: www.forparentsonline.com

FREELANCE POTENTIAL
99% written by nonstaff writers. Publishes 100 freelance submissions yearly; 5% by unpublished writers, 20% by new authors. Receives 500 unsolicited mss yearly.

SUBMISSIONS
Send complete ms. Accepts hard copy and email to editor@mvparentmagazine.com. Retains all material for possible use; does not respond until publication. Include SASE if retaining ms is not acceptable.

- Articles: 1,000–1,800 words. Informational and how-to articles; profiles; and reviews. Topics include regional news, current events, parenting, the environment, nature, health, crafts, travel, recreation, hobbies, and ethnic and multicultural subjects.
- Depts/columns: Word lengths vary. Parenting issues, book reviews, events for kids.
- Artwork: B/W or color prints.
- Other: Submit seasonal material 3 months in advance.

SAMPLE ISSUE
34 pages (70% advertising): 2 articles; 4 depts/columns; 1 special section. Sample copy, free with 9x12 SASE ($.77 postage). Guidelines and editorial calendar available.

- "Ideas to Keep Learning Throughout the Summer." Article provides ways kids can learn while having a blast in the summer.
- Sample dept/column: "Successful Single Parenting" offers tips for reducing one's financial anxiety.

RIGHTS AND PAYMENT
One-time rights. Articles, $20–$50. Pays on publication. Provides tearsheets.

➥EDITOR'S COMMENTS
Your article should feature local sources, local information, and local resources.

The Majellan

Champion of the Family

Maryland Family

P.O. Box 43
Brighton, Victoria 3186
Australia

Editor: Father Michael Gilbert

10750 Little Patuxent Parkway
Columbia, MD 21044

Editor: Betsy Stein

DESCRIPTION AND INTERESTS

A magazine of the Australian Redemptorists, *The Majellan* fosters Christian family life and marriage. Its articles help couples build strong relationships based on Catholic values. Prayers and Bible lessons are also included in each issue. Most of its readers are Catholics living in Australia and New Zealand. Circ: 23,000.

Audience: Parents
Frequency: Quarterly
Website: www.majellan.org.au

DESCRIPTION AND INTERESTS

Updates on regional family events, news of interest to parents, and substantive articles on child health, behavior, and learning appear in this free publication. It targets parents living in and around Baltimore. Circ: 50,000.

Audience: Parents
Frequency: Monthly
Website: www.marylandfamilymagazine.com

FREELANCE POTENTIAL

50% written by nonstaff writers. Publishes 20 freelance submissions yearly; 15% by unpublished writers, 20% by authors who are new to the magazine. Receives dozens of unsolicited mss yearly.

FREELANCE POTENTIAL

75% written by nonstaff writers. Publishes 50 freelance submissions yearly; 10% by unpublished writers, 10% by authors who are new to the magazine. Receives 360–600 queries each year.

SUBMISSIONS

Send complete ms. Accepts hard copy and email submissions to editor@majellan.org (Microsoft Word or RTF attachments). SAE/IRC. Response time varies.

- Articles: 750–1,500 words. Informational articles and personal experience pieces. Topics include marriage, parenting, and Catholic family life.
- Depts/columns: Staff written.
- Other: Filler; readers' prayers and photos.

SUBMISSIONS

Query stating areas of expertise. Accepts hard copy. SASE. Responds in 1 month.

- Articles: 800–1,000 words. Informational and how-to articles; profiles; and personal experience pieces. Topics include family issues, parenting, education, recreation, travel, summer camp, sports, and health.
- Depts/columns: Word lengths vary. News briefs, local events, and health tips. "Family Matters," 100–400 words.
- Artwork: Color prints and transparencies.
- Other: Submit seasonal material 2–3 months in advance.

SAMPLE ISSUE

48 pages (15% advertising): 9 articles; 3 depts/columns.

- "More Here Than Meets the Eye." Article discusses the different sacraments in the Catholic religion and their meanings.
- "Because They're Worth It." Article explains how parents communicate messages to their children with every word, facial expression, and action.
- "A Rich Young Nation." Article distills information released by the Australian Catholic Bishops Conference.

SAMPLE ISSUE

46 pages (50% advertising): 7 articles; 2 depts/columns. Sample copy, free with 9x12 SASE.

- "He Was a Gift." Article chronicles the joy and sadness of a mother who gave birth to a baby with a fatal chromosomal defect.
- "Too Many Mildly Ill Kids Sent Home from Preschool." Article reports on a study that shows too many children are being sent home for just the sniffles.

RIGHTS AND PAYMENT

Rights vary. Written material, $50–$80 Australian. Pays on acceptance.

RIGHTS AND PAYMENT

First and electronic rights. Written material, payment rates vary. Pays on publication. Provides 1 contributor's copy.

➤EDITOR'S COMMENTS

Your submission should support strong Christian family values. Child development issues and teen topics are of special interest. Familiarize yourself with our tone and topics first.

➤EDITOR'S COMMENTS

Articles that have a local angle and are written by freelancers from the Baltimore area have a better chance of being accepted. Send useful information for busy parents.

Massive Online Gamer

4635 McEwen Drive
Dallas, TX 75244

Editor: Douglas Kale

DESCRIPTION AND INTERESTS
Enthusiasts of massively multiplayer online (MMO) games read this magazine for game reviews and descriptions, strategies, and techniques. It covers all types of games, including fantasy, science fiction, adventure, and war games. It also includes interviews and in-game item giveaways. Circ: 100,000.
Audience: YA–Adult
Frequency: 6 times each year
Website: www.massiveonlinegamer.com

FREELANCE POTENTIAL
90% written by nonstaff writers. Publishes 120+ freelance submissions yearly; 20% by unpublished writers, 70% by authors who are new to the magazine. Receives 200+ queries each year.

SUBMISSIONS
Query with writing sample and list of MMO experience. Prefers email queries to dkale@beckett.com; will accept hard copy. SASE. Response time varies.

- Articles: Word lengths vary. Informational and how-to articles; personal experience pieces; and interviews. Topics include MMO game descriptions, strategies, and gaming techniques.
- Depts/columns: Word lengths vary. MMO etiquette, technology, contests, and news.

SAMPLE ISSUE
88 pages: 21 articles; 4 depts/columns. Sample copy and guidelines available upon email request to mog@beckett.com.

- "A Look at Wizard 101." Article reviews a family-style MMO that features a unique method of combat that will appeal to both children and adults.
- "A Look at Going Rogue." Article interviews Melissa Bianco, the lead designer for City of Heroes, about its upcoming expansion.

RIGHTS AND PAYMENT
All rights. Written material, $25–$150. Pays 45 days after publication.

☛EDITOR'S COMMENTS
We're always interested in leveling guides, reviews, previews, and exclusive interviews with personalities in the world of MMO. Your query should demonstrate your extensive knowledge of this field.

MetroFamily

306 South Bryant, Suite C-152
Edmond, OK 73034

Editor: Mari Farthing

DESCRIPTION AND INTERESTS
A parenting magazine for residents of central Oklahoma, *MetroFamily* features articles that educate, inform, and inspire parents and empower families. It covers all areas of parenting, child development, and family relationships. Circ: 35,000.
Audience: Parents
Frequency: Monthly
Website: www.metrofamilymagazine.com

FREELANCE POTENTIAL
60% written by nonstaff writers. Publishes 45 freelance submissions yearly; 10% by unpublished writers, 10% by authors who are new to the magazine. Receives 1,000 queries and unsolicited mss yearly.

SUBMISSIONS
Query or send complete ms. Accepts email to editor@metrofamilymagazine.com (no attachments). Responds to queries in 3 weeks, to mss in 1 month.

- Articles: 300–600 words. Informational and how-to articles; profiles; and personal experience pieces. Topics include parenting, education, health and fitness, travel, and recreational activities.
- Depts/columns: Staff written.

SAMPLE ISSUE
42 pages: 3 articles; 11 depts/columns. Sample copy and guidelines, free with 10x13 SASE. Guidelines also available at website.

- "Get Out There! Why Kids Need Nature." Article examines why something as simple as a walk around the neighborhood can be beneficial for children.
- "The 30-Day Financial Freeze: How a Norman Mom Conducted a Money Makeover." Article reports on a woman who went a full month without spending any money.

RIGHTS AND PAYMENT
First North American serial rights. Articles, $25–$50. Kill fee, 100%. Pays on publication. Provides 1 contributor's copy.

☛EDITOR'S COMMENTS
"Local, local, local," is our editorial mantra. We prefer to work with writers from our region, and all articles must have a local perspective. We do not shy away from humor, so feel free to brighten your message with levity.

MetroKids

1412-1414 Pine Street
Philadelphia, PA 19102

Executive Editor: Tom Livingston

DESCRIPTION AND INTERESTS
The articles in *MetroKids* offer readers a fresh approach to common parenting issues. Its essays and personal experience pieces provide parenting resources, tips, and ideas tailored to parents in the greater Philadelphia region. Circ: 115,000.

Audience: Parents
Frequency: Monthly
Website: www.metrokids.com

FREELANCE POTENTIAL
30% written by nonstaff writers. Publishes 25 freelance submissions yearly; 10% by authors who are new to the magazine. Receives 600 unsolicited mss yearly.

SUBMISSIONS
Send complete ms. Accepts email submissions to editor@metrokids.com (Microsoft Word or text attachments). Availability of artwork improves chance of acceptance. Responds if interested.

- Articles: 550–900 words. Informational, how-to, and self-help articles. Topics include pregnancy, childbirth, parenting, pets, computers, education, health, fitness, nature, the environment, travel, recreation, and social issues.
- Depts/columns: 550–700 words. School news, product recalls, health notes, opinions, book reviews, nature activities, special education information, and local events.
- Artwork: Color prints or transparencies.

SAMPLE ISSUE
52 pages (15% advertising): 5 articles; 8 depts/columns. Sample copy, free with 9x12 SASE. Guidelines available.

- "Rebels with a Cause." Article discusses several ways to curb rebellion during the teen years.
- Sample dept/column: "BabyFirst" offers tips for first-time expectant dads.

RIGHTS AND PAYMENT
One-time and electronic rights. Written material, $35–$50. Artwork, payment rates vary. Pays on publication. Provides 1 contributor's copy.

➥EDITOR'S COMMENTS
We prefer articles with a local angle. General topics will be considered, however, especially if they can be localized with sidebars.

Metro Parent Magazine

22041 Woodward Avenue
Ferndale, MI 48220

Managing Editor: Julia Elliott

DESCRIPTION AND INTERESTS
Metro Parent Magazine mixes ideas for family fun with more serious, substantive pieces on child development, health, education, and family management. Parents can pick it up free of charge at various sites throughout Detroit and southeast Michigan. Circ: 80,000.

Audience: Parents
Frequency: Monthly
Website: www.metroparent.com

FREELANCE POTENTIAL
75% written by nonstaff writers. Publishes 250 freelance submissions yearly; 5% by unpublished writers, 35% by authors who are new to the magazine. Receives 960+ queries and unsolicited mss yearly.

SUBMISSIONS
Query or send complete ms. Accepts email submissions to jelliott@metroparent.com. Responds in 1–2 days.

- Articles: 1,500–2,500 words. Informational, self-help, and how-to articles; interviews; and personal experience pieces. Topics include pregnancy, childbirth, parenting, family life, education, child development, social issues, travel, finance, fitness, health, recreation, entertainment, and nature.
- Depts/columns: 850–900 words. Family fun, new product information, women's health, media reviews, computers, and crafts.

SAMPLE ISSUE
68 pages (60% advertising): 6 articles; 12 depts/columns. Sample copy, free. Guidelines available at website.

- "The Perfect Moms' Night Out." Article explores simple, inexpensive ways to have fun with girlfriends.
- "Babysitter in the Making." Article tells how parents can prepare tweens or teens to successfully take care of younger children.

RIGHTS AND PAYMENT
First rights. Articles, $150–$300. Depts/columns, $50–$100. Pays on publication. Provides 1 contributor's copy.

➥EDITOR'S COMMENTS
We're looking for writing that reflects the communities we cover. Southeast Michigan ideas and sources are preferred. You must include a minimum of two sources.

Midwifery Today

P.O. Box 2672
Eugene, OR 97402

Managing Editor: Cheryl K. Smith

DESCRIPTION AND INTERESTS
Midwifery Today is a professional journal for those whose work is among the most personal of all—natural birth practitioners. Circ: 4,000.

Audience: Childbirth practitioners
Frequency: Quarterly
Website: www.midwiferytoday.com

FREELANCE POTENTIAL
90% written by nonstaff writers. Publishes 80–100 freelance submissions yearly; 35% by unpublished writers, 50% by authors who are new to the magazine. Receives 120–144 queries, 96–108 unsolicited mss yearly.

SUBMISSIONS
Query with author background; or send complete ms. Accepts email submissions to editorial@midwiferytoday.com (Microsoft Word or RTF attachments). No simultaneous submissions. Responds in 1 month.

- Articles: 800–1,500 words. Informational and instructional articles; profiles; interviews; personal experience pieces; and media reviews. Topics include feminism, health, fitness, medical care and services, diet, nutrition, and multicultural and ethnic issues related to childbirth.
- Depts/columns: Staff written.
- Artwork: Digital images at 300 dpi.

SAMPLE ISSUE
72 pages (10% advertising): 27 articles; 7 depts/columns. Sample copy, $12.50. Guidelines and editorial calendar available at website.

- "Supporting Women During Labor and Birth." Article examines the calming effects of massage during a natural birth.
- "Disturbing 'New Trends' in Tear Prevention Threaten Midwives' Autonomy." Article cites Scandinavian studies relating the use of the Ritgen maneuver during childbirth and the reduction of severe perineal tears.

RIGHTS AND PAYMENT
Joint rights. Written material, no payment. Artwork, payment rates vary. Pays on publication. Provides 2 author's copies and a 1-year subscription for articles longer than 800 words.

☙EDITOR'S COMMENTS
We accept technical, objective, instructive, and personal articles regarding natural childbirth. Do not feel constrained by our themes.

Minnesota Conservation Volunteer

500 Lafayette Road
St. Paul, MN 55155-4046

Editor: Kathleen Weflen

DESCRIPTION AND INTERESTS
Published by the Minnesota Department of Natural Resources through donor support, this magazine seeks to entice young naturalists to conserve natural resources. Its articles celebrate the state's natural beauty and environmental activities. Circ: 150,000.

Audience: Middle-grade students and teachers
Frequency: 6 times each year
Website: www.dnr.state.mn.us/volunteer

FREELANCE POTENTIAL
60% written by nonstaff writers. Publishes 25 freelance submissions yearly. Receives hundreds of queries, 40 unsolicited mss yearly.

SUBMISSIONS
Query with synopsis for feature articles and "Field Notes." Send complete ms for essays. Accepts hard copy and email queries to kathleen.weflen@dnr.state.mn.us. SASE. Response time varies.

- Articles: 1,200–1,800 words. Informational articles and essays. Topics include the natural resources, wildlife, state parks, lakes, grasslands, groundwater, biofuels, fishing, and outdoor recreation of Minnesota.
- Depts/columns: "Field Notes," 200–500 words. "A Sense of Place," and "Close Encounters," 800–1,200 words. "Young Naturalists," conservation Q&As, and wildlife profiles, word lengths vary.
- Other: Student activities and teacher guides.

SAMPLE ISSUE
82 pages: 5 articles; 7 depts/columns. Sample copy available at website.

- "Fishing After the Flood." Article reports on how fish adapted to new conditions after torrential flooding reshaped their river.
- Sample dept/column: "Sense of Place" offers an essay about a man's family time with his daughters on a camping trip.

RIGHTS AND PAYMENT
First North American serial rights with option to purchase electronic rights. Articles and essays, $.50 per word plus $100 for electronic rights. Payment policy varies.

☙EDITOR'S COMMENTS
Our mission is to inform readers of the recreational opportunities in our state's wilderness, and to foster an appreciation for them.

Mission

223 Main Street
Ottawa, Ontario K1S 1C4
Canada

Editor: Peter Pandimakil

DESCRIPTION AND INTERESTS
This peer-reviewed journal focuses on the main trends and special concerns of contemporary missiological, interreligious, and intercultural thinking. Written in both English and French, it includes scholarly articles, stories, and book reviews. Circ: 400.

Audience: YA–Adult
Frequency: Twice each year
Website: www.ustpaul.ca

FREELANCE POTENTIAL
95% written by nonstaff writers. Publishes 6–9 freelance submissions yearly; 5% by unpublished writers, 30% by authors who are new to the magazine. Receives 84 mss yearly.

SUBMISSIONS
Send complete ms with résumé. Accepts disk submissions (RTF files), email submissions to ppandimakil@ustpaul.ca, and simultaneous submissions if identified. SAE/IRC. Responds in 1–2 months.

- Articles: 8,000–10,000 words. Bilingual articles; reviews; and personal experience pieces. Topics include current events; history; religion; and multicultural, ethnic, and social issues.
- Fiction: Word lengths vary. Historical, multicultural, ethnic, and problem-solving stories.
- Artwork: 8x10 B/W and color prints.

SAMPLE ISSUE
170 pages (no advertising): 6 articles; 9 book reviews. Sample copy, $12 U.S. with 8x10 SAE/IRC. Guidelines available.

- "'God,' the Heart of 'New Evangelization': A Lesson from Peter's Missionary Discourses." Article examines the role of new evangelization by studying various stories of discourse from Peter's theology.
- "Selflessness and Trust in a Time of Crisis." Article reflects on the importance of selfless love as a basis for communal trust during the current economic crisis.

RIGHTS AND PAYMENT
Rights vary. No payment. Provides 3 copies.

☛ EDITOR'S COMMENTS
We look for interreligious articles that offer reflection on the complex situations that challenge the modern missionary. Personal experience pieces are welcome.

Momentum

National Catholic Educational Association
1077 30th Street NW, Suite 100
Washington, DC 20007-3852

Editor: Brian Gray

DESCRIPTION AND INTERESTS
Momentum focuses on the ideas, trends, and successes of Catholic school education. It is read by Catholic school teachers and administrators. Circ: 23,000.

Audience: Teachers, school administrators, and parish catechists
Frequency: Quarterly
Website: www.ncea.org

FREELANCE POTENTIAL
95% written by nonstaff writers. Publishes 90 freelance submissions yearly; 20% by unpublished writers, 65% by new authors. Receives 60 unsolicited mss yearly.

SUBMISSIONS
Send complete ms with résumé and bibliography. Accepts hard copy, disk submissions (Microsoft Word), and email submissions to momentum@ncea.org. SASE. Responds in 1–3 months.

- Articles: 1,000–1,500 words. Informational and scholarly articles on education. Topics include teacher and in-service education, educational trends, technology, research, management, and public relations—all as they relate to Catholic schools.
- Depts/columns: Book reviews, 300 words. "Trends in Technology," 900 words. "From the Field," 700 words.

SAMPLE ISSUE
80 pages (20% advertising): 15 articles; 7 depts/columns. Sample copy, free with 9x12 SASE ($1.05 postage). Guidelines and editorial calendar available at website.

- "Teachers Are Students, Too." Article relates the importance of ongoing quality professional development options for teachers.
- Sample dept/column: "Technology Trends" discusses how to stimulate religious discipleship in a digital age.

RIGHTS AND PAYMENT
First rights. Articles, $75. Depts/columns, $50. Pays on publication. Provides 2 copies.

☛ EDITOR'S COMMENTS
In addition to articles that support our monthly themes, we're interested in success stories from schools and parish religious education programs, as well as pieces that relate successful ways to encourage vocations.

MOMSense

2370 South Trenton Way
Denver, CO 80231-3822

Editor: Mary Darr

DESCRIPTION AND INTERESTS
Filled with equal parts information, inspiration, and support for mothers of preschool children, *MOMSense* is a parenting magazine with a Christian perspective. Circ: 120,000.

Audience: Mothers
Frequency: 6 times each year
Website: www.MomSense.com

FREELANCE POTENTIAL
70% written by nonstaff writers. Publishes 45–50 freelance submissions yearly; 20% by unpublished writers, 20% by authors who are new to the magazine. Receives 360–480 unsolicited mss yearly.

SUBMISSIONS
Send complete ms. Prefers email submissions to MOMSense@mops.org (Microsoft Word attachments); will accept hard copy. Availability of artwork improves chance of acceptance. SASE. Response time varies.

- Articles: 500–1,000 words. Informational articles; profiles; and personal experience pieces. Topics include parenting, religion, and humor.
- Depts/columns: Word lengths vary. Parenting and family life.
- Artwork: B/W or color prints or transparencies.
- Other: Submit seasonal material 6–12 months in advance.

SAMPLE ISSUE
32 pages: 12 articles; 8 depts/columns. Sample copy, free. Guidelines available.

- "Don't Go It Alone." Article implores mothers to reach out to others when feeling overwhelmed and admit when all is not "fine."
- Sample dept/column: "Next . . ." profiles a woman who is making a big difference in people's lives by running a tiny concession stand.

RIGHTS AND PAYMENT
First rights. Written material, $.15–$.25 per word. Payment policy varies. Provides contributor's copies.

❖EDITOR'S COMMENTS
As a Christian publication, we put an emphasis on helping others. We're always interested in articles that suggest ways in which mothers can help other mothers. While our articles are Christian-based, we are not preachy.

Mothering

P.O. Box 1690
Santa Fe, NM 87504

Articles Editor: Candace Walsh

DESCRIPTION AND INTERESTS
Founded in 1976 to serve a community of parents who believe in natural living and peaceful parenting, this magazine covers such issues as organic living, midwifery, breastfeeding, and topics that support the full potential of family life. Circ: 100,000.

Audience: Parents
Frequency: 6 times each year
Website: www.mothering.com

FREELANCE POTENTIAL
100% written by nonstaff writers. Publishes 40 freelance submissions yearly; 20% by unpublished writers, 70% by new authors. Receives hundreds of queries yearly.

SUBMISSIONS
Query with outline. Prefers email queries to editorial@mothering.com; will accept hard copy. SASE. Responds in 2–4 weeks.

- Articles: 2,000 words. Informational and factual articles; profiles; and personal experience pieces. Topics include pregnancy, childbirth, midwifery, health, homeopathy, teen issues, and organic food.
- Depts/columns: Word lengths vary. Cooking, book and product reviews, health news, parenting updates, and inspirational pieces.
- Artwork: 5x7 B/W and color prints.
- Other: Children's activities and crafts. Poetry about motherhood and families. Submit seasonal material 6–8 months in advance.

SAMPLE ISSUE
104 pages (35% advertising): 3 articles; 9 depts/columns. Sample copy, $5.95 with 9x12 SASE. Guidelines available at website.

- "River School." Article reports on the lessons learned from an eight-day rafting trip.
- Sample dept/column: "Living Treasure" profiles natural-birthing advocate Suzanne Arms.

RIGHTS AND PAYMENT
First rights. Written material, $100+. Artwork, payment rates vary. Pays on publication. Provides 2 copies and a 1-year subscription.

❖EDITOR'S COMMENTS
Our magazine is based on a foundation of reader-submitted work. Our main objective is to be truly helpful, to provide information that empowers our readers to make changes, and to support them in being their own experts.

MultiCultural Review

194 Lenox Avenue
Albany, NY 12208

Editor: Todd Goldman

DESCRIPTION AND INTERESTS
Educators and librarians who are interested in multicultural literature and non-print media subscribe to this magazine. It presents discussions of multiculturalism in America and practical pieces on multicultural pedagogy and librarianship. Circ: 3,500+.

Audience: Teachers and librarians
Frequency: Quarterly
Website: www.mcreview.com

FREELANCE POTENTIAL
80% written by nonstaff writers. Publishes 600 freelance submissions yearly; 10% by unpublished writers, 20% by authors who are new to the magazine. Receives 120 queries yearly.

SUBMISSIONS
Query with résumé and writing samples. Accepts email queries to todd@ggpubs.com. Responds in 2–3 months.

- Articles: 2,000–6,000 words. Informational and how-to articles; bibliographic essays; interviews; and opinion pieces. Topics include multiculturalism in the U.S., ethnography of specific groups, books, authors, media, education, and libraries.
- Depts/columns: Book and media reviews, 200–500 words. News, 1,500–2,000 words.
- Artwork: Line art. Prints, charts, or graphs.

SAMPLE ISSUE
98 pages (10% advertising): 5 articles; 3 depts/columns; 123 book reviews. Sample copy, $15. Writers' guidelines and editorial calendar available.

- "A Look at Multicultural Alphabet Books." Article shows how alphabet books can introduce children to different areas of the world and less familiar ethnic traditions.
- "The Making of *This Is Nollywood*." Article tells how a documentary filmmaker portrayed the African film industry.

RIGHTS AND PAYMENT
First serial rights. Articles, $50–$100. Reviews, no payment. Pays on publication. Provides 2 contributor's copies.

⬧EDITOR'S COMMENTS
Articles must be timely and geared specifically to the issues relative to or impacted by multiculturalism. Perspectives and opinions should demonstrate knowledge of diversity.

MultiMedia & Internet@Schools

14508 NE 20th Avenue, Suite 102
Vancouver, WA 98686

Editor: David Hoffman

DESCRIPTION AND INTERESTS
This magazine bills itself as "the guide to electronic tools and resources" for school library and media specialists for kindergarten through grade 12. Each issue provides information on the technology products that can be used to further teaching and learning. Circ: 12,000.

Audience: School media and technology specialists and teachers
Frequency: 6 times each year
Website: www.mmischools.com

FREELANCE POTENTIAL
90% written by nonstaff writers. Publishes 20–24 freelance submissions yearly; 20% by unpublished writers, 20% by authors who are new to the magazine. Receives 60 queries and unsolicited mss yearly.

SUBMISSIONS
Query or send complete ms. Accepts email submissions to hoffmand@infotoday.com. Availability of artwork improves chance of acceptance. Responds in 6–8 weeks.

- Articles: 1,500 words. Informational and how-to articles. Topics include K–12 education, the Internet, technology, multimedia and electronic resources, and curriculum integration.
- Depts/columns: Word lengths vary. Product news, reviews, and ideas from educators.
- Artwork: TIFF images at 300 dpi.

SAMPLE ISSUE
48 pages (15% advertising): 3 articles; 8 depts/columns. Sample copy and guidelines, $7.95 with 9x12 SASE.

- "The Real and the Virtual: Intersecting Communities at the Library." Article explains how to create virtual communities that will become an asset for libraries.
- Sample dept/column: "In the Spotlight" offers a review of the new HP mini notebook personal computer.

RIGHTS AND PAYMENT
First rights. Written material, $300–$500. Artwork, payment rates vary. Pays on publication. Provides 2 contributor's copies.

⬧EDITOR'S COMMENTS
We like to focus on the tools that are being used today, as well as what's on tap for tomorrow.

Muse

Cricket Magazine Group
70 East Lake Street, Suite 300
Chicago, IL 60601

Submissions Editor: Elizabeth Preston

DESCRIPTION AND INTERESTS
This magazine aims to get kids and teens interested in a wide range of topics, including science and technology, history and culture, and the arts, through lively articles and interviews. Never dull, always enlightening, *Muse* gets to the brain via the funny bone. Circ: 45,000.

Audience: 10+ years
Frequency: 9 times each year
Website: www.musemagkids.com

FREELANCE POTENTIAL
100% written by nonstaff writers. Of the freelance submissions published yearly, 20% are by authors who are new to the magazine.

SUBMISSIONS
All work is assigned. Send résumé and clips. Accepts hard copy and email to muse@caruspub.com. Response time varies.

- Articles: To 2,500 words. Informational articles; interviews; and photo-essays. Topics include science, nature, the environment, history, culture, anthropology, sociology, technology, and the arts.
- Depts/columns: Word lengths vary. Science news, Q&As, math problems, and personal experience pieces.
- Other: Cartoons, contests, and activities.

SAMPLE ISSUE
40 pages (no advertising): 4 articles; 7 depts/columns. Sample copy and guidelines available at website.

- "Garden of Surprises." Article takes a look at an English puzzle garden designed by an Elizabethan spymaster.
- "The Future Is Here." Article reports on the exhibits at the Institute for Human and Machine Cognition in Pensacola, Florida.
- Sample dept/column: "Muserology" tells of the author's fascination with mold development and identification.

RIGHTS AND PAYMENT
Rights vary. Written material, payment rates vary. Payment policy varies.

➡EDITOR'S COMMENTS
We are looking for submissions from writers with expertise in their subject, who can convey that knowledge in language that speaks to the target age group and generates excitement about the topic.

Music Educators Journal

MENC
1806 Robert Fulton Drive
Reston, VA 20191

Submissions: Sage Publications

DESCRIPTION AND INTERESTS
As the official publication of MENC: The National Association for Music Education, this magazine covers all phases of music education in schools and communities. It accepts material from MENC members only. Circ: 80,000.

Audience: MENC members, music teachers
Frequency: Quarterly
Website: www.menc.org

FREELANCE POTENTIAL
90% written by nonstaff writers. Publishes 30 freelance submissions yearly; 10% by unpublished writers, 15% by authors who are new to the magazine. Receives 120 unsolicited mss each year.

SUBMISSIONS
MENC members only. Send complete ms with credentials and affiliations. Accepts submissions via http://mc.manuscriptcentral.com/mej. Response time varies.

- Articles: 1,800–3,500 words. Informational and instructional articles; and historical studies of music education. Topics include teaching methods and philosophy, and current trends in music education and learning.
- Depts/columns: Word lengths vary. Media reviews, teaching tips, technology updates, and association news.
- Artwork: TIFF, EPS, JPEG, or PDF digital files.
- Other: Submit seasonal material 8–12 months in advance.

SAMPLE ISSUE
60 pages (40% advertising): 5 articles; 7 depts/columns. Sample copy, $6 with 9x12 SASE ($2 postage). Writers' guidelines available at website.

- "The Rewards of Teaching Music in Urban Settings." Article offers perspectives from experienced music teachers about the challenges and joys of working in urban classrooms.
- "Strings Got Rhythm." Article offers guidelines for developing rhythmic skills.

RIGHTS AND PAYMENT
All rights. Written material, no payment. Artwork, $10. Provides 2 contributor's copies.

➡EDITOR'S COMMENTS
Please note that we accept submissions from MENC members exclusively.

My Light Magazine

Editor: Jennifer Gladen

DESCRIPTION AND INTERESTS
This e-zine was developed to show children how wonderful a real relationship with God can be. Written for elementary school children who practice the Catholic faith, it includes stories, articles, crafts, poems, profiles of saints, and Bible stories. Hits per month: 1,000.

Audience: 4–12 years
Frequency: Monthly
Website: www.mylightmagazine.com

FREELANCE POTENTIAL
95% written by nonstaff writers. Publishes 180 freelance submissions yearly; 50% by unpublished writers, 75% by authors who are new to the magazine.

SUBMISSIONS
Send complete ms with bibliography and brief author bio. Accepts email submissions to mylightmagazine@msn.com (Microsoft Word attachments). Response time varies.

- Articles: 300–900 words. Informational articles. Topics include prayer, Jesus's teachings and parables, the rosary, Mary, the saints, Holy Mass, God's creation, spiritual experiences, respect for parents and teachers, Catholic values, and the Beatitudes.
- Fiction: 300–900 words. Stories that represent Christian lifestyles and morals.
- Depts/columns: 500 words. Activities, prayers, and crafts.
- Artwork: Color line art.
- Other: Poetry, to 15 lines.

SAMPLE ISSUE
38 pages: 4 articles; 2 stories; 5 depts/columns; 4 poems. Sample copy, guidelines, and theme list available at website.

- "Father Faricy SJ." Article chronicles a young man's journey to the priesthood.
- "Saint Bede." Article tells about the life of a saint who devoted his life to learning, teaching, and writing about God.

RIGHTS AND PAYMENT
One-time electronic rights. No payment.

☛EDITOR'S COMMENTS
Everything we publish is focused on helping children understand their faith. Stories should feature characters that portray good Catholic values. Keep in mind that a good story always has a problem to solve.

Nashville Parent

2270 Rosa L. Parks Boulevard
Nashville, TN 37228

Editor-in-Chief: Susan Day

DESCRIPTION AND INTERESTS
This regional magazine covers topics of interest to parents with school-aged children living in Nashville and environs. Its focus is always on the region. Circ: 85,000.

Audience: Parents
Frequency: Monthly
Website: www.nashvilleparent.com

FREELANCE POTENTIAL
15–20% written by nonstaff writers. Publishes 400 freelance submissions yearly; 40% by authors who are new to the magazine. Receives 1,200 unsolicited mss yearly.

SUBMISSIONS
Send complete ms. Accepts hard copy and Macintosh disk submissions with hard copy. Availability of artwork improves chance of acceptance. SASE. Response time varies.

- Articles: 800–1,000 words. Informational and how-to articles; profiles; interviews; photo-essays; and personal experience pieces. Topics include parenting, family life, current events, social issues, health and fitness, music, travel, recreation, religion, the arts, crafts, computers, and multicultural and ethnic issues.
- Depts/columns: Staff written.
- Artwork: B/W and color prints.
- Other: Submit Christmas, Easter, and Halloween material 2 months in advance.

SAMPLE ISSUE
108 pages (50% advertising): 6 articles; 9 depts/columns. Sample copy, free with 9x12 SASE. Guidelines available.

- "What's a Recession, Mom?" Article offers advice for parents on how to talk with their children about money management and the current economic downturn.
- "Behind the Scenes at Juvy." Article takes readers to the Davidson County Juvenile Detention Center to show its unique approach to education and rehabilitation.

RIGHTS AND PAYMENT
One-time rights. Written material, $35. Pays on publication. Provides 3 contributor's copies.

☛EDITOR'S COMMENTS
We welcome submissions from local writers or writers who know Nashville well. Articles should be lively as well as informative.

National Geographic Kids

National Geographic Society
1145 17th Street NW
Washington, DC 20036-4688

Executive Editor: Julie Agnone

DESCRIPTION AND INTERESTS
This magazine proves that learning is fun. It offers factually accurate, informative articles in an entertaining and lively format that makes readers want to learn more. Circ: 1.3 million.

Audience: 6–14 years
Frequency: 10 times each year
Website:
  http://kids.nationalgeographic.com

FREELANCE POTENTIAL
85% written by nonstaff writers. Publishes 20–25 freelance submissions yearly; 1% by unpublished writers, 30% by authors who are new to the magazine. Receives 360 queries each year.

SUBMISSIONS
Query with clips. Accepts hard copy. SASE. Responds if interested.

- Articles: Word lengths vary. Informational articles. Topics include geography, archaeology, paleontology, history, entertainment, nature, and the environment.
- Depts/columns: Word lengths vary. News and trends, amazing animals, and fun facts.
- Other: Puzzles, games, and jokes.

SAMPLE ISSUE
32 pages (20% advertising): 3 articles; 8 depts/columns; 4 activities. Sample copy, $3.95. Guidelines available.

- "Lifestyles of the Rich and Furry." Article shows the most outrageous ways to pamper your pet.
- "Animal Talk." Article explores how animals and humans communicate with each other.
- Sample dept/column: "Amazing Animals" introduces readers to a tortoise who has been outfitted with a skateboard to compensate for her paralyzed hind legs.

RIGHTS AND PAYMENT
All rights. Written material, payment rates vary. Artwork, $100–$600. Pays on acceptance. Provides 3–5 contributor's copies.

⇒EDITOR'S COMMENTS
Experienced writers who can convey the excitement and wonder of a new discovery, little-known scientific fact, or surprising bit of history are most welcome to submit their ideas with examples of their previously published work.

National Geographic Little Kids

National Geographic Society
1145 17th Street NW
Washington, DC 20036-4688

Executive Editor: Julie Agnone

DESCRIPTION AND INTERESTS
Parents and children enjoy *National Geographic Little Kids* together. Each issue offers interactive activities, stories, and articles that entertain and enlighten. Circ: Unavailable.

Audience: 3–6 years
Frequency: 6 times each year
Website:
  http://littlekids.nationalgeographic.com

FREELANCE POTENTIAL
10% written by nonstaff writers. Publishes 5 freelance submissions yearly.

SUBMISSIONS
Query with résumé. Accepts hard copy. SASE. Responds if interested.

- Articles: Word lengths vary. Informational articles. Topics include nature, animals, the environment, science, history, and world cultures.
- Fiction: Word lengths vary. Rebus stories about animals and other cultures.
- Depts/columns: Basic science experiments, craft projects, and recipes.
- Other: Activities, games, and jokes.

SAMPLE ISSUE
24 pages (no advertising): 4 articles; 1 rebus story; 2 depts/columns; 5 activities. Sample copy, $3.95.

- "Musical Instruments Around the World." Article introduces readers to the major musical instrument groups and explains their roles in different cultures.
- "Arctic Hare Hide-and-Seek." Article shows how the coat of an arctic hare changes with the seasons.
- Sample dept/column: "Activity" offers a recipe for making and decorating heart-shaped gelatin treats.

RIGHTS AND PAYMENT
All rights. Written material, payment rates vary. Pays on acceptance. Provides 3–5 contributor's copies.

⇒EDITOR'S COMMENTS
We're interested in material that will capture the imagination of the budding scientist and explorer in every young child. All articles, stories, and activities should make learning fun, and encourage readers to want to find out more about the topic.

Natural Life

B2-125 The Queensway, Suite 52
Toronto, Ontario M8Y 1H6
Canada

Editor: Wendy Priesnitz

DESCRIPTION AND INTERESTS
This magazine is written for an international audience of families who want progressive information about natural family living. It describes environmentally friendly, sustainable practices and principles while focusing on natural parenting, gardening, and housing. Circ: 85,000.

Audience: Parents
Frequency: 6 times each year
Website: www.naturallifemagazine.com

FREELANCE POTENTIAL
50% written by nonstaff writers. Publishes 40 freelance submissions yearly; 20% by unpublished writers, 20–30% by authors who are new to the magazine. Receives hundreds of queries yearly.

SUBMISSIONS
Query with detailed outline and 50- to 200-word synopsis. Accepts email to editor@naturallifemagazine.com and simultaneous submissions if identified. Responds in 3–5 days.

- Articles: 2,500–3,500 words. Informational and how-to articles; profiles; interviews; and personal experience pieces. Topics include green living, eco-travel, natural parenting, unschooling, lifelong learning, self-directed learning, and social issues.
- Depts/columns: Staff written.
- Artwork: Color prints. High-resolution TIFF images at 300 dpi.

SAMPLE ISSUE
62 pages: 10 articles; 9 depts/columns. Sample copy, $6.95 with 9x12 SAE/IRC ($6 postage). Guidelines available at website.

- "Green, Raw, and Smooth." Article outlines the benefits of green smoothies and offers simple recipes.
- "Raising a Humane Child." Article offers an overview of the Humane Education and Human Parenting movements.

RIGHTS AND PAYMENT
One-time print and non-exclusive electronic rights. No payment. Provides author's copies.

➾EDITOR'S COMMENTS

We look for contributors who can write simply and clearly, in concise, non-academic prose, rather than as professional "experts." Our style is friendly, but not folksy.

Nature Friend

4253 Woodcock Lane
Dayton, VA 22821

Editor: Kevin Shank

DESCRIPTION AND INTERESTS
Nature-themed articles, stories, and activities that foster children's awareness of God are published in this magazine. It is produced by a conservative Christian publisher. Circ: 15,000.

Audience: 8–16 years
Frequency: Monthly
Website: www.naturefriendmagazine.com

FREELANCE POTENTIAL
20% written by nonstaff writers. Publishes 50 freelance submissions yearly; 5% by unpublished writers, 10% by authors who are new to the magazine. Receives 480–720 unsolicited mss yearly.

SUBMISSIONS
Send complete ms. Accepts hard copy and email to editor@naturefriendmagazine.com. SASE. Response time varies.

- Articles: 250–900 words. Informational and how-to articles; profiles; and personal experience pieces. Topics include science, nature, wildlife, and astronomy.
- Fiction: 300–900 words. Themes include adventure, wildlife, and nature.
- Depts/columns: 100–450 words. Seasonal, nature-related stories, activities, and science experiments.
- Artwork: High-resolution digital images with accompanying contact prints.
- Other: Nature-related puzzles and games.

SAMPLE ISSUE
24 pages (no advertising): 7 articles; 5 depts/columns; 3 puzzles; 1 game. Sample copy and guidelines, $9.

- "The Busy Builder." Article follows the very active life of a beaver and tells how and why beavers build dams and lodges.
- Sample dept/column: "Wondernose" provides clues about which animal has such long legs that it appears to walk on stilts.

RIGHTS AND PAYMENT
One-time rights. Written material, $.05 per word. Artwork, $25–$75 per photo. Pays on publication. Provides 1 contributor's copy.

➾EDITOR'S COMMENTS

While we are a Christian publisher, we provide a place for children to simply enjoy what God has made without being directed toward a spiritual application.

The New Era

50 East North Temple Street, Room 2420
Salt Lake City, UT 84150-3220

Managing Editor: Richard M. Romney

DESCRIPTION AND INTERESTS
Full of inspirational articles and profiles, this magazine is written for young adult members of the Church of Jesus Christ of Latter-day Saints. It seeks submissions that depict the way God works in the lives of teens. Circ: 230,000.

Audience: YA–Adults
Frequency: Monthly
Website: www.newera.lds.org

FREELANCE POTENTIAL
40% written by nonstaff writers. Publishes 50 freelance submissions yearly; 5% by unpublished writers, 5% by authors who are new to the magazine. Receives 1,340 queries yearly.

SUBMISSIONS
Query. Accepts hard copy and email queries to newera@ldschurch.org. SASE. Responds in 2 months.

- Articles: 200–500 words. Informational and self-help articles; profiles; and personal experience pieces. Photo features and interviews, to 1,500 words. Topics include Gospel messages, religion, social issues, missionary work, family relationships, testimonies, humor, and Scripture.
- Depts/columns: Word lengths vary. News items, events, and youth church activities.
- Artwork: Digital images at 300 dpi; color transparencies.
- Other: Poetry, to 30 lines.

SAMPLE ISSUE
50 pages (no advertising): 12 articles; 6 depts/columns; 1 poem. Sample copy, $1.50 with 9x12 SASE or at website. Guidelines available at website.

- "Prayer at 30 Feet Down." Article relates the story of a young woman who uses prayer to overcome her fears while scuba diving.
- Sample dept/column: "Instant Messages" tells of a boy who visited the birthplace of Joseph Smith.

RIGHTS AND PAYMENT
All rights. Written material, $.03–$.12 per word. Pays on acceptance. Provides 2 contributor's copies.

➥EDITOR'S COMMENTS
We seek articles that deal with how youth are adapting in wholesome ways to the use of new technology.

New Moon Girls

P.O. Box 161287
Duluth, MN 55816

Executive Editor: Helen Cordes

DESCRIPTION AND INTERESTS
Created by girls for girls, New Moon Girls is dedicated to helping readers discover and honor their true selves. It presents reader-created material along with adult-written articles and fiction, each designed to speak to the thinking girl. Circ: 15,000.

Audience: 8+ years
Frequency: 6 times each year
Website: www.newmoon.com

FREELANCE POTENTIAL
90% written by nonstaff writers. Publishes 200 freelance submissions yearly; 90% by unpublished writers, 95% by authors who are new to the magazine. Receives 720 queries and unsolicited mss yearly.

SUBMISSIONS
Female authors only. Query or send complete ms. Accepts email submissions to girl@ newmoon.com. Responds in 6 months only if interested.

- Articles: 300–600 words. Profiles and interviews. Topics include activism, school, fitness, recreation, science, technology, and social and multicultural issues.
- Fiction: 900–1,200 words. Empowering stories about girls ages 8–12.
- Depts/columns: Word lengths vary. "Go Girl!" (activism and athletics), "Global Village," "Women's Work," "Herstory," "Body Language," and "Science Side Effects."
- Other: Poetry and artwork by girls ages 8–12.

SAMPLE ISSUE
32 pages (no advertising): 5 articles; 1 story; 9 depts/columns; 5 poems; 1 artwork page. Sample copy, $7. Guidelines and theme list available at website.

- "Interviewing Gloria Steinem." Article presents an interview with the author, journalist, activist, and feminist.
- Sample dept/column: "Body Language" examines the pros and cons of piercing one's ears.

RIGHTS AND PAYMENT
All rights. No payment. Provides 3 copies.

➥EDITOR'S COMMENTS
We are looking for nonfiction writing by girls ages 8 to 14. Our magazine is a safe place for girls to exchange dreams and thoughts.

New York Family

79 Madison Avenue, 16th Floor
New York, NY 10016

Editor: Eric Messinger

DESCRIPTION AND INTERESTS
This regional parenting magazine tackles all
the topics usually found in similar publications
—including articles on child development and
educational issues. In addition, it features articles on family getaways, health, and fashion.
Circ: 40,000.

Audience: Parents
Frequency: Monthly
Website: www.newyorkfamily.com

FREELANCE POTENTIAL
50% written by nonstaff writers. Publishes 40
freelance submissions yearly; 40% by authors
who are new to the magazine. Receives 200
queries yearly.

SUBMISSIONS
Query with clips. Accepts hard copy. SASE.
Response time varies.

- Articles: 800–1,200 words. Informational
  articles; profiles; interviews; photo-essays;
  and personal experience pieces. Topics
  include education, music, recreation, regional
  news, social issues, travel, and parenting
  advice and techniques.
- Depts/columns: 400–800 words. News and
  media reviews.

SAMPLE ISSUE
82 pages: 4 articles; 10 depts/columns.
Sample copy, free with 9x12 SASE. Writers'
guidelines available.

- "Stroll Into Spring." Article previews children's spring fashions, highlighting items
  that can be found in New York City stores.
- "Family Health Guide: Top Hospitals." Article
  provides information on New York City's
  leading hospitals and their most family-
  friendly features.
- Sample dept/column: "In the Neighborhood"
  features the Isis Condominium building with
  boutique apartments for families.

RIGHTS AND PAYMENT
First rights. Written material, $25–$300. Pays
on publication. Provides 3 author's copies.

➠EDITOR'S COMMENTS
We prefer articles that are filled with local
information. Our readership consists of afflu-
ent, sophisticated, active parents. Our ideal
author knows the issues related to raising
children in the city.

New York Times Upfront

Scholastic Inc.
557 Broadway
New York, NY 10012-3999

Editor: Elliot Rebhun

DESCRIPTION AND INTERESTS
High school students learn about current
events and the world around them through
New York Times Upfront. It takes articles about
national and international events from *The
New York Times* and combines them with profiles of newsworthy young adults and essays by
teens. It also includes a teacher edition to
guide classroom discussions. Circ: 300,000.

Audience: 14–18 years
Frequency: 14 times each year
Website: www.upfrontmagazine.com

FREELANCE POTENTIAL
10% written by nonstaff writers. Publishes 2
freelance submissions yearly; 10% by authors
who are new to the magazine. Receives 144
queries yearly.

SUBMISSIONS
Query with résumé and clips. Accepts hard
copy. Availability of artwork improves chance
of acceptance. SASE. Responds in 2–4 weeks
if interested.

- Articles: 500–1,200 words. Informational
  articles; profiles; and interviews. Topics
  include current events, politics, history,
  media, technology, social issues, careers,
  the arts, the environment, and multicultural
  and ethnic issues.
- Depts/columns: Word lengths vary. Essays by
  teens, opinion, news briefs, and trends.
- Artwork: Color prints or transparencies.
- Other: Cartoons.

SAMPLE ISSUE
Sample copy and editorial calendar available at
website. Guidelines available.

- "Supreme Decision." Article details the
  process and issues surrounding the appoint-
  ment of a new Supreme Court justice.
- "A Comeback for Nuclear Power?" Article
  explains why nuclear power may be getting
  another chance in the U.S.

RIGHTS AND PAYMENT
All rights. All material, payment rates vary. Pays
on publication.

➠EDITOR'S COMMENTS
Because most of our material comes from
The New York Times, we don't accept much
freelance work. However, we might consider
a submission that shows exceptional talent.

NextStepU Magazine

2 West Main Street, Suite 200
Victor, NY 14564

Editor-in-Chief: Laura Jeanne Hammond

DESCRIPTION AND INTERESTS
With articles designed to help college and college-bound high school students find the right path in life, *NextStepU Magazine* focuses on "real life" issues such as money management and career decisions, as well as topics such as choosing a college and preparing for the SATs. Circ: 800,000.

Audience: 14–21 years
Frequency: 5 times each year
Website: www.nextstepu.com

FREELANCE POTENTIAL
90% written by nonstaff writers. Publishes 40 freelance submissions yearly.

SUBMISSIONS
Query. Accepts email queries to laura@ nextstepu.com. Response time varies.

- Articles: 700–1,000 words. Informational, self-help, and how-to articles; profiles; interviews; personal experience and opinion pieces; humor; and essays. Topics include college planning, financial aid, campus tours, choosing a career, life skills, résumé writing, public speaking, personal finances, computers, multicultural and ethnic issues, sports, and special education.
- Depts/columns: Word lengths vary. Personal experience pieces from college students.

SAMPLE ISSUE
38 pages: 12 articles; 3 depts/columns. Sample copy available at website. Writers' guidelines available.

- "Why You Should Consider Joining the Military." Article outlines three important benefits of a military career, and how one can parlay that experience into a rewarding post-military career.
- "Why Do You Want to Go to College?" Article challenges students to answer the tough question about "why" before they get to "where" and "what" regarding college.

RIGHTS AND PAYMENT
All rights. Written material, payment rates vary. Pays within 1 month of acceptance.

➡EDITOR'S COMMENTS
We encourage queries from professionals within the business or education fields who can share advice and insider tips with our readers.

NJCAA Review

1755 Telstar Drive, Suite 103
Colorado Springs, CO 80920

Executive Editor: Wayne Baker

DESCRIPTION AND INTERESTS
This publication of the National Junior College Athletic Association covers the issues facing the organization, as well as its athletes, schools, coaches, programs, and events. Circ: 3,300.

Audience: YA–Adult
Frequency: 10 times each year
Website: www.njcaa.org

FREELANCE POTENTIAL
30–40% written by nonstaff writers. Publishes 3–5 freelance submissions yearly. Receives 12 unsolicited mss yearly.

SUBMISSIONS
Send complete ms. Accepts hard copy. Availability of artwork improves chance of acceptance. SASE. Responds in 2 months.

- Articles: 1,500–2,000 words. Informational articles. Topics include sports, college, careers, health, fitness, and NJCAA news.
- Artwork: B/W prints or transparencies.

SAMPLE ISSUE
20 pages (25% advertising): 12 articles. Sample copy, $4 for current issue; $3 for back issue with 9x12 SASE. Editorial calendar available.

- "Fond Du Lac Athletic Director Serves as Curling Official at 2010 Winter Olympic Games." Article reports on the curling activities of Donna Statzell.
- "According to Jim . . . It's All About Stats." Article reports on the Miami Dade athletic director who doubles as a statistician for various professional teams.
- "Potomac State College: Success Starts Here." Article profiles the West Virginia college and its eight varsity sport programs.

RIGHTS AND PAYMENT
One-time rights. No payment. Provides 3 contributor's copies.

➡EDITOR'S COMMENTS
We are a great place in which to cut your journalistic teeth, and we're always looking for people who can report on the myriad sporting activities of our nation's junior colleges. If you've got a story about a particular athlete, coach, or program, send it to us. We prefer to work with writers who are familiar with the schools in question and/or the junior college system.

Northumberland Kids

39 Queen Street, Suite 203
Coburg, Ontario K9A 1M8
Canada

Editor: Susan Stanton

DESCRIPTION AND INTERESTS
Topics that are of interest to parents in
Northumberland County can be found in
this magazine, along with information on
local recreational and educational resources.
Circ: Unavailable.

Audience: Parents
Frequency: Monthly
Website: www.northumberlandkids.com

FREELANCE POTENTIAL
40–50% written by nonstaff writers. Publishes
25 freelance submissions yearly. Receives
240–300 queries yearly.

SUBMISSIONS
Query. Accepts email queries to sstanton@
northumberlandkids.com (Microsoft Word or
text file attachments). Response time varies.

- Articles: 1,200–1,400 words. Informational
  articles; profiles; and interviews. Topics
  include parenting, health and fitness, current
  events, nature, the environment, family recreation, social issues, and special education.
- Depts/columns: 750 words. Safety, health
  and nutrition, recreation, media reviews,
  alternative medicine, and the environment.
- Artwork: High-resolution digital images at
  300 dpi.

SAMPLE ISSUE
32 pages: 3 articles; 7 depts/columns. Sample
copy and guidelines available at website.

- "Eating Out with Kids: The 10 Command-
  ments." Article provides 10 tips for making a
  trip to a restaurant less grueling.
- "How Safe Is Your Teen's Summer Job?"
  Article explains how to broach the topic of
  safety with a teen starting his first job.
- Sample dept/column: "Summertime" offers
  simple ideas for avoiding the "I'm bored"
  summertime wail.

RIGHTS AND PAYMENT
First rights. Written material, payment rates
vary. Pays on publication.

▪▸EDITOR'S COMMENTS
We offer a variety of opportunities for freelancers here, and are happy to hear your
ideas. All material must contain information
that Northumberland parents will find helpful
and relatable to their own family, including
local resources.

NYMetroParents

1440 Broadway, 5th Floor
New York, NY 10018

Editorial Director: Phyllis Singer

DESCRIPTION AND INTERESTS
The largest publisher of parenting magazines
in New York, NYMetroParents publishes *Big
Apple Parent,* as well as editions in Brooklyn,
Queens, Westchester, Long Island, and
Connecticut. The focus is on raising happy and
healthy children, and providing regional news.
Circ: 500,000.

Audience: Parents
Frequency: Monthly
Website: www.nymetroparents.com

FREELANCE POTENTIAL
50% written by nonstaff writers. Publishes 300
freelance submissions yearly; 20% by unpublished writers, 10% by authors who are new to
the magazine. Receives 12 queries, 72 unsolicited mss yearly.

SUBMISSIONS
Query or send complete ms with two clips,
sidebar, and sources. Accepts email submissions. Responds if interested.

- Articles: 800–900 words. Informational articles; profiles; interviews; and personal experience pieces. Topics include family issues,
  education, camp, health, nutrition, fitness,
  current events, and regional news.
- Depts/columns: Staff written.
- Other: Submit seasonal material 4 months
  in advance.

SAMPLE ISSUE
66 pages: 11 articles; 10 depts/columns.
Sample copy, free with 10x13 SASE.

- "After School Special." Article lists the steps
  one can take to start an afterschool program
  in the community.
- "City Sprouts." Article is a guide to gardening
  with kids in apartments and the community.
- "Sitcom Mom with Kids Who Care." Article
  profiles actress Joely Fisher and focuses on
  her dedication to community service.

RIGHTS AND PAYMENT
First New York area rights. No payment.

▪▸EDITOR'S COMMENTS
We like articles that pack a punch—we want
submissions that offer a lot of practical
advice and information to parents in a few
words. You don't need previous publishing
credits, but you do have to prove to us that
you know what you're writing about.

OC Family

1451 Quail Street, Suite 201
Newport Beach, CA 92660

Editor: Kim Porrazzo

DESCRIPTION AND INTERESTS
Distributed throughout Orange County, California, this magazine covers general parenting topics. It also includes information on child-related events, goods, and services in the county. Circ: 58,000.
Audience: Parents
Frequency: Monthly
Website: www.ocfamily.com

FREELANCE POTENTIAL
82% written by nonstaff writers. Publishes 50 freelance submissions yearly; 1% by unpublished writers, 1% by authors who are new to the magazine. Receives 144 queries yearly.

SUBMISSIONS
Query. Accepts hard copy. SASE. Responds in 1 month.

- Articles: 800–2,500 words. Informational articles and profiles. Topics include education, health, nutrition, family travel, regional food and dining, youth sports and recreation, and child care and development.
- Depts/columns: Word lengths vary. Parenting advice, children's book reviews, family movie reviews, fashion, and beauty.
- Artwork: B/W or color prints.

SAMPLE ISSUE
204 pages (60% advertising): 3 articles; 20 depts/columns; 2 directories. Sample copy, free with 9x12 SASE. Editorial calendar available.

- "Family Wellness." Article stresses the importance of exercise, and offers suggestions for fitness activities families can do together.
- "Bound by Love." Article examines the rewarding—and sometimes tumultuous—process of adopting a child.
- Sample dept/column: "First Years, 0–2" discusses the work two doctors are doing to help premature babies overcome their greatest challenge: absorption of nutrients.

RIGHTS AND PAYMENT
One-time rights. Articles, $100–$500. Depts/columns, payment rates vary. Artwork, $90. Kill fee, $50. Pays 45 days after publication. Provides 3 contributor's copies.

➬EDITOR'S COMMENTS
Our readers rely on us for helpful information. If you can speak directly to their interests and cite local sources, send us a query.

Odyssey

Cobblestone Publishing
30 Grove Street, Suite C
Peterborough, NH 03458

Senior Editor: Elizabeth E. Lindstrom

DESCRIPTION AND INTERESTS
Budding scientists are the audience for this magazine that combines fascinating articles, challenging activities, poetry, and short stories on science, math, and technology themes. Circ: 25,000.
Audience: 10–16 years
Frequency: 9 times each year
Website: www.odysseymagazine.com

FREELANCE POTENTIAL
70% written by nonstaff writers. Publishes 60 freelance submissions yearly; 2% by unpublished writers, 25% by authors who are new to the magazine. Receives 300 queries yearly.

SUBMISSIONS
Query with outline, author biography, bibliography, and clips or writing samples. Accepts hard copy. Availability of artwork improves chance of acceptance. SASE. Responds in 5 months if interested.

- Articles: 750–1,000 words. Informational articles; biographies; and interviews. Topics include math, science, and technology.
- Fiction: 1,000 words. Science fiction and science-related stories.
- Depts/columns: Word lengths vary. Astronomy, animals, profiles, and science news.
- Artwork: B/W and color prints.
- Other: Activities, to 600 words. Seasonal material about space or astronomical events.

SAMPLE ISSUE
50 pages (no advertising): 9 articles; 9 depts/columns; 3 activities. Sample copy, $4.50 with 9x12 SASE (4 first-class stamps). Guidelines and theme list available at website.

- "1,2,3 . . . Strike Up the Cell Phones!" Article describes the first telesymphony, a concert using cell phones as the instrument.
- Sample dept/column: "Kids Can . . . Do Amazing Science" tells of a program that teaches kids to draw a scientific concept.

RIGHTS AND PAYMENT
All rights. Written material, $.20–$.25 per word. Artwork, payment rates vary. Pays on publication. Provides 2 contributor's copies.

➬EDITOR'S COMMENTS
We would like to see more science-related or sci-fi short stories that correspond to our list of themes.

The Old Schoolhouse

P.O. Box 8426
Gray, TN 37615

Editors: Paul & Gena Suarez

DESCRIPTION AND INTERESTS
This magazine publishes articles on the vital aspects of homeschooling and family life—particularly from a Christian perspective. It also publishes technical and research-based articles on homeschooling. Circ: 50,000.

Audience: Homeschool families
Frequency: Quarterly
Website:
   www.thehomeschoolmagazine.com

FREELANCE POTENTIAL
80% written by nonstaff writers. Publishes 160 freelance submissions yearly; 30% by unpublished writers, 50% by authors who are new to the magazine. Receives 192 queries yearly.

SUBMISSIONS
Query with outline, sample paragraphs, and brief author bio. Accepts queries submitted through website only (homeschoolblogger.com users should note their user name on query). No simultaneous submissions. Responds in 4–6 weeks.

- Articles: 1,000–2,000 words. Informational and how-to articles; and personal experience pieces. Topics include homeschooling, family life, art, music, spirituality, literature, child development, teen issues, science, history, and mathematics.
- Depts/columns: Word lengths vary. Short news items, styles of teaching, opinion pieces, teaching children with special needs, and humor.

SAMPLE ISSUE
220 pages (40% advertising): 2 articles; 21 depts/columns. Sample copy and guidelines available at website.

- "Homeschooling and Adoption: A Winning Combination." Article profiles homeschooling families whose lives have been touched by adoption.
- Sample dept/column: "Little Artists" shows how to draw a hermit crab.

RIGHTS AND PAYMENT
First rights. Written material, payment rates vary. Pays on publication. Provides 2 copies.

➤EDITOR'S COMMENTS
Articles that explore the history, current status, and character of the homeschool movement always get our attention.

On Course

General Council of the Assemblies of God
1445 North Boonville Avenue
Springfield, MO 65802-1894

Editor: Amber Weigand-Buckley

DESCRIPTION AND INTERESTS
On Course is published by the National Youth Ministry of the Assemblies of God. Its mission is to empower teens to grow in a real-life relationship with Christ. Circ: 160,000.

Audience: 12–18 years
Frequency: Quarterly
Website: www.oncourse.ag.org

FREELANCE POTENTIAL
95% written by nonstaff writers. Publishes 32 freelance submissions yearly; 30% by unpublished writers, 40% by authors who are new to the magazine.

SUBMISSIONS
All work is assigned. Send audition ms with résumé. Prefers hard copy and email submissions to oncourse@ag.org; will accept Macintosh-compatible disk submissions. SASE. Response time varies.

- Articles: To 800 words. Informational and how-to articles; profiles; humor; and personal experience pieces. Topics include social issues, music, health, religion, sports, careers, college, and multicultural issues.
- Fiction: To 800 words. Genres include contemporary, humorous, multicultural, and sports-themed fiction.
- Depts/columns: Word lengths vary. Profiles and brief news items.

SAMPLE ISSUE
32 pages (33% advertising): 6 articles; 9 depts/columns. Sample copy, free. Guidelines available at website.

- "Out of the Blue." Article profiles recording artist Molly Jenson.
- Sample dept/column: "Laugh" shares the author's admission that he talks to himself, yet knows that talking to God is wiser.

RIGHTS AND PAYMENT
First and electronic rights. Written material, payment rates vary. Payment policy varies. Provides 5 contributor's copies.

➤EDITOR'S COMMENTS
We look for fresh voices that can convey the Word of God in language that our teen readers can relate to. To that end, we will accept audition manuscripts only, and then assign articles to those writers we feel are a good fit for us.

Organic Family Magazine

P.O. Box 1614
Wallingford, CT 06492-1214

Editor: Catherine Wong

DESCRIPTION AND INTERESTS
Written for families trying to live a more natural, simple lifestyle, this magazine features a mixture of educational, entertaining, and spiritual articles about the process of moving away from the mainstream, consumer-based ideology and into a lifestyle that embraces simplicity and contentedness. Circ: 200.

Audience: Families
Frequency: Twice each year
Website: www.organicfamilymagazine.com

FREELANCE POTENTIAL
90% written by nonstaff writers. Publishes 40 freelance submissions yearly.

SUBMISSIONS
Query or send complete ms. Prefers email submissions to sciencelibrarian@hotmail.com; will accept hard copy. SASE. Response time varies.

- Articles: Word lengths vary. Informational articles; interviews; and personal experience pieces. Topics include nature, organic agriculture, conservation, parenting, natural pet care, herbs, organic gardening, nutrition, progressive politics, health, wellness, and environmental issues.
- Fiction: Word lengths vary. Stories about nature and the environment.
- Depts/columns: Word lengths vary. New product reviews, recipes, profiles of conservation organizations, and media reviews.
- Other: Poetry.

SAMPLE ISSUE
44 pages: 28 articles; 2 depts/columns. Sample copy and guidelines available at website.

- "All I Am Saying Is Give (Locally Grown) Peas a Chance." Article examines the myriad ways people can eat local food, and explains the cost of big-market food production and distribution.
- "Organic Family Interview: Dan Wells." Article provides an interview with the actor on how he maintains an organic diet.

RIGHTS AND PAYMENT
One-time rights. No payment. Provides 1 contributor's copy.

❖EDITOR'S COMMENTS
To us, "organic" refers to much more than food. It refers to a whole lifestyle and philosophical belief in natural, peaceful living.

Our Little Friend

Pacific Press Publishing
P.O. Box 5353
Nampa, ID 83653-5353

Editor: Aileen Andres Sox

DESCRIPTION AND INTERESTS
Stories and Bible lessons for children in Seventh-day Adventist Sabbath school are published in this magazine. Devotionals are also featured. Circ: 35,000.

Audience: 1–6 years
Frequency: Weekly
Website: www.ourlittlefriend.com

FREELANCE POTENTIAL
20% written by nonstaff writers. Publishes 52 freelance submissions yearly; 10% by unpublished writers, 10% by authors who are new to the magazine. Receives 240 unsolicited mss each year.

SUBMISSIONS
Send complete ms. Accepts hard copy, email submissions to ailsox@pacificpress.com, and simultaneous submissions if identified. SASE. Responds in 4 months.

- Articles: 500–650 words. Devotionals, Bible lessons, and true stories that teach Christian values. Topics include school and family.
- Fiction: 500–650 words. Short stories that portray God's love for children, personal faith, and contemporary issues.
- Artwork: Color prints. Line art.
- Other: Submit seasonal material 7 months in advance.

SAMPLE ISSUE
8 pages (no advertising): 5 stories; 2 Bible lessons. Sample copy, free with 9x12 SASE (2 first-class stamps). Guidelines available.

- "Sarah Helps Build Churches." Story relates how a little girl realizes that by contributing to the Sabbath offering she is helping to buy building materials for churches.
- "Digging Together." Story tells about a little boy, his dad, and his much younger cousin who discover that digging in the dirt is something that all ages can enjoy.

RIGHTS AND PAYMENT
One-time rights. Written material, $25–$50. Pays on acceptance. Provides 3 copies.

❖EDITOR'S COMMENTS
An ongoing need is for read-aloud stories with messages of Christian love. Because we are a Seventh-day Adventist publication, all material must be consistent with the teachings of our church.

Pack-O-Fun

2400 East Devon, Suite 292
Des Plaines, IL 60018-4618

Editor: Annie Niemiec

DESCRIPTION AND INTERESTS

Fun projects that are easy to do in a classroom or at home are the focus of this craft magazine. It features a range of party ideas (and projects to go with them), activities, and games, along with crafts suitable for all age ranges. Circ: 15,000.

Audience: Parents and teachers
Frequency: 6 times each year
Website: www.pack-o-fun.com

FREELANCE POTENTIAL

50% written by nonstaff writers. Receives 500 unsolicited mss yearly.

SUBMISSIONS

Send complete ms with instructions, brief materials list, and photographs of project. Accepts hard copy and email submissions to aniemiec@amoscraft.com (attach files). SASE. Responds in 4–6 weeks.

- Articles: To 200 words. How-to articles; craft projects; and party ideas.
- Depts/columns: Word lengths vary. Art ideas, projects for children and adults to do together, vacation Bible school projects, photos of readers' projects.
- Artwork: B/W and color prints; JPEG files. Line art.

SAMPLE ISSUE

66 pages (10% advertising): 39 crafts; 4 depts/columns. Sample copy, $4.99 with 9x12 SASE (2 first-class stamps). Writers' guidelines available at website.

- "Nature Walk Pouches." Article provides instructions for making a felt pouch that can hold treasures found during a hike.
- Sample dept/column: "Bible Creations" explains how to make crosses featuring images of people for whom we are thankful.

RIGHTS AND PAYMENT

All rights. All material, $25–$150. Pays 30 days after signed contract. Provides 3 copies.

❖EDITOR'S COMMENTS

The basic outline that all project articles follow is: tell what it is, the materials needed, and the steps to follow. All projects must be easy to make and made from recyclable or low-cost materials. The best ones will also have a theme or focus relating to a holiday, gift, or curriculum-based subject.

Pageantry

1855 W. State Road 434, Suite 254
Longwood, FL 32750

Editor

DESCRIPTION AND INTERESTS

Written for teens and adults who participate in beauty pageants, this magazine immerses readers in the glamour of the gowns, jewelry, and hairstyles needed to win competitions. Articles also focus on the more demanding side, such as fitness and talent. Circ: Unavailable.

Audience: YA–Adult
Frequency: Quarterly
Website: www.pageantry-digital.com

FREELANCE POTENTIAL

10% written by nonstaff writers. Publishes 5 freelance submissions yearly.

SUBMISSIONS

Query. Accepts hard copy and email queries to editor@pageantrymagazine.com. SASE. Response time varies.

- Articles: Word lengths vary. Informational articles; profiles; interviews; and personal experience pieces. Topics include beauty pageants, celebrities, fitness, modeling, makeup tips, interviewing techniques, dance, winning psychology, judges' perspectives, etiquette, coaching, talent competitions, and fashion.
- Depts/columns: Word lengths vary. Jewelry, makeup, hairstyles, fitness, body shaping, modeling, personal advice, teen issues, winner profiles, etiquette, news, opinions, show business, and celebrities.
- Artwork: JPEG digital images.

SAMPLE ISSUE

144 pages: 4 articles; 25 depts/columns. Sample copy, $4.95. Writers' guidelines available at website.

- "It's All Up to You." Article tells how to stand out from the crowd at the International Modeling and Talent Association convention.
- Sample dept/column: "Makeup" provides instructions for creating a sun-touched look.

RIGHTS AND PAYMENT

First North American serial rights. Written material, payment rates vary. Payment policy varies. Provides 1 contributor's copy.

❖EDITOR'S COMMENTS

We invite you to participate in our magazine by submitting event and program news articles and photos. Check our website for editorial deadline dates.

Parentguide News

419 Park Avenue South, Floor 13
New York, NY 10016

Editor: Jenna Hammond

DESCRIPTION AND INTERESTS
Catering to the needs of parents in the New York metropolitan area, this tabloid-sized publication offers guidance and insight to parents with children under the age of 12. It covers everything from family matters and pregnancy to health and education. Circ: 285,000.

Audience: Parents
Frequency: Monthly
Website: www.parentguidenews.com

FREELANCE POTENTIAL
75% written by nonstaff writers. Publishes 100 freelance submissions yearly; 5% by unpublished writers, 60% by authors who are new to the magazine. Receives 4,200 queries yearly.

SUBMISSIONS
Query. Accepts email queries to jenna@parentguidenews.com. Responds in 4 months.

- Articles: 700–1,200 words. Informational and how-to articles; profiles; interviews; and personal experience pieces. Topics include parenting, pregnancy, child development, health and fitness, special education, recreation, crafts, and nutrition.
- Fiction: Word lengths vary. Genres include humor and inspirational fiction.
- Depts/columns: 200–1,000 words. Crafts, health tips, recipes, and regional news and events.
- Other: Submit seasonal material 5 months in advance.

SAMPLE ISSUE
86 pages: 11 articles; 6 depts/columns; 1 special section. Sample copy, $4. Writers' guidelines available.

- "The Co-Sleeping Habit." Article offers suggestions for establishing good bedtime routines in order to break the co-sleeping habit with young children.
- Sample dept/column: "Travel" offers updates on new hotels and travel products.

RIGHTS AND PAYMENT
Regional rights for 1 year. No payment. Provides 2 contributor's copies.

➻EDITOR'S COMMENTS
New writers are welcome to contact us. Your best bet is to query us on a personal experience piece with important, engaging, or seldom-discussed family concerns.

Parenting

135 West 50th Street, 3rd Floor
New York, NY 10026

Submissions Editor

DESCRIPTION AND INTERESTS
Parenting covers the psychological as well as the practical aspects of raising a child from birth to age 12. Its articles also deal with the emotional issues that mothers face—issues such as maintaining their friendships and juggling their various roles. Circ: 2 million+.

Audience: Parents
Frequency: 11 times each year
Website: www.parenting.com

FREELANCE POTENTIAL
80% written by nonstaff writers. Publishes 10–15 freelance submissions yearly; 5% by unpublished writers, 10% by authors who are new to the magazine. Receives 1,000 queries each year.

SUBMISSIONS
Query with clips. Accepts hard copy. SASE. Responds in 1–2 months.

- Articles: 1,000–2,500 words. Informational, how-to, and self-help articles; profiles; and personal experience pieces. Topics include child development, behavior, and health; pregnancy; and family activities.
- Depts/columns: 100–1,000 words. Parenting tips, child development by age range, work and family, health, fitness, and beauty.

SAMPLE ISSUE
184 pages (50% advertising): 5 articles; 22 depts/columns. Sample copy, $5.95 (mark envelope Attn: Back Issues). Writers' guidelines available.

- "The A+ Study Guide." Article explains how to teach kids test-preparation skills.
- "Kids' Toughest Questions." Article compiles advice from experts on ways to deal with awkward questions.
- Sample dept/column: "Money" looks at high-interest checking accounts and offers advice for moms preparing to return to the workforce.

RIGHTS AND PAYMENT
First world rights with 2 months exclusivity. Written material, payment rates vary. Pays on acceptance. Provides 1 contributor's copy.

➻EDITOR'S COMMENTS
Writers who are new to us have the best chance of acceptance with a query for one of our departments. Be sure to enclose clips.

Parenting Children with Special Needs

30905 East Stony Point School Road
Grain Valley, MO 64029

Publisher: Stephanie Myers

DESCRIPTION AND INTERESTS
Distributed in the Kansas City area through schools, hospitals, medical clinics, and businesses, this magazine is filled with practical articles for parents of special needs children. Each issue spotlights local resources, presents timely information from healthcare and other professionals, and offers poetry written by parents. Circ: 20,000.
Audience: Parents
Frequency: 6 times each year
Website: www.pcwsn.com

FREELANCE POTENTIAL
Publishes several freelance submissions yearly.

SUBMISSIONS
Send complete ms. Accepts email submissions to editors@pcwsn.com. Response time varies.

- Articles: Word lengths vary. Informational articles; profiles; and personal experience pieces. Topics include special education, health, medical care, and nutrition.
- Depts/columns: Word lengths vary. Self-care for parents, educational programs, local resources, and advice from healthcare and education professionals.
- Other: Poetry by parents, line lengths vary.

SAMPLE ISSUE
Sample copy available at website.

- "Siblings Play, Paint, and Heal at Leawood Nonprofit." Article reports on a children's center that offers art, music, relaxation, and pet therapy for children with physical illnesses and their siblings.
- "Seeing the World Through the Eyes of Your Special Needs Child." Article offers advice and support from the mother of a hard-of-hearing child.

RIGHTS AND PAYMENT
Rights vary. Written material, payment rates vary. Payment policy varies.

➥EDITOR'S COMMENTS
Our mission is to facilitate the distribution of materials relevant to parents of special needs children by offering support, information, understanding, encouragement, and guidance. We aim to present the facts as well as share the struggles and emotional turmoil faced by parents raising a special needs child within our community.

Parenting New Hampshire

150 Dow Street
Manchester, NH 03101

Editor: Melanie Hitchcock

DESCRIPTION AND INTERESTS
All aspects of parenting—from childbirth through managing adolescents—are covered in this magazine for New Hampshire families. It also provides updates on family-friendly events and resources. Circ: 27,500.
Audience: Parents
Frequency: Monthly
Website: www.parentingnh.com

FREELANCE POTENTIAL
85% written by nonstaff writers. Publishes 25–35 freelance submissions yearly; 20% by unpublished writers, 50% by authors who are new to the magazine. Receives 1,200 queries, 240–360 unsolicited mss yearly.

SUBMISSIONS
Query or send complete ms with writing samples. Accepts hard copy, disk submissions, and email submissions to news@parentingnh.com. SASE. Response time varies.

- Articles: Word lengths vary. Informational and how-to articles; profiles; and interviews. Topics include parenting, education, maternity, childbirth, special needs, gifted education, fathering, child development, summer fun, birthday parties, holidays, back-to-school issues, and health.
- Depts/columns: Word lengths vary. Child development, parenting issues, and health and wellness.
- Other: Submit seasonal material 3 months in advance.

SAMPLE ISSUE
54 pages (42% advertising): 5 articles; 12 depts/columns. Sample copy, free. Guidelines available at website.

- "Let's Hear It for Dad." Article reports on the critical role fathers play in determining positive outcomes for children.
- "A Helmet Isn't Enough." Article exposes the long-term effects of brain trauma.

RIGHTS AND PAYMENT
All rights. Articles, $30. Other material, payment rates vary. Pays on acceptance. Provides 3 contributor's copies.

➥EDITOR'S COMMENTS
We want articles that offer a local perspective, preferably written by authors who are from New Hampshire.

Parenting Special Needs

310 21st Court SW
Vero Beach, FL 32962

Editorial Office

DESCRIPTION AND INTERESTS
The mission of *Parenting Special Needs* is to provide practical tips, share life lessons, help tackle challenges, and celebrate the joys related to raising children with special needs. Hits per month: Unavailable.

Audience: Parents
Frequency: 6 times each year
Website: www.parentingspecialneeds.org

FREELANCE POTENTIAL
Publishes several freelance submissions yearly.

SUBMISSIONS
Query or send complete ms with brief author bio. Accepts hard copy and email submissions to submit@parentingspecialneeds.org (Microsoft Word attachments). Availability of artwork improves chance of acceptance. SASE. Response time varies.

- Articles: 400–1,000 words. Informational articles and personal experience pieces. Topics include health, discipline, alternative treatments, fitness, nutrition, family travel, and developmental stages—all as they relate to children with special needs.
- Depts/columns: Word lengths vary. New product information, book reviews, essays.
- Artwork: B/W or color prints; JPEG, TIFF, or PDF images at 150 dpi (minimum).

SAMPLE ISSUE
Sample copy and writers' guidelines available at website.

- "Catch the Waves." Article reports on Surfers for Autism, a Boca Raton organization that was created to introduce children on the autism spectrum to the healing powers of the ocean.
- "Time-Out: Does It Work?" Article looks at this popular disciplinary strategy, offers guidelines for using it effectively, and suggests other strategies for improving behavior.
- Sample dept/column: "Healthy Summer Treats" presents ways to get creative with summer's fresh vegetables and fruit.

RIGHTS AND PAYMENT
Rights vary. No payment.

➥EDITOR'S COMMENTS
We're always seeking useful, objective information for our readers. Please note that we may hold submissions for possible future use.

Parent Life

One LifeWay Plaza
Nashville, TN 37234-0172

Content Editor: Jodi Skulley

DESCRIPTION AND INTERESTS
This parenting magazine has a distinctly Christian perspective. Its articles offer help, information, and advice in all the areas in which parents seek godly guidance for their children: health, education, safety, and spiritual development. Circ: 63,000.

Audience: Parents
Frequency: Monthly
Website: www.lifeway.com/parentlifeblog

FREELANCE POTENTIAL
90% written by nonstaff writers. Publishes 12–15 freelance submissions yearly; 10% by unpublished writers, 25% by authors who are new to the magazine. Receives 600 queries, 360 unsolicited mss yearly.

SUBMISSIONS
Query or send complete ms. Accepts hard copy and email submissions to jodi.skulley@lifeway.com. SASE. Response time varies.

- Articles: 500–1,500 words. Informational and how-to articles; and personal experience pieces. Topics include family issues, religion, education, health, and hobbies.
- Depts/columns: 500 words. Age-appropriate advice, fathers' perspectives, expectant parents, single parenting, and medical advice.
- Artwork: Color prints and transparencies.
- Other: Accepts seasonal material for Christmas and Thanksgiving.

SAMPLE ISSUE
50 pages: 8 articles; 13 depts/columns. Sample copy, $3.95 with 10x13 SASE. Writers' guidelines available.

- "Dads at Home." Article posits that fathers carry equal responsibility in parenting, and provides advice for helping them in that role.
- Sample dept/column: "On the Way" advises expectant mothers to keep the baby-focused conversations from becoming too much.

RIGHTS AND PAYMENT
Nonexclusive rights. Written material, $125–$350. Pays on publication. Provides 1 contributor's copy.

➥EDITOR'S COMMENTS
Our focus is on parents of younger children rather than teens. All articles should be informative above all else, as well as upbeat and encouraging.

Parents & Kids

785 North President Street, Suite B
Jackson, MS 39202

Editor: Gretchen Cook

DESCRIPTION AND INTERESTS
Parenting, education, health and safety, and local recreation are among the topics covered in this regional magazine. Circ: 35,000.

Audience: Parents
Frequency: Monthly
Website: www.parents-kids.com

FREELANCE POTENTIAL
80% written by nonstaff writers. Publishes 80 freelance submissions yearly; 50% by unpublished writers. Receives 396 mss yearly.

SUBMISSIONS
Send complete ms. Accepts email submissions to magazine@parents-kids.com (text in body of email and as Microsoft Word attachment). Responds in 6 weeks.

- Articles: 700 words. Informational, self-help, and how-to articles. Topics include parenting, education, the arts, computers, crafts and hobbies, health and fitness, multicultural and ethnic issues, recreation, regional news, social issues, special education, sports, and family travel.
- Depts/columns: 500 words. Travel, cooking, and computers.
- Artwork: Prefers digital images; will accept B/W prints or transparencies. Line art.
- Other: Submit seasonal material 3–6 months in advance.

SAMPLE ISSUE
48 pages (54% advertising): 7 articles; 11 depts/columns. Sample copy, free with 9x12 SASE ($1.06 postage). Guidelines available at website.

- "Nintendo's Wii as Therapy?" Article reports on the benefits of using the Wii video game system in occupational therapy.
- Sample dept/column: "Living Greenly" offers ideas for living a more eco-friendly lifestyle.

RIGHTS AND PAYMENT
One-time rights. Written material, $25. Pays on publication. Provides 1 tearsheet.

➥EDITOR'S COMMENTS
We prefer pieces that have local resources and references. We are a hands-on resource for Jackson parents, and want Jackson-area information. If writing about your own experience, be sure to offer information that can help other parents.

Parents' Press

1454 Sixth Street
Berkeley, CA 94710

Editor: Dixie M. Jordan

DESCRIPTION AND INTERESTS
Published for families that live in the San Francisco area, *Parents' Press* specializes in practical information about the care and development of children. Factual, researched-based articles on topics such as health, education, and relationships appear along with information about local resources. Circ: 75,000.

Audience: Parents
Frequency: Monthly
Website: www.parentspress.com

FREELANCE POTENTIAL
15–20% written by nonstaff writers. Publishes 25–50 freelance submissions yearly; 15% by authors who are new to the magazine. Receives hundreds of unsolicited mss yearly.

SUBMISSIONS
Send complete ms. Accepts hard copy and email submissions to parentsprs@aol.com. SASE. Responds in 2 months.

- Articles: To 1,500 words. Informational and how-to articles. Topics include child development, education, health, safety, party planning, and local family events and activities.
- Depts/columns: Staff written.
- Artwork: B/W prints and transparencies. Line art.
- Other: Submit seasonal material 2 months in advance.

SAMPLE ISSUE
32 pages (63% advertising): 7 articles; 14 depts/columns. Sample copy, $3 with 9x12 SASE ($1.93 postage).

- "A-Camping We Will Go." Article provides details on family-friendly campsites in the San Francisco area.
- Sample dept/column: "Parent-Teen" explores ways teens and their parents can connect by volunteering together on community projects during the summer.

RIGHTS AND PAYMENT
All or second rights. Articles, $50–$500. Pays 45 days after publication.

➥EDITOR'S COMMENTS
Personal experiences and opinions are not what we are looking for. We want well-researched articles that provide practical information for parents and include references to local sources.

Parent:Wise Austin

5501 A Balcones Drive, Suite 102
Austin, TX 78731

Editor/Publisher: Kim Pleticha

DESCRIPTION AND INTERESTS
In addition to fact-filled, interview-based articles about parenting, this magazine features humor, essays, and poetry that reflect the day-to-day concerns of families. It was created specifically for families living in central Texas. Circ: 32,000.
Audience: Parents
Frequency: Monthly
Website: www.parentwiseaustin.com

FREELANCE POTENTIAL
25% written by nonstaff writers. Publishes 15+ freelance submissions yearly; 33% by authors who are new to the magazine.

SUBMISSIONS
Send complete ms. Accepts email submissions to editor@parentwiseaustin.com. Response time varies.

- Articles: To 650 words. Informational articles; essays; and humor. Topics include parenting, family life, education, regional news, and people in the Austin community who work to make life better for other families.
- Depts/columns: To 650 words. Humor about parenting and family life; medical advice.
- Other: Poetry about parenting, children, or families; to 24 lines.

SAMPLE ISSUE
40 pages: 3 articles; 6 depts/columns; 3 calendars. Sample copy and writers' guidelines available at website.

- "The Fall of Family Connections: How Fraud Cheated Families." Article reports on how a well-known family assistance agency in Austin was closed after the executive director allegedly committed fraud.
- Sample dept/column: "My Life as a Parent" offers a humorous glimpse at one mom's experience with a triathlon.

RIGHTS AND PAYMENT
First North American serial and Internet rights. Written material, payment rates vary. Payment policy varies.

❖EDITOR'S COMMENTS
We look for thoughtful, intelligent articles that depict some aspect of the parenting journey. Articles must be well-researched, tightly written, and directed at an audience of parents who want to be educated.

Partners

Christian Light Publications
P.O. Box 1212
Harrisonburg, VA 22803-1212

Editor: Etta G. Martin

DESCRIPTION AND INTERESTS
This children's publication is filled with short stories, articles, poems, and puzzles that reflect the Mennonite faith. Used as a Sunday school take-home piece, it is printed in four weekly sections. Circ: 6,923.
Audience: 9–14 years
Frequency: Monthly
Website: www.clp.org

FREELANCE POTENTIAL
98% written by nonstaff writers. Publishes 200–500 freelance submissions yearly; 5% by unpublished writers, 5% by authors who are new to the magazine. Receives 200–300 unsolicited mss yearly.

SUBMISSIONS
Send complete ms. Prefers email submissions to partners@clp.org; will accept hard copy and simultaneous submissions if identified. SASE. Responds in 6 weeks.

- Articles: 200–800 words. Informational articles. Topics include Bible customs, nature, and church history and teachings.
- Fiction: 400–1,600 words. Feature stories that emphasize Mennonite beliefs and biblical standards.
- Other: Word puzzles and activities with Christian themes. Poetry; no free verse. Submit seasonal material 6 months in advance.

SAMPLE ISSUE
16 pages (no advertising): 6 stories; 2 articles; 4 poems, 4 activities. Sample copy, free with 9x12 SASE ($1.22 postage). Guidelines and theme list available.

- "Grandma Grace." Story tells of a young girl's special relationship with an elderly neighbor.
- "Who Keeps It Going?" Article discusses God's work of creating people.

RIGHTS AND PAYMENT
First, reprint, or multiple-use rights. Articles and stories, $.04–$.06 per word. Poetry, $.50–$.75 per line. Activities, payment rates vary. Pays on acceptance. Provides 1 contributor's copy.

❖EDITOR'S COMMENTS
Submissions should have an age-appropriate, clear spiritual lesson, and they should correlate with one of our planned issue themes.

Pediatrics for Parents

P.O. Box 219
Gloucester, MA 01931

Editor: Richard J. Sagall, M.D.

DESCRIPTION AND INTERESTS
Known as "The Children's Medical Journal for Parents," this publication offers carefully researched information in language accessible to the lay reader. Topics covered include wellness, disease prevention and treatment, and the latest medical advances. Circ: 250,000.

Audience: Parents
Frequency: 6 times each year
Website: www.pedsforparents.com

FREELANCE POTENTIAL
50% written by nonstaff writers. Publishes 30 freelance submissions yearly; 50% by unpublished writers, 50% by authors who are new to the magazine. Receives 50 queries and unsolicited mss yearly.

SUBMISSIONS
Query or send complete ms. Accepts email submissions to articles@pedsforparents.com (Microsoft Word attachments). Response time varies.

- Articles: 750–1,500 words. Informational articles. Topics include prevention, fitness, medical advances, new treatment options, wellness, and pregnancy.
- Depts/columns: Word lengths vary. Article reprints and new product information.

SAMPLE ISSUE
32 pages (no advertising): 20 articles; 6 depts/columns. Sample copy, $5 via website. Guidelines available at website.

- "Asthma Camp." Article recounts a doctor's experience treating asthma patients at a summer camp for chronically ill children.
- Sample dept/column: "Stinging Insects" discusses allergic reactions to insect stings.

RIGHTS AND PAYMENT
First rights. Written material, to $25. Pays on publication. Provides 3 contributor's copies and a 1-year subscription.

➝EDITOR'S COMMENTS
We will publish only material that is medically accurate, contains resource citations where applicable, and is useful to parents of children from prenatal to early teen. Submissions of previously published articles from medical and dental journals will be considered only if rewritten for our lay audience. Remember that we emphasize prevention.

Piedmont Parent

P.O. Box 530
King, NC 27021

Editor: Myra Wright

DESCRIPTION AND INTERESTS
Essays and articles that have a local spin are found in *Piedmont Parent*, a tabloid targeting families in the Winston-Salem and High Point regions of North Carolina. Child care, education, and family entertainment are among the topics it covers. Circ: 39,000.

Audience: Parents
Frequency: Monthly
Website: www.piedmontparent.com

FREELANCE POTENTIAL
50% written by nonstaff writers. Publishes 36–40 freelance submissions yearly; 25% by unpublished writers, 50% by authors who are new to the magazine. Receives 1,000+ queries and unsolicited mss yearly.

SUBMISSIONS
Query or send complete ms. Accepts email to editor@piedmontparent.com (Microsoft Word attachments) and simultaneous submissions if identified. Responds in 1–2 months.

- Articles: 500–1,200 words. Informational and how-to articles; interviews; and personal experience pieces. Topics include child development, day care, summer camps, gifted and special education, local and regional news, science, social issues, sports, popular culture, health, and travel.
- Depts/columns: 600–900 words. Family health and parenting news.
- Other: Family games and activities.

SAMPLE ISSUE
40 pages (47% advertising): 8 articles; 5 depts/columns. Sample copy, free with 9x12 SASE ($1.50 postage). Guidelines and theme list available.

- "Delivery Advice from Experts." Article fills expectant parents in on procedures they will likely encounter upon arrival at the hospital.
- "Temper Taming Tactics." Article offers tips for dealing with angry children.

RIGHTS AND PAYMENT
One time rights. Written material, payment rates vary. Pays on publication. Provides 1 tearsheet.

➝EDITOR'S COMMENTS
Features require thorough research (citing a minimum of three reliable sources) and concise interviewing and writing skills.

Pikes Peak Parent

30 South Prospect Street
Colorado Springs, CO 80903

Editor: George Lewis

DESCRIPTION AND INTERESTS
The latest parenting news of interest to families in greater Colorado Springs appears in *Pikes Peak Parent*. All of its articles focus on the best ways to raise, educate, and entertain the area's children. It is distributed free throughout the region. Circ: 30,000.

Audience: Parents
Frequency: Monthly
Website: www.pikespeakparent.com

FREELANCE POTENTIAL
5% written by nonstaff writers. Publishes 4 freelance submissions yearly; 2% by authors who are new to the magazine. Receives 60 queries yearly.

SUBMISSIONS
Query with writing samples. Accepts hard copy and email queries to parent@gazette.com. SASE. Response time varies.

- Articles: 800–1,500 words. Informational and how-to articles; and profiles. Topics include regional news and resources, parenting issues, family life, travel, health, safety, sports, social issues, and recreation.
- Depts/columns: Word lengths vary. News, opinions, grandparenting, health, family issues, profiles, and events.

SAMPLE ISSUE
20 pages (50% advertising): 8 articles; 5 depts/columns. Sample copy, free with 9x12 SASE.

- "More Summer Fun with a Deck of Playing Cards." Article tells how a deck of cards can offer inexpensive fun, whether it's by playing games or learning new tricks.
- Sample dept/column: "The Father 'hood" offers a perspective from a father who is about to become a stay-at-home dad.

RIGHTS AND PAYMENT
All rights on assigned pieces; second rights on reprints and unsolicited pieces. Written material, payment rates vary. Pays on publication. Provides 1 contributor's copy.

◆EDITOR'S COMMENTS
We would rather see practical articles with local sources than opinions and essays about parenting. Articles about local businesses are okay, as long as they offer insights and information parents can use.

Pittsburgh Parent

P.O. Box 374
Bakerstown, PA 15007

Editor: Patricia Poshard

DESCRIPTION AND INTERESTS
Loads of parenting advice from local resources and experts can be found in each issue of this magazine. It covers a variety of family topics of interest to parents of newborns to teens. Circ: 50,000+.

Audience: Parents
Frequency: Monthly
Website: www.pittsburghparent.com

FREELANCE POTENTIAL
80% written by nonstaff writers. Publishes 120 freelance submissions yearly; 20% by authors who are new to the magazine. Receives 1,500 queries and unsolicited mss yearly.

SUBMISSIONS
Query or send complete ms. Accepts hard copy, email to editor@pittsburghparent.com, and simultaneous submissions if identified. SASE. Response time varies.

- Articles: Cover story, 2,500–2,750 words. Other material, 400–900 words. Informational articles; profiles; and interviews. Topics include family issues, parenting, education, science, fitness, health, nature, college, computers, and multicultural subjects.
- Fiction: 1,000 words. Genres include mystery, adventure, and historical and multicultural fiction.
- Depts/columns: Word lengths vary. Education, teen issues, book reviews, and humor.
- Other: Submit seasonal material 3 months in advance.

SAMPLE ISSUE
60 pages (65% advertising): 11 articles; 4 depts/columns. Sample copy, free. Guidelines and editorial calendar available.

- "Teach Kids How to Study." Article discusses the importance of learning good study habits early.
- Sample dept/column: "Teens" discusses which boundaries to set when teens want more privacy.

RIGHTS AND PAYMENT
First serial rights. Written material, payment rates vary. Pays 45 days after publication. Provides 1 tearsheet.

◆EDITOR'S COMMENTS
Well-written and fresh articles with a local angle will always get our attention.

PKA's Advocate

1881 Little Westkill Road
Prattsville, NY 12468

Publisher: Patricia Keller

DESCRIPTION AND INTERESTS
Fiction, personal essays, and poetry, appealing particularly to horse-, nature-, and animal-lovers, are featured. The Gaited Horse Association Newsletter is also included. Circ: 10,000.

Audience: YA–Adult
Frequency: 6 times each year

FREELANCE POTENTIAL
90% written by nonstaff writers. Publishes 150 freelance submissions yearly; 65% by unpublished writers, 35% by authors who are new to the magazine. Receives 1,500 unsolicited mss each year.

SUBMISSIONS
Send complete ms. Accepts hard copy. SASE. No simultaneous submissions. Responds in 6–10 weeks.

- Articles: To 1,500 words. Informational articles; personal experience pieces; profiles; and essays. Topics include horses, animals, the arts, humor, nature, and recreation.
- Fiction: To 1,500 words. Genres include contemporary, historical, realistic, and science fiction; adventure; fantasy; romance; mystery; suspense; and stories about animals, nature, and the environment.
- Artwork: 8x10 B/W or color prints. Line art.
- Other: Gaited Horse Association Newsletter, published within. Poetry, no line limit. Puzzles and recipes.

SAMPLE ISSUE
20 pages (50% advertising): 1 article; 1 story; 18 poems. Sample copy, $5. Writer's guidelines available.

- "Can You Remember Your First Christmas?" Personal essay is a poignant recollection of the first Christmas that the author's family celebrated when he was very young.
- "Little Oh No." Story tells how the birth of a red lamb changed a herd of sheep.

RIGHTS AND PAYMENT
First rights. No payment. Provides 2 copies.

⇢EDITOR'S COMMENTS
Original, previously unpublished pieces are welcome from beginning writers. We are especially interested in stories and personal essays that capture our animal-loving readers' imaginations and hearts. Remember that we are a family-friendly publication.

Playground Magazine

360 B Street
Idaho Falls, ID 83402

Editor: Lane Lindstrom

DESCRIPTION AND INTERESTS
Professionals and others involved in the design, planning, installation, and operation of playground systems read this magazine for informative articles. Profiles of companies are also published. Circ: 35,000.

Audience: Adults
Frequency: 7 times each year
Website: www.playgroundmag.com

FREELANCE POTENTIAL
25% written by nonstaff writers. Publishes 8 freelance submissions yearly; 30% by authors who are new to the magazine. Receives 24–48 queries yearly.

SUBMISSIONS
Query or send complete ms. Accepts hard copy and email submissions to lindstrm@harrispublishing.com. SASE. Responds in 1–2 months.

- Articles: 800–1,200 words. Informational and how-to articles. Topics include the planning, design, and installation of playgrounds; types of play structures; surfacing; safety; maintenance; skate parks; aquatic features; and fundraising.
- Depts/columns: Word lengths vary. Legal issues, news, industry updates, manufacturer profiles, landscaping, design, and the developmental value of play.

SAMPLE ISSUE
32 pages: 3 articles; 6 depts/columns; 1 directory. Sample copy, $5. Guidelines and editorial calendar available.

- "The Chill Effect." Article offers tips on how to provide the best protection against the elements during winter months.
- "Natural Playgrounds." Article describes six ways to put nature back into play.
- Sample dept/column: "News & Notes" profiles Burke's Nucleus playground system.

RIGHTS AND PAYMENT
First serial rights. Articles, $100–$300. Depts/columns, $50–$175. Payment policy varies.

⇢EDITOR'S COMMENTS
While playground structures play a very important part in our editorial mix, we also look for articles that prove and promote the value of play itself. And we want to provide only up-to-date industry information.

Plays
The Drama Magazine for Young People

P.O. Box 600160
Newton, MA 02460

Editor: Elizabeth Preston

DESCRIPTION AND INTERESTS
Plays for elementary, middle, and high school students are the sole focus of this magazine. Original material, as well as adaptations of well-known plays, are featured. Circ: 5,300.

Audience: 6–17 years
Frequency: 7 times each year
Website: www.playsmag.com

FREELANCE POTENTIAL
100% written by nonstaff writers. Publishes 75 freelance submissions yearly; 25% by unpublished writers, 50% by authors who are new to the magazine. Receives 250 queries and unsolicited mss yearly.

SUBMISSIONS
Send complete ms. Query for adaptations of classics or folktales only. Accepts hard copy. SASE. Responds to queries in 2 weeks, to mss in 1 month.

- Fiction: One-act plays for high school, to 5,000 words; for middle school, to 3,750 words; for elementary school, to 2,500 words. Also publishes skits, monologues, puppet plays, and dramatized classics. Genres include patriotic, historical, and biographical drama; mystery; melodrama; fairy tales; folktales; comedy; and farce.
- Other: Submit seasonal material 4 months in advance.

SAMPLE ISSUE
64 pages (5% advertising): 8 plays. Sample copy, free with 6x9 SASE ($.76 postage). Guidelines available.

- "Balancing Act." Play shows a Native American helping a fellow construction worker to understand the relationship between the Manhattan building they are working on and the Iroquois people.
- "Queen of the Playground." Play tells what happens when the new girl in school, who happens to have Tourette's Syndrome, faces down the school's most popular girl.

RIGHTS AND PAYMENT
All rights. Written material, payment rates vary. Pays on acceptance. Provides 1 author's copy.

➥EDITOR'S COMMENTS
We need plays that are easy to produce, secular, and wholesome, and that address issues relevant to the actors' age groups.

Pockets

The Upper Room
1908 Grand Avenue
P.O. Box 340004
Nashville, TN 37203-0004

Editor: Lynn W. Gilliam

DESCRIPTION AND INTERESTS
This magazine emphasizes that God loves us and calls us into community in order to experience that love. It does this through articles, stories, poetry, and activities. Circ: 58,000.

Audience: 6–12 years
Frequency: 11 times each year
Website: www.pockets.org

FREELANCE POTENTIAL
70% written by nonstaff writers. Publishes 165–200 freelance submissions yearly. Receives 600–1,200 unsolicited mss yearly.

SUBMISSIONS
Send complete ms. Accepts hard copy. SASE. Responds in 2 months.

- Articles: 400–1,000 words. Informational articles; profiles; and personal experience pieces. Topics include multicultural and community issues, and individuals whose lives reflect their Christian commitment.
- Fiction: 600–1,000 words. Stories that demonstrate Christian values.
- Depts/columns: Word lengths vary. Scripture readings and lessons; recipes.
- Artwork: Color prints; digital images to 300 dpi.
- Other: Poetry. Puzzles, activities, and games.

SAMPLE ISSUE
48 pages (no advertising): 1 article; 5 stories; 14 depts/columns; 6 activities; 2 poems. Sample copy, free with 9x12 SASE (4 first-class stamps). Writers' guidelines and theme list available at website.

- "A Peace of Pizza." Story tells how a boy strives to be a peacemaker by making an analogy to different types of pizza toppings.
- "Dana's Dilemma." Story relates a girl's eventual reconciliation with her best friend through prayer.

RIGHTS AND PAYMENT
First and second rights. Written material, $.14 per word. Poetry, $2 per line. Games, $25–$50. Pays on acceptance. Provides 3–5 copies.

➥EDITOR'S COMMENTS
Pockets has undergone a major redesign. We're using shorter fiction now, and we've added several nonfiction features. We continue to cater to readers from a variety of denominations, cultures, and family backgrounds.

Pointe

110 William Street, 23rd Floor
New York, NY 10038

Managing Editor: Carol Rubin

DESCRIPTION AND INTERESTS

Dedicated exclusively to ballet, *Pointe* magazine is read by students, professional dancers, teachers, and amateur enthusiasts. It covers all topics related to ballet, including auditioning; injury prevention; training programs; and profiles of dancers, teachers, and choreographers. Circ: 40,000.

Audience: All ages
Frequency: 6 times each year
Website: www.pointemagazine.com

FREELANCE POTENTIAL

75% written by nonstaff writers. Publishes 1–2 freelance submissions yearly; 10% by unpublished writers, 25% by authors who are new to the magazine. Receives 12 queries yearly.

SUBMISSIONS

Query. Accepts hard copy. SASE. Responds in 2 months.

- Articles: 1,200 words. Informational articles; profiles; interviews; personal experience pieces; and photo-essays. Topics include ballet companies, dancers, choreographers, news, trends, festivals and events, premieres, and auditions.
- Depts/columns: 800–1,000 words. Premieres, news, interviews with directors, profiles of dancers and companies, advice, and tips on technique.
- Artwork: B/W and color prints or transparencies; digital photos. Line art.

SAMPLE ISSUE

80 pages (50% advertising): 5 articles; 14 depts/columns. Sample copy, guidelines, and theme list available.

- "Competitions: Beyond the Medals." Article explores the other rewards to competing, including networking, experience, and proving that you can dance under pressure.
- "Toe to Toe." Personal experience piece by a professional dancer examines the physical and emotional hardships one has to overcome to dance.

RIGHTS AND PAYMENT

All rights. Written material, payment rates vary. Pays on acceptance. Provides 2 author's copies.

❖EDITOR'S COMMENTS

We are looking for people with dance experience and a winning way with words.

Positive Parenting

P.O. Box 1312
Ventura, CA 93002

Owner: Deborah Fox

DESCRIPTION AND INTERESTS

This e-zine is dedicated to providing resources and information that help make parenting more rewarding, effective, and fun. All articles relate to the belief that children should be raised lovingly and non-violently, and with discipline that motivates them through love. Hits per month: Unavailable.

Audience: Parents
Frequency: Updated regularly
Website: www.positiveparenting.com

FREELANCE POTENTIAL

30% written by nonstaff writers. Publishes 2–3 freelance submissions yearly; 10–20% by unpublished writers, 80% by authors who are new to the magazine. Receives 48–72 unsolicited mss yearly.

SUBMISSIONS

Send complete ms. Accepts email submissions to info@positiveparenting.com. Response time varies.

- Articles: 500–1,000 words. Informational and how-to articles; and personal experience pieces. Topics include parenting, discipline, and family relationship issues.
- Depts/columns: Word lengths vary. Success stories, reviews.
- Other: Seasonal and holiday-related parenting tips.

SAMPLE ISSUE

4 articles. Sample copy available at website.

- "Ten Keys to Successful Parenting." Article outlines 10 keys to disciplining children in ways that recognize their feelings and build their self-esteem.
- "Deciding to Spare the Rod." Article examines the benefits of removing hitting or spanking from one's discipline method, and outlines ways to discipline without hitting.

RIGHTS AND PAYMENT

Rights vary. No payment.

❖EDITOR'S COMMENTS

A professional background in child development is not needed to contribute to our site. We are about parents (and professionals) helping parents understand how to raise their children in a loving, self esteem-building manner. Articles on discipline issues and success stories are most open to new writers.

Prehistoric Times

145 Bayline Circle
Folsom, CA 95630-8077

Editor: Mike Fredericks

DESCRIPTION AND INTERESTS
Prehistoric Times unearths facts and offers speculations about dinosaurs and other species. It is read by enthusiasts for its scientific articles, as well as for its how-to modeling instructions, collector news, and media reviews. Circ: Unavailable.

Audience: YA–Adult
Frequency: Quarterly
Website: www.prehistorictimes.com

FREELANCE POTENTIAL
30% written by nonstaff writers. Publishes 20+ freelance submissions yearly; 75% by unpublished writers, 75% by authors who are new to the magazine. Receives 24+ unsolicited mss each year.

SUBMISSIONS
Send complete ms. Accepts email submissions to pretimes@comcast.net (attach file). Response time varies.

- Articles: 1,500–2,000 words. Informational articles. Topics include dinosaurs, paleontology, prehistoric life, drawing, and dinosaur-related collectibles.
- Depts/columns: Word lengths vary. Field news, dinosaur models, media reviews, interviews, and detailed descriptions of dinosaurs and other prehistoric species.

SAMPLE ISSUE
60 pages (30% advertising): 8 articles; 15 depts/columns. Sample copy, $7. Guidelines available via email request to pretimes@comcast.net.

- "Professor Earl Douglass." Article profiles the renowned geologist and paleontologist whose discovery of a dinosaur quarry led to Dinosaur National Monument.
- Sample dept/column: "Spinosaurus" provides a description of the species, model specifications, and instructions on how to paint the model.

RIGHTS AND PAYMENT
All rights. Written material, payment rates vary. Payment policy varies.

⇢EDITOR'S COMMENTS
We are interested in receiving more submissions of interviews with scientists, collectors, and model makers. Our readers are knowledgeable, so our writers must be, too.

PresenTense Magazine

214 Sullivan Street, Suite 2A
New York, NY 10012

Editor: Ariel Beery

DESCRIPTION AND INTERESTS
PresenTense is an international grassroots effort to inspire and enable socially-minded pioneering work amongst the Jewish community. Its magazine covers modern Jewish life, Jewish activism, giving back to society, the arts, and current events. Circ: 30,000.

Audience: YA–Adult
Frequency: 3 times each year
Website: www.presentensemagazine.org

FREELANCE POTENTIAL
80% written by nonstaff writers. Publishes 40 freelance submissions yearly; 40% by unpublished writers, 70% by authors who are new to the magazine.

SUBMISSIONS
Query or send complete ms. Accepts email queries and submissions via the website. Responds to queries in 2 weeks, to mss in 2 months.

- Articles: Features, 800–1,200 words. Profiles, 600–700 words. Sidebars, 50–250 words. Topics include Judaism, the Diaspora, Zionism, Israel, activism, community, education, relationships, and health.
- Fiction: 1,000–3,000 words. Genres vary.
- Depts/columns: "Paradigm Shift" essay, 1,200–2,000 words. "Around the World," 600–800 words. News and pop culture briefs, 400–500 words. Reviews, 300–800 words.
- Artwork: Digital photos and scans of line art, paintings, and cartoons at 300 dpi.
- Other: Photo-essays, 12 photos, 600 words. Poetry, to 300 words.

SAMPLE ISSUE
64 pages: 8 articles; 28 depts/columns. Sample copy available at website.

- "Blazing Saddles." Article reports on the evolution of Jewish settlements in Argentina.
- "Smile: Worthwhile." Article reports on the author's experience with a Jewish humanitarian group working in Rwanda.

RIGHTS AND PAYMENT
First rights. No payment. Provides 3 contributor's copies.

⇢EDITOR'S COMMENTS
We are open to new voices with a story to tell. Exceptional writing is a staple here.

Primary Street

Urban Ministries
P.O. Box 436987
Chicago, IL 60643-6987

Editor: Janet Grier

DESCRIPTION AND INTERESTS
Primary Street, a take-home paper supplementing Sunday school or religious education programs, combines Bible stories and lessons with religious-themed puzzles and other activities. Circ: 50,000.

Audience: 6–8 years
Frequency: Quarterly, with weekly issues
Website: www.urbanministries.com

FREELANCE POTENTIAL
80–90% written by nonstaff writers. Publishes 52 freelance submissions yearly; 25% by unpublished writers, 25% by authors who are new to the magazine. Receives 180 queries each year.

SUBMISSIONS
All material is assigned. Query with résumé and writing samples. Accepts hard copy. SASE. Response time varies.

- Articles: Word lengths vary. Informational and how-to articles; personal experience pieces; photo-essays; and Bible stories. Topics include religion, Christian values, nature, the environment, animals, pets, crafts, hobbies, African history, multicultural and ethnic subjects, regional news, and social issues.
- Other: Bible verses. Puzzles, games, and activities.

SAMPLE ISSUE
4 pages (no advertising): 1 article; 1 Bible lesson; 1 memory verse; 2 activities. Sample copy, free. Guidelines available.

- "Mr. Marsh." Article features a gym teacher who comes to realize that his unfair treatment of girls goes against the will of God, who wants us to love all people.
- "Jonah Did Not Care About Others." Bible lesson teaches that even though Jonah was full of anger, God still loved him.

RIGHTS AND PAYMENT
All rights. Written material, payment rates vary. Pays on publication. Provides 1 author's copy.

➥EDITOR'S COMMENTS
The main article in each of our weekly issues focuses on instilling specific knowledge about God. Our hope is that this will lead to changes in behavior and attitude among the children we serve.

Primary Treasure

Pacific Press Publishing
P.O. Box 5353
Nampa, ID 83653-5353

Editor: Aileen Andres Sox

DESCRIPTION AND INTERESTS
Primary Treasure publishes positive, inspiring stories for young children from a Seventh-day Adventist perspective. It also features Bible stories. Circ: 250,000.

Audience: 6–9 years
Frequency: Weekly
Website: www.primarytreasure.com

FREELANCE POTENTIAL
10% written by nonstaff writers. Publishes 52 freelance submissions yearly; 10% by unpublished writers, 30% by authors who are new to the magazine. Receives 240 unsolicited mss each year.

SUBMISSIONS
Send complete ms. Query for serials only. Accepts hard copy, email submissions to ailsox@pacificpress.com, and simultaneous submissions if identified. SASE. Responds in 4 months.

- Articles: 600–1,000 words. True stories about children in contemporary Christian settings; and true, problem-solving pieces that help children learn about themselves in relation to God and others.
- Other: Submit seasonal material 7 months in advance.

SAMPLE ISSUE
16 pages (no advertising): 4 articles; 1 Bible story; 1 puzzle. Sample copy, free with 9x12 SASE (2 first-class stamps). Writers' guidelines available.

- "Follow the Leader." Story tells about two young girls who, tired of following their guide while hiking in the woods, become lost and then pray to Jesus to lead them to safety.
- "Escape from Prison!" Bible story from the Acts of the Apostles recounts how the Apostles obeyed God by continuing to preach despite the danger.

RIGHTS AND PAYMENT
One-time rights. Written material, $25–$50. Pays on acceptance. Provides 3 copies.

➥EDITOR'S COMMENTS
All material submitted must be consistent with Seventh-day Adventist beliefs and practices, but the tone must not be preachy. Our mission is to teach spiritual truths, not reading skills, so keep it simple.

Principal

1615 Duke Street
Alexandria, VA 22314

Managing Editor: Vanessa St. Gerard

DESCRIPTION AND INTERESTS

As the membership publication of the National Association of Elementary School Principals, *Principal* is a source of practical information on topics related to education and school administration issues. Circ: 28,000.

Audience: K–8 school administrators
Frequency: 5 times each year
Website: www.naesp.org

FREELANCE POTENTIAL

90% written by nonstaff writers. Publishes 20 freelance submissions yearly; 80% by authors who are new to the magazine. Receives 150 unsolicited mss yearly.

SUBMISSIONS

Send complete ms. Accepts hard copy, PC-compatible disk submissions, and email submissions to publications@naesp.org. No simultaneous submissions. SASE. Responds in 6 weeks.

- Articles: 1,000–2,500 words. Informational and instructional articles; profiles; and opinion and personal experience pieces. Topics include elementary education, gifted and special education, parenting, mentoring, and technology.
- Depts/columns: 750–1,500 words. "Parents & Schools," "It's the Law," "Practitioner's Corner," "Tech Support," "A Touch of Humor," "Principal's Bookshelf," "Ten to Teen," "The Reflective Principal," and "Speaking Out."

SAMPLE ISSUE

72 pages (25% advertising): 9 articles; 9 depts/columns. Sample copy, $8. Guidelines and theme list available.

- "Project ELI: Improving Early Literacy Outcomes." Article describes an early literacy and language initiative that works.
- "The Value of Play Interventions in Special Education Classrooms." Article posits that play enhances learning for special ed students.

RIGHTS AND PAYMENT

All North American serial rights. No payment. Provides 3 contributor's copies.

➥EDITOR'S COMMENTS

Our readers are not looking for scholarly articles on theories of education. Instead, they turn to our publication for practical information and ideas they can use.

Rainbow Kids

P.O. Box 202
Harvey, LA 70059

Editor: Martha Osborne

DESCRIPTION AND INTEREST

Rainbow Kids is an adoption advocacy website dedicated to helping people adopt from multiple countries. In addition to its listings of children, agencies, and adoption resources, it features articles on the intricacies of the adoption process and personal essays from those involved. Hits per month: 1.5 million.

Audience: Adoptive families
Frequency: Monthly
Website: www.rainbowkids.com

FREELANCE POTENTIAL

10% written by nonstaff writers. Publishes 10–20 freelance submissions yearly; 50% by authors who are new to the magazine.

SUBMISSIONS

Send complete ms. Accepts email submissions to martha@rainbowkids.com (Microsoft Word attachments). Responds in 2–3 days.

- Articles: Word lengths vary. Informational articles and personal experience pieces. Topics include all matters related to adoption and adoptive families, both domestic and foreign. Also publishes adoption guidelines, adoption events, and photo listings.

SAMPLE ISSUE

Sample copy available at website.

- "Adopting a Child With Hearing Loss." Article follows the decision-making process that one family went through before adopting a deaf child.
- "Finding Me: I Am American." Personal experience piece relates the emotional journey a woman went through to finally be at peace with her Chinese birth but completely American upbringing.

RIGHTS AND PAYMENT

Limited electronic rights. No payment.

➥EDITOR'S COMMENTS

We are not an adoption agency. We are an adoption advocacy group made up of adoptees, adoptive families, adoption professionals and counselors, and birth parents. Our articles are designed to provide information to families interested in adopting who need to understand the process, and to support those who have gone through the process on one side or the other. All writers must have experience—either personal or professional—with adoption.

Rainbow Rumpus

Raising Arizona Kids

P.O. Box 6881
Minneapolis, MN 55406

Editor-in-Chief: Beth Wallace

DESCRIPTION AND INTERESTS
Launched in 2006, *Rainbow Rumpus* presents literature specifically geared to children being raised in lesbian, gay, bisexual, or transgendered (LGBT) families. Published online exclusively, it looks for stories for early readers through teens that celebrate diversity and the LGBT community. Hits per month: 9,000.

Audience: 4–18 years
Frequency: Monthly
Website: www.rainbowrumpus.org

FREELANCE POTENTIAL
40% written by nonstaff writers. Publishes 40 freelance submissions yearly; 10% by authors who are new to the magazine. Receives 12 unsolicited mss yearly.

SUBMISSIONS
Send complete ms. Accepts email submissions to fictionandpoetry@rainbowrumpus.org (Microsoft Word attachments; include "Submission" in subject line). Responds in 2 weeks.

- Articles: Staff written.
- Fiction: Stories for children 4–12 years, 800–2,500 words. Stories for teens, to 5,000 words. Publishes most genres.
- Depts/columns: Staff written.
- Other: Poetry, no line limits.

SAMPLE ISSUE
Sample copy and writers' guidelines available at website.

- "Still Open for Debate: Facing Prop. 8." Article offers a teen perspective on the challenges for LGBT couples in the wake of California's passage of Proposition 8, which bans same-sex marriage.
- "How to Grow a Plant Around Your Neck." Article details a craft project for creating jewelry that shows how seeds grow.

RIGHTS AND PAYMENT
First North American electronic and anthology rights. Fiction, $75. Poetry, payment rates vary. Pays on publication.

➡️EDITOR'S COMMENTS
We're primarily interested in stories that are written from the point of view of children with LGBT parents or other family members who are connected to the LGBT community. Don't specifically focus on the family structure, or on children being teased.

7000 East Shea Boulevard, Suite 1470
Scottsdale, AZ 85254-5257

Assistant Editor: Mary Holden

DESCRIPTION AND INTERESTS
The theme behind *Raising Arizona Kids* magazine is that it be a place for sharing ideas and local resources that support the experience of raising children in Arizona. In addition to being a resource for local family-friendly events and services, it publishes articles that help parents grow in their roles. Circ: Unavailable.

Audience: Parents
Frequency: Monthly
Website: www.raisingarizonakids.com

FREELANCE POTENTIAL
65% written by nonstaff writers. Publishes 12 freelance submissions yearly; 1% by unpublished writers, 1% by authors who are new to the magazine. Receives 44 queries yearly.

SUBMISSIONS
Arizona-based writers only. Query with clips. Accepts hard copy and email queries to editorial@raisingarizonakids.com. SASE. Response time varies.

- Articles: 1,000–3,000 words. Informational and how-to articles; profiles; interviews; personal experience pieces; and photo-essays. Topics include parenting issues, children, health and fitness, college and careers, current events, education, social issues, travel, and recreation.
- Depts/columns: Word lengths vary. News, parenting issues, family matters, profiles.
- Other: Journal articles, 500 words.

SAMPLE ISSUE
46 pages: 2 articles; 6 depts/columns; 1 journal article. Sample copy, $6. Guidelines available at website.

- "Cooling Off in Coconino County." Article profiles some family friendly destinations in and around Flagstaff.
- Sample dept/column: "A Conversation With" presents an interview with Ann Meyers Drysdale, general manager of the WNBA's Phoenix Mercury, about raising her children.

RIGHTS AND PAYMENT
Rights vary. Articles, $150+. Journal articles, payment rates vary. Depts/columns, $25+. Pays 30 days after publication.

➡️EDITOR'S COMMENTS
We are a local publication, so articles should quote local experts and parents.

The Reading Teacher

International Reading Association
800 Barksdale Road
P.O. Box 8139
Newark, DE 19714-8139

Managing Editor: James Henderson

DESCRIPTION AND INTERESTS
This peer-reviewed journal shares current theories, research, issues, and practices among literacy educators to help improve literacy instruction for children up to age 12. It is published by the International Reading Association. Circ: 57,500.

Audience: Literacy educators
Frequency: 8 times each year
Website: www.reading.org

FREELANCE POTENTIAL
95% written by nonstaff writers. Publishes 50 freelance submissions yearly; 20% by unpublished writers, 30% by authors who are new to the magazine. Receives 300 unsolicited mss each year.

SUBMISSIONS
Send complete ms. Accepts online submissions via http://mc.manuscriptcentral.com/rt. Responds in 1–2 months.

- Articles: To 6,000 words. Informational and how-to articles; profiles; and personal experience pieces. Topics include literacy, reading education, instructional techniques, classroom strategies, reading research, and educational technology.
- Depts/columns: 1,500–2,500 words. Reviews of children's books, teaching tips, and material on cultural diversity.

SAMPLE ISSUE
84 pages (17% advertising): 5 articles; 5 depts/columns. Sample copy, $10. Writers' guidelines available.

- "Actively Engaging with Stories Through Drama: Portraits of Two Young Readers." Article explains how weaving drama into literary activities can increase reading comprehension among struggling readers.
- Sample dept/column: "Struggling Readers" discusses the benefits of doing a book orientation to increase monitoring and problem-solving skills.

RIGHTS AND PAYMENT
All rights. No payment. Provides 5 contributor's copies for articles, 2 copies for depts/columns.

➡ EDITOR'S COMMENTS
Submissions focusing on children's literature or the relationship between literacy and other subject areas are also welcomed.

Reading Today

International Reading Association
800 Barksdale Road
P.O. Box 8139
Newark, DE 19714-8139

Editor-in-Chief: John Micklos Jr.

DESCRIPTION AND INTERESTS
Reading Today is a newspaper for professionals in the field of literacy education. It covers the critical issues facing literacy, and highlights current trends. Other features include classroom strategies and ideas for administrators and parents. Circ: 68,000.

Audience: IRA members
Frequency: 6 times each year
Website: www.reading.org

FREELANCE POTENTIAL
30% written by nonstaff writers. Publishes 30 freelance submissions yearly; 10% by unpublished writers, 40% by authors who are new to the magazine. Receives 300 queries, 240 unsolicited mss yearly.

SUBMISSIONS
Prefers query; will accept complete ms. Prefers email to readingtoday@reading.org; will accept hard copy and simultaneous submissions if identified. SASE. Responds in 6 weeks.

- Articles: 500–1,000 words. Informational articles and interviews. Topics include reading, reading education, community programs, staffing, assessment, funding, children's books, and censorship.
- Depts/columns: To 750 words. News; education policy updates; and ideas for administrators, teachers, and parents.
- Artwork: Digital images.

SAMPLE ISSUE
44 pages (30% advertising): 70 articles; 23 depts/columns; 1 special section. Sample copy, $6. Guidelines available.

- "International Discoveries." Article reports on the activities of IRA delegates on a fact-finding trip to China.
- Sample dept/column: "In the Classroom" profiles an award-winning teacher who infuses math with literacy.

RIGHTS AND PAYMENT
All rights. Written material, $.20–$.30 per word. Pays on acceptance. Provides 3 copies.

➡ EDITOR'S COMMENTS
Articles about unusual and successful classroom or library reading programs are always of interest. Please note that our freelance space is limited. This, in turn, limits our nonstaff opportunities.

Red River Family Magazine

P.O. Box 7654
Lawton, OK 73506

Executive Editor: Laura Clevenger

DESCRIPTION AND INTERESTS
Written specifically for parents living in south-west Oklahoma and north Texas, this publication focuses on children's health, development, and education, while also offering features on family fun and recreation. Many of its readers are military families. Circ: 20,000.

Audience: Parents
Frequency: Monthly
Website: www.redriverfamily.com

FREELANCE POTENTIAL
34% written by nonstaff writers. Publishes 100 freelance submissions yearly; 10% by unpublished writers, 80% by authors who are new to the magazine.

SUBMISSIONS
Query with clips or writing samples. Accepts email queries to publisher@redriverfamily.com. Response time varies.

- Articles: Word lengths vary. Informational and how-to articles; profiles; interviews; and personal experience pieces. Topics include parenting and family life, social issues, education, special education, health and fitness, college and careers, technology, nature, the environment, and recreation.
- Depts/columns: Word lengths vary. Military life, education, green living, media reviews, fitness, safety, and regional news.

SAMPLE ISSUE
34 pages: 3 articles; 11 depts/columns. Sample copy available at website. Guidelines available via email request.

- "Five Fun Tips for Teaching Golf to Kids." Article provides practical information for teaching kids how to play and enjoy the game of golf.
- "Party On." Article features birthday party plans for teens and younger children, complete with ideas for activities and food.

RIGHTS AND PAYMENT
One-time print and 2-year electronic rights. Articles, $20–$50. Payment policy varies.

➥EDITOR'S COMMENTS
Many of the parents who read our magazine have spouses who are deployed. We are openly patriotic, and some of the material we use is directly related to the needs of these military families. Shorter pieces are needed.

Research in Middle Level Education Online

Portland State University
Graduate School of Education
615 SW Harrison
Portland, OR 97201

Editor: Micki M. Caskey

DESCRIPTION AND INTERESTS
This peer-reviewed journal, exclusively online, features quantitative and qualitative case studies, research studies, and reviews on middle-grade education. It is published by the National Middle School Association. Circ: 30,000.

Audience: Educators and administrators
Frequency: 10 times each year
Website: www.nmsa.org

FREELANCE POTENTIAL
100% written by nonstaff writers. Publishes 10 freelance submissions yearly; 20% by unpublished writers, 50% by authors who are new to the magazine. Receives 40+ unsolicited mss each year.

SUBMISSIONS
Send complete ms with 150- to 200-word abstract. Accepts submissions through online system, www.editorialmanager.com/rmle. Responds in 1 week.

- Articles: 25–40 double-spaced pages. Quantitative and qualitative studies; case studies; action research studies; research syntheses; integrative reviews; and interpretations of research literature—all pertaining to middle-grade education.

SAMPLE ISSUE
Sample copy and writers' guidelines available at website.

- "I Wish I Had Known the Truth Sooner: Middle School Teacher Candidates' Sexuality Education Experiences." Article discusses the need for teacher preparation programs for sexuality education.
- "Adolescents' Psychological Well-Being and Perceived Parental Involvement: Implications for Parental Involvement in Middle Schools." Article reviews and analyzes recent research that relates to the implications of parent involvement in school based on various parenting styles.

RIGHTS AND PAYMENT
All rights. No payment.

➥EDITOR'S COMMENTS
Each submission is reviewed by our editor first. If it meets our editorial standards, it is then forwarded to three reviewers. Prospective writers should have a thorough knowledge of the field.

Reunions Magazine

P.O. Box 11727
Milwaukee, WI 54311-0727

Editor: Edith Wagner

DESCRIPTION AND INTERESTS
Professionals and others directly involved with
family, military, class, and association reunion
planning find ideas, inspiration, and resource
information in this magazine. Circ: 20,000.

Audience: Adults
Frequency: Quarterly
Website: www.reunionsmag.com

FREELANCE POTENTIAL
75% written by nonstaff writers. Publishes 100
freelance submissions yearly; 60% by unpublished writers, 80% by authors who are new to
the magazine.

SUBMISSIONS
Query. Accepts email queries to editor@
reunionsmag.com (Microsoft Word attachments). Responds in 12–18 months.

- Articles: Word lengths vary. Informational,
  factual, and how-to articles; profiles; and
  personal experience pieces. Topics include
  organizing reunions; choosing locations,
  entertainment, and activities; and genealogy.
- Depts/columns: 250–1,000 words. Opinion
  and personal experience pieces, and
  resource information.
- Artwork: Color digital images at 300 dpi
  or higher.
- Other: Recipes, games, cartoons, and filler.

SAMPLE ISSUE
48 pages (45% advertising): 4 articles; 4
depts/columns. Sample copy, $3. Guidelines
and editorial calendar available.

- "Family Reunites After 150 Years." Article
  describes how two Mississippi families, invol-
  untarily separated after the Civil War, discovered their connection.
- Sample dept/column: "Branch Office" shows
  how professionally produced oral history
  videos can enhance a reunion experience.

RIGHTS AND PAYMENT
One-time and electronic rights. Written material,
payment rates vary. Payment policy varies.
Provides contributor's copies.

⚫➤EDITOR'S COMMENTS
We consider only submissions directly related
to reunions, and particularly about planning
them. Stories about successful reunions,
accompanied by photographs that capture
that success, are always welcome.

Richmond Parents Monthly

1506 Staples Mill Road, Suite 102
Richmond, VA 23230

Editor: Lee Barnes

DESCRIPTION AND INTERESTS
For more than 20 years, *Richmond Parents
Monthly* has provided information and
resources that help parents raise children and
build a better family life. It is distributed free
through more than 400 community sites in
central Virginia. Circ: 30,000.

Audience: Parents
Frequency: Monthly
Website: www.richmondparents.com

FREELANCE POTENTIAL
75% written by nonstaff writers. Publishes
50–60 freelance submissions yearly; 5% by
authors who are new to the magazine.
Receives 600 queries and mss yearly.

SUBMISSIONS
Query with 3–5 clips; or send complete ms.
Accepts email submissions to mail@
richmondpublishing.com. No simultaneous
submissions. Availability of artwork improves
chance of acceptance. Responds in 1–3 weeks.

- Articles: 400–2,200 words. Informational
  and self-help articles. Topics include the
  arts, camps, pets, home and garden, parties,
  education, health, and holidays.
- Depts/columns: "Your Turn" essays, 400–
  900 words. Family-related news, media
  reviews, and technology; word lengths vary.
- Artwork: Color prints or transparencies.

SAMPLE ISSUE
30 pages (15% advertising): 4 articles; 8
depts/columns; 1 calendar; 1 contest. Sample
copy, free. Guidelines and editorial calendar
available at website.

- "This Summer, Take a Virtual Vacation."
  Article tells how parents and children can
  visit national parks, museums, and even
  outer space from their home computers.
- Sample dept/column: "Take Care" stresses
  that safety should be at the top of the list
  when selecting summer programs for kids.

RIGHTS AND PAYMENT
One-time rights. Written material, $52–$295.
Pays on publication.

⚫➤EDITOR'S COMMENTS
We try to facilitate a shared sense of community by telling parents' stories and providing a
forum for dialogue. Writers new to our magazine should start with shorter pieces.

Sacramento Parent

457 Grass Valley Highway, Suite 5
Auburn, CA 95603

Editor-in-Chief: Shelly Bokman

DESCRIPTION AND INTERESTS
Offering timely information on news that
affects parents in the Sacramento region, this
parents' magazine also features articles on parenting issues, education challenges, and the
realities of raising children in a modern world.
Circ: 50,000.

Audience: Parents
Frequency: Monthly
Website: www.sacramentoparent.com

FREELANCE POTENTIAL
75% written by nonstaff writers. Publishes 50
freelance submissions yearly; 10% by unpublished writers, 25% by authors who are new to
the magazine. Receives 780 queries yearly.

SUBMISSIONS
Query with writing samples. Accepts email
queries to shelly@sacramentoparent.com.
Response time varies.

- Articles: 700–1,000 words. Informational and
  how-to articles; personal experience pieces;
  and humor. Topics include parenting, health,
  fitness, finance, family travel, education,
  grandparenting, adoption, sports, recreation,
  learning disabilities, and regional news.
- Depts/columns: 300–500 words. Child development, opinions, and hometown highlights.
- Other: Submit seasonal or themed material
  3 months in advance.

SAMPLE ISSUE
50 pages (50% advertising): 4 articles; 6
depts/columns. Sample copy, free with 9x12
SASE ($1.29 postage). Guidelines and theme
list available at website.

- "Choosing an Online High School Program."
  Article explains the program options available to students looking for online classes.
- "How To Raise Body-Confident Kids." Article
  offers advice from a psychologist regarding
  instilling a healthy body image in your child.

RIGHTS AND PAYMENT
Second rights. Articles, $50. Depts/columns,
$25–$40. Pays on publication. Provides contributor's copies.

➡EDITOR'S COMMENTS
Our goal is to provide articles of interest to
families with children and grandchildren of
all ages, and to families with a variety of
lifestyles and beliefs.

San Diego Family Magazine

P.O. Box 23960
San Diego, CA 92193-3960

Editor: Kirsten Flournoy

DESCRIPTION AND INTERESTS
This magazine provides informative, locally
focused articles for families living in the San
Diego area. Circ: 120,000.

Audience: Parents
Frequency: Monthly
Website: www.sandiegofamily.com

FREELANCE POTENTIAL
90% written by nonstaff writers. Publishes
120–200 freelance submissions yearly; 5% by
unpublished writers, 10% by authors who are
new to the magazine. Receives 120 queries,
120 unsolicited mss yearly.

SUBMISSIONS
Query or send complete ms. Accepts email
to kirsten@sandiegofamily.com. Responds in
1 month.

- Articles: 800–1,200 words. Informational,
  self-help, and how-to articles. Topics include
  parenting, pregnancy, childbirth, child care,
  education, summer camp, health, safety,
  nutrition, gardening, dining out, recreation,
  travel, sports, family finance, local events,
  and multicultural issues.
- Depts/columns: Word lengths vary. News
  briefs, tips, trends, restaurant reviews, book
  reviews, cooking, and gardening.
- Artwork: 3x5 or 5x7 four-color glossy prints.

SAMPLE ISSUE
134 pages (60% advertising): 10 articles; 11
depts/columns. Sample copy, $4.50 with 9x12
SASE ($1 postage). Guidelines and editorial
calendar available at website.

- "Classic Rock 101." Article profiles two local
  radio DJs who talk about their families and
  their careers.
- Sample dept/column: "Mom's World" is a
  mother's reflection about the important lessons she hopes she taught her kids before
  they left for college.

RIGHTS AND PAYMENT
First or second, and all regional rights. Written
material, $1.25 per column inch. Pays on pub-
lication. Provides 1 contributor's copy.

➡EDITOR'S COMMENTS
Our goal is to provide parenting information
and resources that enhance the quality and
emphasize the pleasures of family life.

Santa Barbara Family Life

P.O. Box 4867
Santa Barbara, CA 93140

Editor: Nansie Chapman

DESCRIPTION AND INTERESTS
This community-oriented magazine covers events and resources of interest to families living in the Santa Barbara area of California. It focuses on regional arts and entertainment, local destinations, and health and relationship issues. Circ: 60,000.

Audience: Parents
Frequency: Monthly
Website: www.sbfamilylife.com

FREELANCE POTENTIAL
5% written by nonstaff writers. Publishes 10 freelance submissions yearly; 5% by unpublished writers, 10% by authors who are new to the magazine. Receives 500 queries yearly.

SUBMISSIONS
Query or send complete ms. Accepts email queries to nansie@sbfamilylife.com. Responds if interested.

- Articles: 500–1,200 words. Informational articles; profiles; photo-essays; and personal experience pieces. Topics include regional events and activities, parenting, family life, education, recreation, crafts, hobbies, and current events.
- Depts/columns: Word lengths vary. Love and relationships, arts and entertainment, and health issues.
- Other: Puzzles and activities.

SAMPLE ISSUE
36 pages: 1 article; 6 depts/columns; 1 camp and activities guide. Sample copy available at website.

- "Passing On the Tradition of Service." Article profiles a local mother, businesswoman, and tireless volunteer.
- Sample dept/column: "Health Watch" focuses on the diagnosis and treatment of pelvic pain in women.

RIGHTS AND PAYMENT
Rights vary. Written material, $25–$35. Payment policy varies.

➡◆ EDITOR'S COMMENTS
Please remember that our focus is on the Santa Barbara community. In addition to local arts, entertainment, and children's camps, our readers are interested in health and education topics that are relevant to their daily lives.

Scholastic Choices

Scholastic Inc.
557 Broadway
New York, NY 10012-3999

Editor: Bob Hugel

DESCRIPTION AND INTERESTS
In this magazine, teens read about other teens who are facing the same challenges as they are. Sound and helpful advice to meet those challenges is provided. Circ: 200,000.

Audience: 12–18 years
Frequency: 6 times each year
Website: www.scholastic.com

FREELANCE POTENTIAL
90% written by nonstaff writers. Publishes 30–40 freelance submissions yearly; 10% by unpublished writers. Receives 60 queries, 60 unsolicited mss yearly.

SUBMISSIONS
Query or send complete ms. Accepts hard copy and email submissions to choicesmag@ scholastic.com. SASE. Responds to queries in 2 months, to mss in 3 months.

- Articles: 500–1,000 words. Informational and self-help articles; profiles; and personal experience pieces. Topics include health, nutrition, fitness, sports, personal development, personal responsibility, family issues, relationships, safety, social issues, conservation, the environment, popular culture, careers, and substance abuse prevention.
- Depts/columns: Staff written.
- Other: Quizzes, word games, and recipes.

SAMPLE ISSUE
24 pages (20% advertising): 5 articles; 5 depts/columns. Sample copy, free with 9x12 SASE. Writers' guidelines and editorial calendar available.

- "Second Chance." Article introduces readers to a young man whose binge drinking almost cost him his life.
- "Making Peace with Parents." Article offers suggestions for easing the tension between teens and their parents.

RIGHTS AND PAYMENT
All rights. Written material, payment rates vary. Pays on publication. Provides 10 copies.

➡◆ EDITOR'S COMMENTS
We seek articles that offer solutions to the problems faced by teens. In addition to submitting well-researched articles, writers should provide sidebars that offer additional resources, such as helpline or hotline numbers or websites.

Scholastic DynaMath

Scholastic Inc.
557 Broadway, Room 474
New York, NY 10012-3999

Associate Editor: Carli Entin

DESCRIPTION AND INTERESTS
This magazine strives to make math fun. Geared to kids in grades three to six, it is filled with entertaining articles and interactive activities and puzzles that connect math concepts to the real world. Circ: 200,000.

Audience: 8–12 years
Frequency: 8 times each year
Website: www.scholastic.com/dynamath

FREELANCE POTENTIAL
30% written by nonstaff writers. Publishes 16 freelance submissions yearly; 5% by authors who are new to the magazine. Receives 24 queries, 24 unsolicited mss yearly.

SUBMISSIONS
Query with outline; or send complete ms. Accepts hard copy and simultaneous submissions if identified. SASE. Responds in 2–4 months.

- Articles: To 600 words. Informational articles about math skills. Topics include critical thinking; chart and graph reading; measurement; fractions; decimals; problem solving; and interdisciplinary issues such as popular culture, sports, and consumer awareness—all as related to math.
- Other: Filler, puzzles, games, and jokes. Submit holiday material 4–6 months in advance.

SAMPLE ISSUE
16 pages: 5 articles; 5 activities. Sample copy, $4 with 9x12 SASE. Guidelines and editorial calendar available at website.

- "A Look: Take a Look Back(ward)." Article presents a number of problem solving activities that tie into the life of Abraham Lincoln.
- "Cheetah Math." Article focuses on using division as it tells the story of two baby cheetahs from the San Diego Zoo.

RIGHTS AND PAYMENT
All rights. Articles, $250–$400. Puzzles, $25–$50. Pays on acceptance. Provides 3 contributor's copies.

⇢EDITOR'S COMMENTS
We're always interested in receiving math activities that are geared to the curricula of grades three to six and that tie in with high-interest current events. Our editorial calendar will give you a clear idea of the topics we like to cover.

Scholastic Math Magazine

Scholastic Inc.
557 Broadway
New York, NY 10012-3999

Editor: Jack Silbert

DESCRIPTION AND INTERESTS
This magazine makes learning math fun for students in middle school and high school. It features entertaining and easy-to-follow articles that demonstrate how math concepts are part of daily life, such as with sports, movies, music, and video games. Circ: 200,000.

Audience: 11–15 years
Frequency: Monthly
Website: www.scholastic.com/math

FREELANCE POTENTIAL
30% written by nonstaff writers. Publishes 10 freelance submissions yearly; 10% by unpublished writers. Receives 24 queries yearly.

SUBMISSIONS
Query. Accepts hard copy. SASE. Responds in 2–3 months.

- Articles: 600 words. Informational articles. Topics include real-world math, math-related news, teen issues, sports, celebrities, TV, music, movies, and current events.
- Depts/columns: 140 words. Skill-building exercises, quizzes, practice tests, and Q&As.
- Other: Puzzles, games, activities, comic strips, and mystery photos.

SAMPLE ISSUE
16 pages (no advertising): 4 articles; 1 dept/column; 1 comic strip. Sample copy, free with 9x12 SASE (3 first-class stamps). Guidelines and editorial calendar available.

- "Lightning-Fast Service." Article explains the first-serve percentage in tennis and how players use it to size up their competition.
- "Sandy Solids." Article offers a lesson in geometry while describing a company that creates professional sand-sculpture displays.
- "Count on Math." Article discusses the upcoming MATHCOUNTS national finals and includes some questions from previous competitions.

RIGHTS AND PAYMENT
All rights. Articles, $300+. Depts/columns, $35. Pays on publication.

⇢EDITOR'S COMMENTS
Our goal is to be the best resource for bringing real-life math, literacy, and fun into the classroom. A typical issue will include sections on geometry, pre-algebra, statistics, and theme-related activities.

Scholastic Parent & Child

Scholastic Inc.
557 Broadway
New York, NY 10012-3999

Associate Editor: Samantha Brody

DESCRIPTION AND INTERESTS
Targeting parents of children from birth to age 12, this magazine helps readers celebrate the joy of family living and learning. It covers topics important to parents everywhere, including child development, health, and fitness; juggling work and home; and child-related products. Circ: 7.8 million.

Audience: Parents
Frequency: 8 times each year
Website: www.parentandchildonline.com

FREELANCE POTENTIAL
60% written by nonstaff writers. Publishes 20 freelance submissions yearly; 15% by authors who are new to the magazine. Receives 1,200 queries, 600 unsolicited mss yearly.

SUBMISSIONS
Query or send complete ms. Accepts hard copy. SASE. Responds to queries in 3 months, to mss in 2 months.

- Articles: 500–1,000 words. Informational articles and interviews. Topics include child development, education, and parenting.
- Depts/columns: Word lengths vary. Literacy, health, parent/teacher relationships, arts and crafts, child development, product reviews, travel, cooking, and family issues.

SAMPLE ISSUE
88 pages (33% advertising): 5 articles; 11 depts/columns. Sample copy, $2.95. Writers' guidelines available.

- "Autism in the Family." Article interviews actress Holly Robinson Peete about how she and her family deal with her son's autism.
- Sample dept/column: "First Steps" examines babies' ability to self-soothe, and how parents can coax this instinct along.

RIGHTS AND PAYMENT
All rights. Written material, payment rates vary. Pays on publication. Provides author's copies.

❖EDITOR'S COMMENTS
Our topic list is not set in stone. If a topic is of interest to a parent, we're interested in it as well. All articles must be informative, but they must also offer practical advice that parents can apply to their own situations. We do work with first-time writers occasionally, but generally prefer authors experienced in writing about parenting issues.

Scholastic Scope

Scholastic Inc.
557 Broadway
New York, NY 10012-3999

Executive Editor: Lucy Lehrer

DESCRIPTION AND INTERESTS
Scope is designed to entertain teens with articles and activities that grab their attention while also building vocabulary, writing, and reading comprehension skills. Each issue features fiction, nonfiction, plays, and puzzles. Circ: 550,000.

Audience: 12–18 years
Frequency: 17 times each year
Website: www.scholastic.com/scope

FREELANCE POTENTIAL
10% written by nonstaff writers. Of the freelance submissions published yearly, 2% are by unpublished authors, 10% are by authors who are new to the magazine. Receives 200–300 queries yearly.

SUBMISSIONS
Query with résumé, outline/synopsis, and clips. Accepts hard copy. SASE. Response time varies.

- Articles: 1,000 words. News and features that appeal to teens; and profiles of young adults who have overcome obstacles, performed heroic acts, or had noteworthy experiences.
- Fiction: 1,500 words. Contemporary, realistic stories about relationships and family problems, school issues, and other teen concerns; and science fiction.
- Depts/columns: Staff written.
- Other: Puzzles and activities. Submit seasonal material 4 months in advance.

SAMPLE ISSUE
22 pages (8% advertising): 4 articles; 1 play; 3 depts/columns; 1 puzzle. Sample copy, $1.75 with 9x12 SASE (2 first-class stamps); also available at website.

- "Write." Essay tells how a girl read a number of classics and then attempted to emulate the style of her favorite authors.
- "Heeding the Call." Article discusses President Obama's call to middle- and high-school students to volunteer.

RIGHTS AND PAYMENT
Rights vary. Written material, $100+. Pays on acceptance. Provides 2 contributor's copies.

❖EDITOR'S COMMENTS
Stories and activities should be geared to a sixth- to eighth-grade reading level.

SchoolArts

Davis Publications
2223 Parkside Drive
Denton, TX 76201

Editor: Nancy Walkup

DESCRIPTION AND INTERESTS
Each themed issue of *SchoolArts* shares the successful lessons, ideas, and concepts of art teachers for kindergarten through grade 12. In publication since 1901, it offers material divided into sections by grade level. Circ: 20,000.

Audience: Art teachers, grades K–12
Frequency: 9 times each year
Website: www.schoolartsonline.com

FREELANCE POTENTIAL
75% written by nonstaff writers. Publishes 200 freelance submissions yearly; 60% by unpublished writers, 60% by authors who are new to the magazine. Receives 300 unsolicited mss each year.

SUBMISSIONS
Send complete ms with artwork. Prefers disk submissions with images; will accept email submissions to nwalkup@verizon.net (attach files). Responds in 1–2 months.

- Articles: 300–800 words. Informational, how-to, and self-help articles. Topics include teaching art, artistic techniques, art history, classroom projects and activities, curriculum development, and art programs for gifted and disabled students.
- Depts/columns: 500–1,200 words. Crafts, new product reviews, and opinions.
- Artwork: B/W and color prints and slides; high-resolution digital images. Line art.

SAMPLE ISSUE
68 pages (40% advertising): 9 articles; 12 depts/columns. Sample copy, $5. Guidelines and editorial calendar available at website.

- "Go Fly a Kite." Article relates a 5th- and 6th-grade project in which students constructed and decorated non-flying kites for display.
- Sample dept/column: "Teacher-Student Portfolio" shares the experiences of an art teacher and one of her students.

RIGHTS AND PAYMENT
First serial rights. Written material, $25–$150. Artwork, payment rates vary. Pays on publication. Provides 6 contributor's copies.

➥EDITOR'S COMMENTS
Don't worry about fitting your article to one of our themes; our editors will determine that. It is more important to be passionate about your topic.

The School Librarian's Workshop

1 Deerfield Court
Basking Ridge, NJ 07920

Editor: Ruth Toor

DESCRIPTION AND INTERESTS
Filled with trend information, technology updates, research ideas, and book reviews, this publication serves school media specialists and librarians. It seeks practical articles that deal with all aspects of library media programs. Circ: 7,000.

Audience: School librarians
Frequency: 6 times each year
Website:
www.school-librarians-workshop.com

FREELANCE POTENTIAL
28% written by nonstaff writers. Publishes 20 freelance submissions yearly; 10% by unpublished writers, 10% by authors who are new to the magazine. Receives 24 unsolicited mss each year.

SUBMISSIONS
Send 2 copies of complete ms. Prefers disk submissions (Microsoft Word); will accept hard copy. SASE. Responds in 3 weeks.

- Articles: To 1,000 words. Informational, how-to, and practical application articles; profiles; and interviews. Topics include librarianship, literature, special education, ethnic studies, computers, technology, social and multicultural issues, and the environment.
- Artwork: Line art.
- Other: Submit seasonal material 8 months in advance.

SAMPLE ISSUE
24 pages (no advertising): 13 articles. Sample copy, free with 9x12 SASE. Guidelines and theme list available at website.

- "Library Lessons with Dogs." Article looks at a program in which a therapy dog helps kids with reading and science lessons.
- "Who Was Abraham Lincoln?" Article suggests lesson ideas that teachers can use as mini-units.
- "High School Life." Article reviews three poetry collections that portray high school life.

RIGHTS AND PAYMENT
First rights. No payment. Provides 3 copies.

➥EDITOR'S COMMENTS
We're always interested in hearing about novel ideas and current trends that would interest library professionals.

School Library Journal

360 Park Avenue South
New York, NY 10010

Executive Editor: Rick Margolis

DESCRIPTION AND INTERESTS

School Library Journal offers librarians the timely information needed to integrate libraries into the school curriculum; become leaders in technology, reading, and information; and create high-quality book collections for children and young adults. Circ: 34,500.

Audience: School librarians
Frequency: Monthly
Website: www.slj.com

FREELANCE POTENTIAL

80% written by nonstaff writers. Publishes 25 freelance submissions yearly; 60% by unpublished writers, 60% by new authors. Receives 48–72 queries and unsolicited mss yearly.

SUBMISSIONS

Query or send complete ms. Accepts disk submissions (ASCII or Microsoft Word) and email submissions to rmargolis@reedbusiness.com. SASE. Responds to queries in 1 month, to mss in 3 months.

- Articles: 1,500–2,500 words. Informational articles and interviews. Topics include children's and young adult literature, school library management, and library careers.
- Depts/columns: 1,500–2,500 words. Book and media reviews, descriptions of successful library programs, and opinion pieces.
- Artwork: Color prints. Color tables and charts. Cartoons.

SAMPLE ISSUE

116 pages (25% advertising): 5 articles; 9 depts/columns; 3 review sections. Sample copy, $6.75 with 9x12 SASE. Guidelines available at website.

- "Block Party." Article discusses a library's success with attracting reluctant boys by starting a Lego club.
- Sample dept/column: "The Gaming Life" describes a middle school competition of designing and constructing a future city.

RIGHTS AND PAYMENT

First rights. Articles, $400. Depts/columns, $100–$200. Pays on publication. Provides 4 contributor's copies.

✒ EDITOR'S COMMENTS

Our magazine provides librarians with the tools they need to become indispensible players in their schools.

School Library Media Activities Monthly

3520 South 35th Street
Lincoln, NE 68506

Managing Editor: Deborah Levitov

DESCRIPTION AND INTERESTS

This magazine offers articles that help school library and media specialists develop lesson plans and curricula, as well as their own professional careers. Circ: 12,000.

Audience: School library and media specialists, grades K–12
Frequency: 10 times each year
Website: www.schoollibrarymedia.com

FREELANCE POTENTIAL

90% written by nonstaff writers. Publishes 30 freelance submissions yearly; 20% by unpublished writers, 30% by authors who are new to the magazine. Receives 36 queries, 36 unsolicited mss yearly.

SUBMISSIONS

Query or send complete ms with bibliographic citations and brief author bio. Accepts email submissions to dlevitov@abc-clio.com (Microsoft Word attachments). Responds in 2 months.

- Articles: 1,000–1,500 words. Informational articles. Topics include media education and promotion, information technology, integration of curriculum materials, and library management.
- Depts/columns: Word lengths vary. Activities, lesson plans, tips for professional growth.
- Artwork: B/W prints. Line art.

SAMPLE ISSUE

58 pages: 2 articles; 12 depts/columns. Sample copy and guidelines available at website.

- "Library Media Specialists and Assisted Technology." Article describes how new technologies meet the accessibility challenges of students with physical and cognitive disabilities.
- Sample dept/column: "Notes from the Field" offers ways to reach advanced readers in the middle grades.
- Sample dept/column: "Web Monthly" suggests pairs of websites for professionals to explore during vacation.

RIGHTS AND PAYMENT

All rights. Written material, payment rates vary. Pays on publication. Provides 3+ copies.

✒ EDITOR'S COMMENTS

Experienced school library and media specialists are always welcome to share their successful, classroom-tested activities.

The School Magazine

Private Bag 3
Ryde, New South Wales 2112
Australia

Editor: Suzanne Eggins

DESCRIPTION AND INTERESTS
Comprised of four sections that target different age groups, *The School Magazine* offers a mix of short stories, nonfiction, poems, and activities. Teaching units are available for use in the classroom. Circ: 150,000.

Audience: 8–12 years
Frequency: 10 times each year
Web: www.curriculumsupport.education.
nsw.gov.au/services/schoolmagazine

FREELANCE POTENTIAL
70% written by nonstaff writers. Publishes 100 freelance submissions yearly; 10% by unpublished writers, 10% by authors who are new to the magazine. Receives 96 queries, 360 unsolicited mss yearly.

SUBMISSIONS
Query for nonfiction. Send complete ms for fiction. Accepts hard copy. Material is not returned. Responds via email in 6–8 weeks.

- Articles: 800–2,000 words. Informational articles. Topics include nature, pets, the environment, history, biography, science, technology, and multicultural and ethnic issues.
- Fiction: 800–2,000 words. Genres include adventure; humor; fantasy; science fiction; horror; mystery; folktales; and contemporary, multicultural, and historical fiction.
- Depts/columns: Staff written.

SAMPLE ISSUE
34 pages (no advertising): 1 article; 5 stories; 3 depts/columns; 3 poems. Guidelines and sample issue available at website.

- "A Night to Remember." Story tells a humorous tale of an awards ceremony gone wrong.
- "Chang and Eng: The Siamese Twins." Article relates the life story of the famous Siamese twins who were born in Thailand in 1811.

RIGHTS AND PAYMENT
One-time serial rights. Written material, $270 Australian per 1,000 words. Poetry, payment rates vary. Pays on acceptance. Provides 2 contributor's copies.

☛EDITOR'S COMMENTS
Nonfiction submissions should include information on sources and/or research material consulted. Refer to our guidelines for additional information.

Science Activities

Heldref Publications
1319 18th Street NW
Washington, DC 20036-1802

Managing Editor: Miriam Aronin

DESCRIPTION AND INTERESTS
This magazine of "classroom projects and curriculum ideas" is filled with articles on teaching strategies, hands-on activities, teacher-tested projects, and experiments. It targets science teachers of kindergarten through grade twelve. Circ: 1,286.

Audience: Teachers, grades K–12
Frequency: Quarterly
Website: www.heldref.org

FREELANCE POTENTIAL
95% written by nonstaff writers. Publishes 25 freelance submissions yearly; 25% by unpublished writers, 50% by authors who are new to the magazine. Receives 36–48 unsolicited mss each year.

SUBMISSIONS
Send complete ms through http://mc.manuscriptcentral.com/heldref/sa. Responds in 3 months.

- Articles: Word lengths vary. Informational and how-to articles; profiles; and personal experience pieces. Topics include hands-on projects in behavioral, biological, chemical, Earth, environmental, physical, and technological science.
- Depts/columns: Staff written.
- Artwork: B/W prints and slides. Line art.

SAMPLE ISSUE
40 pages (1% advertising): 6 articles; 2 depts/columns. Sample copy available via email request to SA@heldref.org. Guidelines available at website.

- "Becoming Butterflies." Article presents integrated activities that help children fully grasp the process of metamorphosis by observing, asking questions, and using visual arts.
- "The Darkness of Space." Article examines a teaching strategy that uses a scientific approach to determining whether space is light or dark.

RIGHTS AND PAYMENT
All rights. No payment. Provides contributors with free access to articles online.

☛EDITOR'S COMMENTS
We are interested in ideas that promote inquiry into the physical, environmental, biological, chemical, and Earth sciences, as well as those that integrate math and technology.

The Science Teacher

National Science Teachers Association
1840 Wilson Boulevard
Arlington, VA 22201-3000

Managing Editor: Megan Sullivan

DESCRIPTION AND INTERESTS
This peer-reviewed journal provides education professionals a forum for sharing ideas and practical experiences with their peers. All work must be original. Circ: 29,000.

Audience: Science teachers, grades 7–12
Frequency: 9 times each year
Website: www.nsta.org/highschool

FREELANCE POTENTIAL
100% written by nonstaff writers. Of the freelance submissions published yearly, 70% are by unpublished writers, 50% are by authors who are new to the magazine. Receives 360 unsolicited mss yearly.

SUBMISSIONS
Send complete ms with abstract to 200 words. Accepts submissions only through https://mc.manuscriptcentral.com/nsta. Responds in 1 month.

- Articles: 2,000 words. Informational articles; classroom projects; and experiments. Topics include science education, biology, earth science, computers, social issues, space technology, and sports medicine.
- Depts/columns: 500 words. Science.
- Artwork: 5x7 or larger B/W prints. Line art, tables, and diagrams.

SAMPLE ISSUE
84 pages (40% advertising): 6 articles; 6 depts/columns. Sample copy, $4.25 with 9x12 SASE ($.77 postage). Guidelines available in each issue and at website.

- "Frontloading Classroom Management." Article describes a systematic approach to planning for the first days of school, appropriate for today's demanding science classrooms.
- Sample dept/column: "Idea Bank" offers creative ways to incorporate reading and writing into the science classroom by linking science fiction to science.

RIGHTS AND PAYMENT
First rights. No payment. Provides contributor's copies.

➥EDITOR'S COMMENTS
Our readers are interested in the complete experience of successful programs, including the goals, setup details, and student reactions. All submissions should reflect current issues in science education.

Science Weekly

P.O. Box 70638
Chevy Chase, MD 20813

Publisher: Dr. Claude Mayberry

DESCRIPTION AND INTERESTS
Science Weekly develops and reinforces reading, writing, mathematics, and critical thinking skills through interactive science content. Its six differentiated editions (based on reading levels) help students "put a little science in their week." It is designed as a complementary supplement to classroom science lessons. Circ: 200,000.

Audience: Grades K–6
Frequency: 15 times each year
Website: www.scienceweekly.com

FREELANCE POTENTIAL
100% written by nonstaff writers. Publishes 15 freelance submissions yearly; 70% by unpublished writers, 5% by authors who are new to the magazine.

SUBMISSIONS
All work is assigned to writers living in the District of Columbia, Maryland, or Virginia. Send résumé. Accepts hard copy. Response time varies.

- Articles: Word lengths vary. Informational articles. Topics include space exploration, ecology, the environment, nature, biology, meteorology, oceanography, navigation, nutrition, physical science, and secret codes.
- Other: Theme-related puzzles, games, and activities.

SAMPLE ISSUE
4 pages (no advertising): 1 article; 6 activities. Sample copy, theme list, and writers' guidelines available.

- "Migration." Article explores the reasons why certain animals migrate from one habitat to another, and explains how they know when and where to go.
- Sample dept/column: "Weekly Lab" presents an activity that has readers making their own maps based on the location of the sun.

RIGHTS AND PAYMENT
All rights. All material, payment rates vary. Pays on publication.

➥EDITOR'S COMMENTS
We produce several editions based around the same theme. For example, the kindergarten edition may explain the concept of migration, while the grade three edition explores why and how it happens.

Scouting

Boy Scouts of America
1325 West Walnut Hill Lane
P.O. Box 152079
Irving, TX 75015-2079

Managing Editor: Scott Daniels

DESCRIPTION AND INTERESTS
Scouting's articles inform, instruct, and inspire its readers, the majority of whom are leaders and volunteers with the Boy Scouts of America. Its goal is to strengthen volunteers' abilities so they may better perform their leadership roles. Circ: 1 million.

Audience: Scout leaders and volunteers
Frequency: 5 times each year
Website: www.scoutingmagazine.org

FREELANCE POTENTIAL
50% written by nonstaff writers. Publishes 8 freelance submissions yearly; 5–10% by authors who are new to the magazine. Receives 30 queries yearly.

SUBMISSIONS
Query with outline. Accepts hard copy. SASE. Responds in 3 weeks.

- Articles: 500–1,200 words. Informational and how-to articles; profiles; humor; and personal experience pieces. Topics include Boy Scout programs, leadership, volunteering, nature, social issues, and history.
- Depts/columns: 500–700 words. Family activities, outdoor activities, short profiles, and Boy Scout news.
- Other: Quizzes, puzzles, and games.

SAMPLE ISSUE
48 pages (33% advertising): 4 articles; 6 depts/columns. Sample copy, $2.50 with 9x12 SASE. Guidelines available at website.

- "The Real Game Boys." Article describes the phenomenon of geocaching, the centerpiece of BSA's new Get in the Game! program.
- Sample dept/column: "Roundtable: What I've Learned" profiles longtime Scout leader, Bob Dalton.

RIGHTS AND PAYMENT
First North American serial rights. Written material, $300–$800. Pays on acceptance. Provides 2 contributor's copies.

➥EDITOR'S COMMENTS
We're looking for stories from experienced Scout leaders and volunteers that could make our readers say, "My guys would love to do that!" We are always happy to hear about successful programs and trips. Articles that tackle issues related to leadership and mentoring are also welcome.

Seattle's Child

4303 198th Street SW
Lynnwood, WA 98036

Managing Editor: Liz Gillespie

DESCRIPTION AND INTERESTS
With an emphasis on local resources and services, this magazine provides Seattle-area families with a wealth of relevant parenting information. Each issue also features health, travel, and education information. Circ: 80,000.

Audience: Parents
Frequency: Monthly
Website: www.seattleschild.com

FREELANCE POTENTIAL
80% written by nonstaff writers. Publishes 30 freelance submissions yearly; 10% by unpublished writers, 25% by authors who are new to the magazine. Receives 120+ queries yearly.

SUBMISSIONS
Query with outline. Accepts hard copy, email queries to editor@seattleschild.com, and simultaneous submissions if identified. SASE. Responds in 1 month.

- Articles: Word lengths vary. Informational and how-to articles; and personal experience pieces. Topics include family, parenting, social issues, health, fitness, nutrition, regional news, family travel, and recreation.
- Depts/columns: Word lengths vary. Profiles, cooking, and media reviews.

SAMPLE ISSUE
46 pages (30% advertising): 6 articles; 4 depts/columns. Sample copy, $3 with 9x12 SASE. Guidelines and theme list available.

- "More Families Cut Out Gluten." Article examines the growing number of children affected by celiac disease and explains the key to a gluten-free diet.
- "When in Doubt, Sit Them Out." Article addresses the new law that requires removing children from sports if they are suspected of having a concussion.
- Sample dept/column: "Community Voices" explains why recess before lunch helps with learning and nutrition.

RIGHTS AND PAYMENT
Rights vary. Written material, $100–$450. Pays 30 days after publication. Provides 2 contributor's copies.

➥EDITOR'S COMMENTS
Local issues that relate to national trends are always of interest to us, as long as they include sources from our area.

Seek

Standard Publishing Company
8805 Governor's Hill Drive, Suite 400
Cincinnati, OH 45249

Editor: Margaret K. Williams

DESCRIPTION AND INTERESTS
Seek is a take-home paper designed to supplement religious education or Bible study lessons. It is directed at young adults and adults, and contains inspirational stories and Bible lessons. Circ: 27,000.
Audience: YA–Adult
Frequency: Weekly (on a quarterly basis)
Website: www.standardpub.com

FREELANCE POTENTIAL
80% written by nonstaff writers. Publishes 150 freelance submissions yearly; 50% by authors who are new to the magazine. Receives 500–600 unsolicited mss yearly.

SUBMISSIONS
Send complete ms. Prefers email submissions to seek@standardpub.com; will accept hard copy. SASE. Responds in 3–6 months.

- Articles: 400–1,200 words. Inspirational, devotional, and personal experience pieces. Topics include religious and contemporary issues, Christian living, coping with moral and ethical dilemmas, and controversial subjects.
- Fiction: 400–1,200 words. Stories about Christian living, moral and ethical problems, controversial topics, and dealing with contemporary life challenges.
- Other: Submit seasonal material 1 year in advance.

SAMPLE ISSUE
8 pages (no advertising): 3 articles; 1 Bible lesson. Sample copy, free with 6x9 SASE. Guidelines and theme list available.

- "Victory Over Temptation." Article discusses the fortitude and determination needed to resist temptation of all kinds.
- "Tempted to Quit." Article challenges the reader to evaluate how hard they are working versus how much time they are spending with God.

RIGHTS AND PAYMENT
First and second rights. Written material, $.05–$.07 per word. Pays on acceptance. Provides 5 contributor's copies.

⇢EDITOR'S COMMENTS
We choose work that best encourages our readers in their walk with Jesus Christ and helps them apply biblical truths in their lives.

Seventeen

300 West 57th Street, 17th Floor
New York, NY 10019

Editor

DESCRIPTION AND INTERESTS
From fashion to friendship, and popularity to pop culture, this magazine speaks to girls who are looking for answers to the questions of the day. Fiction is offered as well. Circ: 2 million.
Audience: Girls, 13–21 years
Frequency: Monthly
Website: www.seventeen.com

FREELANCE POTENTIAL
20% written by nonstaff writers. Publishes 20 freelance submissions yearly; 5% by unpublished writers, 40% by authors who are new to the magazine. Receives 46 queries, 200 unsolicited mss yearly.

SUBMISSIONS
Query with outline and clips or writing samples for nonfiction. Send complete ms for fiction. Accepts hard copy and simultaneous submissions if identified. SASE. Response time varies.

- Articles: 650–3,000 words. Informational and self-help articles; profiles; and personal experience pieces. Topics include relationships, dating, family issues, current events, social concerns, friendship, and pop culture.
- Fiction: 1,000–3,000 words. Stories that feature female teenage experiences.
- Depts/columns: 500–1,000 words. Fashion, beauty, health, and fitness.
- Other: Submit seasonal material 6 months in advance.

SAMPLE ISSUE
166 pages (50% advertising): 7 articles; 24 depts/columns. Sample copy, $2.99 at newsstands. Guidelines available.

- "Plan the Best Slumber Party Ever!" Article gives suggestions for snacks, games, and crafts to help girls have a fun night in.
- "Turn Off Your Phone to Save Your Life!" Article explains that talking or texting while driving is a deadly combination.

RIGHTS AND PAYMENT
First rights. Written material, $1–$1.50 per word. Pays on acceptance.

⇢EDITOR'S COMMENTS
Writers should be tuned in to the trends, news, and interests of our demographic, as well as to the best way to get our readers to tune in. Offer sound advice, but avoid any hint of preachiness.

Sharing the Victory

Fellowship of Christian Athletes
8701 Leeds Road
Kansas City, MO 64129

Editorial Assistant: Ashley Burns

DESCRIPTION AND INTERESTS
Sharing the Victory targets athletes and coaches who are members of the Fellowship of Christian Athletes. Its articles, profiles, and first-person pieces are meant to inform and inspire its readers. Circ: 80,000.

Audience: Athletes & coaches, grades 7 and up
Frequency: 9 times each year
Website: www.sharingthevictory.com

FREELANCE POTENTIAL
40% written by nonstaff writers. Publishes 20 freelance submissions yearly; 25% by unpublished writers, 10% by authors who are new to the magazine. Receives 48 queries and unsolicited mss yearly.

SUBMISSIONS
Query with outline and writing samples; or send complete ms. Accepts hard copy. Availability of artwork improves chance of acceptance. SASE. Response time varies.

- Articles: To 1,200 words. Informational articles; profiles; interviews; and personal experience pieces. Topics include sports, athletes, coaches, competition, training, focus, faith, missions, and Christian education.
- Depts/columns: Staff written.
- Artwork: Color prints.
- Other: Submit seasonal material 3–4 months in advance.

SAMPLE ISSUE
30 pages (30% advertising): 4 articles; 9 depts/columns. Sample copy, $1 with 9x12 SASE (3 first-class stamps). Writers' guidelines available.

- "Winter Olympic Preview." Article profiles eight Christian Olympic athletes who competed in the name of God.
- "Baseball in the Bay." Article profiles a California man who organizes baseball clinics that also have a spiritual component.

RIGHTS AND PAYMENT
First serial rights. Articles, $150–$400. Pays on publication.

➡EDITOR'S COMMENTS
Profiles and interviews are most open to freelance writers. All profile articles must contain an authentic spiritual angle depicting the person's struggles and successes while including a strong tie to the FCA ministry.

Shine Brightly

P.O. Box 87334
Canton, MI 48187

Editor: Sara Lynne Hilton

DESCRIPTION AND INTERESTS
This Christian publication focuses on motivating, inspiring, and equipping girls to use their voices to "shine brightly" and change the world. Circ: 15,500.

Audience: Girls, 9–14 years
Frequency: 9 times each year
Website: www.gemsgc.org

FREELANCE POTENTIAL
25% written by nonstaff writers. Publishes 20 freelance submissions yearly; 15% by unpublished writers, 90% by new authors. Receives 500 unsolicited mss yearly.

SUBMISSIONS
Send complete ms. Accepts email submissions to shinebrightly@gemsgc.org (no attachments). Responds in 1 month.

- Articles: 100–400 words. Informational and how-to articles; profiles; humor; and personal experience pieces. Topics include community service, stewardship, contemporary social issues, family and friend relationships, and peer pressure.
- Fiction: 400–900 words. Genres include contemporary and science fiction, romance, mystery, and adventure. Also publishes stories about nature, animals, and sports.
- Depts/columns: Staff written.
- Artwork: 5x7 or larger B/W or color prints.
- Other: Puzzles, activities, and cartoons.

SAMPLE ISSUE
24 pages (no advertising): 4 articles; 1 story; 3 depts/columns. Sample copy, $1 with 9x12 SASE ($.75 postage). Guidelines and theme list available at website.

- "A Girls' Guide to Eco Style." Article provides tips for updating a wardrobe without buying new clothing.
- "The Micah Road Mysteries." Story presents the latest installment of a mystery taking place in a darkened church basement.

RIGHTS AND PAYMENT
First, second, and simultaneous rights. Articles and fiction, $.02–$.05 per word. Other material, payment rates vary. Pays on publication. Provides 2 contributor's copies.

➡EDITOR'S COMMENTS
All material should have a Christian perspective. See our website for upcoming themes.

Sisterhood Agenda

16213 Spring Garden Street
St. John, VI 00830

Editor: Angela D. Coleman

DESCRIPTION AND INTERESTS
This magazine, appearing online and in print, is designed to empower and uplift women and girls of African descent through sisterhood, self-knowledge, self-development, and self-esteem. Circ: 500,000.
Audience: 13–32 years
Frequency: Quarterly
Website: www.sisterhoodagenda.com

FREELANCE POTENTIAL
90% written by nonstaff writers. Publishes 100 freelance submissions yearly; 75% by unpublished writers, 90% by authors who are new to the magazine. Receives 100+ unsolicited mss each year.

SUBMISSIONS
Send complete ms. Accepts email submissions to acoleman@sisterhoodagenda.com (Microsoft Word attachments). Availability of artwork improves chance of acceptance. Response time varies.

- Articles: To 500 words. Informational articles; profiles; and photo-essays. Topics include Africa, ancestry, heritage, history, current events, history, nutrition, music, fashion, beauty, self-esteem, fitness, technology, life skills, celebrities, and community service.
- Fiction: Word lengths vary. Genres include multicultural, ethnic, and inspirational fiction.
- Depts/columns: First-person essays; to 300 words. News briefs, book reviews, hair tips, and affirmations; word lengths vary.
- Artwork: Digital images at 300 dpi.
- Other: Poetry, to 15 lines.

SAMPLE ISSUE
50 pages: 6 articles; 23 depts/columns. Sample copy, guidelines, and editorial calendar available at website.

- "Talk to Your Kids. Tackle Obesity." Article provides tips for keeping children healthy.
- "Things We Take for Granted." Article reports on a program aimed at ending teen violence.

RIGHTS AND PAYMENT
One-time rights. No payment.

☞ EDITOR'S COMMENTS
We are part of a global, nonprofit organization whose mission is to reach a historically at-risk and traditionally underserved population.

Six78th

P.O. Box 450
Newark, CA 94560

Editorial Director: Carol S. Rothchild

DESCRIPTION AND INTERESTS
The title *Six78th* refers to the sixth, seventh, and eighth grades—this magazine's core demographic. It's a lifestyle magazine read by girls in middle and junior high school, and its articles reflect everything these girls are interested in, including fashion, celebrities, pop culture, friendship, and learning to deal with new social situations. Circ: Unavailable.
Audience: Girls, 10–14 years
Frequency: 6 times each year
Website: www.six78th.com

FREELANCE POTENTIAL
12% written by nonstaff writers. Publishes 5–10 freelance submissions yearly; 5% by unpublished writers, 5% by authors who are new to the magazine. Receives 60–120 queries each year.

SUBMISSIONS
Query. Accepts email queries to carol@six78th.com. Responds in 2 months.

- Articles: Word lengths vary. Informational and self-help articles; profiles; interviews; and personal experience pieces. Topics include school, current events, health and fitness, sports, music, entertainment, popular culture, celebrities, and social issues.
- Depts/columns: Word lengths vary. Reviews, nutrition, fashion, and friendship.

SAMPLE ISSUE
58 pages: 6 articles; 13 depts/columns. Sample copy, $4.50 with 9x12 SASE. Writers' guidelines available.

- "Face of a Stranger." Article provides tips for making friends when starting a new school.
- Sample dept/column: "School Woes" explains standardized testing and provides test-preparation tips.

RIGHTS AND PAYMENT
Rights vary. Written material, payment rates vary. Pays on publication. Provides 5 contributor's copies.

☞ EDITOR'S COMMENTS
While on the cusp of growing up, our readers are still little girls. We leave the stories about sex and boys to the other magazines. We are open to a variety of subjects, as long as they are something that will touch our readers' hearts or pique their interest.

Skating

United States Figure Skating Association
20 First Street
Colorado Springs, CO 80906

Director of Publications: Troy Schwindt

DESCRIPTION AND INTERESTS
Figure skating—and the personalities, programs, trends, and events that affect the sport—are the focus of this magazine. It is written for members and fans of the United States Figure Skating Association. Circ: 45,000.

Audience: 5 years–Adult
Frequency: 11 times each year
Website: www.usfigureskating.org

FREELANCE POTENTIAL
70% written by nonstaff writers. Publishes 15 freelance submissions yearly; 10% by unpublished writers, 20% by authors who are new to the magazine. Receives 72 queries and unsolicited mss yearly.

SUBMISSIONS
Query with résumé, clips or writing samples, and photo ideas; or send complete ms. Accepts hard copy, Macintosh zip disk submissions, and email to skatingmagazine@usfigureskating.org. SASE. Responds in 1 month.

- Articles: 750–2,000 words. Informational articles; profiles; and interviews. Topics include association news, competitions, techniques, personalities, and training.
- Depts/columns: 600–800 words. Competition results, profiles of skaters and coaches, sports medicine, fitness, and technique tips.
- Artwork: B/W and color prints, slides, or transparencies; digital images at 300 dpi.

SAMPLE ISSUE
56 pages: 5 articles; 11 depts/columns. Sample copy, $3 with 9x12 SASE. Writers' guidelines available.

- "Where Are They Now?" Article profiles the life of Renée Roca now that she is retired from ice dancing.
- Sample dept/column: "In Synch" offers tips for helping skaters and their families choose the right team.

RIGHTS AND PAYMENT
First serial rights. Articles, $75–$150. Depts/columns, $75. Artwork, payment rates vary. Pays on publication. Provides 5–10 contributor's copies.

✦EDITOR'S COMMENTS
We're always interested in hearing about up-and-coming skaters from around the world, as well as coaches with interesting stories.

Skipping Stones
A Multicultural Magazine

P.O. Box 3939
Eugene, OR 97403-0939

Editor: Arun N. Toké

DESCRIPTION AND INTERESTS
Skipping Stones serves as a communications forum for children from different lands and backgrounds. Each issue features a mix of multicultural articles, stories, poems, and art. Circ: 2,500.

Audience: 7–17 years
Frequency: 5 times each year
Website: www.skippingstones.org

FREELANCE POTENTIAL
90% written by nonstaff writers. Publishes 175–200 freelance submissions yearly; 60% by unpublished writers, 75% by new authors. Receives 3,600–4,800 unsolicited mss yearly.

SUBMISSIONS
Send complete ms with author information. Accepts hard copy, Macintosh disk submissions, and email to editor@skippingstones.org (Microsoft Word attachments). SASE. Responds in 4–6 months.

- Articles: 750–1,000 words. Informational articles; profiles; photo-essays; interviews; humor; and personal experience pieces. Topics include cultural and religious celebrations, architecture, living abroad, family, careers, disabilities, sustainable living, nature, technology, parenting, and activism.
- Fiction: To 1,000 words. Genres include multicultural fiction and folktales.
- Depts/columns: 100–200 words. Health issues, book reviews, school topics, Q&As.
- Other: Puzzles and games. Poetry by children, to 30 lines. Submit seasonal material 3–4 months in advance.

SAMPLE ISSUE
36 pages (no advertising): 15 articles; 3 stories; 7 depts/columns; 8 poems. Sample copy, $6 with 9x12 SASE (4 first-class stamps). Guidelines available at website.

- "Chris and Odie." Article tells how a boy's life changed after getting a service dog.
- "Why It Rains." Story retells a folktale from the Philippines.

RIGHTS AND PAYMENT
First and non-exclusive reprint rights. No payment. Provides author's copies and discounts.

✦EDITOR'S COMMENTS
We seek articles on mentoring and educational experiences in developing countries.

SLAP

High Speed Productions
1303 Underwood Avenue
San Francisco, CA 94124

Editor: Mark Whiteley

DESCRIPTION AND INTERESTS

An online magazine dedicated to the sport, lifestyle, and attitude of skateboarding, SLAP provides users with a forum to exchange tricks, information, and techniques. It also profiles skaters and offers reviews of music and the latest gear. Hits per month: 200,000.

Audience: YA
Frequency: Updated daily
Website: www.slapmagazine.com

FREELANCE POTENTIAL

40% written by nonstaff writers. Publishes 24 freelance submissions yearly; 20% by unpublished writers.

SUBMISSIONS

Send complete ms. Accepts hard copy, disk submissions, and simultaneous submissions if identified. Availability of artwork improves chance of acceptance. SASE. Responds in 2 months.

- Articles: Word lengths vary. Informational and how-to articles; profiles; interviews; and personal experience pieces. Topics include skateboarding techniques, equipment, and competitions; music; art; and pop culture.
- Depts/columns: Word lengths vary. Media reviews, interviews, gear, gossip, and skateboard tricks.
- Artwork: 35mm B/W negatives; color prints and transparencies.
- Other: Photo-essays, cartoons, and contests.

SAMPLE ISSUE

Sample copy available at website. Guidelines and editorial calendar available.

- "Animal Collective." Article interviews Geologist, a member of the popular college jam band Animal Collective.
- "Interview with Tom Karangelov." Article catches up with the winner of the One in a Million contest to find the best new skaters.

RIGHTS AND PAYMENT

First rights. All material, payment rates vary. Pays on publication.

➥EDITOR'S COMMENTS

We are only interested in contributors who are in the skateboard world themselves. If you're not a shredder, or don't know one when you see one, we're not for you. Most of our pieces are audio-based with supporting video.

South Florida Parenting

1701 Green Road, Suite B
Deerfield Beach, FL 33064

Editor: Kyara Lomer

DESCRIPTION AND INTERESTS

Serving three counties in southeastern Florida, this publication provides its readers with the most up-to-date regional information on child development, personal finance, family health, recreational activities, and travel. It prefers to work with local writers. Circ: 110,000.

Audience: Parents
Frequency: Monthly
Website: www.sfparenting.com

FREELANCE POTENTIAL

85% written by nonstaff writers. Publishes 90 freelance submissions yearly; 10% by new authors. Receives 996 queries and unsolicited mss yearly.

SUBMISSIONS

Prefers complete ms; will accept query. Accepts hard copy and email submissions to krlomer@tribune.com. SASE. Responds in 2–3 months.

- Articles: 800–1,500 words. Informational and how-to articles; profiles; interviews; and personal experience pieces. Topics include family life, travel, parenting, education, leisure, music, health, and regional events and activities.
- Depts/columns: To 750 words. Family finances, health, nutrition, infant care, and pre-teen issues.

SAMPLE ISSUE

118 pages (60% advertising): 6 articles; 6 depts/columns. Guidelines available.

- "Labor of Love." Article offers eight suggestions for becoming a more compassionate parent.
- "A Piece of the Action." Article explains how to plan a fitness party for kids.
- Sample dept/column: "Family Health & Safety" explains how best to avoid dental cavities.

RIGHTS AND PAYMENT

One-time regional rights. Written material, $50–$300. Pays on publication. Provides contributor's copies upon request.

➥EDITOR'S COMMENTS

We will consider previously published material as long as it is offered to us on an exclusive basis. We will not consider work that is offered to or has been published by other publications in our area.

South Jersey Mom

P.O. Box 2413
Vineland, NJ 08362-2413

Editor: Adrienne Richardson

DESCRIPTION AND INTERESTS
This regional magazine focuses on providing support and advice for moms with children under the age of 12, including expectant moms. Its articles highlight the joys, wonders, headaches, and heartaches that go along with parenting. Circ: 38,000.
Audience: Parents
Frequency: Monthly
Website: www.southjerseymom.com

FREELANCE POTENTIAL
98% written by nonstaff writers. Publishes 50–75 freelance submissions yearly; 40% by unpublished writers, 10% by authors who are new to the magazine. Receives 180 queries each year.

SUBMISSIONS
Query with 2 writing samples. Accepts email queries to adrienne@southjerseymom.com. Response time varies.

- Articles: To 600 words. Informational articles; profiles; and personal experience pieces. Topics include parenting, trends, family issues, pregnancy, technology, education, exercise, safety, sports, and recreation.
- Depts/columns: Up to 600 words. Health topics, gear, technology.

SAMPLE ISSUE
36 pages: 8 articles; 12 depts/columns. Sample copy available at website. Guidelines and editorial calendar available.

- "Pros and Cons for Parents of Twins." Article looks at both the challenges and benefits of raising multiples.
- "Fitness and Health Tips to Become the Biggest Loser at Home." Article offers valuable fitness and nutrition tips that result in weight loss.
- Sample dept/column: "Green Mama" discusses the hazards of letting a car idle.

RIGHTS AND PAYMENT
Rights vary. No payment.

❖EDITOR'S COMMENTS
Our mission is to empower mothers and recognize all they do for their families. Remember that since we are a regional magazine, we need sources and resources from our local area only.

Southwest Florida Parent & Child

2442 Dr. Martin Luther King Jr. Boulevard
Fort Myers, FL 33901

Editor: Pamela Smith Hayford

DESCRIPTION AND INTERESTS
Parents in Florida's southwestern region will find resources, advice, and other information on raising children in each issue of this magazine. Its content covers relationships, travel, recreational activities, personal finance, and local events. Circ: 23,000.
Audience: Parents
Frequency: Monthly
Website: www.gulfcoast.momslikeme.com

FREELANCE POTENTIAL
55% written by nonstaff writers. Publishes 160 freelance submissions yearly; 5% by unpublished writers, 10% by authors who are new to the magazine. Receives 275 queries and unsolicited mss yearly.

SUBMISSIONS
Query or send complete ms. Accepts email submissions to pamela@swflparentchild.com. Response time varies.

- Articles: To 500 words. Informational articles; profiles; and personal experience pieces. Topics include family issues, parenting, education, travel, sports, health, fitness, computers, and social and regional issues.
- Depts/columns: To 500 words. Dining, travel, parenting, education, and nutrition.

SAMPLE ISSUE
74 pages (40–50% advertising): 3 articles; 19 depts/columns. Guidelines available.

- "No More Scary Dental Visits." Article describes the extra steps some area dentists take to make their young patients feel more at ease.
- "Our Black American Roots." Article profiles three regional African Americans who helped develop southwestern Florida.
- Sample dept/column: "Dining Out with Kids" profiles a local breakfast eatery.

RIGHTS AND PAYMENT
All rights. Written material, $25–$200. Pays on publication.

❖EDITOR'S COMMENTS
Most of the freelance articles we use come from writers within our region. Keep in mind that our readers want to hear about fun things to do in the area. They also want valuable tips on raising children, and information about other issues of importance to them.

Spark Action

Forum for Youth Investment
The Cady-Lee House
7064 Eastern Avenue NW
Washington, DC 20012

Editor: Caitlin Johnson

DESCRIPTION AND INTERESTS
Previously listed as *Connect for Kids*, this e-zine offers advocacy tools for those seeking to make a difference in the lives of children. It covers state and federal policy affecting children, and provides action alerts to help readers make changes in their communities and across the nation. Hits per month: 50,000+.

Audience: Parents & child welfare professionals
Frequency: 26 times each year
Website: http://sparkaction.org

FREELANCE POTENTIAL
40% written by nonstaff writers. Publishes 24 freelance submissions yearly; 25% by authors who are new to the magazine. Receives 150 queries yearly.

SUBMISSIONS
Query via http://sparkaction.org. Response time varies.

- Articles: 900–1,500 words. Informational articles; profiles; reviews; and photo-essays. Topics include state and federal policy affecting children and youth; contacting elected officials; organizing campaigns; volunteering; research on children's advocacy issues; child care and development; juvenile justice; child abuse and neglect; crime and violence prevention; parent involvement in education; out-of-school time; diversity and awareness; and mentoring programs.

SAMPLE ISSUE
Sample copy and writers' guidelines available at website.

- "A (Somewhat Unlikely) Summer Reading Recommendation for Advocates." Article explains why a book on finance is relevant for children's advocates.
- "Obama Surprises Michigan High School Students." Article reports on an unexpected meet-and-greet at Kalamazoo Central High.

RIGHTS AND PAYMENT
First rights. No payment.

➥ EDITOR'S COMMENTS
We welcome original and reprinted feature articles that offer a firsthand take on issues affecting children and families. Remember that we serve a wide audience, ranging from professional child advocates to parents, policymakers, and young people.

Sparkle!

P.O. Box 7259
Grand Rapids, MI 49510

Senior Editor: Sara Lynne Hilton

DESCRIPTION AND INTERESTS
Published by GEMS (Girls Everywhere Meeting the Savior) Girls' Clubs, *Sparkle!* features articles, fiction, and activities that present Christian life realistically, and show its young readers how God's Word applies to their daily lives. Circ: 7,000.

Audience: Girls, 6–9 years
Frequency: 6 times each year
Website: www.gemsgc.org

FREELANCE POTENTIAL
20% written by nonstaff writers. Publishes 6 freelance submissions yearly; 90% by unpublished writers, 90% by authors who are new to the magazine. Receives 100 unsolicited mss each year.

SUBMISSIONS
Send complete ms. Accepts email submissions to sparkle@gemsgc.org (no attachments). Responds 4–6 weeks.

- Articles: 100–400 words. Informational articles. Topics include animals, sports, music, musicians, famous people, interaction with family and friends, service projects, and dealing with school work.
- Fiction: 100–400 words. Genres include adventure, mystery, and contemporary fiction.
- Other: Puzzles, games, recipes, party ideas, short humorous pieces, cartoons, and inexpensive craft projects. Poetry, 5–15 lines.

SAMPLE ISSUE
16 pages (no advertising): 2 articles; 1 story; 5 activities; 1 Bible lesson; 1 poem. Sample copy, $1 with 9x12 SASE. Guidelines and theme list available at website.

- "Life Lesson One." Bible lesson tells of Elijah bringing his people to the mountain to show them the real God.
- "The Cupcake Problem." Story depicts a young girl trying to discover how God would want her to handle a bossy classmate.

RIGHTS AND PAYMENT
Rights vary. Articles, $20. Other material, payment rates vary. Pays on publication. Provides 2 contributor's copies.

➥ EDITOR'S COMMENTS
Material should encourage readers to live as Christ would live, and to serve the needs of others.

Spider
The Magazine for Children

Cricket Magazine Group
70 East Lake Street, Suite 300
Chicago, IL 60601

Submissions Editor

DESCRIPTION AND INTERESTS
Spider features easy-to-read stories, interesting articles, poetry, and activities for beginning and early readers. Part of the Cricket Magazine Group, it seeks top-quality work that is fun and age appropriate. Circ: 50,000.

Audience: 6–9 years
Frequency: 9 times each year
Website: www.cricketmag.com
      www.spidermagkids.com

FREELANCE POTENTIAL
90% written by nonstaff writers. Publishes 50 freelance submissions yearly; 35% by unpublished writers, 35% by authors who are new to the magazine. Receives 1,800 unsolicited mss each year.

SUBMISSIONS
Send complete ms; include bibliography for nonfiction. Accepts hard copy and simultaneous submissions if identified. SASE. Responds in 6 months.

- Articles: 300–800 words. Informational and how-to articles; profiles; and interviews. Topics include nature, animals, science, technology, history, multicultural issues, foreign cultures, and the environment.
- Fiction: 300–1,000 words. Easy-to-read stories. Genres include humor; fantasy; fairy tales; folktales; and realistic, historical, and science fiction.
- Other: Recipes, crafts, puzzles, games, and math and word activities. Poetry, to 20 lines.

SAMPLE ISSUE
34 pages (no advertising): 1 article; 3 stories; 4 activities; 2 poems. Sample copy, $5 with 9x12 SASE. Guidelines available at website.

- "Doodlebug & Dandelion." Story tells of a brother and sister who prepare a time capsule with the help of some friends.
- "Boston's Great Molasses Flood." Article describes this event of 1919.

RIGHTS AND PAYMENT
All rights. Articles and fiction, to $.25 per word. Poetry, to $3 per line. Pays on publication. Provides 2 contributor's copies.

➥EDITOR'S COMMENTS
We're publishing fewer freelance pieces than last year; however, our current needs include science fiction and original fairy tales.

Sporting Kid

2050 Vista Parkway
West Palm Beach, FL 33411

Managing Editor: Greg Bach

DESCRIPTION AND INTERESTS
As the member publication of the National Alliance for Youth Sports (NAYS), *Sporting Kid* is an advocate for positive and safe sports for children. Each issue includes valuable tips to help parents and volunteer coaches in their roles, as well as profiles of outstanding players. Circ: 300,000.

Audience: Parents, coaches, and officials
Frequency: Quarterly
Website: www.nays.org/sportingkid

FREELANCE POTENTIAL
15% written by nonstaff writers. Publishes 10 freelance submissions yearly; 5% by unpublished writers, 15% by authors who are new to the magazine. Receives 180 queries, 60 unsolicited mss yearly.

SUBMISSIONS
Query or send complete ms. Accepts email submissions to sportingkid@nays.org. Responds in 1 month.

- Articles: To 1,000 words. Informational and how-to articles; and profiles. Topics include youth sports, coaching, parenting, officiating, health, and safety.
- Depts/columns: 750 words. New product information, the culture of youth sports, and coaching and parenting tips.

SAMPLE ISSUE
32 pages: 7 articles; 4 depts/columns.

- "How Do Your Coaching Skills Rate?" Article discusses the benefits of a new Coach Rating System that evaluates coaches' skills in 14 areas.
- "It's All About the Kids." Article profiles the Coach of the Year, who coaches three teams at the Fort Campbell Army Base in Kentucky.
- Sample dept/column: "SureShots" offers tips for getting overweight kids back on the healthy track.

RIGHTS AND PAYMENT
First and electronic rights. Written material, payment rates vary. Pays on publication.

➥EDITOR'S COMMENTS
Let us know about creative ideas for making sports safe and fun for children, and clever ways coaches can run quality practices that teach kids skills in a safe and productive manner.

Sports Illustrated Kids

Time & Life Building
1271 Avenue of the Americas, 32nd Floor
New York, NY 10020

Managing Editor: Bob Der

DESCRIPTION AND INTERESTS
This version of the popular sports magazine targets younger sports fans with articles on amateur and student athletes and Olympians. It covers all sports, including the ones that appeal to the younger set, such as skateboarding and BMX racing. Circ: 1.1 million.

Audience: 8–14 years
Frequency: Monthly
Website: www.sikids.com

FREELANCE POTENTIAL
3–5% written by nonstaff writers. Publishes 1–2 freelance submissions yearly. Receives 40–50 queries and unsolicited mss yearly.

SUBMISSIONS
Query or send complete ms. Accepts hard copy. SASE. Responds in 2 months.

- Articles: Lead articles and profiles, 500–700 words. Short features, 500–600 words. Informational articles; profiles; and interviews. Topics include professional and aspiring athletes, sports, fitness, health, safety, hobbies, and technology.
- Depts/columns: Word lengths vary. Event coverage, team and player profiles, news, pro tips, humor, and video game reviews.
- Other: Puzzles, games, trivia, comics, and sports cards. Poetry and artwork by children.

SAMPLE ISSUE
56 pages (24% advertising): 5 articles; 7 depts/columns; 1 comic; 1 puzzle; 1 quiz. Sample copy, writers' guidelines, and editorial calendar available.

- "What a Life!" Article profiles Ryan Sheckler, X Games medalist, skateboarder, and star of his own reality show on MTV.
- Sample dept/column: "Sports Gamer" reviews three new sports video games.

RIGHTS AND PAYMENT
All rights. Articles, $100–$1,500. Depts/columns, payment rates vary. Pays on acceptance. Provides contributor's copies.

•❖ EDITOR'S COMMENTS
We are particularly interested in articles about sports that hold a special appeal for kids, and in articles that profile young athletes. We do not use freelancers often, however. Your best chance to break in here is with a short, interesting item.

Stone Soup
The Magazine by Young Writers and Artists

P.O. Box 83
Santa Cruz, CA 95063

Editor: Gerry Mandel

DESCRIPTION AND INTERESTS
This "magazine by young writers and artists" is made up of stories, poems, book reviews, and art from contributors all over the world. It accepts work from children up to the age of 14. Circ: 15,000.

Audience: 8–14 years
Frequency: 6 times each year
Website: www.stonesoup.com

FREELANCE POTENTIAL
100% written by nonstaff writers. Publishes 72 freelance submissions yearly; 90% by unpublished writers, 90% by authors who are new to the magazine. Receives 12,000 unsolicited mss yearly.

SUBMISSIONS
Send complete ms. Accepts submissions from writers under 14 years of age only. Accepts hard copy. No simultaneous submissions. No SASE. Responds in 6 weeks if interested.

- Fiction: To 2,500 words. Genres include multicultural, ethnic, historical, and science fiction; adventure; mystery; and suspense.
- Depts/columns: Word lengths vary. Book reviews.
- Artwork: B/W and color line art.
- Other: Poetry, line lengths vary.

SAMPLE ISSUE
48 pages (no advertising): 8 stories; 2 book reviews; 3 poems. Sample copy and guidelines available at website.

- "Shadow." Story tells of the strong bond that persists between a girl and a stray dog even after he is adopted into a new home.
- "Building the Pyramids." Story tells of a girl's longing for her parents who have traveled to another town to help harvest crops.
- Sample dept/column: "Book Review" offers a synopsis of *The Dragonfly Pool*.

RIGHTS AND PAYMENT
All rights. Written material, $40. Artwork, $25. Pays on publication. Provides 2 contributor's copies.

•❖ EDITOR'S COMMENTS
We are always looking for new writers and artists to send us their work. If you are interested in reviewing books for us, please tell us about yourself and about the kinds of books you like to read.

Story Mates

Christian Light Publications, Inc.
P.O. Box 1212
Harrisonburg, VA 22803-1212

Editor: Crystal Shank

DESCRIPTION AND INTERESTS
This publication is used in Sunday schools and as take-home papers for after-church reflection. Containing stories that correspond to lessons and conform to the conservative Mennonite doctrine, it is geared toward preschool and primary school children. Circ: 6,425.

Audience: 4–8 years
Frequency: Monthly (in 4 weekly volumes)
Website: www.clp.org

FREELANCE POTENTIAL
90% written by nonstaff writers. Publishes 200 freelance submissions yearly. Receives 600 unsolicited mss yearly.

SUBMISSIONS
Send complete ms. Accepts hard copy and email submissions to storymates@clp.org. SASE. Responds in 6 weeks.

- Fiction: Stories related to Sunday school lessons and true-to-life stories of faith, to 800 words. Picture stories, 120–150 words.
- Other: Bible puzzles and activities. Poetry, word lengths vary. Submit seasonal material 6 months in advance.

SAMPLE ISSUE
16 pages (no advertising): 4 stories; 2 poems; 9 activities. Sample copy, free with 9x12 SASE ($1.20 postage). Writers' guidelines and theme list available.

- "No Easter Eggs?" Story finds a family teaching their foster son about their traditions, and how happiness is found not in Easter eggs, but in the simple things.
- "Just a Little Kindness." Story shares the trepidation Tommy felt when he met a new boy who couldn't speak English, then the excitement and pride he felt when he shared his toys with the boy and became his friend.

RIGHTS AND PAYMENT
First, reprint, or multiple-use rights. Fiction, $.04–$.06 per word. Poetry, $.50–$.75 per line. Puzzles, $10. Other material, payment rates vary. Pays on acceptance. Provides 1 contributor's copy.

➥EDITOR'S COMMENTS
An effective message comes from a good heart. A good life adds credibility and weight to your message. Stories should show children learning to live in ways that please God.

SuperScience

Scholastic Inc.
557 Broadway
New York, NY 10012-3999

Editor: Elizabeth Carney

DESCRIPTION AND INTERESTS
Designed for use in the classroom, *SuperScience* is filled with interesting articles on all aspects of science and how they figure into our daily lives. It also provides teacher guides with classroom experiments and reproducible lesson resources. Circ: 200,000.

Audience: Grades 3–6
Frequency: 8 times each year
Website: www.scholastic.com/superscience

FREELANCE POTENTIAL
80% written by nonstaff writers. Publishes 50 freelance submissions yearly; 15% by authors who are new to the magazine. Receives 60–120 queries yearly.

SUBMISSIONS
Query with résumé and clips. Accepts hard copy. SASE. Response time varies.

- Articles: 100–600 words. Informational and how-to articles; profiles; interviews; and personal experience pieces. Topics include earth, physical, and life sciences; health; technology; chemistry; nature; and the environment.
- Depts/columns: Word lengths vary. Science news, mysteries, and experiments.
- Artwork: 8x10 B/W and color prints. Line art.
- Other: Puzzles and activities.

SAMPLE ISSUE
16 pages (no advertising): 3 articles; 5 depts/columns. Sample copy, free with 9x12 SASE. Editorial calendar available at website.

- "Dangerous Race." Article tells of the adventures and dangers that faced Robert Scott and Roald Amundsen as they raced to see who would be the first to reach the South Pole.
- "Standing Tall." Article explains the more interesting facts about giraffes.

RIGHTS AND PAYMENT
First rights. Articles, $75–$650. Other material, payment rates vary. Pays on acceptance. Provides 2 contributor's copies.

➥EDITOR'S COMMENTS
We seek authors with experience writing fact-based articles for our age demographic. Each article must have several sidebars and entrance points. It helps your case if you are also a teacher, as we create teaching guides that correspond to each article.

Swimming World and Junior Swimmer

90 Bell Rock Plaza, Suite 200
Sedona, AZ 86351

Editor: Jason Marsteller

DESCRIPTION AND INTERESTS
This magazine covers the world of competitive swimming for athletes and coaches. It features instructional tips, competition news, athlete profiles, and a special section written by and for young swimmers. Circ: 50,000.

Audience: All ages
Frequency: Monthly
Website:
  www.swimmingworldmagazine.com

FREELANCE POTENTIAL
60% written by nonstaff writers. Publishes 100 freelance submissions yearly; 5% by unpublished writers. Receives 192+ queries yearly.

SUBMISSIONS
Query. Accepts hard copy and email queries to jasonm@swimmingworldmagazine.com. SASE. Responds in 1 month.

- Articles: 500–3,500 words. Informational and how-to articles; profiles; and personal experience pieces. Topics include swimming, training, competition, medical advice, swim drills, nutrition, dry land exercise, exercise physiology, and fitness.
- Depts/columns: 500–750 words. Swimming news, new product reviews, and nutrition advice.
- Artwork: Color prints and transparencies. Line art.
- Other: Activities, games, and jokes. Submit seasonal material 1–2 months in advance.

SAMPLE ISSUE
62 pages (30% advertising): 13 articles; 6 depts/columns. Sample copy, $4.50 with 9x12 SASE ($1.80 postage). Guidelines available.

- "YMCA Nationals Sarasota Sweep." Article reports on the young swimmers of the Sarasota YMCA Sharks.
- Sample dept/column: "Age Group Swimmers of the Month" profiles two young brothers who are winning competitions.

RIGHTS AND PAYMENT
All rights. Written material, $.12 per word. Artwork, payment rates vary. Pays on publication. Provides 2–5 contributor's copies.

⊷EDITOR'S COMMENTS
We're always looking for news and profiles from the junior competition level, and welcome material written by young swimmers.

Syracuse Parent

5910 Firestone Drive
Syracuse, NY 13206

Editor: Jennifer Wing

DESCRIPTION AND INTERESTS
This parenting magazine is distributed at family-friendly locations around central New York. Its purpose is to arm New York parents with the local information they need as they raise a family there. It also publishes an array of articles on parenting and family issues. Circ: 26,500.

Audience: Parents
Frequency: Monthly
Website: www.syracuseparent.com

FREELANCE POTENTIAL
40% written by nonstaff writers. Publishes 15 freelance submissions yearly; 25% by unpublished writers, 10% by authors who are new to the magazine. Receives 95 queries yearly.

SUBMISSIONS
Query. Accepts hard copy. SASE. Responds in 4–6 weeks.

- Articles: 800–1,000 words. Informational and how-to articles; profiles; interviews; personal experience and practical application pieces; and humor. Topics include parenting, family issues, pets, education, health, current events, regional news, social issues, nature, the environment, technology, music, travel, recreation, and sports.
- Depts/columns: Staff written.
- Other: Submit artwork 3–4 months in advance.

SAMPLE ISSUE
24 pages (50% advertising): 6 articles; 7 depts/columns. Sample copy, $1 with 9x12 SASE. Guidelines and editorial calendar available.

- "Cooperation Key To Solving Marital Conflicts." Article posits that because marriages are more of an equal partnership than ever before, effective communication is more important than ever before.
- "Easing Back-to-School Jitters Takes a Little Know How." Article provides tips for putting little ones more at ease about the impending return to school.

RIGHTS AND PAYMENT
First North American serial rights. Articles, $25–$30. Pays on publication.

⊷EDITOR'S COMMENTS
We want local information for local parents. Articles may be on general parenting subjects, but they must use local sources.

Take Five Plus

General Council of the Assemblies of God
1445 North Boonville Avenue
Springfield, MO 65802-1894

Director of Editorial Services: Paul Smith

DESCRIPTION AND INTERESTS
This daily devotional guide for teens is designed to help them consider how God's Word can be applied in their day-to-day lives. Devotionals describe the challenges faced by teens, and then offer Scripture-based advice to handle those challenges. Circ: 20,000.

Audience: 12–19 years
Frequency: Quarterly
Website: www.gospelpublishing.com

FREELANCE POTENTIAL
98% written by nonstaff writers. Of the freelance submissions published yearly, 10% are by authors who are new to the magazine.

SUBMISSIONS
All material is assigned. Send letter of introduction with résumé, church background, and clips or writing samples. Accepts hard copy. SASE. Responds in 3 months.

- Articles: 200–235 words. Daily devotionals based on Scripture readings.
- Artwork: Accepts material from teens only. 8x10 B/W prints or 35mm color slides. Line art, 8x10 or smaller.
- Other: Poetry written by teens, to 20 lines.

SAMPLE ISSUE
104 pages (no advertising): 90 devotionals; 4 poems. Sample copy and guidelines available.

- "The Haskell Syndrome." Devotional uses the character from a 1950s TV sitcom to illustrate how important it is to be honest in our relationship with God.
- "Staying Pure." Devotional describes the challenges, means, and rewards to being a chaste teen.
- "Lifesaver." Devotional shows that God's Word can be like a life preserver when hard times and disappointment overwhelm us.

RIGHTS AND PAYMENT
Rights vary. Devotions, payment rates vary. Payment policy varies.

➟EDITOR'S COMMENTS
Remember that our readership is made up of teens. Keep language and situations believable, address issues relevant to that age group, and avoid excessive religious jargon and preachiness. Devotionals are meant to be illustrational and applicable, and should help readers mature in their faith.

Tar Heel Junior Historian

North Carolina Museum of History
5 East Edenton Street
Raleigh, NC 27601-1011

Editor: Lisa Coston Hall

DESCRIPTION AND INTERESTS
This publication of the North Carolina Museum of History presents a well-balanced selection of scholarly articles about the state's history that appeal to pre-teens and young adults. Its content is designed to supplement middle school and high school curricula. Circ: 9,000.

Audience: 9–18 years
Frequency: Twice each year
Website: http://ncmuseumofhistory.org

FREELANCE POTENTIAL
50% written by nonstaff writers. Publishes 12 freelance submissions yearly; 20% by unpublished writers, 50% by authors who are new to the magazine.

SUBMISSIONS
Query. Accepts hard copy and email queries to lisa.hall@ncdcr.gov. SASE. Response time varies.

- Articles: 700–1,000 words. Informational articles; profiles; interviews; and personal experience pieces. Topics include regional history; geography; government; and social, multicultural, and ethnic issues pertaining to North Carolina history.
- Artwork: B/W and spot color prints or transparencies. Line art.
- Other: Puzzles, activities, and word games.

SAMPLE ISSUE
38 pages (no advertising): 25 articles. Sample copy, $5 with 9x12 SASE ($2 postage). Guidelines and theme list available.

- "Sid Luck: A Traditional Seagrove Potter." Article profiles a fifth-generation potter who lives in the pottery capital of North Carolina.
- "Talking Feet: The History of Clogging." Article explains the history of this traditional American dance and its roots in the state.
- "George Higgs and the Bull City Blues." Article reviews the history of blues music and profiles a well-known local musician.

RIGHTS AND PAYMENT
All rights. No payment. Provides 10 contributor's copies.

➟EDITOR'S COMMENTS
Most of our articles are written by history scholars or experts. Your best bet is to query us with your qualifications and we will determine if your background fits our needs.

Teacher Librarian

4501 Forbes Boulevard, Suite 200
Lanham, MD 20706

Managing Editor: Corinne O. Burton

DESCRIPTION AND INTERESTS

Targeting librarians who work with children and young adults, this magazine features thought-provoking articles on all aspects of library services. Its articles cover strategies for effective advocacy, techniques for student learning, technology, and management issues. Circ: 10,000.

Audience: Library professionals
Frequency: 5 times each year
Website: www.teacherlibrarian.com

FREELANCE POTENTIAL

60% written by nonstaff writers. Publishes 10 freelance submissions yearly; 25% by unpublished writers, 5% by new authors. Receives 6 queries and unsolicited mss yearly.

SUBMISSIONS

Query or send complete ms with résumé and abstract or bibliography. Accepts hard copy, disk submissions, and email submissions to editor@teacherlibrarian.com. SASE. Responds in 2 months.

- Articles: 2,000+ words. Informational and analytical articles; and profiles. Topics include library funding, technology, leadership, library management, audio/visual material, cooperative teaching, and young adult library services.
- Depts/columns: Staff written.
- Artwork: B/W or color prints. Cartoons and line art.

SAMPLE ISSUE

86 pages (20% advertising): 9 articles; 13 depts/columns; 17 review sections. Guidelines and editorial calendar available.

- "Implementation or Bust!" Article examines the latest AASL standards, how they affect the field, and what was learned from past guidelines.
- "The Impact of Facebook on Our Students." Article discusses the safety concerns that affect students as well as computer systems.

RIGHTS AND PAYMENT

All rights. Written material, $100. Pays on publication. Provides 2 contributor's copies.

➡️EDITOR'S COMMENTS

All articles are blind reviewed by at least two members of our advisory board, all of whom are either scholars or recognized professionals.

Teachers of Vision

227 North Magnolia Avenue, Suite 2
Anaheim, CA 92801

Content Editor: Judy Turpen

DESCRIPTION AND INTERESTS

This magazine from the Christian Educators Association International is written for Christian teachers in public and private school systems. Its goal is to empower them to be better educators. Circ: 8,000.

Audience: Educators
Frequency: Quarterly
Website: www.ceai.org

FREELANCE POTENTIAL

78% written by nonstaff writers. Publishes 70–75 freelance submissions yearly; 5% by unpublished writers, 15% by authors who are new to the magazine. Receives 100 unsolicited mss yearly.

SUBMISSIONS

Send complete ms with brief bio. Prefers email submissions to tov@ceai.org; will accept hard copy. SASE. Responds in 2–3 months.

- Articles: How-to articles, personal experience pieces, and documented reports; 800–1,000 words. Topics include education issues, educational philosophy, and methodology. Interviews with noted Christian educators; 500–800 words. Teaching techniques, news, and special event reports; 400–500 words.
- Depts/columns: 100–200 words. Reviews of books, videos, curricula, games, and other resources for K–12 teachers.
- Other: Submit seasonal material 4 months in advance.

SAMPLE ISSUE

27 pages (1% advertising): 18 articles; 11 depts/columns. Sample copy, free with 9x12 SASE (5 first-class stamps). Guidelines available at website.

- "A Grading System for Composition Papers." Article explores a hybrid grading system.
- Sample dept/column: "In the School of Prayer" advocates offering spiritual, Scripture-based support to principals.

RIGHTS AND PAYMENT

First and electronic rights. Articles $20–$50. Pays on publication. Provides 3 copies.

➡️EDITOR'S COMMENTS

The vast majority of our readers are public school teachers, although some work in Christian or private schools. Note that we also accept general education articles.

Teaching Theatre

2343 Auburn Avenue
Cincinnati, OH 45219

Editor: James Palmarini

DESCRIPTION AND INTERESTS
This is the Educational Theatre Association's quarterly journal for theater educators. It features articles on acting, directing, playwriting, and technical theater; program profiles; curriculum design; teaching methodology; and current trends in theater education. Circ: 5,000.

Audience: Theater teachers
Frequency: Quarterly
Website: www.edta.org

FREELANCE POTENTIAL
65% written by nonstaff writers. Publishes 10–12 freelance submissions yearly; 30% by unpublished writers, 50% by authors who are new to the magazine. Receives 150 queries each year.

SUBMISSIONS
Query with outline. Accepts hard copy. SASE. Responds in 1 month.

- Articles: 1,000–3,000 words. Informational articles and personal experience pieces. Topics include theater education, the arts, and curricula.
- Depts/columns: Word lengths vary. Classroom exercises, ideas, technical advice, and textbook or play suggestions.

SAMPLE ISSUE
36 pages (3–5% advertising): 4 articles; 2 depts/columns. Sample copy, $2 with 9x12 SASE ($2 postage). Guidelines available.

- "Building a Better Theatre Curriculum." Article outlines strategies for teaching and learning the theater arts.
- "A Touch, I Do Confess." Article explains classroom exercises that can teach acting students to believably perform battle scenes without hurting anyone.

RIGHTS AND PAYMENT
One-time rights. Written material, payment rates vary. Pays on publication. Provides 3 contributor's copies.

❖EDITOR'S COMMENTS
If an article can be of use to a theater teacher—either by presenting a model, an innovative idea, or a specific teaching methodology—we're interested in taking a look at it. General interest essays on the value of educational theater are likely to be rejected.

Tech Directions

Prakken Publications
832 Phoenix Drive
P.O. Box 8623
Ann Arbor, MI 48107

Managing Editor: Susanne Peckham

DESCRIPTION AND INTERESTS
A resource for technical and vocational educators, *Tech Directions* covers the latest teaching methods and projects. Circ: 43,000.

Audience: Teachers and administrators
Frequency: 10 times each year
Website: www.techdirections.com

FREELANCE POTENTIAL
80% written by nonstaff writers. Publishes 50 freelance submissions yearly; 50% by unpublished writers, 50% by authors who are new to the magazine. Receives 150 queries, 80 unsolicited mss yearly.

SUBMISSIONS
Query or send complete ms. Accepts hard copy and email submissions to susanne@techdirections.com. Availability of artwork improves chance of acceptance. SASE. Responds to queries in 1 week, to mss in 1 month.

- Articles: To 3,000 words. Informational and how-to articles. Topics include teaching techniques and unusual projects in automotive, building trades, graphics, hydraulics, industrial arts, lasers, manufacturing, radio and television, robotics, software, welding, woodworking, and other vocational education.
- Depts/columns: Word lengths vary. Legislation updates; technology news and history; media reviews; and new product information.
- Artwork: Color prints, slides, and transparencies; B/W prints. B/W art. CAD plots.
- Other: Puzzles, games, and quizzes.

SAMPLE ISSUE
30 pages (40% advertising): 4 articles; 6 depts/columns. Sample copy, $5 with 9x12 SASE (2 first-class stamps). Guidelines available.

- "Environmental Technician." Article guides students through this possible career choice.
- Sample dept/column: "Technology Today" highlights how technology affects driving.

RIGHTS AND PAYMENT
All rights. Articles, $50+. Depts/columns, to $25. Pays on publication. Provides 3 copies.

❖EDITOR'S COMMENTS
Technology-related, hands-on projects must include step-by-step instructions. Material should inform students about technology and careers.

Techniques

ACTE
1410 King Street
Alexandria, VA 22314

Managing Editor: Susan Emeagwali

DESCRIPTION AND INTERESTS
Published by the Association for Career and Technical Education, this magazine offers articles that show the connection between education and the workplace. Circ: 30,000.

Audience: Educators
Frequency: 8 times each year
Website: www.acteonline.org

FREELANCE POTENTIAL
60% written by nonstaff writers. Publishes 10–20 freelance submissions yearly; 15% by unpublished writers, 30% by new authors. Receives 96 queries and unsolicited mss yearly.

SUBMISSIONS
Query or send complete ms. Accepts email to semeagwali@acteonline.org (Microsoft Word attachments). Availability of artwork improves chance of acceptance. Responds in 4 months.

- Articles: 1,000–2,500 words. Informational and how-to articles; case studies; and profiles. Topics include career and technical education programming, practices, and policy; integrating career education and academics; technology; and environmental issues.
- Depts/columns: "Research Report," to 2,500 words. Academic papers.
- Artwork: Digital images at 300 dpi. Charts and graphs.

SAMPLE ISSUE
62 pages (30% advertising): 10 articles; 11 depts/columns. Sample copy, guidelines, and editorial calendar available at website.

- "The Promise of Middle-Skill Occupations." Article posits that as the demand for middle-skill workers increases, wages are likely to increase as well, subject to credentials.
- "Productivity, Social Networks and Net Communities in the Workplace." Article describes how the 21st-century workplace is being shaped by technology, shifting demographics, and globalization.

RIGHTS AND PAYMENT
All rights. No payment.

••EDITOR'S COMMENTS
Our content is primarily journalistic, and we expect writers to know their material thoroughly. We continue to be interested in profiles of individuals making an impact in the field.

Teen Graffiti

P.O. Box 452721
Garland, TX 75045-2721

Publisher: Sharon Jones-Scaife

DESCRIPTION AND INTERESTS
Teen Graffiti aims to become the voice of teenagers across the nation by providing a platform for the expression of their styles, concerns, ideas, talents, achievements, and community involvement. With few exceptions, its articles, essays, and opinions are written by teens for teens. Circ: 10,000.

Audience: 12–19 years
Frequency: 6 times each year
Website: www.teengraffiti.com

FREELANCE POTENTIAL
70% written by nonstaff writers. Publishes 30–40 freelance submissions yearly. Receives many queries and unsolicited mss yearly.

SUBMISSIONS
Teen writers only. Query or send complete ms. Prefers email submissions to sharon@teengraffiti.com; will accept hard copy. SASE. Response time varies.

- Articles: 250–500 words. Informational articles; personal experience and opinion pieces; and essays. Topics include college, careers, current events, popular culture, sex, health, and social issues.
- Depts/columns: 100–200 words. Advice and resources from teachers, teen-to-teen advice, and media reviews.
- Artwork: B/W and color prints from teens.
- Other: Poetry.

SAMPLE ISSUE
30 pages (3% advertising): 4 articles; 4 depts/columns. Sample copy, $2.75 with 9x12 SASE. Guidelines available.

- "Health: You Make the Choice." Article reports on teenage obesity and how teens can perform a dietary and exercise makeover on themselves.
- Sample dept/column: "High School & Beyond" offers advice for getting federal student aid for college.

RIGHTS AND PAYMENT
One-time rights. No payment.

••EDITOR'S COMMENTS
We are open to all article ideas. All material must be submitted with full contact information. However, if your piece is of a personal nature (but important for other teens to read), we will not publish your byline.

Teen Tribute

71 Barber Greene Road
Toronto, Ontario M3C 2A2
Canada

Editor: Toni-Marie Ippolito

DESCRIPTION AND INTERESTS
This lifestyle magazine covers the entertainment world and pop culture for its teen readers. It delivers the latest buzz on movies, TV shows, music, video games, and celebrities; and offers advice and fashion inspirations. Circ: 300,000.

Audience: 14–18 years
Frequency: Quarterly
Website: www.tribute.ca

FREELANCE POTENTIAL
10% written by nonstaff writers. Publishes 5–10 freelance submissions yearly; 1% by authors who are new to the magazine. Receives 24 queries yearly.

SUBMISSIONS
Query with clips or writing samples. Accepts hard copy and email queries to tippolito@tribute.ca. Availability of artwork improves chance of acceptance. SAE/IRC. Responds in 1–2 months.

- Articles: 400–500 words. Informational articles; profiles; interviews; and personal experience pieces. Topics include movies, the film industry, music, the arts, entertainment, popular culture, and social issues.
- Depts/columns: Word lengths vary. Media reviews, fashion and beauty tips, new product reviews, relationship advice, gear and gadgets, and horoscopes.
- Artwork: Color prints or transparencies.

SAMPLE ISSUE
38 pages (50% advertising): 9 articles; 10 depts/columns. Sample copy, $1.95 Canadian with 9x12 SAE/IRC ($.86 Canadian postage).

- "Interview." Article features actress Emilie de Ravin discussing her latest movie role with *Twilight* superstar Robert Pattinson.
- Sample dept/column: "Style File" offers style ideas for prom season based on dresses worn by young celebrities.

RIGHTS AND PAYMENT
First serial rights. Written material, $100–$400 Canadian. Artwork, payment rates vary. Pays on publication. Provides 1 contributor's copy.

⊷EDITOR'S COMMENTS
We are interested in short pieces written just for young teens. Movie promos are a great way to break in here.

Teen Voices

P.O. Box 120-027
Boston, MA 02112-0027

Managing Editor: Becca Steinitz

DESCRIPTION AND INTERESTS
Written by and for teen girls, this magazine empowers its readers with inspiring and thoughtful articles about the real issues that teens face. Circ: 55,000.

Audience: Teen girls
Frequency: Monthly (website); Twice each year (print)
Website: www.teenvoices.com

FREELANCE POTENTIAL
95% written by nonstaff writers. Publishes 100 freelance submissions yearly; 95% by unpublished writers, 95% by authors who are new to the magazine. Receives 2,000 unsolicited mss each year.

SUBMISSIONS
Accepts mss written by girls ages 13–19 only. Send complete ms. Accepts hard copy, email submissions to teenvoices@teenvoices.com, and submissions through the website. SASE. Response time varies.

- Articles: Word lengths vary. Informational and self-help articles; interviews; and profiles. Topics include ethnic and religious traditions, the Internet, multicultural issues, surviving sexual assault, family relationships, teen motherhood, disability, health, nutrition, cooking, the arts, and activism.
- Fiction: Word lengths vary. Humorous, inspirational, contemporary, ethnic, and multicultural fiction.
- Depts/columns: Word lengths vary. Media reviews, arts and culture, international issues, food, and opinion pieces.
- Other: Poetry; comic strips.

SAMPLE ISSUE
56 pages (8% advertising): 3 articles; 10 depts/columns; 5 poems. Guidelines and editorial calendar available.

- "Become a Working Girl." Article offers expert tips on finding a job.
- Sample dept/column: "Food Corner" interviews a popular female chef from Boston.

RIGHTS AND PAYMENT
First or one-time rights. No payment. Provides 5 contributor's copies.

⊷EDITOR'S COMMENTS
We accept original writing, poetry, and artwork from teen girls across the country.

Texas Child Care Quarterly

P.O. Box 162881
Austin, TX 78716-2881

Editor: Louise Parks

DESCRIPTION AND INTERESTS
This is a training journal for child care providers and early childhood education teachers and administrators. Published by the Texas Workforce Commission, it provides information about child growth and development theory and gives caregivers tips for activities to do with children. Circ: 32,000.

Audience: Teachers and child-care workers
Frequency: Quarterly
Website: www.childcarequarterly.com

FREELANCE POTENTIAL
50% written by nonstaff writers. Publishes 12–15 freelance submissions yearly; 10% by unpublished writers, 50% by authors who are new to the magazine. Receives 24–36 unsolicited mss yearly.

SUBMISSIONS
Query with outline; or send complete ms. Accepts disk submissions with hard copy and email submissions to editor@ childcarequarterly.com. No simultaneous submissions. SASE. Responds in 3 weeks.

- Articles: 2,500 words. Informational, theoretical, and how-to articles. Topics include child growth and development, school-family communication, health and safety, program administration, professional development, and hands-on activities.
- Depts/columns: Staff written.

SAMPLE ISSUE
44 pages (no advertising): 6 articles; 5 depts/columns. Sample copy, $6.25 or available at website. Guidelines available at website.

- "Learning Centers for Everyone." Article explains the benefits of learning centers, and advises how to create one in any day care center.
- "Parents as Partners—And Customers." Article reports on the financial benefits of providing good customer service to parents.

RIGHTS AND PAYMENT
All rights. No payment. Provides 3 contributor's copies and a 1-year subscription.

➤ EDITOR'S COMMENTS
If writing about an activity, include all information that readers will need to duplicate it in their center. If submitting an informational article, include all source material at the end.

Thrasher

1303 Underwood Avenue
San Francisco, CA 94121

Managing Editor: Ryan Henry

DESCRIPTION AND INTERESTS
Thrasher is all skateboards and snowboards; all tricks and tattoos; all fearlessness and gnarly injuries. This magazine shares the boarding lifestyle, attitude, and experiences with its readers. Circ: 200,000.

Audience: Boys, 12–20 years
Frequency: 13 times each year
Website: www.thrashermagazine.com

FREELANCE POTENTIAL
20% written by nonstaff writers. Publishes 20 freelance submissions yearly; 100% by unpublished writers. Receives 72–120 unsolicited mss yearly.

SUBMISSIONS
Send complete ms. Accepts email submissions to ryan@thrashermagazine.com (Microsoft Word or RTF attachments) and simultaneous submissions if identified. Responds in 1 month.

- Articles: To 1,500 words. Informational articles; profiles; and interviews. Topics include skateboarding, snowboarding, and music.
- Fiction: To 2,500 words. Stories with skateboarding and snowboarding themes.
- Depts/columns: 750–1,000 words. News, tips, art, 'zines, and profiles.
- Artwork: High-resolution digital images.

SAMPLE ISSUE
220 pages (45% advertising): 12 articles; 10 depts/columns. Sample copy, $3.99. Guidelines available at website.

- "Penh Ching Chode." Article tells of the author's two-week skateboarding trip to China and Vietnam.
- Sample dept/column: "Trash" offers news of skateboarder Arto Saari's new team.

RIGHTS AND PAYMENT
First North American serial rights. Written material, $.15 per word. Artwork, payment rates vary. Pays on publication. Provides 2 contributor's copies.

➤ EDITOR'S COMMENTS
If you're not already familiar with our magazine, your work won't fit here. If you are familiar with us, you skateboard or snowboard with the best of them. That said, you should also be able to write about it and speak to our readers in their own language. If "brazen" defines your style, we'll like it.

Time for Kids

Time-Life Building
1271 Avenue of the Americas, 25th Floor
New York, NY 10020

Editor: Martha Pickerill

DESCRIPTION AND INTERESTS
Distributed through schools to students in kindergarten through seventh grade, *Time for Kids* presents today's top headlines in an age-appropriate format. It is designed as a teaching tool, focusing on the news from around the world, as well as the social and political issues that shape modern life. Circ: 4.1 million.

Audience: 5–12 years
Frequency: Weekly
Website: www.timeforkids.com

FREELANCE POTENTIAL
4% written by nonstaff writers. Publishes 4 freelance submissions yearly.

SUBMISSIONS
All work is assigned. Send résumé only. Accepts hard copy. Responds if interested.

- Articles: Word lengths vary. Informational and biographical articles. Topics include world news, current events, animals, education, health, fitness, science, technology, math, social studies, geography, multicultural and ethnic issues, music, popular culture, recreation, regional news, sports, travel, and social issues.
- Depts/columns: Word lengths vary. Profiles and short news items.
- Artwork: Color prints and transparencies.
- Other: Theme-related activities.

SAMPLE ISSUE
8 pages (no advertising): 2 articles; 8 depts/columns. Sample copy, $3.95.

- "Coral Crisis." Article reports on a large ship that veered off course and slammed into a protected section of the Great Barrier Reef.
- "A Big Oil Disaster." Article tells about the effort to contain the huge oil spill off the coast of Louisiana.

RIGHTS AND PAYMENT
All rights. Written material, payment rates vary. Pays on publication.

➤EDITOR'S COMMENTS
We publish three editions: Big Picture for kindergarten and grade one; News Scoop for grades two and three; and World Report for grades four through seven. Our goal is to provide grade-appropriate, timely, cutting-edge, and accurate news for students and teachers. All material is assigned, so send a résumé.

Today's Catholic Teacher

2621 Dryden Road, Suite 300
Dayton, OH 45439

Editor-in-Chief: Mary Noschang

DESCRIPTION AND INTERESTS
Focusing on issues and trends affecting elementary and junior high Catholic school education, this magazine targets teachers, principals, superintendents, and parents. Its articles offer practical tips and information in a concise and direct manner. Circ: 50,000.

Audience: Teachers, grades K–12
Frequency: 6 times each year
Website: www.catholicteacher.com

FREELANCE POTENTIAL
95% written by nonstaff writers. Publishes 20 freelance submissions yearly; 50% by authors who are new to the magazine. Receives 190+ queries and unsolicited mss yearly.

SUBMISSIONS
Query or send complete ms. Accepts hard copy, disk submissions with hard copy, email to mnoschang@peterli.com, and simultaneous submissions if identified. SASE. Responds to queries in 1 month, to mss in 3 months.

- Articles: 600–1,500 words. Informational, self-help, and how-to articles. Topics include technology, fundraising, classroom management, curriculum development, administration, and educational issues and trends.
- Depts/columns: Word lengths vary. Opinion, news, software, character development, curricula, teaching tools, and school profiles.
- Artwork: 8x10 color prints, slides, or transparencies.
- Other: Reproducible activity pages.

SAMPLE ISSUE
76 pages (45% advertising): 4 articles; 10 depts/columns. Sample copy, $3. Writers' guidelines available.

- "Justice Begins Next Door." Article describes a social justice project that gets teens involved in helping those in need.
- Sample dept/column: "School of the Month" profiles a school that created a resource room for students who need extra help.

RIGHTS AND PAYMENT
All rights. Written material, $100–$250. Pays on publication. Provides contributor's copies.

➤EDITOR'S COMMENTS
Material directed to teachers in grades four through eight is given preference. Please keep your article free of jargon.

Toledo Area Parent News

1120 Adams Street
Toledo, OH 43624

Managing Editor: Gina Sares

DESCRIPTION AND INTERESTS

Distributed through more than 1,000 sites in northwestern Ohio and southeastern Michigan, *Toledo Area Parent News* provides important, up-to-date parenting information in an easy-to-read style. Most of its material has a regional angle. Circ: 81,000.

Audience: Parents
Frequency: Monthly
Website: www.toledoparent.com

FREELANCE POTENTIAL

75% written by nonstaff writers. Publishes 12 freelance submissions yearly; 10% by unpublished writers, 20% by authors who are new to the magazine. Receives 48 queries and unsolicited mss yearly.

SUBMISSIONS

Query with clips; or send complete ms. Prefers email to gsares@toledoparent.com; will accept hard copy. SASE. Responds in 1 month.

- Articles: 700–2,000 words. Informational articles; profiles; and interviews. Topics include family issues, parenting, teen issues, education, social issues, health, and fitness.
- Depts/columns: Word lengths vary. Restaurant reviews, brief news items related to family issues.

SAMPLE ISSUE

48 pages (60% advertising): 2 articles; 9 depts/columns. Sample copy available via email request to kdevol@toledocitypaper.com. Guidelines and editorial calendar available.

- "Born in Convenience." Article reports on the rising trend of elective births, where an infant can be delivered at a prescheduled date and time.
- "Stinky Myths." Article explores the myths associated with cloth diapering and discusses new products that are easier to use.

RIGHTS AND PAYMENT

All North American serial rights. Written material, $30–$200. Pays on publication.

⊷EDITOR'S COMMENTS

We are most interested in articles that provide practical information that parents can use in their day-to-day family lives. Submissions should have some relevance or connection to the Toledo area, and should be written in an accessible style.

Treasure Valley Family

13191 West Scotfield Street
Boise, ID 83713-0899

Publisher: Liz Buckingham

DESCRIPTION AND INTERESTS

This regional magazine targets parents with children under the age of 12. It offers informational articles on education, childcare, and health issues, as well as ideas for family activities and excursions. Circ: 20,000.

Audience: Parents
Frequency: Monthly
Website: www.treasurevalleyfamily.com

FREELANCE POTENTIAL

50% written by nonstaff writers. Publishes 10–15 freelance submissions yearly; 1–2% by authors who are new to the magazine. Receives 1,800 queries and unsolicited mss each year.

SUBMISSIONS

Prefers query with clips; will accept complete ms with 1-sentence author bio. Accepts hard copy and email submissions to magazine@treasurevalleyfamily.com (Microsoft Word attachments). SASE. Responds in 2–3 months.

- Articles: 1,000–1,300 words. Informational and how-to articles. Topics include health, preschool, child care, education, summer camp, sports, travel, recreation, teen issues, college, party planning, crafts, hobbies, and the arts.
- Depts/columns: 700–900 words. Events, activities, advice, news, product reviews, age-specific issues, book reviews, women's health, profiles of local agencies, and interviews with area families.

SAMPLE ISSUE

48 pages (45% advertising): 4 articles; 3 depts/columns. Sample copy, free with 9x12 SASE ($1.50 postage). Guidelines and theme list/editorial calendar available at website.

- "Family Day Trip." Article showcases nearby Shoshone Falls, the "Niagara of the West," as an ideal day trip.
- Sample dept/column: "Time 4 Mom" suggests places that are perfect for retreats.

RIGHTS AND PAYMENT

First North American serial rights. All material, payment rates vary. Pays 10% more for Web rights. Pays on publication. Provides 2 copies.

⊷EDITOR'S COMMENTS

Check our website for information about our upcoming issue themes.

Tulsa Kids Magazine

1820 South Boulder Avenue, Suite 400
Tulsa, OK 74119-4409

Editor: Betty Casey

DESCRIPTION AND INTERESTS
Tulsa parents read this magazine for information on parenting, education, and school-age activities. Most articles are focused on the greater Tulsa region. Circ: 20,000.

Audience: Parents
Frequency: Monthly
Website: www.tulsakids.com

FREELANCE POTENTIAL
90% written by nonstaff writers. Publishes 100+ freelance submissions yearly; 20% by unpublished writers, 10% by authors who are new to the magazine. Receives 900 unsolicited mss yearly.

SUBMISSIONS
Send complete ms. Accepts hard copy, disk submissions, and simultaneous submissions if identified. SASE. Responds in 2–3 months.

- Articles: 500–800 words. Informational articles; profiles; interviews; humor; and personal experience pieces. Topics include family life, education, parenting, recreation, entertainment, college, health, fitness, careers, crafts, and social issues.
- Depts/columns: 100–300 words. News, book reviews, social issues, and family cooking.

SAMPLE ISSUE
64 pages (50% advertising): 5 articles; 11 depts/columns. Sample copy, free with 10x13 SASE ($.75 postage). Guidelines available.

- "Culture Boxes Teach Children About the World." Article reports on a program that teaches cultural awareness.
- "Backpacks for Kids." Article highlights a community outreach program that raises funds to outfit needy children with donated backpacks, clothing, and toiletries at the start of the school year.
- Sample dept/column: "Family Travel" offers suggestions for family boating.

RIGHTS AND PAYMENT
One-time rights. Written material, $25–$100. Payment policy varies. Provides 1 author's copy.

➼EDITOR'S COMMENTS
We need more good, well-researched articles on current topics of interest to parents. We prefer local stories that provide information, support, or humor regarding Oklahoma people and places.

Turtle

U. S. Kids
1100 Waterway Boulevard
P.O. Box 567
Indianapolis, IN 46206-0567

Editor: Terry Harshman

DESCRIPTION AND INTERESTS
Geared to preschool children, *Turtle* is filled with entertaining stories, poems, rebuses, experiments, and recipes that teach children about health, nutrition, safety, and exercise. Circ: 382,000.

Audience: 2–5 years
Frequency: 6 times each year
Website: www.turtlemag.org

FREELANCE POTENTIAL
50% written by nonstaff writers. Publishes 45 freelance submissions yearly.

SUBMISSIONS
Send complete ms. Accepts hard copy. SASE. Responds in 3 months.

- Articles: To 500 words. Informational articles and book reviews. Topics include health, fitness, nutrition, nature, the environment, science, hobbies, and crafts.
- Fiction: 100–150 words for rebus. Genres include adventure; fantasy; humor; problem-solving mysteries; and contemporary, ethnic, and multicultural fiction.
- Depts/columns: To 500 words. Crafts, health tips, and recipes.
- Other: Puzzles, activities, and games. Poetry, 4–8 lines. Submit seasonal material 8 months in advance.

SAMPLE ISSUE
36 pages (6% advertising): 2 articles; 2 stories; 15 activities. Sample copy, $1.75 with 9x12 SASE. Guidelines available at website.

- "A Good Name for You." Rebus tells of two friends walking along the beach and the sea creatures they find.
- "Salty Science." Article describes a science experiment that shows how the sun can be used to separate salt from water.

RIGHTS AND PAYMENT
All rights. Articles and fiction, to $.32 per word. Other material, payment rates vary. Pays on publication. Provides up to 10 contributor's copies.

➼EDITOR'S COMMENTS
We're looking for fun, lively material that promotes healthy living in an age-appropriate way. Activities and puzzles should stimulate young minds, and recipes should be easy to follow and nutritious.

Twins

5748 South College Avenue, Unit D
Fort Collins, CO 80525

Editor-in-Chief: Christa D. Reed

DESCRIPTION AND INTERESTS
Since 1984, parents of twins, triplets, and higher-order multiples have been reading this magazine for the valuable information it provides. From health concerns and child development issues to humorous and touching tales of the joys and challenges, *Twins* covers it all. Circ: 40,000.

Audience: Parents
Frequency: Quarterly
Website: www.twinsmagazine.com

FREELANCE POTENTIAL
50% written by nonstaff writers. Publishes 10–12 freelance submissions yearly. Receives 252 queries yearly.

SUBMISSIONS
Query. Accepts email queries to twinseditor@twinsmagazine.com. Responds in 3 months.

- Articles: 800–1,300 words. Informational and how-to articles; profiles; and personal experience pieces. Topics include parenting, family life, health, fitness, education, music, the arts, house and home, nutrition, diet, sports, social issues, crafts, and hobbies.
- Depts/columns: To 800 words. News, new product information, opinion pieces, and short items on child development.

SAMPLE ISSUE
56 pages (30% advertising): 9 articles; 15 depts/columns. Sample copy, $5.50. Guidelines available at website.

- "The Invitation." Article discusses options when only one twin is invited on an outing.
- "Our Family's Journey with Sensory Processing Disorder." Article tells how one family diagnosed and treated this disorder in one of their twins.
- Sample dept/column: "Health & Wellness" provides tips for minimizing exposure to germs during the summer travel season.

RIGHTS AND PAYMENT
All rights. Written material, $50–$100. Pays on publication. Provides 2 contributor's copies.

➡EDITOR'S COMMENTS
Send us your ideas for our "Mom-2-Mom" or "A Word from Dad" columns. We are also interested in new research specific to twins and multiples, as well as personal experience pieces about growing up as a twin.

The Universe in the Classroom

Astronomical Society of the Pacific
390 Ashton Avenue
San Francisco, CA 94112

Editor

DESCRIPTION AND INTERESTS
This electronic, educational newsletter is for teachers and other educators who want to help their students learn more about the universe. Its articles explain astronomical topics and provide hands-on classroom activities that can make the subject come alive for students. Hits per month: 10,000.

Audience: Teachers
Frequency: Quarterly
Website: www.astrosociety.org/uitc

FREELANCE POTENTIAL
75% written by nonstaff writers. Publishes 8 freelance submissions yearly; 10% by unpublished writers, 75% by authors who are new to the magazine. Receives 12 queries yearly.

SUBMISSIONS
Query. Accepts email queries to astroed@astrosociety.org. Availability of artwork improves chance of acceptance. Responds in 1 month.

- Articles: 3,000 words. Informational and factual articles; and classroom activities. Topics include astronomy and astrobiology.
- Artwork: Color prints and transparencies.
- Other: Hands-on activities.

SAMPLE ISSUE
Sample copy available at website. Guidelines available upon acceptance of article query.

- "Probing Extrasolar Planets with the Spitzer Space Telescope." Article reports on the telescope that finally made it possible to observe light coming from planets in another solar system.
- "Invisible Galaxies: The Story of Dark Matter." Article defines dark matter in terms that non-astronomers can understand, and explains how most of the matter in the universe is dark matter.

RIGHTS AND PAYMENT
One-time rights. No payment.

➡EDITOR'S COMMENTS
The Astronomical Society of the Pacific was formed by a group of Northern California professional and amateur astronomers. It is now one of the largest general astronomy societies in the world. Authors need not be professional astronomers, but they must know of what they write, and write for non-astronomers.

Vancouver Family Magazine

P.O. Box 820264
Vancouver, WA 98682

Editor: Nikki Klock

DESCRIPTION AND INTERESTS

Offering the information and resources needed to raise healthy, well-adjusted children, this magazine serves parents in the Clark County area of Washington State. Its emphasis is on family businesses and events located in the region. Circ: 7,000.

Audience: Families
Frequency: Monthly
Website:
www.vancouverfamilymagazine.com

FREELANCE POTENTIAL

90% written by nonstaff writers. Publishes 25–30 freelance submissions yearly; 30% by unpublished writers, 40% by authors who are new to the magazine. Receives 400+ queries each year.

SUBMISSIONS

Query. Accepts hard copy. SASE. Response time varies.

- Articles: Word lengths vary. Informational articles. Topics include parenting, family-related issues, health and fitness, relationships, and recreation.
- Depts/columns: Word lengths vary. Parenting and family issues, local family-related businesses, local news.

SAMPLE ISSUE

32 pages (50% advertising): 3 articles; 5 depts/columns; 1 calendar. Guidelines and editorial calendar available.

- "Better Children Through Chores." Essay reveals how a father is teaching his children responsibility through the assignment of household chores.
- "Feeding the Hungry in Clark County." Article details the resources available for the needy during the holiday season.
- Sample dept/column: "Your Money's Worth" offers tips on teaching children how to earn, save, and spend money.

RIGHTS AND PAYMENT

Rights vary. Assigned articles, $.10 per word. Payment policy varies.

➥EDITOR'S COMMENTS

At this time, we're especially interested in articles that deal with teen issues. Local writers are preferred; a local angle is required for consideration.

VegFamily

4920 Silk Oak Drive
Sarasota, FL 34232

Editor: Cynthia Mosher

DESCRIPTION AND INTERESTS

Families who are living, or want to live, a vegan lifestyle turn to this magazine for information and encouragement. Hits per month: 10,000.

Audience: YA–Adult
Frequency: Monthly
Website: www.vegfamily.com

FREELANCE POTENTIAL

50% written by nonstaff writers. Publishes 150+ freelance submissions yearly; 90% by unpublished writers, 50% by authors who are new to the magazine. Receives 60 queries each year.

SUBMISSIONS

Query. Accepts email queries to cynthia@ vegfamily.com. Responds in 2 weeks.

- Articles: 700+ words. Informational, self-help, and how-to articles; profiles; and personal experience pieces. Topics include vegan pregnancy and health, vegan cooking, natural parenting, animal rights, the environment, and green living.
- Depts/columns: 700+ words. Nutrition advice, recipes, cooking tips, health issues, vegan news, opinions, family profiles, and parenting issues by age group.
- Artwork: JPEG and GIF files.
- Other: Activities. Submit seasonal material 2 months in advance.

SAMPLE ISSUE

Sample copy available at website.

- Sample dept/column: "Vegan Babies and Toddlers" introduces a vegan mom who has had no medical or any other costs associated with her third child.
- Sample dept/column: "Vegan Teens" offers a mother's account of her teen-aged children's struggles with a vegetarian lifestyle.
- "Healthy School Lunches" gives readers four guiding principles for creative, nutritious lunches.

RIGHTS AND PAYMENT

First and electronic rights. Articles, $10–$30. Pays on publication.

➥EDITOR'S COMMENTS

While not absolutely imperative, a vegan perspective is expected to be evident in submissions. Well-written articles on other healthy-living topics, including organic, green, and sustainable living, will be considered.

VerveGirl

401 Richmond Street West, Suite 245
Toronto, Ontario M5V 1X3
Canada

Editor-in-Chief: Xania Khan

DESCRIPTION AND INTERESTS
VerveGirl is a lifestyle publication that covers both the fun and serious sides of being a Canadian teen girl. Its French and English editions include articles on fashion, beauty, entertainment, social issues, current events, the environment, and relationships. Circ: 150,000 English; 30,000 French.

Audience: Girls, 13–24 years
Frequency: 8 times each year
Website: www.vervegirl.com

FREELANCE POTENTIAL
60% written by nonstaff writers. Publishes 10–20 freelance submissions yearly. Receives 200 queries yearly.

SUBMISSIONS
Query. Accepts hard copy. SAE/IRC. Response time varies.

- Articles: Word lengths vary. Informational and self-help articles; profiles; interviews; and personal experience pieces. Topics include health, nutrition, fitness, fashion, beauty, social issues, current events, the environment, education, careers, and music.
- Depts/columns: Word lengths vary. Entertainment, fashion and beauty, and health and wellness.
- Other: Quizzes.

SAMPLE ISSUE
50 pages: 5 articles; 5 depts/columns. Sample copy available at website.

- "It Happened to Me." Article tells of a girl's remorse over stealing money from the cash register at her school store.
- "A True Story of Regret." Personal essay reveals how a teen transformed herself from one of the "mean girls" to a kind and respectful person.
- Sample dept/column: "Spring Fashion" presents two new Converse shoe collections that raise awareness about AIDS in Africa.

RIGHTS AND PAYMENT
Rights vary. Written material, payment rates vary. Pays on publication.

➡️EDITOR'S COMMENTS
We like to balance fashion and beauty topics with articles that examine current social and cultural issues for our audience of intelligent young women.

Vibrant Life

55 West Oak Ridge Drive
Hagerstown, MD 21740

Editor: Heather Quintana

DESCRIPTION AND INTERESTS
This Christian magazine sets itself apart from the competition by taking a holistic approach that incorporates spirituality with overall health. It features articles that offer practical suggestions for living a healthier, happier, and more satisfied life. Circ: 21,711.

Audience: Families
Frequency: 6 times each year
Website: www.vibrantlife.com

FREELANCE POTENTIAL
95% written by nonstaff writers. Publishes 25 freelance submissions yearly; 30% by unpublished writers, 60% by authors who are new to the magazine. Receives 300 queries, 144 unsolicited mss yearly.

SUBMISSIONS
Prefers complete ms; will accept query. Accepts hard copy and email to vibrantlife@rhpa.org (Microsoft Word attachments). SASE. Responds in 1 month.

- Articles: 450–1,500 words. Informational, how-to, and self-help articles; profiles; and interviews. Topics include health, fitness, nutrition, family, spiritual balance, challenges and triumphs, safety, and environmental stewardship.
- Depts/columns: Word lengths vary. Health news, medical advice, green living, spiritual guidance, family life, and recipes.

SAMPLE ISSUE
32 pages: 3 articles; 9 depts/columns. Sample copy and guidelines, $1 with 9x12 SASE (3 first-class stamps).

- "Your Exercise Excuses—Busted." Article offers solutions to the most common roadblocks that keep people from exercising.
- Sample dept/column: "Vibrant Family" discusses the benefits of families exercising together, and suggests a number of ideas.

RIGHTS AND PAYMENT
Full, non-exclusive rights. Written material, $100–$300. Pays on publication. Provides 3 contributor's copies.

➡️EDITOR'S COMMENTS
Our readers count on us to give them practical, affordable suggestions that fit into their demanding schedules while helping them prevent and fight disease.

The Village Family

501 40th Street S, Suite 201
Fargo, ND 58103

Editor: Laurie Neill

DESCRIPTION AND INTERESTS
Targeting parents living in North Dakota's
Fargo region, *The Village Family* offers positive
stories and valuable information that help
improve the quality of life for families. It is
published by the Village Family Service Center.
Circ: 25,000.

Audience: Families
Frequency: 6 times each year
Website: www.thevillagefamily.org

FREELANCE POTENTIAL
90% written by nonstaff writers. Publishes
18 freelance submissions yearly; 5–10% by
authors who are new to the magazine.
Receives 720 queries, 24 unsolicited mss
each year.

SUBMISSIONS
Query or send complete ms with author bio.
Accepts email submissions to magazine@
thevillagefamily.org. Response time varies.

- Articles: 1,500–2,500 words. Informational,
  self-help, and how-to articles; profiles; interviews; and personal experience pieces. Topics include current events, social issues, relationships, parenting, and health and fitness.
- Depts/columns: Word lengths vary. Crafts,
  health tips, recipes, relationships, and opinion pieces.

SAMPLE ISSUE
46 pages (15% advertising): 7 articles; 6 depts/
columns. Guidelines available at website.

- "A Success Beyond Measure." Essay shares a
  mother's experiences in teaching her teen
  daughter confidence and self-esteem.
- "Accident Alert." Article provides an around-
  the-house guide to child-proofing.
- Sample dept/column: "Media" reviews books
  for children of all ages, along with several
  titles for adults.

RIGHTS AND PAYMENT
First and electronic rights. Written material,
$.07 per word. Reprints, $30–$50. Pays on
publication.

☛EDITOR'S COMMENTS
We're interested in material about family and
social issues, such as personal finance,
health, fitness, education, elderly relatives,
domestic violence, and racism.

VOYA Magazine

4501 Forbes Boulevard, Suite 200
Lanham, MD 20706

Editor-in-Chief: RoseMary Honnold

DESCRIPTION AND INTERESTS
Devoted exclusively to the informational needs
of young people (and the people who provide
it), *VOYA* (Voice of Youth Advocates) is read by
librarians and other professionals who work
with teens. It reports on teens' reading, writing,
and developmental needs. Circ: 7,000.

Audience: YA librarians
Frequency: 6 times each year
Website: www.voya.com

FREELANCE POTENTIAL
95% written by nonstaff writers. Publishes 100
freelance submissions yearly; 5% by unpublished writers, 60% by authors who are new to
the magazine. Receives 60 queries yearly.

SUBMISSIONS
Query with résumé, synopsis, and market
analysis. Accepts hard copy and email queries
to rhonnold@voya.com. Availability of artwork
improves chance of acceptance. SASE.
Responds in 2–4 months.

- Articles: 750–3,500 words. Informational
  and how-to articles; book reviews; and book
  lists. Topics include young adult literature,
  contemporary authors, and library programs.
- Depts/columns: Staff written.
- Artwork: B/W and color prints.
- Other: Submit seasonal material 1 year in
  advance.

SAMPLE ISSUE
174 pages (20% advertising): 6 articles; 9
depts/columns; 176 reviews. Sample copy,
free with 9x12 SASE. Writers' guidelines available at website.

- "Celebrate Kwanzaa: Junior Friends Serve Up
  Yearly Tradition." Article profiles a New York
  library's Kwanzaa celebration that gets the
  teen community involved.
- "The Library Commons." Article explains
  how one library created a specific area for
  teens' social interactions.

RIGHTS AND PAYMENT
All rights. Written material, $50–$125. Pays on
publication. Provides 3 contributor's copies.

☛EDITOR'S COMMENTS
We want to hear about libraries' successful
teen programs, as well as librarians' philoso-
phies, literary analysis, and experiences in
working with teens.

Washington Family Magazine

485 Spring Park Place, Suite 550
Herndon, VA 20170

Managing Editor: Marae Leggs

DESCRIPTION AND INTERESTS
Parents living in the Washington, D.C. area find advice on topics ranging from health and safety to fun and games. Circ: 100,000.

Audience: Parents
Frequency: Monthly
Website: www.washingtonfamily.com

FREELANCE POTENTIAL
75% written by nonstaff writers. Publishes 90 freelance submissions yearly; 50% by unpublished writers, 50% by authors who are new to the magazine. Receives 1,200 queries yearly.

SUBMISSIONS
Query with outline. Accepts email queries to editor@thefamilymagazine.com (Microsoft Word attachments). No simultaneous submissions. Response time varies.

- Articles: 800–900 words. Informational, self-help, and how-to articles; and personal experience pieces. Topics include parenting, family life, relationships, fitness, crafts, hobbies, the arts, education, music, multicultural and ethnic issues, social issues, and travel.
- Depts/columns: Word lengths vary. Health, cooking, activities, tips and trends.
- Artwork: 8x10 B/W prints and transparencies. Line art.
- Other: Submit seasonal material at least 3 months in advance.

SAMPLE ISSUE
126 pages (50% advertising): 14 articles; 9 depts/columns. Sample copy, $4. Guidelines and editorial calendar available at website.

- "Preparing Children for the Summer Camp Experience." Article offers suggestions to help make summer camp more enjoyable.
- Sample dept/column: "Hands-on Kids" gives directions for a homemade slip-and-slide.

RIGHTS AND PAYMENT
Exclusive regional and Web rights. Articles, $50. Depts/columns and artwork, payment rates vary. Pays on publication. Provides 1 tearsheet for contributors.

◆ EDITOR'S COMMENTS
Parenting topics are universal, but content in our magazine must have a regional perspective. We enthusiastically accept submissions from local freelance writers, especially those with expertise in their topic.

Washington Parent

4701 Sangamore Road, Suite N 270
Bethesda, MD 20186-2528

Editor: Margaret Hut

DESCRIPTION AND INTERESTS
Washington Parent serves as a resource and support for families living in D.C., Maryland, and Northern Virginia. Its themed issues include articles written by local professionals in the fields of child development, the arts, education, and special needs. Circ: 75,000.

Audience: Families
Frequency: Monthly
Website: www.washingtonparent.com

FREELANCE POTENTIAL
90% written by nonstaff writers. Publishes 20 freelance submissions yearly. Receives 1,000 queries yearly.

SUBMISSIONS
Query. Accepts email queries to contactus@ washingtonparent.net (Microsoft Word attachments). Response time varies.

- Articles: 1,000–1,200 words. Informational and how-to articles. Topics include regional news and events, parenting and family issues, entertainment, gifted and special education, child development, health, fitness, the environment, and multicultural and ethnic issues.
- Depts/columns: Word lengths vary. Family travel, book and media reviews, education, topics relating to children with special needs, and short news items.

SAMPLE ISSUE
98 pages (63% advertising): 7 articles; 8 depts/columns; 3 special resource sections. Sample copy, writers' guidelines, and editorial calendar available.

- "Artful Animals." Article describes a family exhibit of African art at the Smithsonian that dispels myths and stereotypes.
- "The Best Rx for Relationships." Essay shares a man's point of view about dealing with relationship talks.
- Sample dept/column: "Ages & Stages: Tweens & Teens" discusses the importance of connecting to a community.

RIGHTS AND PAYMENT
First rights. Written material, payment rates vary. Provides 3 contributor's copies.

◆ EDITOR'S COMMENTS
We're interested in topics that appeal to parents of newborns through teens.

Westchester Family

7 Purdy Street, Suite 201
Harrison, NY 10528

Editor: Jean Sheff

DESCRIPTION AND INTERESTS
Targeted to parents living in Westchester County in New York and Fairfield County in Connecticut, *Westchester Family* provides current parenting, health and safety, and education articles. Additionally, the magazine features a comprehensive event and activity calendar. Circ: 59,000.

Audience: Parents
Frequency: Monthly
Website: www.westchesterfamily.com

FREELANCE POTENTIAL
60% written by nonstaff writers. Publishes 20 freelance submissions yearly; 5% by unpublished writers, 5% by authors who are new to the magazine. Receives 1,200 queries yearly.

SUBMISSIONS
Query with clips. Accepts hard copy. SASE. Response time varies.

- Articles: 800-1,200 words. Informational articles; profiles; interviews; photo-essays; and personal experience pieces. Topics include education, music, recreation, regional news, social issues, special and gifted education, travel, and women's issues.
- Depts/columns: 400–800 words. News and media reviews.

SAMPLE ISSUE
82 pages (52% advertising): 3 articles; 10 depts/columns. Sample copy, free with 9x12 SASE. Guidelines available.

- "Are Your Wires Crossed?" Article helps parents examine whether their phone or Interent use interferes with parenting.
- "Lace Up! Tips for Ice Skating Success." Article presents tips for ensuring a happy and successful introduction to this sport.
- Sample dept/column: "Health Notes" offers tips on when and how to talk to children about illegal drug use.

RIGHTS AND PAYMENT
First rights. Written material, $25-$200. Pays on publication. Provides 1 contributor's copy.

➥EDITOR'S COMMENTS
We're open to a variety of parenting and family topics. We demand, however, that they be well-researched and written in an engaging style. All material must have a local angle and pertain to people and events in our area.

West Coast Families

#140-13988 Maycrest Way, 2nd Floor
Richmond, British Columbia V6V 3C3
Canada

Managing Editor: Anya Levykh

DESCRIPTION AND INTERESTS
West Coast Families is a local guide to family-related information in the Vancouver region. It puts a focus on the active, green, West Coast lifestyle that more of the families in this area are choosing. It covers parenting, family, and health issues from birth to tween. Circ: 50,000.

Audience: Parents
Frequency: 9 times each year
Website: www.westcoastfamilies.com

FREELANCE POTENTIAL
80% written by nonstaff writers. Publishes 12–40 freelance submissions yearly; 25% by new authors. Receives 400–800 queries yearly.

SUBMISSIONS
Query with résumé or relevant experience and writing sample. Accepts email queries only to editor@westcoastfamilies.com. SAE/IRC. Response time varies.

- Articles: 600–1,200 words. Informational, self-help, and how-to articles; profiles; interviews; and personal experience pieces. Topics include family life, parenting, recreation, travel, religion, current events, health, fitness, finance, education, sports, hobbies, science, technology, nature, and pets.
- Depts/columns: Word lengths vary. Health, travel, finances, crafts.
- Other: Puzzles, activities, and jokes. Submit seasonal material 3 months in advance.

SAMPLE ISSUE
32 pages (8% advertising): 4 articles; 3 depts/columns. Sample copy, free with 9x12 SAE/IRC ($1.45 Canadian postage) or available at website. Guidelines and editorial calendar available at website.

- "Multi-Age Learning." Article reports on the benefits of multi-age groupings in classrooms, especially in rural areas or districts with declining student enrollment.
- "Creative Parenting." Article provides ideas for letting children's natural creativity shine.

RIGHTS AND PAYMENT
One-time and electronic rights. Written material, $50–$100. Kill fee, 50%. Pays on publication. Provides contributor's copies.

➥EDITOR'S COMMENTS
We look for original article ideas that can provide local, useful information for parents.

Western New York Family Magazine

3147 Delaware Avenue, Suite B
Buffalo, NY 14217

Editor: Michele Miller

DESCRIPTION AND INTERESTS
The articles in this family magazine address current parenting issues, with a western New York tie-in whenever possible. Strong emphasis is placed on local, family-oriented events and services for children. Circ: 25,000.
Audience: Parents
Frequency: Monthly
Website: www.wnyfamilymagazine.com

FREELANCE POTENTIAL
90% written by nonstaff writers. Publishes 150 freelance submissions yearly; 30% by unpublished writers, 30% by authors who are new to the magazine. Receives 1,200 unsolicited mss each year.

SUBMISSIONS
Send complete ms with 2-sentence bio. Accepts email submissions to michele@ wnyfamilymagazine.com (text in body of email along with Microsoft Word attachments) and simultaneous submissions if identified. Response time varies.

- Articles: "UpFront" articles, 2,000–2,500 words. Other features, 750–1,500 words. Informational, how-to, and self-help articles; creative nonfiction; humor; and personal experience pieces. Topics include parenting, education, and children with special needs.
- Depts/columns: Word lengths vary. News briefs, reviews, family travel, recipes, fatherhood, and single parenting.
- Other: Submit seasonal material 3 months in advance.

SAMPLE ISSUE
64 pages (40% advertising): 11 articles; 12 depts/columns. Sample copy, $2.50 with 9x12 SASE ($1.79 postage); also available at website. Guidelines and editorial calendar available at website.

- "Birthday Party Basics." Article provides tips for planning successful birthday parties.
- Sample dept/column: "Single Parenting" offers advice on adjusting to single parenthood.

RIGHTS AND PAYMENT
First or reprint and electronic rights. Written material, $.05 per word. Pays on publication.

➥EDITOR'S COMMENTS
We choose articles that present practical information that relates to parents in our area.

West Virginia Family Magazine

P.O. Box 107
Buckhannon, WV 26201

Editor: Carla Cosner

DESCRIPTION AND INTERESTS
This magazine focuses on all the areas of interest to busy families living in the state of West Virginia. It seeks articles and tips on topics such as safety, travel, education, family traditions, and pets. Circ: 19,000.
Audience: Parents
Frequency: Quarterly
Website: www.wvfamilymagazine.com

FREELANCE POTENTIAL
75% written by nonstaff writers. Publishes 25–35 freelance submissions yearly; 15% by unpublished writers, 25% by authors who are new to the magazine. Receives 600 unsolicited mss yearly.

SUBMISSIONS
Send complete ms. Accepts email submissions to editor@wvfamilymagazine.com. Response time varies.

- Articles: 500–850 words. Informational and how-to articles. Topics include education, current events, health and fitness, recreation, and social issues.
- Depts/columns: Word lengths vary. Child development, safety, parenting issues, finance, and regional news.

SAMPLE ISSUE
30 pages: 3 articles; 9 depts/columns; 1 calendar. Sample copy, free. Guidelines and editorial calendar available.

- "Toy Safety." Article explains potential risks associated with some of the most popular children's toys.
- "Helping Animals Help People." Article describes a local pet food pantry for owners who can't afford to feed their pets.
- Sample dept/column: "Quick Bits" discusses the correlation between television viewing and bullying.

RIGHTS AND PAYMENT
One-time print and electronic rights. Articles, $25. Filler, payment rates vary. Pays on publication. Provides 1 contributor's copy.

➥EDITOR'S COMMENTS
Our issues follow the seasons, not the calendar months, so our editorial content is very specific to the season. Please use local sources in your articles. We especially like articles that offer solutions.

What If?

19 Lynwood Place
Guelph, Ontario N1G 2V9
Canada

Managing Editor: Mike Leslie

DESCRIPTION AND INTERESTS
Sporting a new design, *What If?* is Canada's creative teen magazine. It showcases the finest works of prose and poetry in addition to opinion pieces and reviews. It accepts submissions from writers outside of Canada. Circ: 3,000.

Audience: 12–19 years
Frequency: Quarterly
Website: www.whatifmagazine.com

FREELANCE POTENTIAL
95% written by nonstaff writers. Publishes 100 freelance submissions yearly; 95% by unpublished writers, 90% by authors who are new to the magazine. Receives 3,000 unsolicited mss each year.

SUBMISSIONS
Send complete ms. Accepts hard copy, email submissions to editor@whatifmagazine.com (Microsoft Word attachments), and simultaneous submissions if identified. Availability of artwork improves chance of acceptance. SASE. Responds in 3 months.

- Articles: To 1,500 words. Opinion pieces and personal essays. Topics vary.
- Fiction: To 3,000 words. Genres include contemporary, realistic, inspirational, and science fiction; mystery; suspense; fantasy; and humor.
- Depts/columns: Word lengths vary. Reviews and interviews.
- Artwork: Color prints. Line art.
- Other: Poetry, to 20 lines.

SAMPLE ISSUE
56 pages (3% advertising): 8 essays; 5 stories; 15 poems; 4 depts/columns. Sample copy, $8 with 9x12 SASE. Guidelines available.

- "Guns in Canada." Essay shares the author's ideas for decreasing gun violence.
- Sample dept/column: "What's Your Story?" is an essay about a girl's move from Australia to Canada.

RIGHTS AND PAYMENT
First rights. No payment. Provides 2 contributor's copies.

➥EDITOR'S COMMENTS
Read a few issues of our magazine to familiarize yourself with our new format. New writers have their best chance at acceptance with our new features and columns.

What's Up
Canada's Family Magazine

496 Metler Road
Ridgeville, Ontario L0S 1M0
Canada

Editor-in-Chief: Paul Baswick

DESCRIPTION AND INTERESTS
Each issue of this magazine is filled with ideas for family activities, expert advice on managing personal finance and health issues, and entertaining stories about family life. Entertainment news, technology updates, and ideas for family meals are also featured. It accepts work from Canadian authors only. Circ: 100,000.

Audience: Families
Frequency: 6 times each year
Website: www.whatsupfamilies.com

FREELANCE POTENTIAL
80% written by nonstaff writers. Publishes 30 freelance submissions yearly; 60% by authors who are new to the magazine. Receives 348 queries yearly.

SUBMISSIONS
Canadian authors only. Query. Accepts email queries to paul@whatsupfamily.ca. Response time varies.

- Articles: Word lengths vary. Informational articles; profiles; and interviews. Topics include education, family issues, travel, fitness, nutrition, health, the arts, and entertainment.
- Depts/columns: Word lengths vary. "Mom Time," "Health Matters," "Finances," "Baby Steps," "From the Kitchen," "Learning Curves," "Family Travel," "What's Up with Dad?" "Kid's Space," "Cool Careers," "Kid Craft," and other children's activities.

SAMPLE ISSUE
82 pages (15% advertising): 3 articles; 17 depts/columns.

- "Higher Learning." Article profiles a university that offers a series of programs for grades seven and eight to give students a sneak peek at life on campus.
- Sample dept/column: "Family Finances" discusses the cost of pet ownership.

RIGHTS AND PAYMENT
All rights. Written material, payment rates vary. Payment policy varies. Provides copies.

➥EDITOR'S COMMENTS
Our goal is to provide time-strapped parents with strategies for making precious moments with their children even more special—whether it's at the dinner table, in the garden, or on the playground.

Wire Tap Magazine

Independent Media Institute
77 Federal Road
San Francisco, CA 94107

Associate Editor

DESCRIPTION AND INTERESTS
Featuring "ideas and action for a new generation," this independent news and culture e-zine is a platform for progressive journalists. It covers education, the environment, politics, racial justice, and arts and lifestyle issues. Hits per month: 60,000.
Audience: 18–30 years
Frequency: Updated daily
Website: www.wiretapmag.org

FREELANCE POTENTIAL
95% written by nonstaff writers. Publishes 120 freelance submissions yearly. Receives 300 queries yearly.

SUBMISSIONS
Query. Accepts email queries to submissions@wiretapmag.org (no attachments). Response time varies.

- Articles: Word lengths vary. Informational articles; profiles; interviews; and personal experience pieces. Topics include social issues, politics, culture, current events, the environment, immigration, relationships, peace, education, and youth activism.
- Depts/columns: Word lengths vary. Reviews, politics, and news.
- Other: Poetry.

SAMPLE ISSUE
Sample copy available at website.

- "The Price of Jumping Class." Article interviews the editor of a book of essays that explores the social and emotional cost of moving from a poor background to financial success later in life.
- "Top Youth Activism Victories." Article examines the events and media stories that center around American youths working together for change.

RIGHTS AND PAYMENT
Electronic rights. Written material, $50–$400 for assigned pieces. No payment for unsolicited submissions. Payment policy varies.

➛EDITOR'S COMMENTS
We believe in highlighting, mentoring, and amplifying some of the most compelling and urgent young voices in our country today. We are progressive in tone and respect work that is well researched and accurate, yet fosters a particular call to action.

Writers' Journal

Val-Tech Media
P.O. Box 394
Perham, MN 56573-0394

Editor: Leon Ogroske

DESCRIPTION AND INTERESTS
Writers' Journal wants to be known as the "complete writer's magazine." To that end, it covers such topics as the business side of writing, self-publishing, income venues, and writing skills. Circ: 10,000.
Audience: YA–Adult
Frequency: 6 times each year
Website: www.writersjournal.com

FREELANCE POTENTIAL
50% written by nonstaff writers. Publishes 40 freelance submissions yearly; 20% by unpublished writers, 80% by authors who are new to the magazine. Receives 200 queries and unsolicited mss yearly.

SUBMISSIONS
Query with clips; or send complete ms. Accepts hard copy and email submissions to writersjournal@writersjournal.com (text only). SASE. Responds in 2–6 months.

- Articles: 1,200–2,200 words. Informational and how-to articles; profiles; and interviews. Topics include fiction writing, travel writing, technical writing, business writing, screenwriting, journalism, poetry, writing skills and styles, punctuation, interviewing techniques, research, record-keeping, income venues, finance, and self-publishing.
- Depts/columns: Staff written.
- Other: Poetry, to 15 lines.

SAMPLE ISSUE
64 pages (10% advertising): 5 articles; 6 stories; 4 poems; 10 depts/columns. Sample copy, $6 with 9x12 SASE. Guidelines available at website.

- "Children's Writing Resources." Article outlines the books, newsletters, and websites aspiring children's writers should study.
- "Completing the Assignment." Article details the steps to take when writing one's first nonfiction piece.

RIGHTS AND PAYMENT
First North American serial rights. Articles, $30. Poetry, $5 per poem. Pays on publication. Provides 2 contributor's copies upon request and a 1-year subscription.

➛EDITOR'S COMMENTS
We welcome short, lively, and witty poems, especially if they are about writing.

Yes Mag

501-3960 Quadra Street
Victoria, British Columbia V8X 4A3
Canada

Managing Editor: Jude Isabella

DESCRIPTION AND INTERESTS

Yes Mag is a science magazine for kids ages 8 to 14 that is designed to make science, technology, engineering, and mathematics exciting and fun. Each issue contains entertaining stories, do-at-home projects, brain teasers, and environmental and science news. Circ: 23,000.

Audience: 10–15 years
Frequency: 6 times each year
Website: www.yesmag.ca

FREELANCE POTENTIAL

70% written by nonstaff writers. Publishes 30 freelance submissions yearly; 5% by unpublished writers, 15% by authors who are new to the magazine. Receives 300 queries yearly.

SUBMISSIONS

Query. Accepts email queries to editor@yesmag.ca. Response time varies.

- Articles: Features: 300–800 words. Short, theme-related articles, 300–600 words. Informational articles, 250 words. Topics include astronomy, biology, chemistry, ecology, engineering, math, science, technology, nature, and the environment.
- Depts/columns: 250 words. Science and technology news, entomology, world records, environmental updates, book and product reviews, and experiments.

SAMPLE ISSUE

32 pages (no advertising): 5 articles; 6 depts/columns. Sample copy, $4.50 Canadian with SAE/IRC. Guidelines and theme list available.

- "Ping-Pong to the Moon." Article describes a lunar lander competition organized by NASA in an effort to get people back to the moon.
- "Preserving Polar History." Article profiles a conservation group whose efforts are preserving 100-year-old Antarctic huts and artifacts uncovered in past expeditions.
- Sample dept/column: "What Is It?" explains ozone and the chemicals that destroy it.

RIGHTS AND PAYMENT

First and one-time Korean rights. "Sci & Tech Watch," $100. Articles, $145 per page. Pays on publication. Provides 1 contributor's copy.

⇢EDITOR'S COMMENTS

Since we are a Canadian magazine, we like to highlight Canadian scientists and science whenever we can.

Young Adult Today

1551 Regency Court
Calumet City, IL 60409

Editor: Aja Carr

DESCRIPTION AND INTERESTS

This magazine targets Christian young adults living in urban communities. It presents Bible lessons, study guides, daily devotions, and articles that address issues faced by today's young people. It is published by Urban Ministries. Circ: 25,000.

Audience: 18–24 years
Frequency: Quarterly
Website: www.youngadulttoday.net

FREELANCE POTENTIAL

90% written by nonstaff writers. Publishes 52 freelance submissions yearly; 50% by unpublished writers, 50% by authors who are new to the magazine. Receives 240 queries yearly.

SUBMISSIONS

All material is assigned. Query with résumé. No unsolicited mss. Accepts hard copy. SASE. Responds in 2 months.

- Articles: To 400 words. Informational and inspirational articles; Bible lessons; devotional readings; and Bible study guides that explain how Scripture lessons can be applied to modern life.

SAMPLE ISSUE

80 pages (4% advertising): 1 article; 13 teaching plans; 13 corresponding Bible study guides. Sample copy, $2.25 with 9x12 SASE ($.87 postage). Guidelines available.

- "Five Ways to Look Like Jesus." Article lists ways that readers can live a Christian life and emulate Jesus.
- "Christ as Intercessor." Bible study guide examines how Christ played, and continues to play, the role of intercessor in people's lives.
- "Christ as Healer." Bible study guide presents the evidence cited in the Bible that Christ could heal the sick.

RIGHTS AND PAYMENT

Rights negotiable. Written material, $150 per lesson. Pays on publication.

⇢EDITOR'S COMMENTS

We assign all material to our team of writers. Send us your information if you'd like to be considered for assignments. Before doing so, become familiar with our magazine. We have a very specific style which we expect all writers to follow.

Young Adult Today Leader

1551 Regency Court
Calumet City, IL 60409

Editor: Aja Carr

DESCRIPTION AND INTERESTS
A companion publication to Urban Ministries' *Young Adult Today*, this magazine targets youth ministry leaders and Bible study teachers. It presents topics for Christian discussion groups and lesson plans. Circ: 15,000.

Audience: Religious educators
Frequency: Quarterly
Website: www.youngadulttoday.net

FREELANCE POTENTIAL
90% written by nonstaff writers. Publishes 52 freelance submissions yearly; 50% by unpublished writers, 50% by authors who are new to the magazine. Receives 240 queries yearly.

SUBMISSIONS
All work is assigned. Query with résumé. No unsolicited mss. Accepts hard copy. SASE. Responds in 2 months.

- Articles: Informational and inspirational articles, word lengths vary. Devotionals, 400 words. Topics include current events and social issues as they relate to Christianity and the Bible.

SAMPLE ISSUE
96 pages (no advertising): 1 article; 13 lesson plans; 13 Bible study guides. Sample copy, $2.25 with 9x12 SASE ($.87 postage). Guidelines available.

- "Five Ways to Look Like Jesus." Article outlines some simple and not-so-simple ways to live a life closer to God.
- "Open My Heart." Lesson plan is designed to encourage students to respect all people regardless of their socioeconomic status, and to welcome them to their church.
- "Wise Speakers." Bible study uses verses and stories to help readers recognize the importance of controlling the things we say.

RIGHTS AND PAYMENT
Rights negotiable. Written material, $150. Pays on publication.

➡️EDITOR'S COMMENTS
We choose writers who have experience not only in leading Christian youth in prayer and Bible study, but also in writing and planning such lessons. If we think you will fit in here, we'll be happy to give you an assignment. We do not accept unsolicited article ideas or other queries.

Young Rider

P.O. Box 8237
Lexington, KY 40533

Editor: Lesley Ward

DESCRIPTION AND INTERESTS
This magazine provides profiles, riding techniques, horse care tips, and articles on other topics of interest to young horseback riders and enthusiasts. Circ: 92,000.

Audience: 6–14 years
Frequency: 6 times each year
Website: www.youngrider.com

FREELANCE POTENTIAL
15% written by nonstaff writers. Publishes 12 freelance submissions yearly; 5% by unpublished writers, 5% by authors who are new to the magazine. Receives 60 queries yearly.

SUBMISSIONS
Query. Accepts email queries to yreditor@ bowtieinc.com (Microsoft Word attachments). Responds in 2 weeks.

- Articles: Word lengths vary. Informational and how-to articles; and profiles. Topics include horseback riding, training, careers, English and Western riding techniques; and general horse care.
- Fiction: 1,200 words. Stories that feature horses, ponies, and youth themes.
- Artwork: High-resolution digital images.

SAMPLE ISSUE
48 pages (28% advertising): 5 articles; 1 story; 7 depts/columns. Sample copy, $3.99 with 9x12 SASE ($1 postage). Guidelines and editorial calendar available.

- "Rising to Stardom." Article profiles a champion jockey from the popular Animal Planet documentary *Jockeys!*
- "Understanding Your Mustang." Article provides a guide to adopting and training a wild horse, turning a fearful animal into a loyal one.
- Sample dept/column: "Horse and Pony Problems" offers advice and information concerning common problems.

RIGHTS AND PAYMENT
First serial rights. Written material, $.10 per word. Artwork, payment rates vary. Pays on publication. Provides 2 contributor's copies.

➡️EDITOR'S COMMENTS
Any horse- or riding-related topic that will interest a young rider will interest us. Fiction should be realistic and "not too sugary-sweet." High-quality writing is a must.

Youth & Christian Education & Leadership

1080 Montgomery Avenue
Cleveland, TN 37311

Editorial Assistant: Tammy Hatfield

DESCRIPTION AND INTERESTS

Christian educators and youth ministry workers find useful tips and inspiring stories in each issue of this magazine. Its focus is on discipling readers and instructing them on ways to incorporate acts of Christian living into everyday life. Circ: 10,000.

Audience: Adults
Frequency: Quarterly
Website: www.pathwaypress.org

FREELANCE POTENTIAL

10% written by nonstaff writers. Publishes 10 freelance submissions yearly; 90% by unpublished writers, 10% by authors who are new to the magazine. Receives 30–35 queries, 20–25 unsolicited mss yearly.

SUBMISSIONS

Prefers complete ms with author biography; will accept query. Accepts disk submissions (Microsoft Word files) and email to tammy_hatfield@pathwaypress.org. SASE. Responds in 3 weeks.

- Articles: 500–1,000 words. Informational and how-to articles; profiles; interviews; humor; and personal experience pieces. Topics include current events, music, religion, social issues, psychology, parenting, and multicultural and ethnic subjects.
- Depts/columns: Staff written.

SAMPLE ISSUE

30 pages (2% advertising): 10 articles; 6 depts/columns. Sample copy, $1.25 with 9x12 SASE (2 first-class stamps). Guidelines available at website.

- "When Grace Grows Up." Article discusses the best way to focus a church's ministry to attract and keep the attention of teens.
- "Playground Spirituality." Article describes some playground-type activities that can be used to teach spiritual lessons.
- "Making Small Groups Work." Article offers advice on practicing small group ministry.

RIGHTS AND PAYMENT

First rights. Written material, $25–$50. Kill fee, 50%. Pays on publication. Provides 1–10 copies.

✎ EDITOR'S COMMENTS

We are always interested in featuring individuals or groups who are advancing Christian education with distinctive ministries.

Youth Today

1331 H Street NW
Washington, DC 20005

Editor: Nancy Lewis

DESCRIPTION AND INTERESTS

This industry newspaper is read by professional youth workers and administrators of youth service, youth advocacy, and youth policy programs. It keeps them abreast of news, trends, issues, and programs. Circ: 12,000.

Audience: Youth workers
Frequency: 10 times each year
Website: www.youthtoday.org

FREELANCE POTENTIAL

30% written by nonstaff writers. Publishes 25 freelance submissions yearly. Receives 12 queries yearly.

SUBMISSIONS

Query with résumé and clips. Accepts hard copy and email queries to nlewis@youthtoday.org. SASE. Responds in 3 months.

- Articles: 1,000–2,500 words. Informational articles; news and research projects; profiles of youth workers and youth programs; and business features. Topics include foster care, child abuse, program management, violence, adolescent health, juvenile justice, job training, school-to-work programs, after-school programs, mentoring, and other social issues related to youth development.
- Depts/columns: Word lengths vary. Book and video reviews, news briefs, opinion pieces, and people in the news.

SAMPLE ISSUE

32 pages (50% advertising): 22 articles; 5 depts/columns. Sample copy, $5. Writers' guidelines available.

- "Risky Business: The Challenge of Youth Worker Selection and Supervision." Article examines the many challenges facing youth programs regarding volunteer screening.
- "Youth Work Snapshots." Article offers a brief profile of Oasis Center–Oasis Youth Action in Tennessee.

RIGHTS AND PAYMENT

First and Internet rights. Written material, $.50–$.75 per word. Pays on acceptance. Provides 2 contributor's copies.

✎ EDITOR'S COMMENTS

We choose freelancers who have written for daily newspapers, or who have extensive experience researching and writing pieces for newspapers and magazines.

YouthWorker Journal

750 Old Hickory Boulevard, Suite 1-150
Brentwood, TN 37027

Submissions: Amy Lee

DESCRIPTION AND INTERESTS
This journal for Christian youth workers provides youth ministry resources, games, ideas, fundraiser tools, profiles, and inspirational articles. Circ: 10,000.

Audience: Youth ministry workers
Frequency: 6 times each year
Website: www.youthworker.com

FREELANCE POTENTIAL
100% written by nonstaff writers. Publishes 50+ freelance submissions yearly; 15% by unpublished writers, 25% by new authors. Receives 720 queries yearly.

SUBMISSIONS
Query with short biography. Prefers email queries to alee@salempublishing.com (include "Query" in subject line); will accept hard copy and faxes to 615-385-4412. SASE. Responds in 6–8 weeks.

- Articles: Word lengths vary. Informational and practical application articles; personal experience pieces; and reviews. Topics include youth ministry, theology, spreading Christ's word, student worship, family ministry, education, family issues, popular culture, the media, and volunteering.
- Depts/columns: Word lengths vary. National and regional trends; youth workers' quotes.

SAMPLE ISSUE
64 pages (30% advertising): 12 articles; 11 depts/columns. Sample copy, $8. Guidelines and theme list available at website.

- "Tips on Fundraising." Article outlines the strategies and methods of successful fundraising projects.
- "Project Xcitement—Where Everyone Wants to Hang Out." Article provides tips for turning a boring youth room into a place where teens will want to hang out.

RIGHTS AND PAYMENT
All rights. Written material, $15–$300. Pays on publication. Provides 1 contributor's copy.

➤EDITOR'S COMMENTS
We work with well-established writers as well as those who have never been published before, because we value insights from both. If you are unpublished, you'll need to prove you can execute an idea by providing a detailed outline and sample introduction.

Zamoof!

644 Spruceview Place South
Kelowna, British Columbia V1V 2P7
Canada

Editor/Publisher: TeLeni Koochin

DESCRIPTION AND INTERESTS
It's got a funny name because it's filled with fun. *Zamoof!* publishes the kinds of things kids consider fun and funny—comics, games, activities, and articles that encourage creativity. It accepts short stories, pet horoscopes, and essays by and for parents. Circ: 5,000–7,000.

Audience: 7–12 years
Frequency: 6 times each year
Website: www.zamoofmag.com

FREELANCE POTENTIAL
37% written by nonstaff writers. Publishes 13 freelance submissions yearly; 50% by unpublished writers, 100% by authors who are new to the magazine. Receives 6–8 queries, 5–6 unsolicited mss yearly.

SUBMISSIONS
Canadian authors only. Query or send complete ms. Prefers email submissions to mail@zamoofmag.com; will accept hard copy. SASE. Responds in 2–4 weeks.

- Articles: Staff written.
- Fiction: To 1,200 words. Stories that interest girls and boys ages 11–13.
- Depts/columns: "Feet Up Chronicles," to 350 words; essays for parents about parenting. "Pet Horoscopes," 25 words per sign; humorous horoscopes written for pets.

SAMPLE ISSUE
82 pages: 11 articles; 3 stories; 6 depts/columns; 4 comics. Sample copy, $6.50; also available at website. Writers' guidelines available at website.

- "Meep the Bat." Story tells of a fruit bat's return home after many adventures, and the lessons he learned.
- Sample dept/column: "Feet Up Chronicles" features an essay that draws parallels between parenting and remembering one's own childhood experiences.

RIGHTS AND PAYMENT
Writer retains rights. Written material, $.20 per word. Pays on publication. Provides 3 contributor's copies.

➤EDITOR'S COMMENTS
We are well booked for the coming year, but are open to submissions for publication in upcoming years. Please see our guidelines for our needs.

Additional Listings

We have selected the following magazines to offer you additional publishing opportunities. These magazines range from general interest publications to women's magazines to craft and hobby magazines. While children, young adults, parents, or teachers are not their primary target audience, these publications do publish a limited amount of material related to or of interest to children.

As you review the listings that follow, use the Description and Interests section as your guide to the particular needs of each magazine. This section offers general information about the magazine and its readers' interests, as well as the type of material it usually publishes. The Freelance Potential section will provide information about the publication's receptivity to freelance manuscripts.

After you survey the listings to determine if your work meets the magazine's specifications, be sure to read a recent sample copy and the current writers' guidelines before submitting your material.

The Acorn

138 East Holly Avenue
Pitman, NJ 08071

Editor: Stefanie Collum

DESCRIPTION AND INTERESTS: *The Acorn* offers a place for budding student writers to grow. This quarterly literary magazine, published and distributed by Pitman Middle School in New Jersey, features short fiction, poetry, personal experience pieces, and reviews written by students ages 9 to 18 on topics appropriate for, and of interest to, this age group. Circ: 65+.

FREELANCE POTENTIAL: 100% written by nonstaff writers. Publishes 100 freelance submissions yearly; 95% by unpublished writers, 95% by authors who are new to the magazine. Receives 240 unsolicited mss yearly.

SUBMISSIONS AND PAYMENT: Sample copy, $3 with 6x9 SASE. Guidelines available. Send complete ms. Accepts hard copy and email to scollum@pitman.k12.nj.us (no attachments). SASE. Responds in 6 weeks. No rights. Fiction, to 500 words. Poetry, to 32 lines. Provides 1 copy.

Action Pursuit Games

2400 East Katella Avenue
Anaheim, CA 92806

Editor: Bryan Sullivan

DESCRIPTION AND INTERESTS: Paintball enthusiasts subscribe to this magazine to find out about the latest techniques and cutting-edge strategies. This monthly also includes league information and product reviews. Circ: 80,000. **Website: www.actionpursuitgames.com**

FREELANCE POTENTIAL: 60% written by nonstaff writers. Publishes 150+ freelance submissions yearly; 20% by unpublished writers, 30% by authors who are new to the magazine. Receives 480 unsolicited mss yearly.

SUBMISSIONS AND PAYMENT: Sample copy, $4.99 with 9x12 SASE (15 first-class stamps). Send complete ms with artwork. Accepts hard copy and email to bryansullivanapg@gmail.com. SASE. Responds in 1 month. All rights. Articles, 400–500 words. Depts/columns, 300–500 words. Digital images. All material, payment rates vary. Pays on publication. Provides 1 contributor's copy.

AKC Family Dog

American Kennel Club
260 Madison Avenue
New York, NY 10016

Features Editor: Mara Bovsun

DESCRIPTION AND INTERESTS: *AKC Family Dog* is a lifestyle magazine for busy families who want to enjoy a mutually happy relationship with their pet. Articles highlight common breeds, instead of show dogs and pedigrees, and offer advice on dog behavior, grooming, and canine health. It appears six times each year. Circ: 180,000. **Website: www.akc.org/pubs/familydog**

FREELANCE POTENTIAL: 70% written by nonstaff writers. Publishes 24–30 freelance submissions yearly; 15% by authors who are new to the magazine. Receives 60–120 queries yearly.

SUBMISSIONS AND PAYMENT: Sample copy, $3.95 with 9x12 SASE. Guidelines available. Query with outline. Accepts email queries to mbb@akc.org. Responds immediately. First North American serial rights. Articles, 1,000–2,000 words; $125–$500. Pays on publication. Provides 1 contributor's copy.

Akron Family

TNT Publications
11630 Chillicothe Road
Chesterfield, OH 44026

Editor: Terri Nighswonger

DESCRIPTION AND INTERESTS: Distributed free through schools, child-care centers, libraries, and grocery stores, *Akron Family* offers features on parenting children of all ages, as well as regional activity calendars and resource guides. It appears monthly. Circ: 75,000. **Website: www.neohiofamily.com**

FREELANCE POTENTIAL: 50% written by nonstaff writers. Publishes 40–50 freelance submissions yearly; 33% by authors who are new to the magazine. Receives 500 queries yearly.

SUBMISSIONS AND PAYMENT: Guidelines available. Sample copy and theme list available at website. Query with clips. Accepts email queries to editor@tntpublications.com. Responds if interested. Exclusive rights. Articles, 500+ words. Depts/columns, word lengths vary. High resolution JPEG and TIFF images. All material, payment rates vary. Pays on publication. Provides 1 contributor's copy.

The ALAN Review

Louisiana State University
223 Peabody Hall
Baton Rouge, LA 70803

Editor: Dr. Steven T. Bickmore

DESCRIPTION AND INTERESTS: Published three times each year for an audience of English teachers, authors, librarians, publishers, and others, this peer-reviewed journal concentrates solely on literature for adolescents. Circ: 2,500.
Website: www.alan-ya.org

FREELANCE POTENTIAL: 90% written by non-staff writers. Publishes 38 freelance submissions yearly; 15% by unpublished writers, 15% by authors who are new to the magazine. Receives 60–120 unsolicited mss yearly.

SUBMISSIONS AND PAYMENT: Sample copy, free. Guidelines available in each issue. Send complete ms. Accepts email submissions to alanreview@lsu.edu (Microsoft Word attachments; include "ALAN Manuscript Submission" in subject line). No simultaneous submissions. Responds in 2 months. All rights. Articles, to 3,000 words. Depts/columns, word lengths vary. No payment. Provides 2 contributor's copies.

American History

Weider History Magazine Group
19300 Promenade Drive
Leesburg, VA 20176-6500

Submissions: Sarah Richardson

DESCRIPTION AND INTERESTS: *American History* contains factually accurate articles about U.S. history, presented in an engaging, entertaining format. Published every other month, it focuses on the significant events and people that contributed to the making of the nation. Its readership includes historians and the general public. Circ: 100,000.
Website: www.historynet.com

FREELANCE POTENTIAL: 75% written by non-staff writers. Publishes 30 freelance submissions yearly; 50% by authors who are new to the magazine. Receives 300 queries yearly.

SUBMISSIONS AND PAYMENT: Sample copy and guidelines, $6 with return label. Query with 1- to 2-page proposal. Accepts hard copy. SASE. Responds in 10 weeks. All rights. Articles, 2,000–4,000 words; $.20 per word. Depts/columns, word lengths vary; $75. Pays on acceptance. Provides 5 contributor's copies.

Amazing Kids!

20126 Ballinger Way NE, Suite 235
Shoreline, WA 98155

Editor: Alyse Rome

DESCRIPTION AND INTERESTS: This online magazine is a kid-created publication featuring creative nonfiction, art, and photography. It also publishes reviews of family-friendly books, new products, events, and travel destinations. Its content is created by, and directed toward, children ages 7 through 14 and their parents; its goal is to inspire excellence in children. Hits per month: 640,000.
Website: www.amazing-kids.org

FREELANCE POTENTIAL: 30% written by non-staff writers. Publishes 50+ freelance submissions yearly; 90% by unpublished writers, 70% by authors who are new to the magazine. Receives thousands of queries yearly.

SUBMISSIONS AND PAYMENT: Sample copy and guidelines available at website. Query. Accepts email queries to editor@amazing-kids.org. Response time varies. All rights. Articles, word lengths vary. No payment.

American School Board Journal

1680 Duke Street
Alexandria, VA 22314

Editor-in-Chief: Glenn Cook

DESCRIPTION AND INTERESTS: This professional journal from the National School Boards Association serves as an open forum for opinions about education issues. It also presents features on educational leadership, management, and policy. Published monthly, it is read by school board members, educators, and administrators. Circ: 50,200.
Website: www.asbj.com

FREELANCE POTENTIAL: 50% written by non-staff writers. Publishes 35 freelance submissions yearly. Receives 360 queries yearly.

SUBMISSIONS AND PAYMENT: Sample copy, $5. Prefers query with clips; will accept complete ms. Accepts hard copy. SASE. Responds in 2 months. All rights. Articles, 2,200–2,500 words. Depts/columns, 1,000–1,200 words. Solicited articles, $800. Unsolicited articles and depts/columns, no payment. Pays on publication. Provides 3 contributor's copies.

AMomsLove.com

1308 Midland Beaver Road
Industry, PA 15052

Editor: Caroline G. Shaw

DESCRIPTION AND INTERESTS: Stay-at-home
and working moms of infants through teens
check out this online magazine for articles on
parenting and family issues. Other topics include
women's health and fitness, home and garden,
and travel and entertainment. Book reviews and
recipes are also offered. Hits per month: 30,000.
Website: www.amomslove.com

FREELANCE POTENTIAL: 90% written by nonstaff writers. Publishes hundreds of freelance
submissions yearly; 20% by authors who are
new to the magazine.

SUBMISSIONS AND PAYMENT: Sample copy
and writers' guidelines available at website.
Send complete ms with brief author bio. Accepts
email to submissions@amomslove.com (html or
Microsoft Word attachments). Response time
varies. First rights. Articles, 700–1,100 words.
No payment.

The Apprentice Writer

Writers Institute
Susquehanna University, Box GG
Selinsgrove, PA 17870-1001

Director: Gary Fincke

DESCRIPTION AND INTERESTS: Each
September, this magazine publishes well-crafted
stories, poetry, and personal essays written by
high school students from across the nation.
Circ: 10,500.
**Website: www.susqu.edu/writers/
highschoolstudents.htm**

FREELANCE POTENTIAL: 100% written by
nonstaff writers. Publishes 80 freelance submissions yearly; 95% by unpublished writers, 95%
by authors who are new to the magazine.
Receives 4,000 unsolicited mss yearly.

SUBMISSIONS AND PAYMENT: Sample copy,
$3 with 9x12 SASE ($1.17 postage). Guidelines
available at website. Send complete ms by
March 1. Accepts hard copy and simultaneous
submissions if identified. SASE. Responds in
May. First rights. Articles and fiction, 7,000
words. Poetry, no line limits. No payment.
Provides 2 contributor's copies.

Apples

2920 South Webster Avenue
Green Bay, WI 54302

Editor

DESCRIPTION AND INTERESTS: This monthly
magazine replaces the now-defunct *Fox Valley
Kids* but continues to provide Wisconsin parents
with family-centered information and local
resources. It seeks material on parenting issues,
family relationships, and fun things to do with
children in the region. Circ: 60,000.
Website: www.applesfamilies.com

FREELANCE POTENTIAL: 10% written by nonstaff writers. Publishes 10 freelance submissions
yearly; 10% by unpublished writers, 10% by
authors who are new to the magazine. Receives
20 queries yearly.

SUBMISSIONS AND PAYMENT: Query or send
complete ms. Accepts email submissions to
admin@applesfamilies.com. Response time varies.
Rights negotiable. Articles and depts/columns, to
750 words. Written material, payment rates vary.
Pays on publication. Provides 1 contributor's
copy upon request.

Athens Parent

P.O. Box 465
Watkinsville, GA 30677

Editor-in-Chief: Shannon Howell Baker

DESCRIPTION AND INTERESTS: This regional
publication features original articles on issues
that interest parents, grandparents, educators,
and others living in the Athens, Georgia, area
who are involved in the well-being of children
and families. Published six times each year, it
offers regular columns on health, finances,
fathering, child development, teen issues, and
lifestyle topics. Circ: Unavailable.
Website: www.athensparent.com

FREELANCE POTENTIAL: 85% written by nonstaff writers. Publishes 40 freelance submissions
yearly. Receives 500 queries yearly.

SUBMISSIONS AND PAYMENT: Guidelines
and theme list available at website. Query.
Accepts hard copy and email queries to editor@
athensparent.com. SASE. Response time varies.
First rights. Articles and depts/columns, word
lengths and payment rates vary. Payment policy
varies.

Austin Family

P.O. Box 7559
Round Rock, TX 78683-7559

Editor: Melanie Dunham

DESCRIPTION AND INTERESTS: This free magazine has been providing information about good parenting and raising healthy children since 1992. It is published three to five times per month. Circ: 35,000.
Website: www.austinfamily.com

FREELANCE POTENTIAL: 85% written by non-staff writers. Publishes 18 freelance submissions yearly; 10% by unpublished writers, 50% by authors who are new to the magazine. Receives 1,200 queries and unsolicited mss yearly.

SUBMISSIONS AND PAYMENT: Sample copy, free. Query or send complete ms. Accepts email submissions to editor2003@austinfamily.com and simultaneous submissions if identified. Availability of artwork improves chance of acceptance. Responds in 3–6 months. First and second serial rights. Articles, 800–1,200 words. Depts/columns, 800 words. B/W prints. All material, payment rates vary. Pays on publication.

BabagaNewz

11141 Georgia Avenue, Suite 406
Silver Spring, MD 20902

Editor: Sara Marx

DESCRIPTION AND INTERESTS: Designed for Jewish middle school students and their teachers, this magazine and website offer creative, innovative ways to explore Jewish traditions, holidays, and values. Published eight times each year, it looks for submissions that are novel, fun, and thought-provoking. Circ: 41,029.
Website: www.babaganewz.com

FREELANCE POTENTIAL: 30% written by nonstaff writers. Publishes 20 freelance submissions yearly; 10% by authors who are new to the magazine.

SUBMISSIONS AND PAYMENT: Sample copy and guidelines available by email request to aviva@babaganewz.com. All material is written on assignment. Query with résumé. Accepts hard copy. SASE. Response time varies. All rights. Articles and depts/columns, word lengths and payment rates vary. Pays on acceptance. Provides contributor's copies upon request.

Baton Rouge Parents

11831 Wentling Avenue
Baton Rouge, LA 70816-6055

Editor: Amy Foreman-Plaisance

DESCRIPTION AND INTERESTS: Localized to the Baton Rouge area, this monthly magazine offers articles on parenting issues, children's health topics, education, and family recreation. Circ: 55,000.
Website: www.brparents.com

FREELANCE POTENTIAL: 95% written by non-staff writers. Publishes 50+ freelance submissions yearly; 15% by unpublished writers, 30% by authors who are new to the magazine.

SUBMISSIONS AND PAYMENT: Guidelines available via email request to brpm@brparents.com. Query with outline, source list, brief author biography, and 2 writing samples. Accepts hard copy and email queries to brpm@brparents.com (include "Article Query" in subject line). SASE. Response time varies. First North American serial rights. Written material, word lengths vary; $25–$70. Kill fee, $10. Pays on publication. Provides 2 contributor's copies.

Bay Area Parent

1660 South Amphlett Boulevard, Suite 335
San Mateo, CA 94402

Editor: Peggy Spear

DESCRIPTION AND INTERESTS: Catering to families living in the San Francisco Bay area, this monthly includes features of national scope with a local relevance. Regional family resource and event information are also offered. It is published in three regional editions: one for the East Bay; one for San Francisco and Peninsula; and one for Silicon Valley. Circ: 80,000.
Website: www.bayareaparent.com

FREELANCE POTENTIAL: 50% written by non-staff writers. Publishes 15–20 freelance submissions yearly. Receives 100+ queries yearly.

SUBMISSIONS AND PAYMENT: Prefers submissions from local authors. Sample copy and guidelines available at website. Query. Accepts hard copy. SASE. Responds in 2 months. One-time rights. Articles, 1,200–1,400 words. Depts/columns, word lengths vary. Written material, $.06 per word. Pays on publication. Provides 1 contributor's copy.

Beckett Plushie Pals

4635 McEwen Road
Dallas, TX 75244

Editor: Doug Kale

DESCRIPTION AND INTERESTS: This magazine is written specifically for fans of plush toys and their virtual worlds, such as Webkinz, Ty Girlz, Club Penguin, and Beanie Babies. Read by children ages seven and up, it appears monthly and includes articles on new products, interviews with toymakers, and advice on how to play the online games. Circ: 100,000.
Website: www.beckettplushiepals.com

FREELANCE POTENTIAL: 50% written by non-staff writers. Publishes 20 freelance submissions yearly; 50% by authors who are new to the magazine. Receives 50–100 queries yearly.

SUBMISSIONS AND PAYMENT: Sample copy and guidelines available. Query with 3–5 article ideas. Accepts email queries to plushiepals@beckett.com. Responds in 1–2 months. First rights. Articles and depts/columns, word lengths vary; $25–$100. Pays on publication. Provides 2 contributor's copies.

Berry Blue Haiku

Executive Editor: Gisele LeBlanc

DESCRIPTION AND INTERESTS: Launched in 2010, this quarterly e-zine focuses exclusively on the Japanese poetic form of haiku. Its poems, articles, lessons, and crafts are aimed at children up to the age of 13. Hits per month: Unavailable.
**Website: http://cobaltcrowproductions.
blogspot.com**

FREELANCE POTENTIAL: Publishes several freelance submissions yearly.

SUBMISSIONS AND PAYMENT: Sample copy and guidelines available at website. Query for articles. Send ms for poetry and crafts. Accepts email to berrybluehaiku@gmail.com (no attachments; include age level and "Haiku" or "Article/Craft" in subject line). Response time varies. Exclusive worldwide electronic rights for 3 months. Articles, 50–150 words (to age 5); 150–500 words (6–11 years); 500–1,000 words (12+ years). Haiku, 2–3 lines; limit 5 per submission. Written material, payment rates vary. Payment policy varies.

Birmingham Parent

700-C Southgate Drive
Pelham, AL 35124

Publisher/Editor: Carol Muse Evans

DESCRIPTION AND INTERESTS: This monthly magazine is geared specifically to parents in the Birmingham area of Alabama. Its articles cover parenting news and advice, health and safety, and travel, all with a local slant and almost all written by local authors. Circ: 35,000.
Website: www.birminghamparent.com

FREELANCE POTENTIAL: 50% written by nonstaff writers. Publishes 50+ freelance submissions yearly; 5% by authors who are new to the magazine.

SUBMISSIONS AND PAYMENT: Sample copy and guidelines available at website. Query with résumé, clips, and artwork availability; or send complete ms. Accepts email to editor@birminghamparent.com. Responds in 1 month. First North American serial and electronic rights. Articles, 700–1,500 words; payment rates vary. JPEG files at 300 dpi; no payment. Pays within 30 days of publication. Provides 2 copies.

Bop

330 North Brand, Suite 1150
Glendale, CA 91203

Editor-in-Chief: Leesa Coble

DESCRIPTION AND INTERESTS: *Bop* focuses on the celebrities that tween and teen girls are focused on. It offers the latest news about who's who in the worlds of film and television, music, and fashion. Celebrity insider scoops, profiles, and interviews are featured in each photo-filled monthly issue. While freelance writers with access to celebrities have been published in the past, *Bop* is currently not accepting any submissions from freelancers. Check the website for updates to this policy. Circ: 200,000.
Website: www.bopmag.com

FREELANCE POTENTIAL: 100% staff written.

SUBMISSIONS AND PAYMENT: Sample copy, $3.99 at newsstands. Not accepting queries or unsolicited mss at this time.

The Boston Parents' Paper

51 Morgan Drive, Suite 11
Norwood, MA 02062

Associate Editors: Deirdre Wilson & Susan Flynn

DESCRIPTION AND INTERESTS: This monthly magazine is dedicated to giving Boston-area families the latest information pertaining to parenting and child development issues, and it provides recreational opportunities in the region. All articles feature local resources. Circ: 75,000.
Website: http://boston.parenthood.com

FREELANCE POTENTIAL: 10–12% written by nonstaff writers. Publishes 60–75 freelance submissions yearly; 10% by unpublished writers, 50% by authors who are new to the magazine. Receives hundreds of queries yearly.

SUBMISSIONS AND PAYMENT: Guidelines and theme list available. Query with clips or writing samples. Accepts email to deirdre.wilson@parenthood.com. Availability of artwork improves chance of acceptance. Response time varies. All rights. Articles and depts/columns, word lengths vary. B/W prints; line art. All material, payment rates vary. Pays on publication. Provides 5 copies.

Bread for God's Children

P.O. Box 1017
Arcadia, FL 34265-1017

Editorial Secretary: Donna Wade

DESCRIPTION AND INTERESTS: Six times each year, this Christian publication offers families stories and articles designed to help them apply the Word of God to their everyday lives. Shorter stories for very young children are especially sought. Circ: 5,000.
Website: www.breadministries.org

FREELANCE POTENTIAL: 20% written by nonstaff writers. Of the freelance submissions published yearly, 10% is by unpublished writers, 10% is by authors who are new to the magazine. Receives 240 unsolicited mss yearly.

SUBMISSIONS AND PAYMENT: Sample copy, free with 9x12 SASE (5 first-class stamps). Guidelines available. Send complete ms. Accepts hard copy and simultaneous submissions if identified. SASE. Responds in 2–3 months. First rights. Articles and depts/columns, to 800 words; $25. Fiction, 800–1,800 words; $40–$50. Pays on publication. Provides 3 author's copies.

Brain, Child

P.O. Box 714
Lexington, VA 24450

Editors: Jennifer Niesslein & Stephanie Wilkinson

DESCRIPTION AND INTERESTS: Parents and grandparents read this quarterly for entertaining and enlightening articles and stories about raising children. Its perspective is often humorous, always insightful. Hits per month: 30,000.
Website: www.brainchildmag.com

FREELANCE POTENTIAL: 90% written by nonstaff writers. Publishes 40 freelance submissions yearly; 15% by unpublished writers, 60% by authors who are new to the magazine. Receives 300 queries, 2,400 unsolicited mss yearly.

SUBMISSIONS AND PAYMENT: Sample copy and guidelines, $5. Query or send ms. Prefers email to editor@brainchildmag.com (no attachments; include "Submission" and department in subject line); will accept hard copy. SASE. Responds in 10 weeks. Electronic rights. Articles, 3,000–6,000 words. Personal essays, 800–4,500 words. Fiction, 1,500–4,500 words. Written material, payment rates vary. Pays on publication.

Bull Spec

P.O. Box 13146
Durham, TX 27709

Editor: Samuel Montgomery-Blinn

DESCRIPTION AND INTERESTS: Available in print and as an e-zine, *Bull Spec* is a quarterly journal of speculative fiction. It accepts short stories, poetry, interviews with authors, and book reviews. Though it focuses on fantasy and science fiction, it is open to many genres. Circ: 500.
Website: www.bullspec.com

FREELANCE POTENTIAL: 90% written by nonstaff writers. Of the freelance submissions published yearly, 35% is by unpublished writers, 50% by authors who are new to the magazine. Receives 200 queries, 600 unsolicited mss yearly.

SUBMISSIONS AND PAYMENT: Sample copy, $8. Query or send complete ms. Accepts email submissions to sam@bullspec.com (attach file). Responds to queries in 1 month, to mss in 3 months. First worldwide rights. Articles, 500–5,000 words. Fiction, 1,000–8,000 words. Written material, $.05 per word. Payment policy varies. Provides 1 contributor's copy.

Bumples

Editor

DESCRIPTION AND INTERESTS: This interactive e-zine specializes in illustrated fiction for ages 4 to 10. Each issue features animal stories, mysteries, fantasies, sports stories, and poetry. Puzzles, question games, and activities accompany the stories, providing additional information in an entertaining way. *Bumples* is updated 10 times each year. Hits per month: Unavailable.
Website: www.bumples.com

FREELANCE POTENTIAL: 60% written by non-staff writers. Publishes several freelance submissions yearly.

SUBMISSIONS AND PAYMENT: Guidelines available at website. Send complete ms. Accepts email to editor@bumples.com (PDF attachments). Response time varies. Rights vary. Fiction, to 800 words (ages 4–7), to 2,000 words (ages 8–10); $.20 per word. Poetry, line lengths vary; $3 per line. Low-resolution digital images; payment rates vary. Payment policy varies.

Camping Today

126 Hermitage Road
Butler, PA 16001

Editor: DeWayne Johnston

DESCRIPTION AND INTERESTS: With an audience primarily made up of RVers who are retired, *Camping Today* offers articles that appeal to that demographic. Topics covered in the six issues published yearly include road safety, wildlife, and destinations. Pieces written from personal experience that include the author's opinions and impressions are favored. Circ: 10,000.
Website: www.fcrv.org

FREELANCE POTENTIAL: 40% written by non-staff writers. Publishes 10 freelance submissions yearly; 10% by unpublished writers. Receives 240 unsolicited mss yearly.

SUBMISSIONS AND PAYMENT: Guidelines and theme list available. Send complete ms with artwork. Accepts hard copy. SASE. Responds in 2 months. One-time rights. Articles, 1,000–3,000 words. Depts/columns, word lengths vary. JPEG files. Written material, $35–$150. Pays on publication. Provides 1+ contributor's copies.

Calgary's Child

#723, 105-150 Crowfoot Crescent NW
Calgary, Alberta T3G 3T2
Canada

Editor: Ellen Percival

DESCRIPTION AND INTERESTS: Calgary parents of school-aged children read this magazine for timely, in-depth articles on the issues most important to them, from their children's health and safety to community-wide issues. All content, and most authors, are locally based. *Calgary's Child* appears six times each year. Circ: 60,000.
Website: www.calgaryschild.com

FREELANCE POTENTIAL: 99% written by non-staff writers. Of the freelance submissions published yearly, 20% are by authors who are new to the magazine. Receives 1,000 queries yearly.

SUBMISSIONS AND PAYMENT: Sample copy and guidelines available at website. Query with outline. Accepts email queries to calgaryschild@shaw.ca. No simultaneous submissions. Response time varies. Exclusive Calgary rights. Articles, 400–500 words; to $50 Canadian. Payment policy varies.

Canoe & Kayak Magazine

236 Avenida Fabricante, Suite 201
San Clemente, CA 92672

Managing Editor: Jeff Moag

DESCRIPTION AND INTERESTS: Each issue of this magazine is packed with canoe and kayak destination pieces, the latest paddling techniques, expert reviews of paddle and camping gear, and family paddling tips. It appears six times each year. Circ: 50,000.
Website: www.canoekayak.com

FREELANCE POTENTIAL: 90% written by non-staff writers. Publishes 25 freelance submissions yearly; 5% by unpublished writers, 25% by authors who are new to the magazine. Receives 100 queries yearly.

SUBMISSIONS AND PAYMENT: Sample copy, free with 9x12 SASE (7 first-class stamps). Query. Accepts email submissions to jeff@canoekayak.com. Responds in 6–8 weeks. All rights. Articles, 400–2,000 words. Depts/columns, 150–750 words. Written material, $.50 per word. Pays on publication. Provides 1 contributor's copy.

Catalyst Chicago
Independent Reporting on Urban Schools

332 South Michigan Avenue, Suite 500
Chicago, IL 60604

Editor-in-Chief: Lorraine Forte

DESCRIPTION AND INTERESTS: Published five times each year by the Community Renewal Society, this magazine provides a forum for parents, educators, and policy makers to discuss topics related to education reform and policy, particularly as they relate to Chicago's urban schools. Experienced educational journalists are always sought. Circ: 9,000.
Website: www.catalyst-chicago.org

FREELANCE POTENTIAL: 15% written by non-staff writers. Publishes 6 freelance submissions yearly; 25% by authors who are new to the magazine. Receives 45 queries yearly.

SUBMISSIONS AND PAYMENT: Sample copy and guidelines, $2. Query or send letter of introduction. Accepts hard copy and email queries to editorial@catalyst-chicago.org. SASE. Response time varies. All rights. Articles, to 2,300 words; $1,700. Pays on acceptance. Provides 1 contributor's copy.

Cat Fancy

P.O. Box 6050
Mission Viejo, CA 92690

Query Editor

DESCRIPTION AND INTERESTS: Informative articles on cats and feline behavior are published in this monthly magazine dedicated to the love of cats. Circ: 290,000.
Website: www.catchannel.com

FREELANCE POTENTIAL: 95% written by non-staff writers. Publishes 150 freelance submissions yearly; 10% by unpublished writers, 70% by new authors. Receives 500+ queries yearly.

SUBMISSIONS AND PAYMENT: Guidelines available at website. Query with clips between January 1 and May 1 only (news and trend queries accepted year-round). Accepts hard copy and email to query@catfancy.com. Availability of artwork improves chance of acceptance. Response time varies. First rights. Articles, 600–1,000 words. Depts/columns, 600 words. 35mm slides; high-resolution digital images with contact sheets. All material, payment rates vary. Pays on publication. Provides 2 author's copies.

Chickadee

Bayard Press Canada
10 Lower Spadina Avenue, Suite 400
Toronto, Ontario M4V 2Z2
Canada

Submissions Editor

DESCRIPTION AND INTERESTS: *Chickadee* is for children ages six to nine. Its themed issues contain articles, stories, and activities that make learning fun. Interactive content is designed to engage the imagination, enhance independent reading skills, and help sharpen problem-solving skills. Topics cover a wide range, and include animals, science, sports, and history. It appears ten times each year. Circ: 85,000.
Website: www.owlkids.com

FREELANCE POTENTIAL: 5% written by non-staff writers. Publishes 1 freelance submission each year.

SUBMISSIONS AND PAYMENT: Sample copy, guidelines, and theme list, $4. All work is assigned. Send résumé. Accepts hard copy. No SASE. Responds if interested. All rights. Fiction, 650–700 words; $250. Pays on acceptance. Provides 2 contributor's copies.

Children's Advocate

Action Alliance for Children
The Hunt Home
1201 Martin Luther King Jr. Way
Oakland, CA 94612-1217

Editor: Jessine Foss

DESCRIPTION AND INTERESTS: Parents, teachers, child-care providers, librarians, and others who advocate for children read this tabloid. It covers legislation that affects children and families and related advocacy efforts. Appearing six times each year, it is distributed free throughout California by the nonprofit Action Alliance for Children. Each issue includes articles written in English and Spanish. Circ: 15,000.
Website: www.4children.org

FREELANCE POTENTIAL: 60% written by non-staff writers. Publishes 24 freelance submissions each year.

SUBMISSIONS AND PAYMENT: Sample copy and guidelines available. All work is assigned. Send résumé and writing samples. Accepts hard copy. SASE. Response time varies. First North American serial rights. Articles, 500 or 1,000 words; $.25 per word. Pays on acceptance. Provides 3 contributor's copies.

Chirp

Bayard Press Canada
10 Lower Spadina Avenue, Suite 400
Toronto, Ontario M5V 2Z2
Canada

Submissions Editor

DESCRIPTION AND INTERESTS: Designed for the very youngest readers, *Chirp* fills its pages with short stories, puzzles, rhymes, and games that appeal to children and their parents. Created by the publishers of *Owl* and *Chickadee* and published nine times each year, it targets kids ages two through six. All of the content for *Chirp* is assigned; to be considered, writers should send a brief résumé and list of publishing credits. Circ: 60,000.
Website: www.owlkids.com

FREELANCE POTENTIAL: 10% written by non-staff writers. Publishes 1–3 freelance submissions yearly; 1% by unpublished writers.

SUBMISSIONS AND PAYMENT: Sample copy and guidelines, $3.50. All work is assigned. Send résumé only. Accepts hard copy. No SASE. All rights. Written material, 300–400 words; payment rates vary. Pays on acceptance. Provides 2 contributor's copies.

Cincinnati Parent

1901 Broad Ripple Avenue
Indianapolis, IN 46220

Executive Editor: Lynette Rowland

DESCRIPTION AND INTERESTS: Articles on education, health, and child development appear along with regional service directories in this monthly tabloid. It puts a focus on places to go and things to do with children in the greater Cincinnati area. The editors like well-researched articles on surviving the newborn, preschool, school-age, and adolescent years. Circ: 120,000.
Website: www.cincinnatiparent.com

FREELANCE POTENTIAL: 25–40% written by nonstaff writers. Publishes 30 freelance submissions yearly.

SUBMISSIONS AND PAYMENT: Guidelines available at website. Query with writing sample; state areas of interest. Accepts email queries to editor@cincinnatiparent.com. Responds if interested. First rights. Articles, 1,500–2,000 words. Depts/columns, 800–1,000 words. Written material, $.10–$.15 per word. Reprints, $40–$75. Pays on publication. Provides 1 contributor's copy.

Cincinnati Family Magazine

10945 Reed Hartman Highway, Suite 221
Cincinnati, OH 45242

Editor: Sherry Hang

DESCRIPTION AND INTERESTS: In addition to activity calendars and camp directories, this regional monthly offers news and feature articles about general parenting topics, education, and family health. Circ: 55,000.
Website: www.cincinnatifamilymagazine.com

FREELANCE POTENTIAL: 25% written by nonstaff writers. Publishes 20–24 freelance submissions yearly; 5% by unpublished writers, 5% by authors who are new to the magazine. Receives 100–150 queries, 50–100 unsolicited mss yearly.

SUBMISSIONS AND PAYMENT: Guidelines and editorial calendar available. Query or send complete ms. Accepts hard copy and email submissions to sherryh@daycommail.com. SASE. Response time varies. First rights. Articles, word lengths vary; $75–$125. Depts/columns, word lengths and payment rates vary. Pays 1 month after publication.

Classic Toy Trains

21027 Crossroads Circle
Waukesha, WI 53187

Editor: Carl Swanson

DESCRIPTION AND INTERESTS: This photo-filled magazine, published nine times each year, is read by model train hobbyists for how-to articles and pieces on collecting and history. It also publishes profiles of collectors. Circ: 55,000.
Website: www.classictoytrains.com

FREELANCE POTENTIAL: 60% written by nonstaff writers. Publishes 40–50 freelance submissions yearly; 20% by unpublished writers, 20% by authors who are new to the magazine. Receives 96 queries, 60 unsolicited mss yearly.

SUBMISSIONS AND PAYMENT: Sample copy, $4.95 with 9x12 SASE ($3 postage). Prefers query; will accept ms. Accepts hard copy, disk submissions (Microsoft Word), and email submissions to editor@classictoytrains.com. SASE. Responds in 3 months. All rights. Articles, 500–5,000 words; $75 per page. Depts/columns, word lengths and payment rates vary. Pays on acceptance. Provides 1 contributor's copy.

Coastal Family Magazine

340 Eisenhower Drive, Suite 240
Savannah, GA 31406

Managing Editor: Laura Gray

DESCRIPTION AND INTERESTS: *Coastal Family Magazine* is read by parents living in Savannah, Georgia, and South Carolina's Low Country. Each monthly issue is distributed free of charge and offers readers highlights of the region's recreational and travel opportunities, in addition to timely and informative articles on parenting, education, health and safety, family finances, and child care. This publication is currently not accepting unsolicited freelance submissions. Circ: 18,000.
Website: www.coastalfamily.com

FREELANCE POTENTIAL: 10% written by non-staff writers.

SUBMISSIONS AND PAYMENT: Currently not accepting freelance submissions. Please check website for changes to this policy.

Coins

4700 East Galbraith Road
Cincinnati, OH 45236

Editor: Robert Van Ryzin

DESCRIPTION AND INTERESTS: *Coins* is the go-to publication for timely information on coin market trends, buying and selling tips, and pricing. It also offers articles on the history of coin collecting and how to assemble a collection. Personal experience pieces, profiles, and show coverage round out each monthly issue. All content is authored by coin experts. Circ: 60,000.
Website: www.coinsmagazine.net

FREELANCE POTENTIAL: 40% written by non-staff writers. Publishes 70 freelance submissions yearly; 5% by authors who are new to the magazine. Receives 36–60 queries yearly.

SUBMISSIONS AND PAYMENT: Sample copy and guidelines, free. Query. Accepts hard copy. SASE. Responds in 1–2 months. All rights. Articles, 1,500–2,500 words; $.04 per word. Work for hire. Pays on publication. Provides contributor's copies upon request.

College News

39 South LaSalle, Unit 420
Chicago, IL 60603

Copy Editor: Kandy Williams

DESCRIPTION AND INTERESTS: This quarterly magazine targets college students, ages 18 to 29. Topics range from entertainment to education, spring break to study tips, and campus life to career planning. Queries about the more serious side of college are especially sought. It is written mostly by journalism interns, but considers queries from other writers. Circ: Unavailable.
Website: www.collegenews.com

FREELANCE POTENTIAL: 30% written by non-staff writers. Publishes 20 freelance submissions yearly; 70% by unpublished writers, 20% by authors who are new to the magazine. Receives 600 queries yearly.

SUBMISSIONS AND PAYMENT: Sample copy available at website. Guidelines available. Query. Accepts hard copy. SASE. All rights. Articles, 400 words. No payment. Provides 1 author's copy.

ColumbiaKids

Washington State Historical Society
1911 Pacific Avenue
Tacoma, WA 98402

Manuscript Coordinator

DESCRIPTION AND INTERESTS: The Pacific Northwest is celebrated in the stories, poetry, and articles found in this e-zine, which is updated twice each year. Hits per month: 5,000+.
Website:
http://columbia.washingtonhistory.org/kids

FREELANCE POTENTIAL: 80% written by non-staff writers. Publishes 20 freelance submissions yearly; 10% by unpublished writers, 80% by authors who are new to the magazine. Receives 60–120 queries, 36–84 unsolicited mss yearly.

SUBMISSIONS AND PAYMENT: Sample copy and guidelines available at website. Query or send complete ms. Accepts hard copy and email to columbiakids@wshs.wa.gov (no attachments). SASE. Response time varies. First world electronic and archival rights. Articles, 800–1,200 words; $200. Depts/columns, 200–800 words; $50–$100. Poetry, word games, jokes, and rebuses, $25–$50. Pays on publication.

Community College Week

P.O. Box 1305
Fairfax, VA 22038

Editor: Paul Bradley

DESCRIPTION AND INTERESTS: This magazine is read by faculty and administrators at community, technical, and junior colleges for timely articles on academic issues, technology trends, and newsworthy items. Published twice each month, it also lists employment opportunities. Circ: 18,000.
Website: www.ccweek.com

FREELANCE POTENTIAL: 75% written by non-staff writers. Publishes 75 freelance submissions yearly; 40% by authors who are new to the magazine. Receives 60 queries yearly.

SUBMISSIONS AND PAYMENT: Guidelines available. Query with clips, résumé, and source list. Prefers email to editor@ccweek.com; will accept hard copy. SASE. Responds in 1 month. First serial rights. Articles, 600–1,200 words. Depts/columns, word lengths vary. Written material, $.35 per word. Kill fee, $.15 per word. Pays on publication. Provides 6 contributor's copies.

Complex Child E-Magazine

Editor: Susan Agrawal

DESCRIPTION AND INTERESTS: Parents and guardians of children with special needs, medical conditions, and disabilities read this monthly online magazine. Its articles are particularly valuable because they are authored by writers who are themselves caring for children with these same issues. Topics covered include caregiving, special education, insurance, nutrition, safety, and parenting. Hits per month: Unavailable.
Website: www.complexchild.com

FREELANCE POTENTIAL: 60% written by non-staff writers. Publishes 50 freelance submissions yearly. Receives 100 queries yearly.

SUBMISSIONS AND PAYMENT: Sample copy and writer's guidelines available at website. Query. Accepts email queries to submit@ complexchild.com (Microsoft Word or text file attachments). Responds in 1–2 months. Limited-time electronic rights. Articles, word lengths vary. No payment.

Cookie

4 Times Square, 8th Floor
New York, NY 10036

Acquisitions: Mireille Hyde

DESCRIPTION AND INTERESTS: This parenting magazine covers the usual topics—such as child-rearing and family issues; health, fitness, and nutrition; travel and recreation; and home decorating and entertaining—but with a twist. It is for sophisticated moms and dads who are parenting young children while living a busy and upscale lifestyle. It appears ten times each year. Circ: 400,000.
Website: www.cookiemag.com

FREELANCE POTENTIAL: 50% written by non-staff writers. Publishes 10 freelance submissions yearly. Receives 600–1,200 queries yearly.

SUBMISSIONS AND PAYMENT: Sample copy available at newsstands. Query. Accepts hard copy and email to editor@cookiemag.com (include "Freelance Pitch" in the subject line). SASE. Response time varies. Rights vary. Articles, word lengths and payment rates vary. Pays on publication.

Co-op Thymes

1007 SE Third Street
Corvallis, OR 97333

Marketing Coordinator: Emily Stimac

DESCRIPTION AND INTERESTS: Shoppers at the First Alternative community markets in Corvallis, Oregon, pick up this free newspaper, which appears monthly. In addition to community outreach news, *Co-op Thymes* offers recipes, articles that explore the health benefits of natural products, and coverage of the local organic movement. Queries for articles on food-related or health topics are welcome. Circ: 5,000.
Website: www.firstalt.coop

FREELANCE POTENTIAL: 14% written by non-staff writers. Publishes 24 freelance submissions yearly; 95% by unpublished writers, 50% by authors who are new to the magazine. Receives 24 queries yearly.

SUBMISSIONS AND PAYMENT: Sample copy, free. Query. Accepts email queries to thymes@ firstalt.coop. Responds in 1–3 days. Rights vary. Articles and depts/columns, word lengths vary. No payment.

County Parents Magazine

P.O. Box 1666
Bel Air, MD 21014

Publisher: Joan Fernandez

DESCRIPTION AND INTERESTS: Serving parents in Maryland's Harford County, *County Parents Magazine* provides localized parenting and educational resources, as well as articles on family-friendly recreational opportunities, child care topics, health matters, and child development issues. Because of its emphasis on local information, writers from the region are preferred. It is published monthly. Circ: 22,000.
Website: www.countyparents.com

FREELANCE POTENTIAL: 75% written by non-staff writers. Publishes 20 freelance submissions each year.

SUBMISSIONS AND PAYMENT: Guidelines available at website. Query. Accepts hard copy and email queries to countyparents@aboutdelta.com. SASE. Response time varies. First print and electronic rights. Articles and depts/columns, word lengths and payment rates vary. Pays on publication. Provides 1 copy.

Craftbits.com

P.O. Box 3106
Birkdale, Queensland 4159
Australia

Editor: Shellie Wilson

DESCRIPTION AND INTERESTS: Family-oriented and kid- and senior-friendly, this online magazine has craft projects for all ages and skill levels. Directions for more complicated crafts are presented in detailed step-by-step format. Candle- and soap-making, beading, and scrapbooking, as well as holiday-themed and recycled crafts, are among the projects featured. Hits per month: 60,000.
Website: www.craftbits.com

FREELANCE POTENTIAL: 5% written by non-staff writers. Publishes many freelance submissions yearly.

SUBMISSIONS AND PAYMENT: Sample copy available at website. Query with JPEG images. Accepts email queries to staff@craftbits.com. Responds in 1–2 months. All rights. Articles and depts/columns, word lengths vary; $45 (USD). Kill fee, $10 (USD). Pays on publication.

Crow Toes Quarterly

186-8120 No. 2 Road, Suite 361
Richmond, British Columbia V7C 4C1
Canada

Managing Editor: Christopher Millin

DESCRIPTION AND INTERESTS: Known as "The New Face of Children's Lit," this magazine publishes articles, fiction, poetry, and artwork of the "playfully dark variety, written by, and age-appropriate for, children ages eight to thirteen. Issues are now themed. Stories about aliens are currently sought. Circ: Unavailable.
Website: www.crowtoesquarterly.com

FREELANCE POTENTIAL: 90% written by non-staff writers. Publishes 24 freelance submissions yearly; 75% by unpublished writers, 75% by authors who are new to the magazine. Receives 15 unsolicited mss yearly.

SUBMISSIONS AND PAYMENT: Guidelines and theme list available at website. Send complete ms. Accepts hard copy. SASE. Responds in 4 months. First Canadian serial rights. Articles, word lengths vary. Fiction, to 3,000 words. B/W or color JPEG images at 300 dpi; line art. No payment.

Curriculum Review

Paperclip Communications
125 Paterson Avenue, Suite 4
Little Falls, NJ 07424

Editor: Frank Sennett

DESCRIPTION AND INTERESTS: *Curriculum Review* offers teachers and administrators the latest news and research in the field, highlighting "what works in our schools." Articles on education, lesson plans, reviews of classroom resources, and technology updates are featured in issues appearing nine times during the school year. Circ: 5,000.
Website: www.curriculumreview.com

FREELANCE POTENTIAL: 2% written by non-staff writers. Publishes 10 freelance submissions yearly. Receives 24 queries yearly.

SUBMISSIONS AND PAYMENT: Sample copy, free with 9x12 SASE (2 first-class stamps). Query. Accepts hard copy. SASE. Responds in 1 month. One-time rights. Articles, to 4,000 words. Depts/columns, word lengths vary. Written material, payment rates vary. Payment policy varies. Provides contributor's copies.

Dance Teacher

110 William Street, 23rd Floor
New York, NY 10038

Editor: Karen Hildebrand

DESCRIPTION AND INTERESTS: This monthly is written exclusively for dance educators in a studio, conservatory, or school setting. Its articles address the challenges of teaching dance, provide practical advice from leading educators, and present age-appropriate program and costume ideas for recitals and the classroom. Circ: 25,000. **Website: www.dance-teacher.com**

FREELANCE POTENTIAL: 67% written by non-staff writers. Publishes 100–120 freelance submissions yearly; 10% by unpublished writers, 10–15% by authors who are new to the magazine. Receives 100 queries yearly.

SUBMISSIONS AND PAYMENT: Sample copy, free with 9x12 SASE ($1.37 postage). Query. Accepts hard copy and email to khildebrand@dancemedia.com. SASE. Responds in 2 months. All rights. Articles, 1,000–2,000 words; $200–$300. Depts/columns, 700–1,200 words; $150–$250. Pays on publication. Provides 1 copy.

Dollhouse Miniatures

68132 250th Avenue
Kasson, MN 55944

Editor-in-Chief: Kelly Rud

DESCRIPTION AND INTERESTS: Six times each year, *Dollhouse Miniatures* informs, entertains, and inspires its audience of hobbyists of all levels of experience. It seeks unique projects with clear directions accompanied by step-by-step photos. Contributors must fully understand not only the hobby, but the magazine as well. Circ: 25,000. **Website: www.dhminiatures.com**

FREELANCE POTENTIAL: 30% written by non-staff writers. Publishes 8–10 freelance submissions yearly; 10% by unpublished writers, 30% by authors who are new to the magazine. Receives 60 queries yearly.

SUBMISSIONS AND PAYMENT: Sample copy, $6.95 with 9x12 SASE ($1.95 postage). Query with outline. Accepts hard copy and email queries to kelly@dhminiatures.com. SASE. Responds in 2 months. All rights. Articles and depts/columns, word lengths and payment rates vary. Pays on publication.

Dog Fancy

BowTie Inc.
P.O. Box 6050
Mission Viejo, CA 92690-6050

Editor: Ernie Slone

DESCRIPTION AND INTERESTS: *Dog Fancy* is devoted to all dogs, whether purebred or mixed breed. Published monthly, it seeks articles that cover training, canine health and behavior, and living happily with a dog. New contributors with fresh ideas are welcome to query. Circ: 270,000. **Website: www.dogfancy.com**

FREELANCE POTENTIAL: 95% written by non-staff writers. Publishes 20–25 freelance submissions yearly; 10% by authors who are new to the magazine. Receives 480 queries yearly.

SUBMISSIONS AND PAYMENT: Sample copy, $4.99 at newsstands. Guidelines available at website. Query with résumé, outline, and clips. Accepts email queries to barkback@dogfancy.com. Responds in 1 month. First North American serial rights. Articles, 1,000–1,600 words. Depts/columns, 650 words. Written material, payment rates vary. Pays on publication. Provides 2 contributor's copies.

Dolls

P.O. Box 5000
Iola, WI 54945-5000

Editor: Carie Ferg

DESCRIPTION AND INTERESTS: Doll collectors turn to this magazine for its comprehensive coverage of other doll collectors and collections, as well as articles on doll history and doll making. Product reviews and current prices are also included. This photo-filled magazine is published monthly. Circ: 10,000. **Website: www.dollsmagazine.com**

FREELANCE POTENTIAL: 75% written by non-staff writers. Publishes 50 freelance submissions yearly; 10% by authors who are new to the magazine. Receives 40 unsolicited mss yearly.

SUBMISSIONS AND PAYMENT: Send complete ms. Accepts email submissions to carief@jonespublishing.com. Availability of artwork improves chance of acceptance. Response time varies. One-time rights. Articles, 1,000–2,000 words; $200. Color prints, slides, or transparencies; JPEG images at 300 dpi. Pays on publication.

Dyslexia Online Magazine

P.O. Box 1111
Guilford GU1 9EH
United Kingdom

Submissions: John Bradford

DESCRIPTION AND INTERESTS: Parents, teachers, and caregivers of children with dyslexia turn to this online magazine for information as well as inspiration. Personal experience pieces from parents raising dyslexic children are especially sought at this time. Both current and archived articles are available at the website. Hits per month: 150,000.
Website: www.dyslexia-magazine.com

FREELANCE POTENTIAL: 25% written by non-staff writers. Publishes 10 freelance submissions yearly; 50% by unpublished writers, 50% by authors who are new to the magazine. Receives 12 unsolicited mss yearly.

SUBMISSIONS AND PAYMENT: Sample copy and writer's guidelines available at website. Send complete ms. Accepts email submissions to dyslextest@aol.com (no attachments). Responds in 2 weeks. All rights. Articles, word lengths vary. No payment.

Early Years

128 North Royal Avenue
Front Royal, VA 22630

Editor: Tia Gibbo

DESCRIPTION AND INTERESTS: *Early Years* is a newsletter for parents of preschool and kindergarten-aged children. Its brief articles offer practical advice on how to help youngsters get the most and best out of their early school experience. This newsletter is published nine times each year. Circ: 60,000.
Website: www.rfeonline.com

FREELANCE POTENTIAL: 100% written by nonstaff writers. Publishes 80 freelance submissions yearly; 28% by unpublished writers. Receives 36 queries yearly.

SUBMISSIONS AND PAYMENT: Sample copy, free with 9x12 SASE (2 first-class stamps). Query with résumé and clips. Accepts hard copy. SASE. Responds in 1 month. All rights. Articles, 225–300 words. Depts/columns, 175–200 words. Written material, $.60 per word. Pays on acceptance. Provides 5 contributor's copies.

Eco-Kids Magazine

P.O. Box 3306 Hermit Park
Townsville, Queensland 4812
Australia

Editor: Lynette Stein

DESCRIPTION AND INTERESTS: This monthly print magazine, along with the daily-updated website, form a green and eco-conscious community of readers worldwide. Both offer seasonally themed articles on topics such as healthy lifestyles and diets, and environmental issues. Profiles of young people who are actively involved in environmental causes are also featured. Circ: 30,000.
Website: www.ecobites.com

FREELANCE POTENTIAL: 30% written by nonstaff writers. Publishes 15 freelance submissions yearly; 25% by unpublished writers, 50% by authors who are new to the magazine.

SUBMISSIONS AND PAYMENT: Query or send complete ms. Accepts hard copy and electronic submissions through the website. SAE/IRC. Response time varies. Rights vary. Articles, word lengths and payment rates vary. Pays on publication. Provides 2 contributor's copies.

The Education Revolution

417 Roslyn Road
Roslyn Heights, NY 11577

Executive Editor: Jerry Mintz

DESCRIPTION AND INTERESTS: Read by educators, administrators, and parents alike, *The Education Revolution* offers the latest information on alternative education. Quarterly issues feature profiles of successful alternative schools, both public and private, and offer informative articles on homeschooling trends. News, conference and event details, and information about job opportunities are also included. It is published by the Alternative Education Resource Organization. Circ: 5,000.
Website: www.educationrevolution.org

FREELANCE POTENTIAL: 20% written by nonstaff writers. Publishes 10 freelance submissions yearly; 40% by authors who are new to the magazine. Receives 180 queries yearly.

SUBMISSIONS AND PAYMENT: Query. Accepts hard copy. SASE. Responds in 1 month. Rights vary. Articles and depts/columns, word lengths vary. No payment.

EFCA Today

418 Fourth Street NE
Charlottesville, VA 22902

Editor: Diane McDougall

DESCRIPTION AND INTERESTS: Written primarily by and for members of the Evangelical Free Church of America (EFCA), this quarterly focuses on spirituality and evangelism and the role they play in today's society. It publishes articles of interest to church pastors, elders, and deacons, while also targeting ministry volunteers and religious educators. Each issue focuses on a particular theme. Circ: 40,000.
Website: www.efcatoday.org

FREELANCE POTENTIAL: 80% written by nonstaff writers. Publishes several freelance submissions yearly.

SUBMISSIONS AND PAYMENT: Sample copy and guidelines, $1 with 9x12 SASE (5 first-class stamps). Query. Accepts email queries to dianemc@journeygroup.com. Response time varies. First rights. Articles, 200–700 words. Cover theme articles, 300–1,000 words. Written material, $.25 per word. Pays on acceptance.

The Elementary School Journal

University of Michigan, School of Education
610 East University Avenue, Suite 3210
Ann Arbor, MI 48109-1255

Editor: Joanne Carlisle

DESCRIPTION AND INTERESTS: This academic journal is published five times each year, offering articles on education theory and research. It is read and written by educators as well as researchers, and addresses the practical implications of the work presented. All content is peer-reviewed. Circ: 2,200.
Website: www.journals.uchicago.edu/ESJ

FREELANCE POTENTIAL: 100% written by nonstaff writers. Publishes several freelance submissions yearly.

SUBMISSIONS AND PAYMENT: Sample copy, $13.50. Guidelines available at website. Send 4 copies of complete ms with abstract of 100–150 words. Accepts hard copy. SASE. Response time varies. Rights vary. Written material, word lengths vary. No payment.

Encyclopedia of Youth Studies

130 Essex Street
South Hamilton, MA 01982

Editor: Dean Borgman

DESCRIPTION AND INTERESTS: This website, updated regularly, serves as an innovative educational and ministerial resource to those adults who mentor, minister to, study, or otherwise support the world's youth. Its articles summarize topics related to the education of or service to youth, and provide advice, and offer support. Hits per month: Unavailable.
Website: www.centerforyouth.org

FREELANCE POTENTIAL: 20% written by nonstaff writers. Publishes 5–10 freelance submissions yearly; 85% by unpublished writers, 85% by authors who are new to the magazine. Receives 48 queries, 12 unsolicited mss yearly.

SUBMISSIONS AND PAYMENT: Sample copy and guidelines available at website. Query or send complete ms. Accepts email submissions to cys@centerforyouth.org. Responds to queries in 1 week, to mss in 1 month. All rights. Articles, 600 words. No payment.

Entertainment Magazine

P.O. Box 3355
Tucson, AZ 85722

Publisher: Robert Zucker

DESCRIPTION AND INTERESTS: This online magazine provides daily updates on all aspects of the entertainment industry. Included are profiles and interviews, movie and TV updates, and other entertainment news of worldwide interest. Please note that this e-zine does not publish material promoting products or businesses. Hits per month: 500,000+.
Website: www.emol.org

FREELANCE POTENTIAL: 60% written by nonstaff writers. Publishes dozens of freelance submissions yearly; 75% by unpublished writers, 25% by authors who are new to the magazine. Receives 100+ queries yearly.

SUBMISSIONS AND PAYMENT: Sample copy and guidelines available at website. Query. Accepts email queries to emol@emol.org. Responds in 1–2 days. Author retains rights. Articles, to 1,000 words. B/W digital images. No payment.

Equestrian

4047 Iron Works Parkway
Lexington, KY 40511

Editor: Brian Sosby

DESCRIPTION AND INTERESTS: The United States Equestrian Federation publishes this magazine for its members, offering them comprehensive coverage of federation events, news, and competitions. Appearing 10 times each year, it also features articles on horse health, breeding, and training. Circ: 90,000.
Website: www.usef.org

FREELANCE POTENTIAL: 50% written by non-staff writers. Publishes 50 freelance submissions yearly; 10% by authors who are new to the magazine. Receives 200 queries yearly.

SUBMISSIONS AND PAYMENT: Sample copy and guidelines available. Query with résumé and writing samples. Accepts email queries to bsosby@usef.org. Responds in 1 week. First rights. Articles, 2,000–3,000 words. Depts/columns, 500–1,000 words. Written material, payment rates vary. Kill fee, 50%. Pays on publication. Provides 1 contributor's copy.

Family Health & Life

2680 Matheson Boulevard, Suite 102
Mississauga, Ontario L4W 0A5
Canada

Publisher & Editor-in-Chief: Ian Khan

DESCRIPTION AND INTERESTS: In addition to general articles on health and well-being, this magazine presents information on alternative health modalities for residents of the greater Toronto area. Natural healing and medicine, yoga, massage therapy, green living, and meditation are among the topics covered. Writers who are passionate about health issues are welcome to query; they may also be considered for regular writing or columnist positions. Circ: 5,000.
Website: www.thefamilymag.com

FREELANCE POTENTIAL: Publishes several freelance submissions yearly.

SUBMISSIONS AND PAYMENT: Sample copy and guidelines available at website. Query with clips. Accepts email queries to contact@thefamilymag.com. Response time varies. Rights vary. Articles, 500–2,000 words. Depts/columns, word lengths vary. Written material, payment rates vary. Payment policy varies.

eSchoolNews

7920 Norfolk Avenue, Suite 900
Bethesda, MD 20814

Editor: Gregg Downey

DESCRIPTION AND INTERESTS: *eSchoolNews* is a print and online magazine for teachers and school administrators at all grade levels. Its articles cover technology-related topics such as software, systems, and websites. It offers product reviews, resources for professional development and the classroom, as well as technology industry news and trends. It is published/updated monthly. Hits per month: 100,000.
Website: www.eschoolnews.com

FREELANCE POTENTIAL: 20% written by non-staff writers. Publishes 6–8 freelance submissions yearly. Receives 100 unsolicited mss yearly.

SUBMISSIONS AND PAYMENT: Sample copy available at website. Prefers query; will accept complete ms. Accepts hard copy and email submissions to gdowney@eschoolnews.com. SASE. Response time varies. Rights vary. Articles and depts/columns, word lengths and payment rates vary. Pays on acceptance.

Family Life Magazine

100 Professional Center Drive, Suite 104
Rohnert Park, CA 94928

Publisher/Editor: Sharon Gowan

DESCRIPTION AND INTERESTS: *Family Life* is for families living in California's Sonoma, Mendocino, and Lake counties. Its monthly issues provide information about education, health, parenting, and regional recreation. Professionals who write on a subject of expertise receive credit in lieu of payment. Circ: 40,000.
Website: www.family-life.us

FREELANCE POTENTIAL: 40% written by non-staff writers. Publishes 24–36 freelance submissions yearly; 10% by unpublished writers. Receives 120+ unsolicited mss yearly.

SUBMISSIONS AND PAYMENT: Guidelines and editorial calendar available. Send complete ms. Accepts hard copy and email submissions to sharon@family-life.us (in body of email or as Microsoft Word attachment). Response time varies. All rights. Written material, 650–1,150 words; $.08 per word. Reprints, $35–$50. Pays on publication. Provides 1 contributor's copy.

Family Motor Coaching

8291 Clough Pike
Cincinnati, OH 45244

Editor: Robbin Gould

DESCRIPTION AND INTERESTS: This monthly magazine is for families who travel by motor home and RV. It covers topics from vehicle maintenance to destination ideas. Circ: 110,000.
Website: www.fmca.com

FREELANCE POTENTIAL: 75% written by nonstaff writers. Publishes 50 freelance submissions yearly; 10% by unpublished writers, 10% by authors who are new to the magazine. Receives 600 queries, 300 unsolicited mss yearly.

SUBMISSIONS AND PAYMENT: Sample copy and guidelines, $3.99. Prefers query with résumé, outline, and clips; will accept complete ms with résumé. Accepts hard copy and email submissions to magazine@fmca.com. SASE. Response time varies. First North American serial and electronic rights. Articles, 1,200–2,000 words. Depts/columns, 1,000 words. Written material, $50–$500. Pays on acceptance. Provides 1 contributor's copy.

Family Time for You And Your Crew

P.O. Box 334
Selbyville, DE 19975

Publisher: Caine Boyden

DESCRIPTION AND INTERESTS: Serving families in Delaware's Sussex County region, this magazine is published five times each year in print and online. It features parenting information on everything from finding a preschool to planning for college, plus articles on home and gardening topics, family travel, and the many family-friendly destinations in the area. Although it cannot offer payment for accepted submissions, it hopes to do so in the future. Local articles will trump all others. Circ: Unavailable.
Website: www.familytimemag.biz

FREELANCE POTENTIAL: Publishes 12–24 freelance submissions yearly. Receives 48–60 queries, 4–5 unsolicited mss yearly.

SUBMISSIONS AND PAYMENT: Sample copy available at website. Prefers query; will accept unsolicited mss. Accepts email to info@ familytimemag.biz. Response time varies. Rights vary. Articles, 500–700 words. No payment.

Family Safety & Health

1121 Spring Lake Drive
Itasca, IL 60143

Editor: Tim Hodson

DESCRIPTION AND INTERESTS: Published quarterly by the National Safety Council, *Family Safety & Health* is known as "the official magazine for off-the-job safety," although it does report on all safety concerns relevant to families. Experienced writers should introduce themselves with a résumé and clips in order to be considered for an assignment. Circ: 225,000.
Website: www.nsc.org

FREELANCE POTENTIAL: 1% written by nonstaff writers. Publishes 5 freelance submissions yearly; 20% by authors who are new to the magazine.

SUBMISSIONS AND PAYMENT: Sample copy, $4 with 9x12 SASE ($.77 postage). No queries or unsolicited mss; send résumé and clips only. All assignments are made on a work-for-hire basis. Accepts hard copy. All rights. Articles, 1,200 words; payment rate varies. Pays on acceptance. Provides 2 contributor's copies.

Family Tree Magazine

4700 East Galbraith Road
Cincinnati, OH 45236

Editor: Allison Stacy

DESCRIPTION AND INTERESTS: Readers with a new found interest in family history research find beginner-friendly articles in *Family Tree*. Published seven times each year, it seeks articles written in a non-academic style. Circ: 60,000.
Website: www.familytreemagazine.com

FREELANCE POTENTIAL: 90% written by nonstaff writers. Publishes several freelance submissions yearly; 5% by unpublished writers, 5% by authors who are new to the magazine. Receives 480 queries yearly.

SUBMISSIONS AND PAYMENT: Sample copy, $6 at www.shopfamilytree.com. Guidelines available at website. Query with clips. Accepts hard copy and email queries to ftmedit@fwmedia.com. SASE. Responds in 3 months. All rights. Articles, 2,000–3,500 words. Depts/columns, 300–1,000 words. Written material, payment rates vary. Kill fee, 25%. Pays on acceptance. Provides 2 contributor's copies.

Farm & Ranch Living

5925 Country Lane
Greendale, WI 53129

Editor

DESCRIPTION AND INTERESTS: Farming and ranching families read and write this lifestyle magazine featuring articles, profiles, and photo-essays in issues appearing six times each year. A kids' section is also included. Circ: 350,000.
Website: www.farmandranchliving.com

FREELANCE POTENTIAL: 90% written by non-staff writers. Publishes 36 freelance submissions yearly; 50% by unpublished writers, 50% by authors who are new to the magazine. Receives 120 queries and unsolicited mss yearly.

SUBMISSIONS AND PAYMENT: Sample copy, $2. Query or send complete ms. Accepts hard copy and email submissions to editors@ farmandranchliving.com. Availability of artwork improves chance of acceptance. SASE. Responds in 6 weeks. One-time rights. Articles, 1,200 words. Depts/columns, 350 words. Color prints. Written material, $10–$150. Pays on publication. Provides 1 contributor's copy.

FatherMag.com

P.O. Box 231891
Houston, TX 77223

Managing Editor: John Gill

DESCRIPTION AND INTERESTS: Fatherhood from all angles is explored in this online magazine. Offering articles, short stories, poetry, interviews, reviews, and humor, *FatherMag.com* is a source of practical advice, inspiration, and support for dads living with or without their children. Separate "strife" and "life" sections address the challenges and joys of being a dad. Submissions are welcome from anyone who has something worthwhile to say about fatherhood. Hits per month: 1 million.
Website: www.fathermag.com

FREELANCE POTENTIAL: 95% written by non-staff writers. Publishes 50 freelance submissions yearly; 50% by authors new to the magazine.

SUBMISSIONS AND PAYMENT: Sample copy and guidelines available at website. Query. Accepts email queries through website only. Response time varies. One-time rights. Articles and fiction, word lengths vary. No payment.

Fido Friendly

P.O. Box 160
Marsing, ID 83639

Submissions: Claudine Randazzo

DESCRIPTION AND INTERESTS: Appearing six times each year, this magazine is read by dog owners looking for information about pet-friendly travel destinations in the U.S. and Canada. Also published are articles on canine health and wellness, behavior and training, and even fashions for Fido. Circ: 44,000.
Website: www.fidofriendly.com

FREELANCE POTENTIAL: 75% written by non-staff writers. Publishes 20 freelance submissions yearly; 10% by unpublished writers, 10% by authors who are new to the magazine. Receives 100 queries yearly.

SUBMISSIONS AND PAYMENT: Sample copy, $5 with 9x12 SASE (4 first-class stamps). Query with sample paragraph. Accepts email queries to editorial@fidofriendly.com. Responds in 1 month. First rights. Articles, 800–1,200 words; $.10 per word. Pays on publication. Provides 1 contributor's copy.

FineScale Modeler

21027 Crossroads Circle
P.O. Box 1612
Waukesha, WI 53187

Editor: Matthew Usher

DESCRIPTION AND INTERESTS: Appearing 10 times each year, this magazine is read for its detailed and well-illustrated how-to articles on scale modeling. Readers are beginners as well as advanced enthusiasts. Circ: 60,000.
Website: www.finescale.com

FREELANCE POTENTIAL: 85% written by non-staff writers. Publishes 40 freelance submissions yearly; 20% by authors who are new to the magazine. Receives 200 queries yearly.

SUBMISSIONS AND PAYMENT: Sample copy and guidelines available at website. Prefers query; will accept complete ms with bio. Accepts hard copy and disk submissions with hard copy. No simultaneous submissions. Availability of artwork improves chance of acceptance. SASE. Responds in 1–4 months. All rights. Articles, 750–3,000 words. Digital photos, slides, prints, and scale drawings. All material, payment rates vary. Pays on acceptance. Provides 1 copy.

Fort Lauderdale Family Magazine

7045 SW 69th Avenue
South Miami, FL 33143

Publisher: Janet Jupiter

DESCRIPTION AND INTERESTS: Parents living in Fort Lauderdale and its environs read this magazine for articles on child care, family finances, relationships, education, health, safety, fitness, and pets. Local event coverage, movie reviews, recreation ideas, and product information are also featured in monthly issues. All content has a regional focus. Circ: Unavailable.
Website: www.familymagazine.biz

FREELANCE POTENTIAL: 30% written by nonstaff writers. Publishes 15–20 freelance submissions yearly.

SUBMISSIONS AND PAYMENT: Sample copy available at website. Query. Accepts hard copy and email queries to familymag@bellsouth.net. SASE. Response time varies. One-time rights. Articles and depts/columns, word lengths vary; payment rates vary. Pays on publication. Provides contributor's copies.

Gay Parent Magazine

P.O. Box 750852
Forest Hills, NY 11375-0852

Editor: Angeline Acain

DESCRIPTION AND INTERESTS: Published six times each year, this magazine is filled with articles that address parenting issues faced by LGBT parents. It also provides helpful resources for choosing private schools, day and overnight camps, and vacation spots. Circ: 10,000.
Website: www.gayparentmag.com

FREELANCE POTENTIAL: 3% written by nonstaff writers. Publishes 6 freelance submissions yearly; 1% by authors who are new to the magazine. Receives 75 mss yearly.

SUBMISSIONS AND PAYMENT: Sample copy and guidelines, $3.50. Send complete ms. Accepts email submissions to gayparentmag@gmail.com. Artwork improves chance of acceptance. Response time varies. One-time rights. Articles, 500–1,000 words; $.10 per word. Color prints or digital images; payment rates vary. Pays on publication. Provides contributor's copies.

Georgia Family Magazine

523 Sioux Drive
Macon, GA 31210

Publisher: Olya Fessard

DESCRIPTION AND INTERESTS: This monthly parenting magazine delivers information on all topics related to parenting, child development, family relationships, and family recreation. It looks for well-developed storylines, careful research, and independent reporting, and it prefers articles about parenting concerns in central Georgia. Circ: 20,000.
Website: www.georgiafamily.com

FREELANCE POTENTIAL: 60% written by nonstaff writers. Publishes 100–125 freelance submissions yearly.

SUBMISSIONS AND PAYMENT: Send complete ms. Accepts email submissions to georgiafamilymagazine@gmail.com. Responds only if interested. One-time, reprint, and electronic rights. Articles and depts/columns, word lengths vary. Written material, $20–$90 for original work, $10–$30 for reprints. Pays on publication. Provides 1 tearsheet.

GirlMogul Magazine

309 Main Street
Lebanon, NJ 08833

Editor: Andrea Stein

DESCRIPTION AND INTERESTS: This online community site was created to appeal to tween girls between the ages of seven and thirteen who are interested in becoming community leaders, activists, and entrepreneurs. It looks for age-appropriate, witty content that encourages girls to pursue their dreams. Games, quizzes, do-it-yourself projects, and book clubs are part of the mix. Hits per month: Unavailable.
Website: www.girlmogul.com

FREELANCE POTENTIAL: 15–20% written by nonstaff writers. Publishes several freelance submissions yearly.

SUBMISSIONS AND PAYMENT: Sample copy available. Query with author bio; or send complete ms. Accepts hard copy and email submissions to andrea@girlmogul.com. No simultaneous submissions. SASE. Response time varies. First rights. Written material, word lengths vary. No payment. Provides 2 contributor's copies.

Go! Magazine

2711 South Loop Drive, Suite 4700
Ames, IA 50010

Editor: Marcia Brink

DESCRIPTION AND INTERESTS: This is an online magazine for teens and young adults who are interested in a career in transportation. Updated six times each year by Iowa State University's Institute for Transportation, it covers everything from the infrastructure of vehicles to the people behind the wheel. All articles are staff-written, but young writers (ages 14 to 20) may submit essays or opinion pieces to the "Teen POV" column regarding driving or transportation issues. Hits per month: Unavailable.
Website: www.go-explore-trans.org

FREELANCE POTENTIAL: Publishes 2 freelance submissions yearly.

SUBMISSIONS AND PAYMENT: Sample copy, guidelines, and theme list available at website. Query. Accepts email queries to editor@ go-explore-trans.com. Response time varies. First world electronic and archival rights. "Teen POV" column, 500 words; $50. Payment policy varies.

Good Housekeeping

Hearst Corporation
300 West 57th Street, 28th Floor
New York, NY 10019-5288

Executive Editor: Judith Coyne

DESCRIPTION AND INTERESTS:
Understanding the challenges women face in balancing family, housework, and time for theselves, this monthly informs and supports readers with articles on everything from home and gardening tips to parenting issues. Circ: 25 million.
Website: www.goodhousekeeping.com

FREELANCE POTENTIAL: 80% written by non-staff writers. Publishes 50+ freelance submissions yearly. Receives 18,000–24,000 queries yearly.

SUBMISSIONS AND PAYMENT: Sample copy, $2.50 at newsstands. Query with résumé and clips for nonfiction. Send complete ms for fiction; mss not returned. Accepts hard copy. SASE. Responds in 4–6 weeks. All rights for nonfiction; first North American serial rights for fiction. Articles, 750–2,500 words; to $2,000. Essays, to 1,000 words; to $750. Fiction, to 3,000 words; payment rates vary. Pays on acceptance. Provides 1 contributor's copy.

Grandparents.com

24 Union Square East, 5th Floor
New York, NY 10003

Editor

DESCRIPTION AND INTERESTS: *Grandparents.com* serves as a hub of information for engaged and involved grandparents, offering ideas for entertaining and educational activities that grandparents and grandchildren can do together. It also features essays, interviews, and reviews of toys, games, books, gear, movies, and other family-friendly products. The editors are always looking for fresh, new story ideas and freelance writers to add to their editorial team. Hits per month: Unavailable.
Website: www.grandparents.com

FREELANCE POTENTIAL: Publishes several freelance submissions yearly.

SUBMISSIONS AND PAYMENT: Sample copy and writer's guidelines available at website. Query. Accepts email queries to contribute@ grandparents.com. Response time varies. Electronic rights. Articles, word lengths vary. No payment.

Grand Rapids Family

549 Ottawa Avenue NW, Suite 201
Grand Rapids, MI 49503-1444

Editor: Carole Valade

DESCRIPTION AND INTERESTS: Families living in western Michigan read this publication for news about local events and activities; travel ideas; professional and medical advice; and book, movie, and play reviews. *Grand Rapids Family* also presents feature articles on child care and education, as well as profiles and interviews featuring local personalities. It appears monthly. Circ: 30,000.
Website: www.grfamily.com

FREELANCE POTENTIAL: 20% written by non-staff writers. Publishes 15 freelance submissions each year.

SUBMISSIONS AND PAYMENT: Guidelines available with #10 SASE. Query or send complete ms. Accepts hard copy. SASE. Responds to queries in 2 months, to mss in 6 months. All rights. Articles and depts/columns, word lengths and payment rates vary. B/W or color prints, $25. Kill fee, $25. Pays on publication.

Grit

1503 SW 42nd Street
Topeka, KS 66609-1265

Editor-in-Chief: K. C. Compton

DESCRIPTION AND INTERESTS: Six times each year, *Grit* brings readers articles about living a self-sustaining rural life and raising a family "off the grid." Circ: 150,000.
Website: www.grit.com

FREELANCE POTENTIAL: 90% written by non-staff writers. Publishes 80–90 freelance submissions yearly; 50% by unpublished writers, 50% by authors who are new to the magazine. Receives 2,400 queries yearly.

SUBMISSIONS AND PAYMENT: Sample copy and editorial calendar, $4 with 9x12 SASE. Guidelines available at website. Query. Prefers email queries to grit@grit.com (include "Query" in subject line); will accept hard copy. SASE. Response time varies. Shared rights. Articles, and depts/columns, to 1,500 words; $.35 per word. 35mm color prints and slides, and digital images; $35–$175. Pays on publication. Provides 3 contributor's copies.

Guardian Angel Kids

Editor-in-Chief: Jennifer Bond Reed

DESCRIPTION AND INTERESTS: This interactive e-zine, launched in 2010, offers original fiction, nonfiction, and poetry for children ages 2 to 12. Part of Guardian Angel Publishing, it also features games and activities based on characters from Guardian Angel Books. Themed issues appear monthly. Adventure, multicultural, and problem-solving fiction is welcome; nonfiction topics include science, math, animals, and cooking. Hits per month: Unavailable.
Website: www.guardian-angel-kids.com

FREELANCE POTENTIAL: Publishes several freelance submissions yearly.

SUBMISSIONS AND PAYMENT: Sample copy, theme list, and guidelines available at website. Send ms. Accepts email to submissions@ guardian-angel-kids.com (no attachments). Response time varies. All rights. Articles and fiction, to 500 words; $.03 per word. Poetry, $10. Pays within 30 days of publication.

Healthy Mom & Baby Magazine

1208 Weston Pine Circle
Sarasota, FL 34240

Editor: Carolyn Davis Cockey

DESCRIPTION AND INTERESTS: Designed for expectant and new mothers, this quarterly magazine addresses all the issues, topics, and challenges associated with pregnancy and caring for a newborn. It is usually distributed by nurses to women in a healthcare setting. Prospective writers must be experts in the medical or wellness fields. New authors can find the best chance of acceptance through pitching an expert advice column. Circ: 300,000.
Website: www.Health4Mom.org

FREELANCE POTENTIAL: 50% written by non-staff writers. Of the freelance submissions published yearly, 10% is by authors who are new to the magazine.

SUBMISSIONS AND PAYMENT: Sample copy, $3.99. Query. Accepts hard copy. SASE. Response time varies. Rights vary. Written material, word lengths and payment rates vary. Payment policy varies.

Highlights High Five ✖

807 Church Street
Honesdale, PA 18431-1895

Editor: Kathleen Hayes

DESCRIPTION AND INTERESTS: Designed for use in preschool classrooms and daycare centers as well as in the home, *Highlights High Five* shares the philosophy of the Highlights Foundation that "children are the world's most important people." Its stories and activities, which target kids ages two through six, are created to promote reasoning, problem solving, and creative self-expression; foster a love of language; and encourage a sense of wonder about the world. While most of the magazine's regular features continue to be written in-house, other content is commissioned; therefore, its "no freelance" policy remains in effect for another year. Circ: Unavailable.
Website: www.highlights.com

FREELANCE POTENTIAL: Publishes few freelance submissions yearly.

SUBMISSIONS AND PAYMENT: Not accepting freelance submissions at this time.

The High School Journal

Editorial Office, School of Education
University of North Carolina, CB#6215
116 South Boundary Street
Chapel Hill, NC 27514-3808

Managing Editor: Meredith Sinclair

DESCRIPTION AND INTERESTS: This professional, scholarly journal publishes well-researched articles dealing with adolescent growth, development, interests, beliefs, values, and learning as they affect school practice. Published quarterly, it is read by high school administrators and teachers. Circ: 800.
Website: www.uncpress.unc.edu

FREELANCE POTENTIAL: 100% written by nonstaff writers. Publishes 20–30 freelance submissions yearly; 25% by unpublished writers, 85% by authors who are new to the magazine. Receives 324 unsolicited mss yearly.

SUBMISSIONS AND PAYMENT: Sample copy, $7.50 with 9x12 SASE. Send 3 copies of complete ms. Accepts email submissions to msinclai@email.unc.edu. Responds in 3–4 months. All rights. Articles, 1,500–2,500 words. Depts/columns, 300–400 words. No payment. Provides 3 contributor's copies.

High School Years

128 North Royal Avenue
Front Royal, VA 22630

Submissions Editor: Jennifer Hutchinson

DESCRIPTION AND INTERESTS: Distributed monthly to parents by subscribing high schools, this newsletter features topics such as improving school success, parenting skills, and challenges facing teens. Currently, it is not accepting submissions. Email rfecustomer@wolterskluwer.com for updates to the policy. Circ: 300,000.
Website: www.rfeonline.com

FREELANCE POTENTIAL: 100% written by nonstaff writers. Publishes 80 freelance submissions yearly; 25% by unpublished writers. Receives 36 unsolicited mss yearly.

SUBMISSIONS AND PAYMENT: Sample copy, guidelines, and editorial calendar, free with 9x12 SASE. Query with résumé and clips when submissions reopen. Accepts hard copy. SASE. Responds in 1 month. All rights. Articles, 225–300 words. Depts/columns, 175–200 words. Written material, $.60 per word. Pays on acceptance. Provides 5 contributor's copies.

Hip Mama

P.O. Box 82539
Portland, OR 97202

Editor: Kerlin Richter

DESCRIPTION AND INTERESTS: A reader-written magazine, *Hip Mama* targets parents who are outside of the mainstream. Young parents, gay parents, and homeschooling parents are among its readership. Published on an irregular basis, it looks for daring, honest essays about family life. Circ: 5,000.
Website: www.hipmamazine.com

FREELANCE POTENTIAL: 100% written by nonstaff writers. Publishes 32–48 freelance submissions yearly. Receives 60–70 unsolicited mss each year.

SUBMISSIONS AND PAYMENT: Sample copy, $5.95. Guidelines and theme list available at website. Send complete ms. Accepts email submissions to submissions@hipmamazine.com (Microsoft Word attachments). Responds in 1 month. Rights vary. Articles, 250–1,500 words. B/W prints, digital images in JPEG format; line art. No payment.

Home & School Connection

128 North Royal Avenue
Front Royal, VA 22630

Submissions: Matt McGraff

DESCRIPTION AND INTERESTS: This newsletter written for parents of elementary school students is filled with ideas that families can use to promote school success. Published monthly, it is written by a team of educators and journalists. Although it is not reviewing manuscripts or queries, prospective writers are invited to submit their résumé to be considered for future work. Circ: Unavailable.
Website: www.rfeonline.com

FREELANCE POTENTIAL: 100% written by nonstaff writers. Publishes 80 freelance submissions yearly; 28% by unpublished writers, 14% by authors who are new to the magazine.

SUBMISSIONS AND PAYMENT: Sample copy, free with 9x12 SASE (2 first-class stamps). All work is assigned. Send résumé. Accepts hard copy. Responds if interested. Rights vary. Articles and depts/columns, word lengths and payment rates vary. Pays on acceptance. Provides 5 copies.

Home Times Family Newspaper

P.O. Box 22547
West Palm Beach, FL 33416

Editor: Dennis Lombard

DESCRIPTION AND INTERESTS: This monthly, distributed in the Palm Beach and Treasure Coast areas of Florida, provides "information and encouragement for people of faith and values." It currently seeks parenting advice, articles about young adults, and "people stories." Circ: 4,000.
Website: www.hometimesnewspaper.org

FREELANCE POTENTIAL: 80% written by non-staff writers. Publishes 25 freelance submissions yearly; 10% by unpublished writers, 10% by authors who are new to the magazine. Receives 300 unsolicited mss yearly.

SUBMISSIONS AND PAYMENT: Sample copy and guidelines, $3. Send complete ms. Accepts hard copy and simultaneous submissions if identified. SASE. Responds in 1 month. One-time print and electronic rights. Articles, to 1,000 words; $5–$25. Depts/columns, word lengths and payment rates vary. Pays on publication. Provides contributor's copies upon request.

Horse Illustrated

P.O. Box 8237
Lexington, KY 40533

Editor: Elizabeth Moyer

DESCRIPTION AND INTERESTS: This glossy monthly magazine targets horse owners as well as riders. Both Western and English disciplines are covered. Circ: 200,000.
Website: www.horseillustrated.com

FREELANCE POTENTIAL: 80% written by nonstaff writers. Publishes 10–20 freelance submissions yearly. Receives 480 queries, 240 unsolicited mss yearly.

SUBMISSIONS AND PAYMENT: Guidelines available. Prefers complete ms; will accept query with detailed outline, resources, and clips. Accepts hard copy. No simultaneous submissions. Availability of artwork improves chance of acceptance. SASE. Responds in 2–3 months. First North American serial rights. Articles, 1,500–2,000 words; $300–$425. Depts/columns, 1,000–1,400 words; $50–$100. High-resolution digital images; payment rates vary. Pays on publication. Provides 2 contributor's copies.

Horse & Rider

2000 South Stemmons Freeway, Suite 101
Lake Dallas, TX 75065

Associate Editor: Debbie Moors

DESCRIPTION AND INTERESTS: This monthly magazine seeks to educate, inform, and entertain both competitive and recreational Western riders. It seeks tightly focused articles on training, practical stable management techniques, hands-on health care tips, and safe trail riding practices. Circ: 165,000.
Website: www.horseandrider.com

FREELANCE POTENTIAL: 15% written by non-staff writers. Publishes 20–30 freelance submissions yearly; 3% by unpublished writers, 1% by authors who are new to the magazine. Receives 120 queries yearly.

SUBMISSIONS AND PAYMENT: Sample copy and guidelines, $3.50. Query. Accepts hard copy. No simultaneous submissions. SASE. Responds in 3 months. All rights. Articles, 600–1,200 words. Depts/columns, to 900 words. Written material, $25–$400. Pays on acceptance. Provides 1 contributor's copy.

Houston Family Magazine

5131 Braesvalley
Houston, TX 77096

Editor: Dana Donovan

DESCRIPTION AND INTERESTS: *Houston Family Magazine* focuses on practical information that Texas parents can use in their everyday family life. Published monthly, it offers articles on a wide variety of topics, such as child care, education, recreation, and travel—all written from a regional perspective. Circ: 60,000.
Website: www.houstonfamilymagazine.com

FREELANCE POTENTIAL: 20% written by nonstaff writers. Publishes 20 freelance submissions yearly; 25% by authors who are new to the magazine.

SUBMISSIONS AND PAYMENT: Sample copy and guidelines available at website. Query or send complete ms. Accepts email submissions to editor@houstonfamilymagazine.com. Response time varies. First and limited-time electronic rights. Articles and depts/columns, word lengths and payment rates vary. Pays on publication. Provides 2 contributor's copies.

I.D.

Cook Communications Ministries
4050 Lee Vance View
Colorado Springs, CO 80918

Editor: Doug Mauss

DESCRIPTION AND INTERESTS: High school students are the target audience for this weekly Sunday school take-home paper. Each issue offers Bible stories that are connected to lessons and activities focusing on contemporary topics of importance to teens. Discussions of school issues, community service, careers, and relationships are included. Authors are encouraged to check the website regularly for updated submission information. Circ: 50,000.
Website: www.davidccook.com

FREELANCE POTENTIAL: 20% written by non-staff writers.

SUBMISSIONS AND PAYMENT: Guidelines available. Send résumé only; no queries or unsolicited mss. All work is assigned. Accepts hard copy. SASE. Responds if interested. Rights vary. Articles, 600–1,200 words; $50–$300. B/W and color prints; payment rates vary. Pays on acceptance. Provides 1 contributor's copy.

Impact Magazine

3419 East Broadway, Suite F
Pearland, TX 77581

Marketing Director: Jessica Perro

DESCRIPTION AND INTERESTS: This new monthly regional magazine gives its readers—parents and professionals living in the greater Houston area—articles that are focused on raising a family, owning a home, going out on the town, and running a business in the region. As a start-up publication, it is actively seeking ambitious writers, both previously published and new authors, to add to its editorial mix. Circ: Unavailable.
Website: www.impactmagazinehouston.com

FREELANCE POTENTIAL: 90% written by non-staff writers. Publishes 70 freelance submissions yearly; 70% by unpublished writers, 90% by authors who are new to the magazine.

SUBMISSIONS AND PAYMENT: Guidelines and editorial calendar available at website. Query with résumé. Accepts hard copy and email queries to jessica_perro@yahoo.com. SASE. Response time varies. Rights vary. Written material, word lengths vary. No payment.

I Love Cats

1040 First Avenue, Suite 323
New York, NY 10022

Editor: Lisa Allmendinger

DESCRIPTION AND INTERESTS: For more than 20 years, *I Love Cats* has celebrated feline companionship by offering profiles of owners and cats, articles on health and behavior, and stories about life with cats. Published six times each year, it is more likely to accept articles accompanied by JPEG images. Circ: 25,000.
Website: www.iluvcats.com

FREELANCE POTENTIAL: 50% written by non-staff writers. Publishes 50 freelance submissions yearly; 60% by unpublished writers, 70% by authors who are new to the magazine. Receives 6,000 unsolicited mss yearly.

SUBMISSIONS AND PAYMENT: Sample copy and guidelines, $5.95 with 9x12 SASE. Send complete ms. Accepts email to ilovecatseditor@sbcglobal.net. Responds in 1–2 months. All rights. Articles and fiction, 500–1,000 words; $50–$100. JPEG images; payment rates vary. Pays on publication. Provides 1 author's copy.

Indian Life Newspaper

P.O. Box 3765
Redwood Post Office
Winnipeg, Manitoba R2W 3R6
Canada

Editor: Jim Uttley

DESCRIPTION AND INTERESTS: Published by Indian Life Ministries, this newspaper covers the social, cultural, and spiritual issues facing Native North Americans in the U.S. and Canada. All material should have a Christ-based perspective. Native writers, while not used exclusively, are preferred. It is published six times each year. Circ: 20,000.
Website: www.indianlife.org

FREELANCE POTENTIAL: 80% written by non-staff writers. Publishes 20 freelance submissions yearly; 10% by unpublished writers, 40% by authors who are new to the magazine. Receives 300 unsolicited mss yearly.

SUBMISSIONS AND PAYMENT: Sample copy, $3 with #9 SAE. Prefers query; will accept complete ms. Accepts hard copy and disk submissions. SAE (no IRC). Responds in 1 month. First rights. Articles, 250–2,000 words; $.15 per word, to $150. Pays on publication. Provides 3 copies.

Inkling Magazine

Managing Online Editor: Meera Lee Sethi

DESCRIPTION AND INTERESTS: Self-described as an "offbeat science magazine," *Inkling* is written for science lovers who reject technical jargon. The e-zine, updated frequently, leans heavily toward the life sciences. Tackling scientific research, ideas, history, and people, *Inkling* reveals humorous details that are often omitted from more formal reporting. It currently seeks features, profiles, and Q&As that "have color, context, and a strong narrative." Hits per month: Unavailable.
Website: www.inklingmagazine.com

FREELANCE POTENTIAL: Publishes several freelance submissions yearly.

SUBMISSIONS AND PAYMENT: Sample copy and guidelines available at website. Query or send complete ms. Accepts email submissions to meera@inklingmagazine.com. Responds in 1–2 weeks. Rights vary. Articles, 300–1,500 words. No payment.

Inside Kung-Fu

Action Pursuit Group
2400 East Katella Avenue, #300
Anaheim, CA 92806

Editor: Dave Cater

DESCRIPTION AND INTERESTS: Each monthly issue of *Inside Kung-Fu* offers articles on traditional forms of fighting and weaponry. It also features pieces about the history of this Chinese-style martial art, along with profiles of master martial artists. It is read by beginners and experts. Circ: 65,000.
Website: www.insidekung-fu.com

FREELANCE POTENTIAL: 75% written by non-staff writers. Publishes 120 freelance submissions yearly; 50% by unpublished writers, 50% by authors who are new to the magazine. Receives 1,000 queries yearly.

SUBMISSIONS AND PAYMENT: Sample copy and guidelines, $2.95 with 9x12 SASE. Query. Accepts hard copy and email queries to dcater@beckett.com. SASE. Responds in 4–6 weeks. First rights. Articles, 1,500 words. Depts/columns, 750 words. Written material, payment rates vary. Pays on publication.

Inspired Mother

The Design Center
10816 Millington Court, Suite 110
Cincinnati, OH 45242

Editor: Jennifer Hogan Redmond

DESCRIPTION AND INTERESTS: Both the personal and professional sides of mothers are explored in this monthly online magazine. Readers find profiles of moms who are successfully raising their children in today's world, as well as inspiration for themselves. Humor is always welcome, as are book and product reviews. Hits per month: Unavailable.
Website: www.inspiredmother.com

FREELANCE POTENTIAL: 40% written by non-staff writers. Publishes 15–30 freelance submissions yearly; 15% by unpublished writers, 75% by authors who are new to the magazine.

SUBMISSIONS AND PAYMENT: Sample copy and guidelines available at website. Send complete ms. Accepts hard copy and email submissions to editor@inspiredmother.com. SASE. Response time varies. Limited-time electronic rights. Featured articles, to 1,500 words. Short stories and narratives, to 750 words. No payment.

Irish's Story Playhouse

1500 West Lovers Lane, Apartment 107
Arlington, TX 76013

Editor: Irish Monahan

DESCRIPTION AND INTERESTS: Geared for children ages 3 to 14, this monthly website and print magazine features fiction, poetry, and the occasional informational article, each grouped in age-appropriate sections. Circ: Unavailable.
Website: www.irishstoryplayhouse.com

FREELANCE POTENTIAL: 25% written by non-staff writers. Of the freelance submissions published yearly, many are by unpublished writers and most are by new authors.

SUBMISSIONS AND PAYMENT: Sample copy, $6.99 or available at website. Guidelines available at website. Send complete ms. Accepts hard copy and email submissions to submissions2@irishstoryplayhouse.com (Microsoft Word or PDF attachments). SASE. Responds in 1 month. 6-month exclusive print and electronic rights. Articles, 300–1,000 words; $2. Fiction, 300–7,500 words; $3. Poetry, 12-line minimum; $1. Pays on publication.

Journal of Adventist Education

12501 Old Columbia Pike
Silver Spring, MD 20904-6600

Editor: Beverly J. Rumble

DESCRIPTION AND INTERESTS: Appearing five times each year, this journal is for teachers in Seventh-day Adventist learning institutions. It covers topics relating to Christian education, the integration of faith and learning in the classroom, and educator training. Circ: 15,000.
Website: http://JAE.adventist.org

FREELANCE POTENTIAL: 90% written by non-staff writers. Publishes 30 freelance submissions yearly. Receives 24–48 queries yearly.

SUBMISSIONS AND PAYMENT: Sample copy, $3.50 with 9x12 SASE ($.68 postage). Guidelines available. Query. Accepts email to rumbleb@gc.adventist.org (Microsoft Word attachments). Availability of artwork improves chance of acceptance. Responds in 3–6 weeks. First North American serial rights. Articles, to 2,000 words; to $100. Color prints and slides, JPEG or TIFF images, charts and graphs; payment rates vary. Pays on publication. Provides 2 copies.

Justine

6263 Poplar Avenue, Suite 1154
Memphis, TN 38119

Publisher/Editorial Director: Jana Petty

DESCRIPTION AND INTERESTS: Targeting teenage girls, *Justine* provides articles on topics that interest today's young people without relying on celebrities and gossip. It covers fashion, beauty, and style trends with a focus on reality, affordability, and a healthy lifestyle. Material should be written in a "young" voice without patronizing readers. It appears six times each year. Circ: 250,000.
Website: www.justinemagazine.com

FREELANCE POTENTIAL: 20% written by non-staff writers. Publishes 25 freelance submissions yearly; 25% by unpublished writers, 90% by new authors. Receives 100 queries yearly.

SUBMISSIONS AND PAYMENT: Sample copy, $2.99 at newsstands or available at website. Query with résumé and clips. Accepts hard copy. SASE. Response time varies. Rights vary. Articles and depts/columns, word lengths and payment rates vary. Pays 30 days after publication.

Junior Storyteller

P.O. Box 205
Masonville, CO 80541

Editor: Vivian Dubrovin

DESCRIPTION AND INTERESTS: Appearing online and in print, this quarterly offers stories written for oral presentation by children ages 9 to 14. Articles providing tips for speakers are also offered. Theater pieces are sought. Circ: 500.
Website: www.storycraft.com

FREELANCE POTENTIAL: 50% written by non-staff writers. Publishes several freelance submissions yearly; 25% by unpublished writers, 25% by new authors. Receives numerous queries yearly.

SUBMISSIONS AND PAYMENT: Sample copy, $4. Guidelines available at website. Query. Accepts hard copy and email to jrstoryteller@storycraft.com. No simultaneous submissions. Availability of artwork improves chance of acceptance. SASE. Response time varies. First North American serial rights. Articles and fiction, 350–1,000 words; $50–$125. B/W or color prints or digital photos; payment rates vary. Pays on acceptance. Provides 10 contributor's copies.

JVibe

90 Oak Street, 4th Floor
P.O. Box 9129
Upper Falls, MA 02464

Editor-in-Chief: Lindsey Silken

DESCRIPTION AND INTERESTS: Targeting Jewish teens, *JVibe* offers celebrity interviews, covers pop culture, and reports on issues in Israel. The website features content written mostly by teens. Adult authors may query for publication in the magazine. Though many article ideas are planned by the editors, it welcomes queries year-round. It appears six times each year. Circ: 15,000.
Website: www.jvibe.com

FREELANCE POTENTIAL: 90% written by non-staff writers. Publishes 90 freelance submissions yearly; 10% by unpublished writers, 20% by new authors. Receives 120 queries yearly.

SUBMISSIONS AND PAYMENT: Sample copy, guidelines, and editorial calendar available. Query. Accepts email queries to editor@jvibe.com. Responds in 1 week. All rights. Articles, 1,400 words; payment rates vary. Pays on publication. Provides 2 contributor's copies.

Kaboose.com

Disney Online Mom and Family Portfolio
5161 Lankershin Boulevard, 4th Floor
North Hollywood, CA 91601

Vice President: Emily Smith

DESCRIPTION AND INTERESTS: This online
parenting resource center provides parents and
other caretakers with the information they seek
regarding raising a happy, healthy family.
Updated regularly, it is filled with articles on family health, education, child development, and
finding some "mom time." It also offers a host of
ideas for parties, costumes, and crafts. Hits per
month: 3.6 million.
Website: www.kaboose.com

FREELANCE POTENTIAL: 95% written by nonstaff writers. Publishes 30 freelance submissions
yearly; 10% by unpublished writers, 30% by new
authors. Receives 150 queries yearly.

SUBMISSIONS AND PAYMENT: Sample copy
available at website. Query with outline. Accepts
hard copy. SASE. Response time varies. Rights
vary. Articles, 2,000 words. Depts/columns, 500
words. Written material, $.85 per word. Pays on
acceptance.

Kansas 4-H Journal

116 Umberger Hall
Kansas State University
Manhattan, KS 66506-3714

Editor: Rhonda Atkinson

DESCRIPTION AND INTERESTS: Members of
4-H in Kansas turn to this journal for news and
information about club events and activities.
Published six times each year, it also includes
photo-essays, how-to articles, and personal experience pieces that relate to the club's mission
and purpose. It welcomes submissions from
writers who have a solid understanding of
Kansas 4-H clubs. Circ: Unavailable.
Website: www.kansas4hfoundation.org

FREELANCE POTENTIAL: 60% written by nonstaff writers. Publishes 100 freelance submissions yearly; 10% by unpublished writers, 20%
by authors who are new to the magazine.
Receives 696 queries and unsolicited mss yearly.

SUBMISSIONS AND PAYMENT: Sample copy
and editorial calendar, $5. Query or send com-
plete ms. Accepts hard copy. SASE. Response
time varies. Rights vary. Articles, 500 words; payment rates vary. Payment policy varies.

Kahani

P.O. Box 590155
Newton Centre, MA 02459

Editor: Monika Jain

DESCRIPTION AND INTERESTS: *Kahani* is a
children's literary magazine illuminating the
diversity that South Asian cultures bring to North
America. Each quarterly issue also includes nonfiction articles related to the planned theme.
Kahani is currently on a publication hiatus.
Check the website for news about when publication will resume. Circ: Unavailable.
Website: www.kahani.com

FREELANCE POTENTIAL: 50% written by nonstaff writers. Publishes several freelance submissions yearly.

SUBMISSIONS AND PAYMENT: Guidelines and
calendar available at website. Query with clips for
articles. Send complete ms for fiction. Accepts
email to writers@kahani.com (with "Feature Query"
or "Fiction Submission" in subject line). Responds
if interested for articles; in 1 month for fiction.
Rights vary. Articles, 400–600 words. Fiction, to
950 words. No payment. Provides copies.

Keeping Family First Online

P.O. Box 36594
Detroit, MI 48236

Executive Editor: Anita S. Lane

DESCRIPTION AND INTERESTS: This publication describes itself as "an online community of
moms and dads who are dedicated to building
strong families." Each quarterly issue offers
expert advice on topics such as the challenges
of parenting, education, and family health and
wellness. It also accepts personal experience
and inspirational pieces, as well as material on
home, leisure, and entertainment. Hits per
month: 40,000.
Website: www.keepingfamilyfirst.org

FREELANCE POTENTIAL: 100% written by
nonstaff writers. Publishes 70 freelance submissions yearly; 56% by unpublished writers, 10%
by authors who are new to the magazine.

SUBMISSIONS AND PAYMENT: Sample copy
and guidelines available at website. Query.
Accepts email queries through the website only.
Response time varies. Rights vary. Articles and
depts/columns, word lengths vary. No payment.

Keyboard

1111 Bay Hill Drive, Suite 125
San Bruno, CA 94066

Managing Editor: Debbie Greenberg

DESCRIPTION AND INTERESTS: Written for professional and amateur keyboard players, this monthly provides product reviews, recording and playing tips, and artist profiles. It covers the keyboard in all genres of music. Circ: 61,000.
Website: www.keyboardmag.com

FREELANCE POTENTIAL: 25–35% written by nonstaff writers. Publishes 120 freelance submissions yearly; 35% by unpublished writers, 55% by authors who are new to the magazine. Receives 60–120 unsolicited mss yearly.

SUBMISSIONS AND PAYMENT: Sample copy and guidelines available via email request. Send complete ms with résumé. Accepts hard copy and email submissions to keyboard@musicplayer.com. SASE. Responds in 3 months. All rights. Articles, 500–3,000 words. Depts/columns, 400–600 words. Written material, payment rates vary. Pays on publication. Provides 5 contributor's copies.

Kid Magazine Writers

9 Arrowhead Drive
Ledyard, CT 06339

Editor: Jan Fields

DESCRIPTION AND INTERESTS: *Kid Magazine Writers* is an online publication for writers working in, or trying to break into, the children's magazine market. Its informational articles cover topics such as markets, contests, writing courses, software, writing techniques, and time management. It also publishes media reviews. Fiction is not included. Although not currently accepting submissions, interested writers should check the website for status updates. Hits per month: 2,000.
Website: www.kidmagwriters.com

FREELANCE POTENTIAL: 60% written by non-staff writers.

SUBMISSIONS AND PAYMENT: Sample copy and writers' guidelines available at website. Not accepting queries or manuscripts at this time. Check website for changes to this policy.

KidSpirit Magazine

77 State Street
Brooklyn, NY 11201

Editor: Elizabeth Dabney Hochman

DESCRIPTION AND INTERESTS: This magazine publishes the works of children, ages 11 to 15, who are curious about the meaning of life. Published quarterly, each issue is themed and includes short fiction, poetry, reviews, and feature articles. Circ: 5,000.
Website: www.kidspiritmagazine.com

FREELANCE POTENTIAL: 100% written by nonstaff writers. Publishes 40 freelance submissions yearly; 100% by unpublished writers. Receives 30 queries, 20 unsolicited mss yearly.

SUBMISSIONS AND PAYMENT: Guidelines and theme list available at website. Accepts submissions from children ages 11–15 only. Query with author bio for features; send complete ms for other works. Accepts hard copy and email to info@kidspiritmagazine.com. SASE. Responds in 1 month. Rights vary. Written material, word lengths vary. No payment. Provides 2 contributor's copies.

The Kids' Storytelling Club

P.O. Box 205
Masonville, CO 80541

Editor: Vivian Dubrovin

DESCRIPTION AND INTERESTS: Specifically geared toward children ages 9 to 12, this online magazine publishes articles on oral presentation skills, making and using props, and finding venues for storytelling. It also features stories for kids to read aloud. Writers are encouraged to submit ideas, tips, and hints for class and club meetings for the e-zine's new "Workshop" page. Hits per month: 4,000+.
Website: www.storycraft.com

FREELANCE POTENTIAL: 70% written by non-staff writers. Publishes many freelance submissions yearly; many by unpublished writers, most by authors who are new to the magazine.

SUBMISSIONS AND PAYMENT: Guidelines available at website. Query. Accepts hard copy and email queries to jrstoryteller@storycraft.com. SASE. Response time varies. First rights. Articles, 500 words. Fiction, 250–500 words. Written material, $25. Pays on acceptance.

Kids Off the Couch

Founders: Sarah Bowman &
Diane Phillips Shakin

DESCRIPTION AND INTERESTS: *Kids Off the Couch* is a free, weekly email newsletter and website with an editiorial belief that the best way to get kids off the couch is to first get on the couch with them. Each article pairs a child-friendly film with a complementary local event, exhibit, or idea for a family adventure. The result is kids getting excited about film, culture, and family time. There are multiple editions for cities throughout the country. It welcomes adventure ideas from parents. Circ: Unavailable.
Website: www.kidsoffthecouch.com

FREELANCE POTENTIAL: Publishes many freelance submissions yearly.

SUBMISSIONS AND PAYMENT: Sample copy available at website. Query. Accepts email queries to info@kidsoffthecouch.com or via submission form at website. Response time varies. Rights vary. Articles, word lengths vary. No payment.

Kiki

118 West Pike Street
Covington, KY 41011

Editor-in-Chief: Jamie G. Bryant

DESCRIPTION AND INTERESTS: This quarterly magazine targets girls ages 8–14 who appreciate creativity and style. It rejects the usual subjects of boys and social issues to focus instead on topics relating to fashion, design, personal creativity, and travel. It is for the girl who simply loves to express herself as well as the girl who wants to have a career in design. Circ: Unavailable.
Website: www.kikimag.com

FREELANCE POTENTIAL: 75% written by non-staff writers. Publishes 60 freelance submissions yearly; 15% by authors who are new to the magazine. Receives 240 queries yearly.

SUBMISSIONS AND PAYMENT: Sample copy, $7.95 with 9x12 SASE. Guidelines available at website. Query. Accepts hard copy. SASE. Responds in 3 months. All rights. Articles and depts/columns, word lengths vary. Written material, $.50–$1 per word. Pays on publication. Provides 2 contributor's copies.

Kids X-Press

P.O. Box 374
White Plains, NY 10603

Publisher: Nivia Viera

DESCRIPTION AND INTERESTS: *Kids X-Press* is a non-profit, quarterly magazine devoted to promoting literacy and self-expression. It publishes work by children ages 6 to 14 for their peers to enjoy. It accepts articles, interviews, and personal experience pieces on pop culture, sports, animals, and multicultural topics. Circ: 140,000.
Website: www.kidsxpress.net

FREELANCE POTENTIAL: 90% written by non-staff writers. Of the freelance submissions published yearly, 80% are by authors who are new to the magazine. Receives 60–72 queries yearly.

SUBMISSIONS AND PAYMENT: Child authors only. Sample copy, $4.95 with 9x12 SASE ($1.22 postage). Guidelines and theme list/editorial calendar available. Query. Accepts hard copy. Availability of artwork improves chance of acceptance. SASE. Responds in 1 week. Rights vary. Articles, to 250 words. Color prints or transparencies; line art. No payment.

KIND News

Humane Society Youth
67 Norwich Essex Turnpike
East Haddam, CT 06423

Managing Editor: Catherine Vincent

DESCRIPTION AND INTERESTS: *KIND News* is a classroom newspaper published at three reading levels for children in kindergarten through grade six. Published nine times each year by the Humane Society of the United States, its articles, games, stories, interviews, and profiles all relate to the humane treatment of animals. All material published here supports the concepts of good character, respect for all living things, and environmental conservation. Circ: 1 million.
Website: www.kindnews.org

FREELANCE POTENTIAL: 5% written by non-staff writers. Publishes few freelance submissions yearly.

SUBMISSIONS AND PAYMENT: Sample copy available at website. All material is assigned. Send résumé and clips only. Accepts hard copy. SASE. Responds if interested. Exclusive rights. Articles and depts/columns, word lengths and payment rates vary. Pays on acceptance.

Kittens USA

3 Burroughs
Irvine, CA 92618

Managing Editor: Lisa King

DESCRIPTION AND INTERESTS: The focus of this magazine is on the care and keeping of kittens. Articles cover health, nutrition, grooming, and litterbox training. Appearing annually, this photo-filled magazine also includes product reviews. Circ: 78,350.
Website: www.catchannel.com

FREELANCE POTENTIAL: 80% written by non-staff writers. Publishes 12 freelance submissions yearly; 10–20% by authors who are new to the magazine. Receives 12 unsolicited mss yearly.

SUBMISSIONS AND PAYMENT: Sample copy and guidelines available at website. Send complete ms. Accepts email submissions to lking@bowtieinc.com. Response time varies. Exclusive North American serial rights. Articles and depts/columns, word lengths and payment rates vary. Payment policy varies. Provides 2 contributor's copies.

Kiwibox.com

330 West 38th Street, Suite 1602
New York, NY 10018

Submissions Editor: Bianca Merbaum

DESCRIPTION AND INTERESTS: Teens and young adults, ages 14 to 21, write, edit, and design *Kiwibox.com*, which means this e-zine publishes fiction and creative nonfiction specifically for this age group. Fiction may be any type, including genre, contemporary, experimental, inspirational, and multicultural. Nonfiction articles cover topics from science and technology to fashion and film. All material that appears is well-crafted and age-appropriate. It is updated weekly, although it is not accepting submissions at this time. Check the website for changes to this policy. Hits per month: 10 million.
Website: www.kiwibox.com

FREELANCE POTENTIAL: 90% written by non-staff writers. Publishes numerous freelance submissions yearly.

SUBMISSIONS AND PAYMENT: Teen authors only. Sample copy available at website. Not accepting queries or unsolicited mss at this time.

Kyria

465 Gundersen Drive
Carol Stream, IL 60188

Acquisitions Editor

DESCRIPTION AND INTERESTS: The former *Today's Christian Woman* has been revamped as this "digizine." Published monthly, its articles offer in-depth biblical insight into topics of faith and ministry for mature Christian women. Topics include women's ministry, spirituality, church leadership, and marriage and family. Hits per month: Unavailable.
Website: www.kyria.com

FREELANCE POTENTIAL: 70% written by non-staff writers. Publishes 30 freelance submissions yearly; 20% by unpublished writers, 20% by new authors. Receives 360 queries yearly.

SUBMISSIONS AND PAYMENT: Sample copy, guidelines, and theme list available at website. Query with résumé. Accepts hard copy and email queries through the website. SASE. Responds in 2 months. Exclusive online rights and non-exclusive rights. Articles, 600–1,500 words; $50–$150. Pays on acceptance.

Lacrosse

113 West University Parkway
Baltimore, MD 21210

Editor: Paul Krome

DESCRIPTION AND INTERESTS: Lacrosse players, coaches, and fans read this monthly magazine for athlete profiles, how-to articles on training and playing strategies, and collegiate team coverage. Product reviews and news from US Lacrosse—the national governing body—appear as well. Circ: 275,000.
Website: www.laxmagazine.com

FREELANCE POTENTIAL: 30% written by non-staff writers. Publishes 60 freelance submissions yearly; 5% by unpublished writers, 10% by authors who are new to the magazine. Receives 60 queries yearly.

SUBMISSIONS AND PAYMENT: Sample copy, $5. Guidelines available. Query with clips or résumé. Accepts email queries to pkrome@uslacrosse.org. Responds in 6 weeks. Exclusive rights. Articles, 800–1,000 words; $100–$300. Depts/columns, 300 words; $100–$150. Pays on publication. Provides 1+ contributor's copies.

Lake/Geauga Family

TNT Publications
11630 Chillicothe Road
Chesterland, OH 44026

Editor: Terri Nighswonger

DESCRIPTION AND INTERESTS: Helping parents of tots to teens, this monthly publication provides valuable parenting and child development information alongside regional guides for recreational activities, travel, birthday parties, and summer camps. Circ: 75,000.
Website: www.neohiofamily.com

FREELANCE POTENTIAL: 50% written by non-staff writers. Publishes 40–50 freelance submissions yearly; 33% by authors who are new to the magazine. Receives 6,000 queries yearly.

SUBMISSIONS AND PAYMENT: Guidelines available. Sample copy and theme list available at website. Query with clips. Accepts email queries to editor@tntpublications.com. Responds if interested. Exclusive rights. Articles, 500+ words. Depts/columns, word lengths vary. High-resolution JPEG and TIF images. All material, payment rates vary. Pays on publication. Provides 1 contributor's copy.

Leading Edge

4087 JKB
Provo, UT 84602

Fiction or Poetry Director

DESCRIPTION AND INTERESTS: Published twice each year, *Leading Edge* is a journal of science fiction and fantasy stories. It also accepts poetry, as long as it has a science fiction or fantasy theme. Each submission receives a written critique, whether it is published or not. Circ: 200.
Website: www.leadingedgemagazine.com

FREELANCE POTENTIAL: 95% written by non-staff writers. Publishes 18 freelance submissions yearly; most by unpublished writers. Receives 300 unsolicited mss yearly.

SUBMISSIONS AND PAYMENT: Sample copy, $5.95. Guidelines available in each issue and at website. Send complete ms. Accepts hard copy. No simultaneous submissions. SASE. Responds in 2–4 months. First North American serial rights. Fiction, to 15,000 words; $.01 per word, minimum $10. Poetry, no line limit; $10 for first 4 pages, $1.50 for each additional page. Pays on publication. Provides 2 contributor's copies.

Language Arts Journal

Ohio State University
333 Arps Hall
1945 North High Street
Columbus, OH 43210

Language Arts Editorial Team

DESCRIPTION AND INTERESTS: All facets of language arts learning and teaching are covered in this magazine. Published six times each year, it focuses on preschool through middle school. Circ: 12,000.
Website: www.ncte.org

FREELANCE POTENTIAL: 90% written by non-staff writers. Publishes 60 freelance submissions yearly; 15% by unpublished writers, 30% by new authors. Receives 200 unsolicited mss yearly.

SUBMISSIONS AND PAYMENT: Sample copy, $12.50 from NCTE, 1111 W. Kenyon Road, Urbana, IL 61801-1096. Guidelines and theme list available via email request to langarts@ osu.edu. Send 6 copies of complete ms; include Microsoft Word file on disk. Accepts hard copy and disk submissions. SASE. Responds in 3–12 months. All rights. Articles, 2,500–6,500 words. Depts/columns, word lengths vary. No payment. Provides 2 contributor's copies.

Library Media Connection

130 Cremona Drive, Suite C
Santa Barbara, CA 93117

Editor: Marlene Maxwell

DESCRIPTION AND INTERESTS: Written for and by practicing school librarians, *Library Media Connection* features personal essays and articles on library management operation, as well as reviews of books and other library materials. It appears seven times each year. Circ: 14,000.
Website: www.linworth.com

FREELANCE POTENTIAL: 90% written by non-staff writers. Publishes 215 freelance submissions yearly; 50% by unpublished writers, 50% by authors who are new to the magazine. Receives 144 queries, 144 unsolicited mss yearly.

SUBMISSIONS AND PAYMENT: Sample copy, $11 with 9x12 SASE. Query or send complete ms with résumé. Accepts hard copy, disk submissions (Microsoft Word or ASCII), and email to wmedvetz@librarymediaconnection.com. SASE. Responds in 2 weeks. All rights. Written material, payment rates vary. Pays on publication. Provides 4 contributor's copies.

Literary Mama

1416 11th Avenue
San Francisco, CA 94122

Editor-in-Chief: Caroline Grant

DESCRIPTION AND INTERESTS: Fiction, poetry, and creative nonfiction, written by mom-writers and reflecting the many facets of motherhood, appear in this monthly e-zine. Book reviews are also published. Hits per month: 55,000.
Website: www.literarymama.com

FREELANCE POTENTIAL: 80% written by non-staff writers. Publishes 150 freelance submissions yearly; 15% by unpublished writers, 50% by new authors. Receives 100 queries, 2,500 unsolicited mss yearly.

SUBMISSIONS AND PAYMENT: Sample copy and guidelines available at website. Query for profiles, reviews, and columns. Send complete ms for all other work. Accepts email submissions; see website for appropriate editor and email address. Responds in 1–4 months. Non-exclusive rights. Articles and fiction, to 6,000 words. Depts/columns, 1,000–6,000 words. Poetry, no line limit. No payment.

Little Rock Family

122 East Second Street
Little Rock, AR 72201

Submissions Editor: Jennifer Pyron

DESCRIPTION AND INTERESTS: *Little Rock Family* is written for busy parents in need of timely local information for their families. Distributed monthly throughout Arkansas's capital region, it not only features a comprehensive calendar of events but also articles that cover important parenting issues. Topics include health, religion, education, special needs, recreational activities, and dining. Writers should have a strong knowledge of the region and articles should have a Little Rock focus. Circ: 20,000.
Website: www.littlerockfamily.com

FREELANCE POTENTIAL: 1% written by non-staff writers. Publishes few freelance submissions yearly.

SUBMISSIONS AND PAYMENT: Query. Accepts hard copy. SASE. Response time varies. First rights. Articles and depts/columns, word lengths and payment rates vary. Payment policy varies.

Living with Teenagers

One LifeWay Plaza
Nashville, TN 37234-0174

Editor: Bob Bunn

DESCRIPTION AND INTERESTS: This parenting magazine is designed to give Christian parents of teenagers the information and inspiration they need to raise children who are close to God and who proudly proclaim their faith. In addition to biblical topics, the articles here focus on family matters, parenting issues, and youth culture. It is published monthly. Circ: 35,000.
Website: www.lifeway.com/magazines

FREELANCE POTENTIAL: 90% written by non-staff writers. Publishes several freelance submissions yearly.

SUBMISSIONS AND PAYMENT: Sample copy, free or available at website. All material written on assignment. Send résumé and writing samples to be considered. Accepts hard copy. SASE. Responds if interested. All rights with nonexclusive license to the writer. Articles, 600–1,200 words; $100–$300. Pays on acceptance. Provides 3 contributor's copies.

Long Island Parent

152 West 19th Street
Huntington Station, NY 11746

Editor: Liza Burby

DESCRIPTION AND INTERESTS: Published six times each year for, by, and about Long Island moms and dads, this publication provides valuable information and expert advice for raising children from birth through age 16. Education, travel, health and fitness, family recreation, and regional news are some of the topics covered. Circ: 55,000.
Website: www.liparentonline.com

FREELANCE POTENTIAL: 25–30% written by nonstaff writers. Publishes 20 freelance submissions yearly; 30% by authors who are new to the magazine.

SUBMISSIONS AND PAYMENT: Sample copy and guidelines available. Query or send complete ms. Accepts hard copy and email submissions to editor@liparentonline.com. SASE. Responds in 2–4 months. First rights. Written material, word lengths and payment rates vary. Pays on publication. Provides 2 author's copies.

Lowcountry Parent

134 Columbus Street
Charleston, SC 29403

Submissions Editor: Shannon Brigham

DESCRIPTION AND INTERESTS: Families living in Charleston, South Carolina, and the surrounding area read this magazine. Monthly issues feature articles of regional interest, and cover topics including parenting, family travel and recreation, education, health and safety, and personal finances. Profiles of local personalities are also published. Circ: 41,000,
Website: www.lowcountryparent.com

FREELANCE POTENTIAL: Publishes few freelance submissions yearly; 10% by authors who are new to the magazine. Receives 100 queries each year.

SUBMISSIONS AND PAYMENT: Local writers only. Sample copy, free. Send résumé. Accepts email to editor@lowcountryparent.com. Responds if interested. One-time rights. Articles and depts/columns, word lengths vary. Written material, $15–$100. Pays on publication. Provides 3 contributor's copies.

The Lutheran Digest

6160 Carmen Avenue East
Inver Grove Heights, MN 55076

Editor: Nick Skapyak

DESCRIPTION AND INTERESTS: Inspiration, hope, and even some humor can be found in this general-interest quarterly. Its blend of secular and Christian-based articles include home and family topics. Circ: 70,000.
Website: www.lutherandigest.com

FREELANCE POTENTIAL: 100% written by nonstaff writers. Publishes 80 freelance submissions yearly; 30% by authors who are new to the magazine. Receives 300 unsolicited mss yearly.

SUBMISSIONS AND PAYMENT: Sample copy, $3.50 with 6x9 SASE. Send complete ms with author biography. Prefers hard copy; will accept faxes to 952-933-5708 and email submissions to editor@lutherandigest.com (Microsoft Word or PDF attachments). SASE. Responds in 2–3 months. One-time and second rights. Articles, word lengths vary; $35. Poetry, 2 stanzas, and filler; no payment. Pays on publication. Provides 1 contributor's copy.

Mad Magazine

1700 Broadway
New York, NY 10019

Submissions Editor

DESCRIPTION AND INTERESTS: Each monthly issue of *Mad Magazine* is filled with hard-hitting satire, parodies, and comic strips on such subjects as politics, celebrities, sports scandals, and cultural fads. Writers with a twisted sense of humor and a peculiar way of looking at the world are wanted. Circ: 250,000.
Website: www.madmag.com

FREELANCE POTENTIAL: 90% written by nonstaff writers. Publishes 25 freelance submissions each year.

SUBMISSIONS AND PAYMENT: Sample copy, $4.99 at newsstands. Guidelines available at website. Query or send complete ms. Prefers email to submissions@madmagazine.com; will accept hard copy if submission includes artwork. SASE. Responds if interested. All rights. Written material, word lengths vary; $500 per printed page. Graphic artwork, payment rates vary. Pays on acceptance. Provides 1 contributor's copy.

Metro Parent

P.O. Box 13660
Portland, OR 97213-0660

Editor: Marie Sherlock

DESCRIPTION AND INTERESTS: Parents living in Oregon's Portland area find practical information on education, travel, and recreation, as well as typical child development issues, in each issue of *Metro Parent*. Published monthly, it also features a local event calendar and regional news. Preference is given to writers living in the region. Circ: 45,000.
Website: www.metro-parent.com

FREELANCE POTENTIAL: 75% written by nonstaff writers. Publishes 50 freelance submissions yearly; 20% by unpublished writers. Receives 240 queries yearly.

SUBMISSIONS AND PAYMENT: Sample copy and theme list, $2. Query with outline. Accepts hard copy, email to editor@metro-parent.com, and simultaneous submissions if identified. SASE. Responds in 1 month. Rights vary. Written material, word lengths and payment rates vary. Pays on publication.

Metro Spirit

700 Broad Street
Augusta, GA 30901

Editor: Stacey Eidson

DESCRIPTION AND INTERESTS: Subtitled "Augusta's Independent Voice," *Metro Spirit* targets parents living in and around this Georgia city. Each of its monthly issues features comprehensive coverage of local recreational activities and educational programs, along with parenting advice. Circ: Unavailable.
Website: www.metrospirit.com

FREELANCE POTENTIAL: 80% written by non-staff writers. Publishes 50 freelance submissions yearly; 5% by unpublished writers, 5% by authors who are new to the magazine. Receives 240 queries yearly.

SUBMISSIONS AND PAYMENT: Sample copy and guidelines, free with SASE. Query. Accepts hard copy and email queries to spirit@metrospirit.com. SASE. Response time varies. First rights. Written material, word lengths and payment rates vary. Payment policy varies. Provides 1 contributor's copy.

Minnesota Parent

Minnesota Premier Publications
1115 Hennepin Avenue South
Minneapolis, MN 55403

Editor: Tricia Cornell

DESCRIPTION AND INTERESTS: The articles in *Minnesota Parent* highlight the rewarding, exciting, hectic, and fun times parents have while raising their children. Its editorial content ranges from hard-hitting pieces on education and social issues to interviews with local experts, and book, toy, and movie reviews. Published monthly, it considers submissions with local angles only. Circ: 70,000.
Website: www.mnparent.com

FREELANCE POTENTIAL: 50% written by non-staff writers. Publishes 24 freelance submissions each year.

SUBMISSIONS AND PAYMENT: Query. Accepts hard copy and email queries to tcornell@mnpubs.com. SASE. Response time varies. First serial and electronic rights. Articles and depts/columns, word lengths vary; $50–$350. Pays on publication. Provides 2 contributor's copies.

Miami Family Magazine

7045 SW 69th Avenue
South Miami, FL 33143

Publisher: Janet Jupiter

DESCRIPTION AND INTERESTS: From education, health, and nutrition to home improvement and travel, this monthly magazine provides parents with the information they need to happily raise children in Florida's Miami, Fort Lauderdale, and Boca Raton regions. Local angles and personalities are always preferred. Circ: Unavailable.
Website: www.familymagazine.biz

FREELANCE POTENTIAL: 30% written by non-staff writers. Publishes 15–20 freelance submissions yearly.

SUBMISSIONS AND PAYMENT: Sample copy and editorial calendar available at website. Query. Accepts hard copy and email queries to familymag@bellsouth.net. SASE. Response time varies. One-time rights. Articles and depts/columns, word lengths and payment rates vary. Pays on publication. Provides author's copies.

Model Airplane News

Air Age Publishing
20 Westport Road
Wilton, CT 06897

Executive Editor: Debra Cleghorn

DESCRIPTION AND INTERESTS: This magazine promotes the model airplane hobby through its coverage of new products, building techniques, after-market customization, and competitions and events across the country. It is published monthly. Circ: 95,000.
Website: www.modelairplanenews.com

FREELANCE POTENTIAL: 80% written by non-staff writers. Publishes 100+ freelance submissions yearly; 33% by authors who are new to the magazine. Receives 144–288 queries yearly.

SUBMISSIONS AND PAYMENT: Sample copy and guidelines, $3.50 with 9x12 SASE. Query with outline and biography describing model experience. Accepts hard copy. Availability of artwork improves chance of acceptance. SASE. Responds in 6 weeks. North American serial rights. Articles, 1,700–2,000 words; $175–$600. 35mm color slides. Pays on publication. Provides up to 6 contributor's copies.

MOM Magazine

2532 Santiam Highway SE, #102
Albany, OR 97322

Editor: Krista Klinkhammer

DESCRIPTION AND INTERESTS: Appearing
six times each year, this magazine is written for
mothers with children under the age of twelve. It
welcomes articles on parenting issues and family
recreation, as well as personal experience pieces
that share the joy, challenges, and sometimes
sadness of motherhood. Circ: 60,000.
Website: www.mommag.com

FREELANCE POTENTIAL: 85% written by nonstaff writers. Publishes 50 freelance submissions
yearly; 50% by unpublished writers, 50% by new
authors. Receives 500 queries, 150 mss yearly.

SUBMISSIONS AND PAYMENT: Query or send
complete ms. Accepts email to editor@
mommag.com (Microsoft Word attachments).
Availability of artwork improves chance of
acceptance. Response time varies. Reprint rights.
Articles, to 500 words. Depts/columns, word
lengths vary. 5x7 JPEG or TIFF images at 300
dpi. No payment.

Montessori Life

281 Park Avenue South
New York, NY 10010

Co-Editors: Kathy Carey & Carey Jones

DESCRIPTION AND INTERESTS: Written for
teachers, administrators, and other professionals
working in Montessori education, this peer-
reviewed quarterly covers professional development, provides curriculum ideas, and is a forum
for new ideas. Circ: 10,500.
Website: www.amshq.org

FREELANCE POTENTIAL: 90% written by nonstaff writers. Publishes 40 freelance submissions
yearly; 30% by unpublished writers, 30% by
authors who are new to the magazine. Receives
120–240 unsolicited mss yearly.

SUBMISSIONS AND PAYMENT: Sample copy,
$5 with 9x12 SASE. Guidelines and editorial cal-
endar available at website. Send complete ms.
Accepts email to edmontessorilife@aol.com.
Responds in 3 months. All rights. Articles,
1,000–4,000 words. Depts/columns, 500–1,000
words. Written material, payment rates vary. Pays
on publication. Provides 1–5 copies.

Motivos Bilingual Magazine

P.O. Box 34391
Philadelphia, PA 19101

Publisher: Jenee Chiznick

DESCRIPTION AND INTERESTS: High school
and college students, as well as adults, are invited
to write for this quarterly magazine, which publishes all material in English and Spanish. It
seeks work that inspires and empowers Latino
youth to explore their full potential and make
informed choices about life, college, and career
options. Circ: 75,000.
Website: www.motivosmag.com

FREELANCE POTENTIAL: 50% written by nonstaff writers. Publishes 30 freelance submissions
yearly; 40% by unpublished writers, 50% by
authors who are new to the magazine.

SUBMISSIONS AND PAYMENT: Guidelines
available at website. Send complete ms. Accepts
hard copy and email submissions to editor@
motivosmag.com. SASE. Response time varies.
First North American serial rights. Articles,
400–1,200 words; payment rates vary. Payment
policy varies. Provides 2 contributor's copies.

Mysteries Magazine

P.O. Box 131
Waynesville, NC 28786

Editor: Jeremiah Greer

DESCRIPTION AND INTERESTS: This magazine is interested in true stories about anything
that is odd, unsolved, or intriguing. A wide variety of topics are covered, including the paranor-
mal, the occult, conspiracies, disappearances,
bizarre crimes, and lost treasures. It is published
quarterly. Circ: 15,000.
Website: www.mysteriesmagazine.com

FREELANCE POTENTIAL: 30% written by nonstaff writers. Publishes 12 freelance submissions
yearly; 20% by authors who are new to the magazine. Receives 240 queries yearly.

SUBMISSIONS AND PAYMENT: Sample copy,
$8. Guidelines available at website. Query.
Accepts email to editor@mysteriesmagazine.com.
Responds in 1 month. First North American serial
rights. Articles, 3,000–5,000 words. Depts/
columns, 1,200–1,500 words. Book reviews,
200–500 words. Written material, $.05 per word.
Pays on publication. Provides 2 author's copies.

NASSP Bulletin

Sage Publications
2455 Teller Road
Thousand Oaks, CA 91320

Editor

DESCRIPTION AND INTERESTS: This quarterly is the official journal of the National Association of Secondary School Principals. It accepts scholarly and research-based articles that will advance the vision and performance of middle-level and high school principals. All material is peer-reviewed. Circ: 2,000.
Website: http://bulletin.sagepub.com

FREELANCE POTENTIAL: 100% written by nonstaff writers. Publishes 20–25 freelance submissions yearly; 15% by unpublished writers, 30% by authors who are new to the magazine. Receives 150 unsolicited mss yearly.

SUBMISSIONS AND PAYMENT: Sample copy, free with 9x12 SASE. Guidelines available at website. Send complete ms. Accepts submissions via http://mc.manuscriptcentral.com/bul only. Responds in 4–6 weeks. All rights. Articles, to 30 pages. No payment. Provides 2 contributor's copies.

Natural Solutions

2995 Wilderness Place, Suite 205
Boulder, CO 80301-5408

Editor: Lauren Piscopo

DESCRIPTION AND INTERESTS: Since 1994, this magazine has presented readers with information on natural beauty and health, with an emphasis on herbs, healing foods, and natural household products. Articles must use authoritative resources and offer readers practical advice. It is published 10 times each year. Circ: 225,000.
Website: www.naturalsolutionsmag.com

FREELANCE POTENTIAL: 95% written by nonstaff writers. Publishes 40–50 freelance submissions yearly; 25% by authors who are new to the magazine. Receives 30 queries yearly.

SUBMISSIONS AND PAYMENT: Sample copy, $4.95 at newsstands. Guidelines available at website. Query with clips. Accepts email queries to editor@naturalsolutionsmag.com. Responds only if interested. All rights. Articles, 1,200–2,000 words. Depts/columns, word lengths vary. Written material, payment rates vary. Pays within 45 days of acceptance. Provides 2 contributor's copies.

National Geographic Explorer

1145 17th Street NW
Washington, DC 20036

Editor-in-Chief: Jacalyn Mahler

DESCRIPTION AND INTERESTS: Teachers in grades two through six can use this magazine in their classrooms to augment their science and social studies curricula. The same fascinating treatment of subjects that has enthralled adult *National Geographic* readers can be found here, but with a kid-friendly presentation. It is published seven times each year, and each issue comes with a teacher's guide. Circ: Unavailable.
Website:
http://magma.nationalgeographic.com/ngexplorer

FREELANCE POTENTIAL: 5% written by nonstaff writers. Publishes few freelance submissions each year.

SUBMISSIONS AND PAYMENT: All material written on assignment. Send résumé only. Accepts hard copy. Responds if interested. All rights. Articles and fiction, word lengths and payment rates vary. Pays on acceptance.

Neapolitan Family Magazine

P.O. Box 110656
Naples, FL 34108

Editor: Andrea Breznay

DESCRIPTION AND INTERESTS: With a focus on local events, recreation, and resources, this monthly offers articles on topics of interest to parents of Collier County, Florida. Parenting issues, education, family life, local issues, and family-friendly local events are covered here. Circ: 11,000.
Website: www.neafamily.com

FREELANCE POTENTIAL: 90% written by nonstaff writers. Publishes 40 freelance submissions yearly; 20% by authors who are new to the magazine. Receives 500 unsolicited mss yearly.

SUBMISSIONS AND PAYMENT: Sample copy, free with 9x12 SASE. Guidelines and editorial calendar available at website. Send complete ms. Prefers email submissions to andrea@neafamily.com; will accept hard copy. SASE. Responds in 1 month. Rights vary. Articles and depts/columns, word lengths and payment rates vary. Pays on publication.

New Jersey Family

1122 Route 22 West
Mountainside, NJ 07092

Editor: Farn Dupre

DESCRIPTION AND INTERESTS: *New Jersey Family* covers topics such as children's health and fitness, education trends, and the cultural arts. Its monthly distribution in northern and central New Jersey reflects the regional focus of its contents. Seasonal material must be submitted four months in advance. Circ: 126,000.
Website: www.njfamily.com

FREELANCE POTENTIAL: 60% written by non-staff writers. Publishes 150 freelance submissions yearly; 33% by unpublished writers, 33% by authors who are new to the magazine. Receives 240 queries yearly.

SUBMISSIONS AND PAYMENT: Guidelines available at website. Query with writing samples. Accepts email queries to editor@njfamily.com (no attachments). Response time varies. First rights. Articles, 750–1,000 words. Depts/columns, word lengths vary. Written material, payment rates vary. Payment policy varies.

New Jersey Suburban Parent

Middlesex Publications
850 Route 1 North
North Brunswick, NJ 08902

Editor: Melodie Dhondt

DESCRIPTION AND INTERESTS: In addition to its guide to fun and educational family activities, *New Jersey Suburban Parent* provides valuable information on family health, child care, and education. Published monthly, it is distributed throughout New Jersey. Circ: 77,000.
Website: www.njparentweb.com

FREELANCE POTENTIAL: 80% written by non-staff writers. Publishes 12 freelance submissions yearly; 20% by unpublished writers, 40% by authors who are new to the magazine. Receives 12 queries yearly.

SUBMISSIONS AND PAYMENT: Sample copy, guidelines, and editorial calendar, free with 9x12 SASE. Query with writing samples. Accepts hard copy and simultaneous submissions if identified. SASE. Responds in 1–2 months. Rights vary. Articles, 700–1,000 words; $30. B/W or color prints; payment rates vary. Pays on acceptance. Provides 1+ contributor's copies.

North Star Family Matters

689 East Promontory Road
Shelton, WA 98584

Editor-in-Chief

DESCRIPTION AND INTERESTS: Realizing that there are many magazines devoted to providing information about raising physically healthy children, this monthly magazine was founded to promote "conscious parenting" and to address the emotional health of children. After a short break, it has recently resumed publication as a digital magazine. Hits per month: 32,000.
Website: www.northstarfamilymatters-magazine.com

FREELANCE POTENTIAL: 60% written by non-staff writers. Publishes 50 freelance submissions yearly; 60% by unpublished writers, 80% by authors who are new to the magazine.

SUBMISSIONS AND PAYMENT: Guidelines available. Query. Accepts email queries to info@northstarfamilymattersmagazine.com. Response time varies. First and electronic rights. Articles, 300–1,500 words; payment rates vary. Payment policy varies.

North State Parent

P.O. Box 1602
Mount Shasta, CA 96067

Submissions: Lisa Shara

DESCRIPTION AND INTERESTS: *North State Parent* is a monthly resource for parents, grandparents, and caregivers living in the northern counties of California. It features articles on parenting issues, child development, childhood heath and fitness, family relationships, education, and things to do and see in the region. All material must have a local angle. Circ: 18,000+.
Website: www.northstateparent.com

FREELANCE POTENTIAL: 90% written by non-staff writers. Publishes 20 freelance submissions each year.

SUBMISSIONS AND PAYMENT: Guidelines available at website. Send complete ms. Accepts hard copy and email submissions to lisa@northstateparent.com. SASE. Response time varies. First rights. Articles, 700–1,000 words. Depts/columns, 300–500 words. Written material, $35–$75. Pays on publication. Provides 2 contributor's copies.

The Numismatist

American Numismatic Association
818 North Cascade Avenue
Colorado Springs, CO 80903-3279

Editor-in-Chief: Barbara J. Gregory

DESCRIPTION AND INTERESTS: Members of
the American Numismatic Association read this
magazine for the latest news on coin, medal,
token, and paper money collecting. It is published monthly. Circ: 30,500.
Website: www.money.org

FREELANCE POTENTIAL: 60% written by nonstaff writers. Publishes 36 freelance submissions
yearly; 20% by unpublished writers, 10% by
authors who are new to the magazine. Receives
48 unsolicited mss yearly.

SUBMISSIONS AND PAYMENT: Sample copy
and guidelines, free with 9x12 SASE ($2.50
postage). Send complete ms with biography.
Prefers email submissions to editor@money.org;
will accept hard copy and disk submissions.
SASE. Responds in 8–10 weeks. Perpetual non-
exclusive rights. Articles, to 3,500 words; $.12
per word. Pays on publication. Provides 5 contributor's copies.

Owl

Bayard Press Canada
10 Lower Spadina Avenue, Suite 400
Toronto, Ontario M5V 2Z2
Canada

Submissions Editor

DESCRIPTION AND INTERESTS: *Owl* serves
Canadian children, ages 9 to 13, with timely, reliable, and relevant information on the topics and
issues that concern them. Published nine times
each year, the magazine presents informational
articles, quirky facts, and fun puzzles and activities regarding everything from sports and the
environment to pop culture and peer relationships. Circ: 104,000.
Website: www.owlkids.com

FREELANCE POTENTIAL: 60% written by nonstaff writers. Publishes 1–3 freelance submissions yearly; 5% by unpublished writers, 10% by
authors who are new to the magazine.

SUBMISSIONS AND PAYMENT: Sample copy,
$4.28 Canadian. Guidelines available. Send
résumé only. No queries or unsolicited mss.
Accepts hard copy. Responds if interested. All
rights. Articles, 500–1,000 words; $200–$500.
Pays on acceptance. Provides 1 author's copy.

Our Children

National PTA
541 North Fairbanks Court, Suite 1300
Chicago, IL 60611-3396

Editor: Marilyn Ferdinand

DESCRIPTION AND INTERESTS: With both a
print and an online version, this National PTA
publication is interested in articles on how parents
can become more involved with their children's
education. It is published five times each year.
Circ: 31,000.
Website: www.pta.org

FREELANCE POTENTIAL: 50% written by nonstaff writers. Publishes 20–25 freelance submissions yearly; 75% by authors who are new to the
magazine. Receives 180–240 queries yearly.

SUBMISSIONS AND PAYMENT: Sample copy,
$2.50 with 9x12 SASE ($1 postage) or available
at website. Guidelines and editorial calendar
available at website. Query with credentials and
clips. Accepts email to mferdinand@pta.org.
Responds in 2 months. First North American serial, electronic, and reproduction rights. Articles,
600–1,000 words. Depts/columns, word lengths
vary. No payment. Provides 3 author's copies.

Parenting for High Potential

National Association for Gifted Children
1707 L Street NW, Suite 550
Washington, DC 20036
Editor: Dr. Jennifer Jolly

DESCRIPTION AND INTERESTS: This quarterly
magazine is designed to help parents of gifted
children develop their talents and reach their
highest potential. Expertly written articles and
columns, book and media reviews, and a children's section make up the editorial mix. It is
published by the National Association for Gifted
Children. Writers should have experience working with gifted children. Circ: 4,000.
Website: www.nagc.org

FREELANCE POTENTIAL: 100% written by
nonstaff writers. Publishes 10–12 freelance submissions yearly; 50% by authors who are new to
the magazine. Receives 20–30 unsolicited mss
each year.

SUBMISSIONS AND PAYMENT: Guidelines
available. Send complete ms. Accepts email submissions to jjolly@lsu.edu. Responds in 6–8
weeks. First rights. Articles and depts/columns,
word lengths vary. No payment.

ParentingHumor.com

P.O. Box 2128
Weaverville, NC 28787

Editor-in-Chief

DESCRIPTION AND INTERESTS: This website, updated weekly, is dedicated to the lighter side of parenting. Contributors need not be published writers, just parents willing to reach out and make a peer smile. It accepts humorous anecdotes about life as a parent, funny stories, creative essays, jokes, and even fun ideas for party games and recipes. Hits per month: Unavailable.
Website: www.parentinghumor.com

FREELANCE POTENTIAL: 98% written by non-staff writers. Publishes 100 freelance submissions yearly. Receives 50 unsolicited mss yearly.

SUBMISSIONS AND PAYMENT: Sample copy and guidelines available at website. Send complete ms. Accepts electronic submissions via form at website only. Responds in 4–6 weeks if interested. Author retains rights. Written material, no word limit; no payment. Provides published biography of contributor at end of piece, and a link to author's website.

Parents

375 Lexington Avenue
New York, NY 10017

Editor

DESCRIPTION AND INTERESTS: This monthly magazine is read by parents and parents-to-be for its informative articles as well as personal experience pieces. Topics covered include all aspects of parenting, newborn care, child development, safety, nutrition, education, and behavioral issues. It also features new product reviews, profiles, and interviews. Articles on discipline and baby-related articles are particularly sought at this time. Circ: 15 million.
Website: www.parents.com

FREELANCE POTENTIAL: 80% written by non-staff writers. Publishes 300 freelance submissions yearly; 15% by authors who are new to the magazine. Receives 480–600 queries yearly.

SUBMISSIONS AND PAYMENT: Query. Accepts email queries to mailbag@parents.com. Responds in 6 weeks. Rights vary. Articles and depts/columns, word lengths and payment rates vary. Pays on acceptance.

Parents' Choice

Parents' Choice Foundation
201 West Padonia Road, Suite 303
Timonium, MD 21093

Editor: Claire Green

DESCRIPTION AND INTERESTS: This online publication of the Parents' Choice Foundation strives to provide parents with reliable and unbiased information about tools to help their children learn and grow imaginatively, physically, morally, and mentally. It offers themed articles, written by experts, on books, toys, software, music, websites, magazines, and television. Hits per month: 1 million.
Website: www.parents-choice.org

FREELANCE POTENTIAL: 80% written by non-staff writers. Publishes numerous freelance submissions yearly.

SUBMISSIONS AND PAYMENT: Sample copy available at website. Query or send complete ms. Accepts hard copy, email submissions to info@parents-choice.org, and simultaneous submissions if identified. SASE. Response time varies. All rights. Articles, to 1,500 words; payment rates vary. Pays on acceptance.

Parents Express

290 Commerce Drive
Fort Washington, PA 19034

Editor: Mike Morsch

DESCRIPTION AND INTERESTS: *Parents Express* is a magazine for families living in the Philadelphia region and southern New Jersey. Appearing monthly, it covers parenting issues as well as regional events, news, and resources. Circ: 49,000.
Website: www.parents-express.net

FREELANCE POTENTIAL: 30% written by non-staff writers. Publishes 25–30 freelance submissions yearly; 25% by unpublished writers, 75% by authors who are new to the magazine. Receives several queries yearly.

SUBMISSIONS AND PAYMENT: Sample copy, free with 9x12 SASE ($2.14 postage). Query with clips or writing samples. Accepts hard copy. SASE. Responds in 1 month. One-time rights. Articles, 300–1,000 words; $35–$200. Depts/columns, 600–800 words; payment rates vary. Pays on publication. Provides contributor's copies.

Passport

WordAction Publishing
2923 Troost Avenue
Kansas City, MO 64109

Assistant Editor: Laura Lohberger

DESCRIPTION AND INTERESTS: *Passport* is a weekly Sunday school take-home paper for Church of the Nazarene religion students. Non-staff submissions are accepted for "Survival Guide" (which contains inspirational messages based on church doctrine) and "Curiosity Island" (general interest articles). Circ: 55,000.
Website: www.wordaction.com

FREELANCE POTENTIAL: 90% written by non-staff writers. Publishes 30 freelance submissions yearly; 20% by unpublished writers, 20% by new authors. Receives 240 queries and mss yearly.

SUBMISSIONS AND PAYMENT: Sample copy, free with 5x7 SASE. Guidelines and theme list available. Query with bio; or send complete ms. Accepts hard copy and email to lslohberger@wordaction.com. SASE. Responds in 4–6 weeks. Multi-use rights. "Survival Guide," 400–500 words; $25. "Curiosity Island," 200–300 words; $15. Pays on publication. Provides 1 contributor's copy.

Pathways to Family Wellness

327 North Middletown Road
Media, PA 19063

Editor

DESCRIPTION AND INTERESTS: The purpose of this quarterly is to provide parents with the information they need to make good health care choices for their children and themselves. Guided by a natural wellness philosophy, it explores new approaches to health care, while offering articles on parenting, education, pregnancy, childbirth, the mind-body connection, and nutrition. Circ: 12,000.
Website: www.pathwaystofamilywellness.org

FREELANCE POTENTIAL: 80% written by non-staff writers. Publishes 40–50 freelance submissions yearly. Receives 20 unsolicited mss yearly.

SUBMISSIONS AND PAYMENT: Guidelines available. Send complete ms with 50-word author bio. Accepts email submissions to editor@pathwaystofamilywellness.org and simultaneous submissions if identified. Responds in 3 weeks. First or reprint rights. Articles, 900–2,000 words. No payment. Provides 2 author's copies.

The Pink Chameleon

Editor: Dorothy P. Freda

DESCRIPTION AND INTERESTS: This e-zine provides wholesome reading material for the whole family. Among its current needs are works about "rare moments in time," inspirational stories, and nostalgia pieces. Hits per month: 100.
Website: www.thepinkchameleon.com

FREELANCE POTENTIAL: 95% written by non-staff writers. Publishes 50–100 freelance submissions yearly; 40% by unpublished writers, 60% by authors who are new to the magazine. Receives 300 unsolicited mss yearly.

SUBMISSIONS AND PAYMENT: Sample copy and guidelines available at website. Send complete ms with brief author biography September–October and January–March only. Accepts email submissions to dpfreda@juno.com (no attachments). No simultaneous submissions. Responds in 4–6 weeks. Electronic rights for 1 year. Articles and fiction, to 2,500 words. Poetry, to 36 lines. No payment.

Popcorn Magazine for Children

P.O. Box 9223
Richmond, VA 23227

Editor: Charlene Warner Coleman

DESCRIPTION AND INTERESTS: *Popcorn Magazine for Children* is for kids ages 7 to 14 who are interested in having fun and using their imaginations, and maybe even in learning a thing or two along the way. It features articles on kid-friendly subjects and includes fiction, interviews, craft projects, games, and puzzles. Updated monthly, it appears online and in print. Circ: 250,000.
Website: www.popcornmagazine.net

FREELANCE POTENTIAL: 75% written by non-staff writers. Publishes 1,000 freelance submissions yearly. Receives numerous unsolicited mss each year.

SUBMISSIONS AND PAYMENT: Sample copy, $3.95, downloadable at website. Guidelines available at website. Send complete ms. Accepts hard copy. SASE. Response time varies. Rights vary. Articles, word lengths vary; $75. Fiction, to 800 words; $75. Craft projects; $25+.

Prairie Messenger

Box 190
100 College Drive
Muenster, Saskatchewan S0K 2Y0
Canada

Associate Editor: Maureen Weber

DESCRIPTION AND INTERESTS: This weekly Catholic newspaper covers local, national, and international religious news for readers living in Saskatchewan and Manitoba. Work may be submitted by Canadian writers only. Circ: 5,800.
Website: www.prairiemessenger.ca

FREELANCE POTENTIAL: 60% written by nonstaff writers. Publishes 10 freelance submissions yearly. Receives 30 queries and unsolicited mss each year.

SUBMISSIONS AND PAYMENT: Canadian authors only. Sample copy, $1 with 9x12 SASE. Guidelines available at website. Query or send complete ms. Accepts e-mail submissions to pm.canadian@stpeterspress.ca. Responds in 1 month if interested. First rights. Articles and opinion pieces, 800–2,500 words; $55–$75. Depts/columns, word lengths vary; $3 per column inch. B/W prints, $20. Pays at the end of the month. Provides 1 contributor's copy.

Premier Baby and Child

5100 Windance Place
Holly Springs, NC 27540

Editor & Publisher: Robyn Mangrum

DESCRIPTION AND INTERESTS: This parenting magazine is packed with tips for raising children up to age six. Fresh, fun articles are meant to inspire readers while providing information on local products and resources. Appearing annually, it is distributed to hospitals and pediatrician's offices throughout North Carolina's Triangle region. Circ: 35,000.
Website: www.premierbaby.com

FREELANCE POTENTIAL: 100% written by nonstaff writers. Publishes several freelance submissions yearly; 50% by unpublished writers.

SUBMISSIONS AND PAYMENT: Sample copy and guidelines available. Query with résumé and clips. Accepts hard copy and email queries to publisher@premierbaby.com. SASE. Response time varies. All rights. Articles, 250–500 words. Depts/columns, word lengths vary. Written material, $50–$100. Pays on publication. Provides 2 contributor's copies.

Preschool Playhouse

Urban Ministries
1551 Regency Court
Calumet City, IL 60409

Senior Editor: Judy Hull

DESCRIPTION AND INTERESTS: This is a colorful take-home paper designed to complement Sunday school curricula. Targeting children ages two to five, it features Bible stories and short, fun articles that introduce children to Jesus—each written specifically for an African American audience. It is published quarterly with weekly editions. Circ: 50,000.
Website: www.urbanministries.com

FREELANCE POTENTIAL: 25% written by nonstaff writers. Publishes 12 freelance submissions yearly; 10% by unpublished writers, 25% by authors who are new to the magazine.

SUBMISSIONS AND PAYMENT: Sample copy, free. Guidelines available. All work is assigned. Send résumé with clips or writing samples. Accepts hard copy. SASE. Response time varies. All rights. Articles, word lengths and payment rates vary. Pays on publication. Provides 1 contributor's copy.

PTO Today

100 Stonewall Boulevard, Suite 3
Wrentham, MA 02093

Queries Editor

DESCRIPTION AND INTERESTS: This magazine's mission is to serve as a resource to the leaders of parent groups in elementary and middle schools across the United States. The content focuses on helping parent-teacher organizations be more effective and provide greater impact at their schools. It is published six times each year. Circ: 80,000.
Website: www.ptotoday.com

FREELANCE POTENTIAL: 70% written by nonstaff writers. Publishes 15–20 freelance submissions yearly; 5% by unpublished writers, 15% by authors who are new to the magazine. Receives 90–100 queries yearly.

SUBMISSIONS AND PAYMENT: Guidelines available. Query. Accepts email queries to queries@ptotoday.com. Responds in 2 months. First and electronic rights. Articles, 1,200–1,500 words; payment rates vary. Pays on acceptance. Provides 1 contributor's copy.

Purple Circle Magazine

14200 FM 1062
Canyon, TX 79015

Editor: Melita Cramblet

DESCRIPTION AND INTERESTS: This magazine is read by parents of Junior Livestock Show exhibitors, and by show producers and suppliers. Its articles promote the Junior Livestock Show industry, and cover topics such as breeding, selection, care, and showing of champion cattle, goats, hogs, and sheep. Profiles of youths active in the show circuit are featured regularly. This magazine is published ten times each year. Circ: 3,300.
Website: www.purplecircle.com

FREELANCE POTENTIAL: 50% written by nonstaff writers. Publishes 40 freelance submissions yearly; 99% by unpublished writers.

SUBMISSIONS AND PAYMENT: Sample copy available. Query or send complete ms. Accepts hard copy. SASE. Response time varies. Exclusive rights. Articles and depts/columns, word lengths vary. No payment. Provides 2 contributor's copies.

Ranger Rick

National Wildlife Federation
1100 Wildlife Center Drive
Reston, VA 20190-5362

Editor: Mary Dalheim

DESCRIPTION AND INTERESTS: Since 1967, the National Wildlife Federation has published this monthly magazine for children ages 7 to 12. It features educational yet engaging articles and activities that teach readers about animals and nature, and instill a respect for the natural world. It works mostly with staff writers; however, prospective writers can submit their résumé and clips to be considered for future assignments. Circ: 560,000.
Website: www.nwf.org/rangerrick

FREELANCE POTENTIAL: Publishes few freelance submissions yearly.

SUBMISSIONS AND PAYMENT: Sample copy and guidelines available at website. Send résumé and clips only. No queries or unsolicited mss. Accepts hard copy. SASE. Response time varies. Rights vary. Articles and fiction, 900 words; payment rates vary. Pays on acceptance. Provides 2 contributor's copies.

Racquetball

1685 West Uintah
Colorado Springs, CO 80904

Editor: Jim Hiser

DESCRIPTION AND INTERESTS: This sports magazine, published six times each year, covers the sport of racquetball and the news and events of the U.S. Racquetball Association. For younger readers, it offers articles about the association's junior programs and young players. Circ: 40,000.
Website: www.usaracquetball.com

FREELANCE POTENTIAL: 50% written by nonstaff writers. Publishes 24–30 freelance submissions yearly; 80% by unpublished writers, 20% by authors who are new to the magazine. Receives 100 queries yearly.

SUBMISSIONS AND PAYMENT: Sample copy and guidelines, $4. Prefers query; will accept complete ms. Prefers email queries to jhiser@usra.org; will accept hard copy. SASE. Responds in 9 weeks. One-time rights. Articles, 1,500–2,000 words. Depts/columns, 500–1,000 words. Written material, $.03–$.07 per word. Pays on publication.

Rangers Now

General Council of the Assemblies of God
1445 North Boonville Avenue
Springfield, MO 65802-1894

Editor: John Hicks

DESCRIPTION AND INTERESTS: Published by the National Royal Rangers of the Assemblies of God, this magazine offers boys of all ages articles designed to foster a closer relationship with Jesus Christ. It focuses on leadership skills, fitness and health, nature and the environment, and outdoor activities as ways to grow in that relationship. It also publishes personal testimonies. *Rangers Now* appears annually, in six age-appropriate editions. Circ: 87,000.
Website: www.royalrangers.ag.org

FREELANCE POTENTIAL: 10% written by nonstaff writers. Receives 60 queries yearly.

SUBMISSIONS AND PAYMENT: Sample copy, free with 9x12 SASE. Guidelines available. Query. Accepts hard copy. SASE. Responds in 1–2 weeks. First or all rights. Articles, 1,000 words. Depts/columns, word lengths vary. Written material, payment rates vary. Pays on publication. Provides 2 contributor's copies.

Read

Weekly Reader Publishing
3001 Cindel Drive
Delran, NJ 08075

Editor: Bryon Cahill

DESCRIPTION AND INTERESTS: Each themed issue of this magazine offers a mix of classic and contemporary fiction and nonfiction for use in the classrooms of grades six through ten. Divided into a section for literature and a section for writing, it features excerpts from well-known works and original literature as well as grammar exercises and author interviews. *Read* is published 16 times each year. Circ: 160,000.
Website: www.weeklyreader.com

FREELANCE POTENTIAL: 60% written by non-staff writers.

SUBMISSIONS AND PAYMENT: No queries or unsolicited mss. Send résumé only. All work is assigned. Responds if interested. First North American serial and electronic one-time use rights. Articles, 1,000–2,000 words. Written material, payment rates vary. Pays on acceptance. Provides 5 contributor's copies.

Read, America!

3900 Glenwood Avenue
Golden Valley, MN 55422

Editor & Publisher: Roger Hammer

DESCRIPTION AND INTERESTS: *Read, America!* is designed for professionals working in literacy programs. Each quarterly issue includes informative articles as well as fun and motivational stories and poetry for children. Freelance writers have the best chance for publication by submitting stories and poetry written to be read by students or to students. Circ: 10,000.

FREELANCE POTENTIAL: 100% written by nonstaff writers. Publishes 20 freelance submissions yearly; 100% by unpublished writers, 100% by authors who are new to the magazine. Receives 600 unsolicited mss yearly.

SUBMISSIONS AND PAYMENT: Sample copy and guidelines, $7.50. Send complete ms. Accepts hard copy. No simultaneous submissions. SASE. Responds in 2–3 months. All rights. Articles and fiction, to 1,000 words; $50. Pays on acceptance.

Redbook

Hearst Corporation
300 West 57th Street, 22nd Floor
New York, NY 10019

Submissions: Alison Brower

DESCRIPTION AND INTERESTS: This popular monthly consumer magazine targets women, with articles on relationships, beauty and fashion, careers, sex, home and garden, and health. It also publishes articles on parenting, the trials of being a mother, and childhood development issues. It accepts informative articles, as well as personal experience pieces. Circ: 2.3 million.
Website: www.redbookmag.com

FREELANCE POTENTIAL: 5% written by non-staff writers. Publishes 10 freelance submissions yearly; 2% by unpublished writers. Receives 9,960+ queries yearly.

SUBMISSIONS AND PAYMENT: Sample copy, $2.99 at newsstands. Query with clips and source list. Accepts hard copy. SASE. Responds in 3–4 months. All rights. Articles, 1,000–3,000 words; $.75–$1 per word. Depts/columns, 1,000–5,000 words; payment rates vary. Pays on acceptance.

Reptiles

P.O. Box 6050
Mission Viejo, CA 92690

Editor: Russ Case

DESCRIPTION AND INTERESTS: This monthly magazine is used as a guide for owners of reptiles and amphibians. Geared to the beginner or intermediate hobbyist, articles are written by experts on the care and breeding of these pets. Circ: 40,000.
Website: www.reptilechannel.com

FREELANCE POTENTIAL: 60% written by non-staff writers. Publishes 55 freelance submissions yearly; 50% by unpublished writers, 40% by authors who are new to the magazine. Receives 120 queries yearly.

SUBMISSIONS AND PAYMENT: Sample copy, $4.99 at newsstands. Query with description of herp background. Accepts email queries to reptiles@bowtieinc.com. Responds in 2–3 months. First North American serial rights. Articles and depts/columns, word lengths and payment rates vary. Payment policy varies. Provides 2 contributor's copies.

Richmond Family

7275 Glen Forest Drive, Suite 203
Richmond, VA 23226

Submissions

DESCRIPTION AND INTERESTS: This magazine was launched in 2009 to inspire, inform, and entertain parents in the greater Richmond area. It publishes informational and how-to articles about raising healthy and happy families. Using local information and sources is a requirement for writers. It also accepts personal experience pieces, profiles, and articles on family travel and local recreation. It is published monthly. Circ: Unavailable.
Website: www.richmondfamilymagazine.com

FREELANCE POTENTIAL: Publishes several freelance submissions yearly.

SUBMISSIONS AND PAYMENT: Send complete ms. Accepts email submissions to editor@ richmondfamilymagazine.com. Response time varies. Exclusive print and electronic rights. Articles, 800–1,000 words. Depts/columns, word lengths vary. Written material, payment rates vary. Pays on acceptance.

Rugby

33 Kings Highway
Orangeburg, NY 10962

Editor: Ed Hagerty

DESCRIPTION AND INTERESTS: Rugby isn't just for people in the UK, as this magazine gives fans of American rugby news about their favorite sport. Published six times each year, *Rugby* provides readers with player and team profiles, training tips, and competition coverage for both the college and club levels. Circ: 10,500.
Website: www.rugbymag.com

FREELANCE POTENTIAL: 50% written by non-staff writers. Publishes 400 freelance submissions yearly; 50% by unpublished writers, 50% by authors who are new to the magazine. Receives 600 queries and unsolicited mss yearly.

SUBMISSIONS AND PAYMENT: Sample copy and guidelines, $4 with 9x12 SASE ($1.70 postage). Query or send complete ms. Accepts hard copy and disk submissions. SASE. Responds in 2 weeks. All rights. Written material, word lengths and payment rates vary. Pays on publication. Provides 3 contributor's copies.

The Rock

Cook Communications Ministries
4050 Lee Vance View
Colorado Springs, CO 80918

Editor: Doug Mauss

DESCRIPTION AND INTERESTS: This weekly take-home paper for middle school-age students in religious education classes includes Bible stories, scripture lessons, inspirational stories, and articles that encourage readers to make the right choices. *The Rock* is mostly staff-written, but its editors will occasionally assign work to free-lancers. To be considered for assignments, send your résumé and clips. Circ: 35,000.
Website: www.davidccook.com

FREELANCE POTENTIAL: 10% written by non-staff writers. Publishes 2–3 freelance submissions yearly; 20% by unpublished writers.

SUBMISSIONS AND PAYMENT: Guidelines available at website. Send résumé or writing samples only. No unsolicited mss or queries. Accepts hard copy. SASE. Response time varies. Rights negotiable. Written material, word lengths and payment rates vary. Pays on acceptance. Provides 1 contributor's copy.

Scholastic News

557 Broadway
New York, NY 10012

Submissions Editor, Editions 4–6:
Lee Baier

DESCRIPTION AND INTERESTS: Published weekly, *Scholastic News* is a classroom newsletter filled with kid-focused, curriculum-connected articles and activities. Every issue presents high-interest, late-breaking news in a variety of engaging formats, all designed to help kids to understand and interpret the world around them. Published in six editions, with age-appropriate material for students in grades one through six, the newsletter is complemented by a teacher's edition and interactive website that contains additional instruction material. It is not open to submissions of any kind at this time. Circ: 1 million+.
Website: www.scholastic.com

SUBMISSIONS AND PAYMENT: Not accepting submissions at this time.

Scholastic News English/Español

557 Broadway
New York, NY 10012

Editor

DESCRIPTION AND INTERESTS: This monthly classroom newsletter is designed with a flip format in both English and Spanish to help Spanish-speaking ELL students develop the skills they need to make the transition to English proficiency. Targeting students in first and second grade, it also features take-home pages and reproducibles for teacher use. Circ: 125,000.
Website: www.scholastic.com

FREELANCE POTENTIAL: 10% written by non-staff writers. Publishes several freelance submissions yearly. Receives many unsolicited mss each year.

SUBMISSIONS AND PAYMENT: Sample copy and editorial calendar available at website. Query or send complete ms with résumé. Accepts hard copy and simultaneous submissions if identified. SASE. Responds in 1–3 months. All rights. Articles, to 500 words; $75–$500. Pays on publication. Provides 3+ copies.

Science World

Scholastic Inc.
557 Broadway
New York, NY 10012-3999

Editor: Patricia Janes

DESCRIPTION AND INTERESTS: Designed for classroom use for grades 6 through 10, *Science World* brings science to life with feature articles, hands-on activities, and reproducibles for teachers. All articles are assigned. Writers may submit their qualifications in order to be considered for writing projects. Circ: 40,000.
Website: www.scholastic.com/scienceworld

FREELANCE POTENTIAL: 50% written by non-staff writers. Receives 120 queries yearly.

SUBMISSIONS AND PAYMENT: Sample copy, guidelines, and editorial calendar, free with 9x12 SASE. All articles are assigned. Query with list of publishing credits and clips or writing samples. Accepts hard copy. SASE. Responds in 2 months if interested. All rights. Articles, to 750 words; $250–$650. Depts/columns, 200 words; $100–$125. Written material, $.10 per word. Kill fee, 50%. Pays on publication. Provides 2 contributor's copies.

Scott Stamp Monthly

Scott Publishing Company
P.O. Box 828
Sidney, OH 45365

Editor: Donna Houseman

DESCRIPTION AND INTERESTS: Philatelists of all ages can find articles in this monthly to help them further their collecting hobby. New stamp releases, collecting news, and profiles of collectors are offered here. Circ: 35,000.
Website: www.scottstampmonthly.com

FREELANCE POTENTIAL: 70% written by non-staff writers. Publishes 100 freelance submissions yearly; 15% by unpublished writers, 15% by authors who are new to the magazine. Receives 180 queries and unsolicited mss yearly.

SUBMISSIONS AND PAYMENT: Sample copy and guidelines, $3.50 with 9x12 SASE ($2.07 postage). Prefers query; will accept complete ms. Accepts hard copy and disk submissions (Microsoft Word). SASE. Responds in 1 month. First rights. Articles, 1,000–2,000 words; $75–$150. Depts/columns, word lengths and payment rates vary. Pays on publication. Provides 1 contributor's copy.

Scuola Calcio Coaching Magazine

P.O. Box 15669
Wilmington, NC 28408

Submissions: Antonio Saviano

DESCRIPTION AND INTERESTS: This magazine, published nine times each year, is written for youth soccer coaches in the United States and Canada. It shares coaching tactics, drill instructions, and leadership techniques for improving the skills of young soccer players. Circ: 350+.
Website: www.soccercoachingmagazine.com

FREELANCE POTENTIAL: 20% written by non-staff writers. Publishes 120 freelance submissions yearly; 5% by unpublished writers, 10% by authors who are new to the magazine. Receives 1,000–1,200 queries and unsolicited mss yearly.

SUBMISSIONS AND PAYMENT: Query or send complete ms. Accepts hard copy faxed to 910-795-1674 and email submissions to info@soccercoachingmagazine.com (Microsoft Word attachments). SASE. Responds only if interested. Worldwide rights. Articles and depts/columns, word lengths and payment rates vary. Payment policy varies.

See Jane Fly

1212 Mariner Way, #1
Tiburon, CA 94920

Submissions: Erica Rogers

DESCRIPTION AND INTERESTS: Air travel, whether it's for business or recreation, can be a hassle. This website was created in 2007 to give travelers informational travel guides, how-to's, and scores of helpful tips and advice from people who have learned to travel well. Updated regularly, a portion of its content is geared toward traveling with children. It accepts articles and blogs from travel experts who have seen it all and done it all—with kids. Hits per month: 30,000+.
Website: www.seejanefly.com

FREELANCE POTENTIAL: Publishes several freelance submissions yearly.

SUBMISSIONS AND PAYMENT: Sample copy available at website. Query with author interests, credentials, and writing samples. Accepts email queries to partner@seejanefly.com. Response time varies. Rights vary. Articles and blogs, word lengths vary. Written material, payment rates vary. Payment policy varies.

Shameless

360A Bloor Street W
P.O. Box 68548
Toronto, Ontario M5S 1X1
Canada

Editor: Megan Griffith-Greene

DESCRIPTION AND INTERESTS: Teen girls in Canada have an alternative to the typical teenzine. Instead of focusing on cute shoes and boys, *Shameless* offers inspiring articles on social justice and female empowerment. Topics covered include new media and the arts, technology, feminism, and gender identity. This independent, grassroots publication appears three times each year. Circ: 3,000.
Website: www.shamelessmag.com

FREELANCE POTENTIAL: 30% written by non-staff writers. Publishes 25 freelance submissions each year.

SUBMISSIONS AND PAYMENT: Guidelines available at website. Query with clips. Prefers email queries to submit@shamelessmag.com; will accept hard copy. SAE/IRC. Response time varies. First and electronic rights. Articles, 600–2,200 words. Profiles, 300–500 words. No payment.

Sesame Street Magazine

One Lincoln Plaza
New York, NY 10023

Editor: Rebecca Herman

DESCRIPTION AND INTERESTS: Designed for children ages two to five, this magazine features a colorful array of stories, games, and activities. Each issue uses preschoolers' favorite Sesame Street characters to teach numbers, letters, and other basic concepts. It is published 11 times each year. *Sesame Street Magazine* does not accept queries or unsolicited manuscripts, as all material is produced in-house. Writers interested in working for the magazine may send a résumé with published clips only.
Circ: 650,000.
Website: www.sesamestreet.com

FREELANCE POTENTIAL: 100% staff-written.

SUBMISSIONS AND PAYMENT: All material is written in-house or by assignment. No queries or unsolicited mss. Send résumé and published clips only. Accepts hard copy. SASE.

Sharing Space

Creative Response to Conflict
521 North Broadway
P.O. Box 271
Nyack, NY 10960

Executive Director: Priscilla Prutzman

DESCRIPTION AND INTERESTS: *Sharing Space* is the online newsletter of CRC (Creative Response to Conflict), a nonprofit organization that helps teachers develop the skills necessary to find nonviolent, creative solutions to conflict in order to motivate students to resolve conflicts constructively. In addition to CRC news, it offers informative articles on conflict resolution, mediation, problem-solving, communication, affirmation, bias awareness, diversity, and how to prevent bullying. It also features personal experience stories about teaching nonviolence. Hits per month: Unavailable.
Website: www.crc-global.org

FREELANCE POTENTIAL: 10% written by non-staff writers. Receives 600–1,200 queries yearly.

SUBMISSIONS AND PAYMENT: Query. Accepts hard copy. SASE. Responds in 1–2 weeks. Rights vary. Written material, word lengths vary. Line art. No payment.

Sierra

85 Second Street, 2nd Floor
San Francisco, CA 94105

Managing Editor

DESCRIPTION AND INTERESTS: With the motto "Explore, enjoy, and protect the planet," *Sierra* features articles about our natural world. It prefers to work with professional writers, ideally those who have covered environmental issues. It is published six times each year. Circ: 620,000.
Website: www.sierraclub.org/sierra

FREELANCE POTENTIAL: 45% written by non-staff writers. Publishes 50 freelance submissions yearly; 10% by authors who are new to the magazine. Receives 460–720 queries yearly.

SUBMISSIONS AND PAYMENT: Sample copy, $5 with 9x12 SASE ($1.99 postage). Guidelines available at website. Query. Accepts email queries to Submissions.Sierra@sierraclub.org. Responds in 6–8 weeks. First North American serial, reproduction, and archival rights. Articles, 1,000–3,000 words. Depts/columns, to 1,500 words. Written material, $100–$3,000. Pays on acceptance. Provides 2 contributor's copies.

Simply You Magazine

P.O. Box 284
Phillips, WI 54555-0284

Editor

DESCRIPTION AND INTERESTS: Teens are the primary focus for this online magazine; however, it recently began publishing material of interest to readers in their 20s and 30s, with the intent of "growing with the individual." The content of *Simply You* is centered around relationships and coming-of-age issues, as well as true-life teen and young adult stories. It also includes entertainment reviews. Hits per month: 10,000.
Website: www.simplyyoumagazine.com

FREELANCE POTENTIAL: 25% written by non-staff writers. Publishes 20–40 freelance submissions yearly; 25% by unpublished writers, 50% by authors who are new to the magazine. Receives 12–36 unsolicited mss yearly.

SUBMISSIONS AND PAYMENT: Sample copy available at website. Send complete ms. Accepts email to lynne@simplyyoumagazine.com. Responds in 1–2 months. All rights. Written material, word lengths vary. No payment.

SingleMom.com

Editor

DESCRIPTION AND INTERESTS: A private website, *SingleMom.com* presents free information, support, resources, and tools for single mothers. Areas covered include government grants, scholarships, careers, health care, finances, housing, and legal issues, among many others. Informational pieces that specifically target women adjusting to single parenthood are welcome. A popular feature of the site is its "Amazing Mom Stories" department, which features inspiring accounts of sacrifice, determination, will, and the desire to overcome adversity. Hits per month: Unavailable.
Website: www.singlemom.com

FREELANCE POTENTIAL: Publishes several freelance submissions yearly.

SUBMISSIONS AND PAYMENT: Send complete ms. Accepts email submissions to contact@singlemom.com. Response time varies. Articles, word lengths vary. No payment.

Skiing

5720 Flatiron Parkway
Boulder, CO 80301

Editor: Jake Bogoch

DESCRIPTION AND INTERESTS: Targeting people of all skill levels who just can't get enough of the slopes, *Skiing* features articles on ski destinations, tips on techniques, profiles of skiers, and information on the latest gear. It is published six times each year. Circ: 300,000.
Website: www.skiingmag.com

FREELANCE POTENTIAL: 60% written by non-staff writers. Publishes 50 freelance submissions yearly; 2% by unpublished writers, 5% by new authors. Receives 180 queries yearly.

SUBMISSIONS AND PAYMENT: Sample copy, $2.50 with 9x12 SASE ($1 postage). Query with clips or writing samples. Prefers email to editor@skiingmag.com; will accept hard copy. No simultaneous submissions. SASE. Responds in 2–4 months. First universal and all media rights. Articles and depts/columns, word lengths vary; $1 per word. Pays on acceptance. Provides 2 contributor's copies.

Smithsonian Zoogoer

Friends of the National Zoo
P.O. Box 37012, MRC 5516
Washington, DC 20013-7012

Editor: Cindy Han

DESCRIPTION AND INTERESTS: Members of Friends of the National Zoo read this magazine that is published six times each year. Articles, written by field experts, highlight the zoo's animals, staff, and research and discuss wildlife biology and conservation. Circ: 40,000.
Website: www.fonz.org/zoogoer.htm

FREELANCE POTENTIAL: 15% written by non-staff writers. Publishes 8–10 freelance submissions yearly; 5% by authors who are new to the magazine. Receives 60 queries yearly.

SUBMISSIONS AND PAYMENT: Guidelines available. Query with sources, author bio, and clips. Accepts hard copy and email queries to zoogoer@fonz.org (Microsoft Word or text attachments). SASE. Responds in 1–2 months. First rights. Articles, 2,000 words. Depts/columns, 800–1,500 words. Written material, $.80 per word. Pays on acceptance. Provides 5 copies.

Spigot Science Magazine

P.O. Box 103
Blawenburg, NJ 08504

Editor-in-Chief: Valeria Girandola

DESCRIPTION AND INTERESTS: This online magazine is intended for use in upper-elementary and middle-school science classes and other classes across the curriculum. As such, its contents reflect skill-based classroom practices and familiarity with national science standards. Themed issues are published several times each year. Writers with backgrounds in the education field are encouraged to submit. Hits per month: Unavailable.
Website: www.spigotsciencemag.com

FREELANCE POTENTIAL: 10% written by non-staff writers. Publishes 10 freelance submissions each year.

SUBMISSIONS AND PAYMENT: Sample copy, guidelines, and editorial calendar available at website. Query or send complete ms. Accepts email to vgirandola@spigotsciencemag.com. Response time varies. Limited-time electronic rights. Articles, 300–400 words. No payment.

Spirit

Sisters of St. Joseph of Carondelet
1884 Randolph Avenue
St. Paul, MN 55105-1700

Editor: Joan Mitchell

DESCRIPTION AND INTERESTS: Designed for a Roman Catholic audience, *Spirit* seeks to help young people connect their life experiences with the Sunday Gospels. To this end, it publishes stories and articles about family and social issues, and finding the holy in everyday life. The editors are particularly interested in stories about youth service projects, and those reflecting the cultural diversity of American Catholic children. It appears 28 times each year. Circ: 25,000.
Website: www.goodgroundpress.com

FREELANCE POTENTIAL: 25% written by nonstaff writers. Publishes 1–2 freelance submissions yearly.

SUBMISSIONS AND PAYMENT: Sample copy, free. Query or send complete ms. Accepts hard copy and email to JMCSJ9@aol.com or julie@goodgroundpress.com. Response time varies. All rights. Stories and features, 1,100 words; $300. Pays on publication.

Sporting Youth

P.O. Box 1137
Watkinsville, GA 30677

Editor: Rebecca Mobley

DESCRIPTION AND INTERESTS: The goal of this magazine is to inspire children to get active. Geared to families living in northeast Georgia, its coverage includes local and professional sporting events, tips from coaches, and profiles of local athletes. Published six times each year and distributed to area recreation departments, doctor's offices, and schools, it targets children and young adults ages 10 to 18. Circ: 5,000.
Website: www.sportingyouthga.com

FREELANCE POTENTIAL: 50% written by non-staff writers. Publishes 25 freelance submissions each year.

SUBMISSIONS AND PAYMENT: Sample copy available at website. Query or send complete ms. Accepts email submissions to mail@sportingyouthga.com. Responds in 1 month. One-time rights. Articles and depts/columns, word lengths vary. No payment. Provides contributor's copies.

Stories for Children Magazine

54 East 490 South
Ivins, UT 84738

Submissions Editor

DESCRIPTION AND INTERESTS: This e-zine publishes enlightening articles, short stories, poetry, and activities for children ages 3 through 12. The publication has been on hiatus, but plans are to resume publishing nine issues each year beginning in 2011. In the meantime, it is closed to submissions. Please check the website for changes to this policy. Hits per month: 8,000+.
Website:
   http://storiesforchildrenmagazine.org

FREELANCE POTENTIAL: 95% written by non-staff writers. Publishes 368 freelance submissions yearly; 5% by unpublished writers, 15% by authors who are new to the magazine.

SUBMISSIONS AND PAYMENT: Not reviewing queries or manuscripts at the present time. Freelance writers are advised to check the website for updates to this current submission policy.

The Storyteller

2441 Washington Road
Maynard, AR 72444

Editor: Regina Williams

DESCRIPTION AND INTERESTS: This family magazine offers wholesome reading material only—no erotica, violence, racial or religious bias, or graphic language. Articles, essays, short stories, and poetry are welcome; however, material for children is not accepted. Circ: 700.
Website: www.thestorytellermagazine.com

FREELANCE POTENTIAL: 95% written by non-staff writers. Publishes 300 freelance submissions yearly; 40% by unpublished writers, 50% by authors who are new to the magazine. Receives 4,200 unsolicited mss yearly.

SUBMISSIONS AND PAYMENT: Sample copy and guidelines, $6 with 9x12 SASE ($1.54 postage). Send complete ms. Accepts hard copy and simultaneous submissions if identified. SASE. Responds in 1–2 weeks. First North American serial rights. Articles and fiction, to 2,500 words; $.025 per word. Poetry, to 40 lines; $1 per poem. Payment policy varies.

Storytelling Magazine

National Storytelling Network
P.O. Box 795
Jonesborough, TN 37659

Submissions: Kit Rogers

DESCRIPTION AND INTERESTS: *Storytelling Magazine*, published five times each year, brings National Storytelling Network members news of association events, storytelling trends, and profiles of storytellers. Written by experienced storytellers, its editorial content is geared toward professional storytellers and children's librarians. Each issue also features a small number of stories for readers to use. Circ: 2,000.
Website: www.storynet.org

FREELANCE POTENTIAL: 100% written by nonstaff writers. Publishes 100 freelance submissions yearly. Receives 50 unsolicited mss yearly.

SUBMISSIONS AND PAYMENT: Sample copy, $6. Query. Accepts email queries to kit@storynet.org. SASE. Response time varies. First North American serial rights. Articles, 1,000–2,000 words. Depts/columns, 500 words. No payment. Provides 2 contributor's copies.

Student Assistance Journal

1270 Rankin Drive, Suite F
Troy, MI 48083

Editor: Julie Flaming

DESCRIPTION AND INTERESTS: This quarterly professional journal serves those working with students, particularly students at risk. Its editorial focus includes counseling, violence and substance abuse prevention, social skills, and character education. Circ: 5,000.
Website: www.prponline.net

FREELANCE POTENTIAL: 90% written by non-staff writers. Publishes 12 freelance submissions yearly; 50% by unpublished writers. Receives 36 queries yearly.

SUBMISSIONS AND PAYMENT: Sample copy, free. Guidelines available. Industry professionals should send complete ms. Accepts hard copy, IBM disk submissions, and simultaneous submissions if identified. SASE. Accepts email queries from those outside the field to editorial@prponline.net. Responds if interested. First rights. Articles, 1,500 words. Depts/columns, 750–800 words. No payment. Provides 5 author's copies.

Supertwins

P.O. Box 306
East Islip, NY 11730

Editor: Maureen Boyle

DESCRIPTION AND INTERESTS: Sponsored by Mothers of Supertwins (MOST), this website brings together a network of families, volunteers, and professionals to provide support, education, and research on high-order multiple births. It features articles and research on everything from healthy deliveries to successful parenting during every phase of the children's development. Hits per month: Unavailable.
Website: www.mostonline.org

FREELANCE POTENTIAL: 90% written by non-staff writers. Publishes 80 freelance submissions yearly. Receives 100 queries, 10 unsolicited mss each year.

SUBMISSIONS AND PAYMENT: Query or send complete ms. Accepts hard copy and email submissions to info@mostonline.org. SASE. Response time varies. Rights vary. Articles and depts/columns, word lengths and payment rates vary. Pays on publication.

Susie

3741 Bloomington Street, #4
Colorado Springs, CO 80922

Editor: Susie Shellenberger

DESCRIPTION AND INTERESTS: *Susie* is a monthly magazine designed for Christian girls ages 13 through 19. It publishes both fiction and nonfiction, covering topics such as friendship, family life, fashion, and fitness, all with a "Christian twist." The editors are currently seeking more quizzes, crafts, and general-interest pieces. Circ: 60,000.
Website: www.susiemag.com

FREELANCE POTENTIAL: 90% written by non-staff writers. Publishes 75–100 freelance submissions yearly; 10% by unpublished writers, 25% by authors who are new to the magazine. Receives 300 unsolicited mss yearly.

SUBMISSIONS AND PAYMENT: Guidelines available. Send complete ms. Accepts email submissions to susieshell@comcast.net (include "Freelance" in the subject line). Response time varies. First rights. Written material, word lengths vary. No payment. Provides 2 contributor's copies.

Surfing

950 Calle Amanecer, Suite C
San Clemente, CA 92673

Editor: Travis Ferre

DESCRIPTION AND INTERESTS: Experienced surfers read this monthly for information on surfing destinations, technique, surfer profiles, product reviews, and the surfing lifestyle. With content applicable to all surfers, its targeted audience is young surfers. Circ: 105,000.
Website: www.surfingmagazine.com

FREELANCE POTENTIAL: 20% written by non-staff writers. Publishes 15 freelance submissions yearly; 50% by unpublished writers. Receives 72 unsolicited mss yearly.

SUBMISSIONS AND PAYMENT: Sample copy, $3.99 at newsstands. Query or send complete ms. Accepts hard copy, disk submissions (Quark XPress or Microsoft Word), and simultaneous submissions if identified. SASE. Responds in 1 month. One-time rights. Articles, 2,000–3,000 words. Depts/columns, 135–500 words. Written material, $.10–$.25 per word. Pays on publication. Provides 2 contributor's copies.

Sweet Designs Magazine

Editor-in-Chief: Stephanie Lynn

DESCRIPTION AND INTERESTS: *Sweet Designs Magazine*, an online magazine for (and written by) teenage girls and young adult women, covers teen lifestyle issues. These include family, school, dating, friendships, self-esteem, substance abuse, politics, and college. Fashion, beauty, health and fitness, and entertainment are other topics of interest. Writers passionate about their topics who can commit to submitting fresh, interesting material every month are welcome to query. Hits per month: Unavailable.
Website: www.sweetdesignsmagazine.com

FREELANCE POTENTIAL: Publishes several freelance submissions yearly.

SUBMISSIONS AND PAYMENT: Sample copy and guidelines available at website. Query with writing sample. Accepts email queries to sweet2685@gmail.com. Response time varies. Rights vary. Articles, word lengths and payment rates vary.

Synchro Swimming USA

132 East Washington, Suite 820
Indianapolis, IN 46204

Editor: Taylor Payne

DESCRIPTION AND INTERESTS: The latest information on synchronized swimming can be found in this online member publication of United States Synchronized Swimming. Updated quarterly, it spotlights noteworthy teams, coaches, and judges, and offers competition results, member news, and gear and equipment information. It also features a section dedicated to its younger members. New writers are welcome to send submissions. Hits per month: 7,000.
Website: www.usasynchro.org

FREELANCE POTENTIAL: 50% written by non-staff writers. Publishes 12 freelance submissions yearly; 50% by unpublished writers, 50% by authors who are new to the magazine.

SUBMISSIONS AND PAYMENT: Sample copy available at website. Query or send complete ms. Accepts hard copy. SASE. Response time varies. All rights. Written material, word lengths vary. No payment.

Teachers & Writers

520 Eighth Avenue, Suite 2020
New York, NY 10018

Editor: Susan Karwoska

DESCRIPTION AND INTERESTS: Innovative techniques and practical methods for teaching the art of writing are explored in this quarterly publication. Geared to teachers of kindergarten to grade 12, it is filled with valuable ideas and theories for effective teaching. Circ: 3,000.
Website: www.twc.org

FREELANCE POTENTIAL: 60% written by non-staff writers. Publishes 8 freelance submissions yearly; 5% by unpublished writers, 50% by authors who are new to the magazine. Receives 50 unsolicited mss yearly.

SUBMISSIONS AND PAYMENT: Guidelines available. Send complete ms. Accepts hard copy and simultaneous submissions if identified. SASE. Response time varies. First serial rights. Articles, 700–5,000 words. Depts/columns, word lengths vary. Written material, $20 per printed column. Pays on publication. Provides 10 contributor's copies.

TC Magazine

915 East Market, Box 10750
Searcy, AR 72149

Managing Editor: Laura Edwards

DESCRIPTION AND INTERESTS: *TC Magazine* is for teens ages 13 to 19. It provides a positive, faith-based approach to the issues teens face and the culture in which they live. Pop culture, social issues, music, the arts, and careers are all covered here. It has recently stopped publishing in print and now exists online only, with quarterly updates. Hits per month: 7,000+.
Website: www.tcmagazine.org

FREELANCE POTENTIAL: 35% written by non-staff writers. Publishes 5–10 freelance submissions yearly; 20% by unpublished writers, 30% by authors who are new to the magazine. Receives 60 queries and unsolicited mss yearly.

SUBMISSIONS AND PAYMENT: Query or send complete ms. Prefers email to editor@ tcmagazine.org (Microsoft Word attachments); will accept hard copy. SASE. Response time varies. All rights. Written material, payment rates vary. Payment policy varies.

ThisWeek Community Newspapers

7801 North Central Drive
Lewis Center, OH 43035

Editor: Ben Cason

DESCRIPTION AND INTERESTS: Readers in central Ohio turn to one of the 22 region-specific *ThisWeek* monthly publications for articles on family life, parenting, and education, as well as local news, events, and sports coverage. *ThisWeek* gives preference to local writers who have a strong connection to the community. Circ: 200,000+.
Website: www.thisweeknews.com

FREELANCE POTENTIAL: 100% written by nonstaff writers. Publishes 100 freelance submissions yearly.

SUBMISSIONS AND PAYMENT: Sample copy, free with 9x12 SASE. Query. Accepts email queries to editorial@thisweeknews.com (no attachments). Responds in 1 month. First or reprint rights. Written material, word lengths vary; $.10–$.20 per word. Pays on publication. Provides 2 contributor's copies.

Tidewater Parent

150 West Brambleton Avenue
Norfolk, VA 23510

Editor: Jennifer O'Donnell

DESCRIPTION AND INTERESTS: *Tidewater Parent* is a comprehensive monthly magazine showcasing articles and news for today's active parents and families in the coastal regions of Virginia. It puts an emphasis on local information, giving readers articles on parenting issues and child development along with local resources for education, health care, and recreation. Circ: 48,000.
Website: www.mytidewatermoms.com

FREELANCE POTENTIAL: 90% written by non-staff writers. Publishes 40 freelance submissions yearly; 10% by unpublished writers, 50% by new authors. Receives 72 unsolicited mss yearly.

SUBMISSIONS AND PAYMENT: Send complete ms. Will accept previously published mss that can be reprinted. Accepts hard copy. SASE. Response time varies. Rights vary. Articles, 800–1,200 words; $25. Kill fee, 50%. Pays on publication. Provides 1 contributor's copy.

Toy Farmer

7496 106th Street SE
LaMoure, ND 58458-9404

Editorial Assistant: Cheryl Hegvik

DESCRIPTION AND INTERESTS: *Toy Farmer* offers avid collectors and enthusiasts informative articles on farm toy history, collecting, and pricing. It profiles collectors and collections, as well as manufacturers. Show coverage is also included in each monthly issue. Circ: 27,000.
Website: www.toyfarmer.com

FREELANCE POTENTIAL: 100% written by nonstaff writers. Publishes 50 freelance submissions yearly; 20% by unpublished writers, 20% by authors who are new to the magazine. Receives several queries yearly.

SUBMISSIONS AND PAYMENT: Sample copy and editorial calendar, $5 with 9x12 SASE. Query with writing samples. Accepts hard copy. SASE. Responds in 1 month. First rights. Articles, 1,500 words. Depts/columns, 800 words. Written material, $.10 per word. Pays on publication. Provides 2 contributor's copies.

Toy Trucker & Contractor

7496 106th Avenue SE
LaMoure, ND 58458-9404

Editorial Assistant: Cheryl Hegvik

DESCRIPTION AND INTERESTS: *Toy Trucker & Contractor* is read by model truck and equipment collectors. Each monthly issue offers how-to instruction, profiles of collectors, and articles on collecting. Coverage of model truck shows is also provided. Circ: 8,000.
Website: www.toytrucker.com

FREELANCE POTENTIAL: 100% written by nonstaff writers. Publishes 60 freelance submissions yearly; 10% by unpublished writers, 20% by authors who are new to the magazine. Receives 12 queries yearly.

SUBMISSIONS AND PAYMENT: Editorial calendar available. Query with writing samples. Accepts hard copy. SASE. Responds in 1 month. First North American serial rights. Articles, 1,000–5,000 words. Depts/columns, word lengths vary. Written material, $.10 per word. Pays on publication. Provides 2 author's copies.

Trains

21027 Crossroads Circle
P.O. Box 1612
Waukesha, WI 53187-1612

Editor: Jim Wrinn

DESCRIPTION AND INTERESTS: News stories, feature articles, and personal recollections make up the bulk of this monthly magazine for train buffs of all ages. All types of trains are covered, past and present, in entertaining and edifying articles. Material on trains of the eastern and southern U.S. is currently sought. Circ: 95,000.
Website: www.trainsmag.com

FREELANCE POTENTIAL: 65% written by non-staff writers. Publishes 300–400 freelance submissions yearly; 25% by unpublished writers, 25% by authors who are new to the magazine. Receives 300 queries, 120 unsolicited mss yearly.

SUBMISSIONS AND PAYMENT: Sample copy, $5.95. Guidelines available at website. Prefers query; will accept complete ms. Accepts email to editor@trainsmag.com. Responds in 6 months. All rights. Articles and depts/columns, word lengths vary; $.10–$.15 per word. Pays on acceptance. Provides 2 contributor's copies.

Transworld Snowboarding

2052 Corte del Nogal, Suite B
Carlsbad, CA 92011

Managing Editor: Annie Fost

DESCRIPTION AND INTERESTS: The very best of snowboarding is celebrated in this magazine, published eight times each year. It profiles the raddest boarders and the best snowboarding destinations in the world, covers the latest gear, reports on competitions, and provides insight into the sharpest tricks. Circ: 1.4 million.
Website: www.snowboarding.transworld.net

FREELANCE POTENTIAL: 10% written by non-staff writers. Publishes 10 freelance submissions yearly; 5% by authors who are new to the magazine. Receives 120 queries yearly.

SUBMISSIONS AND PAYMENT: Sample copy, $3.99 at newsstands. Guidelines and theme list available. Query. Accepts email queries to annie.fast@transworld.net. Responds in 1 month. Rights vary. Articles, to 1,600 words. Depts/columns, 300 words. Written material, $.35 per word. Pays on publication. Provides 2 contributor's copies.

Turtle Trails & Tales

P.O. Box 19623
Reno, NV 89511

Editor: Virginia Castleman

DESCRIPTION AND INTERESTS: *Turtle Trails & Tales* is an e-zine dedicated to celebrating the similarities and differences of the children of the world. Multicultural themes run throughout the articles, short stories, and personal experience pieces published. New writers are always welcome. Hits per month: Unavailable.
Website: www.publisher-match.com

FREELANCE POTENTIAL: 80% written by non-staff writers. Of the freelance submissions published yearly, 40% are by unpublished writers, 50% are by authors who are new to the magazine. Receives 60 unsolicited mss yearly.

SUBMISSIONS AND PAYMENT: Sample copy, guidelines, and theme list available at website. Send complete ms. Accepts hard copy and email submissions to virginia@publisher-match.com. SASE. Responds in 3 months. Electronic rights. Articles, 750 words. Fiction, 500–800 words. No payment.

Trumbull County Parent

100 DeBartolo Place, Suite 210
Youngstown, OH 44512

Editor & Publisher: Amy Leigh Wilson

DESCRIPTION AND INTERESTS: This magazine, distributed monthly in the Ohio county of Trumbull, offers parents information on local kid-friendly activities as well as parenting articles. Seasonal material must be submitted 3 months in advance. Circ: 50,000.
Website: www.forparentsonline.com

FREELANCE POTENTIAL: 99% written by non-staff writers. Publishes 100 freelance submissions yearly; 5% by unpublished writers, 20% by authors who are new to the magazine. Receives 500 unsolicited mss yearly.

SUBMISSIONS AND PAYMENT: Sample copy, free with 9x12 SASE. Send complete ms. Accepts hard copy and email submissions to editor@mvparentmagazine.com. SASE. Response time varies. One-time rights. Articles, 1,000–1,800 words. Depts/columns, word lengths vary. Written material, $20–$50. Pays on publication. Provides 1 contributor's copy.

Twist

270 Sylvan Avenue
Englewood Cliffs, NJ 07632

Associate Editor: Tina Donvito

DESCRIPTION AND INTERESTS: Celebrity news and profiles are the focus of this magazine. Designed for teen readers, *Twist* also offers articles on relationships, fashion, music, and entertainment. Celebrity interviews are always of interest. This magazine appears ten times each year. Circ: 230,000.
Website: www.twistmagazine.com

FREELANCE POTENTIAL: 5% written by non-staff writers. Publishes 10 freelance submissions yearly; 5% by unpublished writers, 5% by authors who are new to the magazine. Receives 240 queries yearly.

SUBMISSIONS AND PAYMENT: Sample copy, $3.99 with 9x12 SASE. Guidelines available. Query. Accepts hard copy. SASE. Responds in 2–3 weeks. First North American serial rights. Written material, word lengths and payment rates vary. Pays on acceptance. Provides 2 contributor's copies.

Unique Magazine

Editor & Publisher: Kristine Rademacher

DESCRIPTION AND INTERESTS: This publication of Unique Ministries offers articles that encourage and inspire parents of children with special needs. Each monthly issue includes stories about how families have overcome their challenges and experienced the miracle of God's goodness, with the focus on providing hope rather than medical information. *Unique* also publishes poetry. Hits per month: Unavailable. **Website: www.myuniquekid.com**

FREELANCE POTENTIAL: 20% written by non-staff writers. Publishes 5–10 freelance submissions yearly.

SUBMISSIONS AND PAYMENT: Sample copy and guidelines available at website. Send complete ms with author bio. Accepts email submissions to editor@myuniquekid.com. Responds if interested. Limited time electronic rights. Articles, 500–1,250 words. Poetry, to 15 lines. No payment.

Voices from the Middle

University of Texas at San Antonio
Dept. of Interdisciplinary Learning & Teaching
One UTSA Circle
San Antonio, TX 78249

Editor: Roxanne Henkin

DESCRIPTION AND INTERESTS: *Voices from the Middle* appears quarterly in themed issues, each devoted to a single concept related to literacy and learning at the middle school level. It publishes informative articles, personal experience pieces, and literature reviews. Circ: 9,000. **Website: www.ncte.org/pubs/journals/vm**

FREELANCE POTENTIAL: 70% written by non-staff writers. Publishes 12 freelance submissions yearly; 60% by unpublished writers, 85% by authors who are new to the magazine. Receives 150 unsolicited mss yearly.

SUBMISSIONS AND PAYMENT: Sample copy, $6. Guidelines and theme list available at website. Send 3 copies of ms. Accepts hard copy and email to voices@utsa.edu (Microsoft Word attachments; note issue for which you are submitting in subject line). SASE. Responds in 3–5 months. First and second rights. Articles, 2,500–4,000 words. No payment. Provides 2 copies.

Vegetarian Journal

P.O. Box 1463
Baltimore, MD 21203

Managing Editor: Debra Wasserman

DESCRIPTION AND INTERESTS: Launched in 1982, *Vegetarian Journal* targets well-educated readers of various backgrounds who share a common interest in health, nutrition, animal rights, and ecology. With recipes, cooking tips, and scientific updates, each quarterly issue seeks to make the vegan or vegetarian lifestyle easily accessible at any stage of life. Self-help articles and those that encourage the use of nutritional supplements are not accepted. Circ: 20,000. **Website: www.vrg.org**

FREELANCE POTENTIAL: 50% written by non-staff writers. Publishes 10 freelance submissions yearly; 5% by authors new to the magazine.

SUBMISSIONS AND PAYMENT: Sample copy, $4. Query with brief author biography. Accepts hard copy. Submit seasonal material 1 year in advance. SASE. Responds in 1 week. One-time rights. Articles, word lengths vary; $200. Pays on acceptance. Provides 3+ contributor's copies.

Volta Voices

Alexander Graham Bell Association
for the Deaf and Hard of Hearing
3417 Volta Place NW
Washington, DC 20007-2778

Editor: Melody Felzin

DESCRIPTION AND INTERESTS: *Volta Voices* is read by the deaf and hearing impaired and their families, and by educators, researchers, and other professionals in the field of hearing loss. Its timely articles cover spoken-language education, new technologies, social aspects of hearing impairment, advocacy and legislation, and health issues. It is published six times each year. Circ: 5,500. **Website: www.agbell.org**

FREELANCE POTENTIAL: 90% written by non-staff writers. Publishes 6–8 freelance submissions yearly; 50% by unpublished writers. Receives 24 unsolicited mss yearly.

SUBMISSIONS AND PAYMENT: Sample copy available at website. Send complete ms. Accepts email submissions to editor@agbell.org (Microsoft Word attachments). Responds in 1–3 months. All rights. Articles, 500–2,000 words. No payment. Provides 3 contributor's copies.

The Water Skier

USA Water Ski
1251 Holy Cow Road
Polk City, FL 33868-8200

Editor: Scott Atkinson

DESCRIPTION AND INTERESTS: USA Water Ski publishes this glossy magazine for fans and water skiers alike. Features, athlete profiles, how-to articles, new product reviews, event coverage, and USA Water Ski news updates are offered in photo-packed issues appearing seven times each year. The sports of kneeboarding and wakeboarding are also covered. Circ: 20,000.
Website: www.usawaterski.org

FREELANCE POTENTIAL: 20% written by non-staff writers. Publishes 10–12 freelance submissions yearly; 10% by authors who are new to the magazine. Receives 20–30 queries yearly.

SUBMISSIONS AND PAYMENT: Sample copy, $1.25 with 9x12 SASE. Query. Accepts hard copy. SASE. Responds in 1 month. All rights. Articles, 1,000 words. Depts/columns, 500–1,000 words. Written material, payment rates vary. Pays on publication. Provides 1 contributor's copy.

Women Today Magazine

Box 300 STN "A"
Vancouver, British Columbia V6C 2X3
Canada

Senior Editor: Claire Colvin

DESCRIPTION AND INTERESTS: This online magazine offers a Christian perspective on contemporary issues of relevance to today's women. Relationships, parenting, marriage, careers, personal finances, health, beauty, and fitness are among the topics it addresses each month. Hits per month: Unavailable.
Website: www.womentodaymagazine.com

FREELANCE POTENTIAL: 30–50% written by nonstaff writers. Publishes 20–30 freelance submissions yearly; 15% by unpublished writers, 25% by authors who are new to the magazine. Receives 450 unsolicited mss yearly.

SUBMISSIONS AND PAYMENT: Sample copy, guidelines, and editorial calendar available at website. Send complete ms. Accepts submissions through online submission system only. Responds in 4–6 weeks. One-time rights. Articles, 1,000–1,200 words. Depts/columns, 600–1,000 words. No payment.

Weatherwise

Taylor and Francis Group, LLC
325 Chestnut Street, Suite 800
Philadelphia, PA 19106

Managing Editor: Margaret Benner

DESCRIPTION AND INTERESTS: Six times each year, *Weatherwise* publishes articles and photos chronicling the world's weather phenomena. Writers should be meteorologists. Circ: 5,800.
Website: www.weatherwise.org

FREELANCE POTENTIAL: 50% written by non-staff writers. Publishes 25 freelance submissions yearly; 30% by authors who are new to the magazine. Receives 100 queries yearly.

SUBMISSIONS AND PAYMENT: Certified meteorologists only. Sample copy available; email kaitlynmckeefery@taylorandfrancis.com. Guidelines available at website. Query with outline, résumé, and clips. Accepts queries to margaret. benner@taylorandfrancis.com. No simultaneous submissions. Availability of artwork improves chance of acceptance. Responds in 2 months. All rights. Articles, 1,500–2,000 words. Depts/columns, 800–1,500 words. Payment rates vary. Pays on publication.

Woodall's CamperWays

Woodall Publications Group
2575 Vista Del Mar Drive
Ventura, CA 93001

Managing Editor: Maryanne Sullivan

DESCRIPTION AND INTERESTS: RV and camping enthusiasts in the Mid-Atlantic U.S. turn to this monthly publication for how-to information on vehicle maintenance and safety, recreational activities, and destination ideas. Circ: Unavailable.
Website: www.woodalls.com

FREELANCE POTENTIAL: 90% written by non-staff writers. Publishes several freelance submissions yearly; 10% by authors who are new to the magazine. Receives 300 queries yearly.

SUBMISSIONS AND PAYMENT: Guidelines available. Query. Accepts email queries to editor@woodallpub.com (Microsoft Word attachments). Artwork required for acceptance. Responds in 2 months. First North American serial rights. Articles, 1,000–1,400 words; $50–$200. Depts/columns, by assignment only. High-resolution digital images. Pays on acceptance. Provides 2 contributor's copies.

World Around You

Laurent Clerc National Deaf Education Center
KDES, Suite 3600
800 Florida Avenue NE
Washington, DC 20002-3695

Submissions

DESCRIPTION AND INTERESTS: *World Around You*, also known as *WAY*, focuses on the achievements of young people who are deaf or hard of hearing. Five times each year, it offers inspiring articles, essays, profiles, and personal experience pieces about students and young adults who have succeeded in school and in their careers. It also publishes informative articles on technology and deaf culture. Hits per month: Unavailable.
Website: http://clerccenter.gallaudet.edu/worldaroundyou

FREELANCE POTENTIAL: 10% written by non-staff writers. Publishes 3–5 freelance submissions yearly. Receives 48 queries yearly.

SUBMISSIONS AND PAYMENT: Sample copy available at website. Query. Accepts hard copy. SASE. Responds in 1 month. Rights negotiable. Articles, word lengths and payment rates vary. Pays on publication.

Xtreme JAKES

P.O. Box 530
Edgefield, SC 29824

Editor

DESCRIPTION AND INTERESTS: *XTreme JAKES* is an online teen publication from the National Wild Turkey Federation. Its focus is wildlife preservation, advanced hunting and fishing skills, outdoor sports, and responsible sportsmanship. Most articles are nonfiction, but some fiction is accepted. Hits per month: Unavailable.

FREELANCE POTENTIAL: 50% written by non-staff writers. Publishes 30 freelance submissions yearly; 10% by unpublished writers, 30% by authors who are new to the magazine. Receives 150-200 unsolicited mss yearly.

SUBMISSIONS AND PAYMENT: Prefers queries by mail or email to dearjake@nwtf.net. Complete mss accepted. SASE. Responds to queries in 15 business days. First North American serial and Web rights. Written material, $.05 per word. Artwork, payment rates vary. Kill fee, 25%. Pays on publication. Provides 2 contributor's copies.

YARN

Editor: Kerri Majors

DESCRIPTION AND INTERESTS: This literary journal for young adults over the age of 14 seeks to promote teen literacy and to celebrate young adult literature. Each issue offers fiction, essays, and poetry. Its editors are open to all genres, topics, and poetic forms, and are especially interested in work that features strong narrative voices and emotional honesty. Hits per month: Unavailable.
Website: www.yareview.net

FREELANCE POTENTIAL: Publishes several freelance submissions yearly.

SUBMISSIONS AND PAYMENT: Guidelines available at website. Send complete ms. Accepts email submissions (see guidelines for list of email addresses; no attachments) and simultaneous submissions if identified. Response time varies. Exclusive first-time Internet rights. Essays, to 3,000 words. Fiction, to 6,000 words. Poetry, 3–7 poems per submission. No payment.

Young Bucks Outdoors

P.O. Box 244022
Montgomery, AL 36117

Editor: Linda O'Connor

DESCRIPTION AND INTERESTS: This website for kids interested in outdoor recreational pursuits offers articles on topics such as animal behavior, weather and astronomy, insects and bugs, and forest safety. Hits per month: 200,000.
Website: www.buckmasters.com

FREELANCE POTENTIAL: 60% written by non-staff writers. Publishes 30–40 freelance submissions yearly; 50% by unpublished writers, 50% by authors who are new to the magazine. Receives 24 queries yearly.

SUBMISSIONS AND PAYMENT: Guidelines available. Query with detailed photo information. Availability of artwork improves chance of acceptance. Accepts hard copy and email queries to ybo@buckmasters.com. SASE. Responds in 1 week. First rights. Articles, to 600 words. Prefers digital images; will accept color prints and transparencies. All material, payment rates vary. Pays on publication.

Young Salvationist

The Salvation Army
615 Slaters Lane
Alexandria, VA 22314

Editor: Captain Amy Reardon

DESCRIPTION AND INTERESTS: Published 10 times each year, this magazine deals with the life experiences and social issues that impact teen and young adult Christians. Circ: 48,000. **Website: www.salpubs.com**

FREELANCE POTENTIAL: 5% written by non-staff writers. Publishes 8–9 freelance submissions yearly; 20% by unpublished writers, 30% by new authors. Receives few queries, 50–60 unsolicited mss each year.

SUBMISSIONS AND PAYMENT: Sample copy and guidelines available at website. Prefers complete ms; will accept query. Accepts hard copy, email submissions to ys@usn.salvationarmy.org, and simultaneous submissions if identified. SASE. Responds in 4–6 weeks. First and second rights. Articles, to 1,000 words. Depts/columns, word lengths vary. Written material, $.15 per word for first rights; $.10 per word for reprints. Pays on acceptance. Provides 4 author's copies.

Youth Runner Magazine

P.O. Box 1156
Lake Oswego, OR 97035

Editor: Dan Kesterson

DESCRIPTION AND INTERESTS: Middle school and high school students, their parents, and their coaches turn to this magazine for reporting on cross-country and track and field running. Published 10 times each year, it includes training tips and team and athlete profiles. It encourages submissions from professional writers, students, and coaches. Circ: Unavailable. **Website: www.youthrunner.com**

FREELANCE POTENTIAL: 30% written by non-staff writers. Publishes 100 freelance submissions yearly; 50% by unpublished writers, 30% by authors who are new to the magazine. Receives 60 unsolicited mss yearly.

SUBMISSIONS AND PAYMENT: Sample copy available. Send complete ms. Accepts email submissions to editor@youthrunner.com. Response time varies. First rights. Articles and depts/columns, word lengths and payment rates vary. Payment policy varies.

Your Big Backyard

National Wildlife Federation
11100 Wildlife Center Drive
Reston, VA 20190

Editorial Department

DESCRIPTION AND INTERESTS: *Your Big Backyard* is the National Wildlife Federation's nature magazine for children ages three to seven. Its mission is to introduce wildlife and nature — and the concept of protecting it all — in entertaining and educationally sound ways. It publishes informative articles, short stories featuring animal characters, games, puzzles, and activities. It appears monthly. Circ: 400,000. **Website: www.nwf.org/yourbigbackyard**

FREELANCE POTENTIAL: 10% written by non-staff writers. Publishes 3 freelance submissions yearly. Receives 1,200 queries yearly.

SUBMISSIONS AND PAYMENT: Sample copy and guidelines available at website. All work is assigned. Send résumé and clips only. Accepts hard copy. SASE. Response time varies. Rights vary. Articles and depts/columns, word lengths and payment rates vary. Pays on acceptance. Provides 2 contributor's copies.

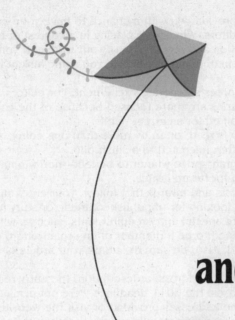

Contests
and Awards

Selected Contests and Awards

Entering a writing contest will provide you with a chance to have your work read by established writers and qualified editors. Winning or placing in a contest or an award program can open the door to publication and recognition of your writing. If you don't win, try to read the winning entry if it is published; doing so will give you some insight into how your work compares with its competition.

For both editors and writers, contests generate excitement. For editors, contests are a source to discover new writers. Entries are more focused because of the contest guidelines, and therefore more closely target an editor's current needs.

For writers, every contest entry is read, often by more than one editor, as opposed to unsolicited submissions that are often relegated to a slush pile.

And you don't have to be the grand-prize winner to benefit—non-winning manuscripts are often purchased by the publication for future issues.

To be considered for the contests and awards that follow, your entry must fulfill all of the requirements mentioned. Most are looking for unpublished article or story manuscripts, while a few require published works. Note special entry requirements, such as whether or not you can submit the material yourself, need to be a member of an organization, or are limited in the number of entries you can send. Also, be sure to submit your article or story in the standard manuscript submission format.

For each listing, we've included the address, a description, the entry requirements, the deadline, and the prize. In some cases, the 2011 deadlines were not available at press time. We recommend that you write to the addresses provided or visit the websites to request an entry form and the contest guidelines, which usually specify the current deadline.

The AAAS Kavli Science Journalism Awards

P.O. Box 2562
Abilene, TX 79604

DESCRIPTION: Begun in 1945, these awards honor distinguished science reporting. They recognize scientific accuracy, initiative, originality, and clarity of interpretation, and they foster public understanding. They include a category for children's science news, for excellence in reporting on science for children to age 14.
Website: www.aaas.org

REQUIREMENTS: The children's award is open to U.S. and international reporters. Entries must have been either published in print, broadcast, or posted online. Submit nine copies, each with an entry form. An entry may consist of a single story; no more than three segments of a thematic series; or a group of three unrelated stories.

PRIZES: Category winners receive $3,000.

DEADLINE: August 1.

All Genres Writing Contest

Buena Vista Enterprises

DESCRIPTION: Buena Vista Enterprises sponsors writing contests in the categories of children's books, YA, poetry, romance, screenplays, and adult fiction and nonfiction. It also has a junior writing contest, all genres, for teens ages 12 to 18. Buena Vista Enterprises is a writing, marketing, and Web design company.
Website: www.allgenreswritingcontest.com

REQUIREMENTS: Entry fees range from $25 to $45, depending on submission date. Submit online only, in pdf, doc, docx, or fdx formats. Multiple entries allowed. Work must be original and unpublished; self-published work is accepted.

PRIZES: First-prize, $3,000 or a three-day writing retreat at Dunton Hot Springs, CO; category prizes, $1,000, or a new computer.

DEADLINE: August 15 to October 14.

Abilene Writers Guild Annual Contest

P.O. Box 2562
Abilene, TX 79604

DESCRIPTION: The Guild's annual contest is open to all writers; its monthly contests are open to members only. The categories for the yearly competition include children's stories for ages 3 to 8, and a novel category that accepts YA fiction. Other categories are flash fiction, general interest articles, poetry, and adult fiction.
Website: www.abilenewritersguild.org

REQUIREMENTS: Guidelines vary for each category. For children, stories can target one age within the range—for preschool, for example, or age 8—and do not have to appeal to all ages. Submit the entire story, which must be original and unpublished. For YA and other novels, send the first 10 pages and a one-page synopsis.

PRIZES: First place, $100; second place, $65; third place, $35.

DEADLINE: Between October 1 and November 30.

Arizona Literary Contest

Contest Coordinator
6145 W. Echo Lane
Glendale, AZ 85302

DESCRIPTION: This annual contest accepts work from writers anywhere in the world. Sponsored by the Arizona Authors Association, it accepts entries of unpublished short stories, poems, articles, essays, and true stories, as well as published books and children's literature.
Website: www.azauthors.com

REQUIREMENTS: Entry fees range from $10 to $30 depending on category. Check website for fees and word length requirements. Accepts hard copy. Manuscripts are not returned. Visit the website or send an SASE for complete guidelines.

PRIZES: First-place winners in each category receive $100. Second- and third-place winners receive $50 and $25, respectively. The top three winners are published or featured in *Arizona Literary Magazine*.

DEADLINE: Entries are accepted between January 1 and July 1.

Atlantic Writing Competition

Writers' Federation of Nova Scotia
1113 Marginal Road
Halifax NS B3H 4P
Canada

DESCRIPTION: Among the categories of this annual contest, open to writers living in Atlantic Canada, are writing for children and juvenile/YA novel. Entries must be unpublished. The competition has been held since 1975.
Website: www.writers.ns.ca

REQUIREMENTS: Entry fees range from $20 to $35. In the children's categories, entries may be fiction, nonfiction, poetry, or stage plays for children up to age 12. Only one entry per category. Do not include your real name on the manuscript itself; select a pseudonym. Also include a one-paragraph description of yourself, and a list of writing credits, if any.

PRIZES: Prizes in each of the categories are $150, $75, and $50. Winners will be announced in September.

DEADLINE: December 3.

Baker's Plays High School Playwriting Contest

Attn: High School Playwriting Contest
45 W. 25th Street
New York, NY 10010

DESCRIPTION: As an advocate for theater in schools for more than 100 years, Baker's Plays sponsors this high school playwriting competition to foster creativity among teens involved in drama.
Website: www.bakersplays.com

REQUIREMENTS: Open to high school students only. No entry fee or length limitations. Plays must be accompanied by the signature of a sponsoring high school English teacher. Manuscripts must be firmly bound and typed. Plays will not be returned. A postcard or email will be sent as notification of receipt of manuscript. Multiple submissions and co-authored scripts are welcome. Visit the website for contest rules and entry form.

PRIZES: First-place winner receives a cash award of $500; second- and third-place winners receive $250 and $100 respectively.

DEADLINE: Entries are accepted between September 1 and January 31.

Waldo M. and Grace C. Bonderman Youth Theatre Playwriting Competition

Indiana Repertory Theatre
140 W. Washington Street
Indianapolis, IN 46204

DESCRIPTION: This annual competition was launched to encourage the development of theatrical scripts that attract young audiences. It accepts plays from adult writers that are intended for audiences in third grade through high school. Scripts must not be committed to publication at the time of submission.
Website: www.irtlive.com

REQUIREMENTS: No entry fee. Scripts for grades 3–5 should have a running time of 30–40 minutes. Scripts for grades 6 and up should have a running time of 45 minutes. Manuscripts must be submitted electronically. Author's name should not appear on the manuscript. Visit the website for complete guidelines.

PRIZES: Prizes vary. Winning plays will be performed at the Bonderman Symposium.

DEADLINE: August 16.

Canadian Writer's Journal Short Fiction Contest

Box 1178
New Liskeard, Ontario P0J 1P0
Canada

DESCRIPTION: Original, unpublished short stories of any genre are accepted for this contest. Submitting writers must be Canadian citizens or landed immigrants.
Website: www.cwj.ca

REQUIREMENTS: Entry fee, $5 per story. Maximum length, 1,500 words. Multiple entries accepted. Accepts hard copy. Author's name must not appear on manuscript. Include a cover sheet with author's name, address, and short biography. Manuscripts are not returned. Visit the website for complete guidelines.

PRIZES: First-place winner receives a cash prize of $150. Second- and third-place winners receive cash prizes of $100 and $50 respectively. Winning entries are published in *Canadian Writer's Journal*.

DEADLINE: April 30.

CAPA Competition

c/o Dan Uitti
Connecticut Authors and Publishers Association
223 Buckingham Street
Oakville, CT 06779

DESCRIPTION: Prizes for poems, short stories personal essays, and children's stories are awarded annually by the Connecticut Authors and Publishers Association. While the competition was previously open to Connecticut residents only, it is now open to all writers.
Website: www.aboutcapa.com

REQUIREMENTS: Entry fees, $10 for one story or essay or up to 3 poems. Children's stories to 2,000 words. Personal essays, to 1,500 words. Poetry, to 30 lines. Multiple entries are accepted. Accepts hard copy. Submit 4 copies of each entry. Manuscripts are not returned. Winning entries are published in a special issue of *The Authority*, CAPA's monthly newsletter.

PRIZES: First-place winners in each category receive $100. Second-place winners receive $50 each.

DEADLINE: December 18.

Delacorte Press Contest

Random House
1745 Broadway, 9th Floor
New York, NY 10019

DESCRIPTION: This contest is open to U.S. and Canadian writers who have not previously published a young adult novel. It looks for stories that feature contemporary settings and plots that appeal to teens.
Website: www.randomhouse.com

REQUIREMENTS: No entry fee required. Length, 100–224 pages. Limit 2 entries per competition. Accepts hard copy. Cover page should include a brief plot summary, the title of the novel, and the author's name, address, and telephone number. Manuscripts are not returned. Visit the website for complete submission information.

PRIZES: Winner receives a book contract from Delacorte Press Books for Young Readers, a $7,500 advance against royalties, and a cash prize of $1,500.

DEADLINE: Entries are accepted between October 1 and December 31.

Children's Writer Contests

Children's Writer
93 Long Ridge Road
West Redding, CT 06896-1124

DESCRIPTION: In 2011, *Children's Writer* is sponsoring two writing contests. One asks for submissions of a fiction or nonfiction story for kindergarteners, to 150 words. The second is middle-grade mysteries, targeted at age eight, to 1,200 words.
Website: www.childrenswriter.com

REQUIREMENTS: No entry fee for subscribers. For non-subscribers, a $15 entry fee includes an 8-month subscription to the newsletter. Manuscripts accepted online or by mail. Manuscripts are not returned. Visit the website for complete contest rules.

PRIZES: Prizes range from $100 to $500. Winning entries are published in *Children's Writer*.

DEADLINE: February 28 and October 31. Check website for details.

Delacorte Yearling Contest

Random House
1745 Broadway, 9th Floor
New York, NY 10019

DESCRIPTION: Unpublished writers of middle-grade fiction are invited to submit their work to the Delacorte Yearling Contest for a First Middle-Grade Novel. Formerly known as the Marguerite de Angeli Contest, this competition accepts contemporary or historical fiction written for children ages 9 through 12.
Website: www.randomhouse.com

REQUIREMENTS: No entry fee required. Length, 96–160 pages. Limit 2 entries per competition. Accepts hard copy. Manuscripts are not returned. Visit the publisher's website for complete submission information.

PRIZES: Winner receives a publishing contract from Delacorte Press Books for Young Readers, a $7,500 advance against royalties, and a cash prize of $1,500.

DEADLINE: Entries are accepted between April 1 and June 30.

Shubert Fendrich Memorial Playwriting Contest

Pioneer Drama Service, Inc.
P.O. Box 4267
Englewood, CO 80155-4267

DESCRIPTION: This annual playwriting contest was established to honor the founder of Pioneer Drama Service. It recognizes outstanding plays that are written for educational and community theater groups.
Website: www.pioneerdrama.com

REQUIREMENTS: No entry fee. Plays should run between 20 and 90 minutes. Accepts hard copy. All entries must include the completed application form (available at website), musical score if applicable, and proof of production. Writers who are currently published by Pioneer Drama Service are not eligible.

PRIZES: Winning entry is published by Pioneer Drama Service; winner receives a $1,000 advance on royalties.

DEADLINE: Ongoing; winner announced each June 1 from plays submitted during the previous calendar year.

H. E. Francis Contest

Department of English
Morton Hall, Room 222
University of Alabama at Huntsville
Huntsville, AL 35899

DESCRIPTION: Judged by a panel of nationally recognized authors, directors of creative writing programs, and editors of literary journals, this contest is sponsored by the Ruth Hindman Foundation and the University of Alabama Huntsville English department. It is for short stories only.
Website: www.uah.edu/hefranciscontest

REQUIREMENTS: Entry fee, $15 per submission. Send 3 copies of manuscript. No identifying information should appear on the manuscript itself. Enclose a cover sheet with story title, word count, and author name and address. Manuscripts are not returned; send SASE for announcement of winner. Visit the website for more information.

PRIZES: First-place winner receives a cash prize of $1,000.

DEADLINE: December 31. Winner is announced in March.

Foster City International Writing Contest

c/o Foster City Parks & Recreation Dept.
650 Shell Boulevard
Foster City, CA 94404

DESCRIPTION: The Foster City International Writing Contest is held each year, and accepts entries of children's stories, fiction, humor, personal essays, and poetry. Only submissions of original, unpublished work will be considered for this contest.
Website: www.fostercity.org

REQUIREMENTS: Entry fee, $20. Multiple entries are accepted. Categorie include hildren's stories, fiction, humor, and personal experience pieces, to 3,000 words. Poetry, to 500 words. Accepts hard copy and email submissions to fostercity_writers@yahoo.com (RTF or Microsoft Word attachments). Visit the website for complete information.

PRIZES: First-place winners in each category receive a cash prize of $150.

DEADLINE: June 1.

Friends of the Library Contest

Decatur Public Library
130 N. Franklin Street
Decatur, IL 62523

DESCRIPTION: Sponsored by the public library in Decatur, Illinois, this writing contest is open to writers from all over the world. It awards prizes for essays, fiction, juvenile fiction, and rhymed poetry. Writers should avoid using the present tense in fiction and near rhyme in rhymed poetry.
Website: www.decatur.lib.i.us

REQUIREMENTS: Entry fee, $3; limit 5 entries per person. Accepts hard copy. Essay, to 2,000 words. Fiction and juvenile fiction, to 3,000 words. Poetry, to 40 lines. Author's name should not appear on the manuscript. All entries must be accompanied by an entry form. Complete contest rules and entry form available at website.

PRIZES: First-place winner receives a cash award of $50. Second- and third-place winners receive $30 and $20 respectively.

DEADLINE: September 25. Winners announced in December.

John Gardner Memorial Prize for Fiction

Harpur Palate
English Department, Binghamton University
Box 6000
Binghamton, NY 13902-6000

DESCRIPTION: Previously unpublished short fiction is accepted for this contest sponsored by Binghamton University. The annual award is given in memory of John Gardner, a fiction writer, dramatist, and teacher.
Website: http://harpurpalate.binghamton.edu

REQUIREMENTS: Entry fee, $15; includes a 1-year subscription to *Harpur Palate*. Length, to 8,000 words. Accepts hard copy. Include a cover sheet with author's name, address, phone number, email address, and the title of the story. Author's name should not appear on entry. Manuscripts are not returned; enclose SASE for contest results.

PRIZES: Winner receives a cash award of $500 and publication in the summer issue of *Harpur Palate*.

DEADLINE: Entries are accepted between January 1 and March 31.

Paul Gillette Awards

c/o Pikes Peak Writers
427 E. Colorado #116
Colorado Springs, CO 80903

DESCRIPTION: The Pikes Peak Writers organization sponsors this contest for unpublished writers of short stories and novels. Short stories can be in all genres. It accepts book-length fiction for children and young adults, as well as historical, mainstream, and science fiction, mystery, suspense, intrigue, and romance.
Website: www.ppwc.net

REQUIREMENTS: Entry fee, $30 per entry for Pikes Peak Writers members; $40 for nonmembers. Up to 2 entries in the same category will be accepted. Word lengths vary for each category. Accepts email submissions only to pgcontest@gmail.com (RTF attachments). Check website for full contest rules and checklist.

PRIZES: First-place winners in each category receive $100. Second- and third-place winners receive $50 and $30, respectively.

DEADLINE: November 15.

Ghost Story Contest

c/o Friends of the Dr. Eugene Clark Library
P.O. Box 821
Lockhart, TX 78644

DESCRIPTION: Each year, the Dr. Eugene Clark Library in Lockhart, Texas, sponsors a ghost story contest in conjunction with its "A Dickens Christmas in Lockhart" festival. The contest accepts unpublished ghost stories of any genre, written on any subject. Prizes are awarded to adult authors, as well as in a junior category for ages 12 to 18.
Website: www.clarklibraryfriends.com

REQUIREMENTS: Entry fee, $20 for adults; $5 for junior category. Limit, one entry per writer. Length, to 5,000 words. Accepts hard copy accompanied by an entry form. Visit the website for full contest rules and entry form.

PRIZES: First-place winners receive $1,000 and a trophy. Second- and third-place winners receive $500 and $250 respectively. Junior contest winners receive $25.

DEADLINE: October 1.

Highlights for Children Fiction Contest

Fiction Contest
803 Church Street
Honesdale, PA 18431

DESCRIPTION: This year's *Highlights for Children* Fiction Contest features stories that involve an embarrassing moment, written for young readers. Writers must be at least 16 years old to submit their work. Stories cannot include derogatory humor, crime, or violence.
Website: www.highlights.com

REQUIREMENTS: No entry fee. Length, to 750 words; to 475 words for beginning readers. Accepts hard copy. Include SASE for return of manuscript. All submissions should be clearly marked FICTION CONTEST. Visit the website for complete guidelines.

PRIZES: Winners receive a cash award of $1,000 or tuition for the Highlights Foundation Writers Workshop at Chautauqua.

DEADLINE: Entries must be postmarked between January 1 and January 31.

Insight Writing Contest

55 West Oak Ridge Drive
Hagerstown, MD 21740-7390

DESCRIPTION: Adults and students up to the age of 22 are invited to enter this contest from *Insight Magazine*. It awards prizes for student short stories and poetry, as well as for short stories written by adults. Submissions must be true, unpublished, and have a spiritual message.
Website: www.insightmagazine.org

REQUIREMENTS: No entry fee. Length, to 7 pages for short fiction; to 1 page for poetry. Accepts hard copy and email to insight@rhpa.org. Multiple entries accepted; each must be accompanied by a cover sheet which includes entry category, author name, address, church name, gender, ethnicity, social security number, and biographical facts. Visit the website for complete guidelines.

PRIZES: Winners receive cash awards ranging from $50 to $220. Winning entries are published in *Insight*.

DEADLINE: June 1.

Memoirs Ink Writing Contest

10866 Washington Blvd., Suite 518
Culver City, CA 90232

DESCRIPTION: Writers of personal essays, memoirs, and stories based on autobiographical experiences are welcome to submit their work to this contest. Writing can be funny, sad, serious, artsy, or fragmented; however, all entries must be written in the first person.
Website: www.memoirsink.com

REQUIREMENTS: Entry fee, $15; $13 for previous entrants. Length, to 1,500 words for February contest; to 3,000 words for August contest. Multiple submissions are accepted; $10 entry fee for each additional submission. Accepts hard copy and submissions through website. Author's name should appear only on entry form. Visit the website for details and entry form.

PRIZES: First-place winner receives $1,000 cash prize. Second- and third-place winners receive $500 and $250, respectively.

DEADLINE: February 15 and August 14.

Magazine Merit Awards

Society of Children's Book Writers & Illustrators
8271 Beverly Boulevard
Los Angeles, CA 90048

DESCRIPTION: This annual award is granted by the SCBWI to recognize outstanding and original magazine writing for young people. It is conferred in the categories of fiction, nonfiction, illustration and poetry. Winning entries genuinely reflect the interests and concerns of young readers.
Website: www.scbwi.org

REQUIREMENTS: No entry fee. Entrants must be members of SCBWI. Members submit four copies of each entry with proof of publication date, indicating the magazine name and date of publication. This may be a table of contents or verification from the editor. See website for details.

PRIZES: Winners in each category, announced in April, are given a plaque. Honor certificates are also awarded.

DEADLINE: December 15.

Milkweed Prize for Children's Literature

Milkweed Editions
1011 Washington Avenue South, Suite 300
Minneapolis, MN 55415

DESCRIPTION: This prize is awarded to novels written for children ages 8 to 13. The publishers of Milkweed Editions choose a winner from the best manuscripts that have been submitted to them during the calendar year, by a writer they have not previously published. It favors books that introduce young readers to memorable characters struggling with the kinds of difficult decisions young people face.
Website: www.milkweed.org

REQUIREMENTS: No entry fee. All children's manuscripts submitted for publication are automatically entered. Submissions should adhere to Milkweed's children's literature submission guidelines available on website.

PRIZES: Winner receives a $10,000 cash prize in addition to a negotiated contract at time of acceptance.

DEADLINE: Ongoing.

National Children's Theatre Competition

Actors' Playhouse/Miracle Theatre
280 Miracle Mile
Coral Gables, FL 33134

DESCRIPTION: Judged by panelists from both professional and academic theatre, this competition seeks original scripts for musicals. Musicals should lend themselves to simplified and suggested settings and be suitable for touring. The target audience is ages 5 to 12, but submissions that also appeal to adults will have an advantage.
Website: www.actorsplayhouse.org

REQUIREMENTS: Entry fee, $10. Multiple entries are accepted; each must be accompanied by entry fee and official entry form. Musicals should have a running time of 45–60 minutes and require no more than 8 adult actors to play any number of roles. Accepts hard copy. Visit the website for complete guidelines and entry form.

PRIZES: Winner receives a cash prize of $500; winning musical will be a featured production of the National Children's Theatre Festival.

DEADLINE: April 1.

New Voices Award

Lee & Low Books
95 Madison Avenue
New York, NY 10016

DESCRIPTION: This publisher awards an annual prize to a picture book that addresses the needs of children of color. Children should be able to relate to, and identify with, the story, and it should promote understanding among cultures and ethnicities. The contest is open to writers of color who are U.S. residents and who have not previously published a children's picture book.
Website: www.leeandlow.com

REQUIREMENTS: No entry fee. Length, to 1,500 words. Limit 2 submissions per entrant. Include cover letter with author name, contact information, and brief biographical note, including cultural and ethnic background. Accepts hard copy. Visit website for complete guidelines.

PRIZES: Winner receives $1,000 and a publishing contract from Lee & Low Books.

DEADLINE: Entries are accepted between May 1 and September 30.

New Millennium Writings Awards

Room M2
P.O. Box 2463
Knoxville, TN 37901

DESCRIPTION: Each year, *New Millennium Writings* sponsors a contest to recognize outstanding fiction, poetry, and nonfiction. Nonfiction can include humor, memoir, creative nonfiction, travel pieces, opinions, essays, interviews, and investigative reporting. It accepts previously published works if they appeared online or in a publication with circulation under 5,000.
Website: www.newmillenniumwritings.org

REQUIREMENTS: Entry fee, $17. Fiction and nonfiction, to 6,000 words. Short-short fiction, to 1,000 words. Poetry, up to 3 poems; limit 5 pages total per entry. Accepts hard copy and submissions through the website. Author name and contact information should appear on cover page only. Visit the website for complete guidelines.

PRIZES: First-place winners in each category receive a cash prize of $1,000.

DEADLINE: November 17.

Pacific Northwest Writers Association Literary Contest

PMB 2717
1420 NW Gillman Boulevard, Suite 2
Issaquah, WA 98027

DESCRIPTION: This contest accepts entries in 12 categories, including mainstream, romance, and historical fiction, screenwriting, children's picture books and chapter books, young adult novels, and poetry. It is sponsored annually by the Pacific Northwest Writers Association.
Website: www.pnwa.org

REQUIREMENTS: Entry fee, $35 for members; $50 for non-members. Limit one entry per category. Word lengths vary for each category. Book-length works may require synopsis. Send 3 hard copies of manuscript, a complete contest registration form, entry fee, and #10 SASE. Author's name should not appear on manuscript. Visit the website for complete guidelines.

PRIZES: Winners in each category receive prizes ranging from $150 to $600.

DEADLINE: February 19.

Pockets Annual Fiction Contest

P.O. Box 340004
Nashville, TN 32703-0004

DESCRIPTION: This annual contest is sponsored by *Pockets*, a magazine designed to connect children to God. Published by Upper Room Ministries, it targets children ages 6 to 12. The contest accepts most types of previously unpublished stories that would be appropriate for publication in the magazine.
Website: http://pockets.upperroom.org

REQUIREMENTS: No entry fee. Length, 750–1,000 words. Manuscripts over 1,000 words will be disqualified; include accurate word count on cover sheet. Multiple submissions are permitted. Entries with an SASE will be returned. Visit website for detailed guidelines.

PRIZES: Winner receives a $500 cash award and publication in *Pockets*.

DEADLINE: Submissions must be postmarked between March 1 and August 15.

Purple Dragonfly Awards

Five Star Publications
4696 West Tyson Street
Chandler, AZ 85226-2903

DESCRIPTION: Focused on children, the Purple Dragonfly Book Awards are given to stories that appeal to young readers of many ages and demonstrate excellence. The categories range from short story collections to board books, picture books, chapter books, YA fiction and nonfiction, and many more.
Website: www.fivestarpublications.com

REQUIREMENTS: Entry fee, $50. Multiple submissions are accepted. Mail two copies of a submission for each category entered, with a completed entry form. Ebooks are not eligible. See website for details and judging criteria.

PRIZES: Grand prize, $300, a marketing consultation with Five Star Publications, and $100 worth of the company's books. First place, $100.

DEADLINE: March 1.

San Antonio Writers Guild Writing Contests

San Antonio Writers Guild
P.O. Box 100717
San Antonio, TX 78201-8717

DESCRIPTION: This contest recognizes exceptional work in the categories of novel, short story, flash fiction, memoir or personal essay, and poetry. It is open to submissions of unpublished work by both members of the San Antonio Writers' Guild and non-members.
Website: www.sawritersguild.com

REQUIREMENTS: Entry fee, $10 for members; $20 for non-members. Word lengths vary according to category. Multiple entries are accepted in up to 3 different categories; each entry must have its own entry form. Submit two hard copies with entry form. Visit the website for complete contest guidelines.

PRIZES: First-place winners receive a cash prize of $100. Second- and third-place winners receive cash prizes of $50 and $25 respectively.

DEADLINE: October 1.

Seven Hills Literary Contest

TWA Seven Hills Contest
P.O. Box 3428
Tallahassee, FL 32315

DESCRIPTION: Sponsored annually by the Tallahassee Writers Association (TWA), this contest accepts entries in categories of short story, creative nonfiction, and flash fiction. It also recognizes children's chapter books or short stories, alternating yearly with children's picture books.
Website: www.twaonline.org

REQUIREMENTS: Entry fee, $10 for members; $15 for non-members. Length, to 2,500 words; to 500 words for flash fiction. Submit 3 hard copies with TWA cover sheet available on website. Author's name should not appear on the manuscript itself. Manuscripts are not returned. Visit the website for complete guidelines.

PRIZES: First-place winners in each category receive $100. Second- and third-place winners receive $75 and $50, respectively. All winning entries appear in *Seven Hills Review*.

DEADLINE: August 31.

Seventeen's Fiction Contest

Hearst Communications, Inc.
300 W. 57th Street, 17th Floor
New York, NY 10019

DESCRIPTION: Fiction writers between the ages of 13 and 21 are encouraged to submit their best stories to this competition. The stories are judged based on originality, creativity, and the author's writing ability. Entrants must be residents of the U.S. or Canada, and all submissions must be unpublished. The winning story appears in *Seventeen* magazine.
Website: www.seventeen.com

REQUIREMENTS: No entry fee. Length, to 500 words. Multiple entries are accepted. Accepts electronic submissions through the website only; each submission must be accompanied by the entry form posted at the website.

PRIZES: Grand-prize winner receives a cash prize of $5,000 and publication in *Seventeen*. Cash prizes and possible publication are awarded to second- and third-place winners.

DEADLINE: December 31.

Kay Snow Writing Contest

Willamette Writers
9045 SW Barbur Boulevard, Suite 5A
Portland, OR 97219-4027

DESCRIPTION: Sponsored by the largest writers' organization in Oregon, and one of the largest in the U.S., this contest accepts fiction and nonfiction for adults; juvenile short stories, novel excerpts, or articles; screenplays; and works written by students.
Website: www.willamettewriters.com

REQUIREMENTS: Entry fee, $10 per entry for members; $15 per entry for non-members. Student entries are free. Send 2 hard copies with entry form and 3x5 card with author name, address, phone, title of entry, and category. Author's name should not appear on the manuscript itself. Manuscripts are not returned. Visit the website for complete guidelines and entry forms.

PRIZES: First-place winners receive a cash prize of $300. Second- and third-place winners receive cash prizes of $150 and $50 respectively.

DEADLINE: April 23.

Skipping Stones Youth Honor Award Program

Skipping Stones
P.O. Box 3939
Eugene, OR 97403

DESCRIPTION: Sponsored by the international multicultural magazine *Skipping Stones,* the Youth Honor Awards recognize creative works by youth, ages 7 to 17. The judges look for essays, interviews, short stories, poems, plays, and artwork that promote multicultural and nature awareness. Non-English and bilingual writings are welcome.
Website: www.skippingstones.org

REQUIREMENTS: Entry fee, $3; low-income entrants and subscribers may enter free. Length, to 1,000 words. Poetry, to 30 lines. Accepts hard copy. Include SASE and certificate of originality from parent or teacher. Visit the website for complete guidelines.

PRIZES: Winners will have their work published in *Skipping Stones*, receive an Honor Award Certificate, a subscription, and five books.

DEADLINE: June 25.

SouthWest Writers Contest

SouthWest Writers
3721 Morris NE, Suite A
Albuquerque, NM 87111

DESCRIPTION: The SouthWest Writers organization offers annual prizes in 14 categories, including middle-grade and young adult novel, children's fiction or nonfiction picture book, adult fiction in a variety of genres, and poetry. The goal is to reward and encourage excellence.
Website: www.southwestwriters.com

REQUIREMENTS: Entry fees, word lengths, and other requirements vary for each category; check website for specific information. Send 2 hard copies of submission with entry form. Author's name and contact information should not appear on the entry itself.

PRIZES: First-place winners in each category receive $150. Second- and third-place winners in each category receive $100 and $50 respectively. All winners are eligible for a $1,000 Storyteller Award.

DEADLINE: May 1.

Sydney Taylor Manuscript Award

Aileen Grossberg
204 Park Street
Montclair, NJ 07042-2903

DESCRIPTION: First awarded in 1985 and sponsored by the Association of Jewish Libraries, this contest recognizes works of fiction for readers ages 8 through 11. Submitted stories should deepen the understanding of Judaism for all children, Jewish and non-Jewish, and present positive aspects of Jewish life. The writer must have no previously published books of fiction.
Website: www.jewishlibraries.org

REQUIREMENTS: No entry fee. Length, 64–200 pages. Accepts hard copy. Manuscripts must be accompanied by a release form, entry form, and cover letter with a short personal statement, synopsis, and curriculum vitae. Visit the website or send an SASE for complete guidelines.

PRIZES: Winner receives a cash prize of $1,000.

DEADLINE: December 15.

Tennessee Williams Fiction Contest

Tennessee Williams/New Orleans Literary Festival
938 Lafayette Street, Suite 514
New Orleans, LA 70113

DESCRIPTION: The judges of this contest seek the best work of fiction from writers who have not yet published a book of fiction. Stories can be of any theme or genre, but those that have won any other writing contest are ineligible.
Website: www.tennesseewilliams.net

REQUIREMENTS: Entry fee, $25. Length, to 7,000 words. Multiple entries and simultaneous submissions accepted. Accepts hard copy and submissions through website. Author's name should not appear on the manuscript. Include a separate page with story title, word count, author's name, address, phone, and email. Visit the website for complete guidelines.

PRIZES: Winner receives a cash prize of $1,500, domestic airfare to attend the literary festival, and publication in *Bayou*.

DEADLINE: November 15.

Tennessee Williams One-Act Play Contest

Tennessee Williams/New Orleans Literary Festival
938 Lafayette Street, Suite 514
New Orleans, LA 70113

DESCRIPTION: The Tennessee Williams/New Orleans Literary Festival sponsors a contest each year to recognize and reward writers of one-act plays. Submissions must not have been previously produced, published, or performed. "Workshopped" readings are accepted.
Website: www.tennesseewilliams.net

REQUIREMENTS: Entry fee, $25. Plays should be no more than one hour in length. Multiple entries are accepted. Electronic entries are preferred and must be in .doc, .rtf, or pdf formats. Will accept hard copy. Include one title page with the play title only and another page with play title and name, address, phone, and email of author. Visit the website for complete guidelines.

PRIZES: Winner receives a cash prize of $1,500, a staged reading at the festival, and publication in *Bayou*.

DEADLINE: November 1.

Utah Original Writing Competition

617 E. South Temple
Salt Lake City, UT 84102

DESCRIPTION: Sponsored by the Utah Division of Arts & Museums, this competition was established to honor the state's finest writers. It is open to Utah residents only, and accepts entries in a number of categories, including novel, general nonfiction, poetry, short story, personal essay, and juvenile book. Entrants must be unpublished in the category they are entering. Submissions are reviewed in a blind process by judges from outside of Utah.
Website: http://arts.utah.gov

REQUIREMENTS: No entry fee. Word lengths vary for each category; check website for specific information. Limit one entry per category. Manuscripts are now being accepted online only. Visit website for submission instructions.

PRIZES: Winners receive cash prizes ranging from $200 to $1,000.

DEADLINE: June 24.

Paul A. Witty Short Story Award

Steven L. Layne, Chairing
Poetry and Prose Awards Subcommittee
Judson University
1151 N. State Street
Elgin, IL 60123-1404

DESCRIPTION: This award is presented to recognize an original work that has appeared during the past year in a periodical that regularly publishes articles and stories for children under the age of 12. Sponsored by the International Reading Association (IRA), it does not consider retellings of folktales, legends, or myths.
Website: www.reading.org

REQUIREMENTS: No entry fee. No word length limitations. Accepts hard copy accompanied by a copy of the periodical in which the article or story appeared. Entries must be mailed separately to each member of the judging committee; visit website or send an SASE for additional information. Nominations may be made by publishers, IRA members, or authors.

PRIZES: Winners receive a $1,000 cash award.

DEADLINE: December 1.

Writers-Editors Network Annual Competition

CNW/FFWA
P.O. Box A
North Stratford, NH 03590

DESCRIPTION: This annual writing competition is sponsored by the Cassel Network of Writers (CNW), and accepts entries from both members and non-members of this writing group. The contest is divided into four categories: nonfiction, fiction, children's literature, and poetry. Within each category there are sub-categories. Except for nonfiction, all submissions must be unpublished or self-published only.
Website: www.writers-editors.com

REQUIREMENTS: Entry fees vary based on membership and length of submission. No stapled entries. Manuscripts are not returned. Visit the website for official entry form, list of categories, category guidelines, and judging criteria.

PRIZES: Each first-place winner receives $100; second-place winners, $75; third-place winners, $50. All winners also receive certificates.

DEADLINE: March 15.

WOW! Women on Writing Flash Fiction Contests

Contest Coordinator

DESCRIPTION: Every three months, the *WOW! Women on Writing* e-zine sponsors a competition for very short stories. Winners of each contest are chosen by a guest judge. While all styles of writing are accepting, it is suggested that writers consider the sensibilities of the guest judge if they wish to be serious contenders.
Website: www.wow-womenonwriting.com

REQUIREMENTS: Entry fee, $10; entry with critique, $20. Length, 250–750. Multiple entries are accepted. Accepts electronic submissions through the website only. Contest closes when 300 stories have been submitted.

PRIZES: First-place winners receive a cash prize of $250. Second- and third-place winners receive $150 and $100 respectively. All winning stories are published in the e-zine.

DEADLINE: Visit website for current quarterly entry deadlines.

Writers' Journal Writing Contest

P.O. Box 394
Perham, MN 56573-0374

DESCRIPTION: Each year, *Writers' Journal* magazine sponsors an array of contests in a number of categories, including fiction, short story, horror/ghost story, romance, science fiction/fantasy, and poetry. The contests it sponsors are open to all writers.
Website: www.writersjournal.com

REQUIREMENTS: Entry fees range from $3 to $15 depending on category. Word lengths and guidelines vary for each contest. Writers may enter as many manuscripts in as many categories as they wish; include a separate entry form and fee for each manuscript. Accepts hard copy. Visit the website or send an SASE for complete contest information.

PRIZES: Winners receive cash prizes ranging from $15 to $500, publication in *Writers' Journal*, and a 1-year subscription.

DEADLINE: Varies for each category.

The Writing Conference, Inc. Writing Contests

P.O. Box 664
Ottawa, KS 66067-0664

DESCRIPTION: Each year, the Writing Conference, Inc. sponsors writing contests for elementary, junior high/middle school, and high school students. Entries must be relevant to each year's contest topic, which is available on the website. The contests recognize outstanding, unpublished student submissions in the areas of poetry, narrative, or essay.
Website: www.writingconference.com

REQUIREMENTS: No entry fee. Visit the website or send an SASE for contest topic, complete guidelines, and entry form. Writers' names should appear on the entry form only.

PRIZES: Winning entries appear in *The Writers' Slate*, an online magazine for students and teachers.

DEADLINE: January 8.

Writing for Children Competition

Writers' Union of Canada
90 Richmond Street, Suite 200
Toronto, Ontario M5C 1P1
Canada

DESCRIPTION: The best writing for children is recognized each year by the Writers' Union of Canada. It accepts any writing up to 1,500 words written in the English language; however, entrants must be Canadian citizens or landed immigrants and cannot have been published by a commercial or university press.
Website: www.writersunion.ca

REQUIREMENTS: Entry fee, $15 per entry. Length, to 1,500 words. Multiple entries are accepted. Accepts hard copy accompanied by separate cover letter with author's name, address, phone number, email address, and number of pages of entry. Visit the website or send an SASE for complete guidelines.

PRIZES: Winner receives a cash prize of $1,500. Entries of winners and finalists will be submitted to 3 children's book publishers.

DEADLINE: April 24.

Writers' Resources

Selected Resources

Working writers do not live only in their own minds. As every writer knows, research of some kind is needed for almost every article or story. Even if it is not, you need the company and feedback of other writers. You need to live in the real world of finding markets, working with editors, handling rights and payment issues, and staying apprised of industry changes. You need to grow in your knowledge of the field. And you—as a language lover and experts—also have an obligation to keep your language skills alive and refined.

This new section of *Magazine Markets for Children's Writers* includes websites and other resources divided into four sections: language and writing, career and writing community, children and children's writing, and research. The resources were selected to offer a balance of practical tools, inspiration, and informational leads. They range from scholarly databases and news sites to social networking sites, writers' associations and groups, editor and writer blogs, sources about children and their reading, and more. Use these resources as a jumping-off point to create your own network of network of connections and ideas. The rich collection that results will be a powerful tool for writing, selling, and promoting your work.

Language & Writing

The Chicago Manual of Style Online

Website: www.chicagomanualofstyle.org

Description
Varying editions of *The Chicago Manual of Style* have been on the shelves of writers, editors, students, and teachers since 1906. It addresses everything about writing from usage to manuscript preparation.

Now published in hardcover and online, the website offers free and subscription services. Among the free resources is a Style Q & A that provides clear, practical information on grammar and syntax. A subscription offers complete access to the *CMOS*, plus the ability to create personalized style guides, make notes, and join the online forums on style, copyediting, professional development, and publishing.

Common Errors in English Usage

Website: www.wsu.edu/~brians/errors/ index.html

Description
A comprehensive list of mistakes even the best of writers may make, Common Errors in English Usage spells out why they are mistakes and offers corrections. The compiler is Paul Brians, English Professor Emeritus at Washington State University.

Clarity and a straightforward format make this an extremely useful reference for the processes of writing, revision, and fact-checking. Brians's introduction to the cross-referenced list of errors—mangled expressions, mistaken terms, mispronunciations, and misuses—is enlightening. The explanations about usage take a balanced view of how language changes, not adhering to the traditional for its own sake.

The Compulsive Copyeditor

Website: http://compulsivecopyeditor. wordpress.com

Description
The Compulsive Copyeditor uses this blog to make "rulings" on language, with good humor and helpful explanations.

Discussions and explorations cover etymology, "English is weird" musings, translations, slang, spelling, language evolution or degeneration, and vocabulary. The blogger writes, "(M)y opinions often feel both ingenious and well founded, like new legal arguments grounded in precedent. Maybe at least some of them will be useful precedents for someone else. Maybe rulings on grammar should be argued and archived like the body of opinion of a court of law."

Expressions & Sayings

Website: http://users.tinyonline.co.uk/ gswithenbank/welcome.htm

Description
The Expressions & Sayings page is one part of a website called Scorpio Tales, and is filled with miscellaneous, fun, and inspiring uses of language. The derivations provided range from "A1" (from Lloyd's of London's eighteenth-century shipping register) to "win hands down" (from horse racing).

Other interesting pages under the Diversions button on Scorpio Tales cover unusual words, collective nouns (a muster of peacocks, a dray of squirrels), ologies (momiologies, the study of mummies), and much more. The site is humorous, informative, and could easily provide writers with ideas and inspiration.

Grammar Girl

Quick & Dirty Tips for Better Writing

Website: http://grammar.quickand dirtytips.com

Description

Started by a magazine and technical writer, the Grammar Girl is Mignon Fogarty, who calls herself a grammar guru. The brightly designed site does not focus as much on grammar blunders as other grammar sites do; rather it takes a more positive slant of improving style through usage.

Tips include "Split Infinitives: It takes boldness to split an infinitive"; "How to Use Transition Words"; and "What Are Run-On Sentences? They don't have to be long." Many of Fogarty's tips on grammar, punctuation, word choice, and style are available in podcasts. The site also includes a section with quick and dirty tips by Legal Lad (law topics) and Math Dude (making math easier).

Slice Magazine

Website: www.slicemagazine.org

Description

Slice is a magazine with the mission of publishing emerging and established writers alongside each other. It has begun We Who Write Workshops, where aspiring authors can develop their writing and gain insights into publishing by working with agents and editors.

Slice is published twice yearly (March and September) by two editors from major publishing houses. Issues focus on themes (villains, metropolis, fear, going home, in translation, heroes), but also include articles, fiction, and poetry on other subjects. The editors "simply look for works by writers who promise to become tomorrow's literary legends." In its CoverSpy feature, "publishing nerds" hit New York City's streets, subways, and bars to see what people are reading.

Sylva Rhetoricae

Website: http://rhetoric.byu.edu

Description

The classic study of persuasion through language is rhetoric—and writers use rhetoric all the time, some better than others. An underlying knowledge of its tools improves writing skills. This site from Brigham Young University wanders "the forest of rhetoric" (*sylva rhetoricae*) to help new and experienced writers.

From abecedarian to zeugma, the devices of rhetoric are explained and illustrated here. The site also includes rhetorical exercises, and addresses issues of audience. Persuading an audience is, after all, the goal of all writing, whether it is a story persuading a reader to believe in its reality and characters, an article arguing a cause, or poetry meant to move.

World Wide Words

Website: www.worldwidewords.org/qa/ qa-pal2.htm

Description

For lovers of language, this is a fun and informative site. Michael Quinlon is a former BBC Radio producer, a writer, and even curator of a regional museum, who also has a wide knowledge of the development of words and phrases. On his site, he "writes on international English from a British standpoint."

World Wide Words includes articles, Q & As, topical words, turns of phrase, weird words, an affixes dictionary, book reviews, and a weekly e-zine. The discussions of words, phrases, and etymologies are so rich that writers may find them full of ideas for their own research and writing. For instance, read the piece on *glebe* or *cucumber time,* or why a *mournival* beats a *gleek.*

Career & Writing Community

Absolute Write

Website: http://absolutewrite.com

Description

Absolute Write is a freelance writer's site that offers articles, publishing news, interviews, reviews, forums, and classes. It comes together to create a community of writers of all levels and interests.

All forms of writing are represented on the site, from children's writers and screenwriters, to greeting card writers. The community includes agents, editors, and publishers. The forums have about 25,000 members, 125,000 threads, and 5 million posts. Absolute Write also lists writers' conferences and contests, publication dates for member publications, archived articles, and a blog.

The Authors Guild

Website: www.authorsguild.org

Description

The Authors Guild is an advocacy organization for writers that focuses on copyright, contracts, and free expression. In recent years it has fought long and hard battles related to electronic rights, and come up against Google and Amazon to represent authors' best interests.

Publications from the Guild include *The Writer's Legal Guide,* and a quarterly *Bulletin* with publishing, copyright, tax, and legal news. Membership gives authors access to health and media liability insurance, contract reviews by attorneys, and other services. Dues are $90 for the first year, and thereafter determined on a sliding scale.

Christian Story Teller

Website: www.christianstoryteller.com

Description

This nonprofit author network provides information, connection, and support for those interested in Christian writing. It helps authors solve publishing problems, gives advice on self-marketing, and reports on scams.

The membership fee is $35 a year, which covers a personal author webpage to showcase writing and other services, as well as templates for ads, press releases, and posters. Christian Story Teller also runs seminars, including a self-marketing seminar cruise.

Editorial Anonymous

Website: http://editorialanonymous. blogspot.com

Description

Editorial Anonymous is a blog written by a children's book editor—obviously anonymously, so she can share stories about authors, editors, publishers, and others in the children's literature community.

The blog author's advice and commentary is straightforward and real-world, and humorous at times. Subjects have included acquisitions, age groups, agents, awards, children's genres and categories, intellectual property, marketing, series, being an editor, rejections, and many others. Editorial Anonymous includes links to other sites of interest for writers.

Education Writers Association

Website: www.ewa.org

Description
The national Education Writers Association (EWA) provides resources, reporting help, a job center, source search, publications, and a contest for educational reporters and writers. It supports professional development, and aims to improve the quality of American education at the same time.

Membership is free, although the organization has charged a fee in the past. The EWA has recently started an online community, and it conducts seminars and regional workshops. Its biweekly newsletter is *Education Reporter* and it also offers a guidebook, *Covering the Education Beat.*

E-zineZ.com

Website: http://e-zinez.com/

Description
An online "handbook of e-zine publishing," this site has "chapters" on preparation, planning, production, publishing, promotion, and profits. It is a free online tutorial on creating email newsletters.

The site argues that e-letters are a powerful tool for marketing. While the site is not directed specifically to writers, it can be used to help create an email newsletter to promote yourself as an author and sell your work. A link leads readers to another useful site, BestEzines, a list of thousands of email newsletters on a multitude of subjects, including writing, publishing, and speaking.

Freelance Writers Report

Website: www.writers-editors.com

Description
FWR is part of the Writers-Editors Network, or Cassell Network of Writers. Its mission is to link writers with editors who are currently looking for editorial content.

Portions of the site are free, and portions are available to paying members only. A basic online membership is $29 a year; premium memberships are also available.

The site regularly updates to include new magazine markets, and posts changes in existing markets, editors, and other personnel. It covers both adult and children's magazines. News is available online, and is also compiled in a monthly email newsletter.

The Freelance Writing Jobs Network

Website: www.freelancewritinggigs.com

Description
This site is all about building a writing career and boosting income. It offers job leads, business information, and writing advice for authors of all kinds.

The site's sections include a networking headquarters, job leads for each business day, a grammar guide, articles on the writing of articles and blogs, job hunting tips, publishing law information, and "Other Stuff." Sample posts include "Don't Lede Me On: Creating a Strong Article to Support an Iron Lede," "Is the Word 'Freelance' Hurting Your Job Search?" and "Join the eBook Revolution."

Funds for Writers

Website: www.fundsforwriters.com

Description

Specializing in providing information and news on grants for writers, this site is put together by author C. Hope Clark. She also highlights contests and markets, and stresses finding the money writers need to create a real career.

Clark's free e-newsletters include *Funds for Writers, FFWSmall Markets,* and *WritingKid.* The site has lists of resources for writers and many links: grant sources, professional organizations, sites for finding writing work, e-books, writing tools, and more. Clark also offers a personal consulting service to writers.

Goodreads

Website: www.goodreads.com

Description

Goodreads is like Facebook for readers—the largest social network for people who love to read and want to connect through their shared interest.

The site is full of member reviews, discussion groups, book clubs, author news, literary trivia quizzes, and even a place to swap books. Goodreads also posts stories and articles written by members. Among the many groups on the site are the 1,225-member Childrens Books group; almost 3,000-member Harry Potter group; more than 1,000-member Wild Things: YA Grown Up group, and countless others relating to children's literature.

A comparable competitive site is LibraryThing (www.librarything.com).

Latinidad

Website: www.marcelalandres.com

Description

Latinidad is a free e-zine from Marcela Landres whose purpose is to help Latinos achieve publication. It offers writing advice, but focuses even more on helping writers to understand the needs of readers and editors, thereby furthering their own publishing career.

Landres is a former Simon & Schuster editor who realized from her experience that many writers are not knowledgeable about the business of publishing. She is the author of *How Editors Think: The Real Reason They Rejected You.* While her advice is directed to would-be book authors, much is also relevant to magazine writers.

LinkedIn

Website: www.linkedin.com

Description

For writers truly serious about their careers, LinkedIn is a business networking site that provides opportunities to research or connect with other writers, editors, and business people. It can further your own writing and publishing efforts.

LinkedIn has more than 75 million members around the world. Members create profiles, manage their professional information, create contacts, create and collaborate on projects, or hold discussions in private group settings. It is a resource for researching people in every kind of professional field, and for job hunting as well.

Magazine Publishers of America

Website: www.magazine.org

Description

To stay knowledgeable about magazine publishing generally, this is the organization to turn to. The MPA offers news, fact sheets, trend analysis, a downloadable *Magazine Handbook*, digital trends, editorial trends, information on magazine launches, growing areas, and more.

While the focus is on the business of magazines and the data is related to many categories of publication, knowledge of the state of the industry is useful to every writer. The *Handbook*, for example, includes articles on the e-reading market, magazine website growth, and the appeal of magazines to young adults.

Mystery Writers of America

Website: www.mysterywriters.org

Description

The Mystery Writers of America is one of the best-known writing organizations in the U.S., and particularly known for its Edgar Awards. The Edgars are given in many categories, including short story, young adult, and juvenile. In addition, the Robert L. Fish Memorial Award is given to the best first short story by an American author.

Members of the MWA and its 11 regional chapters are writers, editors, publishers, and anyone interested in mysteries and crime writing. The MWA also sponsors an active youth literacy program.

My Writers Circle

Website: www.mywriterscircle.com

Description

Sponsored by the WCCL Network, My Writers Circle is an international writers forum that consists of many different discussion groups and boards for posting. Among the categories are All the Write Questions, about editing, grammar, and publishing; Review My Work, where writers can post samples and request critiques; Writing Games & Challenges; and The Coffee Shop, for chat and making writing friends. The site also offers an author's resource center, and a place to post job ads. Check under any of these for even more specific subjects of interest.

Some areas are open to unregistered guests, and some only to registered members.

National Writers Association

Website: www.nationalwriters.com

Description

The nonprofit National Writers Association consists of nationwide and local chapters. The organization's mission is to further writer education through scholarships and free or low-cost seminars and workshops.

The NWA provides its members with contract or agreement reviews; advice on copyrights and issues such as plagiarism; marketing consultations; a complaint service for problems with editors; contests; critiques; member networking; editing services; and a self-publishing arm called National Writers Press. Its publications include a monthly email newsletter, a quarterly magazine, and confidential reports on publications.

PEN Center

Website: www.penusa.org

Description

Founded in 1943, the PEN Center is a renowned writers' organization that encompasses authors in all genres and forms, as well as editors, journalists, historians, and critics. The international arm of PEN has existed since 1921.

PEN USA is an advocacy group that works to protect writers' rights everywhere, and to promote literacy and freedom of expression. The organization hosts literary events, a mentorship project, and annual awards in a variety of categories, including children's literature. The PEN in the Classroom program places professional writers in residencies in California high schools. It also offers a literary fellowship, Emerging Voices, for new writers.

Science Fiction & Fantasy Writers of America

Website: www.sfwa.org

Description

A professional organization made up of authors of science fiction, fantasy, and other speculative fiction, the SFWA informs and advocates for its members. It provides assistance in publishing disputes; has a fund for writers with medical and legal bills; and a mentoring program.

The site has online discussion forums, and an information center for new writers that covers the nuts and bolts of submission, and the craft and business of writing. The SFWA's Nebula Awards (www.nebulaawards.com) acknowledge excellence in science fiction and fantasy in categories that include short stories.

Publishing Law Center

Website: www.publaw.com

Description

The Publishing Law Center is a source of legal information for the professional writing community. It offers legal articles, publishing articles, and trademark, copyright, and intellectual property information. Categories under legal articles include Internet law, electronic rights, contracts, fair use, and privacy. Publishing articles cover editorial, marketing, business, and self-publishing topics.

The sponsor of the site is the Denver, Colorado, law office of Lloyd L. Rich, a publishing attorney.

Writer Unboxed

Website: http://writerunboxed.com

Description

"About the craft and business of genre fiction" is the tag line for this blog, which has more than a dozen contributors who write in the genres of romance, tween fiction, YA, magazine writing, science fiction and fantasy, folklore, historical fiction, and others.

The blog incorporates many interviews with authors and industry experts, and a fair amount of promotion for its authors' publications. It also embraces guest bloggers, and the subjects discussed are not only about career subjects such as whether or not to use a Facebook page, but also craft topics like character reactions to conflict, and inspirational subjects like writers and walking.

On Children & Children's Writing

Booklist

Website: www.booklistonline.com

Description
Booklist is a publication of the American Library Association that all writers, including those writing for children's magazines, should know. It publishes reviews, as well as lists acknowledging quality that can propel authors' careers. These include the *Booklist* Top of the List, *Booklist* Editors' Choice, and Notable Children's Books.

Reading the best children's books is also very wise for magazine writers who want to improve the quality of their own writing and gain a sense of publishing trends in the field.

Cooperative Children's Book Center

Website: www.education.wisc.edu/ccbc

Description
The University of Wisconsin-Madison School of Education is the home of the CCBC. While it was created for students interested in children's literature, it is open to any adult interested in children's and YA writing.

The CCBC is a source of expertise for those who want to know about excellence in literature for children and adolescents. Its libraries have a large collection of historical, as well as contemporary, literature. The CCBC responds to questions from those interested in finding books they remember from their own childhoods—even without the title or author, if the plot and decade of publication are known. The organization also advocates for intellectual freedom and diversity.

Children's Writer

Website: www.childrenswriter

Description
Children's Writer is a 12-page newsletter that promotes better children's writing and helps readers find freelance opportunities. Each issue's lead articles cover a genre or market, such as small presses, picture books, mysteries, YA, and online magazines. Interview-based articles provide editor insights on submissions, style, and subjects. The monthly also includes profiles of publishers, and articles on craft, profession, and more. The Marketplace pages specify additional publishers and their current needs. Two annual writing contests offer prizes up to $500 plus publication in the newsletter. $19 per year.

Cynsations

Website: http://cynthialeitichsmith.
blogspot.com/

Description
Full of informative interviews with children's writers and publishing professionals, Cynsations is the blog of best-selling children's author Cynthia Leitich Smith. She is also on the faculty of the Writing for Children and Young Adults MFA program at the Vermont College of Fine Arts.

Smith's site includes conversations among writers and readers, editors, agents, and others. It provides news and analysis relevant to children's and YA publishing in the vibrant and varying voices of those active in the field. Smith also reviews books and has guest bloggers.

Family Education Network

Website: www.familyeducation.com

Description

A source for parents and educators, the Family Education Network has ideas, advice, stories, events, and resources all about children and families. Writers can use it as a source of information and inspiration.

The site is divided into age ranges—0 to 6, 7 to 11, 12 to 18—which can serve as a useful measure for the writer who wants to target or depict particular stages of child development. Some of the features could also help with character development (NameLab for family and baby names) and targeting literacy levels (Reading Readiness Screening Tool). The parenting message boards are another tool for idea development and information gathering.

The Horn Book

Website: www.hbook.com

Description

The Horn Book covers children's and YA literature with book reviews, genre reviews, interviews, and essays. It aims at librarians, teachers, parents, and writers who want enlightened opinions about the field. A recent issue explored folktales and the picture book genre, singer-songwriter Natalie Merchant's take on childhood poetry, an autistic boy's connection with books, and an interview with YA veteran Patty Campbell. Book reviews are the magazine's *raison-d'être:* A starred review from *Horn Book* always indicates a high-quality read that gets noted in the publishers' marketing and promotion materials. The website has 70,000 reviews archived. $49 per year.

Guys Read

Website: http://guysread.com

Description

Author Jon Scieszka began this site to promote literacy among boys, who are often reluctant readers. The goal is to encourage boys to become self-motivated and eager to pick up a book or magazine, now and for the long-term.

Along with extensive lists of titles that appeal to boys of all ages, Scieszka uses his inimitable humor to discuss news in publishing. He provides links to interesting author websites, and offers suggestions and a process for starting a Guys Read group.

Verla Kay's Message Board for Children's Writers & Illustrators

Website:
www.verlakay.com/boards/index.php

Description

Verla Kay's Message Board is a website with a series of topical threaded discussion groups that contain tens of thousands of postings on hundreds of topics. The board is organized by subject matter: the craft of writing and illustrating, genres, author and illustrator news, URLs of interest, and "off topic" (for everything else). Subcategories in the craft section include writing, illustrating, education, contests, research, professional talk, computer and Web discussions, live chat, and a foreign section. The genre subcategory, as an example, has ten active boards. Like all discussion boards, this one has nuggets and trash, but participants relay considerable information and opinion.

Read Kiddo Read

Website: www.readkiddoread.com

Description
James Patterson's Read Kiddo Read website is dedicated to making kids readers for life. It presents hundreds of book reviews broken down by age group and genre: illustrated books, transitional books, page-turners, and advanced reads. As an example, the illustrated books are further broken down into books for babies, storybooks, easy reads, and factual books. Under storybooks are 43 reviews, from classics to new titles. Each review has links for purchase of the book; excerpts from other reviews by *Horn Book, School Library Journal, Kirkus*, or *Publishers Weekly;* plus listings of additional, similar books.

Society of Children's Book Writers & Illustrators

Website: www.scbwi.org

Description
SCBWI is the gold-standard organization in children's literature, with 22,000 members nationally. It publishes a well-regarded quarterly newsletter and other informational resources. Its two annual conferences are the most important and well-attended conferences in the field. Most of SCBWI's 70 regional groups also publish newsletters and hold conferences and other events. SCBWI promotes and lobbies for its constituents in terms of rights, payment, and other publishing issues. Its Golden Kite Awards for meritorious writing are among the most prestigious in children's literature, and the organization confers other awards and grants as well. Membership, $70 per year.

Teenreads.com

Website: www.teenreads.com

Description
This website promotes reading and good literature for teenagers. It catalogues new releases, does book reviews, profiles authors, recaps award-winning books in the field, and discusses books being made into movies.

Teenreads features reading lists of the best books, including classics, and it promotes the formation of local book clubs for teenagers. The site provides a free, twice monthly electronic newsletter, and blogs. A charming feature is the section If You Ask Me, which has teen readers discussing their favorite books and characters, and why.

YALSA

Website: www.ala.org/ala/mgrps/divs/ yalsa/yalsa.cfm

Description
YALSA is the section of the American Library Association that focuses on young adult literature. While its primary constituency is librarians, media specialists, and educators, writers serious about YA literature can use the YALSA website as a resource for keeping apprised of the best new books for teens, as well as those that are enduring.

Follow the Best Books of the Year list as it unfolds: YALSA members recommend the books their young readers are reaching for. Teens themselves nominate books to a top ten list, and other lists can also prove helpful. The association celebrates Teen Read Week every October, with a different theme each year.

Research

AllExperts.com

Website: www.allexperts.com

Description
This website is an interactive research mecha-nism to match your question to a knowledge-able expert. The inquiry format falls into 36 categories, such as arts/humanities, comedy, and kids. Subcategories refine the search. Under kids are 17 topics, among them health, math, science/nature, which are refined even further. At a selected topic, you can view recent questions and answers, peruse links, or ask a question. Experts' backgrounds are available to help choose one to ask. Experts are also rated by users. Note that many experts are self-nominated.

EurekAlert!

Website: www.eurekalert.org

Description
This website is an online press release data-base and news service operated by the American Association for the Advancement of Science. Universities, medical centers, jour-nals, government agencies, corporations, and other organizations engaged in scientific, medical, and technological research post their news here. The website is good for emerging news, and has voluminous online databases accessible by subject. An inquiry on global climate change turned up 200 press releases. The breaking news section is a good source of ideas.

EyeWitness to History

Website: www.eyewitnesstohistory.com

Description
Subtitled "history through the eyes of those who lived it," this database combines first-hand accounts of historical events with sec-ondary descriptive write-ups. The primary sources are the real bonuses, although the descriptive histories are well researched and well written.

The site also has historical photographs, film clips, and audiotapes. The basic organi-zation is by epoch (ancient world, Middle Ages, etc.) or major event (World War I, World War II, etc.). The home page highlights recent additions and "this month in history." The chronological index can help users to find documents of interest.

Library of Congress

Website: www.loc.gov

Description
The Library of Congress is the largest library in the world, with millions of books, record-ings, photographs, and manuscripts in its many collections, which are housed in three huge buildings in Washington, DC.

The LOC website has an online catalogue with a robust search engine that offers access to all the collections, and links to other major libraries' online catalogues. The website provides good instruction on how to use the Library search engines for maximum efficiency. The LOC is an unmatchable one-stop-shop for all research.

Mondo Times

Website: www.mondotimes.com

Description
This website claims to cover 27,670 news sources in 212 countries through links to the websites of magazines, newspapers, radio and television stations, news agencies, and even other websites. While not every resource in every field is linked, the chances that you find the information you are looking for nonetheless are very high. If Mondo Times comes up short, there is a Google link on every page.

In addition to finding information on current events, or researching archived articles in the various media sources, Mondo Times can help writers research culture, daily life, and people in countries and regions all over the world.

Ready, 'Net, Go!

Website: www.tulane.edu/~lmiller/ ArchivesResources.html

Description
A meta index of archives on the Internet, Ready, 'Net, Go! is a master list for researching collections from around the world. From this database users can link to "almost every archival resource in the metaverse." It was created and is maintained by Tulane University and the special collections division of its library.

The database is organized according to the standards of the Society of American Archivists. The site also provides tools for using archives and search engines. While the site is oriented to archivists themselves, it isa great resource for writers doing serious research.

ProfNet

Website: https://profnet.prnewswire.com

Description
Originally intended to connect journalists with professional communicators (public relations firms), ProfNet expanded to include researchers and 30,000 experts, whose profiles are provided. Once you register, you can describe your interest and request that a topic you are researching be sent to specific resources: activists, analysts, authors, bloggers, colleges and universities, corporations, government, hospitals, legislative offices, media companies, nonprofit organizations, public relations agencies, and small businesses. You can also select a region of the world and a region within North America. Along with a list of potential sources, you get contact information to set up interviews.

Virtual Salt

Website: www.virtualsalt.com

Description
University teacher and writer Robert Harris's website offers expertise and a wide range of resources for writers, students, educators, and others on literature, writing, research, technology, and faith and learning.

Sections include links, lists of resources, and articles. Particularly interesting are: "Evaluating Internet Research Sources"; a current list of Web research tools; software tools; writing tools on vocabulary; and articles on creative and critical thinking, information-processing, and decision-making. Harris has also become an expert on the prevention of plagiarism.

Indexes

Market News

New in 2011

The AAAS Kavli Science Journalism Awards
Abilene Writers Guild Contest
Absolute Write
The Acorn
AllExperts.com
All Genres Writing Contest
Apples
Atlantic Writing Competition
The Authors Guild
Berry Blue Haiku
Booklist
Bull Spec
Bumples
Christian Story Teller
Common Errors in English Usage
Compulsive Copyeditor
Cooperative Children's Book Center
Current Health Kids
Current Health Teens
Cynsations
Editorial Anonymous
Education Writers Association
Eurek Alert!
Expressions & Sayings
EyeWitness to History
E-zineZ.com
Family Education Network

Family Health & Life
Family Time for You and Your Crew
Freelance Writers Report
Freelance Writing Jobs Network
Funds for Writers
Girlworks
Goodreads
Grammar Girl
Guardian Angel Kids
Guys Read
Healthy Mom & Baby
The Horn Book Magazine
Impact Magazine
Inkling Magazine
Irish's Story Playhouse
Verla Kay's Message Board for Children's Writers & Illustrators
Kids Off the Couch
Kids X-Press
Kyria
Lad
Latinidad
Library of Congress
Linked in
Magazine Merit Awards
Magazine Publishers of America
Mondo Times
Mystery Writers of AMerica
My Writers Circle

National Writers Association
NYMetroParents
Parenting Children with Special Needs
Parenting Special Needs
PEN Center
ProfNet
Publishing Law Center
Purple Dragonfly Awards
Read Kiddo Read
Ready, 'Net, Go!
Science Fiction & Fantasy Writers of America
See Jane Fly
SingleMom.com
Slice Magazine
Society of Children's Book Writers & Illustrators
Spark Action
Sweet Designs Magazine
Sylva Rhetoricae
Teenreads.com
Virtual Salt
World Wide Words
Writer Unboxed
Xtreme JAKES
YALSA
YARN

Market News (continued)

Deletions and Name Changes

Abilities: Ceased publication.

African American Family: Ceased publication.

Arizona Parenting: Did not respond to inquiries.

Art Jewelry: Website no longer available; appears to be defunct.

Big Apple Parent: See NYMetroParents.

Biography Today: Publishes books primarily.

BYU Magazine: Alumni magazine; no children's materials.

The Clearing House: Staff-written only.

Clubhouse: No longer accepting freelance submissions.

Creative Child: Ceased publication.

Creative Connections: Ceased publication.

Crinkles: Ceased publication.

Current Health 1: Renamed Current Health Kids.

Current Health 2: Renamed Current Health Teens.

Dirt Rider Magazine: Did not respond; does not appear to accept freelance.

Early Childhood Today: Scholastic website for the magazine uses archived articles.

East Texas Teen: Never produced the announced premiere issue.

Fox Valley Kids, N.E.W. Kids: Renamed Apples.

Henry Parents: Website no longer available; appears to be defunct.

Hot Rod: Did not respond; does not appear to accept freelance.

James Hubbard's My Family Doctor: Ceased publication.

Just 4 Kids: Ceased publication.

Kansas School Naturalist: Infrequent publication schedule.

Kids Discover: Staff-written only.

Kindred: Ceased publication.

KnoWonder!: Ceased publication.

Living for the Whole Family: A local promotional publication.

Michigan History for Kids: Ceased publication.

Mom Writer's Literary Magazine: Ceased publication.

The Northland: Published by, and for, a small Anglican community in Canada; no children's materials.

The Olive Branch: Appears to have ceased publication; nothing new available since 2009.

ParentingUniverse.com: A reference site for parenting publications.

Pocono Parent: Ceased publication.

Queens Parent: See NYMetroParents.

Relate: Ceased publication.

Single Mother: Website no longer available; appears to be defunct.

Small Town: Last issue available in 2009.

Soccer Youth: Appears to be defunct.

Socialist Appeal: Very limited market for children's writers.

Spirit! Magazine: Ceased publication.

Start: New website of publisher (www.eduguide.org) does not appear to include Start.

Story Station: Website no longer available; appears to be defunct.

Street Brand: Website no longer available; appears to be defunct.

TAP: The Autism Perspective: Appears to be defunct.

Teach Kids Essentials: Ceased publication.

Teen Times: Materials appear to be primarily archived.

Tiger Beat: Staff-written only.

U-Turn Magazine: Ceased publication.

Wanna Bet?: Did not respond to inquiries; website materials not regularly updated; appears not to take freelance.

Westchester Parent: Ceased publication.

Wild West: Limited interest for young readers.

Your Child Pub: Ceased publication.

Yummy Mummy: Website no longer available; appears to be defunct.

Fifty+ Freelance for New Writers

Y ou can improve your chances of selling by submitting to magazines that fill their pages with freelance material. We have listed below markets that buy at least 50 percent of their freelance material from writers who are new to the magazine. Of course, there are no guarantees. But if you approach these magazines with well-written manuscripts targeted to their subject, age range, and word-limit requirements, you can increase your publication odds.

The Acorn
The ALAN Review
Alateen Talk
Amazing Kids!
American Secondary
   Education
Autism Asperger's Digest
bNetS@vvy
Brain, Child
Bread For God's Children
Brilliant Star
Calliope
Capper's
Cat Fancy
Child Care Information
   Exchange
Childhood Education
Children and Families
Children's Ministry
The Claremont Review
Dig
Dimensions
Educational Horizons
Education Forum
Education Week
Encyclopedia of Youth
   Studies

Fort Myers & Southwest
   Florida
Girlworks
Group
Highlights for Children
I Love Cats
Indy's Child
Insight
Jack and Jill
Journal of School Health
Justine
Keyboard
Keys for Kids
The Kids' Ark
Learning & Leading with
   Technology
Massive Online Gamer
Momentum
Mothering
My Light Magazine
North Star Family Matters
Our Children
Parents Express
The Pink Chameleon
Positive Parenting
Prehistoric Times
PresenTense Magazine

Principal
Read, America!
Red River Family Magazine
Reunions Magazine
SchoolArts
School Library Journal
Shine Brightly
Sisterhood Agenda
Skipping Stones
Sparkle!
The Universe in the
   Classroom
Voices from the Middle
VOYA Magazine
What If?
What's Up? Canada's Family
   Magazine
Writers' Journal
Zamoof! Magazine

Category Index

To help you find the appropriate market for your manuscript or query letter, we have compiled a category and subject index listing magazines according to their primary editorial interests. Pay close attention to the markets that overlap. For example, when searching for a market for your rock-climbing adventure story for 8- to 12-year-old readers, you might look under the categories "Adventure Stories" and "Middle-grade (Fiction)." If you have an idea for an article about blue herons for early readers, look under the categories "Animals/Pets" and "Early Reader (Nonfiction)" to find possible markets. Always check the magazine's listing for explanations of specific needs.

For your convenience, we have listed below all of the categories that are included in this index. If you don't find a category that exactly fits your material, try to find a broader term that covers your topic.

Adventure Stories
Animals (Fiction)
Animals (Nonfiction)
Audio/Video
Bilingual (Nonfiction)
Biography
Boys' Magazines
Canadian Magazines
Career/College
Child Care
Computers
Contemporary Fiction
Crafts/Hobbies
Current Events
Drama
Early Reader (Fiction)
Early Reader (Nonfiction)
Education/Classroom
Factual/Informational
Fairy Tales
Family/Parenting
Fantasy
Folktales/Folklore
Games/Puzzles/Activities
Geography
Girls' Magazines
Health/Fitness
Historical Fiction

History
Horror
How-to
Humor (Fiction)
Humor (Nonfiction)
Inspirational Fiction
Language Arts
Mathematics
Middle-grade (Fiction)
Middle-grade (Nonfiction)
Multicultural/Ethnic (Fiction)
Multicultural/Ethnic (Nonfiction)
Music
Mystery/Suspense
Nature/Environment (Fiction)
Nature/Environment (Nonfiction)
Personal Experience
Photo-Essays
Poetry
Popular Culture
Preschool (Fiction)
Preschool (Nonfiction)
Profile/Interview
Read-aloud Stories

Real life/Problem-solving
Rebus
Recreation/Entertainment
Regional (Fiction)
Regional (Nonfiction)
Religious (Fiction)
Religious (Nonfiction)
Reviews
Romance
Science Fiction
Science/Technology
Self-help
Services/Clubs
Social Issues
Special Education
Sports (Fiction)
Sports (Nonfiction)
Travel
Western
Writing
Young Adult (Fiction)
Young Adult (Nonfiction)
Young Author (Fiction)
Young Author (Nonfiction)

Computers

Contemporary Fiction

Current Events

Drama

Early Reader (Fiction)

Historical Fiction

Humor (Fiction)

Humor (Nonfiction)

Inspirational Fiction

Multicultural/Ethnic (Fiction)

Multicultural/Ethnic (Nonfiction)

Personal Experience

Poetry

Photo-Essays

Read-aloud Stories

Real life/ Problem–solving

Rebus

Recreation/ Entertainment

Reviews

Romance

Science Fiction

Science/Technology

Self–help

Services/Clubs

Social Issues

Special Education

Sports (Fiction)

Sports (Nonfiction)

Travel

Index

If you do not find a particular magazine, turn to Market News on page 318.

★ indicates a newly listed magazine

C

D